COMPANY LAW

Also by the same author

Constitutional Law in Ireland (1987, Cork & Dublin)
Bankruptcy Law in Ireland (1990, Cork & Dublin)
Reorganising Failing Business (1991, Cork & Dublin)
Industrial Relations Law (1991, Dublin)
Employment Law (1992, Dublin)
Commercial and Economical Law (1992, Devanter, Netherlands)
Law of Company Insolvency (1993, Dublin)
Arbitration Law (1993, Dublin)
Extradition Law in Ireland (2nd ed., 1994, Dublin)
The Law of Extradition in the United Kingdom (1995, Dublin)
Commercial Law (2nd ed., 1997, Dublin)
Commercial Legislation (1998, Dublin)
Cases and Materials on Irish Company Law (2nd ed., 1998, Dublin)

Company Law

3rd Edition

MICHAEL FORDE
B.A. (Mod.) and LL.B (Dublin),
LL.M. (Brussels)
Ph.D. (Cantab.)
of King's Inns and Middle Temple
Barrister-at-Law

ROUND HALL SWEET & MAXWELL
1999

Published in 1999 by
Round Hall Sweet & Maxwell
Brehon House, 4 Upper Ormond Quay,
Dublin 7

Typeset by
Gough Typesetting Services
Dublin

Printed by
MPG Books, Cornwall

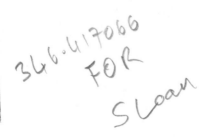

ISBN 1-899738-89-4 pbk
1-85800-151-X hbk

Table of Contents

Preface to the Third Edition

There have been no radical changes in the law since the publication of the second edition in 1992. No Act of particular significance has been passed comparable with the two measures that were enacted in 1990, prompting the second edition. However, there has been a steady accretion of case law, especially in England where the size of the volumes of Butterworth's Company Law Cases (B.C.L.C.) continues to expand every year.

There seems to have been only two judgments of considerable significance given by the Irish Courts in the past seven years but both of them are unsatisfactory, if not wrong. One of them (*Frederick Inns*) has been the subject of a devastating critique in 17 D.U.L.J. 18 (1995). In the other one (*Greendale Developments Ltd. No. 2*) I was Counsel for the losing side (on the appeal), which perhaps may colour the views I express in paragraphs 3–78 and 14–20—14–21. I fail to see what possible wrong there can be in a solvent company distributing part of its assets among one or more of its shareholders/directors/employees, which does not render the company insolvent in any way, where all of the shareholders have assented to that distribution and where there are no debenture-holders. Common sense would suggest that, in company law, such distributions are entirely legitimate, as most modern experts on the subject contend, *e.g.* Whincop, "Of Fault and Default" 21 *Melbourne University Law Review*, 187 (1997), at pages 202–205. I have endeavoured to state the law up to mid-June 1999.

For those of us who practise at the Irish Bar, the loss of Mr Justice Hugh O'Flaherty, who resigned from the Supreme Court earlier this year, will be irreparable. He was the kindest and most generous judge with whom I have ever had dealings and his judgments were always grounded in pragmatism as a well as a good grasp of the law. When the hype that caused him to resign has subsided, one hopes that he will find a suitable avenue for his outstanding talents. In one of the last cases in which I appeared before him, involving a fitness to practise enquiry into allegations of misconduct made against a midwife, he (along with Mr Justice Barron) was quick to see the sheer absurdity of the tribunal preventing expert witnesses being present during the course of a serious judicial-type evaluation of professional matters; his dissenting brethren from a Company Law/Chancery background could see nothing wrong with excluding those experts from the hearing.

Many of the leading cases are reproduced in my *Cases and Materials on Irish Company Law* (second edition) which was published last year, and that book ought to be a useful supplement to the present work. Several of the unreported cases referred to here are reproduced in *Cases and Materials.*

The usual catalogue of "suspects" in my writing endeavours, to whom on this occasion should be added Michael Fealy who practises at the Bar in London, deserve thanks for their assistance in one way or another; *inter alia* Therese Carrick of Round Hall Sweet & Maxwell; Marie Armah Kwantrang, who typed the text; Gilbert Gough, who typeset the book; and of course Catherine, Patrick and Peter who had to put up with me while I endeavoured to complete it.

M.F.
Mountain View Road
Dublin 6
Midsummer's Day, 1999

Table of Cases

Table of Statutes

POST 1922

Companies (Amendment) Act 1990 (No. 27)—*contd.*

Companies (Amendment) Act 1990 (No. 27)—*contd.*

Table of Statutory Instruments

Constitution of Ireland 1937 (Bunreacht na Éireann)

1986 Rules of the Superior Courts (S.I. No. 15 of 1986)

European Union Legislation

Table of International Treaties and Conventions

OTHER JURISDICTIONS

CANADA

ENGLAND

1

Introduction

1–01 Most companies are established in order to engage in some industrial or commercial enterprise; the vast majority of companies are run in order to make profits for their members. But some companies are established for non-commercial or non-profit purposes. With regard to commercial activities, individual business persons may choose to conduct their businesses either in their own names as "sole traders" or under the aegis of registered companies in which they own all or virtually all the shares. Where a number of persons wish to engage in a business in common, they have the choice of either forming a partnership or a registered company. But if a considerable number of persons are involved, the partnership option is not available to them. Among the principal advantages of the sole trader and the partnership forms are that they do not need any special formalities or expenditures to be established. One becomes a sole trader simply by virtue of trading on one's own behalf; the mere fact of doing business in common with others with a view to making some profit constitutes a partnership.[1] At present there are almost 200,000 Irish registered companies and approximately 300 new companies are registered every week.

ATTRACTIONS OF THE REGISTERED COMPANY

1–02 In functional terms, there are three main types of registered company. By far the commonest of these is the company formed to enable a person or a small group of persons to carry on their business; the "one-person" company or family company, or "quasi partnership". There then are companies formed to enable the investing public to put their money in an enterprise; many of these companies are well-known corporate names and have their shares traded on the stock exchange. Thirdly, there is the non-profit company, which is established for social or charitable purposes.[2] There are a number of distinct advantages in running a business under the registered company form.[3]

---

1 Partnership Act 1890, s.1(1).

2 Considered below, paras 14.61 *et seq.*

3 *cf.* Freedman, 'Small Businesses and the Corporate Form: Burden or Privilege?',

Legally Separate from Owners

1–03 The registered company has a legal identity that is entirely distinct from that of its owners. A sole trader's business is part of his own property and its obligations and debts are also that trader's own personal liabilities. A partnership is merely an association of the individual partners; its assets and liabilities are in law those of its members.[4] A registered company, by contrast, exists in law entirely separate from its members or shareholders; company property belongs to it and not to the shareholders and the shareholders are not directly answerable for the company's liabilities. Company property is held in the company's name and legal proceedings are brought by or against the company in its own name. The separate legal personality of companies, therefore, enables business persons to segregate their own private affairs from their business and also to segregate the affairs of their various businesses that are conducted under the aegis of different companies.

Limited Liability

1–04 "Limited liability" means that a company's owners' (*i.e.* the shareholders or members) liability for debts incurred by their company, that it cannot pay, is subject to a limit or ceiling; those owners cannot be held personally responsible for those debts beyond that limit. In any particular company the limit is one the owners agreed to when establishing the company or when they acquired shares in it. If, as often is the case, the company's shares are fully paid, the shareholders cannot then be held personally responsible for their company's debts; in companies limited by shares the shareholders' liability is limited to the amount remaining unpaid on their shares. Thus where Florence owns £1 fully paid shares in Acme Co. Ltd., if the company is wound up as insolvent its creditors cannot claim against him for any of the company's unpaid debts. But if only 60p was paid up on those £1 shares then his liability to the company, and through it to its creditors, is the 40p outstanding on every share that he holds.

1–05 This method of separating business persons' and investors' personal wealth from the fortunes of their enterprises is designed to encourage them to take business risks, without which a capitalist economy and society would stagnate. Limited liability sees to it that, if the particular enterprise fails, its owners' other wealth is not called upon to

---

Mod. L. Rev. 555 (1994).

4 R.C. I'Anson Banks (eds.), *Lindley & Banks on Partnership* (17th ed., 1995), Chaps. 12–14.

satisfy unpaid business creditors. A major concern of company law is to prevent this privilege of limited liability from being abused.[5] The Limited Partnership Act 1907 allows partners to limit their liability in the same way, provided the limited partners do not take part in running the partnership business.[6]

Transferable Shares

1–06 A registered company is comprised of members or shareholders.[7] All that shareholders, who wish to liquidate their investment in the company, need do is to sell their shares to another. This transaction can be effected quite simply; it does not require the assistance of a qualified lawyer and causes no legal disruption to the running of the business. But a sole trader who wishes to dispose of his business must execute conveyances and other elaborate contracts to that end. And as a general rule a partnership must come to an end whenever any one partner retires.[8] The transferable share in a registered company is an administratively simple way of attracting further investment in the company. All that needs to be done is for the company seeking more capital to allot additional shares in return for cash or other assets to those willing to invest in it.

Continuous Existence

1–07 When a sole trader dies his business comes to an end; it may be sold off to satisfy claims by the estate or it may be transferred to one or more legatees under the deceased's will. On the death of any partner generally the partnership is automatically dissolved.[9] A company, by contrast, never dies but continues in existence until it is wound up. Therefore, the business is not disrupted to any like extent when the principal shareholder dies as when the sole trader or a partner dies. In the case of a registered company, the business continues to remain in the same ownership and it is and only the company's shares that change hands.

Borrowing — The Floating Charge

1–08 There is one important method of borrowing, thereby financing the business, that in practice is available only to registered companies,

---

[5] See below, paras 3.28 *et seq.*
[6] See *Lindley & Banks on Partnership*, Chaps. 28–33.
[7] But there are companies which have members who are not shareholders; they are one category of guarantee company — see below, para. 14.65.
[8] See *Lindley & Banks on Partnership*, pp. 728–730.
[9] See *ibid.*, Chap. 26.

namely, the floating charge. A fixed or specific charge constitutes giving the fixed assets of a business (*i.e.* land, buildings and the like) as security for loans.[10] A floating charge, in contrast, constitutes providing the debtor's floating assets as security, *i.e.* assets acquired to be used up in various ways in the business and that ultimately may be disposed of in the course of the business.[11] Some businesses may have a high proportion of floating asset and so a floating charge is a most attractive way to finance its activities. On account of provisions of the Bills of Sale Acts and, until 1988, the Bankruptcy Acts, however, it is very difficult for sole traders and partnerships to resort to this method of secured financing.[12]

Fiscal Advantages

1–09 The company mode of doing business, as opposed to the sole trader or the partnership, may have certain advantages from a taxation point of view.[13] Over the years taxation has played a major role in the choice of a company as a vehicle to either carry on a trade or receive income. At different points along the way the divergence between corporate rates and personal tax rates has been substantial. In the mid 1970s corporation tax rates varied between 40 per cent and 50 per cent while personal tax rates were as high as 80 per cent. In those circumstances the ability to shelter income in a corporate, rather than personal, capacity was a major tax planning point. The ratio between corporate and personal rates has since then varied. The absolute gap is not as great, yet there are still benefits. At present, corporate rates are 28% (25% for the first £100,000) while top personal rates are 32% plus various levies. There is still, at this level, a differential. Clearly, a director must take sufficient income from the company to meet his normal living expenses and on those drawings he will pay a personal tax rate. Income over and above that level can be sheltered at the lower rates.

1–10 Some tax incentives, although not many, are available only to companies; the most significant one in the Irish tax code is the 10 per cent rate for manufacturing companies. The taxation rules governing pension contributions are vastly more generous for company directors than they are for self-employed persons. In addition, it is much easier to offer incentive schemes in a tax efficient manner to employees of companies rather than employees in a sole business or partnership.

---

10 See below, paras 16.09 *et seq.*
11 See below, paras 16.12 *et seq.*
12 See M. Forde, *Commercial Law* (2nd ed., 1997), p. 221.
13 See generally P. Moore and F. Brennan, *Corporation Tax* (9th ed., 1997) and P. Feeney, *Corporation Tax* (1997).

These incentives can vary from bonus payments to share incentive schemes. From a capital tax point of view there are very major benefits in trading as a company. It is easier to move small elements of the enterprise where one is dealing with a company; it suffices to earmark an appropriate number of shares and have them transferred. The ability to transfer equity or value of a company while retaining control through voting shares, which otherwise carry little or no value, has been a major feature of capital tax arrangements for decades.

HISTORICAL CONTEXT

1–11 The registered company as we know it today came into existence in 1844 and in 1855 companies were first permitted to register with limited liability. Prior to then, the principal institution through which persons pooled capital and other factors for the purpose of doing business was the partnership and its derivative, the deed of settlement company. There were other legal forms within which persons could do business, most notably the chartered company and the statutory company; but those in fact were available only to the very wealthy and privileged. One variant of the statutory company that became comparatively common by the middle of the last century was the public utility company, such as railways and waterworks companies established under Companies Clauses Acts. Enthusiastic students of the history of company law should consult the many specialised works on the subject — which, in the light of Ireland's colonial past, is almost entirely the story of how English company law evolved.[14]

Chartered Corporations

1–12 In the past, one way of obtaining legal autonomy for an enterprise was by having it constituted by a royal charter; the charter would establish an incorporated body that was legally distinct from its members. In *Re Commercial Buildings Co. of Dublin*[15] Johnston J. described how the former Commercial Buildings Company, which was located in Dame Street where the Central Bank now stands, obtained its charter; other chartered bodies probably were set up in much the same way:

> "The corporation came into existence in this way. In 1797 a number of business men in the City of Dublin formed themselves into a voluntary

[14] An excellent account is contained in P.L. Davies, *Gower's Principles of Modern Company Law* (6th ed., 1997), Chaps. 2 and 3. See also B.C. Hunt, *The Development of the Business Corporation in England, 1800–1867* (1936).

[15] [1938] 1 I.R. 447.

society for the purpose of 'the founding of buildings to be appropriated to 'the convenience of commercial dealing and intercourse within the City of Dublin.' These gentlemen bore names which are to this day well known and honoured in commercial and professional circles in this city names such a Nathaniel Hone, Randal MacDonnell, Joshua Pim, Pichard Verschoyle, George Maquay and others — and on their application it was referred by Lord Camden, the Lord Lieutenant of the day, to the Attorney-General and Solicitor-General to inquire whether a royal charter ought to be granted. The Attorney-General of the day was none other than Arthur Wolfe, who subsequently became the ill-fated Lord Kilwarden, whilst the Solicitor-General was none other than John Toler, who later was raised to the peerage as Lord Norbury, and became known to fame as 'the hanging judge'. These gentlemen reported in favour of the scheme, and a royal charter was granted on January 1st 1798, erecting a corporation under the name of 'The Commercial Buildings Company of Dublin', with very extensive powers, including that of making bye-laws. The first of these bye-laws ordained that the common seal of the company should be 'kept in an iron repository at the office of the said company, to which there shall be three good locks, each of which shall be materially different in its internal construction from the others', and the keepers of the keys should be three directors of the company, each being responsible for one key.

The commercial building, as we all know, was built on a plot of ground on the North side of Dame Street, ground granted to the Company by the commissioners of Wide Streets, a statutory body which did so much in the eighteenth century to make Dublin the beautiful city that it is today".[16]

1–13 The great majority of chartered bodies were established for other than business purposes. An example of a chartered non-profit corporation is the Law Society of Ireland; it was founded for "facilitating the acquisition of legal knowledge, and for the better and more conveniently discharging of [solicitors'] professional duties".[17] Other such bodies include Dublin University[18] and the Royal College of Surgeons.[19] No new chartered corporations were established since the State was founded in 1922 but Acts of the Oireachtas have been passed on several occasions amending the terms of existing charters.[20]

1–14 Before the "Glorious" Revolution of 1688, it was the Crown that issued charters, so that entrepreneurs would have had to exercise very

---

[16] [1938] 1 I.R. at 480.
[17] Society's Charter of 1852.
[18] *cf. Trinity College Dublin v. Comrs. for Valuation* [1919] 2 I.R. 493.
[19] *cf. Miley v. Attorney General* [1918] 1 I.R. 455.
[20] *e.g.* Universities Act 1997.

extensive political influence in order to get their enterprises constituted in this manner. Subsequently, the Parliament sought to control the issuing of charters and established the practice of passing special legislation authorising the Crown to charter a particular body. By the nineteenth century it was almost unheard of for commercial undertakings to be chartered, which heightened the demand for the deed of settlement form of company. In the 1830s legislation was enacted authorising the Crown by letters patent to confer the privileges of incorporation in place of a full-blown charter.[21] For a time, a major method of establishing commercial companies was by letters patent and it still remains the predominant mode in some Canadian provinces.[22]

Statutory Corporations

1–15 By statutory corporation is meant a company that is established by special legislation other than under the Companies Acts, 1963-1999, and their predecessors. The Bank of Ireland is perhaps the most prominent of those bodies in private ownership, tracing its origin to the Act for Establishing the Bank of Ireland of 1781-82,[23] although it was actually created by a charter issued under the terms of that Act.[24] Several amendments have since been made to the Bank's Charter, all by way of legislation. Private Acts of the Oireachtas were passed in 1929 and in 1935[25] which altered the charter so as to prevent the Bank from being taken over without the Minister of Finance's consent and also introducing limited liability for the Bank's shareholders. Further changes to the Charter were made by the Central Bank Acts.

1–16 Most statutory corporations today that engage in commercial or industrial activity are State-owned or public corporations, like the Central Bank,[26] the Electricity Supply Board,[27] the Irish Gas Board,[28] Radio Telefís Éireann,[29] Coras lompair Éireann[30] and the Voluntary Health Insurance Board.[31] However, not all State-owned public utili-

---

[21] Trading Companies Act 1834 (4 & 5 Will. IV, c. 94).
[22] See B. Welling, *Corporate Law in Canada* (2nd ed., 1991), ch.2.
[23] 21 & 22 Geo. III, c. 16.
[24] Charter issued on May 10, 1783 and enrolled in the Court of Chancery of Ireland on May 15, 1783.
[25] Bank of Ireland Acts of 1929 (No. 4, private) and of 1935 (No. 1, private).
[26] Central Bank Acts 1942–1997, esp. 1942 Act, s.5 and 1971 Act, s. 51.
[27] Electricity (Supply) Act 1927, esp. s.2.
[28] Gas Acts 1976–1987, esp. 1976 Act, s.7,
[29] Broadcasting Authority Acts 1960–1977, esp. 1960 Act, s.3.
[30] Transport Acts 1950–1987, esp. 1950 Act, s.5.
[31] Voluntary Health Insurance Act 1957, esp. s.3.

ties and business ventures are established in this manner.[32] Many of the State businesses are companies registered under the Companies Acts but whose internal regulations contain various provisions specified in the legislation which authorised registration of the company in question. For instance, under the Postal and Telecommunications Services Act 1983, the Minister was required to arrange for two limited companies, named An Post (or the Post Office) and Bord Telecom Éireann (or The Irish Telecommunications Board) to be formed and registered under the Companies Acts. That 1983 Act then went on to set out in considerable detail the principal features of these two companies, like their authorised share capital, their principal objects, the contents of their articles of association, the issue of and subscription for shares in them. Other State-owned bodies which have been constituted in this manner include the A.C.C. Bank plc, the I.C.C. Bank plc, the Irish Forestry Board Ltd and Aer Lingus Teo.

1–17 In the past, special Acts of Parliament were enacted to establish public utilities which, subject to numerous restrictions, were run as private enterprises. Eventually, rather than pass separate statutes constituting each individual utility being set up, Acts known as Companies Clauses Acts were enacted.[33] These Acts established common rules for the various categories of utilities, and they were supplemented by Acts establishing common rules unique to particular utilities, such as the Lands Clauses Consolidation Act of 1845[34] and the Railway Clauses Consolidation Act of 1846,[35] the numerous and Gasworks Clauses Acts.[36] Under the Gas Regulation Act 1982, any private organisation which supplies gas is empowered to adopt a memorandum and articles of association and, thereby, several of the main provisions of the Companies Acts then apply to those bodies. This was enacted principally in order to facilitate the reorganisation of the Alliance and Dublin Gas Consumers Company, which was a deed of settlement company.[37]

Deed of Settlement Companies

1–18 In 1720 the "Bubble Act" of the British Parliament[38] sought to regulate the growing phenomenon of entrepreneurs purporting to es-

---

[32] See Goulding, "The Juristic Basis of Irish State Enterprise" (1978) 13 *Ir. Jur.* 302.
[33] *cf.* Companies Clauses Consolidation Act 1845, 8 & 9 Vict., c. 16.
[34] 8 & 9 Vict., c. 18; consolidated again by 32 & 33 Vict., c. 8. 1869.
[35] 8 & 9 Vict., c. 20.
[36] *e.g.* 10 & 11 Vict., c. 15, 1847 and 34 & 34 Vict., c. 41, 1871.
[37] 10 & 11 Vict., c. xiii, 1847, and 29 & 30 Vict., c. ccv, 1866. 2 5. 6 Geo. I, c. 18.
[38] 6 Geo. I, c. 18.

tablish incorporated trading associations, the shares of which were freely transferable and some of which even claimed limited liability. That Act was a somewhat clumsily drafted measure and precisely what it sought to achieve is far from clear. Its central thrust appears to have been to forbid the establishment of incorporated trading associations, *i.e.* joint business enterprises where it was sought to segregate the business' assets and liabilities from those of its owners. Enactment of the Bubble Act undermined public confidence in many companies, led to extensive litigation aimed at having the charters of numerous existing companies forfeited, all of which caused a collapse in share prices and a long business recession. Thereafter it became increasingly difficult for entrepreneurs to obtain royal charters or legislative backing for incorporating their undertakings; the letters patent system was not introduced until the 1830s. Capitalists and their legal advisers, accordingly, began to experiment with the deed of settlement form of business organisation.

1–19 The deed of settlement company is a hybrid of a partnership and a trust. Entrepreneurs would associate for some common business objective but, instead of drafting up articles of partnership to govern their relationship, they would have drawn up something more akin to a trust deed. Under it, the business property would be vested in trustees; power to manage the business would be conferred on directors, some of whom usually would be trustees as well; the founders' stake in the enterprise would be divided into a specified number of shares; provision would be made for varying the trust deed with the consent of a certain proportion of the shareholders. In this way, the enterprise would have a considerable degree of legal autonomy from its owners. Unlike the registered company or the chartered or statutory company, however, the deed of settlement company was not completely segregated from its owners. That company could neither sue nor be sued in its own name; and save in exceptional circumstances, suit had to be brought in the name of or against all the company's members, which became virtually impossible where there was a large number of members whose identity changed frequently. Nor could members of a deed of settlement company limit their liability in respect of its debts, although the constituting instruments of many such companies used to stipulate that their members' liability was limited.

1–20 While this form of doing business is virtually extinct today,[39] it

[39] A variant, however, is vigorous in Australia. See Ford and Hardingham, "Trading Trusts: Rights and Liabilities of Beneficiaries" in *Equity and Commercial Relationships* (P.D. Finn ed., 1987) Chap. 3; Ford, "Trading Trusts and Creditors'

has had a profound influence on the development of our company law by placing emphasis on the inherently contractual nature of registered companies. Thus, in one of the 1963 Act's central provisions, section 25, it is stated that a company's constitution (its memorandum and articles of association) shall "bind the company and the members thereof to the same extent as if they respectively had been signed and sealed by each member, and contained covenants by each member to observe all the provisions of the memorandum and of the articles."[40]

1–21 Perhaps the principal difference between Irish and British company law on the one hand and that of the United States is that the American law originally developed in a society where the essentially contractual form of constituting companies had not taken root. As the late Professor Gower, writing in 1956, explained,

> "In England . . . incorporation with limited liability by a simple process of registration is only one hundred years old, having attained its centenary (in 1955). Considering the transcendent role played by England in the mercantile community during the nineteenth and early twentieth centuries this is difficult to credit — but so it is. The explanation is that joint-stock enterprise had flourished considerably earlier but had operated principally in the guise of an unincorporated company or partnership under a deed of settlement. It was this familiar form of organisation which the legislation of 1844 and 1855 adopted, successively conferring on it the boons of corporate personality and limited liability. Hence the modern English business corporation has evolved from the unincorporated partnership, based on mutual agreement, rather than from the corporation, based on a grant from the state, and owes more to partnership principles than on rules based on corporate personality. Thus we in England still do not talk about business corporations or about corporation law, but about companies and company law.
>
> In America, on the other hand, the Bubble Act seems, wisely, to have been ignored despite the fact that it had been extended to the colonies by statute in 1741. After the Declaration of Independence, incorporation by special acts of the state legislature was granted far more readily than in England, and the unincorporated joint-stock company, though not unknown, was correspondingly less important. In a number of industrially important states incorporation by registration under a general act came earlier than in England — 33 years earlier in New York — and when it came, the model which the legislative draftsmen had in mind was the statutory or chartered corporation rather than the unincorporated company or partnership. Hence modern American corporation law owes less

---

Rights" (1981) 13 *Melbourne U.L. Rev.* 1 and McPherson, "The Insolvent Trading Trust" in *Essays in Equity* (P.D. Finn ed., 1985), Chap. 8.

[40] See below, para. 10.13 *et seq.*

> to partnership and contractual principles than does the British. This tends to make it less flexible than the English mode."[41]

Incorporation by Registration and Limited Liability

1–22 In 1844 the administratively convenient method of establishing companies by registration with a public official was adopted and ten years later the members of these companies were permitted to have limited liability. The history of company law from that period onwards is, briefly, as follows. The Joint Stock Companies Act 1844[42] was the first law which gave the privilege of incorporation by registration and without a royal charter or a special Act of Parliament. Under this Act, partnerships in which the capital was divided into freely transferable shares, partnerships in which there were more than 25 members and assurance companies were all required to register in a registry of companies. On registration and on filing a deed of settlement, these associations became incorporated and acquired a separate legal existence distinct from that of their members. Thus, for the first time, it became possible for an enterprise to become incorporated as of right by fulfilling prescribed conditions. The deed of settlement corresponded broadly to the modern memorandum and articles of association. However, every member could be made liable for their company's debts as if it had not been incorporated; but a creditor of the company could not sue a member for a debt due by the company without first trying to levy execution against the property of the company as such.

1–23 In 1852 a Commission which was appointed by Parliament to consider whether any alteration should be made to partnership law, so as to give limited liability to partners, reported that such limited liability would not be beneficial. Nevertheless, in the following year the House of Commons passed a resolution as a result of which the Limited Liability Act 1855[43] was passed. This Act amended the 1844 Act and made it possible for registered companies to limit the liability of all their members to the amounts due on their shares provided that certain conditions were observed.

1–24 Under the Joint Stock Companies Act 1856,[44] which consolidated

---

[41] "Some Contrasts Between British and American Corporation Law" (1956) 69 Harv. L. Rev. 1369, pp. 1371–1372. For the most of the last century the principal book on the subject was Lindley's *Treatise on the Law of Partnership and its Application to Companies* (1860). *cf.* B. Welling, *Corporate Law in Canada* (2nd ed., 1991), pp. 60-73.

[42] 7 & 8 Vict., c. 110.

[43] 18 & 19 Vict., c. 133.

[44] 19 & 20 Vict., c. 47.

the 1844 and the 1855 Acts, any seven or more persons were entitled to register a company with limited liability. An annual return had to be filed giving information about the capital of the company and its shareholders, but filing a balance sheet with the auditors' report attached (which had been made compulsory in 1844) became no longer necessary. The Companies Act 1862[45] consolidated existing legislation regarding joint stock, banking and assurance companies, and also made provision for companies limited by guarantee. It required the objects of the company to be stated and prohibited their alteration, and thus introduced the doctrine of *ultra vires.* The principal features of the modern system of company law will be found in the Act of 1862.

1–25 Although the advantages of companies with limited liability are considerable, in its early form the system offered opportunities for fraudulent enrichment to company promoters, as numerous leading cases decided around the turn of the last century testify to. A number of Acts dealing with specific reforms in company law were passed between 1862 and 1900. In 1895 a Committee under the Chairmanship of Lord Davey recommended further legislative amendments.[46] The collapse which had followed the over-optimism of the railway boom had caused many public companies to fail, and in some of those the promoters and the directors had made substantial illicit profits. The Companies Act 1900[47] made provision for a number of matters which had to be stated in every prospectus, and imposed new obligations and liabilities on directors of companies. It also re-introduced the compulsory audit of a company's accounts.

1–26 In 1905 a Committee under the Chairmanship of Sir Robert Reid (subsequently Lord Loreburn, L.C.) was set up to enquire into what additional amendments were necessary to the companies legislation.[48] It recommended that every company should be obliged each year to file a balance sheet, which would be available for inspection by every member of the public. It also made recommendations in relation to accepting the special position of "family" companies. It had been held by the House of Lords in *Salomon v. Salomon & Co.*[49] that there was nothing in the Companies Acts which prohibited the registration of a company with seven members, six of whom held a small number of shares on behalf of the seventh, who owned the rest of the shares. The

---

[45] 25 & 26 Vict., c. 89.
[46] C. 7779.
[47] 63 & 64 Vict., c. 48.
[48] Cd. 3052 (1906).
[49] [1897] A.C. 22; see below, para. 3.09.

Companies Act 1907[50] provided that a private company could be registered with two members only and that it should be exempt from the obligation to file a balance sheet for public inspection. A private company was defined as a company in which restrictions were imposed by the articles of association on the transfer of shares, in which the number of members of the company did not exceed fifty and in which the shares and debentures of the company cannot be offered to the public. Many of the smaller limited companies previously incorporated availed of this legislation by converting themselves into private companies. Another significant development was the emergence of the "holding company" as distinct from the operating company. The holding company was, in the main, the child of the operations of financiers interested in the development of the diamond fields in South Africa before and after the Boer War.

1–27 All the legislation from 1862 to 1907 were consolidated by the Companies (Consolidation) Act 1908.[51] This Act was amended and added to in minor details by the Companies Act 1913,[52] the Companies (Foreign Interests) Act 1917,[53] the Companies (Particulars of Directors) Act 1917,[54] and the Companies (Reconstitution of Records) Act 1924,[55] which was the first company law statute passed by the Oireachtas. This latter Act dealt with the reconstitution of records consequent on the destruction of the Companies Registration Office when the Custom House in Dublin was burned during the Civil War.

1–28 In 1925 in the United Kingdom a Committee was set up to consider and report on what amendments were desirable in the Companies Acts, 1908 to 1917. Mr Wilfrid Greene (subsequently Lord Greene M.R.) was the Chairman of the Committee, and the report is frequently referred to as "the Greene Report".[56] Most of its recommendations were embodied in the Companies Act 1928,[57] and the existing law and the changes made by the Act of 1928 were consolidated in the Companies Act 1929.[58] In 1939 the British Parliament passed the Prevention of Fraud (Investments) Act 1939,[59] the main objects of which were regulating

---

[50] 7 Ed. VII, c. 50.
[51] 8 Ed. VII, c. 69.
[52] 3 & 4 Geo. V, c. 25.
[53] 7 & 8 Geo. V, c. 18.
[54] 7 & 8 Geo. V, c. 28.
[55] No. 21.
[56] Cmd. 2657 (1926).
[57] 18 & 19 Geo. V, c. 45.
[58] 19 & 20 Geo. V, c. 23.
[59] 2 & 3 Geo. VI, c. 16, replaced by an Act of the same name in 1958 and presently part of the Financial Services Act 1986.

the business of dealing in securities, and preventing fraud in connection with dealings in investments.

1–29 In 1943 in the United Kingdom a Committee under the Chairmanship of Mr Justice Cohen (subsequently Lord Cohen) was set up to consider and report on what major amendments were desirable in the Companies Act 1929, and in particular to review the requirements prescribed in relation to the formation and affairs of companies and the safeguards afforded for investors and for the public interest. The Report of this Committee (usually referred to as "the Cohen Report")[60] recommended a number of major alterations in the system of company law. Some of these were not accepted and do not appear in the Companies Act 1947[61] which followed the Report and which was a preliminary step to the Companies Act 1948.[62]

Developments Since 1958

1–30 The Company Law Reform Committee, which was chaired by the late Arthur Cox and whose secretary was Kenny J., reported in 1958[63] to Andreas O'Keeffe, who was then Attorney General. Its remit was to recommend what amendments should be made to the Companies (Consolidation) Act 1908, which at that time was the principal companies legislation in force in the State. Effect was given to some of this committee's principal recommendations in the Companies Act of 1959. Four years later what remains the cornerstone of our present company law was enacted, the Companies Act 1963, which replaced the Act of 1908 and incorporated the 1959 Act and most other recommendations made by the Cox Committee.

1–31 There were few developments of great significance between 1963 and 1990. The Stock Transfer Act 1963 and the Companies (Amendment) Act 1977 introduced administrative reforms to facilitate the transfer of shares. New winding up rules were adopted in 1966. And the Companies (Amendment) Act 1982, amended the 1963 Act in several respects. Other initiatives in this field were mainly the result of Ireland's accession to the E.E.C. in 1973. It was in order to bring domestic law in line with the E.E.C.'s requirements that S.I. No.163 of 1973, S.I. No.282 of 1984 and the Companies (Amendment) Acts of 1983 and 1986 were enacted. Much of the Act of 1983 deals with the capital of limited com-

---

[60] Cmd. 6659.
[61] 10 & 11 Geo. VI, c. 47.
[62] 11 & 12 Geo. VI, c. 38.
[63] Pr.4523.

panies to ensure that they are reasonably adequately captitalised;[64] the Act of 1986 is concerned exclusively with the format and content of company accounts.[65] Undoubtedly, the most significant of all the legislative changes are those contained in the Companies Act 1990,[66] which had a long gestation period. Another measure adopted in 1990, the Companies (Amendment) Act 1990 provides for the protection of companies in serious financial difficulties and the appointment of an examiner who will assess their underlying viability and seek to establish a compromise with the bulk of the creditors.

1–32 In 1999 the Companies (Amendment) Act was passed which amnended the 1990 Act in order that certain measures could be taken to stabilise or maintain the price of traded securities. At the time this book was going to print there was legislation pending in the Oireachtas on several aspects of the law, most notably, providing for exemptions to small companies from the requirement to have audited accounts, tightening the regime for examiners appointed under the 1990 Amendment Act and requiring companies to have at least one Irish-resident director and, for newly registered companies, some additional business connection with the State. There were also proposals to overhaul substantially the entire system for enforcing compliance with companies' legislation but draft legislation to this end had not yet been pubished.

SOURCES OF LEGAL REGULATION

1–33 The legal regime governing registered companies is derived from different sources. What makes parts of company law difficult to grasp is that the legal position on various matters can be contained in an amalgam of common law rules, equitable principles, contractual clauses in the company's own regulations and statutory provisions, to which may be added the rules of the Stock Exchange and standards imposed by the accountancy profession. As the French comparative lawyer, Professor André Tunc, observed:

> "a piece of legislation is sometimes superimposed over an unfortunate judicial rule. But the statute does not eliminate the rule. On the contrary,

---

[64] See generally, Forde, "The Companies (Amendment) Act 1983" (1983) 18 Ir. Jur. 289.

[65] See generally, S. Kelleher, *Companies (Amendment) Act. 1986* (1987).

[66] See generally, M. Forde, D. Hogan, B. O'Neill and F. Brennan, *The New Companies Law* (conference papers, 1991) and G. McCormack, *The New Companies Legislation* (1991).

it takes it for granted and eliminates or alleviates only some of its results. . . . Because the . . . legislator has such a respect for the common law background that it practically never dares to prepare a *tabula rasa* in order to build a new law, its interventions may have the result of increasing the complexities of the law."[67]

The Constitution

1–34 There is no express reference to registered companies in the Irish Constitution. To the extent to which they are necessary for "promot[ing] the welfare of the whole people" and to which they enhance "private initiative in industry and commerce"[68] the policy of the Constitution is to support companies. Registered companies have been accepted as proper plaintiffs in actions to declare legislation unconstitutional.[69]

1–35 There are no major decisions undermining the constitutionality of the Companies Acts.[70] The only instance where a provision of those Acts was struck down was in *Desmond v. Glackin (No.2)*,[71] which concerned section 10(5) of the 1990 Act regarding penalising persons who refused to cooperate with inspectors appointed under Part II of that Act. In such a case, the inspector was authorised to certify that non-cooperation, which would then be investigated by the court and, if the facts warranted, the person would be punished in the same way as if he had committed contempt of court. Because such a sanction could involve a very substantial fine or indeed imprisonment and since section 10(5) did not provide that the matter should be determined by way of a jury trial the subsection was held to be invalid. Whether the system of court-appointed company inspectors in Part II of the Companies Act 1990, would withstand a challenge or separation of powers grounds is debateable.[72] And it would seem that section 22(a) of that Act, purporting to render admissible in evidence the contents of an inspector's report, would be struck down.[73]

---

67 "A French Lawyer Looks at British Company Law" (1982) 45 Mod. L. Rev. 1, pp. 6, 7.

68 Art. 45(1), (3).

69 *Iarnród Éireann Teo v. Ireland* [1996] 3 I.R. 321; see below, para. 3–49.

70 See however *Re R. Ltd.* [1989] I.R. 126, concerning court hearings *in camera; Carway v. Attorney General* [1996] 3 I.R. 30, concerning proof of insolvency in applications to impose restrictions on directors; and *O'Keefe v. Ferris* [1997] 3 I.R. 463, concerning imposing unlimited liability for fraudulent trading.

71 [1993] 3 I.R. 67.

72 *cf. Gould v. Brown* (1998) 72 A.L.J.L.R. 375.

73 *cf. County Glen p.l.c. v. Carway* [1998] 2 I.R. 540 and *Re Employment Equality Bill, 1996* [1997] 2 I.R. 321 at pp. 382–383.

1–36 Provisions that could possibly be struck down, though it is most unlikely that they would be, are section 204 of the 1963 Act under which a company that acquires more than eighty per cent of the shares in another company in a take-over bid may require the remaining shareholders to sell their shares at the bid price;[74] and section 201 of that Act which permits a three-quarters majority of shareholders and creditors to impose settlements on the remaining members of their classes.[75] What should save these from invalidity is that the extensive powers they confer are subject to review by the High Court on broad fairness grounds. The same applies to the "cram down" provisions of the Companies (Amendment) Act 1990, where dissenting members and creditors can be compelled to accept settlements agreed to by specified majorities.[76]

1–37 Some of the above matters were touched on by the European Commission of Human Rights in *Bramelid and Malmstrom v. Sweden*[77] which concerned a provision in Swedish Law that is very similar to the "take out merger" powers in section 204 of the 1963 Act. If, in trying to take over a company, the "bidder" acquires more than 90 per cent of the shares in the "target", the bidder could obtain a court order that the remaining shareholders in the target must sell their shares to the bidder at an independently fixed price. An order was made under this law against the applicants, who held a small stake in a company that was taken over. They then contended that the order contravened inter *alia* the European Convention's private property guarantee, on the grounds that they had been compelled to surrender their property for less than its true value. According to the Commission of Human Rights, the applicants' shares were in principle protected by the Convention's property right. Furthermore, the "take out merger" power could not be justified on the usual grounds of public interest because the Swedish "legislature is pursuing the general aim of reaching a system of regulation favourable to those [private] interests which it regards as most worthy of protection, something which however has nothing to do with the notion of "the public interest" as commonly understood in the field of expropriation."[78] Nevertheless, the "take-out" in these circumstances could not be regarded as a violation of the right to enjoy property. In the first place, provision was made to compensate shareholders whose shares were taken from them. As well as that, compul-

---

[74] See below, paras 12–34 *et seq.*
[75] See below, paras 11–50 *et seq.*
[76] See below, para. 17.65; *cf. Louisville Joint Stock Land Bank v. Radford,* 195 U.S. 555 (1935).
[77] (1983) 5 E.H.R.R. 249.
[78] *ibid.* at 256.

sory transfers of property between individuals is a central feature of the laws of all State parties to the Human Rights Convention, for instance the division of property on succession, the winding up of certain matrimonial settlements, and seizing and selling goods in the course of execution proceedings. In the Commission's view,

> "the right of everyone to the peaceful enjoyment of his possessions cannot form the basis for challenging the right of the legislature to amend, when and how it considers desirable, the rule of private law which can have some effect on the property of individuals, subject of course to the principle of balance [, *i.e.* that] the legislature does not create an imbalance between [individuals] which would result in one person arbitrarily and unjustly being deprived of his goods for the benefit of another." [79]

1–38 An aspect of constitutional law that has been largely unexplored to date is the Constitution's impact on relations between individuals as contrasted with State impositions of burdens on individuals;[80] what may be described as the impact of the Constitution on private law and is known in Germany as the *drittwirkung* question.[81] In what circumstances do shareholders, creditors, employees or directors have constitutionally guaranteed rights *vis a vis* the other shareholders or against the company over and above those rights required by the Companies Acts and by the general law? It is questionable whether attempting to "constitutionalise" problems of this nature greatly assists their proper resolution; the law of contract and of tort, the principles of equity and the extensive provisions of the Companies Act would seem to adequately protect legitimate shareholders' and others' grieviences.[82] In *Glover v. B.L.N. Ltd.*,[83] which concerned the legality of a managing director's dismissal, it was held that, in not telling the plaintiff the charges against him and not giving him some opportunity to rebut them before deciding to dismiss him, the company broke an implied term of the employment contract that the dismissal procedure should be fair. This therefore suggests that some company decisions that affect persons' vital interests may be subject to quasi-constitutional procedural standards.[84]

---

79 (1983) 5 E.H.R.R. 249 at 256, 257.
80 See generally, M. Forde, *Constitutional Law of Ireland* (1987), Chap. 24.
81 See generally, B. Markesinis, *The German Law of Obligations* (3rd ed., 1997), Vol. 2, pp. 352–376 and C. von Bar, *The Common European Law of Torts* (1998), Vol. 1, pp. 569-620.
82 *cf. Crindle Investments v. Wymes* [1998] 2 I.L.R.M. 275.
83 [1973] I.R. 388.
84 *cf. Gaiman v. National Association of Mental Health* [1971] 1 Ch. 317.

Legislation

1–39 The principal statutes that affect registered companies are the Companies Acts of 1963 and of 1990, together with the Stock Transfer Act of 1963 and the Companies (Amendment) Acts of 1977, of 1982, of 1983, of 1986, of 1990 and of 1999; indirectly, the legislation on bankruptcy,[85] on restrictive practices, monopolies and mergers,[86] and on taxation.[87] None of the Companies Acts contain very significant provisions authorising Ministers to set subordinate but general norms by statutory instruments. Although much of our legislation is similar to that in Britain, there are significant differences with the British Companies Act of 1985. There are numerous, and indeed some very important, differences of detail that can easily go unnoticed between the Irish Acts and parallel British provisions.

Mandatory and Optional Rules

1–40 One general feature of the companies legislation that cannot be over-emphasised is the distinction between peremptory and optional provisions.[88] The former are rules that apply irrespective of the wishes of those to whom they are addressed, whereas the latter are rules that persons may agree shall not apply to dealings between themselves. For instance, much of what may be called individual protective employment legislation is peremptory (or *d'ordre public*), whereas the Sale of Goods Act 1893, is a classic optional (or suppletive) measure. Most provisions of the Companies Acts are peremptory; violation of many of their requirements are criminal offences and many other rules stipulate that the obligation being imposed may not be set aside by agreement between the parties, not even by any provision in a company's own regulations. Thus, sections 133 and 137 of the 1963 Act, which concern minimum periods of notice for calling general meetings and demanding polls at those meetings, state that any provision to the contrary in the company's articles of association shall be void. But the Companies Acts also contain numerous optional rules — the most common form being that the Act's requirement in question applies unless the company's own regulations provide otherwise. It has been held

---

85 See generally, M. Forde, *Bankruptcy Law in Ireland* (1990).

86 See generally, M. Forde, *Commercial Law* (2nd ed., 1997), Chap. 8.

87 See generally, P. Moore and F. Brennan, *Corporation Tax* (9th ed., 1997) and P. Feeney, *Corporation Tax* (1997).

88 See generally, B. Cheffins, *Company Law: Theory, Structure and Operations* (1997), Chap. 3 on "classification of company law rules"; "Contractual Freedom in Corporate Law" (1989) 7 Columbia L. Rev. 1395; and Ramsay, "Models of Corporate Regulation: the Mandatory/Enabling Debate" in *Corporate Personality in the 20th Century* (R. Grantham and C. Rickett eds., 1998), Chap. 12.

that companies cannot contract with their creditors that some basic principles of bankruptcy law shall not apply in the event of liquidation.[89]

Interpretation

1–41 There are two principal contrasting methods of interpreting statutes: these may be called the "mischief" and the "literal" approaches. Under the former, the judge is concerned primarily with ascertaining the policy or goals which the provision in question was adopted to promote, and the rules will be applied in the light of that purpose. The other approach focuses entirely on the section's very terms and the judge will give effect to its literal meaning even if that be inconsistent with what it is thought the legislature was trying to achieve. In favour of this latter approach, it can be said that, even though occasionally it may give rise to a nonsense, it nevertheless is preferable because it provides greater certainty than what often amounts to guessing what objective the legislature had in mind when it adopted some provision.

1–42 At least in the British courts, there has been a tendency to interpret legislative provisions that impose detailed restrictions on directors' and shareholders' freedom of action in an exceptionally literal and limited manner, somewhat in the same way as tax laws were construed until very recently there.[90] That is to say, courts have upheld transactions and arrangements that arguably contravened the spirit of the provision in question but were not caught by the section's very terms.[91] Indeed, what perhaps was the most important company law case of all time, *Salomon v. Salomon & Co.*,[92] concerning the separate legal personality of companies and the extent to which proprietors of "one-person" companies can insulate their personal financial situation from that of their companies, reads as an exercise in ultra-literalism. It was contended there, and accepted by a unanimous Court of Appeal, that in exceptional circumstances debts owed by an insolvent company to its general creditors should be paid off before satisfying secured debts owed by the company to its own shareholders. This view was rejected by a unanimous House of Lords, because, in Lord Halsbury L.C.'s words, "I can only find the true intent and meaning of the Act from the Act itself., and the Act appears to me to give a company a

---

89 See below, para. 18–111.

90 *i.e.* until *Furniss v. Dawson* [1984] A.C. 474.

91 Perhaps the best example is *Bushell v. Faith* [1970] A.C. 1099, below, para. 5–41; to a lesser extent, *Russell v. Northern Bank Development Corp.* [1992] 1 W.L.R. 588, below, para. 11–08.

92 [1897] A.C. 22, below, para. 3–09.

legal existence with . . . rights and liabilities of its own, whatever may have been the ideas or schemes of those who brought it into existence".[93]

1–43 A contrary phenomenon, however, and one which may partly explain the literal construction approach to the Companies Acts, is that there are some provisions in those Acts that give the courts remarkably extensive discretions. One of these, section 205 of the 1963 Act sweeps so widely that it could almost be said that many aspects of company law are governed by two separate standards — the "ordinary" rules based on the one hand on the Acts, the memorandum and articles of association and the common law and, on the other hand, the section 205 discretionary standard. It establishes a broad and amorphous criterion of "oppression" for inter-shareholder, company-shareholder and director-shareholder relations; and empowers the court to take appropriate measures whenever the company's or the directors' powers are being exercised "oppressive[ly]" or "in disregard of the interests [of any] member".[94] A somewhat similar and related provision is section 213(f) of the 1963 Act, which empowers the court to order that a company be wound up on "just and equitable grounds".[95] Virtually all the Companies Acts' provisions for drastically altering a company's structure, such as reducing its capital, changing the objects and making schemes of arrangement, either require prior approval by the court or empower the court on the application of dissident members to veto changes; in each instance the governing criterion is some vague standard of justice or fairness.[96]

Common Law and Equity

1–44 "Common law" and "equity" mean rules and principles which, it has been concluded by courts, have the force of law. Much of the judge-made rules concerning companies are the product of equity as distinct from the common law, in that most company matters were heard by the Court of Chancery.[97] However, common law and equity have been merged since the Judiciature Act of 1877, although for purely administrative purposes the bulk of company litigation still takes place on the Chancery side of the High Court.

[93] [1897] A.C. 22 at 31.
[94] See below, paras 10–72 *et seq.*
[95] See below, paras 10–89 *et seq.*
[96] See below, Chap. 11.
[97] See generally, B. Cheffins, *Company Law: Theory, Structure and Operation* (1997), Chap. 7 and Milman, "The Courts and the Companies Acts: The Judicial Contribution to Company Law" [1990] Ll. M. & C.L.Q. 401.

1–47 Some central principles governing the structure and operation of companies were devised by the judges and not the legislature, many of these being incorporated subsequently into the Companies Acts. Thus in a series of cases, of which *Ooregum Gold Mining Co. v. Roper,*[98] *Trevor v. Whitworth*[99] and *Flitcroft's Case*[100] are the best known, the courts laid down a broad principle of capital integrity; in limited companies, shares must not be issued for a price lower than their par value, the company may not purchase its own shares and dividends may not be paid out of capital. This principle and these rules, coupled with analogous rules but subject to some exceptions, are now contained in sections 60 and 72 of the 1963 Act, and are the main subjects of the 1983 Act.[101] In *Ashbury Railway Carriage Co. v. Riche,*[102] it was held that contracts entered into by a company but which are for purposes other than any of those set out in its objects clause are *ultra vires,* void and unenforceable. However, the hardship that unsuspecting outsiders doing business with companies suffered on account of this rule led to its virtual repeal by section 8(i) of the 1963 Act.[103] As happened in the *Salomon & Co.* case, a striking feature of *Ashbury Railway* and to a lesser extent of the capital integrity cases, is that the conclusions reached in them are presented as if they were the automatic consequences of the rules contained in the Companies Acts of the time. Because observers of the business scene then must have been shocked by the implications of *Salomon & Co.* and *Ashbury Railway,* it may have been felt necessary to give the separate legal personality and *ultra vires* principles unquestionable legitimacy by claiming that they arose from the very terms of the Companies Act as a matter of inexorable logic.

Rules of the Stock Exchange

1–46 In order to secure or to retain a quotation for their securities on a stock exchange, or in other words so that their securities may be traded on an exchange, companies must comply with the exchange's own rules. In May 1997 there were 85 Irish companies listed on the Irish Exchange, including most of the major enterprises here like the Allied Irish Banks, the Bank of Ireland, C.R.H. plc. and Jefferson Smurfit plc. But there are some large concerns that have not gone public in this manner, for instance, the Clery's store in O'Connell St., Dublin and the Dunnes stores chain.

---

98 [1892] A.C. 125,
99 (1887) 12 App. Cas. 409.
100 (1882) 21 Ch.D. 519.
101 See below, Chap. 7.
102 (1875) L.R. 7 H.L. 653.
103 See below, para. 13–15 *et seq.*

1–47 At one time there were independent stock exchanges in Dublin[104] and in Cork, and in the major cities of Britain. The Cork Exchange amalgamated with the Dublin Exchange in 1971 and, along with the Exchanges of Belfast, Glasgow, Birmingham and Manchester, in 1973 they merged with the London Stock Exchange.[105] All of those were subject to the same regulations and administrative procedures and the Irish Unit of the International Stock Exchange operated in Anglesea Street, Dublin 2. However, in 1995 the formal links with London were ended and the exchange in Anglesea Street became known as the Irish Stock Exchange. Formerly, those exchanges were self-regulatory, in the sense that their activities did not come under direct Government regulation. But under the Stock Exchange Act 1995, the Central Bank and the Minister for Finance were given extensive regulatory powers over the Irish Stock Exchange and any other such exchange as may be established in the State.[106]

Precedents

1–48 While they may not be a source of law in the narrow sense, established precedents and their accepted meaning in the legal profession are an important feature of company law. The most widely used and influential set of precedents are those collected in *Palmer's Company Precedents*[107] and *Butterworth's Company Precedents.*[108] Of these, Megarry J., who was one of the most meticulous of English judges, observed that

> "[t]he views of a draftsman of precedents, however eminent, cannot of course override the provisions of a statute; but in construing a statutory provision which seems to be devoid of any direct authority on the point, I think I am entitled to pay some regard to a book of precedents of high repute which must have provided a foundation for a very large number of sets of articles [of association] now in use."[109]

1–49 A recent excellent addition to these is Volume 1 *of Longmans' Commercial Law Precedents.*[110]

---

104 Established by 39 Geo. III, c. 40 (Ir.), An Act for the Better Regulation of Stock Brokers (since repealed).

105 Established under Deed of Settlement on December 31, 1875.

106 See generally, B. Clarke, *Irish Investment and Listing Regulation* (loose leaf) (1999).

107 (17th ed., 1956) Parts 1 (general forms) and 11 (winding up).

108 (5th ed., 1988), Vols. 9–11.

109 *Gaiman v. National Association for Mental Health* [1971] 1 Ch. 317 at 328; see also FitzGibbon J. in *Cork Electric Supply Co. v. Concannon* [1932] I.R. 314.

110 Loose leaf (Vol. 1).

APPLICATION OF THE COMPANIES ACTS

1–50 The word "company", standing on its own, signifies a group of persons and encompasses partnerships and most kinds of voluntary associations and clubs, as well as registered companies. But the Companies Acts 1963–1999 do not apply to each and every kind of company. What are companies for the purposes of those Acts are companies which have been registered under them or under any of the earlier Companies Acts. Thus, it has been held that the prohibition against subsidiary companies financing the purchase of their parent company's shares does not apply to foreign-registered subsidiaries.[111] Part IX (sections 328–343) of the 1963 Act sets out a procedure whereby some companies otherwise constituted, for instance by charter, letters patent or statute, can be registered under the Companies Acts.

1–51 Additionally, parts of the Companies Acts are made applicable to certain types of companies that are not registered under those Acts. Section 377 of the 1963 Act defines an "unregistered company" for these purposes and the schedule to the 1990 Act lists all the sections of the companies legislation rendered applicable to those companies.[112] There then are companies which are registered outside the State but either have some establishment or otherwise have some presence in the State. Where they have a business establishment in the State, Part XI (sections 351–360) of the 1963 Act applies to them, as do numerous other provisions of the companies legislation.[113] However, the Acts do not contain any catalogue of those provisions.

IMPLEMENTATION AND ENFORCEMENT

1–52 Legal rules governing companies are implemented and enforced in different ways, the methods of securing compliance running from prosecutions, through civil actions and public and private administrative process, to social sanctions. What does not exist in Ireland and Britain is a public administrative body charged with the special duty of ensuring that the company law is respected, like as the United States'

---

[111] *Arab Bank p.l.c. v. Merchantile Holdings Ltd.* [1994] Ch. 71.

[112] See below, paras 14–82 *et seq*.

[113] See below, para. 14.86 *et seq*.

[114] See generally, L. Loss & J. Seligman, *Securities Regulation* (3rd ed., 1989–90) Vols. 1–4 and J. Seligman, *The Transformation of Wall Street — A History of the Securities and Exchange Commission and Model Corporate Finance* (1982).

Securities and Exchanges Commission[114] and the Australian Securities Commission.[115]

Prosecution

1–53 Non-compliance with many provisions in the Companies Acts is a criminal offence. Quite a number of these crimes are mere administrative or regulatory offences; the maximum fines for them are often too low to deter breaches. Fines were increased considerably by the 1982 Act to compensate for the ravages of inflation since 1963, and there are some hefty fines for breach of parts of the 1990 Act. The maximum fines now are £200,000 for "insider trading"[116] £50,000 for "fraudulent trading,"[117] £10,000 for various frauds and falsifications under the 1990 Act,[118] and there is a maximum of £5,000 for violation of fourteen other provisions. Imprisonment, generally for a term not exceeding two years, is an alternative sanction for some of the most serious violations, such as for failure to keep proper books of account[119] and for circulating a prospectus that contains an inaccurate statement.[120] There is a ten years maximum imprisonment for "insider trading"[121] and a seven years maximum imprisonment for furnishing false information of various kinds which contributes to the company's insolvency or which interferes with its being wound up or facilitates defrauding creditors.[122]

1–54 There are variations in the *mens rea* requirements for some offences. Thus, in many of the offences regarding company accounts, imprisonment will not be imposed unless the offence was "committed wilfully".[123] The burden of proof for false declarations of solvency is partly reversed.; if a declaration of solvency is made and shortly afterwards the company is wound up but cannot pay its debts in full, then any director who made the declaration is deemed not to have had reasonable grounds for his or her opinion until the contrary is shown.[124]

1–55 Until Ernest Saunders, the former chief executive of Guinness,

[115] See generally, H. Ford *et al.*, *Principles of Corporations Law* (9th ed., 1999), Chap. 3.
[116] 1990 Act, s.114.
[117] 1963 Act, s.297 (as amended by 1990 Act, s.137).
[118] 1990 Act, s.203.
[119] *ibid.*
[120] 1963 Act, s.50.
[121] 1990 Act, s.114,
[122] *ibid.*, s.242.
[123] 1963 Act, s.383.
[124] *ibid.*, s.256 (as amended by 1990 Act, s.128).

was sent to Ford Open Prison in Essex in 1990, one rarely read of company directors or managers being jailed for breaking the Companies Acts. Prosecutions under these Acts are rare in Ireland. Although shareholders have the opportunity of bringing private prosecutions or seeking relator injunctions, they do so very occasionally if ever. The Director of Public Prosecutions or the Minister may bring summary proceedings for offences under the Companies Acts;[125] the limitation period for such offences is three years,[126] and the maximum penalties are a fine of £1,000 and imprisonment of 12 months or both.[127] The 1982 Act expanded the number of offences for which the registrar of companies is empowered to prosecute.[128]

1–56 At times, it is only when a company is being wound up that crimes committed by its directors or officers are unearthed. Section 299 of the 1963 Act requires the liquidator who, in the course of the winding up, comes across evidence of offences having been committed, to make a report on the matter to the Director of Public Prosecutions; where the court comes across such evidence it may direct the liquidator to refer the matter to the Director. Company receivers are under a similar duty.[129] During a winding up, the court has extensive power to call before it any company officer or any person suspected of having property belonging to the company, to examine them on oath, and require them to produce any books and papers they may possess relating to the company.[130] Although all questions put by the court must be answered, it is provided that any incriminating answers may not be used against the person who gave them in any other civil or criminal proceedings, apart from prosecution for perjury in respect of their answers.[131] It was held in *Re Aluminium Fabricators Ltd.*[132] that such answers may be used for the purposes of any application to the court in the context of the winding up proceedings, as under section 297 of the 1963 Act on fraudulent and reckless trading and section 298 of that Act on misfeasance.

---

125 1990 Act, s.240.
126 *ibid.*, s.240(5).
127 1990 Act, s.240(2)(a) and (3).
128 s.16; these are all in respect of liquidations and receiverships.
129 1990 Act, s.179.
130 1963 Act, s.245 (as amended by 1990 Act, s.126).
131 s.245(6); contrast 1990 Act, s.18 regarding investigations into companies, providing that answers given by a person may be used in evidence against him.
132 [1984] I.L.R.M. 399; see *Re Aluminium Fabricators Ltd. (No.2)* O'Hanlon J., May 13, 1983.

Civil Claim

1–57 Depending on the nature of the complaint, there are various civil remedies available to persons aggrieved by company law violations. Thus, companies may sue directors for negligence and for breach of their fiduciary duties to the company; shareholders may sue their company, or its controllers, for breach of the contract contained in the memorandum and articles of association, and for breach of numerous provisions of the Companies Acts. Some of these Acts' most significant provisions explicitly provide for a civil remedy against violations.

1–58 Where a statute imposes some obligation on individuals but does not say that persons who suffer financial loss on account of its requirements being violated are entitled to compensation or to an injunction, it depends very much on the circumstances whether persons injured in consequence possess a right of action. In the leading English case dealing with the question of when persons have a private right of action under regulatory legislation, it was said that:

> "the answer must depend on a consideration of the whole Act and the circumstances, including the preexisting law, in which it was enacted... For instance, if a statutory duty is prescribed but no remedy by way of penalty or otherwise for breach is imposed, it can be assumed that a right of civil action accrues.... But this general rule is subject to exceptions. It may be that, though a specific remedy is provided by the Act, yet the person injured has a personal right of action in addition."[133]

In one instance, however, which concerned an unsuccessful attempt to enjoin a building society from doing business, on the grounds that it had been improperly registered under the Building Societies Acts, Barrington J. suggested that constitutional law considerations may dictate deviation from the English principles governing the availability of a civil remedy.[134]

1–59 Those principles may be summed up as follows.[135] Where the statute establishes some special technique for obtaining the benefit arising from its requirements, then almost invariably it does not create a private or civil right of action. Where the obligation imposed is coupled with a criminal sanction, then, as a general rule, there is no civil remedy; there can be situations where persons who stand to lose because of a proposed violation can obtain an injunction although they

---

133 *Cutler v. Wandsworth Stadium Ltd.* [1949] A.C. 389 at 407.
134 *Irish Permanent Building Society v. Cauldwell* [1981] I.L.R.M. 245 at 254.
135 See generally, Buckley, "Liability in Tort for Breach of Statutory Duty" (1984) 100 L.Q.R. 204.

may not be entitled to damages if the offence had been committed. Even where the provision neither provides for a special remedy nor for prosecution, a court may nonetheless treat its breach as a "mere irregularity" and as not entitling persons in the class intended to have the provision's protection to a personal right of action. American developments in securities law in this regard are instructive. In the past the trend was in favour of implying private remedies out of regulatory statutes but this has been significantly reversed in recent years.[136] There is much to be said for the view that, apart from where it is expressly provided for, the Companies Acts do not grant a civil remedy, or at least a remedy in damages, on the grounds that expressly granting that remedy in various provisions of those Acts implies an intention to exclude it elsewhere.

1–60 One of the few modern cases that addresses this matter directly in the context of company law comes from Australia, *Castlereagh Motels Ltd. v. Davies-Roe Motel,*[137] where a company sued its director for *inter alia* breach of what is section 194 of our 1963 Act. Under it, any director who has a financial interest in a contract that the company proposes to enter into must disclose the nature of that interest at the first board meeting at which the contract is considered; the defendant there had not done so in this case. After analysing the major authorities on liability in damages for breach of statutory duty and the relevant section in its context, the court concluded that it could not detect a legislative intendment that a company should have a private right of action for alleged loss sustained in consequence of a director violating the section. Rather, the general intendment was to ensure that a company's affairs are better administered by preventing directors from possibly abusing their positions.[138]

1–61 Civil actions in the company law field are usually heard on the Chancery side of the High Court; in Britain there is a special Companies section in the Chancery Division.[139] Even though shareholders' rights in their companies have been treated as property rights entitled to constitutional protection, it is almost inconceivable that the Civil Legal Aid Board would provide legal aid or assistance for shareholders' suits that do not arise in the context of family disputes. However,

136 Compare *JJ. Case Co. v. Borak*, 377 U.S. 426 (1964) with *Transamerica Mortgage Advisors Inc v. Lewis*, 444 U.S. 11 (1979).

137 [1966] 2 N.S.W.L.R. 79.

138 *cf.* Lord Gough in *Guinness p.l.c. v. Saunders* [1990] 2 A.C. 663. See also *Conway v. Petronius Clothing Co.* [1978] 1 All E.R. 185 and *I.R.C. v. Goldblatt* [1972] Ch. 498.

139 See generally, A. Boyle and P. Marshall, *Practice and Procedure in the Companies Court* (1997).

it is possible in certain cases for the plaintiff at the outset to obtain an indemnity against costs from the company.[140] Is it also arguable that the legal profession's total ban on contingency fees violates the constitutional right to bring a legal claim?

1–62 A somewhat unusual feature of the Companies Acts is that they contain provisions empowering the court to exonerate persons from civil liability for having committed breaches of the law: a kind of pardoning power. The most far-reaching of these is section 391 of the 1963 Act, which deals with where a company director or other officer is found to have contravened a duty owed to the company. If it is determined that he acted "honestly and reasonably" and that in the light of all the circumstances "ought fairly to be excused" from liability, the court may exonerate him wholly or partly on such terms as it thinks fit. A somewhat similar provision is section 34 of the 1983 Act, which enables the court to exempt persons from liability to the company in respect of payments made in violation of some of that Act's capital integrity requirements. Those exemptions may be granted where it is "just and equitable" to do so, and the section sets out a number of matters that ought to be taken into account in reaching that decision.

Inspectors

1–63 The system of Minister-appointed inspectors, whereby the running of a company may be thoroughly investigated, has been in existence since 1862.[141] Court-appointed inspectors with equivalent functions and powers are the product of the 1990 Act, although a serious question mark lies over the constitutionality of Court-appointed inspectors on separation of powers grounds.[142] Both inspection systems are designed to ensure that the full facts relating to allegations of mismanagement and the like are brought to light and disclosed in an official report. That information may then be used either in a civil claim by aggrieved shareholders or creditors, or in proceedings to have directors restricted or disqualified under Part VIII of the 1990 Act, or in criminal prosecutions or otherwise. Even where the information unearthed is not so used, its publication in a report and any criticisms made therein may have a very considerable impact on the future management of the company and on prospects of those persons whose activities have been the subject of comment. Reports of this nature also give the general public a revealing insight into how some companies' affairs are actually conducted.

---

[140] *Wallersteiner v. Moir* [1975] Q.B. 373, below, para. 10–71.
[141] Companies Act 1862, ss. 56 and 57.
[142] cf. *Gould v. Brown* (1998) 72 A.J.L.R. 375.

1–64 Part II of the 1990 Act (sections 7-24) sets out the relevant provisions. Powers contained therein to compel disclosure of confidential information have withstood challenges maintaining that they contravene the constitutional guarantees of private property and of privacy,[143] and the privilege against self-incrimination.[144]

Preliminary Investigation

1–65 Neither the Minister nor the High Court will appoint an inspector until there seems to be good grounds for doing so. To that end, the 1990 Act empowers the Minister to get information relating to the company in question, where he has a concern about its ownership or management. Those enquiries may be sufficient grounds for appointing an inspector.

1–66 Under section 15 of the 1990 Act, any person with information about the true ownership of shares or debentures in a company may be compelled by the Minister to furnish the required information, where it appears necessary that such ownership be investigated on any of three broad grounds, namely for the effective administration of company law; for the effective discharge of the Minister's functions under any Act; or in the public interest.

1–67 Under section 19 of this Act, the Minister can require that any books and records relating to the company be produced to him or to any official designated by him, where the Minister is of the opinion that there are reasons for believing any of the following, namely there are grounds that suggest that an inspector should be appointed; that the company's affairs have been conducted fraudulently: that its affairs were or are about to be conducted in a manner that is or would be "unfairly prejudicial" to some of its members or otherwise unlawfully; or that the company was formed for any fraudulent or unlawful purpose. Any present or past officer or employee can be required to explain features of those books and records and any such statement can be used subsequently in evidence against that person. Documentation held by a bank can be required only where the Minister is of the view that such material is necessary for investigating the affairs of the bank's customers in question to furnish the information required.[145]

1–68 Under section 20 of this Act, the Minister can obtain a search

---

[143] *Chestervale Properties Ltd v. Hoddle Investments Ltd* [1993] 3 I.R. 35 and *Desmond v. Glackin (No. 2)* [1993] 3 I.R. 67.

[144] *Re National Irish Bank,* Supreme Court, January 21, 1999.

[145] s.23(2).

warrant in the District Court in respect of any books and documents that can be required under the above two sections (and section 14). Such force as may be reasonably necessary can be used to enforce that warrant.

Appointment of the Inspectors

1–69 One or more inspectors can be appointed by the Minister or by the High Court, as the case may be. The Ministerial appointee is required to investigate and report on the company's membership:

> "And otherwise with respect to the company for the purpose of determining the true persons who are or have been financially interested in the success or failure (real or apparent) of the company or able to control or materially to influence the policy of the company."[146]

The exact meaning of this remains to be determined and whether, and if so, to what extent it confines the scope of such enquiries as the inspector may carry out and report on. On the face of things, the above seems to be confined to the real or apparent ownership or control of the company. A warrant appointing an inspector may define and limit the scope of his investigation.

1–70 The grounds in section 14(2) for making a Ministerial appointment are extremely wide, namely where there are circumstances suggesting that an inspection is necessary either for the effective administration of company law, for the effective discharge of any of the Minister's statutory functions or in the public interest. It would seem that there is no implied obligation to give the company in question advance notice of an intention to appoint an inspector.[147] Where the appointment is being made on "public interest" grounds, it has been held that the nature of that interest be disclosed in the warrant of appointment.[148]

1–71 Unlike the position in Britain, where otherwise the law is very similar, inspectors can also be appointed by the High Court. This may be done on the Minister's own application where the Court is satisfied that the circumstances suggest any of the following,[149] namely fraud in the formation or the management of the company, or the conduct of its affairs; those affairs being conducted unlawfully or in a manner that "unfairly prejudices" some of the members; persons connected with

---

146 s.14(1) and *Lyons v. Curran* [1993] I.L.R.M. 375.
147 cf. *Century National Merchant Bank v. Davies* [1998] A.C. 628.
148 *Probets v. Glackin* [1993] 3 I.R. 134.
149 s.8.

its formation or management have, in that capacity, been found guilty of fraud, misfeasance or other misconduct; or the company's members not being given all of the information regarding its affairs that they might expect. Further, on the application of the company itself, or any director or creditor, or a substantial minority of its members, the Court has a general discretion to appoint an inspector.[150] No grounds are stipulated for making such appointments; all that the 1990 Act states is that the application must be supported by such evidence as the Court may require, including such evidence as may be prescribed, and the Court may require a sum of money to be lodged to cover security for costs, not exceeding £100,000.

Conduct of Inspection

1–72 Part II of the 1990 Act says comparatively little about how inspections should be carried out, leaving it to the court to lay down such ground rules as the overriding requirement of fair procedures requires. Any officer or agent of the company being investigated can be compelled to produce any book or document he has relating to the company, and to meet the inspector when so requested and to furnish him with all reasonable assistance.[151] A similar obligation rests on any other person the inspector considers has information concerning the company's affairs. Details of any bank account maintained by any of its directors, whether alone or jointly with others and whether in the State or elsewhere, can be required, provided money linked with the company specified has gone through that account; in this context, a director includes any past director, any person "connected with" a director[152] and any present or past "shadow director". Banker-customer confidentiality is overriden by section 10[153] but material covered by legal professional privilege is exempt from compulsory disclosure under this part of the 1990 Act.[154]

1–73 An inspector may interrogate under oath any officer or agent of the company and any other person he regards as having information concerning its affairs.[155] Officers and agents for the purpose of disclosure of documents and of interrogation include the company's bankers, solicitors and auditors.[156] These enquiries are always conducted in

---

150 s.7.
151 s.10.
152 See below para. 5–14.
153 *Glackin v. Trustee Savinges Bank* [1993] 3 I.R. 55.
154 s.23(1); cf. *Corporate Affairs Commission v. Yuill* 172 C.L.R. 319 (1991)
155 s.10(4).
156 s.10(7).

private[157] and information furnished to inspectors is not made public other than in the interim or the final report made to the Minister or to the court. Usually, a transcript is kept of such examinations as are carried out.

1–74 The questioning of a witness should not be done in an oppressive manner.[158] It has been held that a witness cannot be required to sign a confidentiality undertaking before certain factual matters are put to him.[159] Where allegations of wrongdoing by named individuals are being investigated, it is possible that those persons should be given an opportunity to cross-examine their principal accusers who give evidence. At least, it would seem that, in the National Irish Bank inspection of 1999, such an opportunity was furnished by the inspectors when court proceedings on this very question were imminent.

1–75 Information covered by legal professional privilege need not be disclosed.[160] Part II of the 1990 Act is silent about the traditional privilege against self-incrimination, but in *Re National Irish Bank Ltd*,[161] the Supreme Court held that this privilege could not be invoked. Although the privilege has a constitutional dimension, the public interest in combating fraud, and especially in uncovering possible malpractice and illegality in the banking system, was held sufficient to justify displacing the privilege. However, the extent to which answers given to coercive questioning can be used as evidence in subsequent prosecutions was held to be a matter for determination by the trial judge at that stage.

1–76 Although the strict rules of evidence do not apply when persons are being questioned on oath here, in reaching their conclusions inspectors are likely to treat hearsay with considerable scepticism, if not disregard it entirely on central aspects of the enquiry. Unless safeguards are adhered to, hearsay evidence can be extremely unreliable.[162]

1–77 In a series of cases principally arising from an inspection into the events behind Telecom Éireann's purchase of a prominent site at Ballsbridge in 1990, attempts were made to restrict the extent of docu-

---

[157] *Hearts of Oaks Assurance Co. v. Attorney General* [1932] A.C. 392; see too 1990 Act, s.21. cf. *Johns v. Australian Securities Comm.* 178 C.L.R. 408 (1993) and *Britisn Commonwealth Holdings plc. v. Barclays de Zoete Wedd Ltd* [1999] 1 B.C.L.C. 86.

[158] *Re Mirror Group Newspapers plc* [1999] 1 B.C.L.C. 690.

[159] *ibid.*

[160] See above, n.153.

[161] [1999] 1 I.L.R.M. 321.

[162] *Re K.* Supreme Court, January 29, 1999.

mentation being sought and the range of questions being put, but those efforts were rejected.[163]

1–78 Where persons are likely to be criticised in an inspector's report, they are entitled to be given copies of the intended criticism, so that they can comment on it before the report is published.[164]

Aftermath

1–79 The process concludes with the inspector delivering his report. In the case of a Ministerial appointee, no special provision is made for reporting. In the case of a court appointee, he must make his final report to the court.[165] But he may be required by the court to make one or more interim reports before concluding his investigation. If during those enquiries he comes across evidence of an offence being committed, he may so inform the court without making any formal report on the matter. Court-appointed inspectors must also deliver a copy of their report to the Minister and there are a variety of person and bodies to whom the inspector may be directed by the court to furnish copies, namely the persons who sought the inspection; any person whose conduct is referred to in the report; the company's auditors; any member of the company; any other person whose financial interests seem to be affected by the report's contents; and the Central Bank.

1–80 The court may direct that the report should be published. However, in such cases and where the report is to be disseminated among any of the above-mentioned parties, the court may order that certain sensitive matters be omitted from the report.[166] On being so published, the report's contents are privileged.[167]

1–81 In the light of the report's contents, the court may direct that the company be wound up. In addition, section 12(1)(b) empowers the court to make orders:

> "For the purpose of remedying any disability suffered by any person whose interests were adversely affected by the conduct of the affairs of the company, provided that . . . the court shall have regard to the interests of any other persons who may be adversely affected by the order."

What exactly this means remains to be determined. It is unlikely to be

---

[163] Above, n.143 and n.153.
[164] *Maxwell v. Department of Trade and Industry* [1974] Q.B. 523.
[165] s.11.
[166] s.11(4).
[167] s.23(3).
[168] s.18.

regarded as conferring an entirely new discretionary jurisdiction to grant injunctions and to award compensation in the light of the contents of the report. Such a construction may very well render the subsection unconstitutional, as being overborad and void for vagueness. Most likely, it means that the court can give procedural directions that facilitate the bringing of proceedings by aggrieved parties, such as for "misfeasance" under section 298 of the 1963 Act.

1–82 Any answer give to a question put by an inspector may be used against the witness in any subsequent proceedings.[168] Further, by section 22 of the 1990 Act, the report itself is stated to be "admissible in any civil proceedings as evidence of the facts set out therein without further proof unless the contrary is shown". This innovation of 1990, to which there is nothing similar in any comparable jurisdiction, would seem to be unconstitutional[169] because it has had the effect of rendering the inspector the judge in the case and, further, unless the inspector allowed cross-examination and excluded hearsay evidence, enables a case to be made against the person on the basis of hearsay and compounded by no testing through cross-examination.

1–83 Finally, there is the question of the expenses of conducting the inspection. These are borne in the first instance by the Minister but the court has a broad discretion to direct that all or part of those expenses be borne by either the person who is the subject of the report or by the person who applied for the investigation.[170] Additionally, where as a result of the investigation, a person is convicted of indictment of an offence, or is ordered to pay damages or to restore property, or indeed he obtains damages or property is returned to him, he can be required to repay all or part of the expenses incurred.

Banning/Restricting Directors

1–84 Part VII of the Companies Act 1990, (sections 149–168), provides for placing restrictions on directors of companies that were wound up and found to be insolvent; those restrictions can even extend to the outright banning of persons' involvement in the management of companies for a prescribed period. Apart from grounds of fraud and the like, restrictions can be imposed for persistent default in complying with the Companies Acts' requirements. It would seem, however, that the court is not particularly severe in the manner in which it applies

---

[169] *cf. County Glen plc v. Carway* [1998] 2 I.R. 540.

[170] s.12, e.g. *Minister for Industry and Commerce v. Siúcre Éireann c.p.t.* [1992] 2 I.R. 215.

Part VII of that Act. In January 1998, only one person was entirely disqualified from being a director and there were 118 persons who were restricted in so acting.

Public Regulation

1–85 There are a number of public officials whose task, or part of whose function, is to monitor compliance with the company laws.

The Minister

1–86 The Companies Acts assign various functions to the Minister for Industry and Commerce, who now is the Minister for Enterprise, Trade and Employment. For example, the Minister appoints the registrar of companies and is responsible for maintaining and administering the companies' registry;[171] determines what names companies may not be registered with[172] and whether a limited company may omit the term Ltd. from its name;[173] decides which accounting bodies shall be recognised for the purposes of auditors' qualifications;[174] can call an annual general meeting of the company if it has not done so;[175] can appoint an auditor where the shareholders have not appointed one.[176] The Minister must make an annual report to the Oireachtas on matters under the Companies Acts.[177] Perhaps the Minister's most far-reaching powers are under sections 14, 15 and 19 of the 1990 Act to appoint inspectors to investigate the affairs of a company, to require the disclosure of specified information and the production of specified documents; these give the Minister very inquisitorial powers over companies, including foreign-registered companies which are carrying on business in the State.

The Registrar of Companies

1–87 The registrar of companies is responsible for administering the registry of companies, which is located in Parnell Square, Dublin. Before a registered company can be formed, the registrar must be satisfied that all of the statutory prerequisites have been met; he will then issue the certificate of incorporation.[178] Copies of special resolutions

---

171 1963 Act, s.368.
172 *ibid.*, s.21.
173 1963 Act, s.24.
174 1990 Act, s.187(1)(a).
175 1963 Act, s.131(3).
176 *ibid.*, s.160(4).
177 *ibid.*, s.392.
178 *ibid.*, ss. 17-22 and 1983 Act, Pt II.

and the like must be registered,[179] and every company must deliver to the registrar each year an annual return.[180] He can strike off the register companies that are no longer carrying on business or that fail to make returns.[181] The registrar has authority to institute prosecutions for breaches of numerous provisions of the Companies Acts, such as those concerning the annual accounts and returns, and liquidations and receiverships.[182] On payment of the appropriate fee, any person is entitled to inspect the documents kept at the registry of companies and to have certified copies made of them.[183]

The Revenue Commissioners

1–88 The Revenue Commissioners play an indirect role in ensuring that the laws regarding companies are complied with. If, for example, a company's accounts do not satisfy the statutory requirements it is likely that they will not be accepted for the purposes of determining how much corporation tax it must pay. It would appear that *ultra vires* expenditure is not a deductible expense for taxation purposes,[184] but this may no longer be the case in the light of section 8(1) of the 1963 Act.[185]

HARMONISATION OF COMPANY LAW

1–89 A number of significant measures bearing directly on company law have been adopted by the European Communities (E.C.)[186] and it would seem that the future development of Irish company law will be heavily influenced by initiatives from that source. So far, two major Companies Acts have been adopted as a result of E.C. requirements — the Acts of 1983[187] and of 1986[188] — and compliance with E.C. require-

---

179 1963 Act, s.143.
180 *ibid.*, ss. 125–129.
181 1982 Act, ss. 11 and 12 (as amended by 1990 Act, s.245).
182 *ibid.*, s.16.
183 1963 Act, s.370.
184 *cf. Robinson v. Scott Bader Co.* [1981] 1 W.L.R. 1135.
185 See below, para. 13.15 *et seq.*
186 See generally E. Stein, *Harmonisation of European Company Law* (1971); J. Dine and P. Hughes, *E. C. Company Law* (loose leaf); Werlauff, "The Development of Community Company Law" 17 Eur. L.J. 207 (1992); B. Cheffins, *Company Law: Theory Structure and Operation* (1997) Chap. 9; D. Prentice, *E.E.C. Directives on Company Law and Financial Markets* (1991) and Butterworths' *Compendium a E.C. Company Law* (1990).
187 See generally, M. Forde, "The Companies (Amendment) Act 1983" (1983) 18 Ir. Jur. 289.
188 See generally, S. Kelleher, *Companies (Amendment) Act 1986* (1987).

ments also gave rise to Part V of the 1990 Act on insider dealing and sections 90-96 of the 1990 Act regarding disclosing acquisitions of significant shareholdings in quoted companies, as well as to numerous statutory instruments.

Normative Competence

1–90 The legal authority of central government to legislate in the company law domain has been a controversial constitutional matter in a number of federal states, such as Australia,[189] Canada[190] and the U.S.A. The U.S. federal government possesses extensive powers in this area under the Constitution's Commerce Clause but has confined its intervention to mainly regulating public trading in securities.[191] On various occasions calls have been made for a U.S. federal statute governing most major aspects of company law but these have never won widespread support — neither among the general public nor politicians, or even the legal fraternity. A considerable degree of uniformity nevertheless exists among the States in that they tend to follow the model laws laid down in proposed uniform statutes adopted by the influential American Law Institute.

1–91 The general law-making competence of the European Communities may be divided into three broad categories.[192] First, there is the "national treatment" power, which is the authority to prescribe measures aimed at prohibiting discrimination on the grounds of nationality against citizens of E.C. Member States in matters within the Rome Treaty's ambit. Next, there is the "common treaty rules" power, by which is meant authority to adopt measures with a view to putting into effect particular policies contained in the Rome Treaty, for instance Article 51 on the preservation of social security entitlements, equal pay for equal work the right of establishment. As regards companies specifically, there is Article 293 (previously Art. 220) which requires Member States to enter into negotiations on the mutual recognition of companies.

---

189 Culminating in *New South Wales v. Commonwealth* (1990) 64 A.L.J.L.R. 157, striking down provisions of the Corporations Act 1990 (Cwlt.). See generally, H. Ford et al., *Principles of Corporations Law* (9th ed., 1999), pp. 42–49.

190 See generally, B. Welling, *Corporate Law in Canada* (2nd ed., 1991), pp. 11–28..

191 See generally, L. Loss and J. Seligman, *Securities Regulation* (3rd ed., 1989-90), Vols 1–4 vols.; Fleischer, "Federal Corporation Law: An Assessment" (1965) 78 Harv. L. Rev. 1146 and Cary, "Federalism and Corporate Law: Reflections Upon Delaware" (1974) 83 Yale L.J 663.

192 See generally, P. Hogg, *Constitutional Law of Canada* (4th ed., 1997), Chap. 23; B. McMahon and F. Murphy, *European Community Law in Ireland* (1989) Chaps. 9, 20.

Finally, there is the "approximation of laws" power under Article 94 (previously Art. 100):

> "they shall, acting unanimously on a proposal from the Commission, issue directives for the approximation of such provisions laid down by law, regulation or administrative action in Member States as directly affect the establishment or functioning of the common market."

As regards companies, this is supplemented by Article 44(3)(g) (previously Art. 54(3)(g)) from the part of the Treaty dealing with freedom of establishment:

> "the Council shall . . . set out the general conditions under which freedom of establishment is to be attained . . . in particular: by co-ordinating to the necessary extent the safeguards which, for the protection of the interests of members and others, are required by Member States of companies or firms . . . with a view to making such safeguards equivalent throughout the Community."

1–93 An argument had been made that, for instance, the Draft Fifth Directive concerning worker-directors[193] lies outside the E.C.'s powers, because this measure does not deal with primarily economic and commercial matters but with social affairs which, it was said, are a peripheral concern of the communities and do not directly affect the Common Market. Against that, judgments of the European Court of Justice were cited, such as that in April 1967 where it was said that the Community "is not merely an economic union, but is at the same time intended, by common action, to ensure social progress and seek the constant improvement of the living and working conditions of their peoples, as is emphasised by the preamble of the Treaty.[194] In contrast with Directives in the area of employment and social affairs,[195] the normative competence of the E.C. institutions in the field of company law has not engendered litigation before the European Court in Luxembourg.

Legislative Techniques

1–94 The E.C.'s prescribing power may be exercised in four different ways, by Regulation, Directive, Recommendation and Opinion.[196] Since the principal measures adopted so far in the company law field have

---

[193] This draft has gone through several versions; see below, para. 15.11.
[194] *Defrenne v. Sabena* (Case 43/75) [1976] E.C.R. 455, para. 10.
[195] See generally, B. Bercusson, *European Labour Law* (1996),
[196] See generally, T.C. Hartley, *The Foundations of European Community Law* (3rd ed., 1998) ch.7.

been by way of Directive,[197] and because virtually all the existing proposed measures are intended to be Directives, it is not necessary to consider here the other forms. Directives are described in Article 249 (formerly Art. 189) of the Rome Treaty as instruments with which the E.C. Council and Commission "carry out their task" and which are "binding, as to the result to be achieved, upon each Member State to which it is addressed, but shall leave the national authorities the choice of form and methods." Ever since the *Van Duyn* case,[198] which concerned the *ordre public* exception to the freedom of movement for workers, it has been accepted that Directives can have some "direct effect" in national law, in that individuals may possess rights under them against public authorities.

1–95 For several years there was acute controversy about whether, or in what circumstances, Directives possess what has been called "horizontal effect", by which is meant they impose obligations on individuals. This very matter would not arise if Member States always did what they are required to do by Directives, namely, introduce national legislation implementing the Directives' terms. Eventually in the *Marshall* case[199] in 1986, which concerned Directives regarding equal pay for equal work, the European Court held that a Directive "may not of itself impose obligations on an individual" and that "a provision of a Directive may not be relied upon as such against such a person."[200] Thus, companies, their shareholders and directors are not subject to any enforceable legal obligations where a Directive on a particular matter has been made but it has not yet been incorporated into the law of Ireland, either by way of legislation or a statutory instrument.

Measures Adopted

1–96 Most of the E.C. measures in the Company Law field are identified for convenience by reference to numbers — the 1st, the 2nd, etc., Directives. A question that will arise when measures giving effect to various Directives are being considered by the courts is whether, in interpreting the Act or statutory instrument in question, the court should have regard to the very terms of the Directive. Almost certainly, the answer will be yes. In a case involving the "nullity" of companies, the European Court has ruled that, when interpreting any provision of national law, irrespective of whether it was passed before or after a

---

197 The main exception being the proposed Statute for a "European Company" [1990] 1 C.M.L.R. 120.
198 *Van Duyn v. Home Office* (Case 41/74) [1974] E.C.R. 337.
199 *Marshall v. Southampton etc. Health Authority* (Case 152/84) [1986] E.C.R. 723.
200 *ibid.* at 749 and *El Corte Ingles SA v. Rivero (Case* C–192/94) [1996] E.C.R. 1281.

Directive was adopted, the national court must look to the relevant Directive when applying the law.[201] Indeed, in Britain courts have even looked behind the Directives themselves to the national legislation in France and Germany which inspired adoption of a particular measure.[202] It remains to be seen whether Irish courts will resort to comparative law techniques when confronted with such questions.

First Directive

1–97 The First E.C. Company Law Directive[203] was adopted in March 1968. As is explained in detail in Chapter 13 below, it deals mainly with the relations between companies and persons seeking to enter into transactions with them; its primary objective was to remove several legal "traps" in the way of dealing with companies, notably the pre-incorporation contract rule, the *ultra vires* rule and the rule that companies' articles of association could restrict the contracting authority of directors and other agents. In fact the first two of these traps had been removed by sections 37(2) and 8(1) of the 1963 Act, in terms almost identical to those contained in the Directive. The other trap was substantially removed by Statutory Instrument No. 163 of 1973.

Second Directive

1–98 The Second E.C. Company Law Directive[204] was adopted in December 1976. As is explained in detail in Chapter 7 below, it deals mainly with the protection of companies' paid up capital; it aims at ensuring that companies obtain reasonably equivalent consideration for shares they issue and that contributed capital is not improperly repaid or dissipated among the shareholders. Its provisions were implemented by the 1983 Act; some of those provisions do not apply to private limited companies.

Third and Sixth Directives

1–99 The Third and the Sixth E.C. Company Law Directives[205] were adopted in October 1978 and in December 1982, respectively. As is explained below, they will have little practical impact on companies. They deal with a form of merger and of division of a company that is most uncommon in this country. Effect was given to those measures

---

201 *Marleasing S.A. v. La Comercial Int'l de Alimentation* (C-106/89) [1990] E.C.R. 4135.
202 *Phonogram Ltd. v. Lane* [1982] Q.B. 938.
203 [1968] O.J. No. L65/8 (special ed.).
204 [1977] O.J. L26/1.
205 [1978] O.J. L295/36, [1982] O.J. L378/47.

by Statutory Instrument No. 137 of 1987, which applies only to public limited companies.[206]

Fourth Directive

1–100 The Fourth E.C. Company Law Directive,[207] which was adopted in July 1978, is of profound importance to company accountants and auditors. As is explained in Chapter 8 below, it sets out various rules regarding limited companies' accounts, formats for those accounts, the contents of reports that must accompany accounts; it also deals with the annual return of financial information to the registrar of companies. Its provisions were implemented by the 1986 Act.

Eighth Directive

1–101 The Eighth E.C. Company Law Directive, adopted in April 1984,[208] sets out minimum standards of education and competency that persons must possess before they can be entitled to act as a company's auditors. Because the standards presently being applied in Ireland are at least as stringent as those set out in the Directive, implementation of this measure did not demand extensive legislative changes in Part X of the 1990 Act.[209]

Seventh Directive

1–102 The Seventh E.C. Company Law Directive, of June 1983[210] sets out rules regarding the annual accounts of groups of companies, including the contents and formats of those accounts; it complements the Fourth Directive, which deals with the accounts of single companies. The measure acknowledges that many businesses are conducted through groups of companies and that, in order to fully comprehend the financial circumstances of the business, there must be consolidated or group accounts. This was implemented by the European Communities (Accounts) Regulations 1993 (S.I. No. 396).

Eleventh Directive

1–103 Under this Directive, adopted in December 1989,[211] companies which have a branch in one E.C. State but which are registered elsewhere are required to disclose various matters in the State where the

---

[206] Below, para. 12–51.
[207] [1978] O.J. L222/11.
[208] [1983] O.J. L193/1.
[209] As amended by S.I. No. 259 of 1992.
[210] [1984] O.J. L126/28.
[211] [1989] O.J. L395/36.

branch is located, including the company's own annual report. It has been implemented by the European Communities (Branch Disclosures) Regulations 1993 (S.I. No. 395).

Twelfth Directive

1–104 Under this Directive, also adopted in December 1989,[212] it became possible to have private limited companies with one single member only. Several E.C. States' laws already provide for the true "one person" company. In practice there were one person companies in this country and in Britain; the owner of the company would hold all the issued shares but one, and that one share would be held by someone else in trust for the owner. This Directive was implemented by the European Communities (Single Member Private Limited Companies) Regulations 1994 (S.I. No. 275).

Prospectus Directive

1–105 Under this Directive, adopted in April 1989,[213] the contents of every prospectus issued in connection with an offer of securities to the investing public will be subject to uniform requirements across the Community. It was implemented by the European Communities (Transferable Securities and Stock Exchange) Regulations 1992 (S.I. No. 202).[214]

Stock Exchange Directives

1–106 Directives were adopted, in March 1979 and in March 1980,[215] respectively, that deal with stock exchange matters, the conditions to be satisfied for a company obtaining a quotation for its securities on a stock exchange and the information which companies must publish when issuing securities which will be quoted on an exchange. There also is a Directive of February 1982[216] requiring quoted companies to publish interim half-yearly accounts. All of these Directives were implemented by Statutory Instrument No. 282 of 1984.[217]

Insider Dealing Directive

1–107 A Directive of November 1989[218] co-ordinates rules regarding

---

[212] [1989] O.J. L395/40.
[213] [1989] O.J. L124/8 (Directive 89/298).
[214] See below, paras 6–80 *et seq*.
[215] [1979] O.J. L66/21, [1980] O.J. No. L10/11.
[216] [1982] O.J. L48/26.
[217] See below, paras 6–80 *et seq*.
[218] [1989] O.J. L334/30.

what is commonly referred to as insider dealing. Its provisions have been implemented in Part V of the 1990 Act.[219]

Disclosure of the Major Share Transactions Directive

1–108 The Transparency Directive of December, 1988[220] deals with disposals and acquisitions of substantial shareholdings in quoted companies. Those transactions must be disclosed to the company in question and to the Stock Exchange and the beneficial owner of those shares must make himself known. Those provisions were given effect in sections 89-96 of the 1990 Act.[221]

E.C. Measures Not Yet Adopted in Ireland

1–109 The following are the principal E.C. measures in the company law and related fields which have not been adopted in Ireland. The fact that appropriate action was not taken to render them fully effective here does not mean that they are without any significant impact in domestic law. For it has been held that the State and all its agencies are bound by the provisions of Directives if those provisions are unambiguous and are capable of immediate observance. For instance, the U.K. State-owned public utility, British Gas p.l.c., was held to be bound by the provisions of a Directive against sex discrimination in employment even though that Directive had not been brought into force in Britain.[222] As a matter of Community law, public authorities will not be permitted to hide behind their failure to implement Directives. This doctrine, however, is not particularly important in the company law field because it will be very rarely that attempts will be made to enforce these Directives against public agencies; ordinarily, the defendant will be a private company (in the sense of not being an instrumentality of the State), individual directors, investors and the like. A very significant development in late 1991 has been the decision of the European Court of Justice that damages may be awarded against the State for failure to implement a Directive.[223] Liability was said to arise provided three conditions are met. The Directive must purport to confer rights on individuals; the content of those rights must be readily ascertainable from the very terms of the Directive; finally, there must be a causal link between the failure of implementation and the loss suffered.

---

[219] See below, paras 5–150 *et seq*.
[220] [1988] O.J. L348/62.
[221] See below, para. 9–92.
[222] *Foster v. British Gas plc.* (Case C–188/89) [1990] E.C.R. 3133.

1–110 There are some draft Directives still being considered by the E.U. authorities., most notably the controversial Draft Fifth Directive on the Structures of Companies,[224] which provides for employee representation on the boards of public companies, the Draft Ninth Directive on Groups of Companies,[225] the Draft Tenth on Cross Border Mergers of Public Companies[226] and the Draft Thirteenth Directive on Take-Overs[227] which will regulate several aspects of takeovers and mergers. Both the E.C. Council and also the Council of Europe have promulgated conventions on bankruptcy/insolvency.[228]

---

223 *Francovich v. Italian Republic* (C–6/90 and 9/90) [1991] E.C.R. 5357.
224 Doe. Ill/1639/84.
225 [1985] O.J. C 23/11.
226 Doe. XV/63187 rev. 1.
227 E.C. Bulletin, supp. 2 (1982).
228 See generally, I. Fletcher, *The Law of Insolvency* (2nd ed., 1996), pp. 769–782.

2

Company Formation

2–01 By far the most convenient way of setting up business as a registered company is to buy an already-formed company from one of those firms of solicitors or accountants that specialise in selling companies "off-the-shelf". The purchasers would then make whatever alterations to that company they deem necessary, like changing its name, the address of its registered office, directors, capital structure, articles of association. Alternatively, they may decide to form a new company themselves, which in any event is not a particularly onerous or complex task. All that is needed is one or two founders and a signed memorandum and articles of association; these documents must be accompanied by a statutory declaration and a cheque for capital tax, and be registered with the registrar of companies. A number of additional formalities must be complied with before some companies can commence doing business.

THE PRINCIPAL TYPES OF REGISTERED COMPANY

2–02 Like most human institutions, there is an infinite variety of registered companies; there are large and small companies, companies with closely-held and with widely dispersed shareholdings, profit-orientated and non-profit companies, indigenous and transnational companies. Registered companies fall into a number of distinct legal categories: principally, limited and unlimited companies, private and public companies, one-person companies, public limited companies and guarantee companies.

Limited Company

2–03 A company may be registered either with limited liability or with unlimited liability.[1] One of the main reasons why persons choose to do business through the vehicle of registered companies is to obtain

---

[1] 1963 Act, ss. 5(2)(a), 207(1)(d).

the privilege of limited liability. By this is meant that, if the business fails, the owners of the limited company are not personally responsible for all of its unpaid liabilities. Their obligations in respect of the company's debts are measured by how much, if anything, remains unpaid, or outstanding, on the shares they own.[2] An alternative method of limiting liability, which in practice is confined to "non-profit" companies, is by guarantee: the company's shareholders or members undertake to contribute towards its liabilities up to a stated amount in the event of it being wound up.[3] No company, whether limited or unlimited, may increase in any way its members' liability to it or otherwise oblige them to pay it money, unless the member has consented in writing to do so.[4]

Unlimited Company

2–04 It is not surprising that there are comparatively few unlimited companies, since their members can be held liable without limit for the company's debts. There nevertheless are some advantages in having the unlimited form.[5] These companies are exempted from many of the Companies Acts' disclosure requirements, notably disclosing financial information that the 1986 Act requires to be contained in the annual return to the registrar of companies and, accordingly, provide their individual members with greater secrecy about their affairs. Many of the Companies Acts' rules on capital integrity do not apply to unlimited companies, so that it is relatively easy for them to return contributed capital to their members. Tax avoidance schemes often make use of unlimited companies. The Companies Acts place a numerical ceiling on the size of partnerships other than of accountants or solicitors;[6] an unlimited company, therefore, is used where more than twenty persons, or more than ten in the case of bankers, wish to engage in business in common but for one reason or another desire unlimited liability. Unlimited companies do not have to pay *ad valorem* stamp duty on being registered[7] and they enjoy certain other fiscal advantages.[8] Because they possess separate legal personality, unlimited companies are fundamentally different from partnerships, with the consequence that unpaid company creditors have no direct claim

---

2 1963 Act, s.207(1)(d).

3 *ibid.*, ss. 5(2)(b) and 207(1)(e) and (3); see below, para. 14–65.

4 *ibid.*, s.27; see below, para. 9.05.

5 See generally, Rice, "The Unlimited Company — An Anachronism or a Modern Opportunity" (1963) 27 Conv. 442.

6 1963 Act, ss. 372 and 376 (as amended by 1982 Act, s.13). See generally, Calvert, "The Prohibition of Large Associations" (1962) 26 Conv. 253.

7 Finance Act 1973, ss. 67–68.

8 *cf.* Corporation Tax Act 1976, Pt IX.

against the company's members. Instead, those creditors must secure the company's winding up and the liquidator will then attempt to recover outstanding amounts from the members with unlimited liability.[9]

2–05 The 1963 Act allows for limited companies where the liability of the directors, or of the managing director, is unlimited.[10] Any shareholder who knows that the company is carrying on business for more than six months with less than the statutory minimum membership becomes severally liable for company debts contracted during that time.[11]

Private Company

2–06 A company may be registered as either a private or a public company.[12] The paradigm private company is the one-person or the small family trading concern. But some major firms are private too and the portfolios of very rich persons tend to be held by their private companies, which usually have unlimited liability as well. The principal advantages of being private are that, provided the company is small or medium sized, a comparatively restricted amount of information about the company's financial and trading position need be disclosed to the public via the registry of companies.[13] Also many of the rules that derive from E.C. Directives apply only to public limited companies. A public company is defined as any registered company which is not private.[14] By contrast, under the British Companies Act 1985, there is a somewhat elaborate definition of public company and the private company is the residual category there. For the purposes of valuing shares for capital acquisitions tax purposes, there is a special definition of a private company.[15]

2–07 In order to form a private company, there must be a minimum of one or two members[16] and the articles of association must provide for the following:[17] that, apart from worker/shareholders, its membership shall not exceed fifty, that the transferability of its shares is sub-

---

9 1963 Act, s.207(1).
10 *ibid.*, ss. 197, 198, 207(2).
11 *ibid.*, s.36.
12 1963 Act, s.5(1).
13 1986 Act, ss. 11, 12; see below, paras 8–45 *et seq.*
14 1983 Act, s.2(1).
15 Capital Acquisitions Tax Act 1976, s.16(2).
16 1963 Act, s.5(1) and below, n. 22.
17 *ibid.*, s.33

ject to some restriction and that the public should not be invited to subscribe for shares or debentures in it. Part II of Table A, which is in the first schedule to the 1963 Act, contains model articles of association for private companies.

2–08 Where a private company in fact contravenes any of the requirements that its articles of association must contain about maximum membership, share transfers and public offers, it does not thereby lose its private status. Instead, it becomes no longer entitled to several of the legal privileges of this status.[18] But, on application, the court is empowered to permit it retain these privileges where the breach of the articles was accidental or happened through inadvertence or some other sufficient cause, or where it is "just and equitable" to do so.[19] Where a private company offers its shares or debentures to the public, or agrees to allot its securities to members of the public, the company and its responsible officers commit a criminal offence.[20] A private company becomes a public company when any of the above-mentioned three requirements are removed from its articles of association.[21]

2–09 Since 1994, when the E.C. Council Directive of 1989 on single-member companies was implemented,[22] it has been possible to form a private company with just one member only. Further, a private company with two or more members can convert itself into a single-member company.

Public Limited Company — "p.l.c."

2–10 A new kind of company, the public limited company, or "p.l.c." for short, was inaugurated by the 1983 Act. This Act was passed principally in order to give effect to the E.C. Second Directive on Company Law, which expresses itself as applying to the public company limited by shares or limited by guarantee and possessing a share capital. Had this new entity, the p.l.c., not been created, many small firms that were not private companies would have been made subject to various onerous obligations deriving from that Directive. In the past, the law made no distinction, apart from the very obvious one, between public companies with and without limited liability. But from 1983 on, in order to be a public company with limited liability (p.l.c.) a number of requirements, designed principally to protect creditors from being victims of

---

[18] 1963 Act, s.34(1).
[19] *ibid.*, s.34(2).
[20] 1983 Act, s.21.
[21] 1963 Act, s.35.
[22] European Communities (Single Member Private Limited Companies) Regulations, 1994 (S.I. No. 275 of 1994).

under-capitalisation and over-trading, must be satisfied.

2–11 In order to become and remain a p.l.c., the company must have a minimum authorised share capital of at least £30,000;[23] at least one-quarter of the nominal amount must have been paid up on its issued share capital, together with any premium on its shares;[24] it must not have allotted any shares it offered for subscription when the offer was under-subscribed;[25] it must not have allotted shares in return for services contracts[26] or for contracts that can be performed more than five years from the allotment date;[27] an independent valuation must have been made of non-cash consideration transferred in order to acquire shares in it[28] and also of major transactions between it and its first members during its first two years' commercial existence;[29] shares taken by its subscribers must have been paid for in cash;[30] any lien or other charge on its own shares is void;[31] and it may not pay a dividend if it is insolvent in the sense of its net assets being less than its called up share capital and its undistributable reserves.[32] A company that is limited by guarantee and having a share capital cannot become a p.l.c.[33]

Guarantee Company

2–12 In the case of most limited companies, the members of the company will own shares in them and the limit of their liability for the company's unpaid debts will be defined by reference to the amount unpaid on those shares. But it is possible to be a member of a company without holding any transferable shares in it; companies can have a form of personal membership. A guarantee company falls into this category. It has members, who are not shareholders, but those members have undertaken or guaranteed to be responsible for its unpaid debts up to a prescribed amount.[34] The extent of their liability to the company is defined by the terms of their guarantees. Since 1994 it has been

---

23 1983 Act, ss. 5(2), 19(1), 17(1).
24 *ibid.*, s.28.
25 *ibid.*, s.22.
26 *ibid.*, s.26(2).
27 *ibid.*, s.29.
28 *ibid.*, ss. 30, 31.
29 *ibid.*, ss. 32, 33.
30 *ibid.*, s.35.
31 *ibid.*, s.44.
32 *ibid.*, s.46.
33 *ibid.*, s.7.
34 1963 Act, s.5(2)(b).
35 See n. 22, above.

possible to have single-member companies limited by guarantee as well as by shares.[35] Guarantee companies almost invariably are established for reasons other than engaging in commercial activities, such as for sporting, cultural, philanthropic and other non-profit objectives.[36]

2–13 There also is a hybrid form of guarantee company; it has shareholders who also have guaranteed to pay the company's liabilities up to a specified amount. Companies of this hybrid nature cannot become p.l.c.s;[37] but such companies which existed when the 1983 Act came into force are not affected by this prohibition.[38]

MEMORANDUM OF ASSOCIATION

2–14 Every registered company must have a memorandum and articles of association.[39] The 1963 Act's first schedule and the 1983 Act's second schedule set out the forms that the memoranda for the different kinds of company should take, notably as companies limited by shares (Table B), unlimited companies (Table E), guarantee companies (Tables C and D), p.l.c.s limited by shares (1983 Act) and p.l.c.s limited by guarantee (1983 Act). The memorandum must be printed, be duly stamped and be signed by each founder (or "subscriber"), which signature must be witnessed and attested.[40] This document is the company's fundamental law and may be amended only in the circumstances and in the manner as provided by the Companies Acts.[41] The memorandum and articles of association are commonly referred to as the company's regulations or its constitution.

Name

2–15 The memorandum must state the company's name.[42] If it is a limited company, then the name must include that term or its abbreviation "Ltd." — or the Irish equivalent, teoranta or "teo".[43] And if it is a public limited company, this must be stated in the name or with the abbreviation "p.l.c." or with the Irish equivalent.[44] But a limited com-

---

36 See below, para. 14–65.
37 1983 Act, s.7.
38 2nd Sched., Pt II.
39 1963 Act, ss. 5–16.
40 1963 Act, s.7.
41 *cf. Wilson v. Dunnes Stores (Cork) Ltd*, Kenny J., February 22, 1976).
42 1963 Acts s.6(1)(a).
43 *ibid.*, ss. 6(2), (3), 22.
44 1983 Act, s.4(1).

pany that is a "non-profit" organisation, in the sense that any surplus arising from its activities cannot be paid out as dividends and its objects are not commercial in the conventional sense, may be authorised by the Minister to omit the term "Ltd" from its name.[45]

2–16 The registrar of companies may refuse to register a company possessing a name that is deemed inappropriate; any name which in the opinion of the Minister is undesirable will not be accepted.[46] Among such names, presumably, are those that suggest that the company is something fundamentally different from what it purports to be, or suggest close association with the State, or which may lead to it being mistaken for another established company.[47] The registrar of companies' discretion in this matter is not absolute; there is a right of appeal to the court against rejection of a name, although the grounds on which an appeal may succeed are not indicated in the legislation.[48] There do not appear to be any reported decisions that deal with this matter. Where the name the company does business under is one other than its own, then that must be registered as a business name under the Registration of Business Names Act 1963.[49] In order to change its name, a special resolution to that effect must be passed and the Minister must give approval for the new name.[50] Any rights or obligations of the company or legal proceedings by or against it are not adversely affected merely by it changing its name.[51] Where a name that is too like the name of an existing company is registered, the Minister is empowered to require that it be altered.[52]

Authorised Capital

2–17 In Ireland and Britain, and in most European countries, shares are required to have a fixed "par" or "nominal" value, *i.e.* shares must be designed by the company with a particular value — be it £1, 20 pence or £200 each, or whatever. Invariably, a share's actual worth will

---

[45] 1963 Act, s.24; see below, para. 14–66.

[46] *ibid.*, s.21.

[47] Use of a name very similar to another company's name could give rise to liability for passing off or, exceptionally, for breach of trade mark; see generally, M. Forde, *Commercial Law* (1990), pp. 334–340.

[48] *cf. R. (Rowel) v. Registrar of Companies* [1904] 2 I.R. 634; *Abacus Finance Ltd. v. Registrar of Companies* [1985] 2 N.Z.L.R. 607, *Vicom New Zealand Ltd. v. Vicomm System Ltd.* [1987] 2 N.Z.L.R. 600 and *Association of Certified Public Accountants v. Secretary of State* [1997] 2 B.C.L.C. 307.

[49] 1963 Act, s.22; *cf. Re Griffin* (1935) 65 I.L.T.R. 106.

[50] 1963 Act, s.23(1)

[51] *ibid.*, s.23(4); *cf. Singh v. Atombrook Ltd.* [1989] 1 W.L.R. 810.

[52] *ibid.*, s.23(2).

vary with the company's own fortunes. For instance, in a company with shares of £1 par that is earning considerable profits, those shares quite easily might be changing hands in the market at £3 or more. A share's par value has very little bearing on its actual worth. Companies are not allowed to have shares of "no par" value — a practice that is permitted in the U.S.A.[53] Authorised capital is the aggregate par value of the shares that a company has authority to issue to its members; it is a kind of theoretical maximum capital.

2–18 Where, as is usually the case, the company is one with a share capital, the memorandum must state the amount of the authorised capital and how it is to be divided into shares.[54] Public limited companies (or p.l.c.s) must have a minimum authorised capital of £30,000.[55] Provided that some of its share capital is denoted in Irish currency, it would seem that a company can be registered with a multi-currency authorised capital, *i.e.* capital denoted in several currencies. What the Companies Acts say is that the capital must be expressed in a "fixed amount", which it has been held to mean a monetary amount — as distinguished from an amount of gold or of some other metal or commodity.[56]

2–19 Largely non-controversial alterations to the memorandum's capital clause may be effectuated in general meeting, provided the articles of association authorise the change in question.[57] The procedure for reducing the capital is far more elaborate; those articles must authorise the reduction, it must be approved by a special resolution of the members and by the creditors, and be sanctioned by the court.[58] Court sanction is not required where the company purchases its own shares in the manner authorised by Part XI of the 1990 Act.[59]

Objects

2–20 The memorandum of association must state what it is intended that the company shall do, or what are its "objects".[60] Because any shareholder or debenture-holder may apply to have a transaction that transcends the company's objects enjoined,[61] and because outsiders

---

[53] See Reports of "Gedge Committee", Cmd. 9112 (1954), and of "Cox Committee", Pr.4523, paras. 63–72.
[54] 1963 Act, s.6(4)(a).
[55] 1983 Act, ss. 5(2),19(1), 17(1).
[56] *Re Scandinavian Bank Group p.1.c.* [1988] 1 Ch.87.
[57] 1963 Act, ss. 68-70.
[58] *ibid.*, ss. 72–77; see below, paras 11–35 *et seq.*
[59] 1990 Act, ss. 207 and 211–216; see below, paras 7–46 *et seq.*
[60] 1963 Act, s.6(1)(b).
[61] *ibid.*, s.8(2).

generally will not knowingly enter into engagements that are not contemplated by a company's objects, promoters frequently give companies a multitude of objects or have the objects expressed in broad and general terms. On the other hand, some intending shareholders may insist on the objects being drafted in as restrictive a fashion as possible, in order to protect their investment from being put at risk in *ultra vires* ventures. A company's stated objects must not be inconsistent with the Companies Acts or with the general law.[62] The House of Lords in a tax case accepted virtually unlimited objects, viz. "[conducting] all kinds of operations".[63] Having virtually limitless objects cannot be impeached once the company is registered because the certificate of incorporation is "conclusive evidence" that all the Act's requirements regarding registration were complied with.[64]

2–21 At one time companies could never change their objects and then for a time it was necessary to get the prior sanctions of the High Court, but this is no longer so. A special resolution to that effect is required;[65] dissenting members and certain debenture-holders may apply to the High Court to veto the proposed alteration.

Limited Liability

2–22 If the liability of the members is to be limited, that fact must be stated in the memorandum of association.[66] Procedures exist whereby limited companies can change their status to unlimited companies, and where unlimited companies can convert into having limited liability.

Subscribers

2–23 For a private company at least one person and, for a public company, at least seven persons must subscribe to the memorandum, *i.e.* agree to take at least one share each in the company when formed and sign the memorandum opposite the number of shares they are to take.[67] The Companies Acts contain no restrictions on who can be subscribers. Thus, aliens, bankrupts, minors, lunatics and organisations with a legal personality of their own can subscribe; although a minor on attaining full age may repudiate the contract arising from his signature.[68]

---

[62] 1963 Act, s.5(1).
[63] *Newstead v. Frost* [1980] 1 W.L.R. 135.
[64] 1963 Act, s.19(1); 1983 Act, s.4(4).
[65] 1963 Act, s.10; see below, para. 11–13.
[66] *ibid.*, s.6(1)(a).
[67] *ibid.*, ss. 5(1) and 6(4)(b)-(c) (as amended by S.I. No. 275 of 1994).
[68] See below, para. 9–07.
[69] 1963 Act, s.31(1).

There must be at least one (or seven) subscribers, who become the company's members,[69] but one (or six) of them may be mere agents of the person who in fact is founding the company; they may even hold their shares as trustees for the founder.[70]

ARTICLES OF ASSOCIATION

2–24 The second major document needed to form a registered company is the articles of association,[71] which may be regarded as the company's bye-laws; the rules that set down in detail how it is to be governed and managed. These must be printed, divided into paragraphs that are numbered consecutively, stamped in the same way as a deed and signed by each subscriber to the memorandum.[72] The Companies Acts do not stipulate what the articles must contain other than that certain information must be provided in the case of unlimited companies and companies limited by guarantee,[73] and that certain major changes in a company's structure may be made only where there are provisions to that effect in the articles. The articles of companies that are listed on the Stock Exchange are required by the Exchange's rules to contain provisions on matters such as transfers of securities, share certificates, dividends, directors, accounts, rights, notices, redeemable shares, capital structure, voting entitlements and proxies.[74]

2–25 The 1963 Act's first schedule contains a model set of articles, called "Table A",[75] and most companies in fact adopt these for their articles, either in their entirety or subject to some alterations. Where no separate articles are registered, the Table A model becomes the company's articles. Any special articles that are registered are supplemented by the provisions of Table A except to the extent that the model clauses are expressly excluded or modified by the registered articles.[76] The 1963 Act's first schedule also contains model articles for guarantee companies (Tables C and D) and for unlimited companies (Table E). Previous Companies Acts contained earlier versions of Table A and companies

---

[70] *cf. Irish Permanent Building Society v. Cauldwell* [1981] I.L.R.M. 242.
[71] 1982 Act, s.2.
[72] 1963 Act, s.14.
[73] *ibid.*, s.12.
[74] Chap. 13, App. 1 of the rules in the Listing Rules (the "Yellow Book").
[75] As amended by 1983 Act, 1st Sched., para. 24. A very extensive commentary on the case law under these articles is contained in *Palmer's Company Precedents* (17th ed., 1956), Chap. 10 and also in *Buckley's Companies Acts* (14th ed., 1981), pp. 908-1055.
[76] 1963 Act, s.13 and 1982 Act, s.14.

which were registered before 1963, without adopting special articles of association, would still be subject to the model articles in force at the time of their registration. Thus, if the company was registered some time between 1908 and 1963, it is the articles in the Companies (Consolidation) Act 1908, which apply to it. An earlier version still of the model articles is contained in the Companies Act 1862.

2–26 Because Table A is regarded as showing the legislature's view of what articles of association ideally should contain, no article that is substantially similar to any of those in Table A will be held to be *ultra vires*.[77] Although the contents of the memorandum of association take precedence over those of the articles, the latter may be considered in order to clarify ambiguities in the memorandum.[78] Except for restrictions that are inherent in the general law or that are contained in the Companies Acts or the company's memorandum of association, there are no restrictions on what may be included in the articles of association. That particular articles are most unusual or extraordinary does not mean that a company cannot adopt them. Because of the relative ease with which the articles of association can be amended, it is not uncommon for provisions that could be included in the articles instead to be entrenched against alteration in the memorandum of association.[79]

2–27 While the memorandum and articles are defined by section 25 of the 1963 Act as a contract between the company and its shareholders, and between the shareholders *inter se*, there are certain kinds of articles the breach of which does not give rise to a civil right of action between the company and the member or between the members *inter se*.[80] While courts may infer a term into a company's articles by way of purely constructional implication, no term will be implied from existing circumstances, such as the actions and beliefs of the members at the time they incorporated their company. This is because the document is given statutory force by section 25 of the 1963 Act and is open to inspection by anyone considering dealing with the company or taking shares in it.[81] Further, courts will not rectify the terms of articles of

---

77 *New Balkis Eersteling v. Randt Gold Mining Co.* [1904] A.C. 165.
78 *Angostura Bitters Ltd. v. Kerr* [1933] A.C. 550 and *Re Bansha Woollen Mills Co.* 21 L.R. Ir. 181 (1887).
79 1963 Act, s.28; see below, para. 11–11.
80 See below, paras 10–16 *et seq*.
81 *Brattan Seymour Services Co. v. Oxborough* [1992] B.C.L.C. 693.
82 *Scott v. F. Scott (London) Ltd.* [1940] Ch. 794.

association even though those terms do not accord with the members' intentions when they were being adopted.[82]

REGISTRATION

2–28 In order to constitute themselves as a company, the subscribers must deliver to the registrar of companies the signed memorandum and articles of association, together with some other documents and a cheque for capital duty.[83] The requirements for existing companies re-registering under some other form are considered separately in Chapter 11.

Formalities

2–29 All applications for registration as a company must be accompanied by the following. First, there is the statutory declaration by either a solicitor involved in forming the company or by a person designated as first director or secretary of the company, to the effect that all the prerequisites for registration were complied with.[84] Then there is the statement naming the intended first directors and secretary, and indicating where the company's registered office is to be.[85] This statement must give that office's address and such particulars regarding the company's intended officers as are required to be disclosed and to be kept in each company's register of directors and secretaries.[86] As regards directors, these are their names and any former names, usual residential address, nationality if not Irish, business occupation, if any, and particulars of other directorships of Irish companies; as regards the secretaries, their names and any former names, and their usual or registered addresses. This statement must be signed by or on behalf of the subscribers to the memorandum of association and it must be accompanied by signed consents of the persons named as officers to act as such. Where the memorandum is being delivered to the registrar by the subscribers' agent, that fact must be indicated and the agent's name and address stated.

2–30 Thirdly, there must be a statement of the company's assets, liabilities and expenses for the purpose of reckoning the amount of stamp duty to be charged on its formation.[87] The amount of this duty is £1 for

---

[83] 1963 Act, s.5(1).
[84] 1983 Act, s.5 (replacing 1963 Act, s.19(2)).
[85] 1982 Act, s.3.
[86] See below, para. 5–182.
[87] Finance Act 1973, ss. 68–70.

every £100 of the company's net assets, *i.e.* assets to be contributed by the members less liabilities attaching to them and any expenses incurred in the formation. But where this amount is less than the nominal value of shares allotted to members immediately after registration, the charge is on the latter amount instead. The amount of any assets contributed by prospective shareholders with unlimited liability is excluded from this calculation. There is no stamp duty charged on forming certain non-profit companies.

2–31 The company will be registered only when the registrar is satisfied that all the statutory requirements have been complied with.[88] Registration cannot be refused once all those formalities have been met. But registration will be refused because the objects are unlawful, as happened in *R. v. Registrar of Companies*,[89] where it was held that a company being formed in England to deal in Irish hospital sweepstake tickets there could not be registered because those activities constituted an illegal lottery there. Dentists and several other professionals (*e.g.* doctors and lawyers) are prohibited from practising their profession through registered companies and, when the registrar of companies refused to register a company with the name "S.G. Rowell (Dentist) Ltd.", the High Court declined to direct that it be so registered.[90] That was because persons might be deceived and believe that the company had been duly registered to practice dentistry. In 1980 an English court quashed the registration of a company called Lindi St Claire (Personal Services) Ltd., which was engaged in prostitution, on the grounds that its registration was against public policy and was illegal.[91]

2–32 When the certificate of incorporation has been granted, a notice to that effect must be published in the *Iris Oifigiúil*. Similar notices must be published of any alteration in the company's memorandum or articles of association.

Consequences

2–33 A certificate of incorporation issued by the registrar is conclusive evidence that the statutory requirements have been complied with and that the company was duly registered.[92] This gives shareholders and outsiders dealing with registered companies legal security, in that

---

[88] 1983 Act, s.5(1); cf. *R. v. Registrar of Companies ex p. Bowen* [1914] 3 K.B. 1161.
[89] [1931] 2 K.B. 197.
[90] *R. (Rowell) v. Registrar of Companies* [1904] 2 I.R. 634.
[91] *R. v. Registrar of Companies, ex p. Attorney General* [1991] B.C.L.C. 476.
[92] 1983 Act, s.5(4).

it precludes reopening matters that occurred prior to or contemporaneously with registration;[93] no evidence that might show that the company was irregularly incorporated will be admitted. Irish law, therefore, is not bedevilled with problems of defectively-formed companies and nullity of companies.[94] However, the certificate of incorporation does not render lawful a company's objects that otherwise would be unlawful. And if a company is registered with such objects it would appear that the Attorney General can proceed to have it de-registered.[95] From the time of incorporation, the registered company acquires a legal personality of its own and unrelated to that of its members, with all the significant consequences resulting from being a distinct legal entity.[96]

Re-Registration

2–34 Provided they satisfy the various prescribed requirements, companies which register under one form can re-register under a different form. For instance, a private company can go public, a public company can go private, an unlimited company can acquire limited liability. The procedures for these transformations are set out in Chapter 11.[97]

REGISTERED OFFICE

2–35 Every company must have a registered office in the State, to which all communications and notices must be addressed,[98] and some of the company's principal records must be kept at that office. Its location must be given in the statement that is delivered to the registrar of companies prior to incorporation.[99] The company's name must be displayed outside its registered office conspicuously and legibly.[100] Any change in the office's location must be notified to the registrar within

---

93 *cf. Cotman v. Brougham* [1918] A.C. 514.

94 *cf.* E.C. First Directive on Company Law [1968] O.J. L65/41, Arts. 10–2, restricting the doctrine of the nullity of companies and *Ubbink Isolatie B.V. v. Daken Wantecbniek B.V.* (Case 136/87) [1990] 1 C.M.L.R. 262 and *Marleasing S.A. v. La Commercial Internacional de Alimentacion SA* (Case 106/89) [1990] E.C.R. 4135. See generally, Drury, "Nullity of Companies in English Law" (1985) 48 Mod. L. Rev. 644 (1985).

95 above, n. 9; *cf. Bowman v. Secular Society* [1917] A.C. 406.

96 1963 Act, s.18(2).

97 para. 11–67 *et seq.*

98 1982 Act, s.4.

99 *ibid.*, s.3

100 1963 Act, s.114(a).

101 1982 Act, s.4(3).

14 days.[101] Since neither the Companies Acts nor Table A stipulate the procedure for changing the office, any such change would seem to be a matter for determination in general meeting unless the company's own regulations provide otherwise. But a notice of the change in the registered office must be published in the *Iris Oifigiúil* within six weeks of it occurring.[102] A company that does not cause such a notice to be published is estopped from relying, as against others, on the new registered address.[103]

COMMENCING BUSINESS

2–36 Once it is registered, a private company is legally free to commence doing business and to borrow. Public limited companies, by contrast, must comply with a number of formalities before they can do so. An originally incorporated p.l.c. that has not re-registered may do business and borrow only after the registrar of companies has issued a certificate stating that the nominal value of the shares that the company has allotted is not less than £30,000 and that there has been delivered to the registry a statutory declaration concerning capital integrity.[104] This declaration, which one of the company's directors or secretaries has to sign, must state that the nominal value of the allotted share capital does not fall below £30,000; the amount actually paid up on those shares; the amount or estimated amount of the company's preliminary expenses, and the person who has paid or will pay these; and any amount or benefit paid to or given to, or intended to be paid to or given to any promoter, and the consideration therefor. Transactions entered into by a p.l.c. that did not satisfy these requirements are not thereby invalid.[105]

---

[102] S.I. No. 163 of 1973.
[103] *ibid.*, reg. 10.
[104] 1983 Act, s.6.
[105] *ibid.*, s.6(8).

3

Corporate Personality

3–01 The principal attraction that the registered company offers over other legal forms of business organisation is that the company has a separate legal personality from that of its owners.[1] When it is said that an individual or thing possesses legal personality what is meant is that he, she or it enjoys rights and is subject to duties under a given legal system. That is to say, within that legal system he, she or it has a distinctive identity and autonomy in that they or it can acquire rights and/or incur liabilities in respect of themselves or itself, and not merely vicariously on behalf of others. Thus in Ireland neither trees nor dogs possess legal personality, although the law lays down certain rights and obligations that individuals possess and are subject to regarding trees and dogs. But the laws of some societies confer legal rights on certain things, like a religious idol in a famous case concerning Hindu law.[2] In many slave-owning societies, slaves are regarded as not possessing any legal personality.[3] Prior to the Married Women's Property Act 1957, married women did not have quite the same legal capacity to act as their spouses had. And it has been a matter of considerable political as well as legal controversy whether the human foetus is a legal person and, if it is, to what extent and with what effect. Adult citizens of sound mind, by contrast, possess as complete a legal personality as can exist in Irish law. Some of the general principles that are dealt with in this chapter, like *ultra vires*, piercing the corporate veil and limited liability, recur in particular contexts throughout this book.

THE CONCEPT OF CORPORATE PERSONALITY

3–02 In order to determine the nature and extent of registered companies' legal personality one must start with some inescapable facts. A

---

1 See generally, C. Rickett and R. Grantham (eds.), *Corporate Personality in the Twentieth Century* (1998).

2 *Pramatha Nath Mullick v. Pradyumna Kumar Mullick* (1925) L.R. 52 Ind. App. 245; see brief account of this case by P.W. Duff (1927) 3 Camb. L.J. 43; *cf. Bumper Development Corp. v. Commissioner of Police* [1991] 1 W.L.R. 1932.

3 *cf. Dred Scott v. Sandford*, 60 U.S. 393 (1857).

company is an association of at least two or more persons (except for "one-person" companies) who themselves possess a legal personality of their own, so that there is nothing inconsistent with attributing to companies many of the legal characteristics of those who constitute them. Indeed, the Constitution's guarantee of the "liberty for the exercise of the . . . right . . . to form associations" may mean that, subject to public order and morality, associations and companies may be formed that possess a legal autonomy and capacities not that fundamentally different from individuals.[4] On the other hand, there are certain human characteristics that associations and companies by their very nature are incapable of possessing. For instance, they have no distinctive sexual identity, so that they cannot marry; and since they have "no soul to be damned, and no body to be kicked",[5] they cannot be subjected to the penalties of excommunication, imprisonment or corporal punishment. Associations and companies are dependent on human beings to act for them; a company as such, without human intervention, cannot conclude contracts or inflict the kinds of physical and economic damage that form the basis for tortious and criminal liability.

Corporations

3–03 In contrast with the position in continental Europe,[6] the legal personality, or *personnalité morale*, of associations and companies has not attracted much abstract speculation among lawyers in Ireland or Britain. Our inherited legal tradition has been to segregate group institutions into two principal legal types, corporations and unincorporated bodies. Blackstone, writing in the 1780s, described corporations as possessing five characteristics "inseparably incident" to their status, namely:[7]

(a) To have perpetual succession until they are formally dissolved. They are but one person in law, a person that never dies: in like manner as the river Thames is still the same river, though the parts which compose it are changing every instant.

(b) To be capable of suing and being sued in their own name.

(c) Subject to the purposes for which they were created, to be capable of holding in their own right and disposing of property[8] and to

---

[4] *cf.* Decision of French Conseil Constitutionnel, July 16, 1971, J.O. July 18, 1971.

[5] Attributed to Baron Thurlow (1731–1806).

[6] See, *e.g.* J. P. Gastand, *Personnalité Morale et Droit Subjectif* (1977) and S. Bastid et al., *La Personnalité Morale et ses Limites* (1960).

[7] W. Blackstone, *Commentaries on the Laws of England* (1765) Vol. 1, Chap. 18.

[8] *cf. Kathleen Investments (Australia) Ltd. v. Australia Atomic Energy Commission,* (1977) 139 C.L.R. 117.

perform such other acts as human persons may (subject to obvious limitations).

(d) To have a common seal through which they act and speak.[9]

(e) To have internal regulations that bind their members.

It was never established whether, in the absence of express provision to that effect in their instrument of incorporation, corporations possess limited liability;[10] Blackstone does not mention the matter.

3–04 Many of the modern enactments which create statutory corporations reiterate this catalogue of the incidents of corporate status. Thus section 2(2) of the Electricity (Supply) Act 1927 stipulates that the Electricity Supply Board "shall be a body corporate having perpetual succession and may sue and be sued under its said style and name." Under section 3(2) of the Broadcasting Authority Act,1960, which establishes the Radio Telefís Éireann Authority, it is provided that the Authority "shall be a body corporate with perpetual succession and power to sue and be sued in its corporate name and to acquire, hold and dispose of land." A matter to be resolved with these bodies is, where they are not expressly authorised to own land, are they legally capable of becoming land-owners.

3–05 In the past it was not easy for an enterprise to acquire the status of a corporation. As has been explained, only Parliament or the king by charter or by letters patent could create such entities.[11] Why this should have been is a difficult question to answer. Presumably there was some reluctance to facilitate the creation of private power centres with a legal autonomy of their own and that were not regulated by the State. Taxation may have had a bearing on the matter, since a major source of revenue was the passing of property on death, marriage and the like. Because corporations have a potentially limitless life span and they never marry, those taxes could not be imposed directly on them.[12] Enactment of the Joint Stock Companies Act 1844, and the Limited Liability Act 1855, enabled persons by registration to form corporations with limited liability. The central provisions of those Acts are now contained in section 18(2) of the 1963 Act and state that:

---

9 See below, para. 13–05.

10 *cf. J.H. Rayner (Mincing Lane) Ltd. v. Dept. of Trade and Industry* [1990] 2 A.C. 418, where States which were members of an international organisation (the International Tin Council) which became insolvent were held not liable for its unpaid debts by virtue of being its members.

11 See above, para. 1–11 *et seq.*

12 *cf.* Mortmain (Repeal of Enactments) Act 1954.

> "the subscribers of the memorandum, together with such other persons as may from time to time become members of the company, shall be a body corporate, . . . capable forthwith of exercising all the functions of an incorporated company, . . . but with such liability on the part of the members to contribute to the assets of the company in the event of its being wound up as is mentioned in this Act."

3–06 Although the general legal implications of being an incorporated body were established by the middle of the last century, numerous unresolved questions remained. For instance, were registered companies capable of legally effective action beyond the objects for which they were established? Could they be held responsible for committing crimes that require *mens rea*? To what extent did they possess rights and were they subject to obligations arising from statute or from the Constitution? Could sole traders acquire the shield of limited liability merely by incorporating their business under the Companies Acts? Before dealing with these matters, something must be said about the legal personality of partnerships, which is the other major legal form of business organisation in this country.

Partnerships

3–07 As compared with registered companies and with chartered and statutory corporations, the partnership does not possess a legal personality of its own. As a matter of commercial and economic reality, partnerships exist; indeed some of the most influential institutions in Irish and international business are partnerships, like the major accounting firms and solicitor's practices in Dublin and eminent London stockbroking firms. So far as the law is concerned, however, a partnership does not have an autonomy distinct from that of its members. The legal status of partnerships is summarised as follows in the leading work on the subject, *Lindley on Partnership*:

> "There are certain features which characterise most partnerships, in particular the fact that partnerships frequently have a distinctive name which does not necessarily or even usually coincide with the names of the partners, that change of partners often have no visible effect on the continuity of the partnership business and that virtually every partnership operates a separate banking account in the firm's name. Partners may come and go, but the firm appears to go on.
>
> But this is not the legal notion of a firm. The firm is not recognised by . . . lawyers as distinct from the members composing it. . . . Speaking generally, the firm as such has no legal recognition. . . . The law, ignoring the firm, looks to the partners composing it; any change amongst them destroys the identity of the firm; what is called the property of the firm is their property, and what are called the debts and liabilities of the firm are their debts and their liabilities.

> This non-recognition of the firm, in the mercantile sense of the word, is one of the most marked differences between partnerships and incorporated companies."[13]

3–08 Nevertheless, the firm or partnership as a distinct unit is not entirely without some legal identity of its own. The interests of the partnership as a common enterprise is the ultimate criterion against which the relations between partners will be judged. Although each partner is personally liable without limit for the partnership's debts, it is only debts incurred in the course of the common enterprise to which such liability attaches. And the firm's property may not be seized to satisfy any of the insolvent partner's private debts.[14]

SEGREGATION FROM OWNERS

3–09 A distinctive feature of corporate status is that a registered company's legal rights and obligations are wholly separate from its owners' own entitlements and duties. In law, the company and its owners are entirely distinct entities. Property acquired by the company belongs to it and not to its members; debts and obligations incurred by the company are its own liabilities and not liabilities of the members. This principle was endorsed emphatically in the controversial case of *Salomon v. Salomon & Co. Ltd.*[15] The plaintiff, who sued in *forma pauperis*, had owned a moderately successful boot manufacturing business which he decided to incorporate, *i.e.*, to convert into a limited company. To do this he formed the defendant company, in which he held all the shares (2,001) except for a share each held by his wife and five children. He then had transferred to the company his business at an apparent valuation of £30,000, the consideration being 20,000 fully paid shares of £1 in the company and 100 debentures of £100 issued by the company to him. These debentures were acknowledgements by the company of its indebtedness to Salomon to the amount of £10,000, that debt being secured by a floating charge on the company's assets. Subsequently the business failed and the company was put into an insolvent liquidation. The net question was whether the secured debt of £10,000 to Salomon should be paid in priority to debts amounting to about £7,500 owing to the company's unsecured creditors. It was contended that, in the circumstances, the latter should have priority because the entire arrangement "was a mere scheme to enable [Salomon]

---

13 (15th ed., 1984), pp. 33–34.

14 See M. Forde, *Bankruptcy Law in Ireland* (1990), pp. 168–170.

15 [1897] A.C. 22. For information on the general background to this case, see Rubin, "Aaron Salomon and his Circle" in *Essay for Clive Schmitthoff* (J. Adams ed., 1983).

to carry on business in the name of the company with limited liability contrary to the true intent and meaning of the Companies Act . . . and further to enable him to obtain a preference over other creditors of the company by procuring a first charge on [its] assets. . . ."[16] In other words, in reality Salomon owed himself £10,000, which is a logical impossibility. Therefore, in this instance his "loan" ought to make way for sums in fact borrowed from the trade creditors to finance his business.

3–10 A unanimous House of Lords decided that, since legally a company is wholly distinct from its shareholders, priority must be accorded to Salomon's debenture. Referring to what is now section 18(2) of the 1963 Act, Lord Macnaghten remarked that:

> "When the memorandum is duly signed and registered, . . . the subscribers are a body corporate 'capable forthwith . . . of exercising all the functions of an incorporated company.' Those are strong words. The company attains maturity on its birth . . . . I cannot understand how a body corporate thus made 'capable' by statute can lose its individuality by issuing the bulk of its capital to one person. . . . The company is at law a different person altogether from [its shareholders]; and . . . the company is not in law the agent of the [shareholders] or trustee for them. Nor are the [shareholders] as members liable, in any shape or form, except to the extent and in the manner provided by the Act.[17]
>
> The argument that it was not intended that the Companies Acts should be used to enable a person to incorporate any business in order merely to obtain the advantage of limited liability was rejected, with the observation that it is not 'possible to contend that the motive of becoming shareholders or of making [persons] shareholders is a field of inquiry which the statute itself recognises as legitimate'."[18]

The contention that there ought not be a complete segregation between the company and its members when the latter are essentially one person was answered by again referring to the Companies Act: the Act "enacts nothing as to the extent or degree of interest which may be held by each of the [subscribers] or as to the proportion of interest or influence possessed by one or the majority of the shareholders over the others."[19] Thus, once the statutory formalities for registration are complied with, a wholly distinct legal entity comes into being. A logical consequence of this is that companies can be created simply to evade legal obligations and indeed to be engines of fraud. In order to prevent such outcomes, the courts and the legislature have grafted exceptions to *Salomon & Co.'s* "segregation" principle.

---

[16] [1897] A.C. 22 at 26, summarising judgment of the Court of Appeal [1895] 2 Ch. 323.

[17] *ibid.* at p. 51.

[18] *ibid.* at p. 30.

[19] *ibid.*

Instances of Segregation

3–11 The mere fact that, by incorporating their business, persons obtain some legal privilege that would be beyond their reach without such incorporation, or they avoid some statutory obligation that otherwise would fall on them, is not in itself reason for rending aside the wall of incorporation. For instance, in *Irish Permanent Building Society v. Cauldwell*,[20] the registration under the Building Societies Act 1976, of the Irish Life Building Society was challenged on the grounds that the society was not an association of ten or more persons, as required by that Act, but was merely the instrument of a large financial institution. The evidence showed that most of the Society's founders were employees of that institution, and it was contended that they had acted as agents for it and not as independent individuals. Relying extensively on the *Salomon & Co.* case, Barrington J. rejected this argument "as being based on too fine and metaphysical a distinction to be useful in dealing with practical affairs."[21]

3–12 The leading Irish authority on persons being allowed to use the company form with a view to avoiding legal consequences they otherwise would face is *Roundabout Ltd. v. Beirne*,[22] which concerned a picket by bar workers who had been dismissed for joining a trade union. Their employer was the M.P. Co. but, following a dispute about unionisation, M.P. Co.'s directors formed a new company, the plaintiff, and leased the business to it with an option to purchase the entire premises. It was argued that, although for conveyancing and title purposes the plaintiff might be a distinct entity from M.P. Co., the reality was that the ownership of the business had not changed, the plaintiff being dominated by the same persons as owned M.P. Co. Accordingly, it was said, the purported lease was a "sham transaction" merely entered into to extinguish the original trade dispute. In an unreserved judgment, Dixon J. agreed that "there is considerable substance in that view". But speculating that this was not "the sole, or possibly even the primary" purpose of what had happened, the new company was held to be a distinct legal entity from the M.P. Co. and, therefore, was not the barmen's employer for the purposes of the Trade Disputes Act 1906.[23] In England, it was held that a landlord can avoid being made subject to the obligations under the Rent Acts to a "statutory tenant" by letting the premises to an "off the shelf company", which a person owns and con-

---

[20] [1981] I.L.R.M. 242.
[21] *ibid.* at p. 264.
[22] [1959] I.R. 423.
[23] A similar instance is *Dimbleby & Sons Ltd. v. National Union of Journalists* [1984] 1 W.L.R. 427. Compare *Canada Safeway Ltd. v. Local* 373 (1974) 46 D.L.R. (3d) 113.

trols, even though that person then goes into occupation of the premises.[24]

3–13 Nor does the fact that the company is in essence a "one-person" company, with every share held by its creator and driving force, make any difference in principle, as is illustrated by *Lee v. Lee's Air Farming Ltd.*[25] Some social welfare benefits are available only to employed persons as distinct from the self-employed.[26] But it was held in *Lee* that entrepreneurs can participate in such benefits by incorporating their business and then becoming employees of their own company. There the plaintiff's deceased husband held all but one of the defendant company's shares; he was its governing director for life; under its articles of association he was authorised to exercise all the company's powers, including those exercisable in general meeting; and the articles designated him a salaried employee of the company. He was killed while carrying out the company's work. His widow's claim for workmen's compensation on his behalf was resisted on the grounds that in reality he was not an employee; that although a company director is capable of being its employee, a "governing director in whom was vested the full government and control of the company, he could not also be a servant of the company."[27] The Privy Council would not accept this argument. According to it, the criterion of employee status is whether the employer possesses the right of control; following *Salomon & Co.*, "one person may function in dual capacities" and; the broad power the deceased possessed over the company did "not alter the fact that the company and [he] were two separate and distinct legal persons"; the mere fact that control was exercised by the deceased in effect giving orders to himself "would not affect or diminish the right to its exercise."[28] Similarly, what would create a *res judicata* or an estoppel issue between a party and two or more others does not do so as between that party and a company which these others own entirely and of which they are the sole directors.[29] Whether this would invariably be the case with a truly "one-person" company can be debated.

3–14 That the legal segregation of a registered company from its owners is not invariably a boon to them is borne out by *Macaura v.*

---

24 *Hilton v. Plustitle Ltd.* [1989] 1 W.L.R. 149.
25 [1961] A.C. 12.
26 Social Welfare (Consolidation) Act 1993.
27 [1961] A.C. at p. 24, quoting from the New Zealand Court of Appeal [1959] N.Z.L.R. 393.
28 *ibid.* at pp. 26–27. *cf. Buchan v. Secretary of State* [1997] I.R.L.R. 80.
29 *Belton v. Carlow C.C.* [1997] 1 I.R. 172 and *Baracot Ltd. v. Epiette Ltd.* [1998] 1 B.C.L.C. 283.

Northern Assurance Co.[30] The plaintiff transferred his business to a company he controlled but inadvertently allowed the insurance policy on the company's stock to remain in his own name. The stock subsequently having been destroyed in a fire, it was held that he could not claim on the insurance policy because he did not possess an insurable interest in the stock; that belonged to his company and not to him.[31] In *Tunstall v. Steigman*,[32] it was held that a tenant had no claim to the renewal of a lease for carrying on a business in the premises when, in fact, the business was done in the name of a company controlled and virtually wholly owned by the tenant.[33] As one judge there observed, a tenant "cannot say that in a case of this kind she is entitled to take the benefit of any advantages that the formation of a company gave her, without at the same time accepting the liabilities arising therefrom".[34]

3–15 A similar case is *State (McInerney) Ltd. v. Dublin County Council*,[35] which concerned the rights in respect of planning permission within a closely integrated group of companies. The applicant company agreed to buy the land in question but, at its direction, the land was conveyed to one of its wholly-owned subsidiaries. In the interval between the agreement and the conveyance, the applicant applied for planning permission, which in the event was refused. The applicant then sought to have that refusal set aside on several grounds. Under the planning legislation, it is the "owner" of land who is entitled to planning permission, and the County Council contended that, because the applicant did not own the land, it had no *locus standi* to challenge the decision refusing planning permission. Carroll J. would not accept the applicant's claim that it and its wholly-owned subsidiary should be treated as one body for the purposes of the case, observing that instances where the English courts treated wholly-owned subsidiary companies as agents of their parent company, involved "entirely different considerations".[36] Here, there had been some legal and presum-

---

[30] [1925] A.C. 619.

[31] In *Constitution Insurance Co. of Canada v. Kosmopoulos* (1983) 304 D.L.R. 4d 208, the Supreme Court of Canada declined to follow the reasoning in this case, preferring American decisions which hold that having a substantial shareholding in a company can amount to having an insurable interest in its assets. In any event, a shareholder can always insure against the loss or diminution in value of his shares. *cf. Verderame v. Commercial Union Assurance Co.* [1992] B.C.L.C. 793, where directors cum-shareholders were held not to have any claim against the company's negligent insurance broker.

[32] [1962] 2 Q.B. 593.

[33] This is no longer so by virtue of the Landlord and Tenant (Amendment) Act 1980, s.5(3).

[34] [1962] 2 Q.B. 601.

[35] [1985] I.R. 1.

[36] *ibid.* at 7.

ably fiscal advantages in organising the applicant's business under the aegis of numerous subsidiary companies, and the courts should not readily set aside the corporate veil at the request of a company which usually takes advantage of distinct corporate structures. According to Carroll J.:

> "the corporate veil is not a device to be raised or lowered at the option of the parent company or group. The arm which lifts the corporate veil must always be that of justice. If justice requires . . . the courts will not be slow to treat a group of subsidiary companies and their company as one. . . . It is not for a corporate group to claim that the veil should be lifted to illuminate one aspect of its business while it should be left in situ to isolate the individual actions of its subsidiaries in other respects."[37]

3–16 The same conclusion was reached in *Stewarts Supermarkets Ltd. v. Secretary of State,*[38] where the plaintiff sought compensation under the Northern Ireland scheme for criminal injuries to property. The plaintiff was a wholly-owned subsidiary of a major British supermarket chain and its constant practice had been to transfer any surplus cash it had to the holding company. This subsidiary owned a business premises which was destroyed in a terrorist attack. The holding company spent funds on restoring the premises and it was in respect of the interest, which could have been earned on that money if it did not have to be spent on rebuilding, that the compensation was claimed. Since it was the holding company which was being deprived of the opportunity to earn interest and not the plaintiff company, Hutton J. had no hesitation in rejecting the claim. The fact that the parent had complete control of the subsidiary was not sufficient reason, in the circumstances, for piercing the corporate veil.[39]

3–17 A striking example of just how far courts will allow the legal distinction between a company and its shareholders to be stretched is *Northern Counties Securities Ltd. v. Jackson & Steeple Ltd.*[40] One step in an agreed merger between two companies was that the defendant would issue to the plaintiff shares for which there was a stock exchange quotation. In proceedings to enforce that agreement, the defendant was ordered to use its best endeavours to see that a resolution was passed in general meeting authorising the share issue. Because by then the

---

[37] [1985] I.R. 1 at pp. 7, 8.
[38] [1982] N.I. 286.
[39] Following principally *Woolfson v. Stratclyde Regional Council* (1979) 38 P. & C.R. 521; see generally, Rixon, "Lifting the Veil Between Holding and Subsidiary Companies" (1986) 102 L.Q.R. 415.
[40] [1974] 1 W.L.R. 1133.

company would have made a relative loss if the agreed merger went through, and in the light of an opinion obtained from leading counsel, the defendant's directors in effect invited the shareholders to reject the proposed resolution. The contention that the company would contravene the court order if the resolution was not passed was rejected on the grounds that it is the shareholders who determine the outcomes of general meetings, and shareholders and their companies are entirely separate legal entities. A shareholder "who casts his vote . . . is not casting it as an agent of the company in any shape or form. His act, therefore, in voting as he pleases cannot in any way be regarded as an act of the company."[41]

3–18 A person in total control of a company by reason of owning all but one of its shares and controlling the directors can nevertheless be found guilty of stealing the company's property.[42] It was held by the Supreme Court in *Taylor v. Smyth*[43] that the owner and controller of a company can be held liable for engaging in an unlawful conspiracy with it. McCarthy J. saw "no reason why the mere fact that one individual controls the company of limited liability, should give immunity from suit to both that company and that individual in the case of an established arrangement for the benefit of both company and individual to the detriment of others."[44]

Piercing the Corporate Veil

3–19 Where the legislature decrees or a court decides to look behind the corporate screen and identify the company with its owners, it is said that the law "pierces the corporate veil". Although the *Salomon & Co.* case lays down a broad principle of segregation of the company from its owners, there are statutory and other qualifications to that principle, especially in regard to wholly-owned subsidiaries. Indeed, the further we move from 1896 the less reluctant courts are becoming to take account of the economic reality behind the corporate facade.[45] Hard and fast rules for this purpose have not been laid down and perhaps are incapable of being developed. Courts exercising equitable jurisdiction are tending to rely on the amorphous criterion of justice to

---

41 [1974] 1 W.L.R. 1133 at 1144. See also *Re Parnell G.A.A. Club Ltd.* [1984] I.L.R.M. 246.

42 *Attorney General's Reference (No.2 of 1982)* [1984] 2 W.L.R. 447.

43 [1991] I.R. 142.

44 *ibid.* at p. 12. Compare *R. v. McDonnell* [1966] 1 Q.B. 233.

45 See generally, Picketing, "The Company as a Separate Legal Entity" (1968) 31 Mod. L. Rev. 481; Ottolenghi, "From Peeping Behind the Corporative Veil to Ignoring it Completely" (1990) 53 Mod. L. Rev. 338 and Gallagher & Zegler, "Lifting the Corporate Veil in the Pursuit of Justice" (1990) J. Bus. L. 292.

determine whether the corporate veil should be lifted in particular instances. Thus in *Power Supermarkets Ltd. v. Crumlin Investments Ltd.*,[46] where it was sought to identify a subsidiary with its holding company and where the evidence indicated that both companies were merely instruments for carrying out the wishes of their controlling family, Costello J. concluded that:

> "[A] court may, if the justice so requires, treat two or more related companies as a single entity . . . if this conforms to the economic and commercial realities of the situation. It would [moreover] be very hard to find a clearer case than the present one for the application of this principle. [In the circumstances here, t]o treat the two companies as a single economic entity . . . accord[s] fully with the realities of the situation. Not to do so could involve considerable injustice to the plaintiffs as their right under [contract] might be defeated by the mere technical device of the creation of a company with a £2 issued capital which had no real independent life of its own."[47]

The full position in relation to groups of companies is treated separately in Chapter 14.[48]

Statutory Authority

3–20 There are numerous statutes under which controllers or dominant shareholders are expressly made personally accountable for certain activities of their companies. In the 1963 Act itself there is section 297A concerning "fraudulent trading";[49] section 149 requiring public companies to consolidate their accounts with those of their subsidiaries;[50] and section 32 prohibiting a subsidiary from becoming a member of its holding company.[51] Under sections 140 and 141 of the 1990 Act, closely related companies may be required in certain cases to contribute towards payment of each others debts, when one of them is being wound up, and the court may direct that their assets be pooled where several related companies are being wound up. The Income Tax Acts, the Corporation Tax Acts and the Capital Gains Tax Acts contain numerous instances where companies and their owners are treated as one and the same, most notably perhaps transactions with "participators" in "close companies".[52] Under the Landlord and Tenant (Amend-

---

46 Costello J., June 22, 1981; Cases p. 78.
47 *ibid.* at pp. 8 and 9. *Cf. Re Polly Peck International p.l.c. (No. 3)* [1996] 1 B.C.L.C. 428.
48 para. 14–43 *et seq*.
49 See below, paras 18–51 *et seq*.
50 See below, para. 14–31—14–39.
51 See below, para. 14–35—14–41.
52 See generally, Flanagan, "Tax Avoidance and Legal Personality" (1979) 42 Conv. 195.

ment) Act 1980, a tenant of a business premises is entitled to obtain a renewal of the lease where he occupies the premises and also where it is being occupied by his private company, or by its holding company or fellow-subsidiary company, for business purposes.[53]

Discretionary Powers

3–21 Courts exercising broad discretionary powers given by the Companies Acts and by other legislation often take full account of the fact that the company in question is owned by particular individuals or groups and treat the company as if it were its actual owner or owners. Thus, in four major instances where majority shareholders, acting within the the literal terms of the 1963 Act's provisions, were seeking to "squeeze-out" a minority, but where the schemes in question needed court approval before they could become effective, critical inferences were drawn from the actual identity of the majority shareholders: *Re Holders Investment Trust Ltd.*[54] which concerned a section 72 capital reduction; *Re Bugle Press Ltd.*,[55] involving a section 204 "take-out"; *Re Hellenic & General Trust Ltd.*[56] arising out of a section 201 "scheme of arrangement"; and *Scottish Co-op. v. Meyer*[57] concerning "oppression" under section 205.

Fraud

3–22 Judges have stressed continuously that they would disregard the legal segregation of a company and its shareholders where the company was a "sham or a mere simulacrurn", or a "facade concealing the real facts". In the *Salomon & Co.* case emphasis was laid on the fact that there were no fraudulent intentions underlying the creation of the company there. Courts have refused to recognise the separate existence of companies that were formed solely to enable their controllers to avoid their contractual obligations. In *Gilford Motor Co. v. Horne*,[58] for example, the individual defendant was bound by a restrictive covenant under which he could not compete in business against his ex-employer, a garage in a certain area. In order to get around this restriction, he formed a car sales company which he controlled. Because in the circumstances the company was "a mere cloak or sham", the court enjoined him and his company from competing against the plaintiff. Similarly, it was

---

[53] s.5, reversing *Tunstall v. Steigman* [1962] 2 Q.B. 593.
[54] [1971] 1 W.L.R. 583; see below, para. 11–43.
[55] [1961] Ch. 270; see below, para. 12–43.
[56] [1976] 1 W.L.R. 123; see below, para. 11–59.
[57] [1959] A.C. 324; see below, para. 14–45.
[58] [1933] Ch. 935.

held that a person could not escape his obligation of specific performance under an agreement to sell property by incorporating a company or acquiring one "off the shelf" and then conveying the property to it. In *Jones v. Lipman*,[59] where this was attempted, the court said that the company "was a creature" of its owner and was "a device and a sham, a mask which he holds before his face in an attempt to avoid recognition by the eye of equity", and that the "equitable remedy is rightly to be granted directly against the creature in such circumstances".[60] Indeed, it was hardly necessary to resort to veil-piercing analysis there because the company would have acquired the property with notice of the contract and, accordingly, would be deemed to hold it as a constructive trustee for the intending purchaser.

3–23 Where the assets of an insolvent company were transferred by its directors to another company, leaving little from which the transferor's creditors could get paid, it was held that the transferee could be held liable in respect of those debts;[61] but this decision was disapproved by the Court of Appeal.[62] Where a corporate structure was being used as a device to conceal criminal activities, notably extensive evasion of customs duties, the court will readily disregard its separate legal existence and, for example, treat company assets as property of the shareholders.[63]

Agency-Alter Ego

3–24 Instances of separate existence of companies being ignored because they are mere "shams" and "facades" are alternatively explained as *alter ego* situations; in the circumstances the company is merely the agent or instrument of its controllers, so that in justice they should be held directly responsible for its actions. Sometimes greater credibility can be given to the *alter ego* principle by finding that the company acted as an outright agent for its controllers, or vice versa, or that a trustee-*cestui* relationship existed between them. But the existence of an agency or a trust will not be inferred from the mere fact of ownership and control of a company;[64] additional factors must exist which point compellingly to such a legal relationship between the company and its

---

[59] [1962] 1 W.L.R. 832.

[60] *ibid.* at p. 836. *cf. Adams v. Cape Industries p.l.c.* [1990] Ch. 433, where the company was formed to confine future or contingent liabilities within limits.

[61] *Creasy v. Breechwood Motors Ltd.* [1993] B.C.L.C. 480 and in similar vein, *Aveling Barford Ltd. v. Perion Ltd.* [1989] B.C.L.C. 626. *cf. Yukon Line Ltd. v. Rendsburg Investment Corp.* [1998] 1 W.L.R. 294.

[62] *Ord v. Belhaven Pubs Ltd.* [1998] 2 B.C.L.C. 447 at 458.

[63] *Re H.* [1996] 2 B.C.L.C. 500.

[64] *Yukon Line Ltd. v. Rendsburg Investment Corp.* [1998] 1 W.L.R. at pp. 303–305.

owners. Of course, where an express agency agreement exists, the question of piercing the corporate veil does not arise because liability will be based on the ordinary principles of agency. Thus an incorporated club which purchased beer as agent for its members was able to surmount licensing provisions that otherwise would have prevented it from selling beer on its premises.[65] And a foreign company was able to carry on business in England through the agency of its UK-registered subsidiary in order to obtain a tax advantage there.[66]

3–25 *Power Supermarkets Ltd. v. Crumlin Investments Ltd.*[67] provides an excellent illustration of the *alter ego* principle being applied in the context of groups of companies. An agreement was made by a subsidiary of the Dunnes Stores Group, which had leased part of a shopping centre, not to "grant a lease for, or to sell or permit or suffer the sale by any of its tenants" of groceries in a particular manner. Subsequently, the subsidiary conveyed the fee simple interest in that part to its parent company, which then traded in the manner the lease had sought to prevent. Fraud on the contract in the sense described above was not contended. But the evidence disclosed that the subsidiary was never treated as if it were an autonomous legal and economic entity. Costello J. concluded that the two companies were merely vehicles for carrying out the wishes of the Dunne family and that, in the circumstances, justice required that their separate existence be disregarded.[68]

3–26 A similar case is *Munton Brothers Ltd. v. Secretary of State*[69] which involved a claim for compensation in respect of criminal damage to property and where the company that actually suffered the financial loss was the parent company of the one whose property was damaged. Because of the exceptionally close business relations between the two companies here, it was held that the subsidiary was the parent's "agent" or *alter ego* and, accordingly, damage done to the subsidiary was damage done to the parent. The subsidiary never really operated as an independent business entity; its function was to make up cloth supplied by the parent and then return the cloth to it, and the terms on which the subsidiary did this business were such that it never made a profit nor incurred a loss in any year. Gibson L.J. observed that, while the courts are extremely reluctant to hold that a company is its sharehold-

---

[65] *Trebanog Working Men's Club Ltd. v. Macdonald* [1940] 1 K.B. 576; see also *Re Parnell G.A.A. Club. Ltd.* [1984] I.L.R.M. 246.

[66] *Firestone Tyre & Rubber Co. v. Llewellin* [1957] 1 W.L.R. 464.

[67] Costello J., June 22, 1981; Cases p. 78.

[68] *cf. Adams v. Cape Industries p.l.c.* [1990] Ch. 433.

[69] [1983] N.I. 369.

ers' agent or acts as a trustee for them, even for a sole proprietor-shareholder, "the same objections do not apply where it is sought to demonstrate that a subsidiary company is in fact the agent of its parent company because the conception of incorporation is preserved intact".[70] The judge went on to hold that, even in the absence of an agency relationship, there are circumstances where justice demands that closely integrated companies in a group of companies situation should be treated as one.[71] The reported cases do not provide clear guidance as to what those situations are — either regarding the relationship between the companies or the particular context in which the decision to pierce the veil arises. He concluded that the present instance was such a case because, otherwise, compensation would not be paid in respect of extensive consequential loss and the subsidiary was wholly-owned, it had no separate business of its own and the parent company owned the property which it occupied.[72]

Fraud on a Minority

3–27 Where some wrong has been done to the company, it is for the company itself and not its shareholders to bring suit against the wrongdoers, since the members' own legal rights have not been infringed. Where, however, the wrong is done by those who control the company, the majority shareholders, and it amounts to fraud in a loose equitable sense, the individual shareholder is permitted to bring suit in the company's name against the wrongdoers. This complex aspect of company law is often referred to as the rule in *Foss v. Harbottle*[73] and is dealt with in Chaper 10 below.

Limited Liability

3–28 It would appear that limited liability was not a necessary attribute of corporations, although there does not appear to be any authoritative statement that members of a corporation are personally liable for its debts unless the grant of incorporation includes some express limitation on their liability. In any event, the Limited Liability Act of 1855 permitted companies to be registered with the liability of their members limited. The immediate significance of *Salomon v. Salomon & Co.*[74] was that it underwrote the principle that shareholders can en-

---

[70] [1983] N.I. 369 at 379.

[71] Following principally *D.H.N. Food Distributors Ltd. v. Tower Hamlets L.B.C.* [1976] 1 W.L.R. 852.

[72] *cf. Re Polly Peck International p.l.c. (No. 3)* [1996] 1 B.C.L.C. 428.

[73] (1843) 2 Hare 461; below, para. 10–05.

[74] [1897] A.C. 22; above, para. 3–09. See generally, Goddard, "Corporate

tirely insulate their own financial positions from that of their company, in that they themselves are not in jeopardy of being bankrupted if the company is wound up without being able to pay its debts. In the absence of any agreement to the contrary or such exceptional circumstances as are indicated below, shareholders in a limited company are liable to it only in respect of the amounts remaining unpaid on their shares.[75] A number of rules and doctrines exist, however, under which the plight of the limited company's unpaid creditors may be alleviated.

Fraud

3–29 As has been indicated above, in appropriate circumstances the courts will pierce the corporate veil on the grounds that the company is a mere puppet of its controllers, especially where it is being used for fraudulent purposes. This approach is given a degree statutory expression in section 297A of the 1963 Act on "fraudulent trading". Persons managing a company can be made personally liable for its entire debts if it is shown that "any business of the company has been carried on with intent to defraud creditors . . . or for any fraudulent purpose . . ."[76] The question of fraudulent trading and also of reckless trading and other situations where unlimited liability can be imposed is considered in more detail in the chapter on liquidations. Company controllers who in effect give themselves presents of company assets, with the consequence that the company is unable to pay its debts, can be compelled to disgorge those sums to the company's creditors. In *Re George Newman & Co.*[77] it was pointed out that "to make presents out of profits is one thing [but] to make them out of capital or out of money borrowed by the company is a very different matter. Such money cannot be lawfully divided among the shareholders themselves, nor can it be given away by them for nothing to their directors so as to bind the company in its corporate capacity".[78] That is to say, such payments are *ultra vires*. Where capital is repaid to any shareholder other than by the method set out in section 72 of the 1963 Act or an otherwise authorised mode, the funds must be repaid if the member knew or ought to have known that there was a prohibited "distribution".[79]

Personality — Limited Recourse and its Limits" in (C. Rickett & R. Grantham (eds.), *Corporate Personality in the 20th Century* (1998), Chap. 2.

[75] 1963 Act, ss. 27 and 207(1)(d).

[76] See below, paras 18–51 *et seq*.

[77] [1895] 1 Ch. 674.

[78] *ibid*. at 686.

[79] 1983 Act, s.50; below, para. 7.84.

Under-Capitalisation

3–30 It is sometimes overlooked that the core contention in the *Salomon & Co.* case was not that the unsecured creditors should have a direct claim against Mr Salomon but merely that whatever claims he had against the company should be postponed, or subordinated, until other claims were satisfied first. In support of this, it was argued that Salomon had established an insufficiently capitalised entity and that, accordingly, he should suffer the adverse consequences of its over-trading, especially when he exercised complete control over its management and stood to benefit virtually exclusively from any profits arising from the venture. More particularly, it was said that, in return for securities in it, the company had acquired assets from him at a considerable over-valuation, that in consequence the actual capital possessed by the company was seriously over-stated and, therefore, it was unfair for unsecured creditors to bear the entire loss when they may have believed they were doing business with a much more substantial entity. This line of argument foundered on one of the House of Lords' leading cases on promoters' liability.[80] It was cited as supporting the proposition that, where the price paid by a company for a business is an exorbitant one but all the shareholders are perfectly cognizant of the conditions under which the company is formed and the conditions of the purchase, it is impossible to contend that the company is being defrauded.[81] It furthermore was said that the unpaid creditors "if they had thought fit to avail themselves of the means of protecting their interests which the Act provides, could have informed themselves of the terms of the purchase"; and that "the law does not lay any obligations . . . to warn those members of the public who deal with [a company] on credit that they run the risk of not being paid."[82]

3–31 It nevertheless is conceivable that in exceptional circumstances at least the controlling shareholders might be held liable for the debts of their inadequately capitalised companies — as where the creditor is of the "involuntary" category, or where there was some misrepresentation about the company's true worth or the shareholder had "milked" the company of substance.[83] Such an outcome is especially likely where the company is a wholly-owned subsidiary being operated in fact as

---

[80] *Erlanger v. New Sombrero Phosphate Co.* (1878) 3 App. Cas. 1218; below, para. 6.51.

[81] [1897] A.C. at p. 33.

[82] *ibid.* at p. 40. See also, *Henry Brown & Sons Ltd v. Smith* [1964] 2 Ll. L.R. 477.

[83] See generally, Hackney & Benson, "Shareholder Liability for Inadequate Capital" (1982) 43 U. Pittsburgh L. Rev. 837 and Halpern *et al.*, "An Economic Analysis of Limited Liability in Corporation Law" (1980) 30 U.Toronto L.J. 117.

an integral part of the parent's business.[84] Indeed, section 140 of the 1990 Act empowers a court to order that a company contribute towards paying the debts of its insolvent related company.

Involuntary Creditors

3–32 In the *Salomon & Co.* case the argument that, in the circumstances, it would be unjust to give Mr Salomon priority over the unsecured creditors was also met with the answer that they "may be entitled to sympathy, but they have only themselves to blame for their misfortunes. [For] they had full notice that they were no longer dealing with an individual, and they must be taken to have been cognizant of the memorandum and of the articles of association."[85] But what is the position of what is called the involuntary creditor, like the pedestrian who is injured by a company-owned vehicle and has a right of action in negligence?[86] The victim does not choose to be struck by a vehicle owned by an insolvent limited company as opposed to being owned by an individual trader or partnership. Under the bankruptcy rules, which also apply to winding up,[87] the position was that claims for damages in tort were not provable debts against the insolvent tort-feasor.[88] At common law, such claims simply could not be asserted at all, thereby precluding any argument that the company's shareholders should be rendered responsible for those debts because of the very special circumstances of the case. In Britain, this rule was embodied in the bankruptcy legislation (section 30(1) of the 1914 Act). In Ireland, however, the rule was abolished by section 61 of the Civil Liability Act 1961, according to which:

> "Notwithstanding any other enactment or any rule of law, a claim for damages or contribution in respect of a wrong shall be provable in bankruptcy where the wrong out of which the liability to damages or the right to contribution arose was committed before the time of the bankruptcy."[89]

Consequently, involuntary creditors are now entitled to maintain claims against insolvent companies, thereby making it at least possible to argue that the company's shareholders should be held responsible to them because of the special circumstances of the case.

---

84 Lifting the corporate veil in group of company situations is discussed below, paras 14–49 *et seq*.
85 [1897] A.C. at p. 53. Similarly, *H. Brown & Sons Ltd. v. Smith* [1962] 2 L.I.L.R. 476.
86 *e.g. Walkovszky v. Carlton*, 223 N.E. 2d 6 (1966), extracts reproduced in W. Cary & M Eisenberg, *Cases and Materials on Corporations* (5th ed., 1980), p. 83.
87 1963 Act, s.283.
88 See generally, M. Forde, *Bankruptcy Law in Ireland* (1990) at p. 139.
89 See Bankruptcy Act 1988, s.75(1).

3–33 There would be no great difficulty in distinguishing the *Salomon & Co.* case. The argument could be made that the public policy supporting limited liability must be reconciled with, if not forced to make way for, the broad principle that persons who through no fault whatsoever of their own suffer damage as a result to another's fault ought not to go uncompensated.[90] It may even be possible to demonstrate that the economic and social goals that limited liability was intended to achieve are not unduly compromised by allowing recourse in this context against the shareholders, who in any event stand to benefit from the company's risky activities.[91] An inevitable problem with any involuntary creditor doctrine is separating the voluntarily-assumed legal relationships from those imposed by events. Take a Canadian case concerning against whom costs should be awarded when a "one-person" company loses a wholly unmeritorious legal claim brought by it, and is then discovered to be insolvent.[92] In *Sweeney v. Duggan*[93] it was contended that the plaintiff, a former employee of an insolvent company and who was injured at work, fell into the "involuntary" category and that *Salomon & Co.* did not protect the "one man" owner of the company, who (along with his wife) was its director and who managed its business. However, the Supreme Court declined to comment on the proposition, finding against the plaintiff on other grounds.[94]

SCOPE OF LEGAL CAPACITY

3–34 Subject to whatever restrictions are contained in their instruments of incorporation and to obvious limitations as arise from the fact that ultimately they are mere legal constructs, registered companies have almost as complete a legal personality as natural persons and possess the additional attribute of perpetual succession.

Perpetual Succession

3–35 Perhaps the most remarkable feature of the corporate legal personality is that companies continue in existence until they are formally wound up. Shareholders and directors may come and go and, indeed, all of them may die at the one time. But their company remains in

---

[90] *Kirby v. Burke* [1944] I.R. 207.

[91] The argument for imposing liability is made in Hansmann and Kraakman, "Towards Unlimited Shareholder Liability for Corporate Torts" (1991) 100 *Yale L.J.* 1879.

[92] *Rockwell Developments Ltd. v. Newtonbrook Plaza Ltd.* (1972) 30 O.R. (2d) 199.

[93] [1997] 2 I.R. 531.

[94] *cf. Berger v. Willowdale A.M.C.*, 145 D.L.R. (3d) 247 (1983).

existence until its name has been removed from the register of companies through the appropriate procedure.[95] A great advantage of doing business in the corporate form, therefore, is that the incorporated business is not in a legal sense fundamentally affected by the death or retirement of its *de facto* proprietor or proprietors. All that happens is that the company's shares change hands. In contrast, on the death of the sole trader, his executor or the administrator of the estate must sell off the business in order to complete the succession, which can involve expensive conveyancing charges. A sole trader who wishes to retire and dispose of the business will be confronted with those same charges and, moreover, certain contractual rights and obligations may not be capable of assignment, like rights of a personal nature.[96] Where a partner retires or dies, in principle the partnership is dissolved; although the inconvenience of such a state of affairs can be avoided by an appropriate provision in the partnership agreement.[97]

Holding and Disposing of Land

3–36 An unincorporated association cannot actually own land; any land which in a colloquial sense belongs to the association will be vested in its trustees[98] or in its management committee or in its members, as the case may be. Enactments establishing statutory companies usually stipulate that the body in question is authorised to "acquire, hold and dispose of land".[99] In the case of registered companies, the objects clause in their memorandum of association usually empower them to own land. Even where there is no express provision to that effect, if land-owning is a reasonable incident to their general objects, they are empowered to own land for those purposes. In the past there was a "mortmain" restriction on making gifts of land to corporations but it was repealed in 1954.[100]

Suing and Being Sued

3–37 An unincorporated association cannot sue or be sued in its own name. Considerable difficulties, therefore, can arise when associations wish to bring suit or someone wishes to sue them.[101] On occasions, their officers may be entitled to sue or may be liable personally, or the

---

95 Either after being wound up or by being de-registered under s.12 of the 1982 Act (as amended by s.245 of the 1990 Act).

96 *e.g. Griffith v. Tower Publishing Co.* [1897] 1 Ch. 21.

97 *Lindley and Banks on Partnerships* (17th ed., 1995) Chaps. 24, 26.

98 *e.g.* trade unions; *cf.* Trade Union Act 1871, s.8.

99 *cf. Kathleen Investments Ltd. v. Australian Atomic Energy Commission* (1977) 139 C.L.R. 117.

100 Mortmain (Repeal of Enactments) Act 1954.

101 See generally, D. Lloyd, *The Law of Unincorporated Associations* (1938).

strenuous requirements for the representative action may be satisfied. Legislation enabling some of the principal kinds of unincorporated association to be established or registered, like trade unions and friendly societies, provides that actions may be brought by and against the association's trustees or, sometimes, its officers. Thus according to section 94(1) of the Friendly Societies Act 1896:

> "The trustees of a registered society . . . or any other officers authorised by the rules thereof, may bring or defend, or cause to be brought or defended, any action or other legal proceeding . . . touching or concerning any property, right or claim of the society . . . and may sue and be sued in their proper names, without other description other than the titles of their office."[102]

3–38 One of the classic characteristics of incorporated bodies is the capacity to sue and be sued *eo nomine*. However, whereas in civil actions an individual can appear in court *pro se*, a registered company must be represented by counsel or a solicitor; generally, none of its officers will be permitted to appear as an advocate on its behalf.[103] Where a company is charged with an indictable offence, it is provided in section 382 of the 1963 Act that a duly authorised representative may appear for it at all stages of the proceedings, answer any questions put, exercise any right of objection or election conferred on accused persons by an enactment and enter any plea. Section 390 of the 1963 Act authorises a judge, where the plaintiff is a limited company, to require that security be given for costs.[104]

Common Law Rights and Duties

3–39 Registered companies are entitled to sue on contracts and can be held liable for breach of contracts entered into on their behalf; the position of company contractual liability is considered in detail in Chapter 13. Companies are protected by the law of tort just as much as partners and sole traders are.[105] A company has been held competent to sue in defamation;[106] even if the company has never traded, it may in the circumstances of the case succeed in a claim for defamation.[107] On

---

[102] Similarly, Trade Union Act 1871, s.9.

[103] *Battle v. Irish Art Promotion Centre Ltd.* [1968] I.R. 252 and *Radford v. Freeway Classics Ltd.* [1994] 1 B.C.L.C. 445.

[104] *cf. Lismore Homes Ltd. v. Bank of Ireland Finance Ltd.* [1992] 2 I.R. 57; *Irish Press v. Warburg Piacus & Co.* [1997] 2 I.L.R.M. 263; and *Keary Developments Ltd. v. Tarmac Construction Ltd.* [1995] 3 All E.R. 534.

[105] See generally, B. McMahon & W. Binchy, *Irish Law of Torts* (2nd ed. 1990) Chap. 39.

[106] See generally, P. Milmo & W. Rogers (eds.), *Libel and Slander* (9th ed., 1998), pp. 181–187.

[107] *Scott v. Fourth Estate Newspaper Ltd.* [1986] 1 N.Z.L.R. 336.

account of their very nature, companies may not possess some of what are described as rights of personality, like certain aspects of the right of privacy.[108] It has been held that companies are entitled to invoke the plea of self-incrimination, *i.e.* to refuse to give evidence on the grounds that the answers would incriminate them.[109] However, it has been held by the European Court of Justice that, in the course of investigations by E.C. enforcement agencies, companies are not protected by fundamental rights, like the right to silence and the inviolability of their premises.[110]

3–40 As for the liability of companies in tort, although there is little authority squarely on the matter, it is almost universally accepted that the *ultra vires* doctrine does not enable companies to avoid such liability.[111] That a company cannot plead, as a defence to an action for tort or a prosecution, that it had been acting *ultra vires* is now confirmed by section 8(1) of the 1963 Act.[112] In the case of most torts, where it is not necessary to prove a particular mental element on the defendant's part, companies will be held liable where a wrong was done in the course of their employees' or agents' activities, in the same way as non-corporate employers and principals would be vicariously liable.[113] In *Pearson & Son Ltd. v. Dublin Corp.,*[114] which concerned a statutory corporation, the defendant was held liable for a fraud committed by one of its employees in the course of his work although there was no suggestion that the actual members of Dublin Corporation had authorised or consented to the fraud.

3–41 In the case of torts the commission of which requires a distinct mental element, such as malice, the actual mental state of the company's principal agents will be imputed to it. This, it has been said, "results from the fact that a corporation is an abstraction. It has no mind of its own any more than it has a body of its own; its active and directing will must consequently be sought in the person of somebody who for some purposes may be called an agent, but who is really the directing mind and will of the corporation, the very ego and centre of the personality of the corporation."[115] It depends on all of the circumstances

---

[108] See generally, J.G. Fleming, *The Law of Torts* (9th ed., 1998), Chap. 26.
[109] *New Zealand Apple and Pear Marketing Board v. Master & Sons Ltd.* [1986] 1 N.Z.L.R. 191.
[110] *Orkem v. E.C. Commission* (Case 374/87) [1989] E.C.R. 3283.
[111] See McMahon & Binchy, *op. cit.*, n. 105.
[112] See below, para. 13.15 *et seq.*
[113] See McMahon & Binchy, *op. cit.*, n. 105, Chap. 43.
[114] [1907] 2 I.R. 27 at 82, 537.
[115] *Lennards Carrying Co. v. Asiatic Petroleum Co.* [1915] A.C. 705 at 713–714. See

of the case who will be regarded as principal agents for the purpose of attributing their state of knowledge and intentions to the company; a similar point arises for the purpose of breach of statutory duty[116] and for company criminal responsibility.[117]

3–42 For instance, in *The Lady Gwendolen*[118] where, under the legislation in question, ordinary vicarious liability would not suffice to render the company liable, it was held that the company was responsible for breach of shipping safety rules by one of its ship's captains because the head of the company's traffic department was aware of those breaches. The ship, which was owned by the Guinness' brewery and which regularly carried stout from Dublin to Liverpool, collided with another ship in a fog when it had been travelling far too fast. The owners' liability would have been limited if they could prove that the loss did not result from their "actual fault or privity".[119] In other words, even though under the general principles of vicarious liability for negligence the company was responsible, the damages awarded against it would be significantly reduced unless it was privy to the captain's wrongs or was specially at fault for what he had done. In the circumstances, it was held that the company was so responsible because:

> "where, as in the present case, a company has a separate traffic department, which assumes responsibility for running the company's ships, [there is] no good reason why the head of that department, even though not himself a director, should not be regarded as someone whose action is the very action of the company itself, so far as concerns any thing to do with the company's ships."[120]

Statutory Entitlements and Obligations

3–43 Some statutes make it clear that their provisions either apply or do not apply to registered companies. Under the Companies Acts themselves, for instance, a body corporate is not permitted to be either a company's director, examiner, receiver, liquidator or auditor.[121] Under legislation, corporate bodies are forbidden from providing serv-

---

remarks in *Superwood Holdings p.l.c. v. Sun Alliance & London Insurance p.l.c.* [1995] 3 I.R. 303 at 328–30.

116 See below, para. 3–46.

117 See below, paras 3–54 *et seq*.

118 [1965] P. 294.

119 Merchant Shipping Act 1894, s.503(1).

120 [1965] P. at p. 343–344. *cf. Re Supply of Ready Mixed Concrete (No.2)* [1995] 1 A.C. 456 on when a company can be held responsible where its employees have acted in contravention of a court order.

121 1963 Act, ss. 176, 314, 300, and 1990 Act, s.187(2)(g).

ices as solicitors,[122] as medical doctors or dentists[123] or as veterinary surgeons,[124] and special provision is made for companies acting as pharmacists.[125] Certificates of personal fitness to operate bookmaking premises may not be granted to corporate bodies;[126] although it has been held that an individual may hold such a certificate as agent for a company.[127]

3–44 Where the legislation in question does not make it abundantly clear whether or not its provisions apply to companies, in resolving the issue the courts will consider the general background and context of the measure in question. Thus in *The King (Cottingham) v. Cork Justices*,[128] the issue was whether a liquor licence could be granted to a company. On the grounds that one of the prerequisites of getting a licence was that the applicant be of "good character", it was argued that mere legal entities cannot possess any character and, accordingly, can never qualify for a licence. That view was rejected in the light of the history of the Licensing Acts and the purpose of their good character requirement. According to Palles C.B.:

> "I cannot see why a public company cannot have a character. No doubt it has no soul; but it can act by others, and through others do acts which in the case of a natural person would affect conscience, and be the foundation of that reputation which the law knows as 'character', be it good or bad. It can be guilty of fraud, of malice, and of various criminal offences, some of commission, others of omission. . . . 'Character' as used in the section means reputation. Reputation is acquired by conduct. The conduct of the authorised agents of a company is its conduct. Why should not that conduct give rise to a reputation as to its character, good, bad or indifferent?"[129]

3–45 Where the position of companies is unclear under the legislation in question, the matter is often resolved by the Interpretation Act 1937, which generally includes companies within the word "person".

---

[122] Solicitors Act 1954, s.64.

[123] Medical Practitioners Act 1978, ss. 59, 61, and Dentists Act 1985, s.52. *cf. O'Duffy v. Jaffe* [1904] 2 I.R. 27 and *Attorney General (O'Duffy) v. Middletons* [1907] 1 I.R. 471.

[124] Veterinary Surgeons Act 1931, s.47.

[125] Pharmacy Act 1962, s.2(1)(c); *cf. Pharmaceuticals Society of Ireland v. Boyd & Co.* [1899] 2 I.R. 133.

[126] Betting Act 1931, s.4(1).

[127] *McDonnell v. Reid* [1987] I.R. 51.

[128] [1906] 2 I.R. 415.

[129] *ibid.* at pp. 422–423, applied in *McMahon v. Murtagh Properties Ltd.* [1982] I.L.R.M. 342. On other aspects of company ownership of liquor licences, see *The State (Hennessy) v. Commons* [1976] I.R. 238 and *D.P.P. v. Roberts* [1987] I.R. 268.

According to section 11(c) and (i) of this Act: [t]he word "person" shall, unless the contrary intention appears, be construed as importing a body corporate . . . as well as an individual"; and "[r]eferences to a person in relation to an offence. . . shall, unless the contrary intention appears, be construed as including references to a body corporate." The legislature's intention that the word person was not intended to embrace companies may be derived from the nature and structure of, and background to, the measure in question. Although registered companies did not exist at the time it was enacted, it has been held that the Fraudulent Conveyances Act 1634, applies to transactions entered into by companies.[130] In contrast, it was held that the Sunday Observance Act 1677, did not bind companies because they are incapable of performing that Act's declared objective— of "repairing to church and being pious and religious" on one day every week.[131] Reference in Rating Acts to the "persons" occupying premises and to the "occupiers" of a premises were held to connote plural occupation and, accordingly, those provisions did not apply where the occupier was a company.[132] While there is a widespread belief that companies themselves cannot hold liquor licences and it has been the practice for such licences to be held by companies' nominees, companies are "persons" entitled to apply for and to hold such licences.[133] A "club license" for selling liquor can be granted to a company limited by guarantee where all the members are also members of the club;[134] it remains to be seen whether such a licence could ever be granted to a company limited by shares.

3–46 Where it cannot be disputed that a particular statutory obligation or regulatory measure applies to a company, the question remains whether in the circumstances the company could be held responsible for some non-compliance with that duty.[135] There is the separate question of when can individual directors and other company personnel be held personally liable.[136] On the question of vicarious liability under statutory provisions, the matter was considered in the *Meridian Global Funds* case[137] in the context of breaches of an Act designed to regulate

---

130 *Re Kill Inn Motel Ltd.* Murphy J., September 16, 1987. See also *Lawler v. Egan Ltd.* [1901] 2 I.R. 589.

131 *Rolloswin Investments Ltd. v. Chromolit etc. SARL* [1970] 1 W.L.R. 912.

132 *Prior v. Sovereign Chicken Ltd.* [1984] 1 W.L.R. 921; similarly *Real Estate House (Broadtop) Ltd. v. Real Estate Agents Licensing Board* [1987] 2 N.Z.L.R. 593.

133 above, para. 3–44.

134 *Re Parnell G.A.A. Club Ltd.* [1984] I.L.R.M. 246.

135 See generally, Gray, "Company Law and Regulatory Complexity" in C. Rickett and R. Grantham, *Corporate Personality in the 20th Century* (1998) Chap. 8.

136 See *ibid.* and below, paras 5–96 and 5–167 *et seq.*

137 *Meridan Global Funds Management Asia Ltd. v. Securities Commission* [1995] 2 A.C. 500.

transactions on the securities market. Two senior executives knew that the disclosure requirements in question had not been complied with but the board of directors were unaware of that. What had to be decided was whether those executives' actions and knowledge was attributable to the company. To answer this, two principal matters call for consideration. One is the company's own rules for allocating responsibility within itself, being mainly its articles of association, along with common law agency principles. The other is the Act in question and the policy underlying it, which should indicate at what level within the company responsibility is being laid.[138] In the present case, it was held that the policy of the statutory provision there was, in the context of fast-moving stock markets, to compel immediate disclosure of the identity of purchasers of securities. Accordingly, the activities of those who were authorised to initiate buy and sell securities transactions were attributable to the company; otherwise, the policy of the section would be entirely defeated. That the executives there were acting corruptly did not exonerate the company from the breach of statutory duty.

Constitutional Rights and Duties

3–47 Are registered companies "persons" in the constitutional law sense and, in particular, in what circumstances are companies "persons" and "citizens" entitled to the fundamental rights guaranteed in Articles 40–44 of the Constitution? In other countries "moral persons" and corporations enjoy the protection of constitutional human rights provisions. For instance, a matter of great controversy in the United States has been the scope of companies' First Amendment free speech rights.[139] In France the provision of a law on audio-visual communications that excluded profit-orientated companies from the statutory right of response was struck down as violating the principle of equality before the law.[140] There are a number of instances in Ireland of incorporated plaintiffs obtaining judgments that their constitutional rights had been violated.[141] In *Quinn's Supermarket Ltd. v. Attorney General*,[142] where the central issue was whether regulations concerning the sale of Kosher meat contravened the guarantee against religious discrimination, no objection was taken to the fact that the first plaintiff was a company.

---

[138] Similarly in criminal prosecutions; see below, paras 3–54 *et seq*.

[139] *First National Bank of Boston v. Bellotti*, 435 U.S. 765 (1978). See generally, "Constitutional Rights of the Corporate Person", 91 Yale L.J. 1641 (1982) and B. Welling, *Corporate Law in Canada* (2nd ed., 1991), pp. 29-35.

[140] Decision of July 27, 1982.

[141] *cf. National Union of Railwaymen v. Sullivan* [1947] I.R. 77.

[142] [1972] I.R. 1.

3–48 Because of their very nature, however, certain human rights guarantees can have no direct application to companies. It is highly unlikely that companies have legally enforceable claims under Article 41 on the family; indeed, that Article has been held not even to extend to extra-marital families.[143] On a number of occasions, moreover, guarantees that by their general nature are capable of being enjoyed by companies were held not to extend to them on account of the very terms in which those guarantees are formulated. Because of Article 40.1's ambiguous reference to "all citizens . . . as human persons" being equal before the law, in *Quinn's Supermarket*, it was held that companies had no rights under that Article because "under no possible construction of [this] guarantee [can] a body corporate or any entity but a human being be considered to be a human person for the purpose of this provision".[144] Yet there are numerous American cases where claims by companies under the equal protection clause of the Fourteenth Amendment were upheld.[145]

3–49 On account of the way in which property rights are formulated in Article 43 of the Constitution, there was some authority for the proposition that companies did not enjoy the guarantee in it and in Article 40.1.3°,[146] and the practice grew up of the shareholders in the company in question being made plaintiffs in cases where it was sought to vindicate corporate property claims under the Constitution. However, in *Iarnród Éireann v. Ireland*,[147] that theory was rejected and it was held that companies can have *locus standi* to challenge the constitutionality of an Act of the Oireachtas as contravening those Articles. As Keane J. there observed:

> "There . . . would be a spectacular deficiency in the guarantee to every citizen that his or her property rights would be protected against "unjust attack", if such bodies were incapable in law of being regarded as "citizens" at least for the purpose of this Article, and if it was essential for shareholders to abandon the protection of limited liability to which they are entitled by law in order to protect, not merely their own rights as shareholders but also the property rights of the corporate entity itself, which are in law distinct from the rights of its members."[148]

3–50 There, the State-owned railway company challenged the consti-

---

[143] *State (Nicolaou) v. An Bord Uchtála* [1966] I.R. 567.
[144] [1972] I.R. at p. 14.
[145] *e.g. Santa Clara Co. v. Southern Pacific Railway Co.*, 118 U.S. 394 (1886) and *Weeling Steel Corp. v. Glander*, 337 U.S. 562 (1949).
[146] *Private Motorists Protection Society v. Attorney General* [1983] I.R. 339.
[147] [1996] 3 I.R. 321.
[148] *ibid.* at p.345.

tutionality of part of the Civil Liability Act 1961, but in the event failed on the merits. Whether Keane J.'s logic would similarly apply to challenges based on the equality guarantee is debatable because its scope has been narrowly confined by the courts.[149] The fact that they are not human beings does not debar companies from initiating claims under the European Convention on Human Rights and Fundamental Freedoms.[150] But the European Court of Justice in Luxembourg does not extend to companies all the fundamental rights which it recognises individuals as possessing, like the right to silence and to inviolability of their premises.[151]

3–51 The Supreme Court has not yet set out the circumstances in which companies are bound by specific guarantees in the Constitution. In a case concerning the dismissal of a managing director for alleged misconduct, it was held that he should have been afforded an opportunity to meet the charges against him before a final decision to dismiss him was taken.[152] Although Walsh J. there referred to the constitutional guarantee of fair procedure,[153] the decision was based on there being an implied term in the employment contract that he would be afforded some kind of hearing in those circumstances. Since a term to this effect is implied by the common law in comparable situations, it would be wrong to regard the case as an authority for the general proposition being considered here. In many countries with constitutions like that of Ireland, the courts tend to confine constitutional obligations to the State and to other public authorities and not subject private individuals and organisations to such duties.[154] Under the U.S. Constitution, most of the Bill of Rights' guarantees obtain against "state action" only.

3–52 In *Attorney General (S.P.U.C.) v. Open Door Counselling Ltd.*,[155] the plaintiff sought an injunction against two registered companies giving abortion-related advice to pregnant women, on the grounds that this activity contravened the right to life guarantee in Article 40.3.3°. According to this, "[t]he State acknowledges the right to life of the unborn. . . and guarantees in its laws to respect" that right. Since neither of the defendants were agents or instrumentalities of the State, one might have thought that the constitutional provision had no direct application to them; that it instead called on the State, in particular

---

[149] above, para. 3–48.
[150] *e.g. Sunday Times* case, Series A no.30, 2 E.H.R.R. 245.
[151] *Orkhem v. E.C. Commission* (Case 374/87) [1989] E.C.R. 3283.
[152] *Glover v. B.L.N. Ltd.* [1973] I.R. 388; see below, para. 5–43.
[153] *ibid.* at p. 425.
[154] See generally, Forde, "Non-Governmental Interference With Human Rights" (1986) 56 Brit. Y. Bk. Int'l L. 253 and Chap. 1, p. 18, n. 81.
[155] [1988] I.R. 593.

through its legislative organ, to adopt appropriated measures for preventing abortion. But it was held by Hamilton P. that, for the purposes of this guarantee, the courts are as much a part of the State as are the legislature and the executive. Consequently, the courts are constitutionally obliged to combat abortion whenever cases involving that question come before them. According to the learned President:

> "Under the Constitution . . . the State's powers of government are exercised in their respective spheres by the legislature, executive and judicial organs established under the Constitution and the courts will act to protect and enforce the rights of individuals and the provisions of the Constitution. . . . Consequently, the judicial organ of government is obliged to lend its support to the enforcement of the right to life of the unborn, to defend and vindicate that right and, if there is a threat to that right from any source, to protect that right from such threat, if its support is sought."[156]

It would seem that the force of this reasoning was so compelling that the defendants chose not to argue this point on appeal before the Supreme Court.

Criminal Responsibility

3–53 Can companies be convicted of crimes? Where the only penalty for conviction is imprisonment or corporal punishment, this question hardly arises because, as has been observed already, a company has "no body to be kicked" nor can it be incarcerated in a prison.[157] But companies can be fined and the prospect of them being convicted on criminal charges and suffering large fines is a potent deterrent against offences being committed in the course of a company's activities. Applying the criminal law to companies has given rise to two related questions: the extent to which wrongs done by its agents can be attributed to the company and whether there are some offences which never can be attributed to companies.[158]

Attribution

3–54 There is no vicarious criminal liability for serious offences,[159] so that a company can never be held responsible merely by virtue of its

---

[156] [1988] I.R. 593 at 599.

[157] Attributed to Baron Thurlow L.C. (1731-1806).

[158] See generally, L. Leigh, *The Criminal Liability of Corporations in English Law* (1969); C. Wells, *Corporation and Criminal Responsibility* (1993), Khana, "Corporate Criminal Liability: What Purpose Does it Serve?" (1996) 109 Harv. L. Rev. 1477; Leigh, "The Criminal Liability of Corporations and Other Groups" (1977) 9 Ottawa L. Rev. 247 and Developments in the Law, "Corporate Crime" (1979) 92 Harv. L. Rev. 1227.

[159] *R. v. Huggins*, 2 Ray 1574 (1730).

agents, within the scope of their authority, committing an offence. In *Tesco Supermarkets Ltd. v. Nattrass*[160] the House of Lords rejected the doctrine of "enterprise" criminal liability, *i.e.* that offences committed by a company's subordinate officials and employees in the course of the company's general business render the company itself criminally responsible. Instead, the offence must have been instigated by the company's senior management. The proper approach in cases of corporate crimes that require *mens rea* was summed up as follows in that case:

> "A corporation . . . must act through living persons, though not always one or the same person. Then the person who acts is not speaking or acting for the company. He is acting as the company and his mind which directs his acts is the mind of the company. There is no question of the company being vicariously liable. . . . If it is a guilty mind then that guilt is the guilt of the company. It must be a question of law whether . . . a person in doing particular things is to be regarded as the company or merely as the company's servant or agent. . . .
>
> Normally the board of directors, the managing director and perhaps other superior officers of the company carry out the functions of management and speak and act as the company. Their subordinates do not. They carry out orders from above and it can make no difference that they are given some measure of discretion. But the board of directors may delegate some part of their functions of management, giving to their delegate full discretion to act independently of instructions from them. [There is] no difficulty in holding that they have thereby put such a delegate in their place so that within the scope of the delegation he can act as the company. It may not always be easy to draw the line . . . ."[161]

3–55 It will depend on the entire circumstances of the case and the nature of the offence whether the wrong of a particular company functionary will be attributed to the company.[162] In the *Tesco Supermarkets* case, which concerned charges under consumer protection legislation, it was held that the manager of one of the defendant supermarket chain's shops would not be sufficiently close to the board of directors for the purpose of attributing guilt to the company. Similarly, companies have been held not to be responsible for what was done by their depot engineer[163] or their weighbridge operator.[164] By contrast, in a case involving charges of violating war-time fuel rationing, it was held that the accused company's transport manager was sufficiently senior

---

[160] [1972] A.C. 152.

[161] *ibid.* at pp. 170–171. Note comments in *Meridian Global Funds Management Asia Ltd. v. Securities Commission* [1995] 2 A.C. 500.

[162] See generally, Sullivan, "The Attribution of Culpability to Limited Companies", (1996) 55 Cam. L.J. 515.

[163] *Magna Plant v. Mitckell* unreported, Eng. Div. Ct., April 27, 1966.

[164] *John Henshall (Quarries) Ltd. v. Harvey* [1965] 2 Q.B. 233.

for these purposes.[165] Attribution of responsibility is a matter of law, not of fact, but in jury trials the jury must be directed to consider whether sufficient facts were proved as would justify the judge in holding that the company should be made responsible for what was done.[166]

3–56 While the doctrine of vicarious or enterprise criminal liability has been rejected, the legislature has created many offences whereby an employer, or company, is made criminally responsible for designated acts of its agents and employees; what has been called "situational liability".[167] If the offence in question is one which, under the relevant statute, is attributed to individual employers or occupiers when the prohibited acts are done by their employees or agents, a company equally will be held responsible *qua* employer or principal for what its subordinates have done.

3–57 Sometimes the offence in question may be one of strict liability, in the sense that *mens rea* need not be established. For these offences, the legislature often provides a defence where the accused can demonstrate that all that was reasonably possible was done to prevent the prohibited state of affairs from occurring, like issuing appropriate instructions, supervision, improving modes of operation etc. An examples is section 22 of the Consumer Information Act 1978, where taking adequate precautions and exercising all due diligence is a defence. That was the issue in the *Tesco Supermarkets* case, which concerned offences for which an employer or principal, in the course of whose business the offences were committed is criminally liable, notwithstanding that they are due to acts or omissions of his servants or agents which were done without his knowledge or consent or even were contrary to his orders. The question there was whether the employer, who was *prima facie* guilty, had exercised the requisite "due diligence" to ensure that what was done should not occur, which would be a defence.[168] It was held that the company had not done so because it was not enough for it to delegate the task to such subordinate officers as its store managers; the company itself, through its principal officers, should have taken the necessary precautions.[169]

---

165 *Moore v. I. Bresler Ltd.* [1944] 2 All E.R. 515.

166 *R. v. Andrews Weatberfoil Ltd.* [1972] 1 W.L.R. 119.

167 Glazebrook, "Situational Liability", in P.R. Glazebrook (ed.), *Reshaping the Criminal Law* (1978).

168 Under the Trade Descriptions Act 1978, s.24(1)(b) (U.K.), identical to s.22(1)(b) of the Consumer Information Act 1978.

169 *cf. Tesco Stores Ltd. v. Brent L.B.C.* [1993] 1 W.L.R. 1037 and *Seabord Offshore Ltd. v. Secretary of State* [1994] 1 W.L.R. 541, concerning similar questions.

Offences Outside of a Company's Capacity

3–58 There are certain offences which a company cannot be held guilty of committing. In a Scottish case[170] it was held that a company could not be convicted on a charge of conducting itself in a "shameless indecent manner" by selling pornographic materials to young persons. This was because many states of mind have been attributed to companies, through their directors, like malice and an intent to deceive, but a "sense of shame" would not be so attributed; shame was "something which is defined by reference to a type of behaviour of which human beings alone are capable."[171] A company has never been convicted of murder but manslaughter convictions have been recorded.[172] It has been suggested that companies can never be guilty of murder or of perjury;[173] another such possibility is treason.[174]

Procedure

3–59 It was held by the High Court in 1955[175] that a District Judge could not return a company for trial for an indictable offence because witnesses had to be examined in the presence of the accused but, under the then rules, there was no provision enabling a company to be present at the examination. According to Murnaghan J., referring to section 17 of the Indictable Offences (Ireland) Act 1849, he could not "construe the word "person", where it therein appears as including a body corporate" and that it was "impossible to construe this section so as to deal with anything but the case of an individual."[176] This anomaly is now rectified by section 382 of the 1963 Act, which authorises a company to appear at all stages of the proceedings by a representative, who may answer questions for the company; if no such representative appears, the judge is authorised to take the depositions and to return the company for trial. A company's representative for these purposes is also authorised to enter any plea and to exercise any right of objection or of election on its behalf.

---

170 *Dean v. John Menzies (Holdings) Ltd.* (1981) S.C. 23.

171 *ibid.* at p. 38. Similarly, *Rolloswin Investments Ltd. v. Chromolit Portugal S.A.* [1970] 1 W.L.R. 912.

172 *R. v. Murray Wright Ltd.* [1970] N.Z.L.R. 476.

173 *Dean* case, above, n. 170, at p. 35.

174 Constitution Art. 39.

175 *State (Batchelor & Co.) Ireland Ltd. v. O Leannain* [1957] I.R. 1.

176 *ibid.* at p. 17.

ULTRA VIRES

3–60 The inherent capacity of incorporated bodies to make contracts and to enter into various engagements is subject to a number of qualifications. In the first place, a distinction has been drawn between what are called "common law" corporations, *i.e.* corporations created by charter or by letter patent, and `statutory" corporations, *i.e.* corporations created by or that owe their origin to statute. The former possess the legal capacity to do anything other than what they cannot do by virtue of their artificial being (*e.g.* marry, beget, etc.).[177] The latter are subject to the *ultra vires* principle; they can do only what their constituting statute empowers them to do and any transaction they purport to enter into beyond those powers is *ultra vires* and (subject to section 8(1) of the 1963 Act) does not bind them.[178] For example, the Loan Fund Act 1843, enabled Loan Fund Societies to be formed in any district to make loans to the "industrious classes resident therein". In *Enniskillen Loan Fund Soc. v. Green*[179] the plaintiff sought to recover money it had lent to the defendant, who in fact did not live in the Enniskillen district. It was held that, in the light of the 1843 Act's terms, the loan agreement was *ultra vires* and therefore invalid.[180]

Consequences of Ultra Vires Acts

3–61 When it became easy after 1844 to incorporate any kind of lawful business, one burning issue was whether registered companies should be treated in the same way as common law or as statutory corporations, or whether they were *sui generis*. It was not seriously doubted that transactions contravening the very terms of peremptory rules in the Companies Act were illegal and *ultra vires*, such as repaying a company's capital to its shareholders otherwise than by the authorised method,[181] or without their consent attempting to increase the liability of shareholders beyond the amount remaining unpaid on their shares.[182]

---

177 *Case of Sutton's Hospital* (1610) 10 Co. Rep. la, 23a. *cf. Pharmaceutical Society v. Dickson* [1970] A.C. 403.

178 *Attorney General v. Great Eastern Railway* (1880) 5 App. Cas. 473. *cf. Credit Suisse v. Allerdale B.C.* [1997] Q.B. 306 at pp. 336-340, which describes the evolution of the law on *ultra vires*.

179 [1898] 2 I.R. 103.

180 A recent celebrated example of this principle is the "interest swaps" case, *Hazell v. Hammersmith & Fulham L.B.C.* [1992] 2 A.C. 1 and the numerous cases this decision gave rise to, *e.g.* the *Credit Suisse* case [1997] Q.B. 306.

181 *e.g. Trevor v. Whitworth* (1887) 12 App. Cas. 409; below, para. 7–40.

182 *e.g. Bisgood v. Henderson's Transvaal Estates Co.* [1908] 1 Ch. 743; below, para. 11–66.

3–62 Every registered company's memorandum of association is required to state "the objects of the company".[183] What, therefore, is the status of engagements that are entered into and that fall beyond those objects? In *Ashbury Railways Carriage Co. v. Riche*[184] a unanimous House of Lords came down in favour of the statutory analogy, depicting it as the inexorable consequence of the Companies Act's provisions. Lord Cairns L.C. reasoned as follows: that Act

> "does not speak of that incorporation as the creation of a corporation with inherent common law rights . . . but it speaks of the company being incorporated with reference to a memorandum of association . . . .
>
> [T]he memorandum which the persons are to sign as a preliminary to the incorporation [is] to state 'the objects for which the proposed company is to be established'; and the existence, the coming into existence, of the company is to be an existence and to be a coming into existence for those objects and for those objects alone . . . .
>
> [I]f that is so — if that is the condition upon which the corporation is established — it is a mode of incorporation which contains in it both that which is affirmative and that which is negative. It states affirmatively the ambit and extent of vitality and power which by law are given to the corporation, and . . . negatively, that nothing shall be done beyond that ambit, that no attempt shall be made to use the corporate life for any other purpose than that which is so specified."[185]

In other words, because the memorandum of association is a public document, all persons are deemed to know its contents, *i.e.* they have "constructive notice" of what it contains. Accordingly, an *ultra vires* transaction was void and could not he enforced against registered companies.[186]

3–63 It further was held there that an *ultra vires* transaction cannot be rendered effective by all the company's members attempting to ratify it by extending the objects with retroactive effect. Prior to 1963 there was a clear basis for this principle, because (since 1890) companies could not change their objects without the prior sanction of the court. But the logic in continuing the rule since section 10 of the 1963 Act was passed[187] is questionable, especially in view of the emphasis in *Ashbury Railways* on the objects being unalterable in any circumstances before 1890.[188]

3–64 It was to remedy injustices that can arise from the above state of

---

183 1963 Act, s.6(1)(b).
184 (1875) L.R. 7 H.L. 653.
185 *ibid.* at 668–670.
186 *Ashbury Railway Carriage Co.* case, above, n.184.
187 *Northern Bank Finance Corp. v. Quinn* [1979] I.L.R.M. 221 at p. 230.
188 *Ashbury Railway Carriage Co.* case at pp. 660-670, 672 and 684-685.

affairs that section 8(1) of the 1963 Act was enacted, under which *ultra vires* acts are made legally enforceable unless at the time the person dealing with the company was "actually aware" that it was acting beyond its powers. The precise effects and implications of this provision are dealt with in Chapter 13 below. But that section by no means renders the *ultra vires* principle redundant. For any shareholder or debenture holder may apply to the court to enjoin a company from attempting to act beyond its stated objects.[189] Accordingly, the content and meaning of the objects clause remain vital matters in the running of a company.

Construing Objects Clauses

3–65 Most reported cases where construction of an objects clause was the central issue concern a contract between the company and some outside body which one party was seeking to have declared void on the grounds that it was *ultra vires*. In the past, the tendency was to read the objects in a restrictive if not an excessively narrow fashion, because incorporation by registration was regarded as some kind of special privilege and, like statutory corporations, registered companies should be allowed to do only what they had clear authority for. Thus in the *fons et origo* of the voidness principle, the *Ashbury Railway* case,[190] the company, which had agreed to purchase a concession for constructing a railway in Belgium, claimed that it was not bound by that agreement because the entire transaction was *ultra vires*. Its objects clause suggested that it was principally in the rolling stock business, although one of those objects was stated as "to carry on the business of mechanical engineers and general contractors". It was held that the term "general contractors" could not be read so extensively as to cover, and render effective, the contract there because, "according to the principles of construction, the term "general contractors" would be referred to that which goes immediately before, and would indicate the making generally of contracts connected with the business of mechanical engineers — such contracts as mechanical engineers are in the habit of making. . . ."[191] This tendency to "read down" the scope of a particular object in the light of its context among other objects is now usually prevented by inserting what are referred to as "independent objects" clauses into the memorandum, *i.e.* by stipulating that each and every one of the enumerated objects is independent of all the others and stands on its own.

Moreover, in recent years, a more generous approach to construction has been adopted. For instance, objects, "to carry on business as

---

189 1963 Act, s.8(2).
190 (1875) L.R. 7 H.L.
191 *ibid.* at p. 665.

financiers, exporters and importers . . . and merchants generally" were read as extending to all purely commercial occupations, such as running a petrol service station.[192]

Ambiguous Clauses

3–66 Yet loosely worded and ambiguous objects can be a trap for the unwary, as *Northern Bank Finance Corp. v. Quinn*[193] illustrates. There the company, which was the first defendant's unlimited investment vehicle, guaranteed a bank loan made to him. When the bank called in the guarantee the company pleaded *ultra vires*. One of its relevant objects was "to raise or borrow or secure the payment of money". Keane J. had no hesitation in concluding that the guarantee fell outside this object, since:

> "the wording used plainly indicates that it was essentially intended to confer a power of borrowing on the company. Viewed in this context, the words "secure the payment of money" could not reasonably be read . . . as conferring a power to execute guarantees. Th[ose] words. . . are used disjunctively in apposition to 'raise' and 'borrow', clearly indicating that it was intended to confer on the company a power of obtaining money for its own purposes and not a power to guarantee advances made to other persons."[194]

It may well be that in practice some account is taken of the commercial nature of the transaction and of who the other party is, so that if it can reasonably be expected that the other party will employ legal expertise to vet the proposed arrangement, the objects clause will be interpreted in a more legalistic manner.

Subjectively Worded Clauses

3–67 It has become common for companies' objects to be formulated in discretionary and subjective terms, like the company may "carry on any other trade or business whatsoever which can, in the opinion of the board of directors, be advantageously carried on by the company in connection with or ancillary" to its other objects.[195] Among the questions that such provisions give rise to are whether the board's conclusion that a particular line of business is ancillary and would be advantageous can be contested successfully, and whether it is necessary that the transaction embarked upon is of some economic benefit

---

192 *Re New Finance & Mortgage Co.* [1975] Ch. 420. *cf. Halifax Building Society v. Meridian Housing Association Ltd.* [1994] 2 B.C.L.C. 540.

193 [1979] I.L.R.M. 221.

194 *ibid.* at p. 226.

195 From *Bell Houses Ltd. v. City Wall Properties Ltd.* [1966] 2 QB. 656, below.

to the company (other than when it is not a "non-profit" undertaking).[196] On these matters the British and the Irish law would appear not to be at one.

3–68 The only Irish case on the ancillary advantageous evaluation stresses that the decision must be reached "reasonably", whereas what is demanded in Britain is "bona fide"; but this difference may be more one of terminology than of substance. In *Northern Bank Finance Corp. v. Quinn*,[197] another clause within which is was sought to bring the contested guarantee given by the company was one enabling the company to act in the manner just described. But Keane J. concluded that executing the guarantee "could not reasonably be regarded as" and "could not properly be regarded as being fairly" ancillary to the main objects, in that only the bank and Mr Quinn could possibly derive any benefit from the transaction there.[198] In *Bell Houses Ltd. v. City Wall Properties Ltd.*,[199] a construction company, which had an objects clause in the form quoted above, became involved in money-broking for small building companies. The contention that the criterion of what was ancillary and advantageous to its main objects was the "bona fide, but also objective" opinion of the board was rejected. All that was necessary was "the opinion of the directors, if bona fide"; "a clause on the lines of [the above] is able to make the bona fide opinion of the directors sufficient to decide whether an activity of the company is *intra vires*".[200] Nor is it necessary that there be a formal board resolution to this effect. It nevertheless was suggested that transactions involving principally company "insiders" might not be treated as generously. In one instance following *Bell Houses*, a test of the "objective view" and "reasonable[ness]" was used, but that part of the case was largely obiter, and it was held that the contract there easily satisfied even the stringent test.[201]

Objects and Powers

3–69 The distinction is drawn between a company's objects or purposes, in the sense of what it was founded for, its *raison d'etre*, and its powers, meaning the various ways it can go about achieving those objects. Companies possess the legal power to do everything that is

---

196 Non-profit companies are considered generally below, para. 14–61 *et seq.*
197 [1979] I.L.R.M. 221.
198 At p. 226.
199 [1966] 2 QB. 656.
200 *ibid.* at pp. 683 and 688. Similarly, *American Home Assurance Co. v. Timond Properties Ltd.* [1984] 2 NZ.L.R. 452.
201 *Charterbridge Corporation v. Lloyds Bank* [1970] Ch. 62.

reasonably necessary and incidental to advancing their substantive objects,[202] each case turning on the terms of the particular objects clause and the surrounding circumstances. For instance, a company has implied powers to borrow and to give security for loans obtained in order to finance its *intra vires* business.[203] But a mere power cannot be converted into a substantive object simply by the memorandum of association saying so. Whether a stipulation in the memorandum is an object or is only a power turns on whether, by its very nature, it is capable of standing as an independent object. Thus borrowing and giving security can be objects for banks and other financial institutions but may not be for specialised trading companies. In one recent instance the contrast was made between advertising, which, apart from in advertising agencies, can only be an ancillary power, and granting pensions to ex-directors and ex-employees, which it was held was capable of being an object in its own right.[204] Yet paying pensions surely is just as much one method by which a trading company achieves its underlying commercial purposes as are borrowing and advertising?

3–70 A transaction that falls within the terms of a mere power but in fact is for a purpose other than those set out in the substantive objects is void and unenforceable. However (section 8(1) of the 1963 Act aside), such a transaction may confer rights on a third party who dealt with the company in good faith and for valuable consideration, and who did not have notice of the fact that the transaction, while ostensibly within the company's powers, was entered into for an *ultra vires* purpose which was not a stipulated object. Take for example *Re Introductions Ltd.*,[205] where the objects clause stated one kind of business (entertaining foreign visitors) but the company embarked on a wholly different venture (pig breeding). On the strength of one of its independent objects clauses, which read "to borrow or raise money", a bank lent it money. This loan and the security were held to be *ultra vires* because "a power or an object conferred on a company to borrow cannot mean something in the air: borrowing is not an end in itself and must be for some purpose of the company; and since this borrowing was for an *ultra vires* purpose, that is the end of the matter".[206] If the bank had given the loan to enable the company to carry on its entertainment business but, unknown to the bank, the money was spent on pig breeding, then it would have been recoverable. But because the

---

[202] *Attorney General v. Great Eastern Railway Co.* (1880) 5 App. Cas. 473.
[203] *General Auction Estate & Monetary Co. v. Smith* [1891] 3 Ch. 432.
[204] *Re Horsley & Weight Ltd.* [1982] 1 Ch. 442. Similarly, *Simmonds v. Heffer* [1983] B.C.L.C. 298.
[205] [1970] Ch. 199.
[206] *ibid.* at 210.

bank knew that the loan was to be spent on pig breeding, it had notice of the fact that it was being used for an *ultra vires* purpose and, accordingly, did not fall within the above exception.[207] As is explained later, whether the bank there would now be protected by section 8(1) of the 1963 Act is debateable — was it "actually aware" that the company had been acting *ultra vires*?

3–71 A particularly vexed case is one that combines what arguably is a power in the guise of an object, that "object" being expressed in subjective terms and where the transaction in question is of no economic benefit to the company. *Northern Bank Finance Corp. v. Quinn*[208] falls into this mould except that no special emphasis was placed there on the objects/powers distinction. A similar case is *Rolled Steel Products (Holdings) Ltd. v. British Steel Corp.*,[209] the facts of which are quite complex. In brief, the plaintiff company had provided security for loans made to another company, that was owned by the plaintiff's controlling shareholder, and had paid off some debts this associated company owed. Reliance was placed on the following "objects" clause to support these transactions: "to lend and advance money or give credit to such persons, firms or companies and on such terms as may seem expedient and . . . to give guarantees or become security for any such persons, firms or companies." Note that the central criterion is expediency and not some assessment of benefit to the company. It was held, on appeal, that the impugned transactions were "well capable of" falling within those objects.[210]

3–72 Having conducted an extensive review of the cases on the subject, Slade L.J. summarised the governing principles regarding *ultra vires* as follows:

> "(1) The basic rule is that of a company incorporated under the Companies Acts only has the capacity to do those acts which fall within its objects as set out in its memorandum of association or are reasonably incidental to the attainment or pursuit of those objects. Ultimately, therefore, the question whether a particular transaction is within or outside its capacity must depend on the true construction of the memorandum.
>
> (2) Nevertheless, if a particular act (such as each of the transactions. . . in the present case) is of a category which, on the true contraction of the

[207] Similarly, *Re Jon Beauforte (London) Ltd.* [1953] Ch. 131.
[208] [1979] I.L.R.M. 221.
[209] [1986] Ch. 246.
[210] In *Re P.M.P.A. Garage (Longmile) Ltd.* [1992] 1 I.R. 315 at pp. 321–325, Murphy J. upheld guarantees given by companies in respect of the debts of their associated companies.

company's memorandum, is capable of being performed as reasonably incidental to the attainment or pursuit of its objects, it will not be rendered *ultra vires* the company merely because in a particular instance its directors, in performing the act in its name, are in truth doing so for purposes other than those set out in its memorandum. Subject to any express restrictions on the relevant power which may be contained in the memorandum, the state of mind or knowledge of the persons managing the company's affairs or of the persons dealing with it is irrelevant in considering questions of corporate capacity.

(3) While due regard must be paid to any express conditions attached to or limitations on powers contained in a company's memorandum (*e.g.*, a power to borrow only up to a specified amount), the court will not ordinarily construe a statement in a memorandum that a particular power is exercisable 'for the purposes of the company' as a condition limiting the company's corporate capacity to exercise the power; it will regard it as simply imposing a limit on the authority of the directors. . . .

(6) If, however, a person dealing with a company is on notice that the directors are exercising the relevant power for purposes other than the purposes of the company, he cannot rely on the ostensible authority of the directors and, on ordinary agency principles, cannot hold the company to the transaction."[211]

Gratuitous Transactions

3–73 By a gratuitous transaction is meant some arrangement or act that is of no tangible economic benefit to a company. Generally, benevolence that is not authorised by the very terms of the objects clause is nonetheless within a company's powers where is it "reasonably incidental to the carrying on of the [authorised] business" and is dispensed "for the benefit and to promote the prosperity of the company."[212] Gifts to charities and to educational institutions have been sustained on these grounds,[213] and presumably political donations would similarly be upheld.[214] Much depends on the particular facts of the case. The question of gifts in the form of fees, pensions and "golden handshakes" for directors and their dependents is considered separately below.[215]

3–74 A classic instance of benevolence is *Parke v. Daily News Ltd.*,[216] where a newspaper company that was making losses on its publica-

---

[211] [1986] Ch. at p. 295.
[212] *Re Lee Behrens & Co.* [1932] 2 Ch. 46 at p. 51.
[213] *e.g. Evans v. Brunner Mond & Co.* [1921] 1 Ch. 359.
[214] See generally, Ewing "Company Political Donations and the Ultra Vires Rule" (1984) 47 Mod. L. Rev. 57.
[215] below, paras 5–56 *et seq.*
[216] [1962] Ch. 927.

tions sold the copyrights of its papers, its plant and premises for a substantial sum. Rather than sink the proceeds into other ventures or repay it to the shareholders, the board decided to distribute the bulk of it to the employees as compensation for making them redundant, and sought general meeting approval for the scheme. The company was under no legal obligation whatsoever to give its employees these sums; the proposed payments were entirely *ex gratia*. While it appears that the vast majority of the shareholders would have voted for the payments, one shareholder sought a declaration that the proposals were *ultra vires* and illegal, and an injunction. He succeeded on the grounds that:

> "[T]he decision to distribute this enormous sum of money was [not] taken simply in the interests of the company as it would remain after the transfer of the newspaper enterprise. . . . [T]he decision . . . was motivated by other considerations. Predominant among such other considerations was . . . the desire to treat the employees generously, beyond all entitlement, and to appear to have done so. . . . [T]he defendants were prompted by motives which, however laudable, and however enlightened from the point of view of industrial relations, . . . is an application of the company's funds which the law . . . will not allow [and] which a majority of the shareholders is not entitled to ratify."[217]

But the test of *ultra vires* in the classic sense is whether the proposal is incapable of ratification by the entire membership of the company. If the proposed payment there would stand had all the shareholders supported it (the judgment there is silent on this), then the true basis for the decision in *Parke* was "fraud on a minority".[218] Another possible basis might be that the scheme amounted to a distribution of capital other than through the procedures laid down in section 72 of the 1963 Act.[219]

3–75 It has been held that entirely gratuitous transactions that fall four square within the terms of a particular object are not *ultra vires*. In *Charterbridge Corp. v. Lloyds Bank*,[220] a mortgage granted by an associated company, to secure loans made to the central company in the group, was held not to be *ultra vires* the former because its objects clearly envisaged those transactions. Therefore, any question of economic benefit to it was "irrelevant upon this issue". The principle is that:

> "[W]here a company is carrying on the purposes expressed in its memo-

---

[217] [1962] Ch. 927 at 962, 963.
[218] See below, paras 10–44 *et seq*.
[219] See below, paras 7–27 *et seq*.
[220] [1970] Ch. 62.

> randum, and does an act within the scope of a power expressed in its memorandum, that act is an act within the powers of the company. The memorandum of a company sets out its objects and proclaims them to persons dealing with the company and it would be contrary to the whole function of a memorandum that objects unequivocally set out it should be subject to some implied limitation by reference to the state of mind of the parties concerned."[221]

This analysis was endorsed in *Re Horsley & Weight Ltd.*[222] which concerned an objects clause that authorised paying pensions to directors and employees. According to Oliver J.:

> "The objects of a company do not need to be commercial, they can be charitable or philanthropic; indeed, they can be whatever the original incorporators wish, provided that they are legal. Nor is there any reason why a company should not part with its funds gratuitously or for non-commercial reasons if to do so is within its declared objects.... Of course if the memorandum of association expressly or by implication provides that an express object only extends to acts which benefit or promote the prosperity of the company, regard must be paid to that limitation; but where there is no such express or implied limitation, the question whether an act done within the terms of an express object of the company will benefit or promote the prosperity of the company or of its business is ... irrelevant."[223]

3–76 A question that arose in *Greendale Developments Ltd. (No. 2)*[224] was whether it was *ultra vires* and unlawful for a solvent company to give over substantial assets to one or more of its members when, at the time, all of its members were agreeable to that being done. Approximately £450,000 was paid from time to time to one of its directors/ one-third shareholder; the cheques were countersigned by the other director/one-third shareholder and the remaining shareholder, who was the recipient's wife, assented to those payments being made. The company's memorandum of association contained in the objects clauses provisions that the company could "grant... gratuities, bonuses or other payments to the officers ... or the dependents or connections of such persons", and also that the company could "distribute among the members in specie or otherwise as may be resolved any assets of the company. . . ." The company's articles of association contained inter alia clauses 116 and 118 of Table A and a stipulation that a resolution in writing, signed by all of the members, shall be deemed to be a valid and effective resolution of the company as if a members' meeting had

---

[221] [1970] Ch. 62 at 69.
[222] [1982] 1 Ch. 442.
[223] *ibid.* at 450, 452.
[224] [1998] 1 I.R. 8.

been duly convened and the proposal had been passed at it. The Supreme Court there accepted, for argument's sake, that the company was not insolvent when it was wound up and that the liquidation had not become insolvent. If the company had been insolvent when the money was paid over to the director/one-third shareholder, undoubtedly the transactions would have been *ultra vires*.[225] If any one of the members were not in agreement with the company's assets being dealt with in that manner, again undoubtedly there would be a fraud on the minority and the transfer of assets would be unlawful.[226] Such reported authority as there was on the point suggested that all of a company's members are entitled to sanction a very substantial gratuitous disposition of its assets to one or more of them, provided the company was solvent at that time and was not thereby rendered insolvent.[227]

3–77 In the *Greendale* case, the question posed above had not been considered at all by the trial judge, who insisted on the trial going ahead notwithstanding that the defendants had only been given three working days notice of the trial and had no reasonable opportunity to fully instruct a solicitor and counsel in their defence.[228] The Supreme Court decided to determine the question *de novo* but, without hearing argument on that issue,[229] concluded that transactions of this nature are *ultra vires* and unlawful, and that the assets disposed of in the circumstances were recoverable by the company. This decision would seem to be wrong for the following reasons:[230]

---

225 *Re George Newman & Co.* [1895] 1 Ch. 674 and *Re Frederick Inns Ltd.* [1994] 1 I.L.R.M. 387.

226 *Cook v. Deeks* [1916] A.C. 554 and *Re Newbridge Sanitary Steam Laundry Co.* [1917] 1 I.R. 67.

227 *Re S.M. Barker Ltd.* [1950] I.R. 123. Also supportive are *Re Wellington Publishing Co.* [1973] 1 N.Z.L.R. 133, considered below at para. 12–14, and *Multinational Gas & Chemical Co. v. Multinational Gas & Petrochemical Services Ltd.* [1983] 1 Ch. 25.

228 An adjournment was sought, which the liquidator did not oppose, but notwithstanding this was refused by Costello P.

229 Blayney J., who presided, decided at an early stage to deal first with questions in a preliminary motion concerning the mode of trial, the refused adjournment and adducing additional evidence; he directed the Court would later hear full argument on the *ultra vires* point if it ruled against the defendants on those other issues. In the event, in a reserved judgment, the court held against the defendants on those issues but, at the very same time, ruled on the *ultra vires* question without giving them or indeed the liquidator any opportunity to argue it. Within a few weeks, Blayney J. retired from the Court on the grounds of age.

230 The author was the defendants' counsel, which may colour the views expressed here.

3–77 (i) The authorities relied on by Keane J. (for the Court) to support the conclusion were cases where either a minority shareholder was contesting a gratuitous disposition[231] or where the company was insolvent,[232] or it was a non-profit company.[233] It has never previously been held that all of the members of a solvent "for profit" company cannot make a distribution of assets to such one or more of them as they choose.

(ii) The *raison d'etre* of commercial trading companies (except "non-profit" companies) is to distribute surpluses to their members; companies' objects implicitly envisage substantial pay-outs to their members where surpluses exist and are not needed, unless there is an express prohibition to that effect (*e.g.* "non-profit" companies and companies holding charitable status).[234]

(iii) How any surplus is to be shared among a company's members is exclusively a matter for them to decide and has nothing to do with the objects or capacity, or *vires*, of the company as such. Normally, the matter is dealt with in the articles of association, which usually (as is the case in *Greendale*) confer a power on the company to pay dividends to its members, provided they are not paid out of capital.[235]

(iv) Where the articles of association stipulate one formula for dividing up a surplus (*e.g.* pro rata), the members acting unanimously may informally agree to an alternative formula (*e.g.* to one member only), which will be treated as amending the articles to that effect.[236] In any event, the company's articles in *Greendale* placed no restriction on how dividends were to be shared between the members, or on the times when or manner in which dividends should be distributed; the only restriction was that they should not come from capital.

(v) Further, even if the modes in which a surplus is to be divided

---

231 *Hutton v. West Cork Railway Co.* [1883] 23 Ch. D 654 and *Parke v. Daily News Ltd.* [1962] Ch. 927; see observations in P. Davies, *Gower's Principles of Modern Company Law* (6th ed., 1997) at 205 and below, paras. 5–69, 5–116 and 14–20.

232 *Re Lee Behrens & Co.* [1932] Ch. 46; see observations below, paras 5–69 and 14–20.

233 *Roper v. Ward* [1981] I.L.R.M. 408, which concerned how the assets of the Dublin Gas Company Employees' Social and Sports Club Limited should be distributed in the course of its liquidation; moreover, all the company's members had not supported the impugned mode of distribution.

234 For a company to be recognised as charitable, or for a limited company not to have the word "limited" in its name (see below, para. 14–66), it must *inter alia* stipulate in its memorandum of association that any profits it makes or surplus it has will not be divided among its members.

235 Article 116 of Table A (empowering the company in general meeting to declare dividends) and article 118 (no payments from capital).

236 *Cane v. Jones* [1980] 1 W.L.R. 1451; *Re Bradford Investments p.l.c. (No. 2)* [1991] B.C.L.C. 688 at 704 and *Wright v. Atlas Wright (Europe) Ltd*, Times L.R. Feb. 3, 1999; see below, para. 4–41.

up among a company's members indeed relates to the objects clause and corporate capacity, and not just powers, the members acting unanimously may informally agree to permit a large distribution to one of them, which will be treated as amending the objects clause to that effect, at least where there are no debenture-holders.[237] Indeed, the company's articles in *Greendale* stated that the written assent of all of the members is equivalent to a resolution to that effect duly passed by them.

(vi) Further still, the grounds on which one of the cases that supports the lawfulness of such distributions, *Re S.M. Barker & Co.*,[238] are distinguished are thin,[239] to say the least. Curiously, no attempt was made to distinguish the other Irish case that suggests that such distributions are not *ultra vires*, *Peter Buchanan Ltd. v. McVey*.[240] Keane J. relied on a dictum in it to find for the liquidator[241] but the relevant facts there are almost on all fours with *Greendale*, except that the massive distribution made in the *Buchanan* case was done for an unlawful purpose (tax evasion) and it was designed to ensure that (and resulted in) the company would not be able to pay a massive debts to its only creditor, the Revenue. No question of fraud or insolvency arose in *Greendale*.

(vii) Where all the members of a "for profit" company are agreeable to a particular mode of distributing company assets, then unless the memorandum of association contains an entrenched prohibition against that distribution, the true test of legality is whether the provision in the Companies (Amendment) Act 1983, on distributions from capital have been contravened.[242] Lord Hoffman has referred to, as a

---

[237] *Re Home Treat Ltd.* [1991] B.C.L.C. 705. Of course, this could not have been the position before 1963 (or prior to February 1991 in Britain) when the objects clause could never be changed without the prior approval of the court; by virtue of s.10 of the 1963 Act (see below, para. 11–13) prior approval of the court is no longer required. The holding in *Ashbury Railways Carrier Co. v. Richie* (1875) L.R. 7 H.L. 653 at pp. 665-670, 672 and 684-685 is predicated on s.12 of the Companies Act 1862, which rendered companies' objects entirely immutable.

[238] [1950] I.R. 123, discussed below, para. 14–21.

[239] At [1998] 1 I.R. 27. But in the *Barker* case, as in *Greendale*, the alleged wrongdoers were also directors (as well as members) of the company at the time their "wrongs" occurred, which should render the two cases indistinguishable. Unlike in the *Barker* case, the members in *Greendale* did not pass a formal resolution approving the impugned distributions but, since *ultra vires* concerns intrinsic corporate capacity rather than abuse of a power that exists, the formal passing of a resolution can hardly be decisive when all the members are *ad idem*. In any event, the company's articles envisaged informal unanimous resolutions. Further, unlike in the *Barker* case, the company in *Greendale* was not wound up on grounds of insolvency.

[240] [1954] I.R. 89; see below, para. 14–22.

[241] *ibid.* at p. 91.

[242] *Aveling Barford Ltd. v. Perion Ltd.* [1989] B.C.L.C. 626.

primary rule of attribution implied by company law, "the unanimous decision of all the shareholders in a solvent company about anything which the company under its memorandum of association has power to do shall be the decision of the company".[243]

(viii) The analysis set out here accords with the modern case law on *ultra vires*, which emphasises that the doctrine concerns the very capacity of a company to enter into a particular transaction, not the manner in which it executes transactions which it has intrinsic powers to conclude[244] (*e.g.* distribute surplus assets to its members).

(ix) Accepting Keane J.'s distinguishing *Re S.M. Barker & Co.*, on the grounds that the payments made here were not made to the defendant in his capacity as shareholder, and in view of the fact that he was one of the company's principal employees throughout, the transactions would then seem to be insulated from an *ultra vires* challenge by section 52 of the 1990 Act. This section was enacted to change the law as stated in the *West Cork Railways Co.* and similar cases, which were the authorities that Keane J. relied on for his finding of *ultra vires*.

(x) If the Court's decision in *Greendale* is correct, then as a matter of logic it would seem that, unless expressly allowed by the memoranda of association, all dividend payments are *ultra vires*, since there is no reciprocal benefit for the company. Or does it matter that the dividend is quite big rather than comparatively small and, if yes, how is "quite big" to be measured?

(xi) In any event, the company's objects in *Greendale* expressly authorised paying "gratuities" to officers and their dependents and, as well, authorised distributing any assets among the members in such manner as they choose, which under the *Charterbridge* case,[245] would render the contested payments there *intra vires*. Those objects were not relied on in the appeal hearing.[246]

[243] *Meridian Global Funds Management Asia Ltd. v. Securities Commission* [1995] 2 A.C. 500 at 506. See also P. Davies, *Gower's Principles of Modern Company Law* (6th ed., 1997), pp.177–176. *cf. Wright v. Atlas Wright (Europe) Ltd*, Times L.R., Feb. 3, 1999.

[244] *e.g. Rolled Steel Products (Holdings) Ltd. v. British Steel Corp.* [1986] Ch. 246.

[245] *Charterbridge Corp. v. Lloyds Bank* [1970] Ch. 62, above, para. 3–75.

[246] See above, n. 229.

4

Governance and the Members

4–01 The term "governance" in the context of company law means the way in which companies as organisations are run by those who own and control them. It can be contrasted with management, which signifies how a company's ordinary business affairs are conducted, although the lines between overall governance and day-to-day management are not always clearly defined. Different companies possess different methods of governance, just as there is an enormous variety of management systems. The Companies Acts, however, lay down certain minimum ground rules for governance. Ultimate control over companies' destinies is consigned to their members or shareholders. Members' meetings must be convened at least once a year and a significant minority of the membership may call meetings at any time. Various matters concerning the company must be decided at such meetings. It is for companies themselves to determine how votes are to be allocated among their members and what particular powers should be entrusted to the directors. Companies can change their own regulations provided sufficient members support the proposed change. In many small private companies, especially where they are in the nature of joint ventures, their governance may also be regulated by separate shareholders' agreements that purport to override any contrary provisions in their articles of association.[1]

COMPANY MEETINGS AND RESOLUTIONS

4–02 A company's primary organ is its members assembled together in general meeting.[2] Decisions reached at these meetings take the form of resolutions. In the case of single-member companies registered as such, as provided for in the regulations on those companies,[3] the

---

[1] See below, paras 14–10 *et seq*.

[2] See generally, Shearman, *Shackleton on the Law and Practice of Meetings* (8th ed., 1997), Chaps 15–20.

[3] European Communities (Single Member Private Limited Companies) Regulations 1994, S.I. No. 275 of 1994.

position as described here is subject to the very obvious qualification; the one member only will comprise the meeting in question.

Meetings

4–03 A company must hold an annual general meeting every year and not more than 15 months may elapse between these meetings.[4] The principal business to be transacted at AGMs is consideration of the company's audited accounts and of the directors' and the auditors' reports, filling vacancies on the board, appointing auditors and fixing their remuneration, and declaring a dividend.[5]

4–04 There are also "extraordinary" general meetings, which usually are convened when matters of some urgency must be considered by the members.[6] Public companies need no longer hold a "statutory" meeting before they can commence business. Meetings of particular classes of the membership are called "class" meetings.

Convening Meetings

4–05 Ordinarily, it is the board of directors that convenes general meetings.[6] Where the board convenes a meeting in some manner inconsistent with the company's regulations, this may be a "mere irregularity" that does not nullify the outcome of the shareholders' deliberations. It depends on the circumstances and on the nature of the regulation in question whether or not contravening it is fatal to the meeting. For instance, in *Browne v. La Trinidad*,[7] where directors other than the plaintiff met and issued notices of a general meeting to consider inter alia whether the plaintiff should be removed from the board, it was held that not notifying the plaintiff of that board meeting was insufficient reason to stop the ensuing general meeting from taking place. In another instance, where the number of directors fell below the quorum for board meetings but they nevertheless acted as a board and convened a shareholders' meeting, it was held that resolutions passed at the general meeting were not thereby invalid.[8] On the other hand, a notice issued, for example, by the company's secretary and without the board's consent is ineffective.[9] A properly constituted board must meet as such before calling a shareholders' meeting to deal with

---

4 1963 Act, s.131(1) and Table A, art. 48.
5 Table A, art. 53.
6 1963 Act, s.132 and Table A, art. 49.
7 (1887) 37 Ch. D. 1.
8 *Boschoek Pty. Co. v. Fuke* [1906] 1 Ch. 148.
9 *Re Estate of Wyoming Syndicate Co.* [1901] 2 Ch. 431.

"matters of such vital moment" as winding up the company or appointing a liquidator.[10]

Notices

4–06 The periods of notice needed for convening general meetings are usually fixed in the articles of association; the very minimum periods which may be provided for are set out in section 133 of the 1963 Act. In Table A it is 21 days for annual general meetings; it is 14 days for extraordinary general meetings but only seven days for *e.g.*m.s of private companies which have Part II of Table A.[11] It is 21 days where the purpose is to pass a special resolution.[12] Provision, however, is made in the 1963 Act for shorter notice periods. Any general meeting may be called within whatever period the auditors and all the members entitled to attend and to vote agree upon.[13] Except for "extended notice" resolutions, less than 21 days' notice of a special resolution may be given where that is agreed to by enough members as hold 90 per cent of the nominal value of the shares entitling them to attend and vote.[14]

4–07 Although section 134(a) of the 1963 Act stipulates that notices of meetings "shall be served on every member", this is made subject to any contrary provision in the articles of association. It is provided in Table A that notices must be sent to such persons as are entitled under the company's regulations to receive them.[15] These model articles, moreover, state that the proceedings of a meeting shall not be invalid because of the non-receipt of a notice or the accidental omission to give notice.[16] An injunction was once given against holding a meeting because some notices were posted to the shareholders during a postal strike.[17] Even though the company's articles of association expressly deemed the posting of notices as good service, it was held that the distinct likelihood of some shareholders there not being notified in time, thereby being deprived of the opportunity to vote on a proposed transaction, warranted deferring the meeting until an application would be made to the court to discharge the injunction.

4–08 Apart from some special kinds of notices, the Companies Acts

---

[10] *Re Haycroft Gold Reduction & Mining Co.* [1900] 2 Ch. 230.
[11] Arts. 51 and 4 (Part II).
[12] *ibid.* and 1963 Act, s.141.
[13] 1963 Act, s.133(3).
[14] *ibid.*, s.141(2); *cf. Re Pearce Duff & Co.* [1960] 1 W.L.R. 1014.
[15] above, n. 11.
[16] Art. 52.
[17] *Bradman v. Trinity Estates plc.* [1989] B.C.L.C. 757.

do not indicate what notices of meetings generally must contain. According to Table A, they must state the place and time of the meeting and, in the case of special business "the general nature of that business. . . ."[18]

Location

4–09 Every annual general meeting must be held in the State, except where the articles of association do not require meetings to be held in Ireland and, additionally, all the members agree that they should meet abroad or it was resolved at the preceding A.G.M. to hold the next meeting outside the State.[19] Any business transacted at a meeting held in contravention of this requirement is void. There are no statutory restrictions on where extraordinary general meetings can be held; the matter can be determined by the articles of association. Article 47 of Table A requires that all general meetings of the company be held in the State. Arguably this does not apply to general meetings of particular classes of shareholders. Table A does not indicate where within Ireland the meetings must be held, except that any notice must specify, *inter alia,* the "place" of the meeting.[20]

Timing

4–10 In exercising their power to call general meetings, directors will not be permitted to call one at an unusually early date in order to prevent a recent purchaser of shares from voting against the board.[21] In *Kinsella v. Alliance & Dublin Gas Consumers Co.,*[22] in an attempt to wrest control from the existing board, the plaintiff and those who supported him bought a considerable number of shares in the company. Because many of the share transfers were not yet registered, their anti-directors motions at an extraordinary general meeting were defeated. Barron J. confirmed that persons who bought shares had no right to vote until they were registered as shareholders. The argument was made that the outcome of the meeting should nonetheless be declared invalid because the plaintiff's transfers were not registered as a result of a conscious decision by the incumbent directors to thwart his designs. It was concluded, however, that no such decision had been established in evidence and indeed all the indications were that the best reasonable efforts had been made to register those transfers in time. In any

---

18 above, n. 11.
19 1963 Act, s.140.
20 above, n. 11.
21 *Cannon v. Trask* (1875) L.R. 20 Eq. 669.
22 Barron J., October 5, 1982; Cases, p. 168.

event, it was pointed out, there was nothing to prevent the plaintiff calling another extraordinary general meeting once his transfers were registered.[23]

Default Powers

4–11 Default powers exist where the board either refuses or is unable to convene a meeting. In the case of the annual general meeting, any member may apply to the Minister, who may direct that the meeting be called and give such ancillary directions as are deemed appropriate.[24] In the case of extraordinary general meetings, section 132 of the 1963 Act enables members representing at least one-tenth of the paid up capital carrying voting rights to request the board to call a meeting. If the directors do not do so within 21 days, the meeting may be convened by at least half of those requisitionists. Any reasonable costs the requisitionists thereby incur can be recovered from the company and the company in turn can deduct the equivalent from the defaulting directors' remuneration.

4–12 The possibility of the directors undermining these provisions, by convening a meeting but to be held in the very distant future, does not exist because section 132(3) requires that the meeting be convened for not later than two months of receiving the members' requisition. In England, where there is no set deadline for actually holding the meeting, it was held that convening one for a distant date can amount to oppression under the equivalent of section 205 of the 1963 Act.[25]

Court-Ordered Meetings

4–13 Where for any reason it is "impractical" to call or to conduct a meeting in the normal manner the court may intervene.[26] Section 135 of the 1963 Act empowers the court itself, either on the application of a director or of a voting member, or of its own motion, to order that a meeting be held and may give such ancillary directions as it deems appropriate. It has been observed that the jurisdiction under this provision is of "a necessarily wide scope" and, in considering applications under section 135, the court should consider the practicalities of the situation.[27] For example, even though the articles of association of a company did not provide for voting by ballot, an application for an

---

[23] 1963 Act, s.132 and above.
[24] *ibid.*, s.131(3)–(6).
[25] *McGuinness v. Bremner p.l.c.* [1988] B.C.L.C. 673.
[26] See generally, Gertz, "Court Ordered Company Meetings" (1969) 33 Conv. 399.
[27] *Re El Sombrero Ltd* [1958] Ch. 900.

order that a meeting be held to vote by ballot succeeded, on account of the very considerable disruption that had previously occurred when a minority of the members attended at the general meeting.[28] A well-known Australian case where this power was exercised concerned a company of which a husband and wife were the only shareholders and directors, who were killed together in a car crash.[29] The court directed that a meeting of the company be held and that the personal representatives of the deceased should be treated as shareholders entitled to attend and to vote at that meeting. But the section is not restricted to extreme situations, nor to where there is no shareholder opposition to a meeting being held.[30]

4–14 However, this section does not empower the court to make orders that would decisively shape the outcome of any meeting it directs to convene; in particular, in order to resolve a deadlock between members. Thus in *Ross v. Telford*,[31] where the two equal shareholders and the directors of the company were a husband and wife, who had gone through a bitter divorce and the ex-wife declined to attend meetings convened by him, the court refused to direct that a representative of his solicitors could attend the meeting as an additional member. Section 135 was described there as "a procedural section not designated to affect substantive voting rights or to shift the balance of power between shareholders in a case where they have agreed that power should be shared equally and where the potential deadlock is something which must be taken to have been agreed on with the consent and for the protection of each of them".[32] Similarly, in *Harman v. B.M.C. Group Ltd*[33] where the company had two classes of shareholding ("A" and "B" shares) and there was a shareholders' agreement that a representative of the B shareholders must be present at all general meetings, the court refused to direct a meeting to be held without such representative being present; their agreement conferred a "class right" to have some B shareholder present and section 135 does not enable the court to override class rights. If the applicants have a sufficient majority under section 132 to call for a meeting to be convened and the directors have not declined to call one, they should not be applying to the court under section 135.[34] That one or more of the shareholders have sued for "op-

---

[28] *Re British Union for the Abolition of Vivisection* [1995] 2 B.C.L.C. 1.

[28] *Re Noel Tedman Holdings Pty. Ltd* [1967] Q'd L.R. 561.

[30] *E.g. Re Opera Photographic Ltd* [1989] 1 W.L.R. 634.

[31] [1998] 1 B.C.L.C. 82.

[32] *ibid.* at p. 87.

[33] [1994] 1 W.L.R. 893.

[34] *Angelis v. Algemene Bank Nederland (Ireland) Ltd*, unreported, Kenny J., July 4, 1974.

pression" under section 205 of the 1963 Act has been held not a reason for not directing a general meeting to be held, although it is a factor the court will take into account when exercising its discretion.[35]

Resolutions

4–15 There are two principal kinds of resolution, ordinary and special resolutions. Traditionally, in the absence of provision to the contrary, the general meeting acts by a simple majority of those voting.

Ordinary Resolution

4–16 The "ordinary" resolution is not expressly mentioned in the Companies Acts and, although it is referred to in Table A,[36] it is not defined there. An ordinary resolution is understood as meaning one that needs a simple majority of the votes cast.[37]

Special Resolution

4–17 A "special" resolution — previously known as an "extraordinary" resolution — is defined by section 141 of the 1963 Act as one passed by a majority of at least three-quarters of the votes cast, at a meeting of which at least 21 days' notice was given. However, if the holders of more than 90 per cent in value of the voting shares agree, a special resolution may be passed notwithstanding shorter notice. Special business is defined in Table A as all business transacted at extraordinary general meetings and at annual general meetings other than the principal AGM business referred to above[38] but, curiously, it seems that a special resolution is not necessary to determine matters that are "special" in this sense.

Extended Notice Resolution

4–18 Section 142 of the 1963 Act provides for a variant of these, the "extended notice" resolution, which is necessary for certain kinds of drastic decisions, like removing a director from the board and replacing the incumbent auditors.[39] Except where such a resolution is submitted by the board, those moving it must notify the company not less than 28 days before the meeting; the company must then notify the members in the same way as notice of the meeting was given. Where it

---

[35] *Re Sticky Fingers Restaurant Ltd* [1992] B.C.L.C. 84 and *Re Whitechurch Insurance Consultants Ltd* [1993] B.C.L.C. 1359.

[36] *e.g.* Arts. 2, 40, 44, 45, 97, 99, 100.

[37] *Bushell v. Faith* [1970] A.C. 1099; see below, para. 5–41.

[38] Art. 53.

[39] 1963 Act, ss. 182 and 161.

is "not practicable" to do this, within 21 days of the meeting the company must either give notice by advertisement in a newspaper that circulates in the district where the registered office is located or notify the members in such other mode as the articles allow for.

Notices of Proposed Resolutions

4–19 One of the fundamental principles of company law is that notices of ordinary and of special resolutions must sufficiently describe what is being proposed, so as to permit shareholders to form a reasoned judgment. In particular, notices must not be misleading. For instance, in *Kaye v. Croydon Tramways Co. Ltd*[40] notices convening a general meeting stated that the purpose was to approve the sale of the company's undertaking for a specified sum but did not indicate that, as an additional part of the consideration, the buyer was to pay the directors "golden handshakes".[41] On the grounds that, although it did not contain untruths, the notice was "playing with words" and was "tricky", and "most artfully framed to mislead the shareholders", it was held that the ensuing resolution endorsing the sale did not bind absent and dissenting shareholders. As it was put in a later and very similar case,

> "If any attempt is to be made by the directors to get the sanction of the shareholders it must be made on a fair and reasonably full statement of the facts upon which the directors are asking the shareholders to vote. . . . [S]pecial resolutions obtained by means of a notice which did not substantially put the shareholders in the position to know what they were voting about cannot be supported, and in so far as . . . resolutions were passed on the faith and footing of such a notice the [company and directors] cannot act upon them."[42]

Whether a particular notice is misleading or does not provide enough information is essentially a factual matter and depends on the circumstances of each case.[43] If the effect of any resolution is that the directors will obtain some material benefit, which they otherwise would not be entitled to, this fact must be disclosed.[44]

---

[40] [1898] 1 Ch. 358.

[41] *cf.* 1963 Act, s.187, enacted to prohibit this type of deception; see below, paras 5–71 *et seq*.

[42] *Baille v. Oriental Telephone & Electric Co.* [1915] 1 Ch. 503 at 514–515.

[43] See, *e.g.* *Jackson v. Munster Bank Ltd* (1884) 13 L.R. Ir. 118, *Tiessen v. Henderson* [1899] 1 Ch. 861, *Re Dorman Long & Co.* [1934] Ch. 635 and *Rose v. McGivern* [1998] 2 B.C.L.C. 593 at 600–603.

[44] *Kaye* case, above, n. 40, *Baillie* case, above, n. 42, *Jackson* and *Tiessen* cases, above, n. 43 and *Normandy v. Ind. Coope & Co.* [1908] 1 Ch. 84.

4–20 It is not necessary to give the actual text of a proposed special resolution but clear and precise indications of its entire substance must be provided. This is essential because "all the situations in which special resolutions are required are special situations, where the resolutions in question are by their very nature likely either to affect the company's constitution or to have an important effect on its future."[45] Therefore, it is imperative that each shareholder be fully appraised "so that he may decide whether he should attend the meeting or is content to absent himself and leave the decision to those who do."[46] Furthermore, the resolution ultimately passed must not depart in its substance from the one notified, not even *de minimus,* although minor variations of mere form may be tolerated. In *Re Moorgate Mercantile Holdings Ltd*[47] the requirement of "absolute identity at least in substance" was perhaps carried to an extreme. Notices were issued of a resolution that the share premium account, standing at £1,356,900, be cancelled on the grounds that the entire amount had been lost. Due to an oversight, the proposer did not make provision for a premium of £321 obtained shortly before then when the minority interests had been bought out. On discovering this, the chairman proposed to amend the resolution to one reducing the share premium account from £1,356,900 to £321, which was carried. It was held that even this small variation rendered the resolution invalid.[48]

4–21 In order to have a resolution set aside on the grounds that misleading or inadequate information was circulated to the members, the plaintiff does not have to show that it was the misrepresentation that induced members to vote for the resolution.[49] Where, however, the transaction that was approved by the resolution has been executed, it may be too late to have the resolution set aside, even where the transaction involved "insiders". In that leading case on minority shareholders' rights, *Prudential Assurance Co. v. Newman Industries Ltd (No. 2),*[50] it was held that individual shareholders have no "personal" right of action in damages against directors who, by tricky and misleading notices, deliberately caused the company to suffer a loss by buying assets at overvalued prices.

---

45 *Re Moorgate Mercantile Holdings Ltd* [1980] 1 W.L.R. 277 at 283.
46 *ibid.*
47 [1980] 1 W.L.R. 277.
48 *cf. Re Willaire Systems p.l.c.* [1987] B.C.L.C. 67.
49 *Buffin v. Bebarfalds Ltd* (1938) 38 S.R. (N.S.W.) 423.
50 [1982] 1 Ch. 204; see below, paras 10–53 *et seq*.

Conduct of Meetings

4–22 All that the Companies Acts say about the conduct of general meetings is that, unless the articles of association provide otherwise, the quorum for a private company (other than a one-person company[51]) is two and for a public company is three members present in person;[52] the members present can elect any one of their number to the chair;[53] corporate members can be represented in such manner as their own directors or governing bodies determine;[54] a company's articles of association cannot unduly restrict a member's right to demand a poll.[55] Articles 53-62 of Table A sets out the "proceedings at general meetings". These are supplemented by special articles, where they exist, and by the general principles of law relating to meetings.[56] The following are the most important questions that arise.

Place

4–23 On account of modern audio-visual techniques, it has been held that a meeting does not necessarily have to take place in any single room or hall. According to Browne Wilkinson V.C. in *Byng v. London Life Association Ltd*,

> "The rationale behind the requirement for meetings in the [Companies] Act is that members shall be able to attend in person so as to debate and vote on matters affecting the company. Until recently, this could only be achieved by everyone being physically present in the same room face to face. Given modern technological advances, the same result can now be achieved [otherwise]. . . . [I]n cases where the original venue proves inadequate to accommodate all those wishing to attend, valid general meetings of a company can be properly held using overflow rooms provided, first, that all due steps are taken to direct to the overflow rooms those unable to get into the main meeting and, second, that there are adequate audio-visual links to enable those in all the rooms to see and hear what is going on in the other rooms."[57]

Quorum

4–24 The 1963 Act and Table A fix the quorum at three members in the case of a public company and two where the company is private

---

[51] *i.e.* a company registered in accordance with S.I. No. 275 of 1994.
[52] 1963 Act, s.134(c).
[53] *ibid.*, s.134(d).
[54] *ibid.*, s.139; *cf.* Table A, art. 74.
[55] *ibid.*, s.137.
[56] See generally, I. Shearman, *Shackleton on the Law and Practice of Meetings* (8th ed., 1997).
[57] [1990] 1 Ch. 170 at 183.

(other than a "one-person" company).[58] A higher quorum may be fixed by the articles of association. The members must be present in person when the meeting commences. In a private company which has Table A, the meeting can continue provided that at least one member remains present.[59] No company business can be transacted where these requirements are not satisfied. If within a half an hour of a meeting being convened a quorum is not present, the meeting stands adjourned for a full week or to such other time and place as the directors determine; but in such cases the meeting is dissolved if it was one that the members had requisitioned.[60] Where all of a company's members are present then it is probable that the quorum is filled even where the regulations stipulate for a higher number. It is not settled whether one member only can constitute a meeting, other than in a duly registered one-person company.

4–25 If it is "impracticable" to make the quorum, any director or member with voting rights may apply to the court, under section 135 of the 1963 Act, to order that a meeting be held and conducted, and to make any necessary ancillary directions.[61] Thus, in *Re Opera Photographic Ltd*[62] there were two shareholders and directors of a company, one holding 51 per cent of the shares. He wanted to remove the other from the board of directors but that other would not attend at general meetings, where a resolution for his removal could be considered and voted on. The court decided to resolve the deadlock by directing that a meeting attended by the majority shareholder for the purpose of removing the other from the board shall be an effective meeting of the company.

Chairman

4–26 The chairman of the meeting regulates its proceedings. Who occupies the chair and the extent of the chair's powers is determined primarily by the articles of association. Under Table A,[63] general meetings should be chaired by the chairman of the board of directors; failing him, the directors present can choose one of their number to take the chair and, if they do not do so, the members present at the meeting decide who chairs it. Table A gives the chairman a casting vote where there is an equality of votes.

---

[58] 1963 Act, s.134(c) and Table A, arts. 54 and 5 (Pt II).
[59] *Re Hartley Baird Ltd* [1955] Ch. 143; *cf. Re London Flats Ltd* [1969] 1 W.L.R. 711.
[60] Art. 55.
[61] See above, para. 4–13.
[62] [1989] 1 W.L.R. 634.
[63] Art. 56.

4–27 A chairman's powers and responsibilities derive partly from the common law regarding meetings generally as well as from provisions in the articles of association. In *Byng v. London Life Association Ltd*[64] it was held that decisions taken by the chair, even within the general terms of those he undoubtedly possesses, might be set aside if, in the circumstances, he failed to take account of relevant factors or he acted unreasonably. At common law, he has no general right to adjourn a meeting for his own convenience but he can adjourn where unruly behaviour impedes the conduct of the meeting. Table A empowers him to adjourn the meeting with its consent. Where in the circumstances it is possible to ascertain the meeting's view on the matter, he should not adjourn without its consent. Table A requires him to adjourn where the meeting so directs. No entirely new business may be transacted at an adjourned meeting.

4–28 The chairman should ensure that the business before the meeting is properly conducted. His rulings on points of order and related matters are deemed prima facie to be correct.[65] Those members present must be afforded a reasonable opportunity to debate the proposed resolutions and all views on them must be adequately aired. But the chair may stop discussions when enough has been said and, provided minority views get a fair hearing, must do so when so directed by the meeting.[66] One of the chair's most delicate tasks is in deciding whether to allow an amendment to a proposed resolution to be moved. Any amendment must remain within the scope of the notice which was given. In the case of "special" business, proposals may be amended only in form and not in substance.[67]

Voting

4–29 Voting can be done by way of a show of hands or a poll. Usually the question will first be put to a show of hands of the members present. Then one or more members may demand a poll, in which case they can cast whatever number of votes are attached to their respective shareholdings. Where there was no poll, the chairman determines whether or not a proposed resolution was carried on a show of hands; that decision is "conclusive evidence" of the fact.[68]

---

64 [1990] 1 Ch. 170.

65 *cf. John v. Rees* [1970] Ch. 345.

66 *Wall v. London & Northern Assets Corporation* [1898] 2 Ch. 469.

67 *Re Moorgate Mercantile Holdings Ltd* [1980] 1 W.L.R. 277.

68 1963 Act, s.141(3) and Table A art. 59; *cf. Arnot v. United African Lands Co.* [1901] 1 Ch. 518.

Poll

4–30 At common law, every member is entitled to demand a poll in the general meeting. This right could be qualified or excluded by express terms in the articles of association but the scope of any exclusionary provision is now drastically restricted. The right to demand a poll may be excluded only in respect of electing the chairman and decisions about adjournments.[69] Furthermore, the articles of association may not "mak[e] ineffective" any demand for a poll by either not less than five members with voting rights or by a member representing not less than one-tenth of the total voting rights.[70] Under article 59 of Table A, a member is entitled to demand a poll provided he has the support of two other members present at the meeting or else he (and his supporters) hold at least 10 per cent of the voting shares. Apart from motions for selecting who chairs the meeting and for an adjournment, the chairman determines at what stage of the meeting a poll demanded on any question shall be held.[71] He also decides the manner in which any poll is to be taken.[72]

Right to Vote

4–31 Absent any express provision in the company's regulations to the contrary, a precondition of being entitled to vote at a general meeting is registration as a member in the company's register of members. Article 67 of Table A gives whoever is chairman of the meeting an extensive power to determine who shall vote. Under it, no objection to the qualification of any voter may be raised except at the meeting. The chair's decision on the matter is "final and conclusive" and any vote not disallowed is declared "valid for all purposes". In one instance it was said that there was much to commend a regulation that promotes finality in this way.[73] Persons who sell their shares and execute the relevant transfer documents remain entitled to notices of general meetings and to vote as they please at them until the purchaser pays for the shares and is duly registered as a member[74] But a vendor of shares who has received the full purchase price is a trustee for the purchaser of those shares and must vote in the interests of the *cestui* or as the *cestui* directs.[75] Similarly, a mortgagor of shares or a bankrupt whose

---

[69] 1963 Act, s.137(1)(a).
[70] *ibid.*, s.137(1)(b).
[71] Art. 62.
[72] Art. 60.
[73] *Marx v. Estates & General Investments Ltd* [1976] 1 W.L.R. 380.
[74] *Musselwhite v. Musselwhite & Son* [1962] Ch. 964.
[75] *Lyle & Scott Ltd v. Scott's Trustee* [1959] A.C. 763 and *Re Piccadilly Radio p.l.c.* [1989] B.C.L.C. 673.

name remains on the share register must vote as the mortgagee or the Official Assignee, respectively, directs.[76] However, no notice of any trust shall be entered on the register of members.[77]

4–32 Section 137 of the 1963 Act restricts greatly the power companies had to prevent members from calling for a poll in general meeting.[78] The right of every enfranchised member to have his vote recorded was proclaimed in most emphatic terms in *Pender v. Lushington*,[79] where it was held that the plaintiff was "a member of the company, and whether he votes with the majority or the minority he is entitled to have his vote recorded — an individual right in respect of which he has a right to sue".[80] Subject to what is said below about class and minority rights,[81] shareholders may exercise their voting rights for the most selfish reasons, disregarding what other persons may consider are the interests of the company at large.[82] It even has been held that they may vote against a resolution that the court has ordered the company to adopt and implement.[83] Members are not obliged to cast all the votes they possess in the same way.[84]

Proxy Votes

4–33 Since a member of a corporation has no right at common law to vote by proxy,[85] at one time, in order to vote, a shareholder had to attend the general meeting in person unless the articles of association allowed for proxy voting. Today, under section 136 of the 1963 Act, any shareholder who is entitled to attend and vote at a meeting of the company, be it a general meeting or a class meeting, may appoint someone else as their proxy to speak and to vote for them. The proxy may vote either in a poll or on a show of hands. Proxies are not made compulsory for guarantee companies which have no share capital. Unless the articles of association provide otherwise, a member may appoint more than one proxy.

4–34 Every notice calling a meeting of a company possessing share

---

[76] *Wise v. Landsell* [1921] 1 Ch. 420 and *Morgan v. Gray* [1953] Ch. 83.
[77] 1963 Act, s.123 and Table A, art. 7; see below, para. 9–72.
[78] *cf. MacDougall v. Gardiner* (1875) 1 Ch. 13.
[79] (1877) 6 Ch. D. 70.
[80] *ibid.* at 81.
[81] See generally, Chap. 10.
[82] *North-West Transportation Co. v. Beatty* (1887) 12 App. Cas. 589.
[83] *Northern Counties Securities Ltd v. Jackson & Steeple Ltd* [1974] 1 W.L.R. 1133; see above, para. 3–17.
[84] 1963 Act, s.138.
[85] *cf. Harben v. Phillips* (1883) 23 Ch. D. 14.

capital must make it clear that every member entitled to attend and vote may appoint a proxy, who need not be a member of the company. A company may not require that the instrument that evidences the appointment of a proxy be deposited with the company more than 48 hours before the meeting. Article 68 of Table A stipulates that votes may be cast either personally or by proxy, and a number of rules regarding proxies are set down in Articles 69–73. Under these, the instrument of appointment, which must approximate to a particular form, must be signed by the shareholder or his duly authorised agent. It must be deposited at the company's registered office or such other specified place not less than 48 hours before the meeting. A person who is both a member and a proxy can vote only once on a show of hands; the chairman cannot be expected to ascertain how many votes a hand is intended to convey.[86] A duly-appointed proxy is entitled to demand a poll. Unless the company has received prior intimation of the fact, any vote cast by proxy is valid notwithstanding the shareholder's death, insanity or revocation of the proxy.[87] Absent agreement to the contrary, it would appear that a proxy is not obliged to cast the votes with which he was entrusted but company directors who are appointed proxies may not refrain from casting those votes.

4–35 Especially in large companies with widely diffused shareholdings (so-called mega-corporations), there is a danger of directors manipulating proxies in order to entrench their positions and to resist shareholder pressure against them — a phenomenon that also occurs in large building societies. Typically, a resolution critical of the board or its policies will be tabled for a general meeting. In response to those criticisms, the directors will send the shareholders some glowing account of their own accomplishments, and will ask shareholders either to vote against the resolution or to give their proxy to someone (usually one of the directors) who will vote against it. It has been held that the expenses of distributing such circulars and proxy forms may be paid from the company's funds[88] and that it is not necessary for the directors to state the views of their opponents.[89] But directors must not circulate misleading information with proxy forms[90] and the costs of distribution may not be charged to the company where the board policy that is being challenged is one that advances the directors' personal interests.[91]

---

86 *cf. McGratten v. McGratten* [1985] N.I. 28.
87 Art. 73.
88 *Peel v. London & North Western Rly. Co.* [1907] 1 Ch. 5.
89 *Campbell v. Australia Mutual Provident Soc.* (1908) 24 T.L.R. 623.
90 *e.g. Jackson v. Munster Bank Ltd* (1884) 13 L.R. Ir. 118.
91 *Peel* case, above, n. 88.

4–36 One practice that used to be permitted, partial distributions, is now restricted. Where proxies are being solicited at the company's expense, every member entitled to a notice of the meeting and to vote must be sent a copy of the invitation.[92] The board, therefore, cannot invite only those from whom they expect a favourable response, and opponents of the board may learn the grounds on which votes are being sought. Under the Rules of the Stock Exchange, every quoted company's articles of association must allow for the "two way" form of proxy, *i.e.* forms by which the shareholder can direct the proxy to vote either for or against the resolutions.[93]

Irregular Meetings

4–37 Regardless of company size, there is always the danger of irregularities occurring in general meetings. The Companies Acts permit general meetings to take place on short notice provided that all the members entitled to vote and also the auditors so agree.[94] The public law distinction between "mandatory" and merely "directory" rules,[95] and the uncertainty as to where exactly the line between them should be drawn, applies also to the law of company meetings. Some rules on the conduct of meetings are regarded as so vital that any member may bring suit to enjoin their violation or have declared invalid the purported outcome of a violation; for instance, the right to have one's votes counted[96] and that notices of resolutions should not be misleading.[97] But breach of some other rules are regarded as mere irregularities that can be "cured" by an ordinary resolution and, therefore, may not be the subject of a shareholder suit.[98] The question of the basis on which these categories can, or ought to be, distinguished is dealt with below in relation to minority shareholders' rights.[99] Also considered separately is the extent to which outsiders dealing with companies are adversely affected by irregularities that can take place in general meetings.[100]

---

92 1963 Act, s.136(5); *cf. Wilson v. London, Midland & Scottish Rly. Co.* [1940] 1 Ch. 169.
93 Yellow Book, s.13.28.
94 1963 Act, s.133(3).
95 See generally, Wade and Forsyth, *Administrative Law* (7th ed., 1994), pp. 253–255.
96 *Pender v. Lushington* (1877) 6 Ch. D. 70.
97 *Kaye v. Croydon Tramways Co.* [1898] 1 Ch. 358.
98 *e.g. MacDougal v. Gardiner* [1875] 1 Ch. D. 13; see below, para. 10–06.
99 See below, paras 10–17 *et seq.*
100 See below, paras 13–43 *et seq.*

Minute Book

4–38 Every company must keep a minute book of the proceedings at its general meetings.[101] Where they are signed by the person who chaired the meeting in question or the very next meeting, the minutes are prima facie evidence of what took place. Until the contrary is proved, all proceedings at the meeting and all appointments of directors or of liquidators made at it are deemed to be valid. Every member is entitled to inspect these minutes and to have copies made from them.[102]

Registering Resolutions

4–39 Section 143 of the 1963 Act, as amended,[103] requires that copies of various kinds of resolutions be sent to the registry of companies within 15 days of their being passed. These are: special resolutions; decisions made by all the members that have the effect of special resolutions; decisions made by all the members of a particular class that are equivalent to special resolutions of that class; resolutions increasing the company's share capital; resolutions that the company be wound up voluntarily by reason of its liabilities or because the time for which it was incorporated has expired, or the task for which it was incorporated has been achieved; resolutions attaching rights or restrictions to any share or varying any such incidents of the share; resolutions converting shares of one class into shares of another; and resolutions classifying any unclassified share. At one time outsiders dealing with a company were deemed to have notice of the contents of any special resolutions recorded in the registry of companies but that is no longer entirely the case.

Informal Unanimity

4–40 Especially in small companies, general meetings may take place in a most informal manner.[104] In the case of private companies, Part II of Table A provides that a purported resolution in writing that is signed by all the members entitled to vote on it in general meeting is deemed a "valid and effective" resolution, as if it had been passed at a duly convened and conducted general meeting.[105] The logic underlying this principle, that a resolution will be deemed to have been passed where it is shown that the proposal in it had the unanimous support of the

---

[101] 1963 Act, s.145.
[102] *ibid.*, s.146.
[103] By 1982 Act, s.5 and 1983 Act, s.39.
[104] See generally, Grantham, "The Unanimous Consent Rule in Company Law" 52 Cam. L.J. 245 (1993).
[105] Art. 6.

members entitled to vote, was held in *Buchanan v. McVey*[106] to apply to companies generally, in the absence of any contrary provision in their regulations. According to Kingsmill Moore J.,

> "If all the corporators agree to a certain course then, however informal the manner of their agreement, it is an act of the company and binds the company subject only to two prerequisites [namely] 1, that the transaction to which the corporators agree should be *intra vires* the company; 2, that the transaction be honest."[107]

There, payments made to the defendant by way of cheques drawn by him on the company's bank account, were held to have been sanctioned by a resolution of the members, because it was quite clear that those members had agreed to the payments being made. Because those payments were part of an elaborate scheme devised to avoid paying taxes to a foreign revenue authority, the purported resolution were declared invalid on the grounds of dishonesty. In a later English case the principle was stated as follows: that "where it can be shown that all shareholders who have a right to attend and vote at a general meeting of the company assent to some matter which a general meeting . . . could carry into effect, that assent is as binding as a resolution in general meeting would be."[108] The fact that the assents were not given at an actual meeting but were given informally and at different times does not detract from this principle.[109] But a resolution to remove any of the company's directors or to remove its auditors, or to have the company wound up, ordinarily cannot be passed in this manner.[110]

4–41 The principle that the unanimous agreement of all the members of a company is an effective resolution of the company was extended in *Cane v. Jones*[111] to unanimous decisions to alter the articles of association. There all the shareholders of a family company, the shares in which were split evenly between two camps, at one stage agreed in writing that the chairman should no longer have a casting vote.[112] It was argued that, in the light of the equivalent of section 15 of the 1963 Act, for effect to be given to this agreement, then at the least an actual meeting must have taken place between the members and the agree-

---

106 [1954] I.R. 89.
107 *ibid.* at 96.
108 *Re Duomatic Ltd* [1969] 2 Ch. 365 at 373. *cf. Re Bradford Investments Ltd* [1991] B.C.L.C. 224 and *Re New Cedos Engineering Co.* [1994] 1 B.C.L.C. 797 at 813–815.
109 *Parker & Cooper v. Reading* [1926] Ch. 975.
110 1963 Act, s.142, requiring "extended notice" for proposals to remove director or auditor. This section does not apply where the directors themselves resolve to put down the resolution.
111 [1980] 1 W.L.R. 1451.

ment reached must have purported explicitly to alter the articles of association. But it was held that this section "is merely laying down a procedure whereby some only of the shareholders can validly alter the articles: and if . . . all the corporators, acting together, can do anything which is intra vires the company, then [there is] nothing in [section 15] to undermine this principle".[113] Support for the view that the articles of association could be changed in this manner was derived from the equivalent of section 143(4)(c) of the 1963 Act, concerning the compulsory registration of *de facto* special resolutions. In *Re Home Treat Ltd*[114] the informal unanimity principle was held to apply to the *ultra vires* rule, in that where all of a company's members have agreed to a particular course of conduct, it will be deemed to be *intra vires* the company. There the silence of one of the company's members on the matter in question was held, in the circumstances, to constitute acquiescence by him in what was being done by the others. Where, however, the Companies Acts lay down certain steps that must be taken before a resolution is effective and those steps are more than formalities (*e.g.* pre–1963, obtaining court approval for a proposed change of objects), the informal unanimity principle does not apply.[115] Accordingly, the *ultra vires* qualification referred to in *Buchanan v. McVey* signifies something that is prohibited by the Companies Acts or by some other law, or by the memorandum of association,[116] and not merely something outside the company's objects clause.

4–42 Section 141(8) of the 1963 Act permits a written agreement signed by all the shareholders to be treated as a special resolution, provided however that the company's articles of association so authorise it. Presumably it must be quite clear from the signed document that it is to have the effect of a special resolution, although it probably is not necessary for it to proclaim itself formally as such a resolution. All the signatures must be of persons entitled to attend the general meeting and to vote on the subject of the purported resolution. Any purported resolution meeting these requirements will be deemed to have been passed at the time it was signed by the last member to sign it. Because of the express requirement that, in order to be effective, a purported resolution in this form should be permitted by the articles of associa-

---

[112] *cf.* Table A, art. 61.
[113] [1980] 1 W.L.R. at 1459.
[114] [1991] B.C.L.C. 1105.
[115] *Re R. W. Peak (Kings Lynn) Ltd* [1998] 1 B.C.L.C. 193 — purported approval for company purchasing its own shares.
[116] *Meridian Global Funds Management Asia Ltd v. Securities Commission* [1995] 2 A.C. 500 at 506.

tion, it may very well be that an Irish court would not follow *Cane v. Jones*, absent such a provision in the company's articles — for instance, a company which has adopted Table A but not Part II.

DIVISION OF POWERS BETWEEN THE MEMBERS AND THE DIRECTORS

4–43 How in fact power is allocated and exercised inside companies depends on the various relationships and allegiances that exist between groups of shareholders and the factions on the board. The Companies Acts require that some major and mainly constitutive decisions be taken by the members in general meeting. For instance, authorising the issue of additional shares and waiver of pre-emption rights to new shares, where applicable, is the function of the general meeting. Otherwise, the allocation of particular powers is a matter for a company's own regulations to determine, which sometimes are supplemented by separate contractual arrangements. Where authority over some matter is not delegated to the directors or otherwise, it falls to be decided by the general meeting.

Allocations of Particular Powers

4–44 As well as authorising them to manage the company's business generally,[117] the Table A model articles empower the directors, for instance, to allot unissued shares, within the overall authorisation given by the general meeting,[118] to make calls on shares from time to time,[119] to borrow money and give security on behalf of the company,[120] to determine the managing director's remuneration,[121] to recommend a dividend[122] and to carry forward undistributed profits and place them in reserve.[123] In private companies it is usual to give the board a discretion to refuse to register any transfer of shares.[124] Except perhaps for the general managing power, any or all of these powers could be reserved by the articles of association to the general meeting. Under Table A, although the board recommends the dividend it is for the general

---

[117] Art. 80; see below.
[118] Art. 5; see below, paras 6–24 *et seq*.
[119] Art. 15; see below, paras 6–43 *et seq*.
[120] Art. 79; see below, paras 6–09 *et seq*.
[121] Art. 111; see below, para. 5–58 *et seq*.
[122] Art. 116; see below, paras 9–25 *et seq*.
[123] Art. 119; see below, paras 9–27 *et seq*.
[124] *e.g.* Table A, Pt. II, art. 3; see below, paras 9–32 *et seq*.

meeting to decide whether one should be paid;[125] and the board may not borrow more than the nominal amount of the issued share capital without the general meeting's consent.[126]

4–45 Where any particular power is given to the directors, how they are to exercise that power in any instance cannot be dictated by the shareholders. Neither a bare majority nor a 75 per cent majority, nor possibly even all but one of the entire body of members, can lawfully compel the directors to carry out a specific mandate, such as to recommend a dividend[127] or make calls on shares.[128] For so long as there is a validly constituted and effective board of directors, none of those specific powers can be exercised by the members as such. Of course, the members always have the choice of altering the articles of association and withdraw the power in question from the directors. Conversely, the directors can always ratify action which the members took without authority but which could have been taken by the directors.

4–46 The articles of association may even confer powers on certain shareholders or even on outsiders, provided these powers are not reserved by the Companies Acts to the general meeting. Examples include a case[129] where the articles empowered each of two director-shareholders to veto any proposal by the board to buy or sell property; in another case the plaintiff was empowered under the articles to nominate two persons of its choice to the board.[130] Often special allocations of powers in the articles are the subject of parallel contractual provisions.

"Manage the Business"

4–47 Article 80 of Table A, which empowers the board to "manage [the] business of the company", raises a number of important questions to which there are few categorical answers.[131] Stripped of some of the excessive verbiage, it stipulates that:

> "The business of company shall be managed by the directors, who . . . may exercise all such powers of the company as are not, by the Act or by these (articles), required to be exercised by the company in general meet-

---

[125] Art. 116.
[126] Art. 79.
[127] *Scott v. Scott* [1943] 1 All E.R. 582.
[128] *Re Coachman Tavern (1985) Ltd* [1988] 2 N.Z.L.R. 635.
[129] *Salmon v. Quin & Axtens Ltd* [1909] 1 Ch. 311.
[130] *British Murac Syndicate Ltd v. Alperton Rubber Co.* [1915] 2 Ch.186.
[131] See generally, Sullivan, "The Relationship Between the Board of Directors and the General Meeting in Limited Companies" (1977) 93 L.Q.R. 569.

> ing, subject, nevertheless, to any of these (articles), to the provisions of the Act and to such directions, being not inconsistent with the aforesaid (articles) or provisions, as may be given by the company in general meeting . . ."

The conventional interpretation is that this article gives the directors managerial autonomy, in the sense that the general meeting cannot interfere with the board's functions except by altering the articles or, indirectly, by removing the existing directors. But as has been pointed out, the cases do not squarely support this view and, more importantly, the very structure and terms of the article suggest that the general meeting may by ordinary resolution "give . . . directions" to the board.[132] Additionally, the Irish formulation of article 80 is not identical to that contained in the British 1948 version nor in the 1908 version, on which many of the cases were decided. Instead of "regulations . . . prescribed," "directions . . . given" is used, and it is not inconceivable that a court might fasten on this difference in terminology to distinguish the decided cases. Three major categories of decisions ought to be considered separately.

Everyday Affairs

4–48 It would be most impractical if the general meeting could interfere with the board in a company's day-to-day management, like selecting suppliers, determining the terms for which products are to be sold, hiring and firing. For this reason, it is likely that article 80 would be construed to prevent the general meeting from issuing instructions on these matters or from vetoing board decisions regarding them. In *Scott v. Scott*,[133] an attempt by the general meeting to dictate dividend policy to the board was held to be ineffective because it concerned "an ordinary financial matter" and was "purely a matter of the management of the business". The judge deemed the case to be "such an easy one" that it was not necessary for him to consider in detail the authorities.

Strategic Decisions

4–49 By "strategic" matters is meant those major management choices that will have a significant and long-lasting effect on the company's development, for instance, substantial expansions or contractions of capacity, the purchase and sale of major assets, take-overs, etc. They

---

132 *ibid.*

133 [1943] 1 All E.R. 582; see also *Re Olderfleet Shipbuilding Co.* [1922] 1 I.R. 26 at 31–33.

134 See generally, Chap. 11.

are to be contrasted, on the one hand, with everyday business affairs as just described and, on the other, with what may be termed fundamental "structural changes", such as altering the objects clause, repaying capital and drastically re-arranging the company's capital structure. These structural changes require at the minimum the shareholders' overwhelming approval; also many of those changes that obtain the requisite support can nevertheless be vetoed by the court.[134] Precisely how decision-making power over strategic matters is allocated in companies with regulations along the lines of article 80 of Table A is an open question.

4–50 A case could be made that it is more practical for the board to have only initiating power in relation to these matters, but the argument against the general meeting having a veto over them is less convincing. Managements can engage in take-overs, for example, principally to enhance their own prestige and power rather than for the benefit of the company. The leading case on the question is *Automatic Self-Cleansing Filter Syndicate Co. v. Cunninghame*[135] where, by an ordinary resolution, the shareholders sought to instruct the board to sell the company's undertaking. Whether they lawfully could do so, the court stressed, depended on the construction of the articles. In the event, it was concluded that those instructions could not be given there. The case, however, is more important for its affirmation of what may be called a presumption of board autonomy: that in the absence of unambiguous indications to the contrary, "it is not competent for the majority of the shareholders at a [general] meeting to affect or alter the mandate originally given to the directors, by the articles . . ."[136] This arises from the fact that, at least in the Table A scheme, the board are representatives of the entire company and not just the agents of the majority or of a special majority of the shareholders:

> "No doubt for some purposes directors are agents. For whom are they agents? You have, no doubt, in theory and law one entity, the company, which might be a principal, but you have to go behind that when you look to the particular position of directors. It is by the consensus of all the individuals in the company that these directors become agents and hold their rights as agents. It is not fair to say that a majority at a meeting is for the purposes of this case the principal so as to alter the mandate of the agent. The minority also must be taken into account. There are provisions by which the minority may be over-borne, but that can only be done by special machinery in the shape of special resolutions. Short of that the mandate which must be obeyed is not that of the majority — it is

---

[135] [1906] 2 Ch. 34.
[136] *ibid.* at 42.

that of the whole entity made up of all the shareholders. If the mandate of the directors is to be altered, it can only be under the machinery of the memorandum and articles themselves."[137]

4–51 The *Automatic Self-Cleansing* case could be distinguished on the grounds that it did not deal with article 80 of Table A and not even with the then British version of that article. For under the company's regulations there, the board's general powers of management were subject only to the Companies Acts, the articles themselves and any special resolution; and the board's specific power there to sell property was unqualified. Nevertheless, its underlying pro-board autonomy sentiments would most likely be followed today even under the Irish version of article 80. It is possible, on the other hand, that a general meeting veto on a "strategic" decision would be sustained here.[138] However extensive a managerial monopoly article 80 may confer on the directors, it does not extend beyond questions of the company's business and management. Thus, unless duly authorised to do so by the articles of association, directors have no authority to resolve that their company should be wound up.[139]

Litigation

4–52 Where the articles of association do not refer expressly to the matter, the question of who has the power to sue in the company's name is a complex and vexed one. What at least is certain is that, where some loss or damage has been caused to a company, the proper plaintiff is the company itself and not any of its members or directors, no matter how large a shareholding he may have.[140] Further, where the majority shareholders commit what is termed a "fraud on the minority", a matter to be dealt with in detail subsequently, then the minority may sue them in the company's name — in what is called the "derivative" suit. Apart from that, the major authorities are somewhat inconclusive. In one instance it was held that, once the majority shareholders commence an action in the company's name to vindicate its property rights, then the directors cannot intervene to have the action struck out.[141] But the grounds on which *Automatic Self-Cleansing* was distinguished were far from convincing, and the judge indicated that he was not bound by dicta in that case affirming the principle of board au-

[137] *ibid.* at 42–43; see also *Re Gramophone & Typewriter Ltd v. Stanley* [1908] 2 K.B. 89.
[138] *cf. Dowse v. Marks* (1913) 13 S.R. (N.S.W.) 332, upholding a veto power.
[149] *Re Emmadart Ltd* [1979] Ch. 540.
[140] *Stein v. Blake (No.2)* [1998] 1 B.C.L.C. 573.
[141] *Marshall's Valve Gear Co. v. Manning Wardle & Co.* [1909] 1 Ch. 267. *cf. Paramount Acceptance Ltd v. Souster* [1981] 2 N.Z.L.R. 38.

tonomy. Another case is often cited in support of the view that once the board commences an action in the company's name then the shareholders cannot intervene to stop the action.[142] But one judge there dissented and the judgments of the other two do not rest on article 80. When subsequently the matter was raised, it was said that "there are deep waters here", and it was found unnecessary in the circumstances to reconcile whatever conflict as exists between the authorities.[143]

4–53 This uncertainty has now been resolved in England, in *Breckland Group Holdings Ltd v. London & Suffolk Properties Ltd.*[144] The company had articles similar to article 80 of Table A. An action was commenced in its name by its majority shareholder, without any reference to the directors, and the question to be determined was whether the action had been properly commenced. Relying on the pro-board autonomy decisions, Harman J. concluded that only the directors could commence proceedings in the company's name. The principle is that:

> "where matters are confided by articles such as article 80 to the conduct of the business by the directors, it is not a matter where the general meeting can intervene . . . . [T]he action was wrongly brought [and i]f the board do not adopt it, a general meeting would have no power whatever to override that decision of the board and to adopt it for itself."[145]

It furthermore has been held that no individual director, not even a managing director, may authorise bringing proceedings in the company's name unless the directors delegated such authority to him,[146] although the unauthorised commencement of proceedings is something that the directors may subsequently ratify. The directors cannot prevent a true "derivative" claim being brought by one or more members, because what is involved there is not merely management of the business; the allegation is that the directors abused and exceeded whatever powers of management they possessed. But it would seem that a claim of that nature may be prevented by a decision of a majority of the members not directly involved in the dispute.

Deadlock

4–54 Where for one reason or another the board is deadlocked and cannot reach a decision on a matter ordinarily within its competence, then it falls to the shareholders in general meeting to resolve the ques-

---

[142] *John Shaw & Sons (Salford) Ltd v. Shaw* [1935] 2 K.B. 113.
[143] *Re Argentum Reductions Ltd* [1975] 1 W.L.R. 186 and *Paramount* case, above, n. 141.
[144] [1989] B.C.L.C. 100.
[145] *ibid.* at 106.
[146] *Mitchell & Hobbs (UK) Ltd v. Mill* [1996] 2 B.C.L.C. 102.

tion. Thus in one instance where there were but two directors and one of them refused absolutely to discuss company business, it was held that there was "power in the company to do itself that which under other circumstances would be otherwise done".[147] Acts can be done on behalf of a company possessing no directors, and these acts can be ratified subsequently by the shareholders.[148]

---

147 *Barron v. Potter* [1914] 1 Ch. 895 at 903.
148 *Alexander Ward & Co. v. Samyang Navigation Co.* [1975] 1 W.L.R. 673.

5

Management and the Directors

5–01 Every company must have directors[1] and a secretary, and various duties regarding the company's affairs are imposed on these officers. In a typical medium sized company, there will be a board of directors comprised of a managing director, some salaried executive directors, who work full time for the company, and some non-executive directors who have significant business interests elsewhere as well. Especially in large companies, various managerial functions will be assigned to management committees. Occasionally, companies delegate the running of their business to outsiders through what are known as management contracts. Ordinarily, it is the shareholders who select the directors and directors can be removed by a simple majority vote of the shareholders. Directors must not be negligent in exercising their functions and they owe their company extensive fiduciary duties. The Companies Acts have established an elaborate set of rules governing directors' remuneration and disclosing information about directors' affairs to the shareholders and to the general public.

THE SYSTEM OF MANAGEMENT

5–02 How a company's business affairs are managed is determined in the main by its own regulations. The Companies Acts do not insist on any particular organisational structure other than that every company (including "one-person" companies) must have at least two directors and a secretary[2] to whom certain responsibilities are assigned.

The Board of Directors

5–03 In the model articles of association, Table A, the board of directors is given a broad power to "manage . . . the business of the com-

---

[1] See generally, C. Ryan, *Company Directors* (3rd ed., 1990).

[2] 1963 Act, s.174 and *ibid.*, s.175. *cf. Levins v. Clarke* [1962] N.S.W.L.R.

pany"[3] together with a number of particular powers, the most important of which have been indicated already. But a company's regulations could just as easily restrict drastically the directors' powers in ways not envisaged by Table A, such as by insisting that borrowing must first be approved by a resolution of the members,[4] or that certain managerial decisions shall be taken by named shareholders or be subject to their veto.[5] Unless the regulations stipulate otherwise, the board itself must exercise the specific powers conferred on it and must determine general policies about running the company's business affairs.[6] Table A permits delegating powers to a managing director[7] and to committees comprising of at least one director.[8]

The Managing Director

5–04 The everyday business affairs of most commercial companies are run by managing directors. Under the Table A scheme, the board can appoint a managing director from one of its members and determine his terms of service;[9] the retirement by rota system does not apply to the managing director;[10] and he may be entrusted with any of the board's powers, either exclusively or collaterally, and subject to such terms and qualifications as the board deems fit.[11] Article 112 of Table A suggests that it is possible for the board provisionally to divest itself of all its powers and transfer them to a managing director. Whether in fact this can be done has not been determined; it may be of some significance that this article uses the term "all" and not "any"

5–05 Although their "ostensible" or "usual" authority to enter into arrangements that bind the company is most extensive,[12] in *Battle v. Irish Art Promotion Centre Ltd.*[13] it was held that a managing director, who is also a major shareholder in the company, has no inherent authority to represent it in civil proceedings. One consequence of a company's separate legal personality is that it cannot attend court and argue its case personally; its right of audience is confined to counsel or a

---

3 Art. 80; see above, para. 4–47 *et seq*.
4 *e.g. Royal British Bank v. Turquand* (1856) 6 E. & B. 327 and *Irvine v. Union Bank of Australia* (1877) 2 App. Cas. 366.
5 *E.g. Quin & Axtens Ltd. v. Salmon* [1909] A.C. 442.
6 *Re Haycroft Gold Reduction & Mining Co.* [1900] 2 Ch. 230.
7 Art. 110; see below, para. 5–04.
8 Art. 105; see below, para. 5–06.
9 Arts. 110-112. *cf. Runciman v. Walter Runciman p.l.c.* [1992] B.C.L.C. 1084.
10 Art. 110.
11 Art. 112.
12 See below, paras 13–34 *et seq*.
13 [1968] I.R. 252.

solicitor instructed on its behalf.[14] The precise scope of a managing director's authority and entitlements depends on the actual terms of appointment; some are given very extensive powers, others are subject to various constraints. What is said below about directors' status, duties and remuneration applies to managing directors too.

Other Delegations

5–06 How far a board of directors may validly delegate its powers has not been authoritatively established.[15] Under the Table A scheme, the board can delegate any of its powers to committees comprising of at least one director, which may in fact be one-person committees.[16] It is not clear how far these committees may delegate policy-making power. Table A also authorises the board to appoint attorneys for such purposes and with such powers as the directors may think fit, which includes the power to sub-delegate.[17]

The Secretary

5–07 Every company must have a secretary.[18] Neither the Companies Acts nor Table A set down qualifications for holding this office. However, under section 236 of the 1990 Act, the directors of a p.l.c. are obliged to ensure that the secretary is a person who appears to have "the requisite knowledge and experience to discharge the functions of secretary." Thus, if the secretary of a p.l.c. is a person who is demonstrably incapable of doing that job properly, the directors who hired him would be held responsible for any losses the company suffers through his action or inactivity. Additionally, the secretary of a p.l.c. must be someone who either was the secretary of a company during three of the five years before his appointment, or is a member of a body recognised by the Minister for these purposes, for instance, the major accountancy organisations and the Chartered Institute of Secretaries, or appears "capable of discharging his functions" by virtue of his membership of any body or his previous work. Those who were secretaries of p.l.c.s before section 236 of the 1990 Act came into force can continue in that position. What is said below about persons con-

---

[14] However, the court in its discretion can permit the managing director or some other non-lawyer to represent it in exceptional circumstances: *Re G. Mannix Ltd.* [1984] 1 N.Z.L.R. 309 and *Arbuthnot International Leasing Ltd. v. Havelet Leasing Ltd.* [1990] B.C.L.C. 802. *cf. Jonathan Alexander Ltd. v. Proctor* [1996] 2 B.C.L.C. 91 on the question of costs in such cases.

[15] See, however, *Guinness p.l.c. v. Saunders* [1990] 2 A.C. 663; below, para. 5–64.

[16] Arts. 105–107.

[17] Art. 81.

[18] 1963 Act, s.175; see generally, C. Doyle, *The Company Secretary* (1994) and L. Brazil et al., *Jordan's Irish Company Secretarial Precedents* (1999).

victed of an offence involving fraud, undischarged bankrupts and former directors of insolvent companies being restricted from being again company directors[19] also applies to becoming company secretaries.

5–08 A company's first secretary or secretaries are appointed in the same way as its initial directors, *i.e.* by designation in the statement delivered to the registrar of companies along with the memorandum of association.[20] Subject to this, the company's regulations determine his status. Under Table A, the directors are empowered to appoint and remove secretaries and to determine their terms and conditions of employment.[21] The secretary may also be one of the directors; where this is the case, any provision authorising or permitting anything to be done by a director and secretary is not satisfied where it is done by the one person holding both offices.[22] Certain details about the secretary and his beneficial shareholdings in the company must be kept available for inspection at the company's registered office.[23] Although the company secretary's role is primarily administrative, in some companies the secretary is allowed to participate in broader policy and managerial decisions. In recent years, courts have come to accept that the secretary has a somewhat extensive "ostensible" or "usual" authority to bind the company in contract.[24]

5–09 The Companies Acts do not define the secretary's function but it is regarded as principally to ensure that the company's affairs are conducted in accordance with the law and its own regulations. Among the statutory duties that fall on the secretary are to sign the annual return that is made to the registrar of companies;[25] to issue share and debenture certificates; to deliver to the registry of companies a return of allotments; to keep and make available for inspection the minutes of general meetings and the various registers concerning shareholders, debenture-holders, charges, directors and secretaries; to send out copies of the balance sheet and the auditors' and directors' reports; to ensure that the company's name is published on its business letters and the like, and outside all of its places of business. He is required to verify

---

19 below, paras 5–22 *et seq.*
20 1982 Act, s.3. *cf. Eley v. Positive Government Life Assurance Ltd.* (1876) 1 Ex. D. 88; see below, para. 10–21.
21 Art. 113.
22 1963 Act, ss. 175, 177.
23 See below, para. 5–182.
24 *Panorama Developments (Guildford) Ltd. v. Fidelis Furnishing Fabrics Ltd.* [1971] 2 Q.B. 711.
25 1963 Act, s.127.

the statement of affairs filed in court in a compulsory winding up[26] and must also verify the statement of affairs given to a receiver who is appointed by debenture-holders who have a floating charge;[27] there is no similar requirement for the statement of affairs to be given to an examiner within a week of his appointment.[28] The secretary would be liable to a fine where there was default by the company in complying with these requirements unless, of course, the secretary had some special defence. The secretary, as well as the company, can be penalised under Part XIV of the Corporation Tax Act 1976 for failure to supply specified information or make returns to the Revenue Commissioners. Under the V.A.T. legislation, the secretary is answerable for performing all acts required of the company with regard to that tax.[29] It may be negligent for a secretary who knows that the company is in serious financial difficulties not to warn the directors that it is insolvent, but the mere fact of being secretary of a company and knowing that it is insolvent does not render the secretary liable under section 297A of the 1963 Act for fraudulent trading.[30] While there is little authority on the point,[31] company secretaries are subject to the same general fiduciary principles as are company directors, to use their powers for a proper purpose and the benefit of the company, and not to become involved in undue conflicts of interests.

De Facto Directors

5–10 Frequently, persons act as directors without having been properly appointed to or eligible for the office; they are only *de facto* directors.[32] For many purposes, however, these persons are deemed to be directors of the company. The 1963 Act's general definition of director merely speaks of anyone "occupying the position of director".[33] It does not appear to have been decided that a person who is acting as a director, without being duly appointed to the office, is subject to all the duties of a director under the Companies Acts. However, some of these Acts' provisions simply refer to persons who are "carrying on the [company's] business", like section 297A on fraudulent trading;[34] others speak merely of company "officers", like section 298A on the

---

[26] 1963 Act, s.224.
[27] *ibid.*, s.320
[28] Companies (Amendment) Act 1990, s.14.
[29] Value Added Tax Act 1972, ss. 26(3), 33(1).
[30] See below, paras 18–51 *et seq.*
[31] *New Zealand Netherlands Society "Oranje" Inc. v. Kuys* [1973] 1 W.L.R. 1126.
[32] See below, paras 13–37 *et seq.* on their ostensible authority.
[33] s. 2(1).
[34] See below, paras 18–51 *et seq.*

misfeasance summons.[35] A *de facto* director was held to be a director for the purposes of the rules regarding disqualification orders. Whether a person indeed is a *de facto* director depends on all the circumstances of the case.[36]

5–11 It was to protect persons dealing with companies from adverse consequences of internal irregularities that section 178 of the 1963 Act was enacted. According to this, "[t]he act of a director shall be valid notwithstanding any defect which may afterwards be discovered in his appointment or qualification."[37] That is to say, in the absence of notice to the contrary, persons dealing with companies either as shareholders or as outsiders are entitled to assume that those whom the company treats as directors were properly appointed, and that they accordingly act as the board. In the leading case on this section, *Morris v. Kanssen,*[38] its potentially extensive sweep was significantly restricted. The objective underlying the section was described as "to avoid questions being raised as to the validity of transactions where there has been a slip in the appointment of a director";[39] it was not intended to be "utilised for the purpose of ignoring or overriding the substantive provisions relating to such appointment", or to give efficacy to "a total absence of appointment, and still less to a fraudulent usurpation of authority".[40] This analysis does not indicate where the line is to be drawn between "slips or irregularities" and breaches of "substantive provisions". The "vital" distinction is between "an appointment in which there is a defect" and "no appointment at all".[41] Yet the argument could be made that, once a defect exists, then the appointment has not been made; that there can be no such thing as a "defective appointment". Although it was not an issue in the case, it was also said that section 178 does not apply where the term of office of a director has expired but he nevertheless continues to act as a director.[42] Despite the above qualifications, however, a company may be bound by the acts of de facto directors who are usurpers or who overstay their term

---

[35] See below, paras 18–66 *et seq*.

[36] *Re Lo-Line Electric Motors Ltd.* [1988] Ch. 477, *Re Hydrodan (Corby) Ltd.* [1994] 2 B.C.L.C. 180; *Re Richborough Furniture Ltd.* [1996] 1 B.C.L.C. 507 at pp. 519-524; *Re Moorgate Metals Ltd.* [1995] 1 B.C.L.C. 503, *Secretary of State v. Laing* [1996] 2 B.C.L.C. 324 and *Secretary of State v. Tjolle* [1998] 1 B.C.L.C. 333.

[37] See Table A, art. 108.

[38] [1946] A.C. 459.

[39] *ibid.* at p. 472.

[40] *ibid.*

[41] *ibid.* at p. 471. See also *Grant v. John Grant & Sons Property Ltd.* (1950) 82 C.L.R. 1 and *Re New Cedos Engineering Co.* [1994] 1 B.C.L.C. 797.

[42] *ibid.* at p. 472.

of office, where they were "held out" by the company as being authorised to act for it and the other party has no notice of the irregularity surrounding their position.[43]

Shadow Directors

5–12 A shadow director connotes someone who is not appointed to the board of directors or is manifestly involved in running the business, but who nevertheless has a decisive say in managing the company from a distance. Because the actual directors do his bidding, there is no necessity for him to be appointed a director; in that way he would hope to escape many of the liabilities which the law imposes on company directors. He is now defined by section 27(1) of the 1990 Act as "a person in accordance with whose directions or instructions the directors of the company are accustomed to act . . . " Accordingly, it must be shown that there is a well established practice or pattern of the company's directors carrying out someone's directions before he can be regarded a shadow director.[44] An exception is made for persons who advise directors in a professional capacity. In one case[45] it was suggested that, in certain circumstances, even banks could be shadow directors, where many features of the company's business are being run on their instructions; for instance where the debenture sets out in detail how the business is to be run. A handful of provisions of the 1963 Act applied to shadow directors as well as to directors proper.[46] The 1990 Act very significantly extends these obligations, notably in respect of fraudulent or reckless trading and disclosure of any financial interest in a contract with the company.

Alternate Directors

5–13 An alternate director is someone who stands in for a duly appointed director in his absence. Although the office of a director cannot be assigned, if the articles of association so permit, a person can be appointed as an alternate director. A provision to that effect is contained in Part II of Table A, clause 9; but the alternate there must first be approved by a majority of the directors and also by a special resolution.[47] While holding that position, the alternate is entitled to notices of all directors' meetings and to attend and vote at them.

---

[43] See below, paras 13–37 *et seq*.
[44] *cf. Secretary of State v. Laing* [1996] 2 B.C.L.C. 324.
[45] *Re M.C. Bacon Ltd.*, Knox J; see also *Re Tasbian Ltd. (No. 3)* [1991] B.C.L.C. 792 and *Kuwait Asia Bank E.C. v. National Mutual Life Nominees Ltd.* [1991] 1 A.C. 187.
[46] *e.g.* ss. 195(12)(a).
[47] 1963 Act, s.199.

Directors' Families

5–14 One of the distinctive features of the 1990 Act is that several of its key requirements apply as much to immediate members of directors' families as it applies to the directors themselves. One of the most important of these deals with so-called "connected persons" in Part III of that Act, which concerns making loans to directors and entering into several other kinds of contracts with them.[48] Many of these rules also apply to contracts and arrangements with companies that the director controls and with his spouse, parent, brother, sister or child, the trustee of a trust for any of them and the director's partner. In Part IV of that Act, which requires directors and secretaries to disclose to the company any beneficial interest they have acquired in the company's shares, an interest for these purposes includes one acquired by their spouse or minor children.[49] Where persons are disqualified from having certain positions in respect of the company, for instance, being its auditor or liquidator, by virtue of being an officer of the company, the disqualification extends to any parent, spouse, brother, sister or child of a company officer.[50]

DIRECTORS' APPOINTMENT AND TENURE

5–15 A company director is an officer of the company. A director must be properly appointed to the office and the fact that a person's name may be registered as a director has nothing to do with whether he holds or has held the office.[51] Traditionally, office-holders[52] possessed some degree of autonomy as to how they accomplished the duties accompanying their office; they also had extensive procedural rights if it was sought to remove them. Employees, on the other hand, enjoy the protection of modern labour legislation, much of which does not extend to office-holders. It is common for executive directors, especially managing directors, to hold their appointments under contract with their companies. In those circumstances, it was held in *Glover v. B.L.N. Ltd.*,[53] which concerned the dismissal of a managing director, the relevant common law rules are not affected by the person's legal status. According to Walsh J., "once the matter is governed by the terms of a contract between the parties, it is immaterial whether the employee concerned is deemed to be a servant or an officer in so far as the dis-

---

[48] See below, paras 5–76 *et seq.*
[49] 1990 Act, s.64; see below, paras 9–82 *et seq.*
[50] *ibid.*, s.187(2)(c) and 1963 Act, s.300(A)(b).
[51] *POW Services Ltd. v. Clare* [1995] 2 B.C.L.C. 435.
[52] *cf. Edwards v. Clinch* [1981] Ch.l.
[53] [1973] I.R. 388.

tinction may be of relevance depending on whether the contract is a contract for services or a contract of service."[54]

5–16 Whether or not a director is an employee of the company depends on the circumstances, in the light of the criteria that were elaborated on in the *Ready Mixed Concrete case.*[55] The general tendency was against regarding company directors, even executive ones, as employees; but this is not a hard and fast rule. In *Stakelum v. Canning*[56] Kenny J. found that a salaried full-time executive director was an employee; he said that when a person who is a director but is not a managing director is working wholetime with the company, "the inference that he was a . . . salaried employee seems . . . to be justified unless there is evidence that he was a whole-time director only and was paid as such."[57] In other words, unless the circumstances strongly suggest that he was not engaged as an employee, the inference is that he is an employee of the company.[58]

Mode of Appointment

5–17 The Companies Acts do not lay down any set method for appointing directors except for a company's first directors; as is explained below, certain persons are disqualified from becoming directors. Under section 3 of the 1982 Act, before registering a company, the subscribers to the memorandum of association must select at least two persons to be its directors. These must sign consents to act as such and a statement, containing personal particulars together with those consents, must be delivered to the registrar of companies. Once it is incorporated, these persons are deemed to be the company's directors. The only other statutory rules on appointing directors is that qualifying shares, where required, must be taken up within two months.[59] And where appointments are made by the general meeting, any motion to appoint must refer to only one person at a time.[60] This prohibition on "composite" motions is to ensure that an unpopular candidate is not elected on the back of a very strong candidate. However, the prohibi-

---

[54] [1973] I.R. 388 at 427.

[55] *Ready Mixed Concrete (South East) Ltd. v. Minister of Pensions* (1968) 2 QB. 497. See generally, Rubin, "The Director as Employee of the Company" (1978) J. Bus. L. 328.

[56] [1976] I.R. 314.

[57] *ibid.* at 316.

[58] *cf. Lee v. Lee's Air Farming Ltd.* [1961] A.C. 12, *cf. Buchan v. Secretary of State for Employment* [1997] I.R.L.R. 80.

[59] 1963 Act, s.180.

[60] *ibid.*, s.181 and *Moylan v. Irish Whiting Manufacturers Ltd.*, Hamilton J., April 14, 1980.

tion does not apply where the meeting resolves separately to proceed by the composite method.

5–18 Apart from these requirements, companies can appoint their directors by whatever way they choose; there is no legal obligation to select directors in general meeting.[61] Thus companies may in their regulations designate persons by name as directors;[62] or the regulations may empower a shareholder, or even a complete outsider, to appoint one or more of the directors.[63] The power of appointment may even be the subject of contractual arrangements between the shareholders, but those agreements cannot prevent the articles of association from being altered under section 15 of the 1963 Act.[64]

5–19 In companies which have adopted Table A, the size of the board is fixed by the general meeting, which may increase or reduce the number of directors and also fix how they are to retire by rotation.[65] The mode of appointment provided for in Table A is as follows. The first directors are chosen by the subscribers to the memorandum of association.[66] No shareholding qualification is required,[67] *i.e.* the appointees are not required to hold a specified number of shares in the company. But the general meeting may lay down a qualification of that nature.[68] Where it is intended to appoint any new director, notice of between three and twenty-one days must be given to the company of the intention to propose that person and also his written assent to serve, if elected.[69] But this notification requirement does not apply to a candidate who is recommended by the existing directors or to a director who is retiring by rotation and is seeking re-election.[70] Directors who are retiring by rotation and offer to serve again are deemed to have been re-elected, unless the general meeting resolves either not to fill their vacancy or not to re-appoint them.[71] Casual vacancies can be filled by the directors themselves and the person so chosen serves until the next A.G.M.;[72] he is then eligible for re-election, but is not treated as a director retiring by rotation.

---

61 *cf. James v. Eve* (1873) L.R. 6 H.L. 335.
62 *e.g. Punt v. Symons & Co.* [1903] 2 Ch. 506.
63 *e.g. British Murac Syndicate v. Alperton Rubber Co.* [1915] 2 Ch. 186.
64 See below, paras 11–08 *et seq.*
65 Art. 97.
66 Art. 75.
67 Art. 77.
68 *ibid.*
69 Art. 96.
70 *ibid.*
71 Art. 95.
72 Art. 98.

5–20 If annual general meetings are not held for a period, there is a risk that all of the directors will be deemed to have retired by rotation and none of them have been replaced.[73] But whether failure to hold A.G.M.s has this effect depends on the terms of the relevant article. In *Phoenix Shannon p.l.c. v. Purkey*,[74] which concerned the status of persons who were purportedly co-opted as directors after the A.G.M. for 1996 was not held, Costello J. declined to imply into that company's articles a term that the offices should then be deemed vacated. The Article there provided that, at the next A.G.M., those directors "shall retire"[75] but, until an A.G.M. actually took place, it was held that they remained in office.[76]

5–21 Where the full quota of directorships is not filled, the directors can fill any vacancy temporarily until the next a.g.m.[77] But the members too are empowered to fill any vacancies.[78] In private companies that are subject to Part II of Table A, any director, with the approval of a majority of the board, may appoint an alternate or substitute who is acceptable to a majority of his fellow directors.[79]

Disqualifications

5–22 There are no set qualifications for being a company director, although in 1999 a Bill was published under which at least one director of most companies will be required to be resident in the State, unless a bond for £20,000 is posted. Infants,[80] the senile[81] the illiterate and innumerate[82] are all legally eligible to be elected to company boards. It even has been said that there is nothing shareholders can do against the majority placing on the board a bunch of "amiable lunatics",[83] although that probably exaggerates the legal position somewhat. But a body corporate is not allowed to become a company director.[84] Various grounds of disqualification are contained in the Companies Acts[85]

---

[73] *e.g.* in *Re New Cedos Engineering Co.* [1994] 1 B.C.L.C. 797.
[74] Costello P., May 7, 1997.
[75] As in reg. 92 of Table A on rotation; contrast reg. 98 on casual vacancies.
[76] Distinguishing several English cases which might suggest otherwise, *e.g. New Cedos* case [1994] 1 B.C.L.C. 797.
[77] Art. 98.
[78] Art. 100.
[79] Art. 9.
[80] *cf. Re Cardiff Savings Bank (Marquis of Bute's Case)* [1892] 2 Ch.100.
[81] *cf. Re Brazilian Rubber Estates & Plantations Ltd.* [1911] 1 Ch.425.
[82] *cf. Re Denham & Co.* (1884) 25 Ch.D.752.
[83] *Turquand v. Marshall* (1886) L.R. 6 Eq. 112.
[84] 1963 Act, s.176.
[85] See generally C. Ryan, *Company Directors* (3rd ed., 1990), Chap. 3.

and others may be set out in the company's regulations; for instance, Table A prohibits *inter alia* bankrupts and persons of unsound mind. It is an open question whether exclusion on grounds such as race, sex, religion, political affiliation and the like are unconstitutional. A Bill published in 1999 proposes to limit the number of directorships any person can hold to that of 25 companies at any one time.

Bankrupts

5–23 An undischarged bankrupt may not be a director in that, under section 183 of the 1963 Act,[86] he commits an offence if he acts as such or as any other officer of the company or, indeed, in any other way "directly or indirectly" takes part in or is concerned in the management of the company. However, the court has a discretion in an appropriate case to permit a bankrupt to act as a director. This prohibition extends to persons who are undischarged bankrupts under the law of England or of Scotland. Contravening section 183 is an offence involving strict liability, in the sense that *mens rea* is not required.[87] Because the relevant legislation in Northern Ireland has changed, it would appear that undischarged bankrupts under the law there are not now caught by the prohibition. In any event, Table A disqualifies any person who was adjudicated bankrupt in the State, Northern Ireland or Great Britain.[88]

Qualifying Shares

5–24 By qualifying shares is meant the number of shares that the articles may specify each director must acquire in order to hold the office, the rationale behind this being the belief that directors with a direct financial stake in their company are more likely to manage it better than non-investor managers. These shares are not required by Table A but the general meeting may still lay down such a requirement.[89] Any director who, within two months of being appointed or such shorter time as is stated in the articles, does not take up any requisite "qualifying shares" automatically vacates the office and cannot be re-appointed until he acquires those shares.[90]

Disqualification Orders

5–25 One of the earliest declared objectives of what became the 1990

---

[86] As amended by 1990 Act, s.169.
[87] *R. v. Brockley* [1994] 1 B.C.L.C. 606.
[88] Art. 91 (b).
[89] Art. 77.
[90] 1963 Act, s.180. *cf. Pulbrook v. Richmond Consolidated Mining Co.* (1878) 9 Ch.D. 610 and *Holmes v. Keys* [1959] Ch. 199.

Act was to strike at so-called "rogue directors", meaning persons who had been involved in company frauds or had committed other wrongs when managing a company. In order to deter wrong-doing, these persons would be banned from managing companies for a prolonged period. Section 160 of the 1990 Act empowers the court to ban persons, who are convicted of any offence involving fraud or dishonesty, from acting as directors for up to five years or indeed for a longer period in an appropriate case. This ban is called a "disqualification order" and it prohibits the person affected from being appointed or acting as a director or other officer of the company or being in any way, whether directly or indirectly, concerned with or taking part in the management or the promotion or formation of any company. The ban therefore is wide-ranging and indeed extends to being a shadow director, a secretary or other officer of the company, or a company auditor, receiver, liquidator or manager. It extends to any of the above positions in an industrial and provident society.

5–26 Directors can similarly be disqualified in the following circumstances. In any proceedings whatsoever, the Director of Public Prosecutions, any member, officer, employee, creditor, receiver, liquidator or examiner of the company may apply for a disqualification order. If the court is then satisfied of the following, it may make the order and indeed may do so of its own motion:[91] that is, while an "officer" of the company, the person committed a fraud in relation to it, its members or creditors, or was in breach of any of the duties attaching to his office, or was held to have committed fraudulent trading or reckless trading, or whose conduct as such officer made him "unfit to be concerned in the management of a company", or who was "persistently in default" of his obligations under the Companies Acts. Those company officers whose acts may result in disqualification here are any director, including *de facto* director,[92] promoter, auditor, receiver, liquidator and examiner and, presumably, secretary. There is a substantial body of case law in Britain dealing with the circumstances where disqualification orders will be made; several of them deal with what constitutes conduct indicating unfitness to manage a company, which has been held to extend even to gross negligence without any suggestion of dishonesty or contravening commercial morality.[93]

5–27 A register of disqualified persons is kept at the registry of com-

---

[91] s.160(2).

[92] *Re Lo-Line Electric Motors Ltd.* [1988] Ch.477.

[93] Summarised in *Re Landhurst Leasing p.l.c.* [1999] 1 B.C.L.C. 287 at 344-347. See generally, Finch, "Disqualification of Directors: A Plea for Competence" (1990) 53 Mod. L. Rev. 385.

panies.[94] Contravention of a disqualification order is a criminal offence and the court can impose unlimited liability for debts incurred by the company during the period a disqualified person was involved in managing its affairs in the manner proscribed.[95]

Former Directors of Insolvent Companies

5–28 Another objective of the 1990 Act was to deal with the so-called "phoenix syndrome", meaning directors liquidating one company, leaving substantial unpaid debts behind, and then going on and setting up a new company, often in the very same or a similar business. It was felt that certain restrictions should be placed on former directors of insolvent companies. Except where permitted by the court under section 150 of the 1990 Act, a person who was the director of a company which is wound up and is found to be insolvent[96] cannot be a company director for a period of five years, unless the company meets certain minimum capital requirements. This restriction applies only where the company was wound up after 1st August, 1990. But it applies to anyone who was a director or a "shadow director" of the company within 12 months prior to the winding up commencing, including foreign-registered companies with an established place of business in Ireland.[97] And it extends to being appointed or acting in any way, either directly or indirectly, as a company director or secretary, and even being concerned in or taking part in the promotion or formation of any company. This prohibition is founded on the assumption that the former company probably would not have become insolvent if it had been adequately capitalised.

5–29 Accordingly, any company which these persons now wish to manage should have a substantial capital basis. Any p.l.c. must have a minimum capital of £100,000 which, along with any premium on those shares, must be fully paid up in cash. In the case of a private limited company, that minimum is £20,000. Additionally, that company is not allowed to avail of section 60(2)–(11) of the 1963 Act,[98] which permits it to lend money or otherwise assist persons to purchase the company's own shares. Also, the company must comply with the requirements in sections 32–36 of the 1983 Act,[99] regarding having certain acquisitions of substantial assets by the company subjected to independent valua-

---

[94] 1990 Act, s.167.
[95] 1990 Act, s.163.
[96] *cf. Carway v. Attorney General* [1996] 3 I.R. 300 on how insolvency can be proved here.
[97] 1990 Act, s.149(4).
[98] See below, paras 7–75 *et seq.*
[99] See below, paras 6–57 *et seq.*

tion, as if it were a p.l.c. An allottee of shares in a p.l.c. or a private company which are not fully paid up in cash, as required above, remains liable for the outstanding sum.

5–30 The above restrictions do not apply in the following circumstances.[100] If the directorship was held solely by reason of the person being nominated by a licensed bank or other financial institution, in connection with that institution providing credit facilities to the company, ordinarily he will escape the restriction. However, he must have acted "honestly and responsibly" in the office and, additionally, the institution must not hold any personal guarantee from any of the company's directors in respect of the company's liabilities. Directors nominated by prescribed venture capital companies can also be excluded. Apart from these, if the director can satisfy the court that he had acted "honestly and responsibly" in connection with the company and there is no other reason why, in fairness, these restrictions should apply to him, the court can exonerate him. In applying this very broad criterion, it has been said that:

> "The primary purpose of the section is not to punish the individual but to protect the public against the future conduct of companies by persons whose past record as directors of insolvent companies have shown them to be a danger to creditors and others.... Ordinary commercial misjudgment is in itself not sufficient to justify disqualification. In the normal case, the conduct complained of must display a lack of commercial probity, although ... in an extreme case of gross negligence or total incompetence, disqualification could be appropriate."[101]

Finally, within one year of the court declaring the restriction applicable, section 152 of the 1990 Act enables the person to apply to the court to be relieved of the restriction in whole or in part.

5–31 Any director who contravenes a restriction commits an offence[102] and, additionally, is deemed to be subject to a "disqualification order" under section 160 of the 1990 Act.[103] If at that time he was subject to a disqualification order, then the period of the order is extended by an additional ten years and he may not apply to the court under section 160(8) to have that order relaxed or lifted. Moreover, the court is em-

---

[100] 1990 Act, s.150(2).

[101] Re *La Moselle Clothing Ltd.*, Shanley J. May 11, 1998 at p. 9. Other cases on this point include *Re Cavan Crystal Group Ltd.*, Murphy J., April 26, 1997; *Re Outdoor Advertising Services Ltd.*, Costello P., January 28, 1997; *Business Communications Ltd. v. Baxter,* Murphy J., July 21, 1995 and *Re Costello Doors Ltd.*, Murphy J., July 21, 1995.

[102] 1990 Act, s.161.

[103] *ibid.*, s.163(1).

powered to impose unlimited liability on him in respect of any debts incurred by the company during the period he acted as its director or officer while disqualified or, if the company was not adequately capitalised, subject to the restriction.[104]

Service Contracts

5–32 Not all directors have service contracts with their company. But many full-time executive directors have those contracts and the rights and duties of some non-executive directors may be set out in contracts with their company. The various incidents of directors' service contracts raise mainly questions of employment law and are best dealt with in a book on that subject;[105] for instance, the scope of the work obligation, times of work and absences from work, sick pay, holidays, non-disclosure of confidential information, restraints on employment when they cease to be directors, occupational pension schemes and income taxation. As is explained below, the Companies Acts lay down certain requirements regarding directors' remuneration and expenses and also the dismissal of directors.

Authority to Conclude Service Contracts

5–33 Questions of remuneration aside, the Companies Acts do not lay down who is entitled to conclude directors' service contracts for the company. Normally, that power is exercised by a special committee of the board established to deal with these matters. Where a committee of this nature exists, ordinarily it will be comprised entirely or mainly of non-executive directors. Table A does not deal with authority to conclude service contracts as such but provides that the directors' "remuneration", in the sense of fees, is to be fixed by the general meeting.[106] But the managing director's and executive directors' remuneration, in the sense of salary, other terms and conditions and pensions may be fixed by the board of directors.[107] Special statutory procedures are laid down before "golden handshakes" can be paid.[108]

"Golden Umbrellas"

5–34 A golden umbrella is a phrase often used to describe service contracts of a very long duration. The gilded element is that, if the

---

[104] 1990 Act, s.163(3), (4).
[105] See generally, M. Forde, *Employment Law* (1992).
[106] Art. 76.
[107] Art. 85.
[108] See below, paras 5–71 *et seq*.

employer wants to terminate the contract, he must pay the equivalent of the remuneration which would have been earned during the remainder of the contract period. Thus the longer the duration the higher the price to be paid in order to rid the company of the director. In one major Irish case,[109] where the directors sought to prevent a person who inherited shares in the company from being registered as a shareholder, one of those directors had a 20 years service contract. A device used at times to ward off take-over bids is to give the directors golden umbrellas; if an intending bidder then wants to take over the company, it will have to pay large sums of compensation to any of the directors it wants to replace.

5–35 Section 28 of the 1990 Act prohibits the conclusion of golden umbrellas with a duration longer than five years, without the prior approval of an ordinary resolution of the company's members. That approval is required whether the contract is one of service or for services, *i.e.* whether under the contract the director is an employee or is to be treated as self-employed. Approval must be given to any service contract which the company is not completely free to terminate lawfully within five years of the service commencing. In the case of a director of one or more companies within a group of companies, the approval must come from the members of the holding company. Before any approval can be given to these contracts, a written memorandum of the proposed terms must be available for inspection for at least fifteen days prior to the general meeting taking place; that memorandum must also be available at the meeting. The term of any service contract which contravenes these requirements is void and can be determined by the company at any time on giving reasonable notice of dismissal.

Inspecting Service Contracts

5–36 Another of the innovations introduced in 1990 is to entitle every shareholder to inspect a copy or a memorandum of the terms of many directors' service contracts, regardless of who is entitled to appoint directors or determine their remuneration. The right here applies to all contracts with an unexpired duration of three years or more. Section 50 of the 1990 Act requires that a copy or memorandum of the contract be kept at either the registered office, the principal place of business or where the register of members is kept. This information must be open for inspection during business hours by any member, without charge. Similar information regarding directors of subsidiaries must be kept

---

[109] *Re Hafner* [1943] I.R. 426.

by the holding company. In the case of directors who work "wholly or mainly outside" the State, only the name of the director and the duration of the contract need be disclosed in this manner.[110]

Vacating the Office

5–37 Subject to section 182 of the 1963 Act, persons can be appointed to directorships even for the duration of their lives. Most articles of association, however, provide for periodic retirals. Under Table A, all the directors are required to retire at the first annual general meeting;[111] following that, one-third of the board must retire every year on a rota basis. The office is deemed vacated[112] when the director *inter alia* is adjudged bankrupt, makes an arrangement or composition with his creditors generally, becomes of unsound mind, is convicted of an indictable offence (unless the other directors decide that he should stay on) or is absent for more than six months from board meetings without the board's consent. It is probable that companies cannot prohibit directors from ever resigning or impose penalties on the exercise of the option to resign.

Dismissing Directors

5–38 Apart from their disqualifying provisions,[113] the Companies Acts do not set down grounds for removing directors from office. It used to be the case that, in the absence of express provision to the contrary in the company's regulations or in a service contract, shareholders did not possess the "inherent" power to remove directors of registered companies appointed for a definite period until that time had expired.[114] Article 99 of Table A provides that any or all of the directors can be removed by an ordinary resolution of the members. The regulations of some companies empower the directors themselves to remove any of their number from the board. It has been held that where, under such a regulation, directors resolve to remove one of their number but that resolution is unlawful, in the sense that the directors were pursuing extraneous objectives and were not acting for the company's benefit, the resolution nevertheless is legally effective.[115] This result was justified by the need to give "business sense" to the regulation in question and to prevent paralysis of the company's management pending the outcome of any dispute about the removal from office.

---

[110] s. 50(5).
[111] Art. 92.
[112] Art. 91.
[113] above, paras 5–25 *et seq*.
[114] *Imperial Hydropathic Hotel Co. v. Hampson* (1882) 23 Ch.D. 1.
[115] *Lee v. Chou Wen Hsien* [1984] 1 W.L.R. 1202.

Right to Dismiss

5–39 One of the most important rules in company law is section 182 of the 1963 Act whereby shareholders, by passing an ordinary resolution, may remove any or all of the directors from the board before their periods of office expire. That is to say, a simple majority of the members voting may immediately sack any director and even the entire board. Extended notice must be given of an intention to propose such a resolution.[116] Consequently, the ultimate control over the running of companies lies with whoever owns or has influence over 50 per cent of the voting shares. Although the board itself may be legally free to ignore instructions given to it by an ordinary resolution of the general meeting,[117] the fact that a bare majority of the voting members can oust the board means that the directors will pay particular attention to the majority's wishes. Persons seeking to take over a company may be satisfied with a 51 per cent stake, in that this brings them control of the management; although more often they may prefer at least a 75 per cent stake, so that they are in a position to alter the articles of association.

5–40 A director of a private company who, under the articles of association, holds office for life is excepted from this rule.[118] But Table A does not make any provision for life directors. If a company with Table A appointed someone as a life director it therefore is legally free to remove him.

5–41 In order to entrench the principle of simple majority rule on this matter, section 182 of the 1963 Act adds that the power to remove directors by ordinary resolution cannot be excluded by the articles of association or by a service contract; that power exists notwithstanding anything in the articles or in an agreement between the company and the director. But the section does not prohibit a contrary provision in the memorandum of association, nor separate voting agreements between shareholders, or between shareholders and directors, not to exercise their statutory power. And in *Bushell v. Faith*[119] it was held that virtually perpetuating directors' positions by giving them weighted votes on the issue of their removal from office was permissible. The company there had three shareholders, each with an equal number of shares. According to its regulations, on any resolution to remove a director, that director should have three votes for every share he owned.

---

[116] *cf. Currie v. Cowdenbeath F.C.* [1992] B.C.L.C. 1029.
[117] *Automatic Self-Cleansing Filter Syndicate Co. Ltd. v. Cunninghame* [1906] 2 Ch. 34.
[118] *cf. Bersel Manufacturers Co. Ltd. v. Berry* [1968] 3 All E.R. 552.
[119] [1970] A.C. 1099.

A and B with 100 shares each cast 200 votes to remove C; but C, although he held only 100 shares, under that regulation could cast 300 votes and defeat that proposal. It was contended that if such a scheme were sustained it would "make a mockery of the law", in that if "writ large it would set out a director is not to be removed against his will and that in order to achieve this and to thwart the express provision of [s.183], the voting power of any director threatened with removal is to be deemed to be greater than it actually is."[120]

5–42 In answer, the majority of the Law Lords fastened on section 198's insistence on an ordinary resolution, which means a majority of the votes cast, and the fact that the legislature "has never sought to fetter the right of the company (set out in article 2 of Table A) to issue a share with such [voting] rights and restrictions it may think fit".[121] Classes of shares with different voting weights have always been allowed, whether the weighing is for all questions or for particular issues only;[122] there is nothing in the Companies Acts to suggest that the freedom companies have to devise their internal power structures in this way was abrogated. It did not matter that the actual device used here was inconsistent with what it was hoped that section 182 would achieve. This decision is perhaps the most extreme example of literal construction in modern company law, has attracted considerable criticism and, indeed, might not be followed in Ireland.

Oppression and Inequity

5–43 In very exceptional circumstances, removal of a director from the board can amount to "oppression" under section 205 of the 1963 Act or be grounds for winding up the company on "just and equitable" grounds. But that director must also be a member of the company and must show that, in the circumstances, he had a very compelling "legitimate expectation" to remain a director against the wishes of the majority of members. An example might be where the company is what is termed a quasi-partnership and was established on the clear understanding that he would always have a full say in managing the business.[123]

5–44 Even where this is shown to be the case, a court will not grant an injunction restraining the general meeting from considering a proposed resolution under section 182 that the director/shareholder should

---

[120] [1970] A.C. 1099 at 1106, Lord Morris dissenting.
[121] *ibid.* at 1109.
[122] See below, para. 9–22.
[123] *e.g. Re Westbourne Galleries Ltd.* [1973] A.C. 360; see below, paras 10–94 *et seq.*

be removed from office. In *Feighery v. Feighery*,[124] which in any event did not involve a "quasi partnership" and there was little evidence to support a strong "legitimate expectation", Laffoy J. refused to make such an order. This was an account of the importance of the shareholders' statutory right under section 182. Even if passing such a resolution would amount to oppression, the shareholders were entitled to so act albeit the aggrieved member may then become entitled to appropriate redress under section 205. But in *Gilligan v. O'Grady*,[124a] the Supreme Court distinguished that case and made an interlocutory order restraining the plaintiff's removal from the board.

Damages

5–45 A director, especially an executive director, may hold office under a contract that runs for a set period or until terminated on expressly stated or impliedly provided for grounds. Section 182(7) of the 1963 Act and also article 99 of Table A stipulate that the power to remove them by ordinary resolution shall not deprive the directors of any entitlement to damages or compensation they may possess. A director may lawfully be removed from office only in accordance with any service contract's provisions regarding notice and procedures, except where he has broken a major term of the contract, in which case he may be dismissed *instanter* once he has been given a fair opportunity to defend himself. The contractual terms may be express or implied. On account of section 182(7), it can be very expensive for the company to remove directors who have service contracts, especially where the members gave them "golden umbrellas".

5–46 Whether a director was in fact removed from office depends on the circumstances of each case, the question being whether the company's conduct amounted to a repudiation of the service agreement. For instance in *Harold Holdsworth & Co. (Wakefield) Ltd. v. Caddies*,[125] the plaintiff was appointed director of a company for a five-year period, his function being defined as running the company and its associated companies in such manner as may from time to time be assigned to or vested in him by the board. Following differences that arose between them, the board resolved that the plaintiff should confine his attentions to just one company in the group. It was held that this was not a breach of the service agreement because, under its terms, the board reserved the power to limit his responsibilities as it saw fit. The mere appointment out of court by creditors of a receiver and manager to act

---

[124] Laffoy J., February 25, 1998.
[124a] [1999] 1 I.L.R.M. 303.
[125] [1955] 1 W.L.R. 352.

for the company does not *ipso facto* amount to a repudiation of the service contract with a managing director.[126]

5–47 In *Glover v. B.L.N. Ltd.*[127] the plaintiff's contract as managing director provided that he could be removed without compensation for serious misconduct, serious neglect of duties, wilful disobedience of reasonable orders and the like. One issue before the court was whether, when dismissing him, the defendant's board possessed sufficient evidence of serious misconduct and neglect on his part. It was held that only one of the many allegations made against him provided grounds for summary dismissal. At times the required standard of performance must be implied from the surrounding circumstances. A director whose conduct repudiates the service agreement can be removed almost instantaneously. In *Carvill v. Irish Industrial Bank Ltd.*[128] what, to use a neutral term, was unwise conduct on the part of a small bank's managing director was held by Kenny J. to warrant immediate dismissal. But the Supreme Court concluded that, in the circumstances, his indiscretion was not sufficiently repudiatory for that purpose. Unless the contract provides for a fixed term of service or for dismissal only on stated grounds, a director may lawfully be removed for any reason whatsoever if given proper notice. Proper notice means the period stipulated in the contract or, where the contract is silent, a reasonable period. In *Carvill*, for example, it was found that twelve months was a reasonable period.

5–48 Requirements similar to natural justice must he complied with before the members can pass a resolution under section 182 to remove a director. The proposed resolution must follow the section 142 extended notice procedure[129] and a copy of it must be forwarded by the company to the director in advance. Ordinarily, he is entitled to have written representations circulated to the shareholders and to speak at the general meeting on the resolution. It was held in the *Glover* case that it is an implied term of a director's service contract, especially one that lays down grounds for removal from the board, that the removal procedures be fair. If, for example, the grounds stated for dismissal are misconduct or neglect of duty, then the director must be "told of the charges against him [and be] allow[ed] to meet the charges . . . and afford[ed] an adequate opportunity of answering them . . . ."[130] It is of no relevance to this that the director is an employee and not an office-

---

[126] *Griffiths v. Secretary of State* [1974] 1 Q.B. 468.
[127] [1973] I.R. 388.
[128] [1968] I.R. 325.
[129] See above, para. 4–18.
[130] [1973] I.R. 425.

holder. Refusal to accord these procedural rights is a breach of contract regardless of how guilty the director may have been. The court in *Glover* did not consider whether or to what extent these rights could be excluded or waived by contract.

The Articles and the Service Contract

5–49 There remains the question of the relationship between tenure under a director's service contract and removal provisions contained in the articles of association. In the first place, section 15 of the 1963 Act empowers a company to alter its articles of association by special resolution, which could enable it to remove any director. Thus in *Shuttleworth v. Cox Brothers & Co.*,[131] the plaintiff was designated in the articles as a permanent director entitled to hold office for as long as he lived. The articles were later amended to add a new ground for disqualifying a director, viz. a request in writing by all his co-directors that he should resign. A request to resign was then made of the plaintiff and thereafter he was treated as no longer holding office. Because, in the circumstances, there was no evidence of bad faith or discriminatory motives, it was held that alteration made to the articles was valid and, accordingly, his removal under the new article was effective.

5–50 A company cannot waive its power to alter its own regulations,[132] not even by express stipulation in a separate service contract. There is some authority to the effect that a court will enjoin a company from altering its articles where doing so would contravene an earlier contractual obligation undertaken by it;[133] but it most likely would not be followed today, at least in this context. Nevertheless, to act on such an alteration by removing a director may be a breach of contract if doing so is contrary to a term in a contract entered into before the alteration. In *Southern Foundries (1926) Ltd. v. Shirlaw*,[134] where the plaintiff had a ten years service contract as a managing director, the company's articles of association were changed so as to empower the parent company to remove him from office. While the alteration itself could not be impeached, it did not necessarily follow that the company was free to act on the new article by dismissing him.

5–51 Article 110 of Table A stipulates that a managing director's appointment shall be automatically determined if he "ceases from any cause to be a director"; article 99 empowers the general meeting to

---

[131] [1927] 2 K.B. 9.
[132] See below, paras 11–08 *et seq*.
[133] *British Murac Syndicate Ltd. v. Alperton Rubber Co.* [1915] 2 Ch. 186.
[134] [1940] A.C. 701.

remove any director before their period of office expires "notwithstanding anything in . . . any agreement." The question, therefore, has arisen whether a company may lawfully dismiss its managing director through the simple expedient of removing him from the board. Is the managing director's service contract subject to an implied power by the company, under these articles, to terminate it in this manner? The answer is generally no, because of the general principle against self-induced frustration of contracts: that "if a party enters into an arrangement which can only take effect by the continuance of a certain existing state of circumstances, there is an implied engagement on his part that he shall do nothing of his own motion to put an end to that state of circumstances, under which alone the arrangement can be operative."[135]

5–52 Thus, in *Shindler v. Northern Raincoat Co.*[136] the plaintiff was appointed managing director of the defendant company for a ten years period. Following a subsequent take-over of the company and disagreements between the plaintiff and the new controllers, resolutions were passed removing him from office as director and terminating the service agreement in so far as it might still be subsisting. The company's regulations included clauses along the lines of articles 110 and 99 of Table A. The contention that the plaintiff could be removed under the power they conferred was flatly rejected on the grounds that:

> "[a]pplying the [self-induced frustration] principle to the present case, there is an implied engagement on the part of the defendant company that it will do nothing of its own motion to put an end to the state of circumstances which enables the plaintiff to continue as managing director. That is to say, there is an implied undertaking that it will not revoke his appointment as a director, and will not resolve that his tenure of office be determined."[137]

5–53 One line of defence in the earlier *Southern Foundries* case[138] was that, since the power under the articles to remove from office was in effect vested in the defendant's parent company, the defendant fell outside the self-induced frustration principle. But it was held that the defendant there was "sufficiently involved in the removal process to be caught by that principle; "if a wrong . . . if done by [the defendant] it surely must a wrong . . . if done by [the parent] who derives [its] power to do the act from [the defendant] only."[139]

---

135 *Stirling v. Maitland* (1864) 5 B. & S. 840 at 852.
136 [19601] 1 W.L.R. 1038.
137 *ibid.* at 1043.
138 [1940] A.C. 701.
139 *ibid.* at 718.

5–54 It nevertheless can happen that the service contract by implication authorises the company without "cause" to terminate the agreement before its normal expiry date; although there would need to be very persuasive circumstances to raise such an implication when the contract states that it is for a fixed term. In one instance where the contract was for an indeterminate period, *Read v. Astoria Garage (Streatham) Ltd.*,[140] it was held that, although the board would have to give proper notice in order lawfully to remove the plaintiff, he could be removed without notice by a general meeting resolution under articles 110 and 99 of Table A. However, in *Shindler* this case was said to have been wrongly decided.

DIRECTORS' REMUNERATION, EXPENSES AND LOANS

5–55 The question of directors' remuneration[141] is a sensitive matter in many companies. In closely-held companies tax considerations bear heavily on whether the directors are to be rewarded by emoluments that are subject to Schedule E or by generous expenses, both of which are deductible from the company's own tax bill; or else by way of dividends or, indeed, loans. At times, there may be concern that majority shareholders will occupy all the seats on the board, pay themselves handsome directors' fees and leave little or nothing for distribution by way of dividends. In large companies with many shareholders, the dilemma may be whether the directors are being adequately rewarded to ensure that they will give of their best in advancing the company's interests. To this end, part of their remuneration may be options on the company's shares. "Golden handshakes" paid to retiring directors can give rise to concern among shareholders about whose benefit the company in fact is being run – either for the professional directors or for the shareholders.

Ultra Vires

5–56 In *Re Horsley and Weight Ltd.*[142] it was held that a provision in a company's objects clause authorising it to pay pensions was a substantive object and not just a power. Accordingly, such payments could not be set aside as being *ultra vires* simply because they were gratuitous and brought no benefit whatsoever to the company. It remains to

---

140 [1952] Ch. 637.

141 See generally, C. Ryan, *Company Directors* (3rd ed., 1990), Chap. 7 and B. Cheffins, *Company Law: Theory, Structure and Operation* (1997), Chap. 14.

142 [1982] Ch. 442.

be seen whether this reasoning finds favour in Ireland and whether it will be extended to "golden handshakes" and loans to directors. However, a payment that is *intra vires* on this basis is nonetheless unlawful and *ultra vires* where it amounts to an unauthorised repayment of the company's capital. Where, as usually is the case, the company's objects do not deal with remuneration but the articles of association set down the procedure for determining directors' remuneration, it would appear that payment of remuneration cannot then be impeached on *ultra vires* grounds, in the sense of being outside the company's capacity. In *Re Halt Garage (1964) Ltd.*,[143] which concerned a company with Table A as its articles, it was held that remuneration paid for a director's services, even if the rate was excessive, could not be struck down for being *ultra vires*. It may be that the memorandum or articles of non-profit companies must stipulate for remunerating their directors before those payments can be *intra vires*.[144] As is explained below, there are several cases on pensions for directors' widows which were held to be *ultra vires* but which might not be followed today, at least on that ground. None of the cases appear to have considered the relevance of taxation principles to this enquiry, *i.e.*, the view that if the payment would not be allowed as an expense in computing the company's tax bill then it is not a genuine fee or salary.

Fees and Salaries

5–57 The Companies Acts do not state who shall determine whether or how much the directors should be paid in fees and salaries, other than that no such payment may be made free of income tax.[145] The right given by section 50 of the 1990 Act to inspect many directors' service contracts[146] now enables every shareholder to ascertain exactly how much directors are being paid, in what manner and for what services. Every set of annual accounts must contain or be accompanied by a statement showing the aggregate of *inter alia* directors' "emoluments".[147]

Authorised Remuneration

5–58 Where the payment in question is expressly authorised by the company's objects clause then by definition it is *intra vires*. The only qualification to an express power in the articles to pay remuneration is that a company's capital must not be repaid to its shareholders: "a

---

[143] [1982] 3 All E.R. 1016.
[144] *cf. Cyclists' Touring Club v. Hopkinson* [1910] 1 Ch. 179.
[145] 1963 Act, s.185.
[146] See supra, para. 5–36.
[147] 1986 Act, sched., para. 39(6).

gratuitous payment out of the company's capital to a member, *qua* member, is unlawful and cannot stand, even if authorised by all the shareholders".[148] That is to say, remuneration may be paid on any scale provided there are profits available for distribution and the company is solvent. Where, however, there are no such profits and the money in fact is coming from contributed capital, the payment is unlawful if it is shown that the transaction in question is not a "genuine exercise of the power" to remunerate but instead is "a cloak for making payments out of capital to the shareholders as such".[149] Apart from these circumstances, the size of the remuneration, "whether it be mean or generous, must be a matter of management for the company to determine in accordance with its constitution which expressly authorises payment for directors' services. Shareholders are required to be honest but . . . there is no requirement that they must be wise and it is not for the court to manage the company."[150]

5–59 A distinction must be made between where the decision to pay is made by the board and, as is more often the case, by the general meeting or is ratified by it. The board's determination is subject to the general fiduciary standards that bind directors; they must act bona fide and for the company's benefit. Violation of this duty does not render the payment *ultra vires* but payment may be unenforceable, as being beyond the board's authority, and further the company, and possibly minority shareholders in a representative action, can sue the directors for breaking their obligations to the company. Where the determination is made by the general meeting but in reality amounts to defrauding the company for the benefit of the majority shareholders, it can be impeached at the instigation of any shareholder as a "fraud on the minority". But this too does not render the payment *ultra vires* because "the test of bona fides and benefit to the company [is] appropriate, and really only appropriate, to the question of the propriety of an exercise of a power rather than the capacity to exercise it".[151]

5–60 A distinction must also be drawn between fees for non-executive directors and salaries paid to executive directors who have service contracts with the company. In the case of the former, there must be express authority in the memorandum or articles of association to pay them any fee or salary.[152] Article 76 of Table A authorises the general

[148] *Re Halt Garage (1964) Ltd.* [1982] 3 All E.R. 1038; see also *Re Horsley & Weight Ltd.* [1982] 1 Ch. 442.
[149] *ibid.* at 1039.
[150] *ibid.*
[151] *ibid.* at 1034.
[152] *Re George Newman & Co.* [1895] 1 Ch. 674 and *Boschoek Property Co. v. Fuke* [1906] 1 Ch. 148.

meeting to determine directors' remuneration, though this term is not defined. Where all the directors are also the entirety of the shareholders, then their approval of accounts that include amounts drawn by them during the year as remuneration is equivalent to them sanctioning the payments in general meeting.[153] Even though a company is implicitly empowered to do everything incidental to securing its business objects, like paying reasonable salaries, it has been held that directors may not appoint any one of their number to a salaried office in the company without having express power to do so.[154] Under clause 85 of Table A, the board can appoint any director as managing director or to any other office or "place of profit" in the company, and determine the terms on which these positions are to be held, including the remuneration. Although in principle the director in question may not vote on the matter of his own appointment to such a position or even be counted in the quorum for this purpose, this rule is modified by article 86 of Table A, which includes them in the quorum. In companies that have adopted article 7 of Part II of the model regulations, that director is even allowed to vote on this very matter.

5–61 Application of the principles stated here can be illustrated by several relatively recent cases. In *Taupo Totara Timber Co. v. Rowe*,[155] which concerned a combination of a salary and "golden handshake" agreement, the contention that a lavish arrangement with an "outsider" managing director was beyond the directors powers and even the company's powers was rejected on the grounds that "[t]here is no question as to the bona fides of the directors in entering into this particular agreement. It was shown that similar agreements had been entered into with other employees, and that to do so had been the company's policy for several years. The view that inclusion of a provision giving protection in the event of a take-over was in the interests of the company, was clearly one that reasonable and honest directors might take. In its absence, the staff might be likely to go elsewhere."[156]

5–62 In *Re Halt Garage (1964) Ltd.*[157] the first defendant acquired a shelf company and thereafter carried on a garage business through the company. He and his wife owned the only issued share capital in the company and were its only directors. Its articles of association incorporated article 76 of Table A, which gave the company an express power to remunerate a director, the amount to be determined in general meet-

---

[153] *Re Duomatic Ltd.* [1969] 2 Ch. 365.
[154] *Boschoek Property* case, above, n. 152.
[155] [1978] A.C. 537.
[156] *ibid.* at 546.
[157] [1982] 3 All E.R. 1016.

ing; they also included express power for the company to determine and pay directors' remuneration for the mere assumption of the post of director. The husband and wife built up the company together and drew weekly sums from the business as remuneration. Then the wife became ill. She remained a director of the company but soon afterwards it became apparent that she would not be active again in the business. The husband continued to work virtually full-time in the business for several years apart from two periods of three and six months when he was away because of his wife's illness and an accident he sustained. At the start the business was making a substantial trading profit but from then on the profits began to decline and, despite an increase in turnover, the company became insolvent. It went into voluntary liquidation and was subsequently compulsorily wound up. Throughout the entire period the husband and wife drew director's remuneration. The liquidator brought proceedings against both of them, claiming to recover the whole of the remuneration drawn by the wife from the very beginning and such part of the husband's remuneration as exceeded the market value of his services to the company, on the grounds that they were guilty of misfeasance and breach of trust in making the drawings. The liquidator submitted that, although the amounts drawn were either formally determined by the company in general meeting as directors' remuneration or were otherwise sanctioned as such by the company, and although they were made in good faith, nevertheless they were *ultra vires* the company as being gratuitous payments made out of capital otherwise than for consideration, unless it could be shown that they were made for the benefit of the company and to promote its prosperity. He further submitted that, having regard to the amount of the drawings, they could not have been made for the company's benefit when it was suffering a loss and the money was needed for the business.

5–63 Regarding the husband's drawings, it was held that there was no evidence that, in the light of the company's turnover, those payments were patently excessive or unreasonable as director's remuneration, or that they were disguised gifts of capital rather than genuine remuneration. Accordingly, the court would not inquire into whether it would have been more beneficial to the company to have paid him less, since that was a matter for the company alone to determine. As for the wife's drawings, it was held that, although the company's articles included power to award remuneration for the mere assumption of the office of director, even where the director was not active in the conduct of the business, the mere fact that the label of directors' remuneration was attached to her drawings did not preclude the court from examining their true nature. Having regard to her inactivity during the period in question, it could not be said that the whole of the amounts drawn by her in that period were genuine remuneration for holding office as a director. That part of her drawings in excess of what would have been a reasonable award of remuneration amounted to a disguised gift of capital or payment of dividends in recognition of her co-proprietorship of the business; it therefore was *ultra vires* the company and repayable to the liquidator.

5–64 *Guinness p.l.c. v. Saunders*[158] concerned a very large "success fee" which the plaintiff company paid to one of its directors for services he had provided the company in connection with a successful take-over bid. The company sought to recover the money on the grounds that its payment had not been properly authorised. A sub-committee of the directors had been established to implement the bid, which the board had decided to make; the payee of the fee was a member of that committee. It was held that the authority delegated by the board to the committee did not extend to approving payments of that nature. Under the company's articles of association, it was for the board of directors to determine the directors' remuneration and, since the board itself had not given its approval for the large fee, its payment had not been properly authorised. Referring to the article which enabled the board to decide its own members' remuneration, Lord Templeman observed that:

> "The shareholders . . . run the risk that the board may be too generous to an individual director at the expense of the shareholders but the shareholders have . . . chosen to run this risk and can protect themselves by the number, quality and impartiality of the members of the board who will consider whether an individual director deserves special reward. Under [that] article the shareholders . . . do not run the risk that a committee [of the directors] may value its own work and the contribution of its own members . . . . A committee, which may consist of only two or . . . three members, however honest and conscientious, cannot assess impartially the value of its work or the value of the contribution of its individual members."[159]

Several other provisions in the articles which might be regarded as authorising the committee to sanction the payment — like establishing local committees and boards with extensive authority and also permitting directors to be paid for services rendered to the company in a "professional capacity" — were held not to have that effect. Indeed, because the power to fix remuneration was conferred on the board,

---

[158] [1990] 2 A.C. 664.
[159] *ibid.* at 686.

they could not, even if they wanted to, delegate that sensitive matter entirely to one of its committees.

Obligation to Remunerate

5–65 In the absence of an agreement to the contrary, directors have no right against the company to be paid for their services; any remuneration paid to them is in the nature of a gratuity or gift. But the company may be obliged on the basis of *quantum meruit* to pay a reasonable remuneration for services in fact rendered to it. In *Craven-Ellis v. Canons Ltd.*[160] the plaintiff had been appointed managing director but at that time he was not a director of the company, which was held to have rendered his appointment void. He claimed payment for work he had done for the company both before and after his purported appointment. His claim was upheld on the basis of "the implied obligation to pay . . . imposed by law . . . arising from the performance and acceptance of services."[161] Ordinarily, an executive director's right against the company will be based on contract; where in fact no contract exists, he may be entitled to a reasonable sum on a *quantum meruit* basis.

5–66 In one instance, however, a director was found to have fallen between two stools and, in consequence, obtained no payment for his services. In *Re Richmond Gate Property Co.*[162] the plaintiff was a validly appointed managing director and the company's articles stipulated that the holder of that office should be paid "such remuneration . . . as the directors may determine." But the board never decided how much he should be paid. It was held that he was not entitled to any remuneration because his contract left him "at the mercy of the board"; he "gets what they determine to pay him and, if they do not determine to pay him anything, he does not get anything."[163] Furthermore, the existence of the contract excluded any claim founded on *quantum meruit*. Some emphasis was placed on the fact that the articles there designated the plaintiff by name as managing director and the plaintiff was also a member of the company; so that the above reasoning may not be applied to officers who do not find themselves in that very situation. Remuneration on the basis of *quantum meruit* or an equitable allowance was also refused in *Guinness p.l.c.* v *Saunders*[164] for several reasons. Unlike the plaintiff in *Craven-Ellis*, the director there was a validly elected

160 [1936] 2 K.B. 403.
161 *ibid.* at 411.
162 [1965] 1 W.L.R. 335.
163 *ibid.* at 337.
164 [1990] 2 A.C. 664.

director at the relevant time; a very substantial conflict existed between his own personal interests and the company's interests and there was no question of the *Guinness* directors and shareholders having actually approved the payment of the large "success fee".

Pensions

5–67 A pension is a form of deferred salary that an employer may be obliged by contract to pay or that may be paid as a gratuity. It depends on the circumstances whether a sum paid to a retiring or retired director is a pension or more in the nature of a "golden handshake"; although for the purpose of disclosure in the company's accounts, there are elaborate definitions of each of these terms.[165] The same general principles explained above that apply to fees and salaries govern pensions.

5–68 All that the Companies Acts require is that directors' pensions may not be paid free of income tax[166] and the aggregate amount of pensions must be shown in a company's annual accounts.[167] Companies in business have implied powers to agree to pay pensions to executive directors and, after those directors have died, may agree to pay pensions to their dependents.[168] Even in the absence of any express authority in the articles of association, it has been said that "it is within the power of the [directors] of a trading company . . . to grant a pension to a retiring officer or servant, and to do that with or without any reasonable terms which may be bargained for or imposed".[169] But it has also been said that, where the articles are silent, the directors cannot make "a gift or reward . . . out of the company's assets . . . to one of their own body . . . unless authorised . . . by the shareholders at a properly convened meeting . . ."[170] The matter may turn on the size of the payment in question and the extent to which it can be justified by the directors' past service. In any event, the boards of companies subject to article 90 of Table A are authorised to pay pensions to directors who worked for the company in any capacity under a service contract, and to their dependents.

5–69 There are two reported modern instances of agreements to pay pensions to directors' widows being struck down at the instigation of

---

165 1963 Act, ss. 191(3), (4).
166 *ibid.*, s.185.
167 1986 Act, sched., para. 39(6).
168 *Henderson v. Bank of Australasia* (1888) 40 Ch. D. 170.
169 *Normandy v. Ind. Coope & Co.* [1908] 1 Ch. 84 at 104–105.
170 *Re Lee Behrens & Co.* [1932] 2 Ch. 46 at 53.

liquidators. In *Re Lee Behrens & Co.*[171] three years before the company was wound up the board agreed to pay a £500 per annum pension for life to the long deceased managing director's widow. It was argued that the agreement was in effect a gratuitous distribution from the company's capital but there was no evidence to support this allegation. It then appears to have been assumed that, since the company derived no perceptible advantage from its generosity, the payment was *ultra vires* unless expressly authorised by the memorandum of association. In fact, the memorandum there empowered the company to pay pensions and the like to "persons in [its] employment". But it was held that the agreement fell outside these terms because it was made by the directors and had never been ratified by the company in general meeting; additionally, the managing director was not an employee. Two of the three criteria announced there for determining the capacity of companies to make such payments (bona fide and to promote the company's prosperity) have since been held relevant only to questions of directors' powers and minority shareholders' rights, and not to *ultra vires* as it is understood today.[172] Despite this criticism, it could be argued that, even by today's standards, in the circumstances of that case the pension was *ultra vires* as a "gratuitous" transaction falling outside any of the company's express or implied powers, because the agreement took no account of the company's solvency. However, the widow might now, under section 8(1) of the 1963 Act, be able to enforce the agreement against the company if she was not "actually aware" of this defect.[173]

5–70 In the other case, *Re W. & M. Roith Ltd.*,[174] a director who also was general manager of a company and its controlling shareholder, but had no service agreement with it, became anxious about providing for his dependents should he die. Acting on legal advice, the memorandum and the articles of association were changed to authorise the board to pay pensions to *inter alia* director's widows. Then an agreement was made with him appointing him full-time general manager for life, and providing for payment of a substantial widow's pension. In fact, he was in poor health at the time and he died within a year. Following *Lee Behrens*, the pension provision was struck down because, in the circumstances, the entire agreement was neither reasonably incidental to the company's business nor made bona fide to promote its prosperity. Rather "the whole object of the plan of campaign was to

---

171 *Re Lee Behrens & Co.* [1932] 2 Ch. 46 at 53.
172 *Charterbridge Corporation v. Lloyds Bank* [1970] Ch. 62.
173 See below, paras 13–15 *et seq*.
174 [1967] 1 W.L.R. 432.

benefit not the company but [the widow]."[175] While these considerations have a bearing on whether the board's decision was a breach of its fiduciary duties or was a "fraud on a minority", in the light of the power inserted in the company's regulations they are irrelevant to the question of *vires*. The only way the agreement there could be set aside is if it were shown that its true purpose was to return contributed capital to the shareholders or that it was a gift by the board to one of themselves but in breach of their fiduciary duties and which the majority could not ratify.

"Golden Handshakes"

5–71 The term "golden handshake" signifies sizeable payments made to company directors on their retirement other than by way of ordinary pensions. In the 1963 Act these are called "compensation for loss of office or as consideration for or in connection with retirement from office".[176] These payments usually used to be made in lump sums but tax considerations now compel companies to space them out over a number of years.[177] Golden handshakes may be either the estimated cost of removing a director from office prematurely or may be more in the nature of a gratuity.

5–72 The Companies Acts require that these payments must not be made tax free[178] and the aggregate amount of them in any year must be disclosed in or along with the annual accounts.[179] Over and above any questions of *ultra vires* and bona fides, in order to be valid the particulars, including the amount of any proposed payment connected with retirement from the position of a *de facto* or a *de jure* director, must be disclosed to the company's members, who must give their approval in general meeting. Disclosure must be made while the payment is still only a proposal and it must be made to all the company's members, even to those who do not have full voting rights in general meeting,[180] like many preference shareholders. Parallel provisions exist for such payments intended to be made in the context of full or partial takeovers and purchases of sizeable assets from the company in question.[181] A person who does not observe these parallel provisions must disgorge the payment. Section 186 does not stipulate that "ordinary" golden

---

175 [1967] 1 W.L.R. 432 at 439.
176 1963 Act, ss. 186-189.
177 Finance Act 1967, ss. 114–115.
178 1963 Act, s.185.
179 *ibid.*, s.191(1)(c), (4).
180 *Re Duomatic Ltd.* [19691 2 Ch. 365; *cf. Re Greenore Trading Ltd.* [1980] I.L.R.M. 94.
181 1963 Act, ss. 187(2), 188(3).

handshakes are returnable but, since unauthorised payments are declared not lawful, they therefore can be recovered from the directors who were responsible for making them.

5–73 The prerequisite of prior general meeting approval does not apply to "any bona fide payment by way of damages for breach of contract or by way of pension in respect of past services . . ."[182] How an arrangement such as that in the *Taupo Totara Timber Co.* case[183] would fare under this exemption is debatable. There, the plaintiff had been employed as the defendant company's managing director for a five-years period. In the service contract it was provided that, in the event of the company being taken over at any time during that period, he could resign and would thereupon become entitled to a sum equivalent to five times his annual salary. The contention that the New Zealand versions of sections 186 and 189 of our 1963 Act required prior disclosure to an approval by the shareholders of the resignation terms was rejected, because those provisions dealt with "uncovenanted payments" as contrasted with payments which the company is legally obliged to make.[184] That is to say, if, under a separate contract, the company is required to pay sums to a retiring director, then the arrangement is not caught by those sections. Otherwise, it was said, any service agreement with a managing director that provided for a special payment on relinquishing the job would have to be approved in advance in general meeting, which could be very impracticable. Nevertheless, a strong argument could be made that section 186 of the 1963 Act applies to a payment of the kind made in *Taupo Totara*, as the New Zealand version of section 186 did not contain an express exclusion of bona fide damages and pensions. Also an understanding reached at the outset to pay the equivalent of five years' salary in the event of a take-over could not be regarded as damages. There is no compelling reason why the general meeting should be kept in the dark about such unusual, and at times very expensive, compensation terms. Furthermore, if all sums due under contract fell outside section 186, it would take little legal ingenuity to devise golden handshake packages that did not have to be disclosed to and approved by the shareholders.

5–74 It is only in the most exceptional circumstances that golden handshakes endorsed in general meeting would be held unlawful, the classic instance being *Hutton v. West Cork Railway Co.*[185] The general meeting

---

182 1963 Act, s.189(3).
183 [1978] A.C. 537.
184 *ibid.* at 546.
185 (1883) 23 Ch.D. 654.

of a company, that was in the process of going into liquidation, voted to pay appreciable sums to directors in respect of their unremunerated past services. That decision was challenged by a dissenting shareholder/debenture-holder. It was held that, while it would be permissible to make payments "reasonably measured by the services they have rendered in winding up this company and in connection with the completion of the dissolution",[186] because the business by then was defunct, paying remuneration in respect of past services could not conceivably be for the company's benefit and could not be authorised by a majority of the shareholders; it was the company's and not the majority's money. In any event, the special statutory provision governing the closedown and transfer of that company's business[187] did not permit payments of this nature. Authority in the memorandum of association to pay golden handshakes would dispose of any *ultra vires* challenge if such a clause is treated as a substantive object and not an ancillary power. If it is a power, or where authority for such payments is contained in the articles of association, then the criterion of legality is the *Re Halt Garage*[188] one, of disguised repayment of capital. Even if it is *intra vires*, the handshake may nevertheless constitute a "fraud on a minority" or "oppression" within section 205 of the 1963 Act.

Expenses

5–75 Before 1990, the question of directors' expenses was not the subject of legislative provision — apart, of course, from the tax laws. Companies doing business have an implied power to pay those expenses; Table A authorises paying all expenses properly incurred in connection with the company's business.[189] As is explained below, loans and a variety of related payments to directors are prohibited by section 31 of the 1990 Act. An exception to this principle is made by section 36 of that Act for any arrangement whereby vouched expenses properly incurred by a director in the course of his duties will be met by the company. The prohibition on loans and the like does not:

> "prohibit the company from doing anything to provide any of its directors with funds to meet vouched expenditure properly incurred or to be incurred by him for the purposes of the company or the purpose of enabling him properly to perform his duties as an officer of the company or doing anything to enable any of its directors to avoid incurring such expenditure."

---

[186] (1883) 23 Ch.D. 654 at 677.

[187] s.12 of 42 & 43 Vict. c. clxxxvii, Cork & Kinsale Junction etc. Railway Act 1879 (private).

[188] [1982] 3 All E.R. 1016.

[189] Art. 76.

However, where the company incurs a liability that would have been caught by the prohibition against loans and the like but for the exception here for expenses, that liability must be discharged within six months of the date it was incurred.

Loans and Similar Arrangements

5–76 Apart from prohibiting companies from financing the purchase of their own shares[190] and requiring that the aggregate amount of loans to directors be disclosed in the annual accounts,[191] before 1990 the Companies Acts said nothing about a company lending money to its own directors or providing security for its directors' borrowings. Loans to directors, especially at below-market interest rates, can be a convenient method of remuneration. Often executive share option schemes are accompanied by generous loan arrangements. At one time, company controllers could pay themselves what in effect were tax-free dividends by having their company advance them loans that were never called in;[192] but this method of turning the separate legal personality of the company to the shareholders' fiscal advantage has for long been forestalled. Indeed, since 1976 loans to what are known as "participators" in close companies are treated as dividends for income tax purposes.

The Articles

5–77 It is convenient to deal first with the position apart from the 1990 Act's complicated requirements. Depending on the company's objects and the nature of the transaction, a loan made to one of the directors or security provided for such a loan may be *ultra vires*.[193] Moreover, *intra vires* lending to themselves, outside the explicit authority in the company's regulations or without the shareholders' informed consent, can be a breach of directors' duties.[194] Directors who are not parties to such transactions but who are or ought, in the circumstances, to be aware of them and who do not take appropriate action are liable for breach of duty. The *causes celebres* on these matters are the *Jackson v. Munster Bank* cases.[195] There the bank's regulations forbade it from making loans to its directors, even on their personal guarantees, unless there was adequate security. In 1882 rumours began to spread that many of the bank's directors were heavily indebted

---

[190] 1963 Act, s.60; see below, para. 7–60 *et seq*.
[191] 1990 Act, s.41.
[192] *I.R.C. v. Samsom* [1921] 2 K.B. 492.
[193] *Northern Bank Finance Corp. v. Quinn* [1979] I.L.R.M. 221.
[194] *Knight v. Frost* [1999] 1 B.C.L.C. 364.
[195] (1884) 13 L.R. Ir. 118 and (1885) 15 L.R. Ir. 356.

to it without there being any or sufficient security for their liabilities. Following complaints made by numerous shareholders, an investigation into the matter was conducted and some members' meetings were held. Eventually, but at very short notice, the directors called a special general meeting to consider resolutions *inter alia* to alter the articles of association in a way that would facilitate granting loans to themselves; they also sought proxies in support of those resolutions. However, voting on those resolutions was enjoined because the information circulated with the proxy forms was misleading; it was "neither fair nor candid" because it "did not call the attention of the shareholders to the real operation that would be effected by such a change".[196] The Vice-Chancellor observed of the proposed amendment, that sought to allow a unanimous board to lend to any of its members on their personal guarantee, "[c]an anyone say that this would be for the benefit of the company, or that it would be a bona fide exercise of their powers by the directors for the benefit of the shareholders?"[197] In the following year, one of the directors who had not borrowed from the bank was held responsible in negligence for not taking steps to protect the bank from the "fraudulent misconduct of its directors".[198]

5–78 There is no express authority in Table A to make loans to the company's directors or members of their families, nor to provide security for their borrowings.

Part III of the 1990 Act

5–79 Subject to some exceptions, Part III of the 1990 Act introduces very extensive restrictions on companies making substantial loans to their directors. This part goes much further in that it hits at a very wide category of transactions akin to loans, whereby a director obtains substantial credit at ultimately the company's expense; also the restrictions apply to loans and comparable transactions with immediate members of a director's family, companies he controls and other connected persons. Unlike many other restrictions in the 1990 Act, those here on loans are not conditional on the transaction getting prior shareholder approval; the prohibition is absolute, contravention of which is a criminal offence as well as a civil wrong. The central provision is section 31(1) of the Act, according to which, except as provided by sections 32–37, a company shall not:

---

196 (1884) 13 L.R. Ir. at 135, 137.
197 *ibid.* at 136.
198 (1885) 15 L.R. Ir. at 361.

"(a) make a loan or a quasi loan to a director of the company or of its holding company or to a person connected with such a director;

(b) enter into a credit transaction as creditor for such a director or a person so connected;

(c) enter into a guarantee or provide any security in connection with a loan, quasi loan or credit transaction made by any other person for such a director or a person so connected."

Several indirect ways of achieving the same result as that set out here are also prohibited. Sections 41-45 of the Act set out in great detail what information, concerning all loans and comparable arrangements with directors and connected persons, must be disclosed in the annual accounts.

5–80 Several obligations laid down in the 1990 Act apply with reference not alone to directors but also to so-called "connected" persons. Who they are is defined in section 26 of the Act. They are all members of the director's immediate family, being his spouse, parent, brother, sister or child; the trustee of a trust where any of those persons are beneficiaries; and his partner. They also include any company he controls and the trustee of any trust for which a controlled company is a beneficiary. Control for these purposes means where the director, either alone or with any of the above persons, either is "interested in" more than half the equity capital or controls more than half of the voting power in general meeting. The latter includes where those votes are controlled between him and another company he controls. What constitutes an "interest" in shares for these purposes is defined very widely in section 54 of the Act.[199]

5–81 In order to prevent evasion of the requirements, section 31 strikes at loans and also guarantees, other securities and what are called "quasi-loans" and "credit transactions"; these are defined in section 25(2) and (3). A quasi-loan envisages arrangements where some third party is to pay money or to reimburse expenditure incurred by the director or connected person, on the basis that they will be reimbursed by the company. A credit transaction envisages hire purchase and comparable arrangements, like conditional sale, leases and licences in return for periodic payments and any other transfer of land, goods or services on the understanding that payment will be deferred. There then is a definition of when is a transaction or arrangement "made for" a per-

---

[199] See below, para. 9–83.

son,[200] meaning *inter alia* that a loan or quasi-loan is made to him, property or services are transferred to him under a credit transaction, a guarantee or security is given in connection with a loan, quasi-loan or credit transaction made to or for him.

5–82 As well as outlawing a loan etc. to a director or connected person or giving security for such a transaction,[201] the prohibition extends to the company agreeing to assume, by way of assignment, credit obligations incurred by some party in favour of the director.[202] This covers, for example, where X Ltd. guarantees a loan and the company arranges to take over the liability on that guarantee. Also prohibited is an arrangement whereby a third party will receive a benefit from the company, or another company in the group, for entering into a transaction which would be prohibited if the company itself had entered into it.[203] For instance, X Ltd. is given a contract to supply the company with goods and services on the understanding that X Ltd. will guarantee a loan to one of the company's directors or a connected person.

5–83 In order to fall within the prohibition, the aggregate loans or comparable transactions with the directors must exceed 10 per cent of the company's net assets.[204] In other words, the company must not have lent money or become party to other credit-type transactions with the entirety of its directors and their connected persons which in sum exceed 10 per cent of net assets. For this calculation, the relevant accounts are those of the previous financial year. If no accounts for that year were prepared or laid, then the maximum is 10 per cent of the company's called up share capital.[205] A formula is laid down for measuring the value of every loan and the like[206] but if, for some reason, a fixed value could not be put on the transaction, it is deemed to exceed £50,000.[207] Circumstances can arise where the total "directors loans etc." did not exceed that figure but, because of a fall in value of the company's assets or high losses or some other reason, the 10 per cent figure is then exceeded. Where a fall in asset value occurs with that result and they learn or should have become aware of it, the company, the directors and the persons for whose benefit the credit arrangements were

---

200 s.25(6).
201 s.31(1).
202 s.31(2).
203 s.31(3).
204 s.32.
205 s.29(2)(b).
206 s.25(4).
207 s.25(5).

made are given two months to bring these loans etc. within the 10 per cent ceiling.[208]

5–84 The following loans and comparable transactions are not caught by the above provisions. One is vouched expenses properly incurred in the course of the directors' duties, provided that any liability falling on the director is discharged within six months[209] Another is a transaction the company entered into in the ordinary course of its business and in respect of which the director was not treated any better than someone else of comparable standing.[210] This would cover, for example, a house purchase loan made to a bank's director on the usual commercial terms or a hire purchase company selling a car to a director on the usual terms available to persons of his standing. It is most unlikely that loans or comparable arrangements made in connection with share option schemes would be regarded as within the ordinary course of the company's business. Certain transactions with the company's holding company and also within that group of companies are also exempted.[211]

5–85 A loan made in breach of these provisions is voidable at the instance of the company and, therefore, is recoverable by the company irrespective of its terms.[212] It is not a criminal offence on the part of the company itself to make a prohibited loan but every company "officer" who authorises or permits the company to make a loan and any other person who procures the company to make it commit an offence.[213] If the company is wound up and is insolvent and one or more prohibited loans contributed materially to its insolvency, the borrower or person who benefited from the transaction can be declared personally liable for all or part of the company's debts.[214] The director or connected person can be made to account to the company for any gain that resulted from the loan or transaction; they and any director who authorised it can be made indemnify the company for any loss or damage resulting therefrom.[215] Furthermore, to the extent that the company has obligations under any credit-related transaction, it can choose to avoid those obligations.[216] But that option is not open to the company where it is

---

208 s.33.
209 s.36.
210 s.37.
211 ss. 34, 35.
212 s.38(1) and *Tait Consibee (Oxford) Ltd. v. Tait* [1997] 2 B.C.L.C. 349.
213 s.40.
214 s.39.
215 s.38(2).
216 s.38(1).

no longer possible to return the money or property in question, or the company has been indemnified for any loss it suffered, or the rights of any third party bona fide purchaser for value would be prejudiced.

DIRECTORS' POWERS AND RIGHTS

5–86 The question of what powers and rights company directors possess raises two separate matters. One is the extent of their authority and entitlements as a collectivity — as the board of management of the company. The other concerns their positions as individuals. These questions may be dealt with in the articles of association and also in separate contracts; their tenure of office and claims to remuneration have already been considered, as has the question of what powers the articles vest in the directors, notably in article 80 of Table A, to manage the company's business without interference from the shareholders. Important powers like issuing additional shares in the company,[217] registering share transfers[218] and recommending dividends[219] are dealt with separately.

Directors' Meetings

5–87 Directors' collective powers are exercised by way of resolutions passed at their meetings[220] and the articles of association will stipulate how those meetings should be held. According to Table A, it is for the directors to determine "as they think fit" how board meetings are to be conducted,[221] subject to the following qualifications. Any director may at any time summon a board meeting.[222] It is implied that reasonable notice must be given to all directors. But the directors may resolve that any director resident in Ireland but temporarily abroad need not be notified.[223] It is not legally necessary to give notice of the actual business to be transacted. The quorum is set at two, neither of whom may have a financial interest in the resolution under consideration.[224] But if the number of directors falls below the quorum, the remaining board

---

217 See below, paras 6–24 *et seq*.
218 See below, paras 9–31 *et seq*.
219 See below, paras 9–25 *et seq*.
220 See generally, C. Ryan, *Company Directors* (3rd ed., 1990), Chap. 4 and I. Shearman, *Shackleton on the Law and Practice of Meetings* (7th ed., 1983).
221 Art. 101.
222 *ibid*.
223 *ibid*.
224 Art. 102 and *Re Greymouth-Point Elizabeth Railway* [1904] 1 Ch. 32; but cf. Table A, Part III, art. 7 and below, para. 5–139.

member, or members, are empowered to fill vacancies or summon a general meeting.[225] Decisions are taken by majority vote.[226] In the event of a tie the chair, who may be elected by the directors or chosen by those attending the meeting, has a casting vote.[227] It has been held that the casting vote of a chairman who was invalidly appointed is void.[228]

5–88 Every company must keep a minute book of the proceedings of board meetings, and of the proceedings of meetings of committees of directors.[229] When signed by the chair, these are *prima facie* evidence of what took place at the meeting. The Companies Acts do not say who is entitled to inspect these minutes.

5–89 That board meetings may be informal is acknowledged by article 109 of Table A, where it is provided that a written resolution signed by all of those entitled to notice of board meetings shall be as valid as if it had been passed at a properly constituted meeting.[230] Apart altogether from this, a meeting of the entire board can take place without the directors being assembled in the one place at the one time.[231] Moreover, where one director makes an agreement on behalf of the company and all the other directors informally acquiesced on it, that agreement binds the company.[232] However, casual communications or encounters between directors cannot be treated as duly convened meetings over the objections of any director entitled to attend. Thus in *Barron v. Potter*,[233] following discussions that took place on the platform at Paddington Railway Station between the only two directors of a company, it was argued that they had resolved effectively to fill a vacancy on the board. But one of them had constantly maintained that he would not attend a board meeting of the company. It was held that, in those circumstances, no such resolution had been passed and no board meeting at all had taken place because, although "if directors are willing to hold a meeting they may do so under any circumstances, . . . one of them cannot be made to attend the board or to convert a casual meeting into a board meeting . . ."[234]

---

[225] Art. 103.
[226] Art. 101.
[227] *ibid.*
[228] *Clark v. Workman* [1920] 1 I.R. 107.
[229] 1963 Act, s.145.
[230] *cf. Hood Sailmakers Ltd. v. Axford* [1997] 1 W.L.R. 625.
[231] *Parker & Cooper v. Reading* [1926] Ch. 975.
[232] *E.g. Runciman v. Walter Runciman p.l.c.* [1992] B.C.L.C. 1084.
[233] [1914] 1 Ch. 895.
[234] [1914] 1 Ch. 895 at 901.

5–90 Where the board is improperly constituted because not all of its members have been notified of the meeting, or those in attendance fall below the quorum, or it comprises wholly or partly of *de facto* directors, it depends on the circumstances whether or not deviation from the company's regulations renders the outcome of its deliberations legally ineffective. There are instances of breach of the articles on these matters being deemed to be "mere irregularities".[235]

Individual Directors' Rights

5–91 The actual legal rights of individual directors in that capacity are surprisingly limited.[236] For instance, unless he is duly authorised to do so under the articles of association or by the board, no single director (not even managing director) is entitled to sanction the bringing of legal proceedings on behalf of the company.[237]

Participation in Board Meetings

5–92 By definition, every director is entitled to be notified of and to participate in board meetings; the court will enjoin directors against excluding some duly appointed director from their proceedings. Thus in *Coubrough v. James Panton & Co.*,[238] the court ordered that the plaintiff-director ought not be prevented from participating in board meetings. Budd J. there rejected the contention that an injunction should not be granted because the shareholders no longer wished the plaintiff to be a director, pointing to the possibility of the plaintiff being held responsible for decisions made by the board in his absence, to the fact that *qua* shareholder the plaintiff had a substantial interest in knowing what occurred at board meetings, and the possibility of directors' resolutions being invalid because one of their number was excluded improperly. Where, however, there is strong shareholder resistance against a person attending the board and his title to act as a director cannot easily be resolved, the courts tend to hold the matter over to be decided in general meeting.[239]

Inspect all Books and Records

5–93 Every director is entitled to inspect the company's books of ac-

---

[235] *e.g. Browne v. La Trinidad* (1887) 37 Ch.D. 1.
[236] See generally, C. Ryan, *Company Directors* (7th ed., 1990), Chap. 7.
[237] *Mitchell & Hobbs (UK) Ltd. v. Mill* [1996] 2 B.C.L.C. 102.
[238] [1965] I.R. 272. See also *Pulbrook v. Richmond Consolidated Mining Co.* (1878) 9 Ch.D. 610.
[239] *e.g. Harben v. Phillips* (1883) 23 Ch.D. 14. *cf. Lee v. Chou Wen Hsien* [1984] 1 W.L.R. 1202 and *Moylan v. Irish Whiting Manufacturers Ltd.*, Hamilton J., April 14, 1980.

count regarding income and expenditure, sales and purchases, and assets and liabilities.[240] In *Healy v. Healy Homes Ltd.*[241] it was held that a director is entitled to make copies of these accounts and to be accompanied by an accountant when making the inspection. Furthermore, an accountant may inspect alone the books of account if so authorised by a director; but in those circumstances the accountant may be required to give a written undertaking that any information thereby acquired will be used only in order to advise the director in relation to the matter for which the accountant was retained. In an English case[242] it was held that the statutory right to inspect the company's books could not be enforced in a civil action because the sanction provided for violation of the right was prosecution; but that nevertheless a director has a common law right to inspect those books to enable him to fulfil his duties as a director.

Rights Under the Articles

5–94 The company's memorandum and articles of association may purport to confer additional rights on a director. However, when it comes to enforcing those rights, the conventional view is that rights so conferred *qua* director are different from rights *qua* shareholder. While the courts will enforce rights conferred by the articles on the director *qua* shareholder, rights conferred by the articles only in his capacity as director ordinarily will not be enforced. In other words, the articles of association are a contract between the company and the shareholders but third parties, even if they are named in the articles, cannot sue to enforce them; they are third party beneficiaries of a contract.[243] This is so even if they happen to be members of the company if they are seeking to enforce rights other than those of a member — for instance, to hold office in the company.[244] At times the distinction between rights *qua* member and *qua* director is not an easy one to draw. Indeed, where the director has a service contract it is possible that there will be implied into that contract rights which the articles of association purport to give him *qua* director.

DIRECTORS' DUTIES AND LIABILITIES

5–95 The Companies Acts place numerous obligations on company

---

[240] 1963 Act, s.147(3).
[241] [1973] I.R. 309.
[242] *Conway v. Petronius Clothing Co.* [1978] 1 W.L.R. 72.
[243] See below, paras 10–21 *et seq.*
[244] *cf. Eley v. Positive Government Security Life Assurance Co.* (1876) 1 Ex.D. 21.

directors.[245] Additional duties may be laid down in the company's own regulations and further obligations may be imposed in service contracts. On top of all these, directors owe the company a general duty to manage its affairs with reasonable care and skill. Their discretionary powers must be exercised bona fide in what they consider to be in the interests of the company and any particular power conferred on them must not be used for some extraneous purpose. They must not unjustly enrich themselves at the company's expense nor put themselves in a situation where there is a serious conflict or potential conflict between their individual interests and those of the company.

5–96 Ordinarily, it is to the company only and not to its shareholders nor its creditors as individuals that directors' duties are owed, no matter how large the shareholding or liability may be;[246] directors are officers and agents of the company and not of its individual members nor of its creditors. It has been held by the High Court that directors of insolvent companies owe a fiduciary duty to the creditors but it is debatable whether this is good law.[247] If, however, a director enters into direct dealings with a shareholder, supplier or creditor, those arrangements are subject to the general law of contract and tort.[248] Thus, in the case of negligent misstatements made by a director in the course of his duties, which causes financial loss, he is not personally liable unless it is shown that, objectively, the plaintiff could reasonably have taken it that the director was assuming personal responsibility for what he said.[249]

5–97 While the company in general meeting may ratify certain breaches of directors' duties, very serious breaches cannot be "cured" by ratification;[250] or, put differently, in some circumstances directors will not be permitted to vote their own shares *qua* shareholders on a resolution to ratify serious breaches of duty that they have committed.

---

245 See generally, R.R. Pennington, *Directors' Personal Liability* (1987); C. Ryan, *Company Directors* (3rd ed., 1990) Chaps 6, 8 and 9 and Finch, "Personal Accountability and Corporate Control: The Role of Directors' and Officers' Liability Insurance", 57 Mod. L. Rev. 880 (1994).

246 *Circuit Systems Ltd. v. Zuken-Redac (UK) Ltd* [1996] 2 B.C.L.C. 349 at 368–369.

247 *Jones v. Gunn* [1997] 3 I.R. 1, following the logic of *Re Frederick Inns Ltd.* [1994] 1 I.L.R.M. 387; see below, para. 16–08.

248 *E.g. Al-Nakib Investments (Jersey) Ltd. v. Longcroft* [1990] 1 W.L.R. 1390 and *Allen v. Hyatt* (1913) 30 T.L.R. 444.

249 *Williams v. Natural Life Health Foods Ltd.* [1998] 1 W.L.R. 830; *cf. Fletcher v. National Mutual Life Nominees Ltd.* [1990] 3 N.Z.L.R. 641 and *New Zealand Guardian Trust Co. v. Brooks* [1995] 1 W.L.R. 96.

250 See below, para. 10–09.

Certain breaches of directors' duties that the company does not act against can constitute "oppression" for the purposes of section 205 of the 1963 Act.

Care and Skill: Bad Management

5–98 Anyone who works for another is obliged to perform that work with reasonable care and skill; so says the common law of negligence.[251] Company directors, be they executive or non-executive. paid or unpaid, are liable to the company for any foreseeable loss to the company that arises from their negligence.[252] However, it is only in the most exceptional circumstances that companies sue directors who have shown ineptitude in managing the business and what reported decisions as exist mainly concern failure by directors of banks and other financial institutions to detect frauds. More often than not, all that happens is that negligent directors are asked either to resign from the board or not to seek re-election. If the company in question has a widely dispersed shareholding, bad business decisions will render it prey to takeover bidders, who most likely would remove the incompetent directors. Where the company's performance is so bad that it is forced into liquidation, then the liquidator might bring misfeasance proceedings under section 298 of the 1963 Act[253] against the directors if their negligence was compounded by impropriety on their part.

A Duty to Whom?

5–99 The general principle that directors' duties of care are owed only to the company and not to its members is subject to one important statutory qualification, which is discussed fully later. Ever since 1890,[254] where a company issues a prospectus soliciting investment in its securities, the directors are personally liable to persons who subscribed for shares on foot of the prospectus where it contained some inaccurate material statement. A statement is deemed to be inaccurate if it not alone is untrue but if it is misleading in its context. However, section 49 of the 1963 Act now provides for certain defences to claims of this nature.[255]

---

251 See generally, B. McMahon & W. Binchy, *Irish Law of Torts* (2nd ed., 1990), Chaps. 5–7.

252 See generally, Trebilcock, "The Liability of Company Directors for Negligence" (1969) 32 Mod. L. Rev. 499 and Finch, "Company Directors : Who Cares about Skill and Care?" (1992) 55 Mod. L. Rev. 179.

253 See below, para. 18–67 *et seq*.

254 Directors Liability Act 1890; today 1963 Act, s.49.

255 See below, paras 6–103 *et seq*.

The Standard of Care

5–100 In *Re City Equitable Fire Insurance Co.*,[256] the leading case on this matter, the scope of a director's duty of care was summarised as follows:

> "In ascertaining the duties of a director of a company, it is necessary to consider the nature of the company's business and the manner in which the work of the company is, reasonably in the circumstances and consistently with the articles of association, distributed between the directors and the other officials of the company.
>
> In discharging those duties, a director (a) must act honestly, and (b) must exercise such degree of skill and diligence as would amount to the reasonable care which an ordinary man might be expected to take, in the circumstances, on his own behalf. But, (c) he need not exhibit in the performance of his duties a greater degree of skill than may reasonably be expected from a person of his knowledge and experience; in other words, he is not liable for mere errors of judgment; (d) he is not bound to give continuous attention to the affairs of his company; his duties are of an intermittent nature to be performed at periodical board meetings, and at meetings of any committee to which he is appointed, and though not bound to attend them he ought to attend when reasonably able to do so; and (e) in respect of all duties which, having regard to the exigencies of business and the articles of association, may properly be left to some other official, he is, in the absence of grounds for suspicion, justified in trusting that official to perform such duties honestly."[257]

5–101 Therefore, there is no fixed minimum standard of care for all directors; the standard that a director must satisfy is what one can reasonably expect of that person with his own background and experience. In other words, what may be negligent for an accountant-director may not render a dilettante or a "country gentleman" liable.[258] For instance, in one of the very few modern reported cases on directors' negligence, the court took account of the fact that two of them were chartered accountants and that the third director had considerable accountancy experience.[259] When the position of directors of that or comparable calibre is being determined, the general principles governing professional negligence would apply.[260]

5–102 Trustees are required to manage the trust fund with extreme caution. Company directors, especially those in industrial and trading

---

256 [1925] Ch. 407.

257 *ibid.*, headnote.

258 *cf. Re Denham & Co.* (1884) 25 Ch.D. 752.

259 *Dorchester Finance Co. v. Stebbings* [1989] B.C.L.C. 498; below, para. 5–106.

260 See generally, McMahon & Binchy, above, n. 251, Chap. 14.

companies, by contrast, are expected to demonstrate entrepreneurial skills that involve risk-taking. From this arises what Americans call the "business judgment" defence to negligence claims. That is to say, if at the critical time it was not patently unreasonable to take a particular business decision, like investing in some enterprise or disinvesting, the director will not be held responsible because that transpired to be the wrong decision. In other words, there must be some room for reasonable business error. How extensive that room would be depends on variables like the director's own background and experience and the information reasonably available at the time when the wrong decision was taken. There do not appear to be any modern reported cases that illustrate the range within which directors are legally free to run commercial risks. Almost all of the reported cases in this century have concerned failure to supervise the day-to-day management of the business.

5–103 Thus in *Jackson v. Munster Bank,*[261] most of the Bank's directors, in breach of its regulations, had authorised the making of loans to themselves without providing adequate security — which the court described as a "nefarious system" and a "systematic fraudulent misappropriation" of the bank's funds. A director not involved in these transactions, who did nothing to investigate them after some shareholders had made allegations to him about them, was held to have been negligent in not looking into the matter fully and raising it at the general meeting. The defendant was based in Dublin and his principal job was to look after the Bank's Dublin business, but all the misappropriations were taking place down in Cork, where the bank had its headquarters. Had the defendant not been appraised of the shareholders' concern and there was no other special reason why he should have known about what was occurring in Cork, he would not have been held liable.

5–104 Directors should ensure that proper systems of management and controls are established in the company. Where tasks are delegated to a suitable person, then, unless there are reasons to be suspicious, a director is entitled to assume that the delegate will perform those tasks honestly and diligently. Thus in *Land Credit Co. of Ireland v. Lord Fermoy,*[262] an executive sub-committee of the board lent two associates money to buy the company's own shares, thereby enhancing its image in the stock market. The board approved the loans on being satisfied of the borrowers' credit-worthiness, but without being told why the

---

261 (1885) 15 L.R. Ir. 356.
262 (1870) L.R. 5 Ch. App. 763.

funds were being lent. It was held that "it would be carrying the doctrine of liability too far to say that the directors are liable for negligence . . . because they did not enquire what [the borrowers] were going to do with the money."[263] In the *City Equitable* case, by contrast, directors were held liable for permitting a managing director to control, without any supervision at all, large sums of the company's money, which were lost.

5–105 Directors do not have to attend each and every board meeting, although they ought to attend where they reasonably can. Absence from a meeting at which the negligent decision was taken is a defence. In one notorious instance,[264] the president of the Cardiff Trustee Savings Bank was exonerated from liability for irregularities in the way the Bank was run because he had attended only one board meeting in thirty-eight years. On the other hand, it is no answer for directors in attendance to say that they were not paying attention. As one judge put, "It is their duty to be awake, and their being asleep would not exempt them from the consequences of not attending to the business of the company."[265] Today a professional director probably would be held responsible for major miscalculations made at board meetings which he consistently declined to attend. Indeed, it is possible that the titled gentleman and absentee president of the Cardiff T.S.B. for nearly four decades might not be exonerated if his case were heard today. A difficulty with holding an individual absentee liable in damages is, since his fellow-directors were fully aware of the absences but did not make a major issue of the matter, could the company not be regarded as condoning the absences? Additionally, under clause 91(g) of Table A, a director's office becomes vacated if he is absent from meetings for more than six months continuously without the other directors' permission. There is also the problem of causation; for instance, could it be said that the 38 years absence of the president of the Cardiff T.S.B. actually caused the losses it incurred? As was said in a leading American case "when a business fails from general mismanagement, . . . how is it possible to say that a single director could have made the company successful, or how much in [money] he could have saved?"[266]

5–106 These difficulties were overcome in the only modern reported case, *Dorchester Finance Co. Ltd. v. Stebbing*.[267] Two defendants, who

---

263 (1870) L.R. 5 Ch. App. 763 at 772. See also *Dovey v. Corey* [1901] A.C. 477.
264 *Re Cardiff Savings Bank (Marquis of Bute's Case)* [1892] 2 Ch. 100.
265 *Land Credit Co.* case (1870) L.R. 5 Ch. App. at 770–771.
266 *Barnes v. Andrews*, 298 F.614 (S.D.N.Y. 1924).
267 [1989] B.C.L.C. 498.

each had considerable accounting experience, were non-executive directors of a company. They visited the company's office infrequently, left the management of its affairs to a third director and often signed blank cheques to be counter-signed by that other director at a later date. But he grossly mismanaged the company's affairs, which caused it to suffer a very large loss. The other two defendants were held responsible for failing to exhibit the necessary care and skill and indeed failing to perform any duty as directors.[268]

Enforcement, Exemption and Indemnity

5–107 Where the gravamen of the complaint against a director is negligence, ordinarily only the company can sue him for damages. If the company does not do so, then, unless what may loosely be called some breach of trust was also involved, a shareholder cannot bring proceedings against him, not even the so-called "derivative" claim.[269] Nor can a liquidator succeed against him on a "misfeasance" claim under section 298 of the 1963 Act; mere negligence is not misfeasance.[270] But any provision in the company's articles or in his service contract which purports to exonerate him from liability in negligence is invalidated by section 200 of the 1963 Act.[271] And it would seem that an insurance policy indemnifying directors for any damages they must pay in this regard is also invalid if the premium was being paid by the company.

Fiduciary Duties and Disabilities

5–108 What are called fiduciary duties and disabilities are imposed by principles of equity on trustees and others who hold similar positions, most notably on executors with reference to their beneficiaries, on solicitors with reference to their clients, on agents with reference to their principals and on partners to each other.[272] In comparatively recent times it became recognised that many of these duties had a common thread and could be classified under a logically coherent set of fiduciary principles. Because the function of directors is very similar to that of trustees, executors and business agents — to manage other

---

[268] Contrast *Norman v. Theodore Goddard* [1991] B.C.L.C. 1028; cf. *Re Barings p.l.c. (No. 5)* [1999] 1 B.C.L.C. 433 at 486-489.
[269] See below, paras 10–56 *et seq*.
[270] *Re Mont Clare Hotel Ltd.*, Costello J., December 2, 1986.
[271] See below, paras 5–172 *et seq*.
[272] See generally, P. Finn, *Fiduciary Obligations* (1977); Shepherd, "Towards a Unified Concept of Fiduciary Relationships" (1981) 97 L.Q.R. 51; Sealy "Fiduciary Relationships" (1962) Cam. L.J. 69; Sealy, "Some Principles of Fiduciary Obligation" (1963) Cam. L.J. 119 and Frankel, "Fiduciary Law" (1983) 71 California L. Rev. 795.

persons' property on their behalf — they are also regarded as falling within the general principles of fiduciary obligation.[273] The precise extent of that obligation varies somewhat from one category of fiduciary to another. For instance, because managing a business requires some risk-taking, directors are not expected to exhibit quite the same degree of caution in certain matters as would be expected of trustees. On the other hand, requirements that trustees keep proper accounts,[274] that they use their powers in the interest of their *cestuis*[275] that they do not make any profit from their office without the *cestuis'* consent[276] and that they avoid situations where a significant conflict may arise[277] apply also to the company directors — the company being their *cestui*. As is explained below, subject to certain requirements and limits, the company can exonerate directors for breach of many of these duties, either by way of an ordinary resolution or a provision to that effect in the articles of association.

5–109 Fiduciary duties are owed to the company, not to its individual members, and ordinarily the director is not bound by any additional fiduciary obligations in any direct dealings with the members.[278] In exceptional circumstances, where the transaction is vitally important to the company but its full implications have not been explained to a shareholder, he may be entitled to insist on being given additional information about it.[279] Furthermore, where the director-shareholder relationship is a particularly close one, directors may have a duty to disclose to the shareholders special information acquired by virtue of their position in the company.[280]

Interests of the Company and Proper Purpose: Abuse of Power

5–110 Every fiduciary is obliged to act fairly for the benefit of their *cestuis* and, in particular, not to use their powers for their own benefit or to benefit some third party.[281] Company directors are subject to an identical obligation which, in *Re Smith & Fawcett Ltd.*,[282] was formu-

---

273 *E.g. Regal (Hastings) Ltd. v. Gulliver* [1967] 2 A.C. 134n; below, para. 5–131.
274 See generally, D.J. Hayton, *Underhill & Heyton's Law Relating to Trusts and Trustees* (15th ed., 1995) "rule 62" — p. 657.
275 *ibid.* "rule 50" – p. 500.
276 *ibid.* "rule 60" – p. 639.
277 *ibid.* "rule 61" – p. 646.
278 *Crindle Investments v. Wymes*, Supreme Court, March 5, 1998.
279 *Securities Trust Ltd. v. Associated Properties Ltd.*, McWilliam J., November 19, 1980; Cases, p. 552.
280 *Coleman v. Myers* [1977] 2 N.Z.L.R. 225; see below, para. 12–11.
281 See generally, Finn, above, n. 272, Pt 1.
282 [1942] Ch. 304.

lated as follows: directors must exercise their discretion "bona fide in what they consider . . . is in the interests of the company, and not for any collateral purpose".[283] Since a company in fact is the generality of its members, what this really means is that directors must act for the advantage of the members as a whole and not to serve their own selfish interests or other external interests, or the interests of a discrete section of the membership. Moreover, any powers that are conferred by a company's regulations on directors for a particular purpose must not be used for wholly extraneous reasons.

5–111 While it is easy to generalise about directors, and indeed it is relatively easy to apply the bona fide principal in the most egregious of cases, one runs into difficulty in trying to pin down more precisely what is envisaged by the interests of the company's membership as a whole. When dealing with large companies it may be possible to speculate on what is to the advantage of the average shareholder. But what approach can be taken to the closely-held company with only two members, or where the membership is split into two distinct factions,[284] or into two or more distinct classes of shareholder?[285] At times courts can avoid answering questions like these by reverting to a principle somewhat similar to the business judgment standard in the law on directors' negligence. Where the power in question concerns a "matter of management", which means in effect most matters, considerable deference will be paid to the directors' own judgment or assessment.

5–112 Thus, it is only where the directors are unashamedly pursuing their own or some external interest, or are discriminating blatantly between groups of shareholders, or are acting in a wholly capricious manner, that the courts tend to intervene. The best approach to these matters, as formulated by Lord Wilberforce, in what perhaps is the leading case on the subject, *Howard Smith Ltd. v. Ampol Petroleum Ltd.*,[286] is:

> "to start with a consideration of the power whose exercise is in question. . . . Having ascertained, on a fair view, the nature of this power, and having defined as can best be done in the light of modern conditions the, or some, limits within which it may be exercised, it is then necessary for the court, if a particular exercise of it is challenged, to examine the substantial purpose for which it was exercised, and to reach a conclusion whether that purpose was proper or not. In doing so it will necessarily give credit to the bona fide opinion of the directors, if such is found to

---

[283] [1942] Ch. 304 at 306.
[284] *e.g., Clemens v. Clemens Brothers Ltd.* [1976] 2 All E.R. 268; below, para. 10–34.
[285] *e.g., Mills v. Mills* (1938) 60 C.L.R. 150.
[286] [1974] A.C. 821; below, para. 5–121.

> exist, and will respect their judgment as to matters of management; having done this, the ultimate conclusion has to be as to the side of a fairly broad line on which the case falls."[287]

The exercise of certain powers tends to be more strictly policed than that of other powers; for instance, the power to issue additional shares[288] is scrutinised far more carefully than the power to veto share transfers,[289] which is often found in the regulations of private companies.

5–113 Different parts of this book deal with abuses of particular powers, such as those regarding directors' remuneration[290] the dividends-reserves option[291] and the supposedly absolute discretion which directors may have to refuse to register a transfer of shares.[292] Certain general aspects of this question call for mention here.

Furthering Own Interests

5–114 A fiduciary who uses his powers simply to further his own personal interests almost always contravenes his fiduciary duties.[293] A problem that arises frequently, however, is actually proving that the powers in question were being exercised in the interest of the director or the directors in question. For often their own personal interests and those of the company will coincide. If evidence can be presented of self-serving motives, that should resolve the matter. But evidence of that nature is often difficult to find; there are very few self-dealing directors who leave behind them a trail of incriminating documents. As the cases on vetoing share transfers illustrate, it is not enough to make allegations against the director and then not challenge his explanations for his conduct. For instance, in *Re Smith & Fawcett Ltd.*,[294] where a director was accused of refusing to register a share transfer because he wanted those shares for himself, the plaintiff did not apply to cross-examine the defendant on his affidavit. For that reason, the court declined to find that defendant's inaction was for the wrong motives. However, if sufficient circumstantial evidence is assembled which strongly suggests self dealing,[295] especially in connection with such vital matters as issuing new shares, the court will readily find

---

287 [1974] A.C. 821 at 835.
288 See below, para. 5–119 *et seq*.
289 See below, para. 9–34 *et seq*.
290 See above, para. 5–57 *et seq*.
291 See below, para. 9–27 *et seq*.
292 See below, para. 9–33 *et seq*.
293 See generally, P. Finn, *Fiduciary Obligations* (1977), Chap. 11.
294 [1942] Ch. 304.
295 *e.g. Re Hafner* [1943] I.R. 426; see below, para. 9–38.

wrong motives unless the directors can give a fully satisfactory explanation.

Furthering the Interest of Third Parties

5–115 The classic view of the company has been that of a closed community devoted to financial gain for its shareholders, and of the directors' role as essentially to manage the business so that it will earn profits for the shareholders. Absent express authority in the company's own regulations and distinct statutory duties, like those in the Companies Acts designed to protect creditors, directors must not exercise their powers principally to benefit persons other than the shareholders. They may not bestow lavish gifts on others, except where that largesse is designed to bring a substantial benefit to the company. Indeed, non-advantageous gifts may even constitute a "fraud on a minority" or amount to "oppression" of a minority, except of course where all the members entitled to vote on the matter are in agreement. Nor may directors bind themselves to advance the interests of third parties over those of the company as a whole although, as is explained below, the exact boundaries of this principle remain to be fixed.

5–116 Formerly, it was a breach of directors' duty for them to use their powers in the exclusive interests of the company's employees where the company would not receive any reciprocal advantage. For instance in *Parke v. Daily News Ltd.*,[296] which was an extreme case, the board of a newspaper company that had sold off its entire undertaking proposed to distribute the bulk of the proceeds of sale among its employees in the form of gratuitous compensation for being made redundant. That generosity was held to be beyond the directors' powers.[297] Nevertheless, boards of companies that envisage continuing in business are entitled to be benevolent on a relatively small scale, provided the company stands to benefit to some extent, and it would appear that directors of one company in a "group" may take some account of the group's overall interests.[298] Additionally, under section 52(1) of the 1990 Act, the employees' interests are made a matter of legitimate concern for the directors. It states that among the matters they should "have regard [to] in the performance of their functions shall include the interests of the company's employees in general, as well as the interests of its members".[299] Therefore, what happened in the *Daily News* case would no longer be a breach of the directors' duties, although a minor-

---

[296] [1962] Ch. 927.
[297] Similarly, *Re Lee Behrens & Co.* [1932] 2 Ch. 46.
[298] See below, paras 14–44 *et seq*.
[299] See below, para. 15–04.

ity shareholder in such a case might still succeed in having a payment of that nature blocked on the grounds of "fraud on a minority", "unfair discrimination" or "oppression" under section 205 of the 1963 Act.[300] Although directors are now required to take account of the interests of the employees, that duty is owed only to the company and cannot be enforced by any or all of the employees.

Fettering Discretion

5–117 Fiduciaries must not, without the consent of their *cestuis*, unduly fetter their discretion, *i.e.* tie themselves down as to how in the future they will exercise their discretionary powers. It would appear to be generally accepted that, without the company's consent, directors may not enter into agreements with outsiders or with a section of the members under which they undertake to vote in a particular way at board meetings. Yet authority on this matter is sparse except for a handful of Commonwealth decisions and *Clark v. Workman*.[301] This case concerned protracted negotiations in which an English-based syndicate sought to buy control of a Belfast shipbuilding company that was owned by two families. The chairman of the board promised the syndicate that he would use his best endeavours to ensure that their bid would succeed and, to that end, exercised his casting vote to facilitate transfers of shares to them. It was held that his vote was invalid because "he had fettered himself by a promise . . . and [thereby] had disqualified himself from acting bona fide in the interests of the company . . ."[302] In one case[303] the analogy was drawn between the company director and the Member of Parliament who would be acting unlawfully if, for payment from some outside body, he agreed to vote in a particular way.

5–118 Difficulties arise in determining what kinds of understandings between directors and others amount to fetters and in what circumstances they can be justifiable. Take, for example, the nominee director, *i.e.* one who is nominated by a large shareholder to represent his interests in the company. It has been said that there is nothing wrong with this "so long as the director is left free to exercise his best judgment in the interests of the company which he serves. But if he is put upon terms that he is bound to act in the affairs of the company in accordance with the directions of his patron, it is beyond doubt unlaw-

---

300 See below, Chap. 10.
301 [1920] 1 I.R. 107.
302 *ibid.* at 117–118.
303 *Boulting v. A.C.T.A.T.T.* [1963] 2 Q.B. 606 at 627.

ful."[304] Somewhat general understandings existing between directors and outsiders should not automatically be assumed to constitute proscribed fetters; any such contract is to be construed "in the light of the presumption that the parties to it contemplate and intend performance in a lawful manner only."[305] A distinction has been drawn between three types of voting agreements: those between directors and others, which are forbidden; those with or between the shareholders themselves, which are permissible;[306] and agreements made in good faith between the company and some outside interest that envisages the directors exercising their powers in a specified manner. In one Australian case,[307] for example, in order to finance a project, a small property company agreed to allot shares to another company for cash and undertook *inter alia* to reorganise its capital structure, pay dividends in a specified manner, execute certain contracts and the like. As a defence to a claim for damages for wrongfully repudiating the agreement, it was contended that the agreement itself was voidable as an undue fetter on the directors' discretion. This was rejected by the court because, assuming the directors initially decided that it was in the company's interest to enter into the contract, it therefore could not be argued that they had improperly fettered the exercise of their future discretion. Where at the time all of the directors concerned are also members of the company or where the "fetter" in question has been assented to by all of its members, it is legally effective and enforceable.[308]

Issuing and Allotting Further Shares

5–119 The power to allot unissued shares in the company has been the subject of considerable litigation. Frequently, it is alleged that the directors' objective was not to raise additional capital but was some improper purpose, such as to alter a delicate balance of voting power in the company or to ward off a take-over bid which, if successful, could lead to the existing directors being replaced. Most articles of association give the board the exclusive power and a wide discretion over allotting further shares. Under article 5 of Table A, for instance, "the shares shall be at the disposal of the directors, and they may . . . dispose of them to such persons, on such terms and conditions and at such times as they may consider to be in the best interests of the company and its shareholders." Leaving aside the vitally important require-

---

304 [1963] 2 Q.B. 606 at pp. 627-628. *cf. Levins v. Clark* [1962] N.S.W.L.R. 686 and *Re Broadcasting Station 2 G.B. Pty.* [1964–5] N.S.W.L.R. 1648.
305 [1963] 2 Q.B. at p. 649.
306 *Ringuet v. Bergeron* (1960) 24 D.L.R. (2d) 449.
307 *Thorby v. Goldberg* (1965) 112 C.L.R. 597.
308 *Fulham F.C. v. Cabra Estates p.l.c.* [1994] 1 B.C.L.C. 363.

ments of prior shareholders' authority and pre-emption, introduced by the 1983 Act, it has been held that existing shareholders are not always entitled to be given the opportunity to subscribe for additional shares in the company before those shares are offered to others. Except as is otherwise provided for in legislation or in the company's regulations, no shareholder has any right "to expect that his fractional interest in the company will remain for ever constant."[309] Cases dealing with improper exercise of the share-allotting power must now be read in the light of sections 20 and 23 of the 1983 Act.

5–120 One kind of case may be described as the corporate *coup d"état*: where the directors, who own a minority of shares, allot additional shares to themselves or their associates in order to secure control of the company. The classic instance is *Piercy v. S. Mills & Co.*,[310] where a proposed share allotment was enjoined because its "purpose [was] converting a minority into a majority, and . . . defeating the wishes of the existing majority . . ."[311] A very similar Irish instance is *Nash v. Lancegaye Safety Glass (Ireland) Ltd.*,[312] where the personal defendant and his supporters held about 49 per cent of the voting shares and dominated the board, whereas the plaintiff and the proxies he had obtained controlled about 51 per cent. Major differences about policy arose between them, which led to the plaintiff requisitioning an extraordinary general meeting at which he would propose to increase the size of the board and to appoint new directors. In the meantime, the board decided to issue £16,000 of unissued voting shares, £5,000 of which were to be allotted to the defendant and the remaining to be allotted to the existing members on a *pro rata* basis. Two reasons were given for allotting the £5,000 shares to the defendant: much of the company's commercial success was a result of his endeavours and the board wished to reward him for past services or to meet some supposed claim on moral grounds for compensation. It also was said that new capital was needed. But Dixon J. found from the evidence that, while " [t]here can be a legitimate difference of opinion as to whether fresh capital was necessary", it was "hard, however, to see how the [share] issue could reasonably be regarded as an urgent necessity"; he considered that "the suggestion of urgency [was] wholly unconvincing and quite inadequate to explain the somewhat indecent haste with which the matter was put through."[313] Therefore, in his judgment, the decision to issue additional shares was not made "in good faith in what [was] believed to be in the

---

309 *Mutual Life Insurance Co. v. Rank Organisation Ltd.* [1985] B.C.L.C. 11 at 24.
310 [19201] Ch. 77.
311 *ibid.* at 85.
312 (1958) 92 I.L.T.R.
313 *ibid.* at 22.

interests of the company", but was "primarily inspired by the dual desire to confer a privilege or benefit on [the defendant] and to increase the voting strength of [his] interests."[314] This was sufficient to warrant granting the declarations of invalidity which the plaintiff sought.

5–121 A number of the leading cases concern take-over bids, where additional shares in the "target" company were allotted either to ward off a bid or to favour one bidder over another. For instance, in *Hogg v. Crampborn Ltd.*,[315] the board decided to resist a bid in the firm belief, which was not contested, that leaving the existing board to manage the company's affairs would be more advantageous to the shareholders, the company's staff and its customers. To this end, a trust for the employees was established, which was under the directors' control, and the company lent the trust money to enable it to purchase a block of shares that the company would allot to it.[316] With their own shares and those of their supporters, and being in a position to determine how the employees' trust shares would be voted, the directors could then defeat the bid. It was held that the allotment and the loan in the circumstances were made for an improper motive, viz. "the primary object . . . was to deprive those members who were not recognised supporters of the board of their position as a majority in the company."[317] In a later case, *Howard Smith Ltd. v. Ampol Petroleum Ltd.*,[318] a company that was short of funds was the subject of a take-over bid from its principal shareholder. In order to prevent that bid from succeeding and, as well, to raise further capital, new shares were issued to another company, which then was to launch a take-over bid. It was held that, since the substantial purpose of that share issue was "simply and solely to dilute the majority voting power held by the first bidders so as to enable a then minority of the shareholders to sell their shares more advantageously",[319] the board acted improperly. The governing principle is that:

> "[I]t must be unconstitutional for directors to use their fiduciary powers over shares . . . purely for the purpose of destroying an existing. majority, or creating a new majority that did not previously exist. To do so is to interfere with that element of the company's constitution which is separate from and set against their powers."[320]

---

[314] *ibid.* at 23.
[315] [1967] Ch. 254.
[316] *cf.* 1963 Act, s.60(13)(b), (c).
[317] [1967] Ch. at 271.
[318] [1974] A.C. 821.
[319] *ibid.* at 837.
[320] *ibid.* See also, *Whitehouse v. Carlton Hotel Property Ltd.* (1987) 61 A.L.J.R. 216.

Mixed Motives

5–122 It sometimes happens that directors act both for genuinely proper as well as for improper purposes. For instance, the company may badly need additional capital but the minority shareholders are impecunious and for the time being cannot pay for additional shares they are offered, a fact that the majority well know and take advantage of.[321] Or the inevitable and, for the directors, happy consequence of an allotment of shares may be to defeat a take-over bid that was poised to succeed.[322] Reported cases on these questions should be treated with caution because the outcome in many of them turned on inferences the judges drew from evidence on affidavit and appellate courts must accept the trial judge's findings of fact that are not patently erroneous. Separate proper purposes were asserted in the *Lancegaye Glass*[323] and the *Ampol Petroleum*[324] cases, but were held not to have been established by the evidence or, to the extent that they may have existed, were very much secondary or incidental. Most cases say that the best approach is to ascertain what the directors' principal or dominant purpose was. Yet this does not resolve the cases where the various purposes are somewhat evenly balanced.

5–123 There is authority to the effect that the judge should then fall back on the overriding criterion of what, in good faith, the directors consider to be the best interests of the company. If this approach were to be followed, it would leave the matter to be determined on the merits on a case by case basis. Some commentators urge that, while this approach may be acceptable as regards business decisions that do not fundamentally alter the power structure within companies, it is too lenient in the context of, for instance, allotting additional shares. The argument is made that, given the effect a share allotment can have on relative voting strengths within a company, an improper motive, whether primary or secondary, should render invalid an exercise of that power. In the *Lancegaye Glass* case, Dixon J. appears to have endorsed this latter analysis. According to him:

> "having the two-fold object . . . is it of any avail to the defendant directors that they may have had the object, other things being equal, of benefiting the company . . . Even if (this latter object) contributed to their

---

321 *e.g. Pennell v. Venida Investments Ltd.*, Templeman J., July 25, 1974 analysed in Burridge, "Wrongful Rights Issues" (1981) 44 *Mod. L. Rev.* 40.

322 *e.g. Harlowe's Nominees Property Ltd. v. Woodside (Lakes Entrance) Oil Co.* (1968) 42 A.L.J.R. 123 and *Teck Corp. v. Millar* (1973) 33 D.L.R. (3d) 288; see below, para. 12–23.

323 above, n. 312.

324 above, n. 318.

decision . . . that would not suffice to validate the resolutions if the motives were partly improper."[325]

Fidelity: Unjust Enrichment and Conflict of Interests

5–124 Not only must fiduciaries not enrich themselves at their *cestui's* expense, but they are required not to put themselves in situations where their personal interests and those of their *cestui* conflict significantly.[326] In exceptional circumstances, however, they may be allowed to retain for themselves profits they earned in situations of potential conflict but not at the *cestui's* expense. Directors who unjustly enrich themselves at their company's expense also risk being convicted of fraud or of conspiracy to defraud.[327] The question of "insider trading" is considered separately below.[328]

Taking Company "Property"

5–125 A director may not without the shareholders' consent take and use for his own benefit what belongs to the company. In *Cockburn v. Newbridge Sanitary Steam Laundry Co.*,[329] for instance, the managing director of a laundry company entered into a substantial contract in his own name to do work for one customer, the military authorities based in the Curragh. Under an arrangement he made with the other directors, the actual work was done by the company, but he would get £3,000 on the contract and £1,000 of that was paid over to the company. Most of the difference apparently was paid in bribes. It was held that he had to account to the company for that difference. Similarly, where one of the sons of the later Robert Maxwell was party to a transfer of shares, held by the company as trustee for its pensioners, to a company controlled by his father and for no consideration whatsoever, he was held liable because he was a director of the transferor trustee company.[330]

5–126 There is no exhaustive definition of what constitutes company property in these circumstances. Often confidential information will he treated as property, the governing principle being that "a person who had obtained information in confidence is not allowed to use it as a springboard for activities detrimental to the person who made the confidential communication, and springboard it remains when all the

---

[325] (1958) 92 I.L.T.R. 11 at 26. See also, *Whitehouse* case, above, n. 320, at p. 219.
[326] See generally, P. Finn *Fiduciary Obligations* (1977) Chap. 21.
[327] *E.g. Adams v. R.* [1995] 1 W.L.R. 52.
[328] below, paras 5–149 *et seq.*
[329] [1915] 1 I.R. 249.
[330] *Bishopsgate Investment Management Ltd. v. Maxwell (No.2)* [1993] B.C.L.C. 1282.

features have been published or can be ascertained by actual inspection by any member of the public."[331] But not every single piece of information acquired by a director in the course of duty must *ipso facto* be regarded as received in confidence and remaining confidential. At times, information acquired by a director in the course of duty, which could not be regarded as confidential but which he used to acquire some personal benefit, is characterised as property, although in fact use of the term "property" may be simply to justify the court's conclusion on the merits,[332] *i.e.*, that the director should disgorge the profit to the company.

Competing Against the Company

5–127 There is little authority on the extent to which directors may participate in a business that competes with that of their company.[333] It would seem that it is not always a breach of trust for a fiduciary to have a share in a business which competes with a business belonging to the trust.[334] In the absence of an express prohibition to the contrary or some exceptional circumstances, employees in their spare time may work for an enterprise that competes with their employer's.[335] A partner, on the other hand, is not permitted to compete against the partnership without the consent of the other partners.[336] In a case decided in 1891,[337] an application made to restrain one of the plaintiff's directors from becoming a director of a rival concern was rejected on the grounds that, since the company's regulations did not prohibit him from doing so and it was not established that confidential information acquired in the plaintiff's service would be passed on to the rival, the director was at liberty to join the rival's board. This decision was cited with approval in *Bell v. Lever Bros. Ltd.*,[338] where it was added that "[w]hat he could do for the rival company, he could of course, do for himself."[339] It, therefore, would appear that, in the absence of a contractual prohibition or of a strong likelihood of confidential information being passed on, mere management of a rival is not incompatible with a directorship.

---

331 *Cranleigh Precision Engineering Co. v. Bryant* [1965] 1 W.L.R. 1293 at 1318.
332 *cf. Phipps v. Boardman* [1967] 2 A.C. 46.
333 See generally, Christie, "The Director's Fiduciary Duty Not to Compete", 55 Mod. L. Rev. 506 (1992).
334 *Moore v. M'Glynn* [1894] 1 I.R. 74.
335 *Hivac v. Park Royal Scientific Instruments Ltd.* [1946] 1 Ch. 169.
336 Partnership Act 1890, s.30.
337 *London & Mashonaland Exploration Co. v. New Mashonaland Exploration Co.* [1891] W.N. 165.
338 [1932] A.C. 161.
338 *ibid.* at 195.

5–128 Of course, there are significant restrictions on the extent to which an executive director may work for a rival and whatever freedom to do so as exists under the general law most likely would be the subject of an express or implied prohibition in the service contract.[340] In exceptional circumstances a company that tolerates a director competing against it may commit "oppression" under section 205 of the 1963 Act.[341]

"Corporate Opportunities"

5–129 By a corporate opportunity is meant the chance for a company to become involved in some business project that stands to yield it a sizeable profit.[342] Occasionally, fiduciaries intercept, for their own personal gain, opportunities through which the *cestui* stood to derive a substantial gain. The classic instance in Company Law is *Cook v. Deeks*,[343] which concerned a major Canadian construction company that had prospered from contracts it carried out for a railway enterprise. When a new railway construction contract was being negotiated, the defendants, who were some of the company's directors, succeeded in having the contract eventually awarded to themselves rather than to the company. They never gave the company even an opportunity of obtaining the contract and they concealed from their co-directors all the circumstances regarding the negotiations. In other words, "while entrusted with the conduct of the affairs of the company they deliberately designed to exclude, and used their influence and position to exclude, the company whose interest it was their first duty to protect."[344] The Privy Council had no hesitation in concluding that they violated their fiduciary duties, observing that persons "who assume the complete control of a company's business must remember that they are not at liberty to sacrifice the interests which they are bound to protect, and, while ostensibly acting for the company, divert in their own favour business which should properly belong to the company they represent."[345]

5–130 Difficulties arise, however, where it cannot be said that the directors were acting in bad faith; or where the board fully considered

---

[340] *e.g. Irish Microfilms Ltd. v. Browne*, Murphy J., April 3, 1987.
[341] *Re Stewarts (Brixton) Ltd.* [1985] B.C.L.C. 4.
[342] See generally, Brudney & Clark, "A New Look at Corporate Opportunities" (1981) 94 Harv. L. Rev. 997.
[343] [1916] 1 A.C. 554.
[344] *ibid.* at 562.
[345] *ibid.* at 563. A very similar instance is *Canadian Aero Services Ltd. v. O'Malley* [1974] 40 D.L.R. (3d) 371; noted in (1974) 37 Mod. L. Rev. 464.

the opportunity and rejected it; or where, from lack of resources or other reasons, the company in fact could never have availed of the opportunity. In some of these situations, moreover, the company may have been taken over in the meantime and it could be argued that the new owners obtain an unfair windfall when they act against ex-directors who, in good faith, had availed of a corporate opportunity. The authorities on these matters are not wholly consistent, which may be explained by the lack of a coherent underlying theory of fiduciary obligation or that divergent outcomes are inevitable when the contexts vary so much. There are no reported Irish cases that go into these issues in any depth. In the relatively few English cases, the underlying principle appears to be that where one makes a personal profit, either as a result of one's position as a director or in any situation where there is a conflict or a potential conflict of one's duty to the company and one's personal interests, the company is entitled to recover the profit. This is the case regardless of whether one acted in good faith or whether the company rejected the opportunity, or in fact could not have earned the profit.[346] In other words, there is a strict rule against directors profiting from their office.

5–131 Thus in *Regal (Hastings) Ltd. v. Gulliver*,[347] in order to enhance a cinema company's asset value, with a view to selling the entire business, the board decided to take a lease on an additional cinema. Because the company did not have sufficient funds to provide the lessor with security, the directors came to its assistance by putting some of their own funds into a subsidiary, which then would take the lease. Subsequently, the company and its subsidiary were taken over at a price which earned those directors substantial profits from their investment. But the company, then under new management, claimed that those ex-directors had thereby contravened their fiduciary duties. A unanimous House of Lords held that they must account for those profits regardless of the fact that they "acted with bona fides, intending to act in the interests of" the company.[348] The governing rule, it was held, is:

> "the rule of equity which insists on those, who by use of a fiduciary position make a profit, being liable to account for that profit, in no way depends on fraud, or absence of bona fides; or upon such questions or considerations as whether the profit would or should otherwise have gone to the plaintiff, or whether [the profiteer] was under a duty to obtain the source of the profit for the plaintiff, or whether he took a risk or

---

[346] *cf. Phipps v. Boardman* [1967] 2 A.C. 46; *cf. Holder v. Holder* [1968] Ch. 353.
[347] [1967] 2 A.C. 134.
[348] *ibid.* at 143.

> acted as he did for the benefit of the plaintiff, or whether the plaintiff has in fact been damaged or benefited by his action."[349]

5–132 Although this principle has never seriously been questioned and indeed reiterates what has always been the rule applicable to trustees, its application in the precise situation as arose in *Regal (Hastings)* has been modified for most companies today. Directors of companies with articles of association containing a clause similar to article 78 of Table A are exempted to some extent from liability. They are permitted to acquire shares in or become directors of a company that their company promotes or is interested in and they are not accountable for any remuneration or benefits they thereby receive. But the company reserves the option of directing them to account for those benefits. This regulation has not yet been interpreted by the courts.

5–133 In *Industrial Development Consultants Ltd. v. Cooley*,[350] the duty to account for profits made was held to apply even where an executive director comes across the opportunity entirely in a private capacity. The defendant, who was managing director of an engineering firm, was approached privately and offered a lucrative engineering contract which, under no circumstances, would have been offered to his company. He then resigned his position on the pretext of being ill and took up the contract for himself. It was held that he ought to account for the profit he made on the grounds that he allowed himself to be placed in a situation where his legal obligations and his personal interests conflicted and, additionally, he:

> "had not been wholly honest with the company. He had one capacity and one capacity only in which he was carrying on business at that time. That capacity was as managing director of the plaintiffs. Information which came to him while he was the managing director and which was of concern to the plaintiffs to know, was information which it was his duty to pass on to [them . . . Furthermore,] he embarked on a deliberate policy and course of conduct which put his personal interest as a potential contracting party . . . in direct conflict with his pre-existing and continuing duty as a managing director of the plaintiffs."[351]

Whether a non-executive director in an analogous position would be liable to account would turn on the policy underlying the rule. If, as it appears to be, the objective is deterrence — that drastic and over-broad proscriptions are necessary in order to discourage directors from the

---

349 *ibid.* at 144, citing *inter alia, Keech v. Sandford* (1726) Sel. Cas. Ch. 61.

350 [1972] 1 W.L.R. 443.

351 [1972] 1 W.L.R. 443 at 451. *cf. Island Export Finance Ltd. v. Umunna* [1986] B.C.L.C. 460 and *Framlington Group p.l.c. v. Anderson* [1995] 1 B.C.L.C. 475.

natural temptation to profit at their company's expense — then he would be held liable.

5–134 In at least two Commonwealth cases it was held that directors,[352] even managing directors,[353] of small companies have a defence where full disclosure about the project is made to the board, which is given the opportunity to take it up but then rejects the opportunity because the company lacks the necessary resources.[354] It is questionable whether that reasoning would be followed in Ireland. Superficially, these decisions conflict with *Regal (Hastings)*[355] but it may be significant that the *Regal* directors did not offer the company's fifteen independent shareholders the chance of investing in what was virtually guaranteed to be a very profitable enterprise. In the circumstances there, a gain of almost 300 per cent was made from a three weeks' investment carrying practically no risk whatsoever. Whether they really did act entirely bona fides is debatable. *Regal Hasting* can be contrasted with a leading trusts case[356] where trustees profited from an investment they made in a trust asset but in circumstances where their bona fides could not seriously be questioned. They nevertheless were compelled to hand over the profit they made on the basis of well-settled equity principles. What remains to be determined in this country is whether the full rigours of those principles always apply to corporate opportunities or whether, exceptionally, the deserving director, who revealed everything to his fellow directors and did his best in the circumstances, will be permitted to retain his profit. While those directors ordinarily would have no authority to exonerate him from his breach of duty, it may be that in a special case full disclosure to them and unquestionable bona fides may provide a complete defence to an action for breach of fiduciary duty.

Contracts Where Directors Have a Financial Interest

5–135 There is always a great danger of directors abusing their positions to make a profit for themselves when, directly or indirectly, they have dealings with their company. For instance, they might sell their property or goods to the company at an excessive price or they might

---

[352] *Peso Silver Mines v. Cropper* (1966) 58 D.L.R. (2d) 1, noted in (1979) 30 Mod. L. Rev. 450.

[353] *Queensland Mines v. Hudson* (1978) 52 A.LJ.R. 399; noted in (1979) 42 Mod. L. Rev. 711.

[354] Compare *Abbey Glen Property Corp. v. Stumborg* (1976) 65 D.L.R. (3d) 235, (1978) 85 D.L.R. (3d) 35; noted in (1979) 42 Mod. L. Rev. 215.

[355] above, para. 5–131.

[356] *Phipps v. Boardman* [1967] 2 A.C. 46.

buy something from it at a knock-down price. Accordingly, contracts with the company in which directors possess a financial interest are subject to a number of restrictions that fall into three tiers. In equity, those contracts may be avoided by the company unless full disclosure of the essential details about them is made to the general meeting, which then ratifies them.[357] But this rule is not always a very effective deterrent against unjust enrichment; the transaction may be concluded in its entirety before the fact of a conflict of interests comes to light[358] or the interested directors may be the majority shareholders or otherwise control the general meeting.[359] On the other hand, especially in large companies with numbers of outside directors, serious administrative difficulties could arise if every contract in which a director had some financial interest had to be voted on in general meeting. As one judge put it, the shareholders "may think in . . . matters of this description it is better to have directors who may advance the interest of the company by their connection, and by the part which they themselves take in large money dealings, than to have persons who would have no share in such transactions as those in which the company is concerned."[360]

5–136 Almost invariably, therefore, the equitable principle is set aside by the articles of association in favour of, usually, a requirement that disclosure of any interest must be made to the board, coupled with certain other safeguards. There is now a minimum degree of disclosure that cannot be waived by the articles; under section 194 of the 1963 Act, the director must "declare the nature of his interest" to the board. One of the most important features of the 1990 Act is that it introduces rigid safeguards aimed at preventing companies from entering into potentially disadvantageous contracts with their directors, members of their families and certain other close associates.

The Equitable Rule

5–137 In *Aberdeen Railway Co. v. Blackie Brothers*[361] it was laid down that, in principle, all contracts between a company and its directors or with one of their partners can be avoided by the company, should it choose to do so. As explained by Lord Cranworth:

---

357 *Aberdeen Rly. Co. v. Blaikie Brothers* (1854) 1 Macq. 461.
358 *e.g. Prudential Assurance Co. v. Newman Industries Ltd. (No.2)* [1982] 1 Ch. 204.
359 *ibid.*
360 *Imperial Mercantile Credit Association v. Coleman* (1871) L.R. 6 Ch. App. 558 at 568.
361 (1854) 1 Macq. 461.

> "The directors are a body to whom is delegated the duty of managing the general affairs of the company. A corporate body can only act by agents, and it is of course the duty of those agents so to act as best to promote the interests of the corporation whose affairs they are conducting. Such agents have duties to discharge of a fiduciary nature towards their principal. And it is a rule of universal application, that no one, having such duties to discharge, shall be allowed to enter into engagements in which he has, or can have, a personal interest conflicting, or which possibly may conflict, with the interests of those whom he is bound to protect. So strictly is this principle adhered to, that no question is allowed to be raised as to the fairness or unfairness of a contract so entered into. It obviously is, or may be, impossible to demonstrate how far in any particular case the terms of such a contract have been the best for the interest of the cestui que trust, which it was possible to obtain. It may sometimes happen that the terms on which a trustee has dealt or attempted to deal with the estate or interests of those for whom he is a trustee, have been as good as could have been obtained from any other person — they may even at the time have been better."[362]

This principle applies even if it is shown that the company obtained good value or indeed more than full value from the transaction; "[s]o inflexible is the rule that no inquiry on the subject is permitted."[363]

5–137 Today, however, the articles of association of most companies modify this principle in one way or another, the commonest requirement being that the directors' financial interests in the transaction with the company be disclosed to an independent board of directors. The articles of some companies, however, impose far more stringent requirements and, as has been said, substantial additional safeguards are contained in the 1990 Act.

Table A

5–139 In companies which have adopted Part I of Table A, these matters are regulated by clauses 83-86; only some of those requirements apply to companies with Part II of Table A, *i.e.* to the great majority of private companies registered in the State. Article 85 is common to both types of company and provides that, in principle, contracts with the company in which the directors are "in any way interested" are not voidable nor constitute breaches of fiduciary duty. Although *Aberdeen Railway Co.*, therefore, does not apply to these companies, article 83 requires full disclosure of the director's interest to the board that:

---

[362] (1854) 1 Macq. 461 at 471–472.
[363] *ibid.* at 472.

> "A director who is in any way, whether directly or indirectly, interested in a contract or a proposed contract with the company shall declare the nature of his interest at a meeting of the directors in accordance with section 194 of the Act."

This article does not refer to "shadow directors" but they are brought within section 194 by the 1990 Act.[364] However, even though shadow directors who do not make due disclosure may contravene section 194, it does not follow that they have contravened article 83. What is required here is as follows.

5–140 To begin with, the director must be in some way or another, "whether directly or indirectly, interested" in the contract. Almost always the interest in the contract will be a financial one; what other kinds of interest are caught by clause 83 could be debated. Clearly a director would be directly interested where he or his partnership were one of the parties, as in *Aberdeen Railway Co*. It would depend on all the circumstances of the case whether the director had an indirect financial interest in a contract with the company. To an extent the burden is on the director to show that he did not have an interest, when the matter is challenged.[365] An interest most likely would be found where the party was the director's spouse or a company in which he had a substantial shareholding. How far the net should be cast among his relations and other companies in which he has some involvement may depend on the nature of the contract in question and the extent of the director's relationship with his family and those companies.[366] The 1990 Act defines a category of "connected persons" for the purpose of its requirements regarding contracts with the company[367] and guidance may be obtained from that definition in an appropriate case. Even where the director holds shares in the other contracting company in trust, he still has a financial interest for these purposes; in one instance, a director held 1,000 shares in trust under his father-in-law's will and his wife was beneficially interested in a 100 of them, subject to her mother's life interest.[368] Since 1990, loans and equivalent arrangements with connected persons are brought within section 194 of the 1963 Act and, most likely, within these articles.

---

364 s.27(2).

365 *Lee Panavision Ltd. v. Lee Lighting Ltd.* [1991] B.C.L.C. 575.

366 *cf. Re Dominion International Group p.l.c. (No.2)* [1996] 1 B.C.L.C. 572 at 589: funding scholarships which a director's children availed of.

367 s.26; see above, para. 5–14.

368 *Transvaal Lands Co. v. New Belgium (Transvaal) Land & Development Co.* [1914] 2 Ch. 488. *cf. Wilson v. London, Midland & Scottish Railway* [1940] 1 Ch. 169 and *Costa Rica Railway Co. v. Forwood* [1900] 1 Ch.746.

5–141 There is some authority which suggests that merely being a director of the other contracting company is not a sufficient interest and that view seems to be accepted by section 194(3) of the 1963 Act. Under this, a director can declare his interest in all contracts with a particular company simply by giving a general notice which states his membership of that company, which is to be regarded as being interested in all contracts with it. There is no similar notice procedure for where he is merely a director of the other company, although all other directorships they hold are one of the matters which directors must disclose to the company and have entered in the register of directors.[369] Against all of this, clause 84(d) of Table A implies that being an officer of the other contracting company always constitutes a financial interest in contracts with that company. This latter view would seem to be the better one.

5–142 Once the requisite interest exists, it must be disclosed to the board at the first meeting which considers entering into the contract. If the director only became interested in the contract at a later date, that interest must be declared at the very next board meeting after the interest arose. While the making of some formal declaration may be envisaged, it has been said that sufficient disclosure is made where there is genuine informal consent by all the directors.[370] A general notice can be given where the nature of the interest is membership of the other contracting company or firm (partnership). This notice must be given either at a board meeting or else read at the next meeting after it was given to the company. The making of the declaration of interests should be recorded in the minutes of the meeting, although the absence of any such record does not preclude other proof that a declaration was duly made.[371] Further, the company is required to keep a book which records every declaration of interest made by a director.[372] Beyond this, the requirements for Table A private companies and public companies diverge.

5–143 Where clause 7 of Part 11 of Table A applies, nothing further is required. Clause 7 adds that the director "may vote in respect of any contract, appointment or arrangement in which he is interested, and he shall be counted in the quorum present at the meeting". What is the position if the director does not declare his interest but he votes for the

---

369 *cf.* 1963 Act, s.195; below, para. 5–182.

370 *Re Dominion International Group p.l.c. (No.2)* [1996] 1 B.C.L.C. 572 at 598–600. See also *Runciman v. Walter Runciman p.l.c.* [1992] B.C.L.C. 1084 at 1093–1097.

371 *Neptune (Washing Vehicle Equipment) Ltd. v. Fitzgerald* [1996] Ch. 274.

372 1963 Act, s.194(5).

contract — or he remains silent and, having made the quorum, leaves the meeting when it comes up for consideration? As the *Rolled Steel Products* case[373] demonstrates, the contract can be avoided by the company[374] and in many cases the director can be obliged to account to the company for whatever profit he made on the contract.

5–144 Where clause 84 of Table A applies, in addition to the duty to declare his interest, the director cannot be counted in the quorum of the meeting which considered the contract, nor is he allowed to vote on the contract. However, these restrictions can be relaxed or waived at any time by the company in general meeting, presumably by way of an ordinary resolution. Additionally, there are four types of arrangement which are not caught by these quorum and voting restrictions.[375] One is where the director's interest is by virtue of being an officer of the other company or holding shares or other securities in it.[376] The others are where the contract is for him to subscribe for or underwrite securities in the company, or an arrangement to give any security or indemnity to him for liabilities he undertook for the company, or an arrangement to give any security or indemnity to a third party for certain liabilities he undertook on the company's behalf.[377] In *Cox v. Dublin Distillery Co. (No.2)*[378] the directors decided to issue debentures to several of their number as security for advances they had made to the company. It was held that those directors could not have made up the quorum and, accordingly, their debentures were held to have been invalidly given and therefore were worthless. An arrangement like that would now be protected by the exception to clause 84. Where a director does not comply with the above requirements, the company is entitled to avoid the contract and usually can recover any profit he made on the contract. While the articles relax the *Aberdeen Railway Co.* principle,[379] if they are not scrupulously complied with that relaxation is lifted and the general equitable principle applies.[380] A further foundation for liability could be breach of the articles themselves.

---

373 *Rolled Steel Products (Holdings) Ltd. v. British Steel Corp.* [1986] 1 Ch. 246 at 282–286.
374 *Movietex Ltd. v. Bulfield* [1988] B.C.L.C. 104 at p. 125. Contrast *Cowan de Groot Properties Ltd. v. Eagle Trust p.l.c.* [1991] B.C.L.C. 1045 at pp. 1113-1117.
375 These are expressly excluded by Art. 84 (a)–(d).
376 *e.g. Movietex* case, above, n. 374.
377 *e.g. Re Olderfleet Shipbuilding & Engineering Co.* [1922] 1 I.R. 26.
378 [1915] 1 I.R. 345.
379 The requiring of disclosure to and approval by the members.
380 *Movietex* case [1980] B.C.L.C. at p. 114.

S. 194 of the 1963 Act

5–145 Because many companies used to place clauses in their articles of association exonerating directors from practically all obligations of disclosure of their interest in contracts, section 194 of the 1963 Act imposes a minimum disclosure requirement for all companies without exception. Where a director has an interest in a contract with the company, be it direct or indirect, the nature of that interest must be declared at the board meeting which considered the contract or at the very next meeting after that interest arose.[381] As has been explained, a "general notice" can be given where the interest is a shareholding in another company[382] and the company must keep a book which records every declaration of interest made.[383] What is said above about an indirect interest applies equally to section 194, except it is conceivable that, if the company has nothing comparable to clause 84 of Table A, merely being a director of another company is not of itself sufficient to constitute a financial interest in that company. Perhaps a distinction might be drawn between executive and non-executive directorships for these purposes.

5–146 These requirements have been extended by section 47 of the 1990 Act, whereby loans and the like made to any "connected person" are deemed to be arrangements in which the director is interested.[384] Additionally, a "general notice" can be given of who any "connected persons" are for these purposes and also "shadow directors" are brought within the above requirements.[385]

Substantial Property Transactions

5–147 Section 29 of the 1990 Act marks a significant departure from previous legislative attitudes in that it requires general meeting approval for substantial disposals or acquisitions of assets to or from a director or person closely connected with him. For this requirement to apply, the value of the asset in question must exceed either £50,000 or ten per cent of the company's net assets, *i.e.* its total assets less its total liabilities together with provisions for liabilities and charges. A director for these purposes includes a shadow director; a "connected person" here has the meaning in section 26 of the 1990 Act, considered above with reference to loans. Before the company enters into any ar-

---

381 *cf. Lee Panavision Ltd. v. Lee Lighting Ltd.* [1991] B.C.L.C. 575 and *Knight v. Frost* [1999] 1 B.C.L.C. 364.
382 1963 Act, s.194(3)(a) (as amended by 1990 Act, s.47(3)).
383 *ibid.*, s.194(5).
384 See above, paras 5–79 *et seq.*
385 1990 Act, s.27(3).

rangement for acquiring or for disposing of an asset of that value (other than cash) from a director or connected person, the proposal must have been sanctioned by a resolution of the general meeting.[386] If the person is a director of the holding company, the resolution must be passed by its members. Any arrangement which is not so approved is voidable at the company's instance and the party to that arrangement is liable to account to the company for any resulting gain he made and to indemnify the company for any resulting loss or damage it suffered.[387] Any director of the company who authorised that arrangement is similarly obliged to account to the company and to indemnify it. But there is no liability under these heads where the person took all reasonable steps to secure compliance with the Act or he did not know the circumstances which constituted the breach of section 29.

5–148 These requirements do not apply to where the person gets property from the company "in his capacity as a member",[388] for instance a distribution *in specie* to members as provided for in the articles of association. Nor do they apply where the company is being wound up, other than in a members voluntary liquidation, nor to certain inter-group acquisitions and disposals.[389] An arrangement as described above is no longer voidable where, within a reasonable period, it was sanctioned in general meeting.[390] Nor is it voidable where the company is indemnified, as provided for above, for any loss it suffered, or restitution is no longer possible, or the rights acquired by third party bona fide purchasers without notice would be affected by the avoidance.[391]

Insider Trading

5–149 The term "insider trading" connotes a person buying or selling some asset in a market place who, by virtue of his unique position or other special circumstances, possesses information concerning that asset's value which is unknown to others in the market. What is objectionable about insider trading is that the person with the inside knowledge has an overwhelming advantage over others in the market and it is regarded as unfair for him to exploit that advantage at the expense

---

[386] *cf. Joint Receivers & Managers of Niltan Carson Ltd. v. Hawthorne* [1988] B.C.L.C. 298 at 320–328.

[387] *e.g. Re Duckwari p.l.c.* [1997] Ch. 201 and *Re Duckwari p.l.c. (No. 2)* [1999] 2 W.L.R. 1059. *cf. British Racing Drivers' Club Ltd. v. Hextall Ekskine & Co.* [1997] 1 B.C.L.C. 182, a claim for damages for giving negligent advice about this section.

[388] s.29(8).

[389] s.29(6), (7)(a), (b).

[390] s.29(3)(c).

[391] s.29(3)(a), (b).

of those others.[392] Although it arises in other contexts too, the phenomenon of insider trading is most often associated with take-overs and mergers. Armed with the special knowledge of an expected bid, which they obtained by virtue of their position, the bidder's or the target company's directors may buy, or may purchase options on, the target's shares. Once the bid is announced publicly, the value of those shares should rise significantly and the directors would then sell out at a handsome profit for themselves. Or alternatively, the target's shares may be at a relatively high price due to a take-over bid that is rumoured or that has been announced. But with inside knowledge that the bid will fail, directors may sell, or take options to sell, the target's shares and, when the failure becomes known generally, the share price would fall, with the directors making a sizeable profit. A common reaction to such practices is one of condemnation because it offends against market egalitarianism, it involves use by the insiders of something that is not really theirs, and it smacks of persons getting something for nothing.

5–150 Insider trading is roundly condemned by the City Code and in 1980 was made a criminal offence in Britain.[393] It is now unlawful in most industrial countries and the campaign against the practice has advanced to the stage that there is an E.C. Directive which outlaws the practice[394] and the Council of Europe has adopted a Convention which deals with international co-operation in combating insider trading.[395] The practice was made a criminal offence and an actionable wrong in Part V the 1990 Act.

Fiduciary Principles

5–151 While it is almost universally assumed that directors violate their fiduciary duties when they engage in insider trading, curiously there is no major reported Irish or British decision that deals with the rationale for and scope of this liability. It would appear that insider dealing cannot be categorised as a fraud on the company for the purposes of a derivative suit because, exceptional circumstances aside, it

---

[392] See generally, M. Ashe and Y. Murphy, *Insider Dealing* (1992); White, "Towards a Policy Basis for the Regulation of Insider Dealing" (1974) 90 L.Q.R. 494 and Brudney, "Insiders, Outsiders and Informational Advantages Under the Federal Securities Laws" (1979) 93 Harv. L. Rev. 322.

[393] Presently, Criminal Justice Act 1993, Pt V; see generally, B. Hannigan, *Insider Dealing* (2nd ed., 1994).

[394] [1989] O.J. L334/30; see generally, Hopt, "The European Insider Dealing Directive" (1990) 27 Comm.Mkt. L. Rev. 51.

[395] Eur. T.S. No. 130 adopted, April 20, 1989; see generally, Lowry, "The International Approach to Insider Trading: the Council of Europe Convention" (1990) Eur. L. Rev. 460.

cannot be said that the company *qua* corporation suffers any tangible loss due to dealings in its securities. The alternative mode of redress for the aggrieved shareholder who either sold securities to, or bought them from, an insider (the "personal" claim) is usually blocked by *Percival v. Wright*.[396] It was held there that directors ordinarily have no fiduciary duties to their company's shareholders; put the other way, the rights that shareholders possess under the articles of association do not extend to rights against the directors arising from their dealings in the company's shares.

5–152 In that case shareholders of a private company, the shares of which could not be transferred without the board's consent, offered to sell their shares at a stated price. The company's directors agreed to buy them, although at the time negotiations were under way with the board to take over the company at a much higher price per share. On discovering this, the plaintiffs sought to have the sale set aside, contending that the defendants should not have made the purchase without disclosing the "special information". Their claim was rejected on three grounds. The general principle that directors' duties are owed only to the company does not admit of an exception in these circumstances, because "a shareholder is fixed with knowledge of all the directors' powers, and has no more reason to assume that they are not negotiating a sale of the undertaking than to assume that they are not exercising any other power".[397] Nor was there any question of unfair dealing here; the approaches were made by the plaintiffs and it was they who named the price.[398] Finally, a general obligation of disclosure prior to directors purchasing shares would be most impracticable in that it would "place directors in a most invidious position, as they could not buy or sell shares without disclosing negotiations, a premature disclosure of which might well be against the best interests of the company."[399]

5–153 This decision has been criticised as an insider dealers' charter and indeed has been said to have been wrongly decided. But some central matters of fact were conceded by the plaintiffs. They conceded that the directors would not have been obliged to disclose a large casual profit that is made on the discovery of a new deposit of ore; secondly, that there was no unfair dealing or any purchase at an undervalue. Thus, the case is far from being authority for the proposition that in-

---

396 [1902] 2 Ch. 421.

397 *ibid.* at 426. Similarly, *Chase Manhattan Equities Ltd. v. Goodman* [1991] B.C.L.C. 897.

398 Contrast *Allen v. Hyatt* (1914) 30 T.L.R. 444.

399 [1902] 2 Ch. at 426.

sider trading can never give rise to liability. A selling or purchasing shareholder will succeed where the insider furnished him with misleading information to induce him to enter into the transaction.[400] And in some very special circumstances the relationship between director and shareholder can be so intense that the former is subject to fiduciary constraints *vis-à-vis* the shareholder.[401]

Directors Dealing in Options

5–154 Even where it cannot be shown that they actually abused their position by trading with valuable inside knowledge, dealings by directors in options in their companies' shares is now prohibited. On account of the many difficulties in proving a case of insider trading and because of the great temptation and potentially very high profits arises from dealing in options in their own company's securities, it was thought best to prohibit that practice entirely. Section 30 of the 1990 Act applies to directors and shadow directors and makes it a criminal offence for them to deal in "put" or "call" options on their company's shares, and shares in its subsidiary or holding company, or in another subsidiary of that company. Those shares must be listed on a stock exchange, whether in the State or elsewhere. The prohibition here applies to dealing in options in debentures and extends to persons who buy options for or at the instigation of a director. But it does not apply to buying an option to subscribe for securities or buying convertible debentures.[402]

Insider Dealing

5–155 Insider trading proper is now regulated by Part V of the 1990 Act (ss. 107-121), which makes the practice as defined therein both a civil wrong and a criminal offence. The securities which are the subject of these prohibitions are not confined to those of Irish registered companies. They must, however, be listed on a stock exchange which has been prescribed by the Minister.

5–156 Insiders for these purposes are, primarily, persons connected with the company. They are defined as including anyone who, within the preceding six months, was a director, shadow director, secretary, employee, auditor, liquidator, receiver, examiner, person administering a compromise or scheme made with the creditors, a shareholder,

---

[400] *e.g. Allen v. Hyatt* (1914) 30 T.L.R. 444 and *Coleman v. Myers* [1977] 2 N.Z.L.R. 225.

[401] *Coleman v. Myers, ibid.*; see below, para. 12–11.

[402] s.30(3).

the officer of a substantial shareholder in the company and someone who, by virtue of some professional or business or other relationship with the company, holds a position which may reasonably be expected to give him access to "inside" information. The net is cast wider still in that it extends to each of the above categories of person who has any of the above relationships with a "related company" — that being the company's subsidiary or holding company or another subsidiary.[403] Even so-called "tipees" come within the net; these are any person who receives price-sensitive information from any of the above individuals and who is or ought reasonably to be aware that they are prohibited from making use of that information for share dealing.[404] Subject to several exceptions, where a company "officer" is prohibited from dealing in securities, that company is also prevented from dealing in them.

5–157 What exactly constitutes insider dealing here is defined principally by section 108(1) and (2). It is unlawful for any of the above persons to deal in the company's shares, debentures or other debt securities if, by reason of his connection with the company,

(1) he is in possession of information that is not generally available, but, if it were, would be likely materially to affect the price of those securities [or]

(2) he is in possession of information that –
  (a) is not generally available but, if it were, would be likely materially to affect the price of those securities, and
  (b) related to any transaction (actual or contemplated) involving both [that and another company] or involving one of them and securities of the other, or to the fact that any such transaction is no longer contemplated.

Under section 2 of the Companies (Amendment) Act 1999, this prohibition does not apply to specified dealings that occur during a "stabilisation period" as defined in that Act.

5–158 Thus three critical questions under (1) are whether the person concerned possesses information that is not available generally, whether that information is price-sensitive and whether he obtained that information due to his connection with the company. It is a matter for evidence whether that information is price-sensitive, *i.e.* if more generally available the price of the securities would be noticeably higher or lower, as the case may be. Para (2) also raises the same three critical questions, except that the securities being dealt with there are those of a

---

403 See below, para. 14–36.
404 s.108(3).

different company and the price-sensitive information involves some transaction involving both companies (*e.g.* a joint venture) or involving one company and the securities of the other (*e.g.* a take-over bid). A "tipee" who gets price-sensitive information caught by paras (1) and (2) is also prohibited from dealing in those securities if he should have known that the person who imparted that information falls within either of those paragraphs.[405] Section 108 (4) and (5) make it unlawful for any such person or their tipee to cause another person to deal in those securities or to communicate that information to someone else who will then use the information to deal in those securities or will cause someone to deal in them. Certain specified transactions are exempt from these provisions.[406]

5–159 There is a two years period within which civil claims must be brought for breach of these provisions. As well as compensating for any loss caused by insider trading, any profit thereby made must be accounted to the company which issued the securities.[407]

Disclosing Interests in Securities and Transactions

5–160 Under the 1963 Act most companies were required to keep a register of all shares in the company held by the directors and secretary and their immediate families, including shares held in trust for them or in which they have some other beneficial interest.[408] That information enabled other shareholders to ascertain the true extent of the directors' financial stakes in the company and to monitor dealings in those shares. To an extent, insider trading could thereby be policed. These requirements are now elaborated on in Part IV of the 1990 Act (ss. 53-106).

5–161 For these purposes, the relevant securities are shares or debentures in the company, its holding or subsidiary company, or a subsidiary of its holding company — in short, group companies. The nature of the interest to be notified is defined in sections 54-55 extremely widely; almost every conceivable legal or equitable interest is included. And an interest is notifiable even if it is held by the director's or secretary's spouse or minor child. The duty to notify is set out principally in section 53. On becoming a director or secretary, the existence of any such interest must be notified within four days of becoming aware of the interest. Thenceforth if he ever becomes or ceases to be interested

---

[405] s.108(3).
[406] s.110 and s.4 of the Companies (Amendment) Act 1999.
[407] s.109(1).
[408] See *Company Law* (1st ed., 1985), pp. 166–168.

in the company's securities in the ways set out in section 53(2), he must also notify the company within five days. Because this topic overlaps considerably with the mechanism for ascertaining the true beneficial owners of a company's shares, it is considered further in Chapter 9.[409]

Keeping Proper Books of Account

5–162 As, is explained later,[410] section 202 of the 1990 Act requires all companies to keep proper books of account, which must comply with the requirements laid down there and give a "true and fair view" of the company's position. Any director who either fails to take all reasonable steps to secure compliance or who, by his own wilful act, causes the company to contravene these requirements commits an offence. If the company is wound up and is found to be insolvent, any director who was in breach of section 202 may be fastened with unlimited liability for all or part of the company's debts where that breach either contributed to the insolvency or resulted in substantial uncertainty regarding the company's assets or liabilities, or otherwise impeded an orderly liquidation.[411]

Miscellaneous Duties

5–163 The above are the principal duties and liabilities that are imposed on company directors; there are several others that call for brief mention.[412] Unlimited liability for reckless and for fraudulent trading is dealt with in Chapter 18 on Liquidations.[413]

Prohibited Distributions and Share-Purchases

5–164 As is explained later, dividends can only be paid by solvent companies and from distributable profits.[414] Any director responsible for paying an unauthorised dividend can be held liable to the company.[415] Where a company acquires shares in its holding company but, within six months, is wound up and is found to be insolvent, the directors are jointly and severally liable to repay the company the price it paid for those shares.[416] However, the court has a discretion to relieve one or more of them from this liability.

---

409 See below, paras 9–80 *et seq*.
410 below, paras 8–05 *et seq*.
411 *e.g. Meighan v. Duignan* [1997] 1 I.R. 340.
412 See generally, C. Ryan, *Company Directors* (3rd ed., 1990), Chap. 9.
413 below, paras 18—51 *et seq* and 18—61 *et seq*.
414 1983 Act, s.45; see below, para. 7–27 *et seq*.
415 *Re Exchange Banking Co., Flitcroft's Case* (1882) 21 Ch.D. 519.
416 1990 Act, s.225.

Relations with Auditors, Examiners and Inspectors

5–165 Directors and other "officers" of a company must provide information requested by the auditors and also by examiners appointed over a company under the Companies (Amendment) Act 1990, or inspectors appointed under Part II of the 1990 Act. Regarding the auditors, they are "entitled to require from the officers . . . such information and explanations that are within their knowledge or can be procured by them as [are] necessary for the performance of the duties of the auditors".[417] It is an offence not to provide that information within two days of its being sought.[418] It is also an offence to give information which, knowingly or recklessly, is false, deceptive or misleading in a material particular.[419] A court-appointed examiner is entitled to the same degree of co-operation from company officers as auditors are entitled to.[420] An examiner can require any present or past director to produce all documents he has relating to any bank account in his name, whether solely or jointly or severally, into which money connected with the company or any transaction with it has been paid.[421] Any officer or agent of the company may be examined on oath by the examiner.[422] Inspectors appointed by the court to investigate the affairs of a company have similar powers to obtain information from all officers or agents of the company.[423] But inspectors appointed by the Minister normally do not have the power to see all documents concerning officers' own bank accounts.[424]

Format of Cheques and Orders

5–166 Whenever a company issues a bill of exchange, order, business letter, notice, invoice or receipt, section 114 of the 1963 Act requires that the company's name must be mentioned on the document in legible characters. Where a director or other "officer" of the company causes a bill of exchange or cheque, or an order for money or goods, to be issued but which does not adequately identify the company, he will be made personally liable for the amount on that bill or order. For instance, in *Rafsanian Pistachio Producers Co-Op v. Reiss*,[425] the plaintiffs obtained a default judgment against the company but then settled the

---

[417] s.193(3).
[418] s.197(3).
[419] s.197(1), (2).
[420] Companies (Amendment) Act 1990, s.5.
[421] s.8(3).
[422] s.8(4).
[423] 1990 Act, s.10.
[424] *ibid.*, s.14(5).
[425] [1990] B.C.L.C. 352.

dispute, whereby the company gave them several post-dated cheques. These were dishonoured. Because the cheques did not have the company's full name (although they bore its bank account number), the plaintiffs sued the director who had signed them. It was held that he was personally liable on the cheques and that, in the circumstances, the plaintiffs were not estopped from relying on section 114(4). Even where the company's name is mentioned but not the entire name, or the words "limited" or "ltd." are omitted, liability can arise under this section.[426] But a mis-spelling of the company's name on the cheque, that does not mislead parties about the company they are dealing with, does not incur liability.[427]

Wrongs Committed by the Company

5–167 Except where it is expressly provided so by statute, the mere fact that the company has committed a wrong does not make its directors personally responsible for that wrong. Something more is required before individual directors can be rendered accountable. Thus in *Dun Laoghaire Corp. v. Parkhill Developments Ltd.*,[428] the plaintiff obtained a "section 27" order against a property development company for contravening the planning legislation. But Hamilton P. refused to make any order against the company's managing director and effective controller because there was no evidence of impropriety on his part.

5–168 However, if a director actually commits a tort on the company's behalf or he authorises a company employee to do something which is tortious, he then will be personally liable.[429] If his instructions did not authorise the tortious act, he will not be held responsible. Similarly with contempt of court; a director is not personally liable merely by virtue of his office where the company broke a court order, even though he knew of the making of that order.[430] But if he committed some act of omission which caused the company's contempt or he showed wilful disregard of what was going on, he then could be held in contempt.[431] There are numerous provisions in the Companies Acts which set out the various circumstances in which directors can be con-

---

[426] *Durham Fancy Goods Ltd. v. Michael Jackson (Fancy Goods) Ltd.* [1968] 2 Q.B. 839 and *Lindholst & Co. AIS v. Fowler* [1988] B.C.L.C. 166.

[427] *Jenice Ltd. v. Dan* [1993] B.C.L.C. 1349. *cf. Bondina v. Rollaway Shower Blinds Ltd.* [1986] B.C.L.C. 177 on a similar requirement in s.26 of the Bills of Exchange Act 1882.

[428] [1989] I.R. 447.

[429] *E. Evans Ltd. v. Spritebrand Ltd.* [1985] 1 W.L.R. 317 and *Mancetter Developments Ltd. v. Gormanson Ltd.* [1986] 1 Q.B. 1212.

[430] *Director General of Fair Trading v. Buckland* [1990] B.C.L.C. 162.

[431] *Attorney General for Tivalu v. Philatelic Distribution Corp.* [1990] B.C.L.C. 245.

victed of an offence where the company has contravened a penal section of those Acts.[432] Where directors act dishonestly or illegally in relation to their company, but in their defence claim consent, knowledge by them of their wrong-doing will not normally be imputed to the company; this principle applies in the criminal law just as much as in civil law.[433]

5–169 One frequently encounters in regulatory legislation, that imposes liability on companies, a rider that directors and officers who were aware of the breach in question shall also be liable for the statutory penalties. For instance, section 34(2) of the Organisation of Working Time Act 1997 provides that

> "where an offence under this Act has been committed by a body corporate and is proved to have been committed with the consent or connivance of, or to be attributable to any neglect on the part of, a person being a director, manager, secretary or other officer of that body corporate, or a person who was purporting to act in that capacity, that person shall also be guilty of an offence. . . ."[434]

Authorising and Exonerating Breaches of Directors' Duties

5–170 One of the most difficult questions in company law is in what circumstances directors may be exonerated from breaking, or indeed may be authorised to break, what ordinarily would be their duties to the company. In the absence of explicit authority in the company's regulations to do so, the board itself does not possess any power to relieve individual directors from liability. Any effective exemption must arise either from the company's regulations or be given by the shareholders in general meeting.

Exemption Clauses

5–171 In the past, sweeping exemption clauses in articles of association were a common phenomenon; they could exonerate directors from liability in negligence and for breach of several other duties, even from losses resulting from *ultra vires* actions provided the directors were not acting dishonestly. In support of extensive exempting powers, an eminent judge once observed that:

> "It is not for me to say which was the wiser or better course nor do I think that this Court professes to lay down rules for the guidance of men

---

[432] *cf. Hamilton v. Whitehead* (1988) 63 A.L.J.R. 80.

[433] *Attorney General's Reference (No.2 of 1982)* [1984] 1 QB. 624.

[434] *cf. R. v. Boal* [1992] Q.B. 591 and *Woodhouse v. Walsall Metrop. B.C.* [1994] 1 B.C.L.C. 435 on who is a "manager" under similar provisions.

> who are adult, and can manage and deal with their own interests. It would be a violent assumption if any thing of that kind were attempted. It must be left to such persons to form their own contracts and engagements, and this Court has only to sit here and construe them, and also to lay down certain general rules for the protection of persons who may not have been aware of what the consequences would be of entrusting their property to the management of others where nothing is expressed as to the implied arrangement. . . ."[435]

This absolute *laissez-faire* philosophy suggests that, in so far as the shareholders are concerned, company directors can be permitted to engage in all kinds of skulduggery once there is clear authority to do so in the company's own regulations. In fact, the courts would read any ambiguity in regulations against so wide a mandate, and it has always been the position that company officers may not be exempted from liability for their own dishonesty.[436]

5–172 Section 200 of the 1963 Act would appear to abrogate entirely the *laissez-faire* approach, by proscribing any provisions in a company's regulations or in some other contract "exempting any officer . . . from, or indemnifying him against, any liability which by virtue of any rule of law would otherwise attach to him in respect of any negligence, default, breach of duty or breach of trust of which he may be guilty in relation to the company. . . ." The *City Equitable* case[437] on directors' and auditors' negligence was fresh in the legislature's mind when this section was first adopted. There the directors, who were found to have managed the company incompetently and negligently, were held nevertheless not to be accountable because of an exclusion clause in the company's articles of association. The justification for section 200 is that *laissez-faire* in this context operates unjustly, by allowing what often are company promoters and controllers of companies to exonerate themselves from obligations that one normally expects from company directors. Especially in companies with many shareholders, there is no genuine freedom of contract, since small investors do not have sufficient contracting power of their own to negotiate about an exemption clause. Yet it can be argued that when persons acting in a position of relative bargaining equality form a company, they should be free to exonerate their directors from at least some of the more stringent standards imposed by equity. Section 200 has generated some

---

[435] *Imperial Metal Credit Association v. Coleman* (1871) L.R. 6 Ch. 558 at 568. See too *Costa Rica Railway Co. v. Forwood* [1900] 1 Ch. 746.

[436] *Re City Equitable Fire Insurance Co.* [1925] Ch. 407.

[437] *ibid.*; see above, para. 5–100.

academic comment[438] but appears only once to have been subject of authoritative interpretation.

5–173 While the central thrust of section 200 is clear enough, does it go so far as condemning clauses that permit directors to have certain conflicts of interest, contracts which compromise an action which is brought against a director and even professional indemnity liability policies taken out either by the company or by the directors themselves? Its apparently extensive scope may be confined in several ways. Since Table A is part of the 1963 Act, none of the exclusion clauses in the model articles can be proscribed by section 200. This would resolve some question about article 78, the so-called *Regal (Hastings)* regulation.[439] Section 200's reference to "liability" could be read as not including doctrines and rules the breach of which renders a transaction merely voidable by the company. One such rule is against being in a position of potential conflict of interest without in any way unfairly profiting from that conflict; articles 78 and 85 of Table A waive requirements for being in two potential conflict situations.[440] In *Movietex Ltd. v. Bulfield,*[441] Vinelott J. reconciled articles similar to those articles 78 and 85 on the following grounds. These deal with the general equitable principle against self-dealing. But it is inaccurate to describe them as rules which imposes a duty to avoid all conflicts of interests, except where the *cestui's* informed consent is obtained. The true rule is that there is no duty as such; rather, fiduciaries, including directors, are under a disability in that, if they place themselves in a conflict situation, the transaction with the company becomes voidable and they can be called to account for any profit made. However, the company's articles can exclude or modify application of this principle.

5–174 A strong case could be made for section 200 not insulating two categories of breach of duty from any *ex ante* exemption. Negligence is expressly mentioned by the section and its history demonstrates that it was adopted partly to strike at the kind of exclusion clause that exonerated the directors in the *City Equitable* case. The other is deliberate fraud. It would be surprising if fraud were deemed to fall outside the section's strong words; in any event, it was widely accepted that the old *laissez-faire* analysis did not allow exemption from liability for fraud. The question that then arises is what precisely does "fraud" mean in

---

[438] See generally, Birds, "The Permissible Scope of Articles Excluding the Duties of Company Directors" (1976) 39 Mod. L. Rev. 394 and Gregory, "The Scope of the Companies Act 1948, Section 205" (1982) 98 L.Q.R. 413.

[439] See supra, para. 5–132.

[440] See supra, para. 5–60.

[441] [1988] B.C.L.C. 104.

this context: *Derry v. Peek*[442] type deceit or some broad equitable notion of fraud? Although directors' liability insurance would seem to be caught by section 200, it is possible that it only applies to indemnity arrangements where it is the company itself which pays the premium. Most likely the section would not be construed to prohibit directors themselves from taking out insurance against liability for bona fide breaches of fiduciary duty and perhaps negligence as well.

Members "Ratifying" or Remedying Officers' Wrongs

5–175 Use of the term "provision" suggests that section 200 does not strike at *ex post facto* exemptions in the form of the general meeting ratifying some breach of duty that has already occurred. The argument that general meeting resolutions authorising in advance directors to contravene a duty to the company are not "provisions" and, therefore, fall outside the section, is plausible although hardly persuasive.

5–176 There are numerous instances where the courts have upheld general meeting resolutions that ratified, after the event, breaches of various directors' duties, such as allotting additional shares to forestall a take-over and voting for a contract with the company in which the director had a financial interest. But there are other kinds of breaches of duty that cannot be ratified, at least over the objections of a minority of the members, such as unfair discrimination against that minority or defrauding the company. Much confusion exists about what wrongs are capable of so-called ratification and the legal consequences of shareholders' approval for directors' wrongs. Certain elementary principles and distinctions are often overlooked when considering this complex subject.[443]

5–177 Many of the cases do not involve the company suing the errant director but are proceedings being brought by aggrieved minority shareholders. In those instances, the issue then is when does general meeting approval or "ratification" of the breach of duty prevent those shareholders' actions being heard. As is explained in Chapter 10, depending on the circumstances of the case, majority approval for what was done may be a bar to shareholders' claims, requiring analysis of the principles and exceptions associated with the early Victorian case,

---

[442] (1889) 14 App. Cas. 337.

[443] See generally, Partridge, "Ratification and Release of Directors From Personal Liability" (1987) 46 Cam. L.J. 122 and Whincop, 'Of Fault and Default: Contractarianism as a Theory of Anglo-Australian Corporate Law', 21 Melbourne U.L. Rev. 187 (1997).

Foss v. Harbottle.[444] However, the fact that majority approval for the directors' wrongs may block a shareholder's own action does not mean that the company may not at some later stage change its mind and sue the directors for their wrongs. It would be different if the company and the directors reached an enforceable agreement putting an end to all claims between them. But a mere "ratifying" resolution, which can have the effect of rendering binding otherwise voidable contracts or deficient decisions of the directors, is not an enforceable agreement to waive all claims. For there has been no consideration given. Nor normally would that resolution operate as an effective estoppel against the company subsequently bringing proceedings. For practical purposes, however, provided there is no major change in the membership, it is unlikely that, having passed a resolution exonerating the directors, the company will later turn around and bring proceedings against those directors.

5–178 If, at the general meeting's behest, a contract under seal was made with the directors exonerating them, the question then arises whether the company is legally capable of making such an agreement. On the basis of the *Re Duomatic Ltd.*[445] principle, that agreement would be effective if it had the backing of all the shareholders, provided it is not *ultra vires* the company. But where it has the backing of a majority only, it would be set aside if it fell within the circumstances where aggrieved minority shareholders' claims would succeed. These same considerations apply in *ex ante* exonerations. If, before the wrong was done or at the very time it was done, the shareholders signified their approval, that would amount to a waiver of the directors' duty to the company. As the duty would not then exist, the directors could not then be in breach of duty. However, as with the sealed contract not to sue, an *ex ante* waiver is only fully effective if it was in respect of a matter which would not give rise to an aggrieved minority shareholders' claim. If the matter did not indeed fall within the so-called exceptions to *Foss v. Harbottle*, the purported waiver would be a "fraud on the minority" and not binding on the company.

5–179 Accordingly, the question of the legal enforceability of directors' duties is closely related to the issue of minority shareholder protection.[446] This is particularly so in companies with relatively few members — the great majority of registered companies — where the directors usually hold a majority of the shares as well. Where the di-

---

[444] (1843) 2 Hare 461; see below, para. 10–05.
[445] [1969] 2 Ch. 365.
[446] See generally, C. Ryan, *Company Directors* (3rd ed., 1990), Chap. 11.

rectors as a group or a majority of them are negligent or otherwise in breach of duty, if they are also the majority shareholders there is little real prospect of the company suing them for breach of duty. In those companies, therefore, for practical purposes the directors' wrongs which can be redressed in court are the breaches of duty which also are a basis for a minority shareholders' action, namely most breaches of the memorandum and articles of association and what falls under the rubic "unfair discrimination" and "fraud on the company". Another mode of redress against errant directors is an action under section 205 of the 1963 Act for "oppression". All of these are dealt with in Chapter 10.

Court Exonerating Officers from Liability

5–180 Section 391 of the 1963 Act gives the court a discretionary power to exonerate any officer of a company, be they directors or auditors, from liability for breach of a duty owed to the company. Relief will be granted provided three conditions are satisfied, viz. that the officer acted "honestly", that he acted "reasonably" and that "having regard to all the circumstances of the case he ought fairly to be excused".[447] Thus any dishonesty or unreasonableness entirely prevents the officer from even being considered for relief. Having a personal interest in a transaction that contravened section 29 of the 1990 Act and intending to profit from it has been held as grounds for not exonerating liability.[448] Having taken certain action on foot of counsel's opinion has been held to indicate reasonableness,[449] as has acting consistently with past practice.[450] On the other hand, engaging in somewhat complex transactions, such as paying "golden handshakes", without having obtained legal advice has been found not to be reasonable.[451] The section's scope is most extensive in that the court can even exonerate from liability for *ultra vires* acts.[452] But the section does not apply to penal proceedings brought to enforce the Companies Acts.[453] Relief granted may be in whole or in part. It is not necessary in advance to plead this section; it can be raised at the trial for the first time.[454]

---

[447] *Re Duomatic Ltd.* [1969] 2 Ch. 365; *e.g. Re D'Jan of London Ltd.* [1994] 1 B.C.L.C. 561.
[448] *Re Duckwari p.l.c.* [1997] 2 W.L.R. 48 at p.56.
[449] *Re Claridge's Patent Aspbalte Co.* [1921] 1 Ch. 543.
[450] *Re Duomatic Ltd.* [1969] 2 Ch. 365.
[451] *ibid.*
[452] *Re Claridge's etc.*, above, n. 449.
[453] *Customs & Excise Commissioners v. Hendon Alpha Ltd.* [1981] 1 Q.B. 818.
[454] *Re Kirby Coaches Ltd.* [1991] B.C.L.C. 414.

RECORDS REGARDING OFFICERS

5–181 Mention has already been made of records that must be kept about a company's officers and some of their activities. A director in the context of these requirements usually includes any person under whose instructions the company's directors are accustomed to act.

Register of Directors and Secretaries

5–182 Section 195 of the 1963 Act[455] requires every company to keep a register of its directors and secretaries containing the following particulars. As regards every director, there must be stated their present and any former name or names, their usual residential address, their nationality, their business occupation and particulars of any other directorships they hold in companies incorporated in Ireland or abroad. All directorships held during the preceding ten years must also be shown, other than directorships of any of the company's wholly-owned subsidiaries. As regards every secretary, all that need be recorded is their present and any former name or names, and their usual address; where the secretary is a company, its name and registered address should be shown. For the purposes of keeping this register up to date, every director and secretary is obliged to notify the company promptly of any relevant change in their circumstances. This register must be kept at the company's registered office and be open to inspection during business hours to any member without charge, and to any other person on payment of not more than one pound.

Interests in Contracts Book

5–183 Section 194(5) of the 1963 Act requires every company to keep a book in which is recorded every declaration made by a director of his interest in a contract with the company and of every general notice that a director's membership of a company shall be regarded as an interest in any contract made with that company.[456] The book must be kept at the registered office and be open for inspection without charge by every director, secretary, auditor and member of the company. It must be produced at every general meeting and, where a director so requests, it must be produced at board meetings.

Register of Interests in Company's Shares and Debentures

5–184 What was formerly known as the register of director's shareholdings has been replaced by a register of directors' and secretaries'

---

[455] Amended by 1990 Act, s.51.
[456] See supra, para. 5–145.

interests in the company's shares and debentures. As is explained more fully later,[457] whenever a director or secretary or any shadow director acquires or disposes of an "interest" in their company's own securities, they must notify the company promptly of that matter. Sections 59-62 of the 1990 Act require every company to keep a register wherein will be recorded every such interest obtained or relinquished. There must also be entered therein details concerning every right to subscribe for shares given to a director and also details whenever that right has been exercised. The nature and extent of the interest in the securities must be recorded. This register can be inspected by any member of the company free of charge and by anyone else on paying a very modest charge; they can require that copies be made from this register. Provision is made for removing names from the register where more than six years elapsed since they held an interest in the securities.

---

[457] See below, paras 9–80 *et seq*.

6

Raising Capital

6–01 There are several ways in which companies finance their operations. The Companies Acts contain elaborate provisions about companies issuing their shares and debentures, especially where securities are offered to the general investing public. Among the principal concerns of these rules are to ensure that existing shareholders control allotments of unissued shares being made by the directors and to ensure that investors are not deceived or misled into acquiring shares of negligible value.

SOURCES OF FINANCE

6–02 One of the first things that must be determined when embarking on a business venture is how to finance it. Various options present themselves, like equity investment by shareholders, long-term and short-term borrowings, grants of various kinds that can be obtained from the State and financing expansion from profits generated by the business.[1] If the company seeks to raise additional share capital it must choose whether first to approach its existing shareholders or to offer its securities to others — even to the general public. It is most unusual today for newly-formed companies to approach the investing public immediately for funds.

Share Capital

6–03 To begin with, how much should shareholders themselves invest in the business as equity or risk capital? Whatever sum that is will be represented by shares they subscribe for and which will be allotted to them. For instance, if £50,000 is needed initially as risk capital, the original shareholders will take up shares in the company representing that sum — exchanging cash or other assets for those shares. Thus if

---

[1] See generally, M. Sabine, *Corporate Finance* (2nd ed., 1993) and R. Burgess, *Corporate Finance Law* (2nd ed., 1992).

the shares are to be fully paid up and have a nominal value of £1 each, 50,000 shares of £1 will be allotted in return for the company obtaining consideration worth at least £50,000. Shares are commonly referred to as equity.

6–04 A number of general points must be made at this stage about a company's share capital, although the actual rules pertaining to many of these matters are dealt with in different parts of this book. Mention has already been made of the fact that in most Western European countries shares are required to have some fixed nominal or par value, *i.e.* be assigned a specific theoretical value, be it £1.00, 20 pence, £200 or whatever. Although persuasive reasons can be advanced for permitting companies to issue shares without having to assign them some par value, there would appear to be little demand for such innovation. A company's authorised capital (sometimes called nominal capital) is the aggregate par value of the shares that its memorandum of association permits it to issue to subscribers: its theoretical maximum capital. The issued capital means the aggregate par value of the shares that have been issued to subscribers; in other words, the total par value of the company's shares that have been acquired by its members. Usually, companies will not issue all of their authorised capital but will retain some of it unissued. Allotted capital means the same as issued capital. The Companies Acts generally speak of allotting rather than of issuing shares; allotting is the technical term for appropriating to a person a certain number of shares.

6–05 By paid up capital is meant the amount in money or money's worth that has been paid to a company in return for shares allotted by it. The laws in most Western European countries prohibit allotting shares at a discount, *i.e.* at the very least, the par value must be paid up on shares. Frequently, shares are allotted for more than their par value, *i.e.* at a premium; where this happens the paid up capital is the aggregate par value of the shares that have been allotted together with the total premiums paid on them. Where a company does not require to be paid over to it immediately the entire par value and any premium on shares it allots, it will require its shareholders to pay over only part of the amount due by them and will call up part or all of the remainder at some later stage. The amount that it requires to be paid over to it is the called up capital; the remainder is the uncalled capital. Shares may be divided into different classes — often into ordinary and preference shares, where the latter are given certain preferential rights over the former, such as in respect of dividends and repayment of capital on a winding up.

Borrowing

6–06 How much the company should borrow depends on the circumstances of each case, like how much funds the shareholders themselves possess to invest in risk capital, the nature of the business, the company's creditworthiness and the like. It is trite financial wisdom that a company should not borrow more than it comfortably can repay. Borrowing can take various forms; it can be mainly from the company's own shareholders, from personal investors who do not wish to be exposed unduly to risk, or from financial institutions such as banks and insurance companies which usually will require security.

Modes of Borrowing

6–07 Banks and other financial institutions offer a wide variety of borrowing facilities, like overdrafts, term loans and credit factoring.[2] A method of financing that has become especially popular due to taxation considerations is equipment leasing. Borrowing may even be the consequences of the company's cash flow. That is to say, if the company can get paid for the goods or services it produces before it is required to pay for its principal inputs, the suppliers of those inputs in fact finance its business. A dangerous variant of this is relying on employees' social insurance contributions, sums deducted for PAYE purposes and VAT collected that have not yet been paid over to the State. Where a company borrows funds and issues the lenders documents evidencing the right to be repaid, these documents are called debentures. Although transferable debentures can resemble shares in various respects, they are fundamentally different from shares.

Power and Authority

6–08 A power to borrow for the purposes of the company's business is usually included in the memorandum of association's objects clause; where no such power is expressly given, borrowing for business purposes would usually be *intra vires* a registered company as an implied power. However, in *Re Introductions Ltd.*[3] it was held that an express "object" of borrowing does not necessarily empower a company to borrow in order to finance transactions that are not contemplated by its other objects. In those circumstances, if the lender knows or ought to have known that the funds are to be spent on some *ultra vires*[4] matter, then the loan and the security for it are *ultra vires*. Borrowing or providing security for loans that are of no economic benefit to the company are *ultra vires* unless they are expressly authorised by the

---

2 See generally, J. Breslin, *Banking Law in the Republic of Ireland* (1998).
3 [1970] 1 Ch. 199.
4 See above, para. 3–62 *et seq*.

memorandum, as *Northern Bank Finance Corp. v. Quinn*[5] illustrates. *Ultra vires* borrowing may be rendered legally effective by virtue of section 8(1) of the 1963 Act.[6]

6–09 How a company's borrowing powers are to be exercised is almost invariably determined by its articles of association. Article 80 of Table A, under which the "business of the company shall be managed by the directors",[7] empowers the board to borrow for business purposes. While this power is subject to article 79, which states that the aggregate of funds borrowed or secured shall not at any time exceed the total nominal amount of the shares that the company has issued, it adds that borrowing or security in excess of that amount shall not be "invalid or ineffectual" unless the lender or security-holder at the time had "express notice" of that ceiling.[8] Where the articles require some internal formality to be satisfied before funds can be borrowed by the company, like approval by an ordinary resolution in general meeting, the lender is under no positive obligation to ensure that the requirement was fully satisfied.[9] Provided that it is not *ultra vires*, unauthorised or irregular borrowing may be ratified in general meeting and therefore made binding on the company.[10]

Security

6–10 Where the memorandum of association contains an express power to borrow, it usually will be accompanied by a power to give security; where borrowing falls within a company's implied powers almost invariably the company will have an implied power to give security for those borrowings. Security given for *ultra vires* borrowings is itself *ultra vires*. In *Re Bansha Woollen Mills Co.*,[11] for example, where with the shareholders' approval the company mortgaged its property to secure a loan from one of its directors, it was held that, since in the circumstances part of the loan was *ultra vires*, the mortgage was ineffective insofar as it secured that part. It would appear that a power in the objects clause to provide security for loans which are of no economic value to the company itself will be construed narrowly, especially where the lender is a sophisticated financial intermediary.[12]

---

5 [1989] I.L.R.M. 221.
6 See below, para. 13–15 *et seq*.
7 See above, para. 4–47 *et seq*.
8 cf. *Bank of Ireland Finance Ltd. v. Rockfield Ltd.* [1979] I.R. 21; see below, para. 7–87.
9 *Royal British Bank v. Turquand* (1856) 6 E. & B. 327; see below, para. 13–47.
10 *Irvine v. Union Bank of Australia* (1877) 2 App. Cas. 366.
11 (1887) 21 L.R. Ir. 181.
12 *Northern Bank Finance Corp. v. Quinn* [1979] I.L.R.M. 221.

6–11 Ordinarily, the articles of association will set out how the power to grant security is to be exercised. Article 79 of Table A authorises the directors to "mortgage or charge [the] undertaking, property and uncalled capital . . . and to issue debentures . . . whether outright or as security for any debt, liability or obligation of the company or of any third party". But this is subject to the aggregate of borrowings and security not exceeding the issued capital's nominal amount; and it is unlawful to take security with "express notice" that this ceiling has been breached. Charges made on specific assets are "fixed charges" and charges on current assets as the company possesses from time to time are called "floating charges".[13]

Gearing

6–12 The term gearing means the ratio between a company's equity and its debt. A company that has borrowed heavily in comparison with its share capital is said to be highly geared. The main attraction of high gearing is that, if the business is very successful, the shareholders (the equity investors) will get a much higher return on their investment. Take a business that needs £50,000 in capital and that is being inaugurated by three persons, each with £8,300 to invest in it (*i.e.* £25,000 in aggregate); assume that it would earn £10,000 in each year. If the remaining £25,000 could be borrowed at say 10 per cent per annum, this would require £2,500 per annum to service, leaving a surplus of £7,500 at the end of the year to be divided among the three shareholders — or £2,500 each. If however, instead of borrowing they bring in other shareholders who invest £25,000, at the end of the year the original three will be entitled, between themselves, at most to only half of the £10,000 annual profits — or £1,666 each.

6–13 These figures demonstrate the principal argument for borrowing in order to finance a business. The more highly geared a company is the greater is the proportion of profits available for distribution as dividends on the equity. Another attraction of high gearing is taxation; interest on loans is a business cost and therefore can be deducted from the trading surplus, leaving even more to be distributed as dividends. The main argument against high gearing is simply the case against heavy borrowing. If the business runs into difficulties, it may not be possible to meet the interest charges, which could easily result in the company being put into receivership or into liquidation. Moreover, companies that are highly geared may experience some difficulties in attracting further equity investment on account of there being

---

[13] See below, paras 16–09 *et seq.*

prior charges on earnings and also because of lenders' tendency to close down businesses in bad times.

Hybrids of Debt and Equity

6–14 There are various intermediate solutions to resolving the debt-equity dilemma. One is that the company borrows from its own shareholders, assuming they have the funds to lend. In this way there is less likelihood of creditors shutting the business down as soon as it encounters temporary difficulties. Another option is the "preference" share, which in fact, though not in law, is a hybrid of debt and equity. This is a special class of share the owners of which have prior claims against the company over the "ordinary" shareholders.[14] A common form of preference share is one the holders of which, if profits are earned and dividends are being declared, are entitled to be paid a fixed dividend before any dividend can be paid to the other shareholders. Preference shares usually carry a prior claim over other shares in the return of capital, in the event of the company being wound up. With preference shares, therefore, the company can obtain the principal advantage of high gearing without the main disadvantage.

6–15 The "convertible" security is another intermediate solution. It is a claim against or in the company of one kind that either can be converted or must be converted into a claim of another kind on or after some specified time or event. The commonest form is the convertible debenture, *i.e.* a loan to the company that at some stage can be converted into equity investment in it. A major attraction of this form of security is that it enables a company to obtain investment at a time when persons are reluctant to acquire shares in it and, should the company prosper, to convert those borrowings into equity.

State Grants and Aids

6–16 A major source of company finance today is the grant and aid schemes offered by various public bodies, especially the Industrial Development Authority.[15] State assistance can take the form of outright cash grants, loans, the purchase of shares in the company and several other methods. How much and what types of aid a company can obtain will depend on the bargaining power it possesses, such as how risky its business is, the likelihood of it expanding, its contribution to exports and to import-substitution and, perhaps of greatest importance, how many persons it plans to employ.

---

[14] See below, paras 9–45 *et seq.*

[15] See generally, *Comprehensive Guide to Government and E.C. Support Programmes* (1991–C.11/S.K.C.)

Retained Earnings

6–17 Next is the question of self-financing; how much should the company rely on profits generated by the business to finance expansion? Among the advantages of what is referred to as "ploughing back" profits is that the immediate dependence on banks and other lending institutions is greatly reduced and there is less need to go to the existing shareholders or to outsiders for further equity capital. Indeed, few businesses prosper and endure without retaining an appreciable proportion of their earnings in good trading years. Especially in "close" companies, taxation is an important consideration influencing the dividend decision.

6–18 The Companies Acts leave it almost entirely to companies themselves to determine their dividend policies — when should a dividend be paid, how much should be paid, and who decides these questions. These and related questions will be dealt with in the articles of association. All that the Acts insist on is that a dividend (now called a "distribution") must not be paid from the subscribed capital nor be paid if the company is insolvent;[16] also that the directors' report to the annual general meeting shall state how much the board recommends should be paid in dividends and how much should be retained in the company or placed in reserve.[17] Because determinations about how earnings are to be disposed of are very much matters of business policy, courts have shown a marked reluctance to interfere with decisions about dividends that comply with the articles of association's requirements. The governing rule is that there is

> "no principle which compels a company while a going concern to divide the whole of its profits amongst its shareholders. Whether the whole or any part should be divided, or what portion should be divided and what portion retained, are entirely questions of internal management which the shareholders must decide for themselves. . . . And it makes no difference whether the undivided balance is retained to the credit of profit and loss account, or carried to the credit of a rest or reserve fund, or appropriated to any other use of the company. These are questions for the shareholders to decide subject to any restrictions or directions contained in the articles of association . . . "[18]

In very exceptional circumstances, however, decisions regarding the payment or the non-payment of dividends may be upset by the courts on the grounds of "oppression".[19]

---

[16] 1983 Act, Pt IV; see below, para. 7–25 *et seq.*
[17] 1963 Act, s.158 (1).
[18] *Burland v. Earle* [1902] A.C. 83 at 95. *cf. Re Buck Dec'd* [1964] V.R. 284.
[19] *Re Sam Weller & Son Ltd.* [1990] Ch. 682; see below, para. 9–28.

ISSUING SECURITIES

6–19 Those persons who subscribe to a company's memorandum of association become its first shareholders.[20] Subsequent shareholders are either persons to whom the company allots shares, *i.e.* persons who put cash or other assets into the company in return for shares, and those persons' successors-in-title.[21] Debenture-holders are persons who have made loans to the company and their successors-in-title. The term securities, which is commonly used in company law practice, although rarely mentioned as such in the Companies Acts,[22] signifies both shares and debentures. This section deals with various aspects of companies issuing their securities to investors. Protecting investors against fraud and negligence and the like is treated separately below; protecting creditors against shares being issued for worthless or for grossly overvalued consideration is considered in the next chapter.

Application and Allotment

6–20 Occasionally investors will search for a company into which they can put funds at their disposal. More often it is the company, or its shareholders or directors, or persons promoting the company, who will seek out potential investors. As regards shares, usually the investor will apply to the company to subscribe for them, *i.e.* will offer to acquire its shares in return for some consideration. If the offer is accepted, the company will allot shares to that person and enter his name on its register of members. These shares are then said to have been issued. The term "issue" with regard to shares has slightly different meanings according to the context.[23] The term "allotted" is now defined by the 1983 Act as "when a person acquires the unconditional right to be included in the company's register of members in respect of those shares".[24] The general principles of contract law govern the offer and acceptance,[25] such as informal and conditional offers, acceptance within a reasonable time, by post or otherwise; notification of acceptance; revocation of the offer and acceptance; mistake etc.

Minimum Payment

6–21 There are a number of statutory provisions designed to ensure that a minimum amount becomes payable to a company before it al-

---

[20] 1963 Act, s.31(1).
[21] See below, para. 9–63 *et seq*.
[22] But see, *e.g.* "equity share" in 1963 Act, s.155(5) and "equity security" in 1983 Act, s.23(13).
[23] *National Westminster Bank p.l.c. v. Inland Revenue* [1995] 1 A.C. 119.
[24] s. 2(2).
[25] See generally R. Friel, *The Law of Contract* (1995), Chaps 2–6.

lots shares. Except in the case of p.l.c.s, at least five per cent of a share's nominal value must be payable on application,[26] *i.e.* if say £1.00 shares are being allotted, they must be paid up to at least 5 pence per share. P.l.c.s, however, may not allot shares unless at least one-quarter of their nominal value, together with any premium on them, is immediately payable to the company.[27] Where a p.l.c. offers its shares for subscription but the offer is undersubscribed (*i.e.* the entire offer is not taken up), it is forbidden to allot those shares that are subscribed for unless the offer stated that allotments would be made in those circumstances.[28] The 1983 Act's "anti-watering" measures, which are considered in Chapter 7, forbid companies to allot shares at less than their par value[29] and contain numerous provisions aimed at ensuring the p.l.c.s get approximately equivalent value for any shares they allot.[30]

Following Prospectus Offer

6–22 Where a company offers shares to the public for the first time, no allotment may be made on that offer until at least the "minimum amount" was raised.[31] By minimum amount is meant the sum stated in the prospectus and which, in the directors' opinion, it is necessary to raise in order to pay for the company's preliminary expenses, any commissions owed in respect of subscriptions, the purchase price to be paid for any property it is intended to buy with the issue's proceeds and any working capital.[32] Where a prospectus has been issued generally, *i.e.* to persons other than the company's existing shareholders and debenture-holders, the company is not permitted to allot shares on foot of that prospectus until at least the fourth day after it was issued or such later time as is specified in the prospectus.[33] The general principle that an offer may be revoked unless it has been accepted is subject to an exception in the case of applications made for securities in pursuance of a prospectus issued generally; offers to take shares or debentures are irrevocable until at least nine days following the time the prospectus was issued.[34] This restriction is to prevent speculators from unfairly "stagging" a new issue, *i.e.* applying for far more shares than they intend to take up, in the hope that this will help the price to rise, and then withdrawing their excess applications at the last minute. But

---

26 1963 Act, s.53(3); for sanction, see s.55.
27 1983 Act, s.28; see below, para. 7–06.
28 *ibid.*, s.22; see below, para. 7–07.
29 See below, para. 7–10.
30 See below, paras 7–11 *et seq.*
31 1963 Act, s.53(1); for sanction, see s.55.
32 *ibid.*, 3rd. schedule, para. 4(a).
33 1963 Act, s.56(1).
34 *ibid.*, s.56(5).

an application for securities may be revoked when any person who was responsible for the prospectus issues a public notice disclaiming or limiting their liability under it.[35] Where a prospectus states that an application has been or will be made for permission to deal in the securities on the Stock Exchange, but the application is not made or permission has not been granted, any allotment made in pursuance of the prospectus is void.[36]

Return as to Allotments

6–23 Whenever a limited company allots shares (other than to its members in a bonus or a rights issue — even if renounceable), section 58 of the 1963 Act requires it to deliver to the registrar of companies within one month what is called the return as to allotments. This must state the number and the nominal amounts of the shares allotted, the allottees' names and addresses, and the amount if any paid on each share. Where the shares were allotted for a consideration other than cash, the duly stamped contracts constituting the allottees' title to those shares and dealing with the consideration given to the company for them must be delivered to the registrar. A stamped statement of the particulars suffices where those contracts are not written. The registrar, moreover, must be furnished with a return stating details of the shares being allotted and the non-cash consideration obtained for them. Where the allotment is made by a p.l.c. and it is one in respect of which the 1983 Act requires an independent expert's valuation report,[37] a copy of this report must be included in the return as to the allotments.

Authority to Issue Additional Shares

6–24 Virtually every business that is growing will need to raise further equity capital at one or more stages of its existence; it is only rarely that a firm can expand entirely on the strength of retained earnings or borrowings. Section 68(1)(a) of the 1963 Act gives companies a broad discretion to increase their share capital, if their articles of association so provide, but exercise of this power can in effect be blocked by appropriate provisions in a shareholders' agreement.[38] Power to issue additional shares is usually conferred by the articles, either on the members in general meeting or on the board of directors. Under articles 2 and 4 of Table A, the general meeting is empowered to issue new shares, be they identical to those already issued or some entirely new

---

[35] 1963 Act, s.56(5).
[36] *ibid.*, s.57
[37] s.31; see below, paras 7–23 *et seq.*
[38] *Russell v. Northern Bank Development Corp.* [1992] 1 W.L.R. 588; see below, para. 11–08.

class of shares. Before 1983, by virtue of article 5 of Table A the board had a wide discretion about to whom and on what terms unissued shares should be allotted. As was explained above when considering directors' duties, the directors could easily change the balance of power within the company by allotting additional shares to themselves or to their favourites. The courts intervened on occasion to prevent the share allotment power from being abused; examples include *Nash v. Lancegaye Safety Glass (Ireland) Ltd.*,[39] *Howard Smith Ltd. v. Ampol Petroleum Ltd.*[40] and *Clemens v. Clemens Brothers Ltd.*[41] One of the E.C. Second Directive's main objectives is the "equal treatment of the shareholders in the same position" and, to that end, it requires E.C. Member States to introduce into their laws measures restricting the freedom that company boards and even shareholders had in respect of issuing additional shares. The two most important of these, the requirement of specific shareholder authority and compulsory pre-emption, are now provided for in the 1983 Act. Instances such as *Nash* and *Howard Smith*, therefore, will become less prevalent, but they will not disappear entirely from the legal landscape.

6–25 According to section 20 of the 1983 Act, a company's directors shall not allot additional shares[42] unless they are authorised to do so as follows. Such authority must be contained either in an ordinary resolution of the general meeting[43] or in the articles of association, and must state the maximum amount of shares that may be allotted. This authority may be particular or general, conditional or unconditional; that is to say, it can leave it entirely to the directors to determine to whom and on what terms the shares may be allotted, or it may set out who the allottees are or what the terms of allotment are to be. Any such authority, moreover, must state how long it is to last, which period cannot exceed five years, although it may be renewed for a further five years period at most. The general meeting retains the power by ordinary resolution to vary or revoke any such authority.[44] These requirements do not apply to an allotment made in pursuance of an employees' share scheme. These requirements do not affect a right to subscribe for or to convert into shares other than those being allotted, but they apply to the grant of such a right. An allotment made contrary to section 20 is not thereby invalid.[45]

---

[39] (1958) 92 I.L.T.R. 11; see above, para. 5–120.
[40] [1974] A.C. 821; see above, para. 5–121.
[41] [1976] 2 All E.R. 268; see below, para. 10–34.
[42] *i.e.* "relevant securities" as defined in subs. (10).
[43] Subject to s.143 of the 1963 Act.
[44] As defined in s.2(1) of the 1983 Act.
[45] 1983 Act, s.20(8).

Rights Issues and Pre-Emption

6–26 Having decided to raise further capital by issuing additional shares, the question that then confronts the company is to whom should it look for the funds. Should it ask its existing shareholders to subscribe for the additional equity, or should the shares be offered to outsiders, even to the general public? Usually in the case of small companies and often with big companies, the new shares are offered initially to the existing shareholders before being offered to outsiders. This is called a "rights" issue; the existing shareholders are given a prior right to subscribe for the new shares. Where the company is public, especially where its shares are quoted on the Stock Exchange, it is common to offer such rights at a price substantially below the market value of the already issued shares and to make the rights renounceable in favour of anybody.[46] For instance, a company with 100,000 issued shares of £1 par value, that are worth £1.90 on the market, may decide to offer an additional 50,000 shares of £1 par to its shareholders on a pro rata basis at, say, £1.20 a share. The relative attractiveness of this price and the desire to maintain their proportionate stake in the company will induce many of the shareholders to take up their rights by applying for the new shares. Some, however, may not wish to do this and, if the rights are fully renounceable, they can sell them to outsiders wishing to invest in the company. Depending on the demand from outsiders, it may be possible to sell the rights at an appreciable profit. For instance, investors may be prepared to pay 40 pence a share for the right to acquire shares in the above company at £1.20 each.

6–27 Pre-emption in this context means compulsory "rights issues", *i.e.* obliging companies when they issue new equity to do so by giving their shareholders a first option on the shares in proportion to their existing holdings. Shareholders value pre-emption because it enables them to protect their stake in the company from dilution. They can retain what proportionate voting strength they possess and, if the company becomes progressively more profitable, they have an exceptionally favourable outlet for funds at their disposal.

6–28 It used to be left to companies themselves to determine who should make decisions about issuing and allotting further shares. There is no general common law principle that requires giving existing shareholders a pre-emptive claim on any new shares. In *Mutual Life Insurance Co. of New York v. Rank Organisation Ltd.*,[47] it was said that, in the

---

[46] *cf.* Yellow Book, 4.16 *et seq.*
[47] [1985] B.C.L.C. 11.

absence of a contrary stipulation in a company's regulations, "no shareholder . . . has any right . . . to expect that his fractional interest in the company would remain for ever constant."[48] In that case, the defendant proposed to issue further shares without giving all of its shareholders a first option on them. Principally in order to avoid having to comply with United States securities regulations, it proposed to offer the shares to all its members except the American shareholders. This was challenged as being unfairly discriminatory. But it was upheld on the grounds that company law does not invariably require identity of treatment and there was no evidence, nor indeed any allegation, that the decision there was prompted by some improper motive. A court might possibly prohibit directors offering further shares to all members on a pro rata basis where the directors knew that a minority shareholder who would dearly like to take up his proportion of shares is temporarily short of funds. Such action was held to be unlawful in the special circumstances of one English unreported case, *Pennell v. Venida Investments Ltd.*[49] Yet in a well known American case, decided in a State where pre-emption was compulsory, it was said that directors are "not to blame for a shareholder's failure to obtain the money necessary for him to avail himself of his pre-emption rights."[50]

6–29 The 1983 Act makes pre-emption compulsory for every company and pre-emption must apply to equity securities for which a Stock Exchange listing is sought. According to section 23 of the 1983 Act:

> "a company proposing to allot any equity securities shall not allot any of those securities on any terms to any person unless it has made an offer to each person who holds relevant shares . . . to allot to him on the same or more favourable terms a proportion of those securities which is as nearly as practicable equal to the proportion in nominal value held by him of the aggregate of [the] shares. . . ."

Thus, for example, in a situation like that in the *Rank Organisation* case above, the American shareholders also would now be entitled to a first option on the new shares. The offer need not be a mathematically exact *pro rata* one; a proportion that is "as nearly as practicable" equal suffices. An offer under the section must remain open for at least 21 days.[51] Any shareholder may renounce his pre-emption rights in favour of

---

[48] [1985] B.C.L.C. 11 at 24. In *Kerry Co-Operative Creameries Ltd. v. An Bord Bainne* [1991] I.L.R.M. 851 this principle was applied to industrial and provident societies.

[49] Templeman J., July 25, 1984; discussed in Burridge, "Wrongful Rights Issues" (1981) 44 Mod. L. Rev. 40.

[50] *Hyman v. Velsical Corp.* (1951) 342 111; App. 489, 97 N.R. (2d) 122.

[51] *cf. Re Thundercrest Ltd.* [1995] 1 B.C.L.C. 117.

somebody else.[52] This statutory pre-emption right does not apply, or applies only partly, in the following circumstances.

6–30 A private company by its memorandum or articles of association may exclude or vary the right; any provisions in a private company's regulations that are inconsistent with the right take precedence over it.[53] Some might argue that private companies should not be allowed to contract out of the statutory requirements so easily.

6–31 The right does not apply to shares that are being allotted for a consideration wholly or partly other than cash.[54] This leaves companies relatively free to acquire property and other non-cash assets in return for their shares. But this also presents opportunities for easily evading what the section broadly seeks to achieve.

6–32 Where authority exists under section 20 of the 1983 Act to make an allotment, then the articles of association or the general meeting by special resolution may waive, either wholly or partly, the pre-emption requirement.[55] In order that such a waiver be effective, the authority to make the allotment must be in force; waiver must have been recommended by the directors; and the notice proposing the special resolution must be accompanied by the directors' written statement, giving reasons for waiving the right, telling the price to be paid for the shares in question and justify[ing]" that amount.

6–33 Only "equity securities" carry the right of pre-emption.[56] By these are meant shares that are not subject to any ceiling on the amounts that may be distributed to their holders by way of dividends and capital, and rights to subscribe for or to convert into such shares. Equity securities, therefore, are principally "ordinary" shares and "preference" shares where the preference is only in respect of dividends or capital.

6–34 There then is a special provision for equity securities of a particular class where the company's regulations give their holders a preemptive right in any further issues of those shares. Where the company offers any additional shares in the class to the class members on a pro rata basis and the offer is accepted, or alternatively the offeree renounces

---

[52] Subject, of course, to any restrictions in the company's regulations against admitting new shareholders into the company.
[53] s. 23(10).
[54] s. 23(4). *cf. Siemens A.G. v. Nold* (Case C–42/95) [1997] 1 B.C.L.C. 291.
[55] s. 24.
[56] For definition, see s.23(13).

his right to them, there is no general obligation to offer those shares to all equity shareholders proportionately.[57]

6–35 Special provision is also made for shares held under an employees' share scheme, *i.e.* a scheme designed to encourage or facilitate a company's employees to acquire its shares. According to section 23(1)(a), the holders of those shares must be offered a proportionate amount of any further equity that is being issued. But where it is proposed to allot shares under such a scheme, there is no obligation to offer them to the other shareholders on a pro rata basis.[58] In *Hogg v. Cramphorn Ltd.*[59] it was held that it was a breach of their fiduciary duties for directors, in an attempt to defeat a take-over bid, to establish an employees' share scheme of which they themselves were the trustees, and arrange for the company to lend money to the scheme so that it could subscribe for a large block of shares in the company.

6–36 A company that contravenes the statutory pre-emption requirements and every officer knowingly involved in the breach is liable jointly or severally to compensate shareholders for all loss, damages and expenses arising therefrom; which right of action is subject to a two years' limitation period.[60] But this statutory remedy does not preclude having the register of members rectified in an appropriate case where, under the pre-emption rules, the shares in question should have been allotted to the plaintiff rather than to the persons in whose name they stand registered.[61]

"Bonus" Shares

6–37 Except where the articles of association provide otherwise, or the company is insolvent or its accumulated losses exceed retained profits, profits earned in the past and that were placed in reserve may be drawn upon in order to pay dividends.[62] Often, however, sizeable sums that build up in the profit and loss account or the reserves are capitalised. That is to say, those funds are used in order to finance a further issue of the company's shares, which are then distributed free to the existing members. By free here means that the reserves are used to pay for those shares either entirely or in part. For example, say over £30,000 has accumulated in the profit and loss account and it is de-

---

[57] s.23(2), (3).
[58] s.23(6).
[59] [1967] Ch. 254.
[60] s.23(11).
[61] *Re Thundercrest Ltd.* [1995] 1 B.C.L.C. 117.
[62] 1983 Act, Pt IV (ss. 45-51).

cided that this sum should be capitalised; and say the company's issued share capital is 25,000 shares of £1 each. Capitalisation would mean every shareholder being given one and one-fifth shares for each share that he owns. A similar method can be used to pay up unpaid amounts outstanding on shares. Take the same figures as above but say that only 10 pence has been paid up on the £1 shares. In a capitalisation, 90 pence per share could be taken from the profit and loss account to pay up the unpaid amount on each of these shares.

6–38 Companies capitalise retained earnings principally to prevent the balance sheet from appearing to be misleading, so that the figure representing capital corresponds more closely to the amounts originally invested and what has been ploughed back into the business. Some shareholders, moreover, may be pleased with their apparent windfall and the more impecunious of them may be tempted to sell off what they obtain as a bonus. Another motive for capitalising is to deter take-over bidders with their eyes on the company's bank balances, in that capitalised reserves can only be paid out *in specie* to the shareholders under the elaborate sections 72-77 capital reduction procedure[63] or through the special procedures for companies purchasing or redeeming their own shares.[64]

6–39 Article 130 of Table A empowers the general meeting, on the directors' recommendation, to capitalise reserves and other amounts that are available for distribution as dividends. Sums that are capitalised in this way must be "applied on behalf of the members who would have been entitled to receive the same if the same had been distributed by way of dividend and in the same proportions. . ." In other words, the amounts of the bonus shares allotted, or amounts paid on shares that were not fully paid up, are to be in the same proportion as shareholders are entitled to on distributions of dividends. Article 131 of Table A gives the directors authority to take various measures to give effect to a resolution to capitalise. The 1983 Act inserts a new regulation here, article 130A, which authorises capitalisation of retained earnings, which on account of that Act's rules against paying dividends from capital are not available for distribution; but this can be done only by way of financing an allotment of fully paid bonus shares.

Share Premiums

6–40 It is common in successful companies to issue shares at a premium, *i.e.* at a price above their par or nominal value, *e.g.* £1 shares at

---

[63] See below, paras 11–35 *et seq*.
[64] See below, paras 7–49 *et seq*.

£1.60. The excess over par is called the share premium. These premiums are subject to the same general principles as apply to calls. Under article 5 of Table A, it is for the directors to decide whether to issue shares at a premium and the size of any premium. Although the courts hesitate to interfere with essentially business decisions, like the issue price for shares (provided it is above par), it cannot be doubted that flagrant abuse of the share-issuing power for discriminatory or self-serving reasons would be deemed to be a breach of fiduciary duties and, in appropriate circumstances, might provide the basis of "oppression" under section 205 of the 1963 Act.[65] A very low issue price could be evidence of discrimination that calls for justification in that, apart from any impact the share issue may have on relative voting strengths within the company, the exceptionally favourable issue terms prevent the company from raising more funds than it otherwise could have and gives the new shareholders an extremely lucrative investment opportunity. But there is no overriding duty on the directors or the company to allot shares for as high a premium as can be obtained in the market; nor is it *per se* wrong to allot shares at par even though other investors are prepared to pay a substantial premium for them. In *Hilder v. Dexter*[66] a company, in order to raise working capital, issued shares at par and gave options to take further shares at par at some later stage. When the price of its shares rose significantly in the market the holders of those options sought to exercise them. It was held that there is no "law" which obliges a company to issue its shares above par because they are saleable at a premium in the market.[67]

6–41 How a company deals with the premium it obtains on issuing shares is regulated by section 62 of the 1963 Act. The aggregate amount or value of any premium received must be placed in a share premium account and that sum is treated mostly in the same way as contributed capital. It can only be repaid to the shareholders through the cumbersome capital reduction mechanism set out in sections 72-77.[68] This sum, however, may be used either to finance the issue to existing members of fully paid up "bonus" shares; or to defray the company's preliminary expenses or the cost of issuing shares or debentures in the company, or to pay any commission or discount on such an issue.

---

[65] See below, paras 10–73 *et seq*.
[66] [1902] A.C. 474.
[67] *ibid.* at 480.
[68] For where the company proposes to purchase its own shares which have been issued at a premium, see 1990 Act, s.207(2)(f).

Brokerage and Commissions

6–42 Where a company uses a financial intermediary to attract subscribers for its shares, it is permitted to pay the customary brokerage.[69] Companies, moreover, are permitted by section 54(1) of the 1963 Act to pay commission of at most 10 per cent, not alone to persons who procure or agree to procure subscribers, but also to those who subscribe for or agree to subscribe for its shares. Although this provision envisages primarily paying underwriting commissions, *i.e.* commissions to financiers who agree to take up any shares being offered to the public that the public do not subscribe for, it is not by its terms confined to this situation. Any commission paid must be authorised by the articles of association; must not exceed 10 per cent of the share's issue price or such lower amount as the articles may stipulate; and the amount and rate of commission, and the number of shares involved, must be disclosed in the prospectus or in the statement in lieu of prospectus as the case may be.[70] Any commission paid, either with the company's own shares or from its "capital money", that does not satisfy these requirements is an unlawful application of the company's capital and is *ultra vires*.[71] The 1963 Act permits applying funds standing in the share premium account to pay these commissions.[72] It would appear that companies may use undistributed profits to this end.

Calls

6–43 When a company allots shares to a subscriber it does not invariably insist on the full amount due on them being paid up there and then. Instead, the shares may be only partly paid up and further payments are deferred until shareholders are called upon to make them; although the practice of having partly paid shares is dying out. Often questions about the accuracy of statements contained in the prospectus[73] and about ownership of and title to shares[74] arise in the context of disputes about liability for calls. A member who disposes of his shares is no longer liable for calls on them.[75] It has been held that, where a shareholder petitions for an arrangement with his creditors and subse-

---

[69] 1963 Act, s.59(3).

[70] *Quere* whether this is consistent with Art. 8(2) of the E.C. Second Directive on Company Law?

[71] 1963 Act, s.59(2).

[72] s. 62(2)(b).

[73] *e.g. Aaron's Reefs v. Twiss* [1896] A.C. 273.

[74] *e.g. Blackstaff Flax Spinning & Weaving Co. v. Cameron* [1899] 1 I.R. 252.

[75] *Re Discoverers' Finance Corp., Lindlar's Case* [1910] 1 Ch. 207, affirmed 1 Ch. 312; see below, para. 9–31.

quently the company makes calls on those shares, the call is not a debt provable in the arrangement.[76]

6–44 The 1963 Act allows companies, whose articles of association so provide, to differentiate between shareholders in the amounts of and times for paying calls, and to accept payments of unpaid amounts although they have not been called up.[77] Provisions to this effect are contained in articles 20 and 21 of Table A. The latter article authorises the company to pay not more than 5 per cent interest on uncalled amounts that have been paid up. Article 15 of Table A authorises the directors from time to time to make calls on unpaid amounts on shares, provided that no call shall exceed a quarter of the share's nominal value or be payable within a month of the time when the last preceding call should have been paid. While the courts will not interfere with most determinations regarding calls, on the grounds that they are primarily matters of business policy to be decided by the board, on a number of occasions calls have been set aside on the grounds that they were unfairly discriminatory. In *Galloway v. Hallé Concerts Society*,[78] the plaintiffs had been in dispute with the directors, had been slow in paying up calls in the past and had not paid anything on a third call. Because of this, the directors resolved to call up all outstanding amounts on their shares. It was held that these circumstances did not furnish sufficient justification for treating the plaintiffs so differently from other shareholders — for violating the "implied condition of equality between shareholders in a company".[79] Not alone will a court declare void and enjoin a call made in those circumstances, but it was held in *Alexander v. Automatic Telephone Co.*[80] that shareholders who had paid up over half the nominal amount on their shares could sue directors who, without disclosing it to the plaintiffs, allotted a considerable number of the company's shares to themselves and made no calls whatsoever on them. Procedural irregularities in the way directors make calls can render them invalid, like where directors were not properly appointed, where there was no quorum when they met and where the number of members fell below what the articles required; but not every procedural slip-up is fatal to a call.

---

[76] *Re Ligoniel Spinning Co.* [1900] 1 I.R. 250.
[77] s.66.
[78] [1915] 2 Ch. 233.
[79] *ibid.* at 239.
[80] [1900] 2 Ch. 56; see below, para. 10–32.

INVESTOR PROTECTION

6–45 One of the earliest major concerns of company law, which was the focus of many of the leading decisions in the field around the end of the last century, was to protect investors against being duped into putting their money into financially unsound companies. Before the Companies Acts addressed themselves to this matter, there were two governing principles. Where the investor simply acquires securities from an existing shareholder or holder of debentures, the maxim *caveat emptor* applies; the purchaser buys at his own risk and there is no legal obligation on the seller to disclose material information that might influence the decision to buy. However, the seller who provided inaccurate information in order to make the sale might in the circumstance be liable in tort for deceit or for negligent misrepresentation, or for breach of contract.

6–46 Where, on the other hand, the securities are acquired directly from the company in question, by way of application and allotment or from some intermediary who is disposing of them on the company's behalf, the company or intermediary and their agents must not make material misrepresentations and are under some duty to disclose relevant material information to the prospective investor. As Palles C.B. explained in one of the leading Irish cases on investor fraud, *Components Tube Co. v. Naylor*,[81] there is a

> "distinction between an ordinary purchase [of shares] and the purchase from a company of some of its shares. It is utterly immaterial to an ordinary purchaser to know what the vendor will do with the purchase money when he gets it. The purchaser has no further interest in it. But an applicant for shares in a company Is in a totally different position. His money becomes part of the capital of the company, and to him it is all important to know what sort of persons are to have control of his money when he has paid it, and how that money is to be applied, whether upon the enterprise itself or in remunerating, perhaps with lavish extravagance, those who have brought the company into existence."[82]

Or as FitzGibbon L.J. put it in another of the leading cases, *Aaron's Reefs Ltd. v. Twiss*,

> "Though *uberrima fidei*, *i.e.* the obligation to disclose everything known that could influence an intending subscriber, is not demanded of the authors of a prospectus, no case has, as yet, applied the rule of caveat emptor to an invitation to the public to take shares."[83]

---

[81] [1900] 2 I.R. 1.
[82] *ibid.* at 651, quoting Lindley L.J. in *Twycross v. Grant* (1877) 2 C.P.D. 469 at 483.
[83] [1895] 2 I.R. 207 at 269.

Although strictly speaking agreements to allot shares are not *uberrimae fidei*, they are so in practice because non-disclosure by a company that solicits investment in itself is sufficient basis for the court to set aside the allotment where rescission remains possible.

Promoters

6–47 A company promoter is simply someone who plays an instrumental role in forming a company and getting it going. Sometimes promoters are professionals, like merchant banks and investment houses that specialise in establishing companies and getting the public to invest in them. But a sole trader who, like Mr Salomon in the *Salomon & Co.* case[84] takes steps to convert a business into a registered company, is just as much a promoter. In the past the duties and responsibilities of company promoters generated a very sizeable quantity of litigation. Many of those cases concerned elaborate schemes devised by fraudsters to persuade individuals to invest in worthless enterprises. In the popular mind, the word promoter had connotations of a high-living crooked financier who prospered from complex schemes of questionable financial merit. The classic definition of the word is anyone who "undertakes to form a company with reference to a given project, and to get it going and . . . takes the necessary steps to accomplish that purpose."[85] Whether a person is a promoter and when does a promotion begin and end are questions of fact, although there are numerous authorities indicating where the lines have been drawn.[86] Promotion includes "floating off" a company's capital to the general public, such as by publishing a prospectus offering shares or debentures for sale or for subscription.[87]

Remuneration

6–48 Professional promoters especially will require remuneration for their services to the company in getting it going. Their payment can take various forms, for instance, a fixed sum of money, an option on the company's shares[88] or a commission or a direct profit on sales of property to the company. The *Salomon*-type promoter may look to some paper profit by transferring the business to the new company at a favourable price. Any contract for either reimbursing expenses or for remuneration made, on the company's behalf, before it was incorpo-

---

[84] [1897] A.C. 22; see above, para. 3–09.

[85] *Twycross v. Grant* (1877) 2 C.P. D. 469 at 541.

[86] *e.g. Erlanger v. New Sombrero Phosphate Co.* (1878) 3 App. Cas. 1218 and *Gluckstein v. Barnes* [1900] A.C. 240.

[87] *Lagunas Nitrate Co. v. Lagunas Syndicate* [1899] 2 Ch. 392 at 428.

rated will not bind the company unless it subsequently ratifies the contract.[89] It would appear that any contract for services must be made before those services were rendered, because past services are not consideration;[90] although the promoter may be entitled to some payment on a *quantum meruit* basis. Article 80 of Table A authorises the directors to pay the expenses incurred in promoting and registering the company. Where securities are being offered to the public, the prospectus must disclose promoters' profits and remuneration.[91]

Duties-Transactions with the Company

6–49 On account of the tremendous influence over embryo and infant companies that promoters possess, there are significant opportunities for and, indeed, temptations to make a profit for themselves at the company's or the investors' expense. The law reports record countless instances of promoter fraud, the commonest kind perhaps being the sale by them to the company of their own property at inflated prices. Promoters are subject to the same general fiduciary standards[92] as apply to those other instruments of vicarious capitalism, company directors. They are not permitted to make secret profits from their activities; in view of their situation of at least potential conflict of interests, they must disclose all relevant matters to the company.

6–50 Because promoters frequently are a company's first shareholders and directors, a particularly vexed question has been in what circumstances does disclosure to the company constitute disclosure to themselves and, accordingly, is not effective disclosure. The rule is that it is "incumbent upon the promoters to take care that in forming the company they provide it with an executive, *i.e.*, with a board of directors, who shall both be aware that the property which they are asked to buy is the property of the promoters, and who shall be competent and impartial judges as to whether the purchase ought or ought not to be made."[93] In one case a promoter-director's contention that the company had been informed of all the profits he had made was rejected as absurd, because disclosure "[i]s not the most appropriate word to use when a person who plays many parts announces to himself in one character what he has done and is doing in another."[94] It nevertheless has

88 *e.g. Hilder v. Dexter* [1902] A.C. 474.
89 See below, paras 13–07 *et seq.*
90 *Re Eddystone Marine Insurance Co.* [1893] 3 Ch. 9
91 1963 Act, 3rd schedule, para. 13
92 See generally, P. Finn, *Fiduciary Obligations* (1977).
93 *Erlanger v. New Sombrero Phosphate Co.* (1878) 3 App. Cas. 1218 at 1236.
94 *Gluckstein v. Barnes* [1900] A.C. 240 at 249.

been held that informing all the initial shareholders, even though they are dominated by the promoters, satisfies the disclosure rule where the then shares have not changed hands afterwards and new shares are not issued to outsiders. This was in the *Salomon & Co.* case,[95] where the plaintiff had promoted a company that acquired his boot manufacturing business at what may have been an excessive price. Assuming that the price was exorbitant, it was said that "when all the shareholders are perfectly cognizant of the conditions under which the company is formed and the conditions of the purchase, it is impossible to contend that the company is being defrauded."[96] In stressing that the disclosure rule is satisfied where approval for an acquisition from promoters is given "by all the shareholders who ever were, or were likely to be, members of the company".[97] Lord Watson intimated that disclosure of a promoter's profit to all the then shareholders does not discharge the fiduciary responsibility where it is envisaged, for instance, that the promoters will dispose of their shares in the company in the not too distant future.[98]

6–51 Section 32 of the 1983 Act introduced new rules in order to protect p.l.c.s from promoter fraud.[99] These apply where any person who is a subscriber to a p.l.c.'s memorandum of association and who, within two years of the company becoming entitled to do business, sells it some non-cash asset in return for a consideration worth at least one-tenth of the company's issued share capital. This requirement may prevent recurrence of the kind of events as arose in one of the classics of promoter fraud, *Erlanger v. New Sombrero Phospbate Co.*[100] There a syndicate bought leases on mines and later formed a company with "dummy" directors, which acquired those leases. The directors then offered shares in the company to the general public without the full history of the leases being disclosed. If this happened today and the acquisition took place within two years of the company being entitled to do business, and assuming that the vendors of the leases would be treated as the "subscribers", an independent account of the entire arrangement would be a matter of public record, so that investors would then know exactly the risk they were undertaking.

---

95 [1897] A.C. 22.
96 *ibid.* at 33.
97 *ibid.* at 37.
98 *cf. Old Dominion Copper Mining & Smelting Co. v. Lewisohn*, 210 U.S. 206 (1907) with *Old Dominion Copper Mining & Smelting Co. v. Bigelow*, 89 N.E. 193 (1909), affirmed 225 U.S. 111 (1912).
99 For details, see below, paras 6–57 *et seq.*
100 (1878) 3 App. Cas. 1218.

The Company's Remedies

6–52 In *Lagunas Nitrate Co. v. Lagunas Syndicate,*[101] promoters made a sizeable profit in forming a company, of which they became the directors and original shareholders, and then issued a prospectus for the company, on foot of which many investors acquired shares in the company. Subsequently, the company sued its promoters to recover their profit on the grounds that full disclosure had not been made to the shareholders. Upholding the judgment against the promoters, Lindley M.R. drew attention to one remarkable aspect of the case, that not one individual who in response to the prospectus had subscribed for shares had brought a claim against the company or the promoters. Since, in principle, a company is legally separate from its shareholders and since the real complaint in cases like this is that investors have been duped into buying the company's shares, one might have expected that the action by the company itself would be struck out. It, however, was concluded that:

> "it does not follow that the . . . company, in its corporate capacity, may not prove a case entitling it to relief. It may prove such concealment of material facts or such misrepresentations as to entitle it to repudiate the contracts [with its promoters] unless [they] can show that the members of the company knew the real truth, and were not, therefore, imposed upon [because] [tlhe . . . company, although, in one sense formed when registered, was not completely formed as contemplated by the promoters, until a prospectus had been issued and a large capital had been subscribed. The issue of the prospectus was the last act of promotion."[102]

6–53 A company's principal remedies for breach of promoters' duties is rescission of any contract with them and disgorgement of their profits. One of the best known instances of disgorgement is *Gluckstein v. Barnes,*[103] where the defendant was a member of a syndicate that bought the Olympia exhibition hall for £140,000, then formed a company and sold it the hall for £180,000, disclosing a profit of £40,000. But there was no mention of an additional profit of £20,000 made by previously having bought up various charges on the property. In an action brought by the liquidator, it was held that an impermissible secret profit had been made and that an equivalent amount had to be returned to the company.

6–54 Provided it acts promptly after discovering the secret profit and that *restitutio in integrum* remains possible, the company can have the

---

[101] [1899] 2 Ch. 392.
[102] *ibid.* at 428, 429.
[103] [1900] A.C. 240.

contract to purchase property from the promoters rescinded and set aside. For instance in the *Erlanger* case,[104] when the new shareholders discovered the truth, they had the original directors removed and replaced by independent directors, who then sought to have the contract to acquire the leases set aside. Rescission was ordered, one Law Lord observing that "those who deal inequitably with a company know that it must necessarily be slow in its proceedings, and are not entitled to complain that time elapes . . . unless the delay is excessive."[105] By contrast, in the *Lagunas* case"[106] which was identical in most respects except that all allegations of fraud against the defendants were withdrawn, the court by a majority declined to order rescission because the assets acquired from the promoters had been transformed so much in the meantime that it was impossible to restore the parties to their original positions. There is authority to the effect that secret profits made on property the promoter owned before the promotion actually commenced are not recoverable by the company; in such a case the only remedy is rescission provided that *restitutio in integrum* is still possible.[107] Where, however, this principle would lead to injustice, there is a tendency to hold that the promotion in fact commenced before the property was bought[108] or that the promoters committed deceit or "equitable fraud" and, therefore, are liable in damages or for equitable compensation.[109]

Investors' Remedies

6–55 Promoters' legal obligations are owed primarily to the company and investors are indirectly protected against promoter fraud to the extent that a company can sue promoters who violate their duties to it.[110] If it is shown that a promoter defrauded the company but it does not sue him because he controls it, it is said that there has been a "fraud on a minority" and an individual shareholder will be permitted to commence an action against the promoter in the company's name.[111] Where the promoter deals directly with individuals and induces them to invest in the company, they may have a direct right of action against the promoter.[112] Where the promoter defrauds the company, such as by

---

104 above, n. 100.
105 (1878) 3 App. Cas. 1218 at 1282.
106 above, n. 101.
107 *Re Cape Breton Co.* (1885) 29 Ch.D. 795 and *Burland v. Earle* [1902] A.C. 83.
108 *e.g. Gluckstein v. Barnes* [1900] A.C. 240 at 252.
109 *cf. Re Leeds & Hanley Theatre of Varieties Ltd.* [1902] 2 Ch. 809.
110 *e.g. Lagunas* case, above, n. 101.
111 *e.g.* the classic cases on "fraud on a minority", *Atwool v. Merryweatber* (1867) L.R. 5 Eq. 464n and *Foss v. Harbottle* (1843) 2 Hare 461.
112 *e.g. Jury v. Stoker* (1882) 9 L.R. Ir. 385.

selling it property at an inflated price and, while under the promoter's control, the company then induces others to acquire securities in it without fully disclosing the promoter's profit, the investor who acted on the misrepresentation may have a remedy against the company. In *Components Tube Co. v. Naylor*,[113] for example, the defendant subscribed for shares in the plaintiff company on foot of a prospectus issued on its behalf but which, fraudulently, suppressed the fact that the company had acquired its bicycle tube manufacturing business from its promoters, who stood to make handsome profits from the flotation. Accordingly, the promoters had contravened their obligation of full disclosure to directors "who shall be competent and impartial judges as to whether the purchase ought or ought not to be made."[114] It was held that the defendant ought to be able to rescind his agreement to take the shares because the promoters/directors had a duty to "the future shareholders who were to form the real company";[115] the company accepted funds from the defendant to enable it to complete an acquisition "which in fact was an unreality and a fraud, [and] was not binding upon the company."[116]

6–56 It would appear, however, that damages will not be awarded against a company that wrongfully induced persons to subscribe for shares in it; in such circumstances the only remedy against it is rescission .[117] But the investor may be able to recover damages from the promoters or directors who were responsible for the inducement.[118] Persons who invest in consequence of an offer contained in a prospectus also have a statutory right of action for misstatement under section 49 of the 1963 Act;[119] they may possibly have an action under section 44 of that Act in respect of omissions from the prospectus.[120]

Acquisitions from p.l.c.'s First Members

6–57 There are numerous instances of companies getting into financial difficulties because they paid excessive prices to buy property from their promoters or controlling directors.[121] While such transactions may be voidable, any right to rescind is lost when considerable time elapses

---

113 [1900] 2 I.R. 1.
114 *ibid.* at 69, referring to the *Erlanger* case, above, n. 100.
115 *ibid.* at 71, referring to the *Erlanger* case.
116 *ibid.* at 70.
117 *Houldsworth v. City of Glasgow Bank* (1880) 5 App. Cas. 317, below, para. 6–65.
118 See below, paras 6–67 *et seq.*
119 See below, paras 6–103 *et seq.*
120 See below, para. 6–107.
121 *e.g. Salomon & Co.* case [1897] A.C. 22; above, para. 3–09.

or third party rights would be prejudiced.[122] And so long as the vendors retain control of the company, it is unlikely that they will institute a claim for negligence or breach of fiduciary duty against themselves. Sections 32 and 33 of the 1983 Act now impose on p.l.c.s valuing and reporting requirements in order to prevent one-sided transactions from occurring during the company's first two years' commercial existence. The transactions affected must also be approved by an ordinary resolution of the company. These provisions apply to an agreement between a new p.l.c. and any subscriber to its memorandum of association, or between a company that registered as a p.l.c. under section 18 and any of its members at the time of registration, whereby during the initial period that person is to transfer what may be called a costly asset. It is hard to understand why this requirement was not extended to agreements with all promoters. The initial period is either two years from the time the new p.l.c. became entitled to do business or two years from the date the company was registered under section 18. A costly asset in this context means any property or interest in property, other than cash, and that is worth at least one-tenth of the nominal value of the company's issued share capital.[123] These requirements do not apply to agreements made by the company in the ordinary course of its business or to arrangements made under the court's supervision.

6–58 The valuer's qualifications and powers are the same as those set down for valuations under sections 30 and 31 of the 1983 Act.[124] His report must be given to the company during the six months immediately preceding the date of the agreement and must be circulated to all the company's members who are entitled to all notices of ordinary resolutions, and to the intended transferor. There must be stated in the report the consideration to be received by and given by the company, specifying what cash amounts are involved and the method and date of valuation. The report must contain or be accompanied by a note on the same matters as must be specified where shares are being allotted for a non-cash consideration,[125] including a statement that the company is obtaining in exchange not less than what it is giving. A copy of the report and of the resolution approving the transfer must be delivered to the registrar of companies.

6–59 Where, in the sense of section 32 of the 1983 Act, a p.l.c. agrees within the initial period to buy a costly asset from any of its first members, and the seller had not received the relevant report or knew or

[122] See below, paras 6–61 *et seq.*
[123] *cf.* 1983 Act, s.2(3), (4); definition of cash and of non-cash assets.
[124] See below, paras 7–23 *et seq.*
[125] See below, para. 7–24.

ought to have known that the statutory provisions were violated, the agreement, so far as it is not carried out, is void and the company may recover either the consideration it gave or its monetary equivalent.[126] Where the consideration for any such agreement is or includes an allotment of shares in the company, the allottee is liable to reimburse the company the same amount as must be paid by other persons to whom shares are allotted improperly for a non-cash consideration[127] as must subsequent holders of shares unless they are protected by the section 26(4) defence for good faith purchasers for value.[128]

Rescission of Agreements to Buy Shares

6–60 Rescission is one of the principal remedies where parties have entered into a transaction under some material mistake.[129] It involves having the entire transaction cancelled and any purchase money refunded together with interest and expenses — which in this context usually means obliging the company to repay the investment and requiring that the shareholder's name be removed from the register of members. One rationale for this remedy here is that, since an innocent principal is not liable in damages for the fraud of an agent who exceeds the scope of his authority, and since in any event a shareholder cannot recover damages against the company in respect of the shares,[130] "in relation to retaining a benefit obtained through the fraud [the company] cannot be in a better position than the fraudulent agent himself."[131] Rescission, however, may be awarded even in the absence of any fraud; it has been said that "a contract to [subscribe for] shares may be rescinded if it has been induced by a material allegation which was not true, even if there was no fraud in the matter."[132] The main advantages of this remedy is that it can be obtained against the company itself and it is not dependent on proving fraud. It is often sought by investors seeking to disclaim liability for calls, on the grounds that they were unlawfully induced to subscribe for shares, *Aaron's Reefs Ltd. v. Twiss*[133] and *Components Tube Co. v. Naylor*[134] being the leading Irish examples.

---

[126] 1983 Act, s.32(7).

[127] See below, para. 7–83.

[128] See below, para. 7–92.

[129] See generally, Lord Gough & G. Jones, *The Law of Restitution* (4th ed., 1993), Chap. 8 and A.K. Turner & R. Sutton, *Actionable Non-Disclosure* (2nd ed., 1990).

[130] *Houldsworth v. City of Glasgow Bank* (1880) 5 App. Cas. 317.

[131] *Components Tube Co. v. Naylor* [1900] 2 I.R. 1 at 37.

[132] *ibid.* at 26, referring to *Karberg's Case, Metropolitan Coal Consumers Association* [1982] 3 Ch. 1.

[133] [1895] 2 I.R. 207, [1896] A.C. 273.

[134] [1900] 2 I.R. 1.

6–61 In order to succeed in a claim for rescission, the following conditions must be satisfied. The defendant's representation of fact must have been addressed to the plaintiff or it must have been known that the plaintiff's application for the securities was based on it. The inaccuracy must have been material or must have induced the plaintiff to acquire the securities. While as a general rule mere non-disclosure of some fact exclusively within a seller's knowledge is not a sufficient basis for rescission, this is not so where suppression of certain facts distorts the meaning of information that is volunteered;[135] nor is it so where the representation is a continuing one that, although originally correct, later becomes untrue.[136] Where the securities are acquired in response to a prospectus, then virtually no distinction is drawn between non-disclosure and misrepresentations.[137]

6–62 If an undue amount of time elapses before an investor looks for rescission or he deals with the securities in a manner that suggests affirmation of the purchase (such as attempts to sell the securities, acceptance of dividends, participating in general meetings etc.), the right to rescind is lost. In the *Aaron's Reefs* case the rule about delay and its rationale were stated as follows:

> "Lapse of time without rescinding will furnish evidence of an intention to affirm the contract. But the cogency of this evidence depends upon the particular circumstances of the case and the nature of the contract in question. Where a person has contracted to take shares in a company and his name has been placed on the register, it has always been held that he must exercise his right of repudiation with extreme promptness after the discovery of the fraud or misrepresentation for this reason: the presence of his name on the register may have induced other persons to give credit to the company or to become members of it."[138]

There, a prospectus was issued in February 1890 offering 200,000 shares in a company that had acquired a gold mine of doubtful value in Venezuela. It was promised in so many words that dividends of 100 per cent per annum would be paid once work on the mine got under way. Only one shilling per share was to paid up in that year. The defendant, a resident of Co. Limerick, subscribed for 100 shares. When, a year later, a call of four shillings per share was made, he refused to pay it, which led to his shares being forfeited. In September 1891 the company sued him for the unpaid calls, to which in December of that year he entered the defence that the prospectus was untrue in material re-

---

[135] *e.g. Aaron's Reefs Ltd. v. Twiss* [1896] A.C. 273.
[136] *e.g. Breiss v. Woolley* [1954] A.C. 337.
[137] *e.g. Component Tube Co. v. Naylor* [1900] 2 I.R. 1.
[138] [1896] A.C. 294.

spects. The fraud practised on him was unearthed only at the trial of the action, which was lengthy. It was held that he had not lost his right to rescind, since where there is fraud or breach of fiduciary duty time begins to run from when the truth is discovered. But in the case of innocent misrepresentation, it would appear that the right to rescind is barred by mere lapse of time — of such time as would enable a reasonably diligent person to discover the truth.[139]

6–63 Nor will rescission be ordered where *restitutio in integrum* becomes impossible or would disrupt third party rights.[140] But a change in the value of shares is no bar to rescission.[141] Where the acquisition of shares was induced by fraud the courts are particularly ready to grant the innocent party rescission.[142] It was held in *Oakes v. Turquand*[143] that rescission will not be ordered once proceedings have commenced to wind up a company, because third parties may have been dealing with the company on the basis that the person now claiming rescission was a shareholder. And in *Seddon v. North Eastern Salt Co.*[144] it was held that, in the absence of fraud or of total failure of consideration, once a contract to transfer shares is executed rescission will not be awarded against the vendor. There the defendant bought all the shares in a company having, he alleged, been led to believe that it was just about breaking even, when in fact it was incurring sizeable losses. His claim for rescission was defeated because by then the sale was completed. It is provided by section 51 of the 1963 Act, however, that one who buys shares from an intermediary to whom they were allotted with a view to them being offered to the public is to be treated as a subscriber for shares with all the rights of a subscriber.[145] Section 122 of the 1963 Act provides for machinery whereby a person who is entitled to rescind against the company can apply to have the register of members rectified.

Compensation

6–64 By compensation is meant financial recompense for the loss suffered, this being principally in the nature of damages either for breach of contract, in tort or for breach of statutory duty; it also includes indemnity and equitable compensation. A person who succeeds in ob-

---

139 *cf. Leaf v. International Galleries* [1950] 2 K.B. 86.
140 *Northern Bank Finance Corp. v. Charlton* [1979] I.R. 149.
141 *Armstrong v. Jackson* [1917] 2 K.B. 822.
142 *Spence v. Crawford* [1939] 3 All E.R. 271.
143 (1867) L.R. 2 H.L. 325; see *Tennant v. City of Glasgow Bank* (1879) 4 App. Cas. 615.
144 [1905] 1 Ch. 326.
145 See below, para. 6–87.

taining rescission will also be entitled to an indemnity against liabilities incurred by having made the investment—such as where the shares acquired carried unlimited liability.[146] The court's equitable jurisdiction includes the power to award compensation, as distinct from damages, where fiduciaries misapply property or otherwise violate their duties of good faith, and also where misrepresentations were made by persons other than strict fiduciaries;[147] though much of this latter area is now occupied by common law damages.

No Damages against the Company

6–65 It would appear that the investor who was defrauded or otherwise misled into subscribing for shares in a company will not be permitted to claim damages against the company itself. Accordingly, if he cannot obtain rescission, the only remedy is against the promoters, directors or whoever wrongfully induced him to buy the shares. This somewhat anomalous rule was laid down in *Houldsworth v. City of Glasgow Bank*,[148] where the plaintiff claimed damages against a company because its directors fraudulently induced him to subscribe for shares in it. Even though the purchaser of a chattel who is defrauded is allowed to retain it and sue for damages,[149] it was held that this option is not open to those who obtain shares by subscription. The reasons given were that to award damages here would be "[i]nconsistent with the contract [with the company] into which [the member] has entered, and by which he wishes to abide";[150] and for a member to claim damages here "[I]n truth. . . is trying to reconcile two inconsistent positions, mainly, that of shareholder and that of creditor of the whole body of shareholders including himself."[151]

6–66 This rule runs against the fundamental principle of the company's separate legal personality. Its real justification, however, would appear to be that rescission and indemnity will not be ordered because that would unduly prejudice outsiders; awarding damages against the company would have a similar effect in that the damages would deplete whatever fund the company has for paying its third party creditors. For the company to pay damages to disappointed subscribers for

---

146 *cf. Newbigging v. Adam* (1886) 34 Ch.D. 582.
147 See generally, R.P. Meagher et al., *Equity* (3rd ed., 1992), Chap. 23 and I.C. Spry, *Equitable Remedies* (3rd ed., 1984), Chap. 7.
148 (1880) 5 App. Cas. 317.
149 Sale of Goods Act 1893, s.53.
150 (1880) 5 App. Cas. at 325.
151 *ibid.* at 333. *cf.* Hornby (1956) 19 Mod. L. Rev. 54 and Gower, *ibid.* at 185. The principle in *Houldsworth* was reversed in Britain in s.11A of the Companies Act 1985.

its shares would be the equivalent of it repaying its capital in a manner not authorised by the Companies Acts. In *Houldsworth* the bank, which failed leaving enormous debts and whose shares carried unlimited liability, was being wound up when the plaintiff commenced his claim for damages (rescission then being impossible).[152] Another justification is the principle[153] that the fraud of an agent acting outside the scope of his authority does not bind the innocent principal and the view that, in situations like that in *Houldsworth*, where directors fraudulently induced the public to acquire the bulk of a company's shares, those directors should in this context be treated as acting beyond their authority.[154] It, nevertheless, is possible that damages would be awarded against the company where the duped shareholders are only a minority and where paying the award would not prejudice the company's creditors. Further, where the shares have been purchased from a third party, as contrasted with being subscribed for, it has been held that the *Houldsworth* principle does not preclude a right of action in damages nor subordinate any claim against the company.[155] The following are the principal heads under which damages may be claimed against those other than the company and, subject to *Houldsworth*, perhaps against the company too.

Deceit/Fraud

6–67 Persons who acquire securities in consequence of some fraudulent misrepresentation made to them have a cause of action in damages for deceit. In one of the early Irish examples, *Jury v. Stoker*,[156] the plaintiff acquired shares in the newly formed Cork Milling Co. on foot of a prospectus which stated, wrongly, that the vendor from whom the company purchased its mills would be investing £7,500 in the company. Subsequently, the company was wound up and the plaintiff lost his entire investment. It was held that in the circumstances the directors responsible for the prospectus were liable for his entire loss because they had deliberately misled the investors.

---

152 *Oakes v. Turquand* (1867) L.R. 2 H.L. 325.
153 *Armstrong v. Strain* [1952] 1 K.B. 232.
154 *cf.* Lord Blackburn in *Houldsworth* case (1880) 5 App. Cas. 317 at 338–341, discussing *Barwick v. English Joint Stock Bank* (1867) L.R. 2 Exch. 259. The *Houldsworth* case was decided before *Barwick* was overruled in *Lloyd v. Grace Smith & Co.* [1912] A.C. 716.
155 *Soden v. British & Commonwealth Holdings p.l.c.* [1998] A.C. 298.
156 (1882) 9 L.R.Ir. 385. A more recent instance is *Northern Bank Finance Corp. v. Charlton* [1979] I.R. 149, concerning the purchase of shares from an existing member.

6–68 The tort of deceit is somewhat narrowly defined. It must be shown that the defendant made, or authorised the making of, a false statement of fact so as to induce the plaintiff to acquire the securities in question and that the inducement worked. In *Derry v. Peek*[157] it was held that the misleading statement must have been made knowing it to be false or recklessly as to its truth or falsity. While mere omission to state some material fact,[158] or even gross negligence on the maker's part,[159] is not enough to establish deceit, non-disclosure in particular circumstances can be fraudulent. The governing principles on this matter were summed up as follows:

> "many facts and circumstances may be lawfully omitted, although some subscribers might be of opinion that these would have been of materiality as influencing the exercise of their judgment. But the statement of a portion of the truth, accompanied by suggestions and inferences which would be possible and credible if it contained the whole truth, but became neither possible nor credible whenever the whole truth is divulged, is . . . a false statement.
>
> [T]he true test [is], taking the whole thing together, was there a false representation? [It does not matter] by what means it is conveyed — by what trick or device or ambiguous language. . . If by a number of statements you intentionally give a false impression and induce a person to act upon it, it is not the less false although if one takes each statement by itself there may be a difficulty in showing that any specific statement is untrue."[160]

As regards causation, a person who reads a glowing prospectus and thereupon subscribes for shares in the company is not "bound to be able to explain with exact precision what was the mental process by which he was induced to act."[161]

6–69 The measure of damages for deceit is the difference between what was paid for the securities in question and their true value at the time they were bought.[162] But the actual market price will not invariably be used to fix the latter sum; account will be taken of subsequent events because they may well show that the shares in fact were worth far less than they appeared to be.[163] On the other hand, if the enterprise

---

157 (1889) 14 App. Cas. 337.

158 *Peek v. Gurney* (1873) L.R. 6 H.L. 377.

159 *Derry v. Peek* (1889) 14 App. Cas. 337.

160 *Aaron's Reefs Ltd. v. Twiss* [1896] A.C. 277 at 287, 281. A recent example of investor fraud is *Smith New Court Securities Ltd. v. Scrimgeour Vickers (Asset Management) Ltd.* [1997] A.C. 254.

161 [1896] A.C. 277 at 280.

162 *Davidson v. Tulloch* (1860) 3 Macq. 783; *McConnell v. Wright* [1903] 1 Ch. 546; *Northern Bank* case [1979] I.R. 149.

163 *Potts v. Miller* (1940) 64 C.L.R. 282.

proves to be a failure for reasons entirely extrinsic to the deceit or misrepresentation, a purchaser of its securities is not entitled to be compensated for losses arising from this fact;[164] although in practice it is difficult to distinguish between the causes of failure that were due to and that were wholly extrinsic to the wrong. Although the amount recoverable in damages is subject to the usual principles regarding causation, remoteness and mitigation, the victim of a fraud is entitled to be compensated for all loss directly flowing from the deceptive transaction, including consequential loss, and not merely loss that was reasonably foreseeable.[165] Where the deceptive statement is a term of the contract to buy the securities then the damages will cover any loss of expected profit.[166] Recently there has been movement toward giving some compensation in tort for loss of the bargain.

Negligent Misrepresentation

6–70 Many of the authorities on the liability of those who sell company securities to investors were decided long before *Donoghue v. Stevenson*[167] established a general obligation not to do what foreseeably may damage another and before *Hedley Byrne & Co. v. Heller & Partners Ltd.*[168] confirmed that this duty of care applied to economic or financial loss as well as to physical damage caused by another's negligence. Thus, in appropriate circumstances, a company offering shares for subscription, or a promoter who is seeking to induce another to buy shares in a company, must not through carelessness and possibly inadvertence give misleading relevant information. This duty may extend in special circumstances to one of taking reasonable steps to ensure that only correct information is given. In what particular circumstance liability under this head will arise depends on the precise nature of the relationship that exists between the purchaser and the defendant.[169] The same principles govern the measure of damages here as in deceit.

6–71 In *Securities Trust Ltd. v. Hugh Moore and Alexander*[170] a shareholder of the defendant company applied for and obtained from it a

---

[164] *Potts v. Miller* (1940) 64 C.L.R. 282.

[165] *Smith New Court* case [1997] A.C. 254.

[166] *cf. Archer v. Brown* [19841] 3 W.L.R. 356.

[167] [1932] A.C. 562.

[168] [1964] A.C. 465.

[169] Where the shares are purchased on the stock market, compare *Al Nakib Investments (Jersey) Ltd. v. Longcroft* [1990] 1 W.L.R. 1391 with *Possfund Custodian Trustees Ltd. v. Diamond* [1996] 1 W.L.R. 1351; see below, paras 6–102 *et seq. cf. Bank of Scotland v. 3i p.l.c.* [1993] B.C.L.C. 968, where the bank advanced funds for investment to a venture capital company.

[170] [1964] I.R. 417.

copy of its memorandum and articles of association. He held his shares in the company as trustee for the plaintiff. His application for the memorandum and articles was in his own name and the company was unaware that he held his shares in trust. The copy of the articles supplied to him contained an error which suggested that, on a winding up of the company, both its ordinary and its preference shareholders would participate in a distribution of surplus assets. On the faith of this, the plaintiff made several purchases of preference shares in the defendant at prices in excess of their true value. Subsequently, the error was discovered by the defendant and it notified the shareholder that the error existed in the copy of the articles supplied to him. On the winding up of the defendant, the plaintiff claimed to be entitled to participate in the distribution of surplus assets in respect of its holding of preference shares, which claim was rejected by the liquidator. Proceedings were then commenced for damages for negligent misrepresentation. This claim was dismissed on the grounds that the requisite degree of proximity, or relationship, between the plaintiff and the company did not exist. Davitt P.'s judgment hints obliquely that the liability-triggering relationship would have existed had the actual purchaser and plaintiff been the shareholder who was given a copy of the articles, especially in the light to the statutory obligation to provide all company members with copies of the memorandum and articles.[171] But even if this were so and causation was established, it still would have to be shown that the defendant was negligent or did not adopt such precautionary measures as were reasonably necessary.

Innocent Misrepresentation

6–72 As a general rule, a person who by a material misrepresentation, made innocently and not negligently, induces another to acquire shares is not thereby liable in damages.[172] If, however, the misrepresentation amounts to a warranty, then the party making it can be made liable in damages for breach of contract.[173] And liability for simple misrepresentation can arise where some exceptional relationship exists between the parties; for instance, equitable compensation has been awarded for breach of a fiduciary's duty of confidence.[174]

Criminal Penalties

6–73 Defrauding investors may constitute a criminal offence. Of spe-

[171] *cf. New Zealand Motor Bodies Ltd. v. Emslie* [1985] 2 N.Z.L.R. 569.

[172] See generally, R. Meagher et al., *Equity* (3rd ed., 1992), Chap. 13 and A.K. Turner & R. Sutton, *Actionable Non-Disclosure* (2nd ed., 1990).

[173] *Bank of Ireland v. Smith* [1966] I.R. 646 at 657–659.

[174] above, n. 172.

cial relevance to frauds in this context is section 84 of the Larceny Act 1861:

> "Whosoever, being a director . . . of any body corporate or public company, shall make, circulate or publish, or concur in making, circulating, or publishing, any written statement or account which he shall know to be false in any material particular, with intent . . . to induce any person to become a shareholder or partner therein shall be guilty of a misdemeanour. . . ."

That is to say, it is an offence for any director knowingly to issue a deceptive document with a view to inducing a person to invest in a company.[175] It would appear that private companies are "public" for the purposes of this section, since they are registered under a public Act.[176] In the leading case on this section, *R. v. Kylsant*,[177] it was held that a document can be false, even though no one statement in it is untrue, if the statements combined give a false impression; and that the criteria of deceit set out in the *Aaron's Reefs* case[178] are just as applicable. In *Kylsant* the company raised funds on foot of a prospectus that gave a comparatively favourable view of its financial position and, in particular, emphasised that substantial dividends had been paid every year over the previous twenty years. What the prospectus did not say was that for some years the company had been incurring losses in its business and the dividends came from exceptional profits that had been earned during the First World War. It was held that the defendant, the company's chairman, had been properly convicted in these circumstances.

INVESTOR PROTECTION IN PUBLIC SECURITIES ISSUES

6–74 It is almost unheard of for a company immediately after its incorporation to go straight to the general public in order to raise capital. As a general rule, a company will have been doing business for some time and, if it is proving to be a commercial success and wishes to expand further, it may choose to raise additional funds by appealing to the investing public to put money into the company. At times, the major shareholders may wish to divest themselves of all or part of their stake in the company for cash and, to that end, may offer their

---

175 See generally, J.W.C. Turner (ed.), *Russell on Crime* (12th ed., 1964), Vol. II, pp. 1122–1125 and A. Arlidge et al., *Arlidge and Parry on Fraud* (2nd eds., 1996), Chap. 8.

176 *R. v. Davies* [1955] 1 Q.B. 71.

177 [1932] 1 K.B. 442.

178 [1896] A.C. 273.

securities for sale to the public. An offer to the public of a large block of securities is called a flotation.[179] Where a company either directly or through an intermediary offers its shares or debentures to the public for subscription, a prospectus that complies with the 1963 Act's requirements must be issued and that Act's and the 1983 Act's rules regarding allotments must be satisfied.[180]

Modes of Issuing Securities to the Public

6–75 There are a number of different ways in which securities can be issued to the public, which in law includes any part of the public, and does not necessarily entail having those securities listed on the Stock Exchange or traded on an unlisted securities market.

Direct Offer

6–76 One method is for the company itself to draw up a prospectus and offer its securities directly to the public. A prospectus is a detailed statement of the company's business history, present financial situation and other matters regarding the company that would concern investors. If investors conclude that the company has good prospects and its shares are going at a reasonable price, they will apply to the company for the shares they wish to acquire. Usually, the offer will be made at a fixed price, so that the applications received may exceed the quantity of securities being offered. Where there has been an over-subscription in this sense, the company will have to decide on what basis the securities should be allocated among the various applicants. Sometimes the company and its advisers may misjudge the market and not attract sufficient applications for the quantity being offered; the offer is said to be under-subscribed. A company, however, will usually insure itself against this eventuality by having what is called an underwriting arrangement with the bank or other financial intermediary that agrees to acquire the surplus shares.

6–77 Very occasionally, the securities will be offered not at a fixed price but by tender, which is a form of auction. In this way the company avoids disposing of its securities at what transpires to be an unduly low price (resulting in over-subscription) or an excessively high price (causing under-subscription). Instead, it obtains a price that approximates to their true market value. The most common tendering technique is to fix a minimum price and to announce that the securities will be allotted at the highest price above that at which all the securities are applied for.

---

179 See generally, R. Burgess, *Corporate Finance Law* (2nd ed., 1993), Chap. 6.
180 1963 Act, ss. 43–58 and 1983 Act, Pt III.

Offer for Sale

6–78 An alternative method is the offer for sale, which involves the company initially allotting its securities to some financial intermediary, which then offers them to the public. Therefore, instead of the investor subscribing for the securities and the company allotting them to him, the investor makes an application to the intermediary and, if accepted, buys the securities. Many companies prefer this method to the direct offer because it throws the entire risk of the offer on the intermediary, which also assumes most of the accompanying administrative burdens. The offer for sale may be at a fixed price or by way of tender. Section 51 of the 1963 Act requires these offers for sale to the public to comply with that Act's prospectus rules.

Placing

6–79 Another method, that is availed of especially by relatively small companies, is placing. This usually involves a financial intermediary acquiring the securities and then selling blocks of them to a small number of financial institutions — banks, insurance companies, pension funds and the like. Alternatively, the intermediary may simply arrange with the financial institutions that they will take blocks of securities directly from the company. At the time the securities are placed in one or other of these ways, there is no intention that shortly afterwards they will be offered for sale to the public. However, those institutions may on occasion sell all or part of their holdings to other institutions or to select groups of private investors. Sometimes a placing is accompanied by the securities being introduced on the Stock Exchange — either by obtaining an official listing or by being traded on an unlisted securities market. Where such an introduction is being sought, an adequate number of securities must be available for dealing so that a market can be maintained in them.

The Regulatory Framework

6–80 Ever since the Companies Act of 1867, virtually all such offers have had to be accompanied by a prospectus which discloses information about various matters affecting the company; since 1890,[181] directors and promoters have been personally liable for losses caused by any misleading statement contained in a prospectus unless they proved they had reasonable grounds for believing the statement to be true. Because of uncertainty in the common law about where to draw the line between what a company must and need not disclose to persons

---

[181] Directors' Liability Act 1890.

wishing to apply for securities in it, the 1963 Act requires most offers of securities to the public to be accompanied by a prospectus, which must contain specified information and a copy must be registered with the registrar of companies. Securities being made available to the public via the Stock Exchange or otherwise must satisfy the additional requirements of the Yellow Book's listing agreement and the E.C. Directives on Listing Particulars[182] and on Prospectuses,[183] which were implemented in 1984[184] and in 1992[185] respectively. The philosophy underlying these provisions is that investors should be free to put their money wherever they choose, but those who solicit investment from the public must disclose all relevant information about the undertaking and those who control it. However, it is only the deterrent effect of possibly being prosecuted or being sued for providing inaccurate or inadequate information that induces companies and their agents to make such disclosure.

6–81 Irish company law does not regulate the market in securities by requiring that professional dealers in shares register with public authorities and be licensed, as happens in Britain.[186] Nor has a public authority been established with the mission of actively investigating the truth of information provided by companies seeking to attract investment, and to make some qualitative assessment of their claims, as for instance is done by the Securities and Exchange Commission in the United States.[187] In his report, *Review of Investor Protection* (1984),[188] Professor L.C.B. Gower proposed sweeping changes in the already elaborate mechanisms for protecting investors in Britain and the present legislation there concerns Irish investors since much of their funds are invested in U.K. securities.

Prospectuses

6–82 Where securities are being offered for subscription or for sale to the public, the offeror must comply with the 1963 Act's requirements

---

182 [1980] O.J. L100/1 (Directive 80/390), amended by Directive 87/345, [1987] O.J. L185/81.

183 [1989] O.J. L124/8 (Directive 89/298); see generally, Warren, "The Common Market Prospectus" 26 Comm. Mkt. L. Rev. 687 (1989).

184 European Communities (Stock Exchange) Regulations 1984, (S.I. No. 282 of 1984) (amended by S.I. No. 18 of 1991).

185 European Communities (Transferable Securities and Stock Exchange) Regulations 1992 (S.I. No. 202 of 1992).

186 Financial Services Act 1986.

187 See generally, L. Loss & J. Seligman, *Securities Regulation* (3rd ed., 1989–90), Vols. 1–4.

188 Cmnd. 9125 (1984); see note in (1984) 47 Mod. L. Rev. 553.

regarding prospectuses[189] and the 1989 E.C. Directive.[190] The term prospectus is defined loosely as "any prospectus, notice, circular, advertisement or other invitation, offering to the public for subscription or purchase any shares or debentures of a company";[191] it includes what may be termed primary market offers for sale.[192] According to section 44(3) and (1) of the 1963 Act:

> "It shall not be lawful to issue any form of application for shares in or debentures of a company, unless the form is issued with a prospectus which complies with the [Act's] requirements . . . [and] every prospectus issued by or on behalf of a company, or [promoter], must state the matters specified . . . and set out the reports specified in . . . the Third Schedule. . . ."

When Required — Offer to the "Public"

6–83 In order for it to fall within the 1963 Act's and the 1989 Directive's prospectus rules, the offer of securities must be made to the public,[193] although an exception is made for some public offers. Section 61 of the Act contains a definition of the term public in this context but it may not be a comprehensive definition and it may not fully displace interpretations of the term under the 1908 Act and its predecessors. There is no definition in the 1989 Directive but it does not apply to offers to persons in the context of their businesses, nor to offers to "a restricted circle of persons". Section 61 reiterates generalisations of the kind made in earlier cases, that public offerings include offers of securities "to any section of the public, whether selected as members or debenture holders of the company concerned or as clients of the person issuing the prospectus or in any other manner. . . ." Thus the offer made to a stockbroker's or a merchant bank's clients, or to a company's employees or even to a company's existing securities-holders, is capable of being an offer to the public. All depends on the surrounding circumstances. Sub-section (2) classifies two broad categories as not being offers to the public, but these require further elaboration before they can provide practical guidelines. These are an offer that is not "calculated to result" in the securities being acquired "by persons other than those receiving the offer or invitation"; also an offer "otherwise of a domestic concern of the persons making and receiving it". This part furthermore states, somewhat clumsily, that a rights issue by

---

[189] 1963 Act, ss. 43–61.
[190] Directive 89/298, implemented by S.I. No. 202 of 1992; see above, n. 183.
[191] 1963 Act, s.2(1).
[192] *ibid.*, s.51.
[193] *ibid.*, s.44(4)(b) and in the definition of a prospectus.

a company the regulations of which prohibit it from making offers to the public does not *ipso facto* prevent such an offer from being one made to the public.

6–84 There are few modern cases that attempt to analyse the concept of an offer to the public with any great precision. One of the leading decisions is that of the Australian High Court, *Lee v. Evans*,[194] where the following remarks were made:

> "The essence of an invitation to the public is not in the manner of its communication or in the number of the persons to whom it is communicated. The criteria are rather, are the recipients of the invitation persons chosen at random, members, that is, of the general public, the public at large, all and sundry; or are they a select group of whom and to whom alone the invitation is addressed, so that if an outsider sought to respond to it he would be told that he was not one invited to come in?
>
> [A]n invitation even to one person only may be seen when considered in the light of all the circumstances, to be part of, even though only the first step in, the communication of the invitation to the public generally, so that if the lone hearer were to tell some stranger of it the stranger would be right in treating it as open to acceptance by him no less than by the hearer."[195]

There, where a company promoter approached individually a handful of persons he did not know and offered them shares, a divided court held that in the circumstances the offerees were "merely individuals in the general mass of citizens", and that therefore there had been no offer to the public. In another Australian instance it was held that an offer by a subsidiary company to more than 12,500 employees of related companies, inviting them to invest in itself, was not to the public, since the invitation was not capable of being accepted by anybody other than a defined section of the community, *i.e.* employees of those companies.[196]

6–85 In the only modern English authority, *Governments Stock etc. Co. v. Christopher*,[197] one major shipping company sought to take over two others and the bidder sent circulars to all of the "target" companies' shareholders, offering to exchange its shares for their shares in the tar-

---

194 (1965) A.L.R. 614.

195 The public nature of an ofer is no longer of key significance in Australia: H. Ford et al., *Principles of Corporations Law* (9th ed., 1999), Chap. 22.

196 *Corporate Affairs Comm. v. David James Finance Ltd.* [1975] 2 N.S.W.L.R. 710. See also, *Corporate Affairs Comm. v. Australian Central Credit Union* (1985) 59 A.L.J.L.R. 785.

197 [1956] 1 W.L.R. 237.

get. It was held *inter alia* that this was not an offer to the public because "the test is not who receives the circular, but who can accept the offer put forward. In this case it can only be persons legally or equitably interested as shareholders in shares of [the "target" companies]. In the case of those who accept, non-renounceable letters of allotment will be issued. In these circumstances the case appears to fall within [section 61(2) of the 1963 Act]."[198]

Excluded Securities Offers

6–86 There are certain kinds of offers of securities to the public that nevertheless do not have to satisfy some or all of the prospectus rules. These rules do not apply to advertisements that are made exclusively for the purpose of general information, as opposed to soliciting applications for securities. Nor do they apply to offers of any item that is not a security. The term security as such is not used in the 1963 Act; the reference is to shares in and debentures of a company, both of which are defined somewhat extensively — the former "mean[ing] share in the share capital of a company, and includes stock";[199] the latter as "includ[ing] debenture stock, bonds and any other securities of a company. . ."[200] The term security is used in the 1989 Directive and is defined as corresponding to shares and debt securities, but those securities itemised in Article 2(2) are excluded from the requirements.

6–87 Only first-time offers to the public come within the 1963 Act and this Directive. What may be called genuine secondary market transactions are excluded, for instance, offers for sale by investors in the conventional sense who simply wish to divest themselves of securities they possess. In order to fall within the prospectus rules, there must be a "form of application for" securities or the offer must be made by or on behalf of the company or a promoter,[201] or be made in consequence of a previous allotment or agreement to allot securities with a view to them being offered for sale to the public.[202] Offers for sale as described above, therefore, are included. But excluded are placings that are purely of a domestic concern and do not involve an introduction on the Stock Exchange. It could be argued that where existing shareholders, who are not in fact conduits for the company or promoters, make an offer of their shares to the public accompanied by an application form, a pro-

---

198 [1956] 1 W.L.R. 237 at 242.
199 1963 Act, s.2(1).
200 *ibid.*
201 *ibid.*, s.44(3), (1).
202 *ibid.*, s.51.

spectus that complies with the statutory form must be published, though it need not be registered.[203]

6–88 A form of application for securities issued in connection with a bona fide invitation to enter into an underwriting agreement in respect of those securities does not require a prospectus that meets the statutory requirements.[204] There are two ways in which satisfying the Stock Exchange's prospectus rules exonerates a company from having to comply with most of the 1963 Act's requirements. Where securities are offered that in all respects are identical to securities that were issued within the preceding two years and are listed on the Exchange, then application forms issued for those securities need not have a prospectus.[205] The other excluded offer is where the Exchange has certified that, having regard to the size and circumstances of the offer, full compliance with the formalities laid out in the Third Schedule would be "unduly burdensome". In that event, if the prospectus published satisfies the Exchange's own prospectus requirements, this is deemed to be compliance with the Third Schedule.[206]

6–89 An offer to exchange securities, as often happens in a take-over bid, may not fall outside the prospectus rules. In the *Government Stock* case,[207] where the bidder made an offer of its own securities in exchange for those in the "target" company, not only was the offer there not to the public but it was held not to be an offer "for subscription or purchase" because that phrase was held to connote payment in cash. However, that analysis is regarded as wrong and has been rejected by an Australian court.[208] The actual outcome in that case was still correct because, since the shares in question were not yet issued at the time, they could not even be the subject of an offer to purchase.

6–90 The manner in which an offer of securities to a company's own members and debenture-holders, notably "bonus", "pre-emptive" and "rights" offers, is treated is somewhat confusing. Indeed, greater clarity could be given to the entire provisions regarding which kinds of offers fall within and outside the prospectus rules; these sections are a notorious example of unnecessarily convoluted draftsmanship. Offers to existing securities-holders can be to the public, especially offers that

---

203 1963 Act, s.44(3) and 47(1).

204 *ibid*, s.44(4)(a).

205 *ibid*, s.44(7)(b) and S.I. No. 198 of 1975 Companies (Stock Exchange) Regulation.

206 *ibid*, s.45 and S.I. No. 337 of 1990 Companies (Stock Exchange) Regulation. *cf.* s.45(2)(c) which has no parallel in the British Act.

207 [1956] 1 W.L.R. 237; see supra, para. 6–85.

208 *Broken Hill Property Co. v. Bell Resources Ltd.* (1984) 8 A.C.L.R. 609.

are renounceable; but offers by or for a private company that are not renounceable are most likely not offers to the public.[209] However, the requirement to issue a prospectus that complies with the forms set out in the 1963 Act's Third Schedule does not apply to offers by a company of its securities to existing shareholders or holders of debentures (*i.e.* a prospectus not issued generally) whether or not applicants can renounce their rights in favour of others.[210]

Material Contracts

6–91 A material contract is defined as a contract entered into by the company within five years of the prospectus being issued "not being a contract entered into in the ordinary course of the business carried on or intended to be carried on by the company. . . ."[211] What is material in this sense depends very much on the circumstances of each case. In *Jury v. Stoker*,[212] which concerned an earlier version of the rules about material contracts, the test formulated by Sullivan M.R. was "[i]s the contract a thing which a man who was about to subscribe his money to the concern ought to have known?"[213] It was held that an arrangement whereby a prominent business person, a "man of credit and position in the city of Cork", was to be paid £750 for allowing himself to be named as a director of the newly formed Cork Milling Co. satisfied the test; for any investor who became aware of that arrangement would have hesitated before putting money into the company. A contract is material, therefore, where knowledge of its existence or contents would influence an average investor's decision whether or not to acquire the securities being offered.

6–92 Every prospectus issued generally must state the dates, parties and general nature of any material contracts with the company.[214] Additionally, a copy of any such contract, or a memorandum of its contents if the contract is unwritten, must be attached to the copy of the prospectus that is given to the registrar of companies.[215]

Form and Contents

6–93 How a prospectus should be laid out and what it should contain in order to conform with the 1963 Act is set out in that Act's Third

---

209 1963 Act, s.61.
210 *ibid.*, s.44(7)(a); see also s.47(1).
211 *ibid.*, Third schedule, reg. 14.
212 (1882) 9 L.R. Ir. 385.
213 *ibid.* at 403.
214 1963 Act, Third schedule, reg. 14.
215 *ibid.*, s.47(1)(b).

Schedule.[216] According to the Regulations giving effect to the 1989 E.C. Prospectus Directive, every prospectus

> "shall contain the information which, according to the particular nature of the issuer and of the securities concerned, is necessary to enable an informed assessment to be made of the assets and liabilities, financial position, profits and losses and prospects of the company and of the rights attaching to the securities."[217]

Part 1 of the Third Schedule lists the matters that must be specified, which, briefly, are as follows. The names, addresses and descriptions of directors and proposed directors must be stated, together with any provisions in the articles of association regarding qualification shares and directors' remuneration – which includes options on shares or debentures. Where the prospectus was issued within two years of the company becoming entitled to commence business, there must be provided full particulars of any interest a director has in promoting the company and in any property it has bought or intends to acquire; of all sums paid to induce him to become a director; and of sums paid in connection with promoting and forming the company. Any payment or benefit made or given, or intended to be made or given, to a promoter in the preceding three years must be specified, together with the consideration. The name and addresses of the company's auditors must be stated.

6–94 As regards the company's capital, the nominal share capital must be stated; the amount of and numbers of any class of shares; details concerning any founders', management or deferred shares and any shares that are redeemable. Where shares are divided into classes, the members' voting rights and rights regarding capital and dividend must be given. Details must be provided of any options persons are entitled to on any of the company's securities, including who those persons are, the period in which the options are exercisable, and the price to be paid and the consideration, if any, to be given. Information must be provided about securities offered for subscription in the preceding three years, such as the amounts offered and actually allotted, and the amounts, if any, paid on those shares. If within the preceding five years securities were issued or were agreed to be issued otherwise than for cash, there must be stated the consideration for them and, if not fully paid, the extent to which they are paid up. The amounts and rates of any commission paid in the preceding three years in respect of subscribing for the company's shares must be specified.

---

[216] Amended by reg. 8(3) of the European Communities (Transferable Securities and Stock Exchange) Regulations, 1992 (S.I. No. 202 of 1992).

[217] Reg. 8(1).

6–95 Details must be given of what it is proposed to do with the money raised by the offer; in particular, about property purchased or acquired, or it is proposed to buy, whether wholly or partly, from the proceeds of the offer, together with acquisitions not completed at the date of issue — apart from contracts entered into in the ordinary course of business and unrelated to the issue, or where the amounts are not material. The vendors' names and addresses must be specified, as must the amounts to be paid to each of them, and whether it is payable in cash, shares or debentures, and the amount, if any, payable for goodwill. Moreover, there must be set out particulars about any transactions relating to that property over the preceding five years in which the vendor to the company, or a promoter or a director or proposed director, had an interest, whether direct or indirect — this being designed principally to reveal any promoters' profits. Where the company's business or the business to be acquired was carried on for less than three years, the duration of the business must be given. And if the prospectus was issued within two years of the company becoming entitled to commence business, the preliminary expenses, *i.e.* expenses of forming the company, must be disclosed, together with who has paid or is to pay them.

6–96 Regarding the offer itself, the time the subscription lists open and the amounts payable on application and allotment must be stated, as must the expenses of the issue and whoever has paid or is to pay them. The "minimum amount" must be stated, *i.e.* the amount that has to be raised by the issue of shares in order to pay for any property that was or is to be purchased from the proceeds of the issue, any preliminary expenses, any commission payable in relation to subscribing for shares in the company, and working capital. And if any of these sums are to come from some other source, the source or sources must be stated.

6–97 Of crucial importance are "material contracts".[218] The dates, parties and general nature of these contracts must be specified. What reports must be set out in the prospectus are indicated in Part II of the Third Schedule. There must be a report by the company's auditors on the company's profits and losses over the preceding three years, on its assets and liabilities as at the last time the accounts were made up, and on dividends paid over the previous three years. Greater detail must be provided where the company has subsidiaries. Where all or part of the proceeds of the issue are to be used to purchase a business or acquire shares in some other company so that it will become a subsidi-

---

[218] See above, para. 6–91.

ary, there must be an accountants' report on that business or company's profits and losses over the preceding three years, and on its assets and liabilities. Accountants who make up this report must be qualified to be appointed as auditors to the company itself.

Registration

6–98 Before a prospectus may be issued by, for or in respect of a company, a dated and signed copy of it must be delivered to the registrar of companies.[219] It must be signed by or for every person named in it as a director or a proposed director. If it contains any statement purporting to have been made by an expert, or an engineer, valuer or accountant, copies of the required consents of those experts must be given to the registrar.[220] In the case of a prospectus issued generally, *i.e.* issued to persons other than the company's existing members or debenture-holders, two further documents must be attached to the registered prospectus. Where any adjustment has been made to figures contained in the accompanying auditors' and accountants' reports, a copy of a statement must be attached in which those adjustments and the reasons for them are set out, and it must be signed by the persons concerned.[221] Copies of any "material contracts" must also be provided.[222]

Listing Agreement and Particulars

6–99 Where a Stock Exchange quotation is being sought for securities, then the requirements of the Exchange's own Listing Agreement and of the E.C.'s 1980 Directive on Listing Particulars[223] must be satisfied. Sections 3 and 4 of the "Yellow Book" set out the information that the Exchange insists must be supplied, regarding the company in question, its directors, auditors and advisers, its capital, its management, its financial record, its recent developments and prospects, and about the securities in question. The Listing Particulars Directive covers much the same ground. According to its central provision, article 4:

> "The listing particulars shall contain the information which, according to the particular nature of the issuer and of the securities . . . is necessary to enable the investors and their investment advisers to make an informed assessment of the assets and liabilities, financial position, profits and losses, and prospects of the issuer of the rights attaching to such securities."

---

[219] 1963 Act, s.47.
[220] *ibid*, s.46.
[221] *ibid*, s.47(1)(b)(ii).
[222] *ibid*, s.47(1)(b)(i).
[223] [1980] O.J. L100/1 and S.I. No. 282 of 1984, First schedule, amended by Directive 87/345, [1987] O.J. L185/81 (S.I. No. 18 of 1991).

This Directive obliges persons who are responsible for listing particulars to provide the requisite information.

Rescission of Agreement to Acquire Shares

6–100 As was explained above,[224] one mode of redress available to investors who were misled into subscribing for securities is to rescind the agreement under which those securities were acquired. Many of the leading cases on rescission in this context have involved erroneous information contained in prospectuses, for instance, the *Aaron's Reefs Ltd.*[225] and the *Components Tube Co.*[226] cases. However, this remedy is no longer available where undue time has elapsed since the securities were obtained and also where *restitutio in integrum* is no longer possible, as when the company goes into liquidation.

Compensation

6–101 For the reasons given in *Houldsworth v. City of Glasgow Bank,*[227] ordinarily a disappointed or even a defrauded investor will not be able to recover damages from the company in respect of the loss he incurred by subscribing for its shares. It is possible that damages would be recoverable where paying compensation would not worsen the general creditors' position, but instances of that nature would be unusual and there is no reported authority which deals with the matter. However, the investor may have a claim promoters and against some or all of the directors for the torts of deceit and of negligent misstatement, as described earlier in this chapter. In addition, there is at least one statutory remedy whereby damages may be recovered.

Director's "Misstatement"

6–102 In 1889 civil liability for negligent misstatement as we know it today did not exist and, in *Derry v. Peek,*[228] decided in that year, it was held that for there to be liability in deceit it must be shown that the defendant acted fraudulently or with disregard for the truth of what was said. Because of the considerable practical difficulties for plaintiff — investors in meeting this stringent requirement, the Directors' Liability Act 1890,[229] was enacted. It made directors and promoters liable to investors in respect of any material inaccuracy contained in a pro-

---

[224] See above, paras 6–60 *et seq.*
[225] [1896] A.C. 273; see above, para. 6–62.
[226] [1900] 2 I.R. 1; see above, para. 6–55.
[227] (1880) 5 App. Cas. 317; see above, para. 6–65.
[228] (1889) 14 App. Cas. 337; see above, para. 6–68.
[229] 53 & 54 Vict., c. 64.

spectus, unless the defendants proved that they acted diligently and honestly in the circumstance.

6–103 Under the current version of this, section 49 of the 1963 Act, every director, person named as director, promoter or other person who authorised the prospectus being issued[230] is liable to compensate any person who subscribed for shares in or debentures of the company "on the faith of" the prospectus for any "loss or damage they may have sustained by reason of any untrue statement included therein", unless the defendants prove that they satisfy a defence set out in sub-section (3) or (5). For the purposes of this section (and section 50, its criminal equivalent), a statement is deemed to be untrue if it is misleading in the form and context in which it is included.[231] Thus, liability can be incurred even where the statement in question is literally correct or is ambiguous.[232] Depending on the circumstances, moreover, a statement of belief, intent or expectation may amount to a representation of fact.[233] It is no defence that documents existed and could have been inspected by the investor to verify the accuracy of what was stated.[234] But it must be established that it was the untruth in the prospectus that to a significant extent induced the subscription and the losses incurred arose from the subject matter of the untruth.[235] It has been held that use of the term "liable to compensate" victims of section 49 violations does not mean that damages are to be measured by criteria other than the traditional ones for determining damages in tort.[236]

6–104 It is an open question whether persons other than those to whom the prospectus is addressed have a statutory right of action where it was reasonably foreseeable that they would rely on it in making their decision to acquire the securities. In any event, it is only persons who subscribe for the securities who can claim under this section. In this context subscribers include those in favour of whom letters of allotment or of rights are renounced, and also those who purchase securities from an intermediary to whom they were allotted with a view to them being offered for sale to the public.[237] It would appear that the prospectus must have been issued by the company or on its behalf, as by a promoter or by an intermediary in an offer for sale. While the

---

230 *cf.* s.49(6)–(8).
231 1963 Act, s.52(a).
232 *cf. Aaron's Reefs Ltd v. Twiss* [1896] A.C. 273.
233 *Edgington v. Fitzmaurice* (1885) 29 Ch.D. 459.
234 *cf. Aaron's Reefs Ltd v. Twiss.*
235 *ibid.*
236 *Clark v. Urquhart* [1930] A.C. 28.
237 1963 Act, s.51.

right of action is against *inter alia* "every person" who authorised the prospectus being issued, the company itself is not contemplated as a defendant.

6–105 Having acted diligently and honestly is a defence to a claim under section 49. But the burden of proof is on the defendant and it is for him to demonstrate that he had reasonable grounds to believe, and up to the time of the allotment did believe, that the inaccurate statement was true. Whether that belief had a reasonable basis is determined by objective standards. As one judge put it, reasonableness is established by "proof of any facts or circumstances which would induce the belief in the mind of a reasonable man, that is to say, a man who stands midway between the careless and easy-going man on the one hand and the over-cautious man and straw-splitting man on the other".[238] In the absence of grounds for being put on inquiry, a director therefore may rely on the company's professional advisers, especially its auditors and solicitors.

6–106 A number of other defences to liability under section 49 are provided for. It is a defence not to have authorised or consented to the prospectus being issued, or that on becoming aware of the untruth prior to the allotment to have withdrawn one's consent to the prospectus. Where the untruth purports to be founded on some expert's[239] statement, report or valuation, it is a defence if it is shown that the expert's utterances were fairly and correctly relayed, that he had consented to them being contained in the prospectus and that there were reasonable grounds to believe the the expert was competent in the field. If the statement was made by an "official person" or was contained in some "public official document", it suffices if the statement was a correct and fair representation of what was said.

Omission from Prospectus

6–107 It is an open question whether a cause of action can arise where a person is induced to invest, not by a false statement, but simply by something material being omitted from the prospectus that section 44(1) and the Third Schedule of the 1963 Act or the 1989 E.C. Directive requires to be stated or contained in it. In *Re South of England Natural Gas Co.*[240] it was held that a director or persons responsible for issuing a prospectus were liable in damages for a loss resulting from a material

---

[238] *Adams v. Thrift* [1915] 1 Ch. 557 at 565.
[239] *cf.* 1963 Act, s.46.
[240] [1911] 1 Ch. 573.

omission from the prospectus, unless the defences set out (in what are subsections (5)(a)-(c) and (6) of the 1963 Act's section 44) are satisfied. As was explained in the introductory part of this book,[241] the entire question of implying a civil remedy from statutory provisions is a complex one. While an Irish court could decide to follow the English Chancery Division, there are a number of grounds on which this case can be distinguished.

6–108 In the first place, the case does not consider in any great detail the arguments for and against the damages remedy. The criteria for determining if a right of action arises for exclusively economic loss resulting from breach of some statutory duty by a private individual or organisation were not settled in 1911 when the English case was decided. Giving a right of action under this section has been criticised to an extent by such eminent commentators as Gower.[242] The architecture of what now is section 38 of the British 1948 Act is different from section 44 of the 1963 Act; although these differences are not a conclusive argument, they suggest at least that the Oireachtas intended that the matter should be dealt with *de novo* here. Founding civil liability on mere omission to state something when general liability for negligent misstatement is still struggling to establish itself, and liability for innocent misstatement is very limited, could give rise to anomalous results. A parallel provision in a Canadian law was construed restrictively by the British Columbia Court of Appeal.[243] On the other hand, contrary to what was held in *Re South of England Natural Gas*,[244] it could be argued that any material breach of the duty imposed by section 44 entitles investors to whom the prospectus was aimed to rescind the allotment.

6–109 Insofar as omitting information that the 1989 E.C. Directive requires to be in a prospectus, the position is most confusing. Although there is an affirmative obligation to include the information in question,[245] it is not stated that damages do not ensue if there is a breach of that duty,[246] with one exception. That is where the obligation in Article 4 of the Directive is contravened.[247] But all that this article states is that Member States shall ensure that those offering securities to the public

---

[241] See above, paras 1–58 *et seq*.
[242] 4th ed., pp. 387–391.
[243] *Ames v. Investo Plan* (1973) 35 D.L.R. 3d 613; *cf.* note in (1974) 52 Can. Bar Rev. 589.
[244] See above, n. 240; also *Re Wimbledon Olympia Ltd.* [1910] 1 Ch. 630.
[245] S.I. No. 202 of 1992, reg. 8.
[246] *ibid.*, reg. 10(3).
[247] *ibid.*, reg. 10(1).

shall publish a prospectus.[248] To confound matters, liability under this heading does not arise where the person in question either did not know the matter not disclosed, or had made an honest mistake of fact, or the contravention is immaterial or, in the circumstances, he ought to be excused.

Omission of Listing Particulars

6–110 The 1984 Regulation on listing particulars[249] obliges persons who are responsible for listing particulars to provide the information set out in the 1980 E.C. Directive.[250] Contravention of Article 4(1) of this is a breach of statutory duty[251] and, it would seem, actionable where causation and loss can be established. However, any person responsible for the particulars has a defence where it is shown that he did not know of the matter not disclosed, or that the omission arose from an honest mistake of fact, or it was in respect of some immaterial matter or otherwise ought to be excused.[252] But this defence does not protect persons from any liability for common law negligent misrepresentation where the matter carelessly suppressed was something that ought to have been disclosed in the listing particulars; nor does it cut back on liability for misstatement under section 49 of the 1963 Act.[253]

The Non-Statutory Remedies Compared

6–111 Because it identifies certain parties as in a sense owing a duty of care and places on their shoulders the burden of proving that they acted honestly and reasonably, there are great advantages in investors founding their claim on section 49 of the 1963 Act rather than on common law or equity. In some respects, however, the torts of deceit and of negligent misrepresentation, and the actions for rescission and for breach of contract and of fiduciary duty, throw their nets wider, especially as regards plaintiffs and defendants. Section 49 has no application where the plaintiff acquired the securities otherwise than by subscription or from a conduit for an offer to the public as envisaged by section 51; in other words, it does not apply to genuine secondary market transactions. The purchaser in the market may have a *Hedley Bryne*[254]-type action for misrepresentation arising from the prospectus against promoters and directors, but there are two initial hurdles to be

---

[248] reg. 89/298.
[249] S.I. No. 282 of 1984 (amended by S.I. No. 18 of 1991).
[250] [1980] O.J. L100/1 (amended by [1987] O.J. L185/81.
[251] reg. 4(4).
[252] reg. 4(2).
[253] reg. 4(3).
[254] [1964] A.C. 465.

cleared in such a claim. At least where the prospectus takes the form of a Stock Exchange advertisement, the opening statement that the directors "have taken all reasonable care" about the accuracy of the information presented and "accept responsibility" accordingly would suggest that there is the requisite degree of proximity or neighbourhood with those who buy on foot of the prospectus that caused the plaintiff to buy the shares. In *Peek v. Gurney*[255] it was held that persons who buy securities in the market on foot of a prospectus that was produced to solicit subscriptions cannot recover damages. But the Lords there did not exclude the possibility of liability where it is shown that the prospectus was published with an eye to encouraging transactions on the market and that the purchaser actually relied on its contents.[256] In the *Al-Nakib* case,[257] it was held that, under the general principles governing liability for economic loss, directors are not liable in negligence to in-the-market purchasers who relied on some inaccuracy in the company's prospectus. However, circumstances can arise where there might be such liability to buyers in the unlisted securities market.[258]

6–112 Today, the Stock Exchange rules require that most kinds of new issues of securities must be accompanied by a prospectus that is published as an advertisement, so that in the early days of public trading it could fairly be said that the prospectus was intended to encourage purchases. The difficulty is in determining for how long it was intended to have this effect.

6–113 It seems that the company is not liable for any breach of section 49. It furthermore has been held that the only remedy available to a shareholder against a company that wrongfully induced one to subscribe for shares in it is *restitutio in integrum,* whether the wrong be deceit, negligent misrepresentation or breach of a contractual term.[259] Therefore, it would appear that the investor who was defrauded or misled by the company into buying its shares has no remedy against it in damages. And once the company goes into liquidation it is too late to rescind.

6–114 If section 44 of the 1963 Act, which forbids omissions, is found to give a right of action in damages, then every person responsible for issuing a non-exempted prospectus to the public is subject to the high

---

[255] (1873) L.R. 6 H.L. 377.
[256] *cf. Andrews v. Mockford* [1896] 1 QB. 372.
[257] *Al-Nakib Investments (Jersey) Ltd. v. Longcroft* [1990] 1 W.L.R. 1390.
[258] *Possfund Custodian Trustee Ltd. v. Diamond* [1996] 1 W.L.R. 1351.
[259] *Houldsworth v. City of Glasgow Bank* (1880) 5 App. Cas. 317.

standard of *uberrimae fidei*: of disclosing everything that the Third Schedule requires to be contained in a prospectus. But the section would not appear to admit of a right of action against the company itself. Presumably, the omission would have to be material and at least the partial cause of the plaintiff acquiring the securities. Directors and others who are sued would appear to have defences of (culpable) ignorance and honest (even if unreasonable) mistake.[260]

6–115 The great advantage of rescission is that it is not dependent on the incorrect material statement being made deceitfully or negligently, and it can be invoked by subscribers against the company. On the other hand, it is a right that can easily be lost through delay or change of circumstances.

Criminal Penalties

6–116 It is an offence to solicit investment from the public, as described above, without issuing and duly registering a prospectus.[261] In addition to the Larceny Act offence of fraudulently inducing persons to become shareholders, which features in *R. v. Kylsant*,[262] the 1963 Act establishes other offences for misleading and incomplete prospectuses. There is a criminal side to the Directors' Liability Act 1890, which is now section 50 of the 1963 Act. It is an offence to issue a prospectus that contains an "untrue statement", which is defined as including a statement that is "misleading in the form and context in which it is included."[263] Every person who authorised the issue of the prospectus is made liable. Although the normal burden of proof is reversed, the offence is not one of strict liability; it is a defence to show that either the statement was immaterial or that it was believed to be true and there were reasonable grounds for believing so.

6–117 Non-disclosure of what section 44 and the Third Schedule of the 1963 Act requires to be included in a prospectus is a criminal offence on the part of any director or other person responsible for issuing the prospectus, which would include promoters and issuing houses, but probably not the company itself. Ignorance or honest mistake are defences; it must be proved that the defendant had knowledge of the matters not disclosed as required by the Third Schedule's paragraph

---

260 1963 Act, s. 44(5). See generally, A. Arlidge et al., *Arlidge and Parry on Fraud* (2nd ed., 1996), Chap. 8.
261 *ibid.*, s.44.
262 [1932] 1 K.B. 442; see above, para. 6–73.
263 1963 Act, s.52.

16. The court is given a discretion to waive liability because the matter omitted was immaterial or because in the circumstances the defendant had acted reasonably. Breach of the requirements in the E.C. Directives can also be a criminal offence which can be prosecuted by the Minister and carries a maximum fine of £1,000.

7

Capital Adequacy and Integrity

7–01 One of the fundamental doctrines of company law is that of capital integrity, which has spawned a number of sub-principles and subrules. Many of these were discovered by the judges between 1880 and 1900, the evidence for their existence being the underlying scheme of the Companies Acts. Their principal objective is to provide company creditors with a degree of security. As Jessel M.R. explained:

> "[t]he creditor has no debtor but that impalpable thing the corporation, which has no property except the assets of the business. The creditor, therefore . . . gives credit to that capital, gives credit to the company on the faith of the representation that the capital shall be applied only for the purposes of the business . . ." [1]

That is to say, the law enables persons to do business under the aegis of registered companies which are legally segregated from their owners and almost invariably have limited liability. Accordingly, all that persons dealing with limited companies can look to for satisfaction of obligations owing to them is the company's own assets. However, there is always a danger of the shareholders withdrawing funds from the company in the shape of dividends or otherwise, with the resultant diminution of the amount creditors can claim against. It, therefore, is necessary to provide that the subscribed capital be protected against the depredations of shareholders and to the detriment of creditors, and indeed of minority shareholders as well.

7–02 We have already come across one distinctive manifestation of the capital integrity principle in *Houldsworth v. City of Glasgow Bank*,[2] which was decided long before most of the leading cases in this field. It was held there that persons who were wrongfully induced by a company to subscribe for shares in it have no remedy in damages against the company once the shares have been allotted to them. One justification for the rule, which flies in the face of the principle of separate legal personality, is that awarding damages against the company depletes

---

[1] *Re Exchange Banking Co., Flitcroft's Case* (1882) 21 Ch.D.519 at 533–534.

[2] (1880) 5 App. Cas. 317; above, para. 6–65.

the fund to which outsider creditors can look for satisfaction of the company's obligations to them.

7–03 The rules regarding capital integrity have been extended significantly by the 1983 Act, which was adopted in response to the E.C. Second Directive,[3] it being based on some major features of French and German law. That Directive's central objective is summed up in its preamble:

> "Whereas Community provisions should be adopted for maintaining the capital, which constitutes the creditors' security, in particular by prohibiting any reduction thereof by distribution to shareholders where the latter are not entitled to it and by imposing limits on the company's rights to acquire its own shares."

Some of this Directive's requirements were already incorporated in the 1963 Act, such as the restrictions on companies buying and financing the purchase of their own shares. But other parts of that Act had to be drastically amended, notably in respect of paying dividends from capital, requiring that p.l.c.s have a minimum capital and that consideration paid for shares in p.l.c.s must be shown to be adequate. Because of the very nature of these matters, it is best to deal separately at the end of this chapter with the sanctions for violation of the various rules.

MINIMUM AMOUNTS

7–04 A major cause of company failure is under-capitalisation, by which is meant having a volume of turnover and of debtors that is far in excess of what the firm's contributed capital can sustain. It, therefore, is often argued that companies should not be permitted to trade unless the subscribers and members pump a minimum amount of capital into them. Persons who decry the ease with which the corporate entity can be availed of to evade, if not avoid, legal obligations also look to a peremptory minimum capital as the panacea. Under the 1963 Act, there was no specific legal duty to ensure that the company had sufficient capital to finance the business embarked upon, other than that a company may not allot shares to the public for the first time until it has raised the "minimum amount"[4] and corporate officers become personally liable for the company's debts where they permit it to

---

[3] [1977] O.J. L26/1; see generally, Temple Lang, "The Second E.E.C. Company Law Directive" (1976) 11 Ir. Jur. 37.

[4] s.53(1) and Third schedule, para. 4(a), above, para. 6–22.

trade when there is no reasonable prospect of its debts being paid.[5] In many Continental European countries, by contrast, it is necessary in order to do business as any of the more important categories of company to have a minimum authorised capital and a minimum paid up capital; where a company's capital is seriously depleted, a general meeting must be convened to consider what should be done. Rules along these lines were adopted by the 1983 Act for p.l.c.s and even for private companies so that they are not unduly under-capitalised.

Minimum Authorised Capital

7–05 In order to be registered as a p.l.c., the memorandum of association must stipulate that the authorised capital is at least £30,000.[6] The Minister is empowered to vary this minimum amount and to require existing p.l.c.s either to increase their capital to the new minimum or else to apply for re-registration as another form of company.

Minimum Paid-Up Capital

7–06 In contrast to the position in some countries and to what at times is advocated, there is no requirement that companies have a truly sizeable minimum actual capital. A step in this direction, however, is section 28 of the 1983 Act which stipulates that a p.l.c. may not allot shares unless the allottee has paid up at least one-quarter of their nominal value, together with the full amount of any premium payable on them.[7] Since one of the prerequisites of a p.l.c. becoming entitled to do business or borrow is that it has allotted shares valued at least £30,000 nominally, no new p.l.c., therefore, may act until it has at the very minimum £7,500 in paid-up capital.

7–07 Section 22 of the 1983 Act embodies another move in the direction of an adequate minimum paid-up capital. Where a p.l.c. offers its shares for subscription but the offer is under-subscribed, the company is forbidden to allot those shares that were subscribed for unless the offer stated that allotments would be made in such circumstances and those very circumstances occurred.

Capital Haemorrhage

7–08 At times a company may start out with adequate funds but may find that years of unprofitable trading erode its capital base. In addi-

---

5 s.297A; see below, paras 18–51 *et seq*.
6 1983 Act, ss. 5(2), 17, 19.
7 *cf.* s.2(2)'s definition of "allotted". This requirement does not apply to shares allotted under an employees' share scheme.

tion now to the rules on "fraudulent" and "reckless" trading,[8] section 40 of the 1983 Act obliges the directors of every limited company, who find that its financial position has deteriorated to the extent that net assets (*i.e.* aggregate assets minus total liabilities) are worth not more than half of its called-up share capital, to convene an extraordinary general meeting. This must be done within 28 days of a director learning of the deficiency and the meeting must be convened for not later than 56 days from that same day. The matter for deliberation at that meeting is "whether any, and if so, what measures be taken to deal with the situation." A director who "knowingly and wilfully" contravenes section 40 of the 1983 Act's requirement to convene a shareholders' meeting to consider the capital haemorrhage is guilty of an offence. It remains to be seen what impact this requirement will have on section 297A of the 1963 Act concerning "fraudulent and reckless trading". Every auditors' report on a company's accounts must state an opinion whether the company is in a "section 40" situation.[9]

ISSUING SHARES AT DISCOUNTS

7–09 The Anglo-European tradition in company law has been one of fixed par value shares. While companies usually prefer to allot their shares for the highest premium over the nominal value that can be obtained, occasions can arise where, without any suggestion of fraud, shares can be allotted only at a discount, *i.e.* for less than their nominal par value. The company, for instance, may have been doing so badly that its £1 shares now stand at 40 pence in the market; if it wishes to raise further capital by issuing additional shares of that class, it will not attract subscribers if it fixes the price at more than what those shares can be obtained for in the market. However, in *Ooregum Gold Mining Co. v. Roper*[10] it was held that it was implicit in the very structure of the Companies Acts that limited companies may not allot shares for less than their par value. As Lord Macnaghten explained, the then Act "proceeds on the footing of recognising and maintaining the liability of the individual members to the company until the prescribed limit is reached. [Accordingly,] the liability of a member continues so long as anything remains unpaid upon his shares. Nothing but payment, and payment in full, can put an end to the liability".[11] An exception to this principle was allowed by section 63 of the 1963 Act in special circum-

---

8 1963 Act, s.297A; see below, paras 18–51 *et seq.*

9 1990 Act, s.193(4)(g).

10 [1892] A.C. 125.

11 *ibid.* at pp. 144 and 145.

stances and with the court's approval; but it was rarely availed of and has been repealed.

Allotment at a Discount

7–10 By virtue of section 27 of the 1983 Act, which applies not alone to p.l.c.s but to all registered companies, "the shares of a company shall not be allotted at a discount." This iron rule admits of no exceptions or qualifications other than the brokerage and commissions authorised by section 59 of the 1963 Act[12] and, possibly, though most unlikely, where the company was formed with the express object of acquiring a particular asset by allotting its shares to the vendor. This latter situation arose in *Re Leinster Contract Corp.*,[13] where the company was incorporated to acquire certain patent rights in return for its shares, but the patents proved to be valueless. It was held that, as there was no fraud here, the allotment to the vendor could not be set aside. Since the shares were issued as fully paid, the allotment was not regarded as *ultra vires* because the entire transaction "was not only contemplated, but imperatively required by the very constitution of the company."[14] However, this decision may not represent the law today since it did not deal with explicit statutory provisions like sections 27 and 26 of the 1983 Act. The sanctions for breach of these provisions are considered separately below.[15]

"Watering" Shares

7–11 By "watering" shares is meant a company allotting its shares for a consideration less than their issue price and, in particular, for less than their par value. The objection to that practice is that it gives a wholly misleading picture of a company's true worth and can be a device for defrauding shareholders and creditors. In order, therefore, to ensure some equivalence between the value of shares issued to subscribers and the consideration that the company receives in return, the 1963 Act prohibited issuing shares at a discount and struck at transactions where the discrepancy in value was patent or there was fraud. These standards are now supplemented by exacting provisions of the 1983 Act, the thrust of which is to prohibit p.l.c.s from allotting shares for consideration of dubious value and to ensue a degree of equality in exchange when allotting p.l.c.s' shares, and in transactions between p.l.c.s and their initial members.[16]

---

[12] See above, para. 6–42.
[13] [1902] 1 I.R. 349.
[14] *ibid.* at p. 359. *cf. Re British Seamless Paper Box Co.* (1881) 17 Ch.D. 467.
[15] below, para. 7–82.
[16] On the similar U.K. rules, see D. Prentice, *The Companies Act 1980* (1980), Chap. 10.

7–12 Subject to the conditions and exceptions outlined below, companies may allot their shares for a consideration other than cash, for instance, in return for property the company acquires from a promoter or investor, or for some service that someone has undertaken to perform for the company. This principle is now endorsed by section 26(1) of the 1983 Act, which stipulates that "£1 shares allotted by a company and any premium payable on them may be paid up in money or money's worth (including goodwill and expertise)." Until recently, when any company proposed to allot shares in return for some consideration other than cash, it was for the company itself to determine what that consideration was worth. In companies subject to clause 5 of Table A, this discretion was consigned to the board of directors, who could allot shares "on such terms and conditions . . . as they may consider to be in the best interests of the company and its shareholders." But this state of affairs made it relatively easy for companies to evade the proscription against allotting shares at a discount; acquiring property at a greatly over-valued price in consideration for its shares is no different in substance from allotting those shares for less than their par value.

Registering the Contracts

7–13 Where any limited company allots shares for a non-cash consideration, section 58 of the 1963 Act obliges it, within one month, to deliver to the registrar of companies the relevant stamped contracts and returns.[17] By these are meant a written contract constituting the allottee's title to the shares in question; the contract for the consideration, be it the sale of property or of goods, or the exchange of services or of other consideration; and a return stating the number and nominal amount of the shares allotted, the extent to which they are treated as paid up and the consideration for them. If any of these contracts is not written, then a duly stamped statement of its particulars must be registered. In this way shareholders and the public generally can be informed of precisely what consideration shares have been allotted for.

7–14 However, these requirements do not apply where the company already owes money to the allottee and it simply sets-off that sum against the price of the shares. For a cash payment has traditionally been regarded as including the exercise of a right of set-off.[18] Where there are mutual debts between the company and an applicant for its

---

[17] An earlier version was s.25 of the 1867 Act; *cf. Re Dublin United Transways Co. (1896) Ltd.* [1901] 1 I.R. 340.

[18] See *Buckley on the Companies Acts* (14th ed., 1981), pp. 144–146. *cf.* 1983 Act, s.2(3)(a).

shares, it is "not necessary that the parties should go through the form of handing the money over and receiving it back or giving cross cheques."[19] Accordingly, registration of the contract can be avoided by the company first issuing the shares for cash, the allottee then selling the assets to the company for cash and the company then setting these debts off against each other.

Bona Fides and Honesty

7–15 In determining the value of property or some other advantage that the company will acquire on issuing its shares to the vendor, the directors must not violate their general duties of acting with due care and skill, and not abuse their powers or put themselves in a situation where serious conflicts of interests arise. However, these duties are owed to the company and not to its shareholders and creditors; and within limits, the company may exonerate directors from liability for breach of their duties.[20]

7–16 So far as the company itself is concerned, it has an extensive discretion to place a value on the consideration it will accept for its shares. As it was put in *Re Wragg Ltd.*,[21] where the previous authorities on this controversial question were reviewed:

> "the obligation of every shareholder in a limited company to pay the company the nominal amount of his shares [can] be satisfied by a transaction which amount [s] to accord and satisfaction as distinguished from payment in cash. As regards the value of the property which a company can take from a shareholder . . . unless the agreement [can] be impeached for fraud, the value of the property or the services [can] not be inquired into. In other words, the value at which the company is content to accept the property must be treated as its value as between itself and the shareholder whose liability is charged by its means.
>
> It has . . . never been decided that a limited company cannot buy property or pay for services at any price it thinks proper, and pay for them in fully paid up shares. Provided a limited company does so honestly and not colourably, and provided that it has not been so imposed upon as to be entitled to be relieved from its bargains [such] agreements are valid and binding on the company and their creditors."[22]

---

[19] *North Sydney Investments etc. Co. v. Higgins* [1899] A.C. 263 at 273.
[20] See below, para. 10–09.
[21] [1897] 1 Ch. 796.
[22] *ibid.* at 826, 827 and 830, applied in *e.g. Park Business Interiors Ltd. v. Park* [1992] B.C.L.C. 1034. For an interesting critique of *Re Wragg Ltd.*, see Guigni, "Consideration for Share Issues: Price or Value?" (1991) Australian L.J. 379.

7–17 There are three circumstances where the courts will set aside the valuation placed by a company on non-cash consideration received for its shares. One is where fraud has been established; but fraud is notoriously difficult to prove. Another is where the consideration given is wholly "illusory".[23] The third is where it is patently obvious from the very terms of the contract that the property is worth less than the nominal value of the shares being allotted and any premium, if there is one. Sometimes for this reason schemes of arrangement or other measures for reorganising companies' capital structure can fall foul of the anti-watering rule.[24] Apart from these cases, the court will not inquire into the value of the consideration; the general principle is that it is for the contracting parties alone to judge the adequacy of consideration being exchanged. Indeed the *Salomon & Co.* case,[25] which was decided in the same year as *Re Wragg Ltd.*, was a licence for over-optimism in valuing assets that are acquired in return for shares. Lord Macnaghten described the price of £39,000, at which Mr Salomon valued his business when he transferred it to his company in exchange for shares and debentures, as an "extravagant" price, "a sum which represented the sanguine expectations of a fond owner rather than anything that can be called a business like or reasonable estimate of value."[26] But fraud was not alleged, the consideration given was not entirely illusory and the value placed on the business was not demonstrably insufficient on the face of the contract.

7–18 These cases were decided at a time when there was no express statutory prohibition against allotting shares at a discount. It is possible that the approach adopted in *Salomon & Co.* no longer fully reflects the law; that where the evidence points persuasively to a substantial over-valuation of assets, the burden then falls on the allottee to demonstrate that there was no hidden discount.

Requirements for p.l.c.s

7–19 The above requirements regarding registering contracts for non-cash consideration and bona fides in valuing that consideration apply just as much to p.l.c.s as to private limited companies. However, a number of substantive as well as procedural safeguards have been introduced by the 1983 Act to prevent the shares of p.l.c.s from being

---

[23] *e.g. Re Eddystone Marine Insurance Co.* [1893] 3 Ch. 9; compare *Re Theatrical Trust Ltd.* [1951] 1 Ch. 771 and *Re Leinster Contract Corp.* [1902] 1 I.R. 349.

[24] *e.g. Re White Star Line Ltd.* [1938] Ch. 458 and *Moseley v. Koffyfontein Mines Ltd.* [1904] 2 Ch. 108.

[25] [1897] A.C. 22.

[26] *ibid.* at 49.

allotted for inadequate consideration. The sanctions for breach of these provisions are dealt with separately below.[27]

Cash Only

7–20 Section 35 stipulates that shares taken by every subscriber to a p.l.c.'s memorandum of association, in pursuance of his undertaking in it to take shares, and any premium on them must be paid for in cash. Cash is defined to include a cheque the company receives in good faith and which the directors have no reason for suspecting will not be paid; cash also includes the release of a liability for a liquidated sum and an undertaking to pay cash at a future date.[28]

Work or Service Contracts

7–21 Section 26(2) of the 1983 Act prohibits a p.l.c. from accepting in payment for its shares an "undertaking [to] do work or perform services", whether or not the person who is to work or to act is the allottee of the shares or another person, and whether the performance is to be done for the company or for another person. That is to say, a p.l.c. may not accept service contracts and the like as consideration for its shares. Since the Act does not define the terms work or services, difficulties will arise about what exactly these terms mean.[29] That the draftsman did not follow the formulation "undertaking to perform work or supply services" that is used in Article 7 of the Second Directive may be significant. Remuneration packages for management that contain share incentive schemes will have to be designed with this prohibition in mind.

Five Years Contracts

7–22 A p.l.c. is prohibited by section 29 of the 1983 Act from allotting any of its shares in return, either wholly or partly, for an "undertaking which is to be or may be performed more than five years after the date of the allotment." In other words, a p.l.c. may not allot shares where the *quid pro quo* is some contract that will be or can be performed more than five years after the allotment date. This section goes on to provide that any variation in a contract to be performed within five years that extends the time of due performance beyond that period is void. The company is entitled to claim the consideration plus interest where a contract to be performed within five years is not performed within

---

[27] See below, paras 7–79 *et seq.*
[28] 1983 Act, s.2(3)(a).
[29] A similar distinction exists for the purposes of the Sale of Goods Acts.

that period. Where, however, the undertaking is simply to pay cash it is not affected by the prohibition.

Independent Valuation

7–23 The discretion that p.l.c.s possess in determining the worth of property and advantages being acquired in exchange for their shares, as set out in *Re Wragg Ltd.*,[30] is substantially constricted by sections 30 and 31 of the 1983 Act: the independent valuation and reporting requirements. These ensure that the company will have an objective assessment of what the consideration is worth and it can be assumed that shares will not be issued for substantially less than that amount unless there are very good reasons for doing so.[31] These provisions also apply where the company both allots shares and at the same time transfers some other asset or benefit in return for some non-cash consideration. But they do not apply to allotments made in connection with an arrangement or merger as defined there.[32] Nor would it seem do they apply where the company resorts to two separate cash contracts and then operates a set-off. That is to say, the company allots shares for cash, the allottee separately agrees to sell the company assets for cash and the reciprocal debts are then set-off against each other. Section 2(3) of the 1983 Act contains a definition of what is "cash" for the purposes of the Companies Act but does not expressly reject the long-established principle that set-off is the equivalent of a cash payment.[33] An assignment of a debt, on the other hand, is not deemed to be a cash payment for these purposes.[34]

7–24 Where a p.l.c. proposes to allot shares in exchange wholly or partly for something other than cash, the consideration must be valued by someone who would be eligible to be the company's auditor;[35] although where it is reasonable to do so, he may delegate all or some of the task to such person as he believes is competent to do that job and who is neither an officer nor servant of the company nor of an affiliate (but may be its auditor). The valuer is entitled to demand from the company's officers such information and explanations as are needed. The report must be made to the company within six months prior to the allotment taking place and a copy of it must be sent to the intended allottee.[36] It must state the nominal value of the shares in question; the

---

30 [1897] 1 Ch. 796; see above, para. 7–16.
31 *cf.* s.30(8)(d) and (10); *cf.* s.32(6)(d).
32 s.30(2)–(4).
33 See above, para. 7–14.
34 *System Control p.l.c. v. Munro Corporate p.l.c.* [1990] B.C.L.C. 659.
35 s.30(5); for auditors' qualifications, see below, paras 8–13 *et seq.*
36 *cf. Re Ossory Estates p.l.c.* [1988] B.C.L.C. 213.

amount of any premium payable on them; a description of the non-cash consideration, the method used for valuing it and the date of valuation; the extent to which the shares are being paid for in cash and in other consideration; and limited details about any delegate who valued some or all of the assets. It must contain or be accompanied by a note stating that the method of valuation used was reasonable in the circumstances; that there appears to have been no material change in value since the valuation was made; if a person other than one eligible to be the company's auditor was used to do some valuation, that it was reasonable to have him do it and to accept his assessment. Perhaps most importantly of all, it must contain a note that the assets valued, together with any cash that is being paid, are worth not less than the nominal value of the shares to be allotted plus any premium on them. There is no requirement to disclose the valuer's report to the shareholders generally, but a copy of it must be delivered to the registrar of companies along with the return of the allotments.[37]

DIVIDENDS FROM CAPITAL

7–25 Another basic principle of the capital integrity doctrine is that a limited company's capital, once contributed, must be "maintained" in the company and not be redistributed to shareholders, except in the cumbersome manner provided for in sections 72-77 of the 1963 Act or under Part XI of the 1990 Act. The rule that dividends must not be paid out of subscribed capital but only from profits gained general recognition in *Flitcroft's Case*.[38] Given the special statutory procedures for capital reduction, it was said, "a company cannot reduce its capital except in the manner and with the safeguards provided by statute, and looking at the Act . . . it clearly is against the intention of the legislature that any portion of the capital should be returned to the shareholders without the statutory conditions being complied with".[39] This conclusion was reinforced by the requirement that every company must have an objects clause, "which is a statement that the capital shall be applied for the purposes of the business, and on the faith of that statement, which is sometimes said to be an implied contract with creditors, people dealing with the company give it credit".[40] The related rule, that companies may not purchase their own shares, was first proclaimed in *Trevor v. Whitworth*.[41] Its existence too was inferred from the proce-

---

[37] s.31(2).
[38] *Re Exchange Banking Co.* (1882) 21 Ch.D. 519.
[39] *ibid.* at 533.
[40] *ibid.*
[41] (1887) 12 App. Cas. 409.

dures for returning capital to shareholders, "the effect of [which] is to prohibit every transaction between a company and a shareholder, by means of which the money already paid to the company in respect of his shares is returned to him, unless the court has sanctioned the transaction".[42] These two rules were incorporated into the 1963 Act, which also prohibits companies from financing the purchase of their own shares, and they have been extended and amended in places by the 1983 Act and Part XI of the 1990 Act.

7–26 Of course a company cannot maintain its capital in an absolute sense, in that if, for example, it commences trading with a capital of say £50,000 but incurs losses of £5,000 each year for its first three years doing business, then its capital in fact is depleted by £15,000 and stands at £35,000. The law does not require companies to preserve their contributed capital intact against trading losses. Thus in *Re Horsley & Weight Ltd.*[43] where it was contended, unsuccessfully, that pension arrangements made by the company were *ultra vires*, it was argued as well that, in the circumstances, the payments contravened the requirement that companies must maintain their capital. This contention was rejected because:

> "It is a misapprehension to suppose that the directors of a company owe a duty to the company's creditors to keep the contributed capital of the company intact. The company's creditors are entitled to assume that the company will not in any way repay any paid up share capital to the shareholders except by means of a duly authorised reduction of capital. . . . On the other hand, a company and its directors acting on its behalf, can quite properly expend contributed capital for any purpose which is intra vires the company."[44]

Pre-1983 Position

7–27 Occasionally, companies have good reasons for repaying part of their capital. For instance, large profits may have been made on the sale of a major asset and there may be no commercial justification in re-investing in the existing business, so that the shareholders may prefer to have part of their investment returned to them. Or one or more shareholders may want to realise their investment but there is no market for the shares and the company may have plenty of funds. The 1963 Act in sections 72-77 sets out a procedure under which capital may be repaid.[45] Briefly, each class of shareholder whose class rights

---

[42] (1887) 12 App. Cas. 409 at 423.
[43] [1982] 1 Ch. 442.
[44] *ibid.* at 453–454. See also *Dale v. Martin* (1882) 9 L.R. Ir. 498.
[45] See below, paras 11–35 *et seq*.

would be affected by the reduction must consent by a special resolution of the class to the proposal; creditors must be given adequate assurances that their claims against the company will not be jeopardised; and the entire arrangement must be confirmed by the court. A limited company may not "reduce its capital in any way" other than through the sections 72-77 procedure or, since 1991, by purchasing or redeeming its own shares under Part XI of the 1990 Act.

7–28 An example of the breadth of this prohibition is the New Zealand case *Jenkins v. Harbour View Courts Ltd.*,[46] which concerned a condominium organised in the form of a limited company, under which any holders of a certain number of the company's shares were entitled to live in one of its apartments. It then was proposed that the company should grant the holders of the relevant number of shares 99-year leases on their apartments, the rent to be fixed annually by the directors at an amount no greater than was needed to meet outgoings and place something in reserve. An objection to this proposal was upheld by the court, on the grounds that in substance it amounted to an unauthorised return of capital to the members. In *Re Halt Garage (1964) Ltd.*,[47] the payments made by an insolvent company to one of the two shareholders-directors, who was suffering from a long-term illness, were characterised not as remuneration but as repayments of capital; the recipient was therefore obliged to re-imburse the company. Similarly, in the "asset stripping" case, *Aveling Barford Ltd. v. Perion Ltd.*,[48] the company, which was insolvent and had no profits from which it could have paid any dividends, sold a property for far less than its market value; both the company and the purchaser were controlled by the one individual. The sale was held to be *ultra vires* as an unlawful return of capital to the company's owner and in substance a fraud on its creditors. And in *Barclay's Bank v. British & Commonwealth Holdings p.l.c.*,[49] covenants the company had with the plaintiff and other banks to maintain certain asset rates, as security for completing a capital restructuring, were held to contravene the principle against paying dividends from capital. Furthermore, the broad principle applies even if the recipient of the distribution is not a member of the company who takes the money or assets in that capacity.

7–29 The classic formulation of the rule was that limited companies may not pay dividends from capital and that dividends may not be

---

[46] [1966] N.Z.L.R. 1; see below, para. 14–71.
[47] [1982] 3 All E.R. 1016.
[48] [1989] B.C.L.C. 626.
[49] [1996] 1 B.C.L.C. 1.

paid if, in consequence, the company would be rendered insolvent. As they were applied, however, these formulae give somewhat inadequate protection to creditors. The approach to what amounted to capital, and accordingly was undistributable, was the *res* theory. By this is meant that capital was identified, not by the monetary quantum stated in the memorandum of association and balance sheet, but connoted the assets contributed by the shareholders in exchange for their shares, or assets into which those original assets had been converted. Consequently, it was concluded, there was no obligation to make up for fixed capital that had depreciated or was lost in trading.[50] The criterion of solvency was not that of assets exceeding liabilities but that of cash flow, *i.e.* whether the company could pay its debts as they fell due.[51] In the cases where some of the ground rules were laid down, it was emphasised that many aspects of dividend policy were more matters of good business or accounting practice than of law, and that the Companies Acts themselves allowed companies an extensive discretion as regards paying dividends.[52]

7–30 Major changes in the requirements were initiated by the E.C. Second Directive and are now incorporated in the 1983 Act.[53] For all companies, the fund from which dividends can be paid has become the aggregate net earned surplus, *i.e.* current profits and any profits carried forward less current losses and any losses carried forward. For p.l.c.s, the test of solvency has become one of balance sheet surplus, *i.e.* the company's net assets must not be less than the subscribed capital together with any undistributable reserves. There are variations on these rules for investment companies and for industrial and life assurance companies.[54]

"Distribution"

7–31 Instead of the term dividend, which has somewhat narrow connotations, the 1983 Act uses the word "distribution". This is defined in section 51 as "every description of distribution of a company's assets to members of the company, whether in cash or otherwise, except [certain itemised] distributions." Therefore, declared dividends and all payments and transfers of assets to shareholders that are analogous to

---

50 *Verner v. General & Commercial Investment Trust* [1894] 2 Ch. 239 and *Kehoe v. Waterford & Limerick Railway Co.* (1888) 21 L.R. Ir. 221.

51 *cf. Re Peter Buchanan Ltd. v. McVey* [1954] I.R. 89 and *Re Castleisland Railway Co.* [1896] 2 I.R. 661.

52 *Verner* and *Kehoe*, above, n. 50 and *Re National Bank of Wales* [1899] 2 Ch. 629.

53 See generally, Prentice, *The Companies Act 1980* (1980), Chap. 12.

54 ss. 47 and 48; see below, paras 14–79 and 14–77.

dividends are distributions. The proposed leases of flats in the *Harbour View Courts* case[55] would be a distribution. It could be argued that the *ultra vires* payment to the director/shareholder in the *Halt Garage* case[56] and the asset disposal in the *Aveling Barford* case[57] are not distributions as defined here, because they were made to one member only and not to "members". But that contention is most unlikely to succeed. It was emphasised in the *British & Commonwealth Holdings* case[58] that what matters is the substance and economic effect of the transaction in question and not its technical form. However, the complex reconstruction of capital, which was in dispute there, was held not to contravene the statutory prohibition because it had previously obtained the approval of the court. Those distributions that are excepted from the rules against repaying capital are the issue of bonus shares as fully or partly paid; the purchase or redemption of shares under Part XI of the 1990 Act; the reduction of capital within sections 72-77 of the 1963 Act; and distributions to members on a winding up.

Solvency

7–32 Companies other than p.l.c.s remain subject to the cash flow, or equitable, test of solvency. But this does not adequately safeguard creditors' interests, in that firms whose liabilities exceed their assets are nevertheless permitted to pay dividends if they succeed in meeting their debts as they fall due. For p.l.c.s, however, the criterion is now that of balance sheet surplus. According to section 46 of the 1963 Act, a p.l.c. may make a distribution only when "the amount of its net assets is not less than the aggregate of [its] called-up share capital and its undistributable reserves" and the distribution will not have the effect of reducing net assets below this aggregate figure. That is to say, the value of the company's assets, less its liabilities, must exceed its called-up share capital together with any undistributable reserves. Uncalled share capital may not be treated as an asset for this purpose. Called-up share capital is defined broadly in section 2(1) as to include calls made but not yet paid up, and capital the company will become entitled to but it has not yet received. Undistributable reserves are defined as the share premium account, the capital redemption reserve fund, any reserve the company is not allowed either by statute or by its memorandum or articles to distribute and the excess of any accumulated unrealised profits that have not been capitalised[59] over any accumu-

---

55 See above, n .46.
56 See above, n. 47.
57 See above, n. 48.
58 [1996] 1 W.L.R. 1.
59 ss. 46(2), 51(3).

lated unrealised losses that have not been duly written-off. The expansive concept of called-up share capital and the inclusion of unrealised profits in undistributable reserves enhances the protection afforded to p.l.c.s' creditors.

Available Profits

7–33 It used to be said that, since "the word 'profits' is by no means free from ambiguity, [the law is] more accurately expressed by saying that dividends cannot be paid out of capital, than by saying that they can only be paid out of profits."[60] This is no longer the case. The 1983 Act focuses on profits, the governing principle as stated in section 45 being that a company "shall not make a distribution except out of profits available for the purpose." Profits available for distribution are defined as a company's "accumulated, realised profits, so far as not previously utilised by distribution or capitalisation, less its accumulated, realised losses, so far as not previously written-off in a reduction or reorganisation of capital duly made." An end, therefore, has been put to the system under which "nimble dividends" could be paid, *i.e.*, although the company had sizeable accumulated losses, if it made a profit in any one year it could pay a dividend from those profits; even though it made a sizeable loss in any one or more years, it could pay a dividend out of profits it previously had earned but never distributed. Since 1983, any current profits and distributable reserves carried forward must exceed aggregate present and past losses that have not been written-off in a capital reduction or reorganisation. Thus, the revenue account is treated as one continuous stream and dividends cannot be paid until all deficits have been eliminated — which in any event is the normal accounting practice.

7–34 It is realised profits and losses that are relevant to this calculation, *i.e.*, profits that in fact are earned and actual losses incurred.[61] Moreover, unrealised profits may not be used to pay up debentures or any amounts unpaid on issued shares,[62] but this does not preclude using unrealised profits to pay up allotments of fully or partly paid bonus shares. Except for a number of particular contexts, the Act does not differentiate in principle between revenue and capital profits and losses.[63]

---

[60] *Verner*, above n. 50, at p. 266; *Bond v. Barrow Haematite Steel Co.* [1902] 1 Ch. 353.
[61] *Re Cleveland Trust p.l.c.* [1991] B.C.L.C. 424.
[62] But see s.51(1), where, prior to the appointed day, the articles of association authorised issuing bonus shares on the basis of unrealised profits.
[63] s. 51(4); *cf. Lubbock v. British Bank of Soutb America* [1892] 2 Ch. 198.

Accounting Rules

7–35 The 1983 Act introduces three categories of accounting rules that govern determinations of whether a company has profits available and is solvent as described above.

Relevant Accounts

7–36 Firstly, there is the matter of the relevant accounts.[64] Normally, these are the properly prepared last annual accounts about which the auditors made a report under section 193 of the 1990 Act and a copy of which was laid before a general meeting. Where that report was not unqualified, the auditors must have stated their opinion whether the matter giving rise to the qualification was relevant to the legality of the distribution in question. If those accounts would cause a distribution to contravene the Act, reliance may be placed on properly prepared more recent interim accounts, provided a copy of them was delivered to the registrar of companies. If it is proposed to make the distribution in the company's first financial year, then properly prepared initial accounts suffice, provided that certain safeguards are complied with. Any accounts being relied on for these purposes must not alone comply with the strict accounting standards in the Companies Acts but must also give a "true and fair view" of the company's trading or capital position, as the case may be.

7–37 That strict compliance with these accounting rules will be insisted on is illustrated by the *Precision Dippings Ltd.* case,[65] where the accounts indicated that there were sufficient funds from which a dividend could be paid. However, those accounts were qualified and the auditors had not provided the statement required, as above. It was held that the company's liquidator was entitled to recover the dividend paid on foot of those accounts. Moreover, even though the auditors subsequently gave the requisite statement and the members passed a resolution purporting to ratify the dividend payment, the breach of section 49(3) was not thereby cured. These rules are designed to protect creditors and the shareholders, therefore, cannot waive any breach of the safeguards.

Difficulties in Determination

7–38 Then there are rules for where it is not possible to say whether a profit or loss was made, or whether some profit or loss was realised.[66]

---

[64] s.49.
[65] [1986] Ch. 447.
[66] s.45(7).

Where no record exists or can be traced of a particular asset's original cost, it is deemed to be worth the amount which was first entered into the company's books. Where the directors cannot determine whether a profit made or a loss incurred before the appointed day is realised or unrealised, they are permitted to treat the profit as realised and the loss as unrealised.[67] There is a special rule of thumb for determining when surpluses and deficits constitute realised profits and losses in the case of companies carrying on industrial or life assurance business, or both.[68]

Depreciation

7–39 Finally, there are the vexed questions of depreciation and other changes in the values of fixed assets.[69] While the law does not strictly require companies to make provision for depreciation or for contingent liabilities, any such provision made must now be treated as a realised loss, with the exception of a provision made in consequence of a decline in value discovered in the course of revaluing all the fixed assets.[70] Indeed, because the relevant accounts must give a "true and fair view" and because failure to provide for depreciation might very well distort that view, it is fair to say that for practical purposes appropriate provision should be made for writing down the values of depreciating assets. The extent of that write down would depend on the normal accountancy practice. The rule in section 149(6)(a) of the 1963 Act,[71] that an unrealised surplus arising in a revaluation of fixed assets may not be distributed as dividends, is now subject to a qualification. A company may treat as a realised profit any difference between the sum set aside for depreciation of a fixed asset which has been revalued and the amount of the unrealised profit thereby discovered.[72]

ACQUIRING OWN SHARES

7–40 The rule first announced in *Trevor v. Whitworth*,[73] that limited companies may not purchase their own shares, is reiterated in the 1963 Act and the 1983 Act. Among the objections to this practice are that it endangers creditors' security, since it is a disguised way of returning

---

67 s.45(8).
68 s.48.
69 See definition in s.45(9) of 1983 Act; *e.g. Bond v. Haematite Steel Co.* [1902] 1 Ch. 353.
70 s.45(4).
71 Repealed by 1987 Act but replaced by *ibid.*, s.45(2).
72 s.45(6).
73 (1887) 12 App. Cas. 409.

capital to the shareholders; it enables company controllers to manipulate the company's share price; and it makes it easier for controllers to entrench their positions of power in a company. Yet there are arguments in favour of allowing companies to purchase their own shares, subject to sufficient safeguards for creditors and against abuse of power by company controllers. Tax considerations aside, it is a much simpler method of returning capital to some shareholders than the procedure under sections 72-77 of the 1963 Act. Individual shareholders may wish to liquidate their investment but there may be no ready market for it; or the management may wish to reduce the number of shareholders below a certain figure, for instance, to under 50 in order to "go private"; or a majority may wish to be in a position where they can expel particularly troublesome members by the company repurchasing their shares. Finally, this method can be used to prevent a stake in a company from going outside a family or some other narrowly defined group. In *Trevor v. Whitworth*, for instance, the reason the company sought to buy its own shares was to keep it a family concern. Even though the E.C. Second Directive allows for this practice where persons concerned in the company are not adversely affected,[74] it remained proscribed in this country until Part XI of the Companies Act 1990, came into force.[75] Part XI was not in several early versions of the 1987 Bill and was included in it only at a comparatively later stage of its journey through the Oireachtas.

The Prohibition

7–41 Subject to the exceptions and qualifications set out below, section 41(1) of the 1983 Act prohibits any limited company having a share capital from "acquir[ing] its own shares (whether by purchase, subscription or otherwise)." *Vision Express (UK) Ltd. v. Wilson*[76] vividly illustrates the thrust of this prohibition. A dispute between the company and a senior employee concerning his alleged fraud was settled on terms that, *inter alia*, the company would purchase shares he held in and options he had on shares in the company; the terms of settlement were annexed to what is known as a "Tomlin order". It was held that this part of the settlement could not be enforced because it involved a breach of section 41 and did not fall within any of the stipulated exceptions. But section 41(1) does not apply where a company acquires shares in a company and the latter already owns shares in the acquiring company;[77] there are special rules for cross-shareholdings between parent

---

[74] Arts. 19–22.
[75] On July 1, 1991.
[76] [1995] 2 B.C.L.C. 419.
[77] *Acatos & Hutcheson p.l.c. v. Watson* [1995] 1 B.C.L.C. 218.

and subsidiary companies.[78] A limited company may acquire its own fully paid shares "otherwise than for valuable consideration"; in other words, by way of gift and the like. But this exemption would not seem to cover the kind of situation that arose in *Re Irish Provident Assur. Co.*,[79] which was one of a series of cases concerning the transformation of a friendly society into an insurance company. The central issue concerned a compromise made of various claims between the company and its former managing director, which was ratified in general meeting. One of the terms was that he would transfer without payment all his shares in the company to such person as the company should direct, and that the company would pay him a lump sum. It was held that this agreement was void in that "the real transaction, notwithstanding the conveyancing effort to conceal its true nature, included a sale to the company of the shares, not a gift of them."[80]

7–42 Where a company issues its own shares to its nominee or where the nominee acquires partly paid shares in the company from some third party, provision is made in section 42(2) of the 1983 Act to ensure that the company recovers any sums due to it on those shares. And where its own shares are acquired by or for a p.l.c. in a number of enumerated ways and are not disposed of, voting rights in respect of them must not be exercised, and the company is required to cancel those shares and reduce its share capital by their nominal value.[81]

Charge and Lien on Own Shares

7–43 In *Re Balgooley Distillery Co.*,[82] on the authority of a case that afterwards was overruled,[83] it was held that a limited company could accept its own fully paid up shares as security for an ordinary business transaction with one of its shareholders and later enforce that security by cancelling those shares. Stating that, under the *stare decisis* system, he had no choice but to uphold the transaction, FitzGibbon L.J. expressed the view that an absolute prohibition against all dealings by companies in their own shares would be preferable. There was "no satisfactory ground for determining the validity of a purchase of its own shares by a company on considerations of motive or intention"; and he "fail[ed] to see any satisfactory distinction between 'trafficking in shares' as it is called . . . and acquiring them for valuable considera-

---

[78] See below, para. 14–41.
[79] [1913] 1 I.R. 352.
[80] *ibid.* at 369.
[81] s.43.
[82] (1886) 17 L.R. Ir. 239.
[83] *Re Dronfield Silkstone Co.* (1880) 17 Ch.D. 76.

tion for other motives".[84] Acceptance by a company of its own shares as security for a debt owed to it is not a violation of section 72 of the 1963 Act's prohibition against companies "purchas[ingl" their own shares or otherwise reducing their share capital. Whether it amounts to "acquir[ing]" their own shares as prohibited by section 42(1) of the 1983 Act is arguable since the word acquiring is not defined.

7–44 The position as regards p.l.c.s is made clear by section 44 of the 1983 Act. Subject to one main exception, a p.l.c. is not allowed to have a lien or any other charge over its own shares, regardless of how that security interest may arise. This does not apply to transactions entered into by banks and by hire purchase companies in the ordinary course of their business. The articles of association of companies often contain an express prohibition against them taking their own shares as security for liabilities of their shareholders to the company.

7–45 A lien is a possessory security and strictly is not a charge. Table A of the 1963 Act gives companies a lien sanctioned by section 44(2)(a) of the 1983 Act, viz. over partly paid shares in respect of sums payable on those shares.[85] Especially in light of that very provision, the validity of articles purporting to grant a lien over the company's fully paid shares in respect of all kinds of debts to the company must be doubted, especially where there is no ready market for those shares.

Permitted Acquisitions of Own Shares

7–46 One of the major innovations in the 1990 Act was to permit limited companies to purchase or otherwise acquire their own shares, or shares in their holding company, subject to the conditions laid down in Part XI of that Act.[86] Changes in the tax rules to make re-purchase of shares a fiscally realistic option for companies and their members were adopted in the following year.[87] In addition to the straightforward share purchase by the company, Part XI of the 1990 Act also permits companies to issue redeemable shares of any class and even to convert their normally irredeemable shares into redeemable ones. This Part also allows subsidiary companies to acquire shares in their own holding company, subject to the certain safeguards.[88]

---

[84] (1886) 17 L.R. Ir. 239 at 264.
[85] See below, para. 9–73.
[86] See generally, *The Purchase by A Company of Its Own Shares*, Cmnd. 7944 (1980).
[87] See generally, F. Brennan, *A Company Purchasing its own Shares* (1991).
[88] See below, paras 14–42—14–43.

7–47 Certain common prerequisites for each of these kind of share acquisitions are laid down.[89] The company's articles of association must permit the company to make the kind of acquisition envisaged. The shares being acquired must always be fully paid shares. Generally, the funds used to pay for the shares the company is acquiring must come from profits which the company is free to distribute by way of dividend; the same applies to any premium being paid on the shares. Finally, not more than a certain proportion of the company's shares may be acquired within these terms. Any acquisition by the company of its shares otherwise than as provided for in Part XI of the 1990 Act remains unlawful. Special rules are laid down for acquisitions by investment companies which resemble unit trusts.[90]

7–48 Where a company acquires its shares in the manner provided for here, ordinarily it has an option. It may cancel those shares; in that event, the share capital is deemed to have been accordingly reduced.[91] Alternatively, it may retain the shares as what are called "treasury" shares[92] — terminology borrowed from the United States. Throughout the period while the company holds its shares in that form they are virtually frozen, in the sense that the votes attaching to them cannot be exercised and no dividend or other distribution may be made in respect of them.[93] If those shares could be voted, the company's management might thereby obtain too influential a say in its affairs and there is little point in the company paying itself a dividend. When the desirable circumstances arise, treasury shares can be re-issued by the company. A return must be made to the registrar of companies of all transactions under these sections.

Purchasing Own Shares

7–49 Section 211 of the 1990 Act allows a limited company to purchase its own shares, provided its articles of association so permit. The maximum number of shares which can be purchased in this manner is measured by reference to any redeemable shares it may have in its share capital. Share purchases by the company must not reach the state that the irredeemable shares in its capital fall below ten per cent of the redeemable shares.[94]

---

89 s.207(2).
90 ss. 254 and 255; see below, para. 14–79.
91 s.208.
92 s.209.
93 s.209(3).
94 s.211(3).

7–50 The common conditions set out above must be met, regarding the shares being fully paid and the purchase money coming from distributable profits; additional preconditions may be laid down in the company's own articles.[95] Moreover, the Minister is authorised to prescribe additional conditions in regulations regarding, for example[96] the kinds of shares which may or may not be purchased, prices, timing, methods and the volume of trading companies may carry out in their shares. Where it is proposed to cancel the shares, their purchase may be financed by a fresh issue of shares made for this very purpose and also by drawing from the share premium account.[97] What authority is needed to go ahead with a proposed re-purchase depends on whether or not the shares are being traded on the stock market.

7–51 Section 215 applies to what are called "market" purchases, *i.e.* purchases of shares on a recognised stock exchange and which are listed on that market or in respect of which dealing facilities have been afforded.[98] Purchases of this nature must have been authorised by a resolution passed in general meeting. This resolution must specify the maximum number of shares which can be acquired and the maximum and minimum prices to be paid, but need not authorise each individual contract for purchase. The expiry date must be specified in the resolution but this authority may never exceed 18 months.[99] A copy of this resolution must be filed with the registrar of companies.

7–52 What are called "off market" purchases are regulated by section 213, *i.e.* purchases other than stock-market transactions.[100] Principally because it is far more difficult to ascertain a fair price for these shares, the conditions laid down are more stringent and each particular purchase contract must have been authorised in advance. A copy of that contract or a memorandum of its terms must have been available for inspection by the members for at least 21 days before the meeting which considers it. If the contract relates to any present shareholder, he must be identified in a memorandum if his name does not appear on the contract. Not alone must the purchase be authorised by a special resolution but the intending seller is not permitted to vote his shares on that resolution in that, if he votes and the proposal is ultimately carried by virtue of his votes, they will not count. Notwithstanding

---

95 s.207(2), (3).
96 s.228.
97 s.208(b)(2).
98 s.212(1)(b), (2).
99 s.216.
100 s.212(1)(a).

anything in the company's articles of association, any member can demand a poll on these proposals. In the case of a p.l.c., any authority given to purchase shares cannot last longer than 18 months.[101]

7–53 Where the company wishes to cancel the shares it has acquired, the position is regulated by section 208 of the 1990 Act. In consequence, the issued share capital is deemed to have been reduced. Where the purchase was funded entirely from distributable profits, an amount equivalent to the nominal value of the shares purchased must be credited to a capital reserve fund; that fund will be treated as if it were fully paid up capital in the company. Accordingly, in an accounting sense, the company's aggregate capital was never diminished. Where a fresh issue of shares funded the share purchase, either entirely or in part, then the difference between the nominal value of the shares purchased and the proceeds of the fresh issue must be credited to a capital reserve account. The capital reserve fund here can be used to finance an issue of bonus shares.

7–54 The treatment of "treasury shares" purchased by the company is provided for in section 209 of the 1990 Act. No more than 10 per cent of the company's issued shares may be held by it at any time in this form. For the purpose of calculating this ratio, shares which its subsidiary holds in the company and also shares held by someone else acting on the company's behalf are included with the treasury shares.[102] As was said above, those shares cannot be voted nor can any dividend or any other payment be made by the company in respect of them. At some later stage the company may decide to cancel all or some of its treasury shares; in that event the rules set out above apply.

7–55 Alternatively, the company may decide to re-issue all or some of those shares. In that case, the normal rules for issuing additional shares apply, for instance, sections 20 and 23 of the 1983 Act regarding prior authority and pre-emption.[103] Where they are being re-issued on the stock market, no special procedure is laid down for fixing the issue price. But in the case of a non-market re-issue, the issue price range must be stipulated in the resolution which authorised the purchase of those shares at the outset.[104] However, the price fixed there can always be varied by a special resolution.[105]

---

[101] s.216.
[102] Also, shares held by a subsidiary in pursuance of s.9 of the Insurance Act 1990.
[103] See above, paras 6–25 and 6–29.
[104] s.209(6)(b).
[105] s.209(6)(d).

7–56 Even though it may have been fully authorised to buy them, a company will not be held liable in damages for breach of a contract to purchase its own shares.[106] However, that does not prejudice any other rights the contracting party may have against the company, notably an action for rescission. Moreover, a court may award specific performance of the contract, but will not do so if the company does not possess sufficient available profits to cover the purchase price. In the event of the company being wound up, its liability under a contract to purchase its own shares ranks after all debts and liabilities to non-members and to any claims by preference shareholders.[107]

7–57 Where a company purchases its own shares, as provided for above, it is required to retain for the next ten years a copy of the purchase contract or, if an oral contract, a memorandum of its terms.[108] Any member of the company is entitled to inspect those records; in the case of a p.l.c., they may be inspected by any member of the public.

Issuing Redeemable Shares

7–58 Formerly, companies could only issue redeemable preference shares, subject to the conditions laid down in section 64 of the 1963 Act. Now, under section 207 of the 1990 Act, they may issue redeemable shares of any class, provided that at least one-tenth of their share capital is comprised of non-redeemable shares. The general conditions described above for purchasing shares also apply to redeeming these shares;[109] additional requirements may be laid down in the articles of association. Once redeemed, the shares may be cancelled or instead held as treasury shares. Where they are subsequently re-issued off the stock market, the issue price range must be fixed in advance by a special resolution.[110]

Converting Irredeemable Shares into Redeemable Shares

7–59 Companies may now convert shares which formerly could not be redeemed into redeemable shares, and then go on and redeem them as provided for above. However, that power, given by section 210 of the 1990 Act, is subject to certain restrictions. As well as the articles of association enabling a conversion of this nature to be made, the power is subject to such "class rights" as may exist, *i.e.* special rights which

---

[106] s.219.
[107] s.219(6).
[108] s.222.
[109] s.207(2); above, paras 7–46 *et seq.*
[110] s.209(6)(c).

attach to any distinctive classes of shares.[111] Furthermore, conversion cannot be forced on any member, but one who objects to having his shares being made redeemable must notify the company before the date fixed for any conversion to take place. Additional requirements may be laid down in the articles of association. What is said above regarding cancelling the shares or holding them as treasury shares also applies here.

FINANCING THE PURCHASE OF OWN SHARES

7–60 It was held in *Re MJ. Cummins Ltd.*[112] that ordinarily it is *ultra vires* for a company to lend money or to guarantee a loan to enable the borrower to purchase shares in that company. There, the shareholders wanted to sell their company but the intended purchaser was not in funds at the time. So the local bank manager devised an "ingenious plan" whereby the bank would advance a substantial sum to the company, which in turn would lend that money to the purchaser, with which he could then buy the shares. Johnston J. held that the bank could not recover the loan from the company. The position there would not have been affected by section 8(1) of the 1963 Act (if in force at the time) because the bank would have been "actually aware" of the improper application of its loan. Transactions of the kind entered into in that case are now the subject of express statutory prohibition, breach of which constitutes a criminal offence. It was for the offence of enabling Guinness p.l.c. to finance the purchase of its own shares, during a take-over battle for Distillers p.l.c., that several leading English financiers were prosecuted in 1990. But for this prohibition, the restriction on companies purchasing their own shares could be avoided very easily. The prohibition was first adopted in England in 1928, in consequence of recommendations in the Greene Report,[113] and was adopted here in 1959.[114] The arguments against financial assistance in this context are the same as those against a company acquiring its own shares; while some situations where such assistance can be beneficial are covered by exceptions under section 60.

7–61 The prohibition does not affect payment of a properly declared dividend, discharge of a liability lawfully incurred by the company or a repayment of capital under sections 72-77 of the 1963 Act. There are

---

[111] See below, para. 11–11.
[112] [1939] I.R. 60.
[113] Cmnd. 2657 (1926).
[114] Companies Act 1959, s.3.

also exceptions for employees' shares, for bank loans and for certain loans made by private companies. Where part of a contract consists of an agreement to provide the proscribed assistance, it may be possible to "sever" that offending part and enforce the remainder of the contract.[115]

The Prohibition

7–62 According to section 60 of the 1963 Act, which applies to all registered companies whether or not they are limited:

> "it shall not be lawful for a company to give, whether directly or indirectly, and whether by means of a loan, guarantee, the provision of security or otherwise, any financial assistance for the purpose of or in connection with a purchase or subscription made or to be made by any person of or for any shares in the company. . . ."

Although this prohibition was aimed principally at preventing persons from taking over companies by using those companies' very own resources for that purpose, the net is cast much wider than that. If section 60 were always to be given a purely literal interpretation, it would condemn some arrangements which actually benefit the company and its members and do not jeopardise the creditors' interests. The view that the very broad scope of this section should be narrowed in the light of the mischief it seeks to remedy has received some judicial support in New Zealand[116] and in 1981 led to modifications in the legislation in Britain.[117] Especially because a criminal provision which casts its net almost indiscriminately widely might be unconstitutional, a purposive and narrow construction most likely would be adopted here.

7–63 Section 60 deals with financing the acquisition of a company's own shares or of shares in its holding company,[118] either by way of subscription or purchase, whether made before or after the actual assistance was provided. Assistance rendered must be financial. But it does not matter whether it is given gratuitously or on commercial terms; transactions entirely at arm's length can fall foul of section 60.[119] For instance, it has been held that the payment by a subsidiary company of its holding company's debt is not excluded from the prohibition.[120]

---

115 *Carney v. Herbert* [1985] A.C. 301.
116 *Re Wellington Publishing Co. Ltd.* [1973] 1 N.Z.L.R. 133; see below, para. 12–14.
117 *cf. Brady v. Brady* [1989] A.C. 755.
118 But not where the subsidiary providing the finance is registered abroad: *Arab Bank p.l.c. v. Merchantile Holdings Ltd.* [1994] Ch. 71.
119 *Belmont Finance Corp. v. Williams Furniture Ltd. (No. 2)* [1980] 1 All E.R. 393.
120 *Armour Hick Northern Ltd. v. Whitehouse* [1994] Ch. 71.

There is no requirement about the form the prohibited assistance must take; it may be a loan, a guarantee or other kind of security, or some other method of putting the purchaser of the shares in funds, like buying assets from him. Assistance may be indirect as well as direct, *i.e.* the initial recipient of the funds or whatever need not be the person who acquired the shares. As one judge put it, the prohibition "is directed to financial assistance to whomsoever given, provided that it be for the purpose of . . . or in connection with a purchase of shares".[121] In a notorious case that involved circular cheques, strings of puppet companies and other stratagems, Lord Denning, M.R. recommended that the corporate veil be cast aside and you "look to the company's money and see what has become of it. You look to the company's shares and see into whose hands they have got. You will soon see if the company's money has been used to finance the purchase".[122]

7–64 It is in determining the precise scope of section 60's *scienter* requirement that the greatest difficulties arise, which are compounded by the fact that companies have no minds of their own, the beneficiaries of their subsidies for share buying are often their own directors, contravention of the section is a criminal offence, as well as a civil wrong, and there are complications about the appropriate civil sanction. A breach occurs where the impugned transaction's sole or primary objective is to finance an acquisition of the company's or its holding company's shares. But it depends very much on the inferences drawn from the established facts whether that very purpose can be shown.

7–65 *Re C.H. (Ireland) Inc.*[123] concerned a complex series of transactions involving a Swiss bank and its Canadian subsidiary, and a Montreal based finance company and its New Brunswick subsidiary; £stg18.8 million was deposited in Switzerland by an Irish company and, in due course, the financier's subsidiary subscribed for shares in the company paying that amount. McCraken J. concluded that the only or main purpose of the company making that deposit was to assist its shares being acquired in that manner and, accordingly, declared that the deposit and the payment obligation arising from it contravened section 60. On the other hand, he found that a guarantee given by the financier's subsidiary was not made principally for that purpose, as it

---

[121] *E.H. Dey Property Ltd. v. Dey* [1966] V.R. 464 at 470.

[122] *Wallersteiner v. Moir* [1974] 3 All E.R. 217 at 238. *cf. Mercato Holdings Ltd. v. Crown Corp.* [1989] 3 N.Z.L.R. 704 on not entirely disregarding the corporate veil in their cases.

[123] McCracken J., December 12, 1997.

was one of several guarantees given by all the subsidiaries at the time when the group was in serious financial difficulty. The judge also declined to declare that other steps in the circular scheme were unlawful, because the only "transactions" that section 60 condemned were those directly involving the company in question; further, some of the parties to them were not involved in the proceedings brought by the company's liquidator.

7–66 In determining whether there has been a breach of section 60, McCracken J. endorsed the following statement of principle:

> "There is no definition of giving financial assistance in the section, although some examples are given. The words have no technical meaning and their frame of reference is in my judgement the language of ordinary commerce. One must examine the commercial realities of the transaction and decide whether it can properly be described as the giving of financial assistance by the company, bearing in mind that the section is a penal one and should not be strained to cover transactions which are not fairly within it.
>
> [T]he sale of an asset by a company at a fair value can properly be described as giving financial assistance if the effect is to provide the purchaser of its shares with the cash needed to pay for them. It does not matter that the company's balance sheet is undisturbed in the sense that the cash paid out is replaced by an asset of equal value. In the case of a loan by a company to a credit worthy purchaser of its shares, the balance sheet is equally undisturbed but the loan plainly constitutes giving financial assistance. It follows that if the only or main purpose of such a transaction is to enable the purchaser to buy the shares, the section is contravened."[124]

7–67 Whether surrendering tax losses can constitute the prohibited financial assistance arose in *Charterhouse Investment Trust Ltd. v. Templest Diesels Ltd.*[125] In most of the cases under section 60 it is the buyer of the shares who gets the assistance; here the alleged assistance was given to the seller. The case arose out of a somewhat complex management buy out from its parent company of a company in financial difficulties. The terms of the agreement involved the parent conferring several financial advantages on the subsidiary, notably injecting around £750,000 in cash into the company, converting considerable outstanding indebtedness into an interest free loan repayable on advantageous terms, not charging any interest and paying redundancy compensation to its

---

[124] *ibid.* at 15–16, quoting Hoffman J. in the *Charterhouse Investment Trust Ltd. v. Templest Diesels Ltd.* [1986] B.C.L.C. 1 at 10.

[125] [1986] B.C.L.C. 1.

managing director. In return, the subsidiary agreed, *inter alia,* to surrender its tax losses to the parent company. At the time, those losses were of little benefit to the subsidiary because of its unpromising financial situation, although in the event the subsidiary became a commercial success and the losses would have been quite valuable if it had retained them. Hoffman J. rejected the contention that the surrender of those losses contravened section 60, holding that the transaction should not be looked at in isolation; it was part of a scheme in which, if anything, the subsidiary received considerable financial assistance rather than gave any such assistance.

7–68 In determining if section 60 has been breached, Hoffman J. there counselled a pragmatic approach, observing that "[t]he need to look at the commercial realities means that one cannot consider the surrender [here] in isolation . . . It was in truth part of a composite transaction under which [the subsidiary] both received benefits and assumed burdens. It is necessary to look at the transaction as a whole and decide whether it constituted the giving of financial assistance".[126] There, the subsidiary did not pay over any cash which facilitated the transfer of its shares. And the balance of advantages in the entire arrangement was predominantly in the subsidiary's favour.[127] Undoubtedly, the most important point made in the case was that, because of the criminal sanction, the vague terms in section 60 should not be construed too broadly. The case also imparts a blessing on management buy outs.

Permitted Transactions

7–69 The following financing arrangements are permitted by section 60.

Paying Dividends

7–70 Section 60 does not apply to "a dividend properly declared by a company . . ."[128] Even if there was no express exception for dividends, it was held that there was no offence committed where a company, which had been bought by a speculator with borrowed money, paid a large dividend from revalued assets so that its new owner could repay his borrowings.[129] Because the transaction there did not prejudice the creditors or any minority shareholders, it was upheld.

---

[126] [1986] B.C.L.C. 1 at 11.
[127] *Barclay's Bank p.l.c. v. British & Commonwealth Holdings p.l.c.* [1996] 1 B.C.L.C. 1 and *Parlett v. Guppys (Bridport) Ltd.* [1996] 2 B.C.L.C. 34 are in similar vein.
[128] s.60(12).
[129] *Re Wellington Publishing Co. Ltd.* [1973] 1 N.L.R. 133.

Discharging Liabilities

7–71 Nor does section 60 apply to "the discharge of a liability lawfully incurred by" the company.[130] Again, even if there were no express exception of this nature, it would seem that the proscription does not apply where a "debt is presently due and payable and the [company] can have no answer to the creditor's demands for payment [and] by paying his debt the [company] gave the creditor financial assistance."[131] The question still arises of how is this exclusion to be reconciled with the wide sweep of the prohibition. If a substantial liability is incurred simply to enable a person to finance the acquisition of shares in the company, has an offence been committed? If the answer is no, then some modes of objectionable financial assistance are permitted, like entering a guarantee to repay funds advanced for that purpose — provided the guarantee is *intra vires* and, perhaps, not a breach of directors' duties. Similarly, purchasing property in order to put the seller in funds, so that he can purchase the shares, would also be permissible. Perhaps the answer is an intermediate position; that guarantees and purchases of this nature are lawful if the entire arrangement is entered into in the ordinary course of business and is in the company's best interests. Whether such arrangements are lawful when providing assistance for share acquisitions is their sole *raison d'etre* is questionable, especially where the objects clause does not expressly authorise the transaction.

7–72 In *Belmont Finance Corp. v. Williams Furniture Ltd. (No.2)*[132] it was held that the section was contravened in England where the company acquired an asset at a fair price from a third party so as to enable him to acquire its shares. Funding the purchase of its shares was the sole purpose of the transaction there; emphasis was placed on the fact that the company had no genuine need in its business for what it bought and had entered into the transaction without regard to its own commercial interests. The court there declined to rule on the position where "the transaction is of a kind which A Ltd. could in its own commercial interests legitimately enter into, and . . . is genuinely entered into . . . in its own commercial interests and not merely as a means of assisting B financially to buy shares of A Ltd., the circumstances that A Ltd. enters into the transaction with B partly with the object of putting B in funds or with the knowledge of B's intended use of the proceeds of the

---

[130] s.60(12).
[131] *Armour Hick* case, above, n. 120, at p. 1525.
[132] [1980] 1 All E.R. 393.

sale . . ."[133] Transactions which fit this description most likely are excluded from the scope of the prohibition in section 60.

Employees' Shares

7–73 The exception for enabling the company's employees to acquire its shares or shares in a subsidiary, either individually or under the aegis of some employees' share scheme, is dealt with separately below.[134]

Loans by Financial Institutions

7–74 Another exception is "where the lending of money is part of the ordinary business of the company, the lending of money . . . in the ordinary course of [that] business."[135] This envisages ordinary bank loans and the like; it depends on the circumstances whether the loan in question can fairly be described as being made in the ordinary course of the company's business. Presumably, a company must be licensed or otherwise authorised by the State to lend money before it can come within this exception. Where the lending company is a p.l.c., the funds must be provided out of the profits available for distribution as a dividend.[136] Alternatively, the p.l.c. can give the assistance provided that its net assets are not thereby reduced.

Permitted Assistance by Private Companies

7–75 Section 60(2)–(11) sets out a mechanism under which private companies may subsidise purchases of their shares, provided there is shareholder approval for the proposal and that the creditors will not be jeopardised. In brief, the directors must make a statutory declaration concerning the proposed payment, the company must pass a special resolution approving the proposal and dissident shareholders may apply to the court to have the proposal vetoed. The statutory declaration must be made by the directors within 24 days before the shareholders' meeting; it must specify the form, the beneficiaries and the purposes of the assistance, and that the declarants after making due inquiry believe that the proposal will not affect the company's ability to meet its debts as they fall due.[137] Copies must be sent to every mem-

---

133 [1980] 1 All E.R. 393 at 402.

134 s.60(13)(b) and (c); see below, para. 15–08.

135 s.60(13)(a). *cf. Steen v. Law* [1964] A.C. 287.

136 s.60(15b) and (15c), inserted by 1983 Act, schedule, para. 10.

137 *cf. Re S.H. & Co. (Realisations) 1990 Ltd.* [1993] B.C.L.C. 1309 and *Re N.L. Electrical Ltd.* [1994] 1 B.C.L.C. 22 on the need for strict compliance with these procedures.

ber and to the registrar of companies. Every shareholder is entitled to notice of and to attend the meeting in question. Unless the resolution gets unanimous support from those members who are entitled to vote, the proposal cannot be put into effect until at least 30 days have elapsed. In the meantime objecting members who comprise at least ten per cent of the issued shares' nominal value or of any class may apply to the court and the proposal fails except to the extent that it is confirmed by the court. There are no authorities on the criteria the court will be guided by in such instances or on the burdens of proof.

7–76 *Lombard & Ulster Banking Ltd. v. Bank of Ireland*[138] is the first major case on compliance with those procedures and the consequences of non-compliance. In brief, the company in question owned valuable property, on which it ran a private school. An arrangement was made whereby several individuals, through a trust company, would acquire the bulk of the shares in the company. However, since the prospective purchasers did not have sufficient funds, it was agreed that they should borrow the funds from the plaintiff bank and that the company would guarantee the loan, giving a charge over its property as security. Because this was a classic instance of the company financing the purchase of its own shares, it was necessary to follow the procedures laid down in subsections (2)–(11) for the transaction to be fully effective. Two major issues arose, namely, was there compliance with these procedures and what are the legal consequences of non-compliance?

7–77 One of the company's shareholders swore an affidavit that he never attended a shareholders' meeting at which it was claimed that the proposed transaction had been sanctioned. The company had not kept minute books of those meetings nor of the directors' meetings. The company's file at Dublin Castle was produced but the documents in it were not proof of their contents, in particular, they were not proof that the requisite resolution had been passed. Indeed, those documents said that the shareholders' resolution had been passed on May 21 and the statutory declaration was made on May 22, which, if correct, was wholly improper. Because of this and other circumstantial evidence, Costello J. concluded that no statutory declaration was made on or before May 21 and no special resolution had been passed subsequently approving the transaction. The judge stressed that the court requires strict compliance with the procedure laid down in subsection (2)–(11); that if exemption from a breach of section 60(1) is claimed, "then strict compliance with the procedures is necessary . . . If the procedural re-

---

[138] Costello J., June 2, 1987.

quirements were not adopted the transaction is an illegal one . . ."[139] The procedures were not satisfied where all of the shareholders authorised an agent, such as their solicitor, to look after all the formalities and subsequently they ratified what had been done.

7–78 In *Re Northside Motor Co. Ltd.*,[140] with the full knowledge of its bankers, the company in question guaranteed a bank loan for the purpose of assisting the purchase of its own shares. Some time later the bank realised that the procedures in section 60(2)–(11) had not been followed and, accordingly, prevailed on the company to make a statutory declaration and pass a special resolution approving the guarantee. But since these steps must be taken before the actual assistance is given, there was not compliance with the requisite procedures and, consequently, the guarantee was ineffective because the bank had actual notice of all the circumstances. Additionally, the special resolution which was passed was inaccurate and misleading and, for that reason also, failed to comply with section 60.

SANCTIONS AND REMEDIES

7–79 Violation of many of the capital integrity provisions are criminal offences on the part of the company and the responsible officers. Criminalising the wrong poses a serious dilemma in that, as a general rule, the transactions that are proscribed in this way are void and unenforceable. But if some transaction that depletes a company's capital is rendered wholly null, then the company stands to lose and so too do its creditors and shareholders, for whose benefit the prohibition was enacted. Take the rule that has caused the greatest difficulties — providing financial assistance to acquire the company's own shares. If a loan or a guarantee by the company to that end is absolutely void, then that assistance once given can never be recouped and the fund to which creditors must look is permanently diminished. It nevertheless has been argued that such an apparently unjust result is preferable in its deterrent effect: that it "is likely to deter potential lenders from lending money on security which might be held to contravene the Act and is likely to be more efficacious in achieving the policy of the section than the very small maximum penalty on the company.[141] Against this view, it may be asked whether in fact widespread violations are pre-

[139] *ibid.* at 9–10.
[140] Costello J., July 24, 1985.
[141] *Heald v. O'Connor* [1971] 1 W.L.R. 497 at 502.

vented by the transactions in question being rendered absolutely void. Especially in the context of section 60 of the 1963 Act, deterrence which takes that drastic form can operate extremely unfairly. In any event, the view that the proscribed transaction must be void is an over-simplification of the general rule of law, because it overlooks the qualification that" [a]lthough . . . no action can arise from a prohibited and illegal act, if a plaintiff can show that he is a member of the class for whose protection the statutory prohibition was imposed, then as an exception such a person can enforce rights or recover property transferred under the illegal transaction."[142] Additionally, as is explained below, the court is given authority to validate otherwise invalid share issues and to exempt persons from liability for breach of most of these provisions in an appropriate case.

Minimum Amounts

7–80 Possession of the "authorised minimum" is a prerequisite to being registered as a p.l.c.[143] Where, in breach of section 28 of the 1983 Act, a p.l.c. allots shares and less than one-quarter of the nominal value and any premium on them is not paid up, the allotment is not invalid but the allottee is liable to the company for the outstanding differences.[144] As for transferees of those shares, previously the matter would be dealt with under the doctrine of estoppel, *i.e.* as a general rule, if the share certificate said that the shares were fully paid then the company would be estopped from denying this.[145] The question is now dealt with by section 26(4) of the 1983 Act, according to which subsequent holders of the shares are equally liable to the company except where they satisfy what may be called the "bona fide purchaser for value defence", explained below.[146]

7–81 Where, in breach of section 22 of the 1983 Act, a p.l.c., whose offer of shares was under-subscribed, allots any of the shares that were applied for, the allottee can avoid the allotment and have whatever he paid to the company refunded. Any director responsible can be held liable for that amount.[147]

---

[142] *Nash v. Halifax Building Society* [1979] 1 Ch. 384 at 390.
[143] 1983 Act ss. 4(3), 5(2), 17.
[144] *ibid.* s.28(2).
[145] See below, para. 9–59.
[146] See below, para. 7–92.
[147] 1983 Act, ss. 22(2) and 1963 Act, ss. 53(4), 55.

Allotting Shares at a Discount

7–82 It was held in the *Ooregum Gold Mining* case[148] that the original allottees who hold shares that were allotted at a discount are liable to pay the company the difference between the issue price and the par value. Under section 27 of the 1983 Act, the allottees of such shares are liable in the same way, as are subsequent holders in the extended sense unless they satisfy the section 26(4) defence for bona fide purchasers for value, as described below.

Allotting Shares for Non-Cash Consideration

7–83 In the light of *Ooregum Gold Mining*, it would appear that where, to the knowledge of the board and the allottees, over-valued consideration is exchanged for shares, the company may recover any deficiency from the allottees, at least where they are still owners of the shares. Where, in breach of section 26 or section 29 of the 1983 Act, a p.l.c.'s shares are "watered" by being allotted for an undertaking to do work or provide services, or for an undertaking capable of being performed in more than five years, or the shares were allotted for some non-cash consideration and the allottee either did not receive a copy of the requisite valuer's report or was aware of some other breach of section 30, the company has a claim for reimbursal by the allottee.[149] Subsequent holders in the extended sense of the shares are equally liable unless they satisfy the section 26(4) defence for bona fide purchasers for value, as described below.

Distributions from Capital

7–84 In *Flitcroft's Case*[150] it was held that the company or the liquidator can recover any unauthorised distribution from those directors responsible for making it. It would appear that there is a right of recovery against shareholders who knowingly accept such distribution.[151] In any event, it is now stipulated that a member who, knowing or with reasonable grounds for believing that it is unlawful, receives a distribution that contravenes sections 45, 46 or 47 of the 1983 Act, is liable to the company for that amount.[152]

---

148 [1892] A.C. 125.
149 1983 Act, ss. 26(3), 29(2), 30(10). *e.g. Re Bradford Investments p.l.c. (No.2)* [1991] B.C.L.C. 688.
150 (1882) 21 Ch.D. 519.
151 1983 Act, s.50(2); *Welton v. Saffery* [1897] A.C. 299.
152 *ibid.*, s.50(1). *cf. Re Cleveland Trust p.l.c.* [1991] B.C.L.C. 424.

Acquiring Own Shares

7–85 It was not necessary in *Trevor v. Whitworth*[153] to determine the consequences of a limited company owning its own shares because the transaction there was inchoate. Nor did the 1963 Act deal directly with this matter. But it does stipulate that any unauthorised allotment or transfer of shares in a holding company to its subsidiary is void.[154] Acquisitions by a company of its own shares that contravene section 41 of the 1983 Act are rendered void by the Act, as are any liens or charges taken by a p.l.c. on its own shares that are not permitted by section 44(2) of that Act. Where, in breach of section 42 of that Act, a company's shares are issued to its nominees, or they are called upon to pay up any outstanding amounts on them but fail to do so within 21 days, then the company's other subscribers or other directors, as the case may be, become jointly and severally liable to pay those amounts. Section 43 of the 1983 Act sets out how shares that are held by or for a p.l.c. should be treated.

Financing the Purchase of Own Shares

7–86 The appropriate civil consequences of contravening the rule against financing the purchase of a company's own shares has been a source of controversy in practically every common law jurisdiction. Generally, the transaction by which the assistance is, or is to be, given is void and unenforceable. Thus, for instance in *Heald v. O'Connor*,[155] where H agreed to sell a company's shares to C and to lend C money to make the purchase, which loan was guaranteed by a charge on that company's assets, it was held that the charge and guarantee could not be enforced. The principle of consequent invalidity is qualified by section 60(14) of the 1963 Act, under which "[a]ny transaction in breach of this section shall be voidable at the instance of the company against any person (whether a party to the transaction or not) who had notice of the facts which constituted such breach".

7–87 Although it is not stipulated expressly, the implication is that the company cannot avoid the transaction where the other party did not have the requisite notice. That interpretation was accepted in *Bank of Ireland v. Rockfield Ltd.*[156] The bank had agreed to advance money to two individuals to enable them to buy a certain piece of land and an equitable mortgage of the certificate of title was intended to be the

---

153 (1887) 12 App. Cas. 409.
154 s. 32(1); see below, para. 14–41.
155 [1971] 1 W.L.R. 497
156 [1979] I.R. 21.

security. In the event, the money was advanced to the order of the defendant company, the land was in its name and it deposited the certificate of title with the bank. Those individuals then used the money to acquire control of the company. It not being contested that section 60 had been violated, the issue was whether the company could avoid its agreement to secure the bank loans. A unanimous Supreme Court concluded that the bank did not have sufficient actual knowledge of how the money was to be used. It was held that notice in this context means actual knowledge and not the equitable "constructive notice". It is not necessary that the person must be aware of the existence of section 60 or that the transition is in breach of this section.

7–88 This issue arose again in *Lombard & Ulster Banking Ltd. v. Bank of Ireland,*[157] which concerned an agreement whereby control could be acquired of a private school that owned valuable land. As was explained above, the procedures under which private companies are permitted to finance the purchase of their own shares had not been followed there. The question then was the effect of non-compliance and, it was held, this is governed by section 60(14) of the Act. Costello J. construed this provision as "mean[ing] (a) that although a transaction in breach of the section is illegal it is only, voidable, not void, and (b) it is only voidable against a person who had notice of the facts which constituted the breach."[158] In other words, the company cannot avoid the transaction unless the other party to the transaction had the requisite notice. Where no attempt was made to go through the subsection (2)–(11) procedures, the notice means actual notice that section 60(1) had been contravened, *i.e.* knowledge of facts which clearly point to the conclusion that the prohibition was breached. Where it was sought to have the transaction sanctioned by the shareholders but their approval was not given in the manner required by subsection (2)–(11), the transaction can be avoided by the company only where it is shown that the other party had actual notice that the statutory procedures had not been followed to the letter. As Costello J. put it:

> "it is not sufficient . . . to show that if [the other party] had made proper inquiries that they would have ascertained that the company had failed to comply with the sub-sections. It must be shown that [the party] had "actual notice" of the facts which constituted the breach, that is (a) that they or their officials actually knew that the required procedures were not adopted or that they knew facts from which they must have inferred that the company had failed to adopt the required procedures, or (b) that

---

157 Costello J., June 2, 1987; see above, paras 7–76—7–77.
158 at p. 10.
159 at p. 11.

> an agent of theirs actually knew of the failure or knew facts from which he must have inferred that a failure had occurred."[159]

It was found that, in the circumstances, the plaintiff bank did not have that kind of notice.

7–89 Where the company itself seeks to sue on the transaction, such as to recover money lent for the proscribed purpose, the courts tend to grant enforcement because the prohibition was enacted for its benefit. Especially when the beneficiaries of its assistance happen to be its own directors acting improperly, it is not in *pari delicto* and, accordingly, should be allowed to recover.[160] While this trend is not universal.[161] some countries have amended their companies legislation to incorporate it.[162] It is not settled whether the agreement itself to acquire the shares is tainted with the illegality.[163] Directors who are responsible for a company becoming a party to a proscribed transaction are liable to it for consequent losses that the company may incur.[164] Additionally, anyone who receives a company's funds that are so misapplied and has knowledge of the breach will be liable to the company as a constructive trustee.[165] In appropriate circumstances, the responsible directors and those who receive the assistance may be liable for the tort of conspiracy.[166]

7–90 Breach of section 60 also can amount to "oppression" under section 205 of the 1963 Act in appropriate circumstances. That was held to be the case in *Re Greenore Trading Co.*,[167] where a majority shareholder bought out one of the other shareholders. But the cheque paying for those shares was drawn on the company's own bank account. Because relationships between the petitioner and the majority holder had broken down, because the petitioner had not been told that company funds would be used for that purchase and on account of the general circumstances in the company, Keane J. held that making the payment constituted oppression.

---

160 *e.g. Wallersteiner v. Moir* [1975] Q.B. 373.

161 *e.g. Central & Eastern Trust Co. v. Irving Oil Ltd.* (1980) 110 D.L.R. (3d) 257.

162 *e.g.* Canadian Business Corporation Act, s.42(3): "A contract made by a corporation in contravention of this section may nevertheless be enforced by the corporation or by a bona fide lender for value without notice of the contravention." In New Zealand the matter is now dealt with under a more general provision, the Illegal Contracts Act 1970; *cf. Catley v. Herbert* [1988] 1 N.Z.L.R. 606.

163 *cf. South Western Mineral Water Co. v. Ashmore* [1967] 1 W.L.R. 110.

164 *e.g. Belmont Finance Corp. v. Williams Furniture Ltd. (No. 2)* [1980] 1 All E.R. 393.

165 *ibid.*

166 *ibid.*

167 [1980] I.L.R.M. 94.

Validating Improper Transactions and Relieving Parties from Liability

7–91 On account of the very complexity of many of the capital integrity rules, occasions are going to arise where they are broken but, in all fairness, the company or third parties should not have to suffer loss in consequence. For this reason the 1963, 1983 and 1990 Acts make provision whereby certain bona fide purchasers of shares are not to be held liable and also whereby the court can validate certain transactions and exonerate individuals from liability.

7–92 Section 26(4) of the 1983 Act is designed to protect persons who have acquired shares in respect of which the original allottees are liable to pay sums to the company under that Act's requirements regarding minimum amounts and allotting shares at a discount or for a non-cash consideration. This applies where the holder of the shares was a purchaser for value of them and at the time he bought them had no "actual notice" of the violation, or he derived title to the shares from a person who had acquired them and was not so liable. Notice here is "of the facts which constitute the contravention. It does not require the offending [persons] to be learned in the law".[168] A holder of shares in this context has an extended meaning, including as well as transferees who are registered members, persons who are unconditionally entitled to be but are not so registered, and also persons unconditionally entitled to have an instrument of transfer executed in their favour.

7–93 Section 89 of the 1963 Act, as amended in 1990,[169] authorises the court to declare valid any issue of shares which is invalid or any acquisition of shares which does not fully comply with the requirements in Part XI of the 1990 Act. In considering an application under section 89, the governing consideration is whether it is just and equitable to grant the order being sought. But an acquisition by a company of its shares otherwise than out of distributable profits, as prescribed, or in breach of its own articles of association cannot be validated in this manner.[170]

Relief from Liability

7–94 Section 34 of the 1983 Act empowers the court to relieve from liability persons made liable to the company by sections 26, 29, 30 and

---

[168] *System Control p.l.c. v. Munro Corporate p.l.c.* [1990] B.C.L.C. 659 at 663.
[169] 1990 Act, s.227.
[170] *cf. Re Sugar Distributors Ltd.* [1995] 2 I.R. 194.

32 of that Act, *i.e.* regarding an undertaking to do work or provide services, an undertaking that can be performed in five years or longer, and in relation to allotting shares for non-cash consideration where independent valuations etc. must be made. On application to it, the court may exempt such persons from liability, either wholly or partly, where it is "just and equitable" to do so and provided certain other criteria are met.[171] There is a somewhat similar provision for where subscribers or directors become liable for calls made on a company's nominee. Under section 42 of that Act, the court may exonerate the persons from liability, wholly or partly, on the grounds that they "acted honestly and reasonably" and in the circumstances ought fairly to be excused.

[171] *e.g. Re Ossory Estates p.l.c.* [1988] B.C.L.C. 213. *cf. Re Bradford Investments p.l.c. (No. 2)* [1991] B.C.L.C. 688.

8

Accounts, Audit and Disclosure of Information

8–01 One of the principal techniques used by the Companies Acts to safeguard investors and persons who deal with companies is the compulsory disclosure of information. In exchange for the privilege of separate legal personality and limited liability, registered companies are required to disclose certain facts about themselves to the general public, usually via the registry of companies. Additional information must be made available to their shareholders and the holders of debentures. As the late Professor Gower explained:

> "On the basis that "forewarned is forearmed" the fundamental principle underlying the Companies Acts has been that of disclosure. If the public and the members were enabled to find out all relevant information about the company, this, thought the founding fathers of our company law, would be a sure shield. This shield may not have proved quite so strong as they had expected, and in more recent times it has been supported by [other measures]. But, basically, disclosure still remains the principal safeguard on which the Companies Acts pin their faith, and every succeeding Act since 1862 has added to the extent of the publicity required, although, not unreasonably, it has varied it according to the type of company concerned.
>
> [M]embers and the public (which, for practical purposes, means creditors and others who may subsequently have dealings with the company and become its members or creditors) are supposed to be able to obtain the information which they need to make an intelligent appraisal of their risks, and to decide intelligently when and how to exercise their rights and remedies which the law affords them."[1]

8–02 The rules regarding company accounts underwent very extensive change with the adoption of the Companies (Amendment) Act 1986, which gives effect to the E.C. Fourth Directive on Company Law,[2] and some additional requirements were adopted in 1990[3] and in sev-

---

[1] *Principles of Modern Company Law* (4th ed., 1979), p. 497; see 6th ed., 1997, p. 505.
[2] [1978] O.J. L222/11 (1978).
[3] Pt X of the 1990 Act (ss. 182–205).

eral statutory instruments implementing other E.C. Directives.[4] The 1986 Act deals almost entirely with companies' accounts and with the directors' and auditors' annual reports. Its central purpose is to ensure that the shareholders and also the general public get a better picture of companies' overall financial situation. However, because requiring companies, especially small companies, to disclose extensive financial information could make them vulnerable to competitors, small companies and also medium-sized companies are not obliged to disclose as much as are large companies and p.l.c.s. The 1986 Act's requirements apply only to limited companies, be they private companies or p.l.c.s; the term company as defined in this Act does not include an unlimited company. Additionally, certain non-profit companies are outside the Act's requirements[5] and some of those requirements do not apply to certain banks and other financial institutions and insurance companies.[6] Because many of the 1986 Act's features are of far more direct concern to accountants than to lawyers and since this book is legal text and not an accountant's manual, only a brief description of that Act's principal requirements will be given here.[7]

8–03 On top of the law, in the sense of legislation and regulations, the Stock Exchange rules and the conventions of the accountancy profession play a significant role in this area. Accounts of companies listed on the Stock Exchange must comply with the requirements of the Exchange's listing agreement.[8] A joint accounting bodies' Accounting Standards Committee has been in existence since 1970. It is comprised of representatives from the Chartered Institutes of Accountants (the Irish, the English and the Scottish Institutes), the Institute of Certified Accountants, the Institutes of Cost and Management Accounts, and the Institute of Public Finance and Accountancy. This Committee's function is to promulgate conventions (called statements of standard accounting practice, or "SSAPs") to govern various difficult accounting questions.[9] On matters that are still the subject of some controversy, it issues a lower form of pronouncement, known as a statement of recommended accounting practice, or "SORP". Members of the affiliated bodies are expected to follow the SSAPs when auditing company accounts.

---

4 Notably S.I. No. 259 of 1992 (auditors' qualifications), S.I. No. 201 of 1992 (group accounts), S.I. No. 294 of 1992 (banks' accounts), S.I. No. 396 of 1993 (unlimited companies' and partnerships' accounts) and S.I. No. 23 of 1996 (insurers' accounts).

5 1986 Act, s.2(1); see below, para. 14–68.

6 *ibid.*, s.2(2) and (3); see below, paras 14–75, 14–78.

7 See generally, N. Brennan & A. Pierce, *Irish Company Accounting* (1996).

8 Yellow Book 3.3–5.

9 See Brennan & Pierce, *op. cit.*, pp. 6–10 and Chap. 2.

ACCOUNTS AND TRADING INFORMATION

8–04 All registered companies must keep proper books of account. Ever since 1879 in the case of banks and since 1900 in the case of all companies, their accounts have had to be audited by persons independent of the company;[10] since the 1908 Act, at least some of their accounts have had to be registered at the registry of companies.[11]

Duty to Keep Proper Books of Account

8–05 The duty to keep proper accounts is now set out in section 202(1) of the 1990 Act, according to which

> "Every company shall cause to be kept proper books of account, whether in the form of documents or otherwise, that:
>
> (a) correctly record and explain the transactions of the company,
>
> (b) will at any time enable the financial position of the company to be determined with reasonable accuracy,
>
> (c) will enable the directors to ensure that any balance sheet, profit and loss account or income and expenditure account of the company complies with the requirements of the Companies Acts and
>
> (d) will enable the accounts of the company to be readily and properly audited."

These books must be kept on a "continuous and consistent basis". Among the matters for which accounts must be kept are assets and liabilities, day-to-day receipts and expenditures, purchases and sales, services provided (where the company's business involves providing services) and stock held, together with records of stocktaking. These books must be kept by the company for at least six years after any event to which they relate occurred.[12] They are normally kept at the company's registered office but may be kept somewhere else as the directors deem fit.[13] As is explained below, these books must give "a true and fair view of the state of affairs of the company . . . " Articles 125–127 of Table A require directors to keep "proper books of account" which shall be available at times for inspection by members.

8–06 Any director of the company who does not take reasonable steps to secure compliance with the above statutory requirements commits

---

[10] Companies Act 1900, ss. 21–23.

[11] Companies Act 1907, s.21. *cf. Caparo Industries p.l.c. v. Dickman* [1990] 2 A.C. 605 at 630–631, which sets out the history.

[12] s.202(9).

[13] s.202(5).

a criminal offence.[14] But courts will not readily entertain proceedings brought by individual shareholders alleging breach of the above articles,[15] If the company is wound up and is found to be insolvent, and inadequate book-keeping either contributed towards its insolvency or otherwise impeded the orderly winding up, every company officer who did not take reasonable steps to ensure compliance with section 202 can be convicted of a serious offence.[16] Additionally, the court may impose unlimited liability for all or part of the company's debts on any company officer or former officer who was in default in this regard,[17] as was done in *Meighan v. Duignan,*[18] where a director of a comparatively small company was made liable for in excess of £90,000 on account of defective bookkeeping. Shanley J. held there that the duty imposed by section 202 was not merely to be a passive custodian of records but was a positive and continuing obligation to create books and records in a particular form and with specified contents.

8–07 Section 202(1)(c) above refers to *inter alia* a profit and loss account and a balance sheet. How these documents are to be laid out and what they should contain has for many years been governed by accounting conventions. In the case of limited companies, however, although the 1986 Act does not deal with the above general duty to keep proper accounts, it indirectly affects that duty insofar as it concerns the profit and loss account and balance sheet. For that Act lays down formats and other requirements which these accounts must meet when being circulated to the sharcholders.[19] Its requirements may be regarded as a general statement of what ordinarily is required to provide a "true and fair view" of the company's position; where necessary in special circumstances, those requirements can be departed from. Accordingly, section 202(4) of the 1990 Act's insistence that the books kept, as described above, must give a true and fair view means that, ordinarily, the 1986 Act's requirements for the profit and loss account and balance sheet must be met except where there was very good reason to depart from them.

"True and Fair View"

8–08 The general question of what exactly is meant by a "true and fair view" is best dealt with at this stage. This concept is not defined

---

[14] s.202(10).
[15] *Devlin v. Slough Estates Ltd.* [1983] B.C.L.C. 497.
[16] s.203.
[17] s.204.
[18] [1977] 1 I.R. 340.
[19] Schedule to the Act, Pt 1.

anywhere in the legislation, nor has it been the subject of much judicial elaboration. Although it is given particular emphasis in the 1986 Act and in the E.C. Fourth Directive, it has been in the legislation since 1963. What is meant by a true and fair view is that the accounts in question properly reflect the actual financial situation of the company. There are numerous accounting rules and conventions which, if rigidly applied in certain circumstances, would produce a somewhat distorted picture of the company's position. The overriding true and fair requirement demands that those accounting standards should not be used in that particular case. [20]

8–09 In 1983 the British Accounting Standards Committee obtained a carefully reasoned Counsel's opinion on the meaning of the concept and its relationship with the many S.S.A.P.s promulgated by that body. Among the observations made by Counsel there, are that true and fair:

> "is an abstract or philosophical concept expressed in simple English . . . representing a very high level of abstraction which has to be applied to an infinite variety of concrete facts. . . . Accounts will not be true and fair unless the information they contain is sufficient in quantity and quality to satisfy the reasonable expectations of the readers to whom they are addressed. On this question, accountants can express an informed professional opinion on what, in current circumstances, it is thought that accounts should reasonably contain. But they can do more than that. The readership of accounts will consist of businessmen, investors, bankers and so forth, as well as professional accountants. But the expectations of the readers will have been moulded by the practices of accountants because by and large they will expect to get what they ordinarily get and that in turn will depend upon the normal practices of accountants."[21]

THE AUDIT

8–10 Every company must have an auditor or auditors, whose principal task is to examine the company's accounts and to make an auditors' report on them. It is the requirements of a professional and independent audit that should give credibility to a company's accounts. In March 1999 the Tánaiste published a Bill, under which small companies could elect not to have audited accounts, provided 90% of the voting shareholders so agreed.

---

[20] See generally Lasok and Grace, "The True and Fair View" (1989) 10 Co. Law. 13 and McGee, "The 'True and Fair View' Debate: A study in the Legal Regulation of Accounting" (1991) 54 Mod. L. Rev. 874.

[21] L. Hoffman Q.C. and M. Arden, B.L., September 13, 1983

Auditors' Status and Remuneration

8–11 For many purposes a company's auditor is deemed by the Companies Acts to be one of its "officers".[22] It is common to appoint a firm of accountants as the auditors; where this is done, the firm's partners who are qualified to be the company's auditors are deemed to have been appointed to the office.[23]

Appointment

8–12 The auditor or auditors are appointed by a resolution of the annual general meeting.[24] Requiring that they be appointed by the shareholders is to ensure that the auditors give primary consideration to the shareholders' interests and are not subject to the directors' influence. Auditors cannot be appointed for a duration longer than between one A.G.M. and the next. But they are deemed to be reappointed at each subsequent A.G.M. unless they become ineligible to hold the office or resign, or are removed from office or somebody else was duly appointed to the office.[25] Where the shareholders fail to appoint an auditor, the Minister is empowered to fill the vacancy.[26] The directors themselves are permitted to appoint the first auditors pending the first A.G.M. being held;[27] they also may fill a casual vacancy in the office.[28]

Qualifications

8–13 In order to ensue that the auditor is professionally competent to do the job, is independent of the company and is honest, the law sets down rigorous qualifications that must be met. These are contained in sections 187–192 of the 1990 Act.

8–14 *Independence* Auditors are required to be independent of the company and its officers, so that they can more easily give an objective assessment of its accounts. What constitutes complete independence can be hard to define and occasionally difficult to achieve, especially within the comparatively small Irish economy. For instance, it is often contended that auditors' firms should not provide management consultancy services to the company, lest a conflict of interests arise which threatens the auditors' independence. The present requirements are set out in section 187(2) of the 1990 Act, which disqualifies the following from being appointed as a company's auditors:

---

[22] *Mutual Reinsurance Co. Ltd. v. Peat Marwick Mitchell & Co.* [1997] 1 B.C.L.C. 1.
[23] 1963 Act, s.160(9).
[24] *ibid.*, s.160.
[25] *ibid.*, s.160(2).

i. Any officer or employee of the company. Who exactly are "officers" for the purposes of this provision is not defined.

ii. Any former officer or employee of the company during any part of the period to which the accounts being audited would relate.

iii. Any partner of or employee of a present officer of the company.

iv. Any immediate member of the family of any of the company's officers, being the parent, spouse, brother, sister or child.

v. Where a person falling within any of the above categories would be disqualified from being an auditor of certain connected companies; they are any of the company's subsidiaries, its holding company or another subsidiary of the holding company.

8–15 *Professional Competence* Formerly, a person could be appointed as auditor without holding any accountancy qualification. In 1963 and again in 1982 more stringent rules were laid down regarding professional qualifications. Most of sections 187-192 of the 1990 Act is devoted to this subject, where the principal requirement is practising membership of a professional accounting body or holding professional qualifications which are recognised by the Minister for these purposes.

8–16 A person is qualified to be a company's auditor where "he is a member of a body of accountants for the time being recognised by the Minister for th[is] purpose . . . and holds a valid practising certificate from such a body."[29] The principal conditions on which recognition by the Minister is granted to an accountancy body are:

i. its standards for awarding practising certificates, relating to training, qualifications and repute are up to the level laid down in the E.C. 8th Directive of 1984.[30]

ii. the Minister is satisfied with its standards regarding ethics, codes of conduct and practice, independence, professional integrity, technical standards and disciplinary procedures.[30]

Any recognised body may be required by the Minister to draw up a code of professional ethics for its members and he may introduce regu-

---

[26] *ibid.*, s.160(4).
[27] *ibid.*, s.160(6).
[28] *ibid.*, s.160(7) (as amended by 1990 Act, s.183(b)).
[29] 1990 Act, s.187(1)(a)(i) and Companies Act 1990 (Auditors) Regulations 1992 (S.I. No. 259 of 1992).
[30] 1990 Act, s.191.

lations for monitoring compliance with that code. The accountancy bodies recognised by the Minister on June 1, 1999 are the Institutes of Chartered Accountants in Ireland, in England and Wales and in Scotland, also the Association of Chartered and Certified Accountants, the Association of Certified Public Accountants and the Institute of Incorporated Public Accountants.

8–17 Any person who was a member of any of the above bodies on December 31, 1990 is also deemed to be qualified provided he holds a valid practicing certificate.[31] So too is any person who, on February 3, 1983, was authorised by the Minister to be a company auditor.[32] A person is also qualified to be an auditor where:

> "he holds an accountancy qualification that is, in the opinion of the Minister, of a standard which is not less than that required for membership [of any recognised professional body] and which would entitle him to be granted a practising certificate by that body if he were a member of it."[33]

In other words, he holds qualifications which are up to the standard required for membership of any of the recognised accountancy bodies and for obtaining a practising certificate from that body. Those who might benefit principally from this provision are persons with accountancy degrees from universities in Ireland or abroad, and those who qualified under some foreign accountancy body. It remains to be seen whether this provision will be administered on an entirely *ad hoc* basis or whether the Minister will publish a list of the qualifications which are deemed to satisfy the above requirement.

8–18 Apart entirely from this provision, section 189 of the 1990 Act empowers the Minister to declare that holding specified foreign accountancy or auditing qualifications shall be sufficient to act as a company auditor in this country. This is designed to facilitate, in particular, the mobility of auditors within the European Community. Before any foreign qualification is so recognised, the Minister must be satisfied that it is at least up to the standard required by the recognised professional bodies. Certain additional educational qualifications may be insisted on before any particular foreign qualification will be accepted under this section.

8–19 Certain persons undergoing training on January 1, 1990 are rendered eligible by section 188 of the 1990 Act who became members of a

---

[31] 1990 Act, s.187(1)(a)(iii) and Companies Act 1990 (Auditors) Regulations 1992, reg. 3.

[32] *ibid.*, s.187(1)(a)(iv).

[33] *ibid.*, s.187(1)(a)(ii).

recognised body before 1996 and who later obtained practising certificates from that body.

8–20 *Register of Qualified Persons* Sections 198–201 of the 1990 Act provide for the registrar of companies keeping a register of everyone who is qualified to be a company auditor. A person's name and address must be registered in it before he can audit a company's books and records.

8–21 *Honesty* Requiring the auditors to be honest persons is now satisfied by reference to the disqualification orders made under Part VII of the 1990 Act, as described earlier in this book.[34] Anyone against whom a disqualification order was made, under section 160 of that Act, cannot act as a company auditor for such period as the court directs. Section 195 of that Act goes further and forbids any such person from becoming a partner in a firm of auditors, giving directions or instructions regarding any audit or working in any capacity in the conduct of an audit.

Removal

8–22 As is also the case with company directors, auditors can be removed from office relatively easily, without prejudice to any rights they may have for breach of contract or otherwise. Section 160(5) of the 1963 Act renders an ordinary resolution of the company sufficient for this purpose. But extended notice, as contemplated by section 142 of that Act, must be given of the resolution and a copy of the resolution must be sent to the auditors. They may wish to contest any such proposal, either to protect their own reputation or in the wider interests of the company. To that end, they are entitled to submit written representations to the company concerning the situation and to have copies of those forwarded to the members for consideration. Auditors facing a resolution for their removal are not entitled to speak in their defence at the meeting which is considering the proposal as such. But they are entitled to attend and be heard at the meeting which is considering to fill the vacancy and at the next annual general meeting when their office would have expired unless it was renewed.

8–23 It is hoped that by giving auditors, threatened with removal, what in effect is a right of reply might protect them and, through them, the company from efforts to get rid of them because they were doing their job perhaps too well. Auditors are thereby encouraged to rebut

---

[34] See above, paras 5–25 *et seq*.

pretexts to have them replaced and to disclose to the shareholders matters that aroused their suspicion. It is possible that, where auditors were improperly removed in suspicious circumstances but they chose not to avail of this right, they might later be held liable in negligence to the shareholders for not disclosing significant information they obtained during their audit, which would have prompted an investigation into the company's affairs.

Resignation

8–24 If the auditors were not happy with the state of affairs in a company, in the past often they would simply resign without disclosing their reasons for doing so. Sections 185 and 186 of the 1990 Act put an end to that practice. Where auditors either intend to resign or do not wish to be re-appointed, they must first notify the company and state that there are no circumstances connected with their decision which should be drawn to the notice of the members of the company or its creditors. If circumstances of that nature indeed exist, these must be disclosed in the notice of resignation and copies of that notice must be forwarded to all the members and debenture-holders. A copy of every notice of resignation should be sent to the registrar of companies.

8–25 Where the notice refers to circumstances which would concern the members or the creditors, the auditors may require that a general meeting be convened to consider the entire matter. That meeting must then be convened by the directors and, if so requested by the auditors, the directors must circulate any further statement made by the auditors concerning the circumstances of their resignation. An auditor who has resigned has the same right as a dismissed auditor to attend and speak at the next annual general meeting or meeting at which his vacancy is proposed to be filled.

Remuneration

8–26 How much the auditors should be paid for their services is controlled by the shareholders. Their remuneration, including expenses, must be fixed either by the annual general meeting or in such manner as that meeting determined.[35] Where the directors filled a temporary vacancy or the appointment was made by the Minister, the appointers also determine the remuneration and expenses to be paid. In appropriate circumstances, the auditor may have a lien on the company's books

---

[35] 1963 Act, s.160(8).

in his possession in respect of the audit fee.[36] Without prejudice to any such lien, however, all books and other papers relating to the company can be demanded by an examiner appointed to the company or by its liquidator and must be delivered up to that person.[37]

Auditors' Powers and Rights

8–27 In order to carry out their task, the auditors are given extensive powers to obtain books and records and to demand information. According to section 193(3) of the 1990 Act, the auditor:

> "shall have a right of access at all reasonable times to the books, accounts and vouchers of the company and shall be entitled to require from the officers [and employees] of the company such information and explanations that are within their knowledge or can be procured by them as he thinks necessary for the performance of the duties of the auditors."

The extent to which this power can be enforced by civil proceedings is not stated. But failure to provide, within two days of the request, any information or explanation being sought is an offence, except where it was not reasonably possible to comply.[38] Giving false or misleading information to the auditors is an offence where that is done knowingly or recklessly and it is information to which the auditors are entitled.[39]

8–28 Additionally, the auditors are entitled to attend any general meeting of the company and to speak and be heard at the meeting on any matter which concerns their function as auditors.[40] All notices and other communications regarding general meetings must be sent to them. Where the company is a holding company with one or more subsidiaries in the State, both the subsidiaries and their auditors are obliged to give the holding company's auditors such information and explanations as they need in order to carry out their audit.[41] Where the subsidiary is incorporated abroad and information concerning it is required by the holding company's auditors, the holding company is required to take such steps as are reasonably necessary to obtain that information.[42]

---

[36] *Re J.J. Hopkins & Co.* (1959) 93 I.L.T.R. 32; *Re Darien Fashions Ltd.* [1981] 2 N.Z.L.R. 47; *DTC (CNC) Ltd. v. Grey Sargeant & Co.* [1996] 1 B.C.L.C. 1529.
[37] 1963 Act, s.244(a) (inserted by 1990 Act, s.125); *e.g. Kelly v. Scales* [1994] 1 I.R. 42.
[38] 1990 Act, s.197(3), (4).
[39] *ibid.*, s.197(1), (2).
[40] *ibid.*, s.193(5).
[41] *ibid.*, s.196(1)(a).
[42] *ibid.*, s.196(1)(b).

Auditors' Duties and Liabilities

8–29 Being appointed by the company, the auditors' primary duty is to it and is to make the auditors' report as described be low.[43] That requires them to audit the company's books and records. In doing so, section 193(6) of the 1990 Act places them "under a general duty to carry out such audit with professional integrity." The very extent and nature of the audit to be carried out may be stipulated in the "letter of engagement" entered into between the auditors and the company. When making their report, the auditors must consider whether the information contained in the directors' annual report is consistent with the information in the company's accounts for that year.[44]

Company Not Keeping Proper Books of Accounts

8–30 The only specific statutory obligation imposed on auditors is where proper books of account are not kept, as required by section 202 of the 1990 Act. In that event, section 194 of that Act requires the auditors to notify the company promptly that proper books are not being kept. They must also notify the registrar of companies to that effect unless, within seven days, the matter has been rectified. If the auditors fail to take these steps and the company is later wound up and found to be insolvent, the consequences can be very serious. If the inadequate book-keeping contributed to the insolvency or caused substantial uncertainty about the company's worth, or substantially impeded the orderly liquidation, the auditors can suffer severe penal sanction[45] and even be made liable without limit for all or part of the company's liabilities.[46]

Negligence — A Duty to Whom?

8–31 If the auditors negligently certify that the accounts presented give a true and fair view of the company's affairs, the company is entitled to be compensated for any ensuing economic loss to it. In what circumstances auditors have a duty of care to persons other than the company is a vexed question. For instance, is a duty owed to the shareholders as such, to creditors and to persons who acquired the company or a majority of the shares in it? These and related questions have been the subject of extensive litigation in recent years, culminating in the House of Lords' decision in 1990, *Caparo Industries p.l.c. v.*

---

[43] 1990 Act, s.193(1), (4).
[44] 1986 Act, s.15.
[45] 1990 Act, s.203.
[46] *ibid.*, s.204.

Dickman,[47] which in turn has generated several interpretations and elaborations in the lower courts in England. The present position there may be summarised briefly as follows. There is a contractual duty of care to the company and a statutory duty to its shareholders as a body but not to any individual member, no matter how large his stake in the company may be.[48] But where there is sufficient "proximity" between the auditors and the plaintiff and no special considerations of public policy arise, there is a duty of care. Thus, there was held to be such a duty owed by the auditors of the wholly-owned Singapore subsidiary of the failed Barings Bank to its English parent company, who were acting on the parent company's instructions.[49] Ordinarily, there is no duty of care to potential purchasers of shares in the company,[50] although circumstances can exist where such a duty will arise, notably to a bidder for control who the auditors know will rely on the accounts for that purpose.[51] Ordinarily, there is no duty of care owed to those who lend to the company[52] but such a duty has been held to exist in favour of trustees for depositors of an investment company,[53] although not in favour of trustees for investors in a company.[53] These questions been the subject of numerous decisions in Australia,[55] Canada[56] and New Zealand.[57]

8–32 Perhaps the only modern Irish case to discuss the question of principle to any extent is *Kelly v. Haughey, Boland & Co.*[58] where the plaintiffs acquired a small private crystal manufacturing company from the widow of its recently-deceased owner. They then alleged that the company's accounts had been negligently audited, in particular, that the figure disclosed for stock in trade was wrong. Assuming they were correct, the question remained whether the auditors owed them a duty of care. According to Lardner J., the answer depends on:

---

[47] [1990] 2 A.C. 605. See generally, Jackson and Powell, *Professional Negligence* (4th ed., 1997) Chap. 8 and R. Bernstein, *Economic Loss* (2nd ed., 1998), pp. 556-602.

[48] *Caparo Industries p.l.c. v. Dickman* [1990] 2 A.C. 605.

[49] *Barings p.l.c. v. Coopers & Lybrand* [1997] 1 B.C.L.C. 427.

[50] *James McNaughton Paper Group Ltd. v. Hicks Anderson & Co.* [1991] 2 Q.B. 113; *Galoo Ltd. v. Bright Grahame Murray* [1994] 1 W.L.R. 1360.

[51] *Morgan Crucible Co. v. Hill Samuel & Co.* [1991] Ch. 295; *Galoo* case, above.

[52] *Al Saudi Banque v. Clarke Pixley* [1990] 1 Ch. 313; *Berg, Son & Co. v. Adams* [1993] B.C.L.C. 1045; *Galoo* case above, n. 50.

[53] *Deloitte Haskins & Sells v. National Mutual Life Nominees Ltd.* [1993] B.C.L.C. 1174 (but no breach of duty found).

[54] *Anthony v. Wright* [1995] 1 B.C.L.C. 236.

[55] *Cambridge Credit Corp. v. Hutcheson* (1985) 9 A.C.L.R. 545.

[56] *Haig v. Bamford* (1976) 72 D.L.R. (3d) 68.

[57] *Scott Group Ltd. v. Macfarlane* [1978] 1 N.Z.L.R. 553.

[58] [1989] I.L.R.M. 373.

> "whether the defendants knew or should have reasonably foreseen at the time the accounts were audited that a person might rely on those accounts for the purpose of deciding whether or not to take over the company and therefore could suffer loss if the accounts were inaccurate. Such an approach does place a limitation on those entitled to contend that there has been a breach of duty owed to them. First of all, they must have relied on the accounts and, secondly, they must have done so in circumstances where the auditors either knew that they would or ought to have known that they might. If the situation is one where it would not be reasonable for the accounts to be relied on, then, in the absence of express knowledge, the auditor would be under no duty. This places a limit on the circumstances in which and the period for which they can be relied on. The longer the period which elapses prior to the accounts being relied on, from the date on which the auditor gave his certificate, the more difficult it will be to establish that the auditor ought to have foreseen that his certificate would, in those circumstances, be relied on."[59]

Negligence — The Standard of Care

8–33 Where, as undoubtedly is the case *vis-à-vis* the company, there is a duty of care, what standard of care are its auditors held to? The overall approach to this question is determined by the common law principles governing professional negligence. Being professionals, occasionally with exceptionally deep pockets, auditors will be judged by the same general standards as the law applies to medical practitioners, solicitors, architects, surveyors and the like. However, many of the leading decisions in this area were given before the accountancy and auditing professions had even begun to aspire to their present level of expertise and sophistication, and perhaps should be treated in the light of this. It has been held that "the quality of the auditor's duty has [not] changed in any relevant respect since 1896. Basically that duty has always been to [act] with reasonable care and skill. [Nevertheless] the standards of reasonable care and skill are, upon expert evidence, more exacting today than those which prevailed [then]."[60]

8–34 Auditors must pursue their activities in a manner one would reasonably expect of them. But it remains to be established whether, for example, compliance with the auditing standards set down by the professional bodies is in itself sufficient performance of the legal duty, or whether any breach of those standards is tantamount to violating the legal duty as well. Machinery for investigating allegations of bad auditing has been established by the accountancy bodies. A question that, therefore, arises is whether censure or criticism of an auditor by

---

[59] At p. 25, quoting Woolf J. in *J.E.B. Fasteners Ltd. v. Marks Bloom & Co.* [1981] 3 All E.R. 289.

[60] *Re Thomas Gerrard & Co.* [1968] Ch. 455.

such investigators is sufficient to establish that he has been negligent in the legal sense. While one reads occasionally in the newspapers of some of the largest accounting firms reaching six-figure and indeed seven-figure settlements of claims made against them, suits on this scale rarely go to trial. A much cited summary of the standard of care is that:

> "It is the duty of an auditor to bear on the work he has to perform that skill, care, and caution which a reasonably competent, careful and cautious auditor would use. What is reasonable skill, care and caution must depend on the particular circumstances of each case. An auditor is not bound to be a detective, or, as was said, to approach his work with suspicion or with a foregone conclusion that there is something wrong. He is a watchdog, but not a bloodhound. He is justified in believing tried servants of the company in whom confidence is placed by the company. He is entitled to assume that they are honest, and to rely upon their representations, provided he takes reasonable care. If there is anything calculated to excite suspicion he should probe it to the bottom; but in the absence of anything of that kind he is only bound to be reasonably cautious and careful."[61]

8–35 With regard to the standard of care to be observed when conducting an audit, Lardner J. in the *Haughey Boland* case[62] was guided by expert evidence of the current practice in the profession and by the S.S.A.P.s which are promulgated by the accounting bodies. More recently in *Lloyd Cheeham Ltd. v. Littlejohn & Co.*[63] Woolf J. observed that S.S.A.P. are not rigid rules, but they are very strong evidence of what is the proper standard to be adopted and, unless there is some justification for doing so, a departure from them will be regarded as a breach of duty. The relevant S.S.A.P in the *Haughey Boland* case was the one concerning stocktaking and in the *Littlejohn* case that concerning depreciation.

8–36 The auditors' function is not that of management consultants; they cannot be held responsible for not attempting to ensure that the company is properly managed. But they must take due care to ensure that the books and accounts are properly kept, and present a true and fair view. To this end, auditors may rely on representations made by company employees. For instance, they do not have to physically check all the stocks or to value independently all the major fixed assets. Pronouncements in many of the older cases about particular practices may very well no longer reflect today's accepted standards in the auditing profession.

---

[61] *Re Kingston Cotton Mills Co. (No. 2)* [1896] 2 Ch. 279 at 288–289.
[62] [1989] I.L.R.M. 373.
[63] [1987] B.C.L.C. 303.

8–37 If auditors come across material that arouses their suspicion or that in the circumstances should demand inquiry, they must investigate it further. Thus in *Re Thos. Gerrard & Son Ltd.*[64] the managing director had for some time been secretly falsifying the accounts and defrauding the company by *inter alia* constantly attributing the prices of stock bought in one accounting period to the following period. The auditor came across some altered purchase invoices but did not follow up the matter. It was held that he was liable in negligence because, in those circumstance,

> "he should have examined the suppliers' statements and where necessary have communicated with the suppliers. Having ascertained the precise facts so far as it was possible for him to do so, he should then have informed the board. It may be that the board would then have taken some action. But whatever the board did he should in each subsequent audit have made such checks and such inquiries as would have insured that any mis-attribution in the cut-off procedure was detected. He did not take any of these steps.... [The court concluded] that he failed in his duty. It is important in this connection to remember that this is not a case of some isolated failure in detection. The fraud was repeated half-yearly on a large scale for many years."[65]

In an Irish case decided at the turn of this century, *Irish Woollen Co. v. Tyson*,[66] it was held that even minor irregularities in the books can be enough to call for some thorough investigation. It was sought there to hold the auditor responsible for approving accounts that in fact had been falsified, thereby causing the company to pay dividends from capital. Three breaches of duty were alleged, namely, 1. that he failed to discover that the stock had been overvalued; 2. that he failed to discover that the book debts had been overvalued; 3. that he failed to discover that the trade liabilities had been understated. Holmes L.J. found in favour of the auditor in respect of 1. and 2. With respect to 1, he said that he did:

> "not understand how the carrying over of the invoices (thus understating the trade liabilities) could have escaped detection by the auditor, who should have used due care and skill and who was not a mere machine. The invoices carried over were ultimately posted to the ledger. If they were posted to their true dates it would have been at once apparent that they were not entered in at the proper time. If they were posted under false dates, why was this not detected when the ledger accounts were checked with the invoices?"

---

[64] [1968] Ch. 455.
[65] *ibid.* at 476.
[66] (1900) 26 Accountant L.R. 13.

ANNUAL ACCOUNTS AND REPORTS

8–38 Every year, a company must have prepared accounts which, along with prescribed reports, must be circulated among all the members and debenture-holders and an annual return must be filed with the registrar of companies.

Duty to Present Accounts

8–39 Section 148 of the 1963 Act requires the directors of every company to draw up and present to the annual general meeting a profit and loss account and a balance sheet. The profit and loss account must deal with the year ending not earlier than nine months prior to the date of the meeting; the balance sheet must be made up to the date of the profit and loss account. The company's very first set of accounts must be presented not later than 18 months from when it was incorporated. A director who does not take all reasonable steps to ensure compliance with these requirements commits an offence. Where the company has one or more subsidiary companies, sections 150–155 of the 1963 Act requires the preparation and presentation of group accounts in most circumstances.[67]

8–40 Two directors must sign the profit and loss account and the balance sheet on behalf of all of the directors[68] after the board approved the accounts.[69] Copies of the following documents must be sent to the company's members and debenture-holders and anyone else entitled to receive them at least 21 days before the annual general meeting:[70] the profit and loss account, the balance sheet, group accounts insofar as they are not incorporated into these two accounts, the auditors' report on those accounts and the directors' annual report. Every member of the company and debenture-holder is entitled, on demand, to be furnished with copies of these.[71]

Contents and Formats of Accounts

8–41 For most limited companies, the lay out and contents of the annual profit and loss account and balance sheet must meet the requirements of section 4 of the 1986 Act.[72] However, some companies need not comply with all of these requirements, nor with that Act's pred-

---

[67] 1963 Act, ss. 150–155; see below, paras 14–39-40.
[68] *ibid.*, s.156(1).
[69] *ibid.*, s.157.
[70] *ibid.*, s.159.
[71] *ibid.*, s.159(4).
[72] See generally, N. Brennan and A. Pierce, *Irish Company Accounts* (1996).

ecessor, the 1963 Act's Sixth schedule. Small and medium-sized private companies are subject to a less exacting regime.

Accounting Principles and Rules

8–42 Certain elementary and widely accepted accounting principles' are stated in section 5 of the 1986 Act, which are complemented by "historical cost rules" and "alternative cost rules" set out in Parts II and III of that Act's schedule. The governing principles are as follows:

> "The company is presumed to be carrying on business as a going concern. Accordingly, assets will be valued on a going concern basis rather than on the assumption that the business has ended and they are being disposed of piece meal. However, circumstances can arise which warrant dealing with the company's affairs other than as a going concern.
>
> Consistency from one year to the next is required in accounting policies.
>
> Prudence is required in determining the amount or value of any item; over-optimism is not allowed. In particular, only profits which were realised, *i.e.* in fact earned, at the balance sheet date can be included in the profit and loss account.
>
> Additionally, where there is a distinct likelihood of a liability or loss having arisen in the year in question or in the previous year, full account should be taken of that matter. This also applies to liabilities and losses which only became apparent after the accounts were made up and before they were signed by the directors.
>
> Once an item of income or expense relates to the financial year, it should be dealt with in that year's accounts regardless of the actual date of receipt or payment. Departure from any of these principles must be stated in a note to the accounts."[73]

8–43 Perhaps the greatest and most enduring controversy in accounting is the basis on which items should be costed; in particular, should items be included in the accounts on a historic cost basis. The main argument against historic cost is that, given the endemic nature of inflation over the past 30 years or so, that approach exaggerates the amount of profits earned. This issue arose in *Carroll Industries p.l.c. v. O'Culachain*,[74] where the company returned profits ascertained on a current cost basis but the Revenue sought to tax its profits computed in accordance with historic cost. Dealing with the general debate, Carroll J. concluded that no single approach was obligatory for all companies. The very nature of a company's business would determine which approach was the most appropriate for it. But for the purpose of

---

[73] 1986 Act, s.6

[74] [1988] I.R. 705.

computing income tax, the legislation presupposed use of historic cost. For the purpose of companies' accounts generally, the 1986 Act does not take sides in this debate. Instead, companies can choose which method is most appropriate for them. If they opt for historic cost, Part II of the Act's schedule lays down several rules to be followed in making the computation. If instead they follow current cost, appropriate computation rules are set out in Part III of that schedule.

True and Fair View

8–44 One of the main features of the 1986 Act is that it sets out the formats which companies' balance sheets and profit and loss accounts should take, as well as the above guidelines. The objective of these is to ensure that the accounts provide an entirely accurate representation of the company's position. However, in several places the Act emphasises that these rules are subject to the overriding requirement that the accounts shall give a "true and fair view" and, where it is necessary to do so for that purpose, the accounts should depart from the statutory formats and guidelines. According to section 3(1)(b) and (4) of the Act, regarding the format of annual accounts:

> "every . . . balance sheet of a company shall give a true and fair view of the state of affairs of the company as at the end of its financial year and every . . . profit and loss account of a company shall give a true and fair view of the profit and loss of the company for the financial year. [This obligation] overrides [most] requirements of . . . the Companies Acts . . . as to the matters to be included in the accounts of a company or in notes to those accounts; and accordingly where a balance sheet or profit and loss account of a company drawn up in accordance with [the format] requirements would not provide sufficient information to [give a true and fair view], any necessary additional information shall be provided in that balance sheet or profit and loss account or in a note to the accounts."

Similarly with the general "accounting principles" in section 5,

> "If it appears to the directors . . . that there are special reasons for departing from any of the[se] principles . . . they may so depart, but particulars of the departure, the reasons for it and the effect on the balance sheet and profit and loss account of the company shall be stated in a note to the accounts. . . ."

Small and Medium-Sized Private Companies

8–45 For the purpose of the annual accounts, companies are divided into three categories — small, medium-sized and large companies. Small private companies need only provide their members with an abridged balance sheet and an abridged profit and loss account;[75] medium-sized private companies can supply an abridged profit and loss account and need not provide the details of their turnover.[76] In their annual returns, small companies can annex an abridged balance sheet, omitting some of the notes,[77] and need not annex a profit and loss account. Medium-sized companies can annex abridged balance sheets and abridged profit and loss accounts to their annual return.[78] Where the company falls within the small or the medium-sized private company exception, a statement to that effect must be filed with the annual return.[79] A company can be quite large by Irish standards and still be a small company for these purposes.

8–46 A small private company is one which satisfies any two of the following criteria:[80] the balance sheet total is less than £1,500,000, the turnover is less than £3,000,000 and it employs less than 50 persons. A medium-sized private company is one that satisfies any two of the following criteria:[81] its balance sheet total is less than £6,000,000, its turnover is less than £12,000,000 and it employs less than 250 persons. Section 8 of the 1986 Act contains various rules for calculating these criteria, such as for determining the balance sheet total, the amount of turnover and the average number of employees, and section 9 of that Act provides for movement from one of these categories to another.

Exemptions

8–47 The 1986 Act does not apply to unlimited companies[82] unless one or more of the members is itself a company or partnership limited by shares or by guarantee, or is an unlimited company or partnership comprised of any of those companies, partnerships or bodies.[83] Nor does that Act apply at all to the following non-profit companies, namely, a company that does not trade "for the acquisition of gain by [its] members", a company controlled by and that acts in accordance with the prescripts of any of several religions and a company exempted for the time being by the Commissioners of Charitable Donations and Bequests.[84] Nor does the 1986 Act's requirements regarding the format

---

75 1986 Act, ss. 10(1), 11(1); see Brennan and Pierse, *op. cit.*, Chap. 37.
76 *ibid.*, ss. 11(1), 12(2); Brennan & Pierse, *op. cit.*, Chap. 37.
77 *ibid.*, ss. 10(2), 12(1)
78 *ibid.*, ss. 11(2), (3).
79 *ibid.*, s.18(2).
80 *ibid.*, s.8(1)(a), (2); European Communities (Accounts) Regulations 1993, reg. 4.
81 *ibid.*, s.8(1)(b), (3); European Communities (Accounts) Regulations 1993, reg. 4.
82 s.1(1).
83 European Communities (Accounts) Regulations 1993, Pt III.
84 s.2(1).

and contents of accounts apply to the following financial companies, namely, authorised life and non-life insurance companies, licensed banks, certified trustee savings banks, companies engaged only in the business of hire purchase or credit sale, the A.C.C. p.l.c. and the I.C.C. p.l.c.[85] Instead, those financial companies' (other than insurers) profit and loss accounts must satisfy the 1963 Act's sixth schedule.[86] But these companies (except insurers) must comply with sections 13-16 of the 1986 Act, regarding information in the directors' report, recording in the accounts acquisitions of the company's shares and publishing information concerning associated companies. The E.C.'s Directive on the Accounts of Banks[87] was implemented in 1992;[88] there are elaborate requirements under E.C. Directives for the accounts of insurers,[89] which were implemented in 1996.[90] Since 1990 unregistered companies' annual accounts must satisfy almost all of the 1963 Act's Sixth schedule.[91]

Profit and Loss Account

8–48 A company's profit and loss account shows the company's overall trading record for the period in question: what it earned, what its outgoings and liabilities assumed were, and its ultimate profit or loss.[92] For companies fully within the scope of the 1986 Act, the requisite formats and accounting principles and rules are contained in that Act's Schedule. Section 11(1) of that Act sets out what items can be abridged in small and medium-sized companies' accounts. There are some special provisions for the accounts of holding companies and subsidiary companies (section 16 and paragraphs 45–55 of the schedule)[93] and there are also some special rules for investment companies (paragraphs 56–59 of the schedule).[94]

8–49 Four different alternative formats exist of the profit and loss account, subject, of course, to the overriding "true and fair view" requirement. While these differ in their order of presentation and in some details, there is considerable identity in what they should contain. Format 1 requires that the following be shown, namely, turnover, cost of

---

85 s.2(2), (3).
86 1963 Act, s.149(2).
87 [1985] O.J. L375/3.
88 S.I. No. 294 of 1992.
89 [1991] O.J. L374/7.
90 S.I. No. 23 of 1996.
91 1990 Act, schedule; see below, paras 14–82 *et seq*.
92 See generally, Brennan & Pierce, *op. cit.*, Chaps. 11–13.
93 See below, paras 14–39-40.
94 See below, para. 14–80.

sales, gross profit or loss, distribution costs, administrative expenses, other operating income, income from shares in group companies, income from shares in related companies, income from other financial assets, other interest receivable and similar income, amounts written off, financial assets and investments held as current assets, interest payable and similar charges, tax on profit or loss on ordinary activities, after-tax profit or loss on ordinary activities, extraordinary income, extraordinary charges, extraordinary profit or loss, tax on extraordinary profit or loss, other taxes not shown under any of the above items, profit or loss for the financial year. Formats 2 and 4 require, in addition to most of the above items, entries for raw materials, depreciation and staff costs. Abridged accounts can combine as one item turnover, cost of sales, other operating income and gross profit or loss (Format 1). The corresponding amounts for the previous financial year must always be given. Paragraphs 39–43 of the Act's schedule sets out information and particulars which must supplement these accounts, in particular with regard to directors' remuneration and golden handshakes, auditors' remuneration, interest and similar charges, tax, turnover, staff and their remuneration, details of any extraordinary or exceptional items, and expenditure on research and development.

8–50 There are various rules and principles in the 1986 Act regarding the items contained in the profit and loss account. The amount of pretax profit or loss on ordinary activities must always be shown. Amounts representing income must not be set-off against amounts representing expenditure. The following must always be shown: the aggregate amount of dividends paid and proposed to be paid; any transfers to and from reserves; the increase or reduction in the balance from the previous year; any profit or loss brought forward and any carried forward. The accounting principles in section 5 relative to the profit and loss account are as follows: only profits which were realised at the balance sheet date should be stated; the liabilities and losses which must be stated are all those which have arisen or are likely to arise in respect of the accounting year and also the previous financial year, together with any liabilities and losses which arose between the balance sheet date and the date on which the accounts were signed; and account should be taken of all income and charges relating to the accounting year regardless of when the money was received or paid.

Balance Sheet

8–51 A company's balance sheet is the account that shows its overall financial position: what its issued and actual capital is, what reserves it has, its assets and liabilities.[95] It should be possible to judge what a company is in fact worth from a perusal of its balance sheet. The 1963

Act's provisions regarding the balance sheet are supplanted by the 1986 Act's formats and other requirements. As is the case with the profit and loss account, there are special rules for holding and subsidiary companies,[96] for investment companies[97] for banks and other credit institutions,[98] and also for insurers.[99] Small and medium-sized companies can have abridged balanced sheets.

8–52 The 1986 Act's schedule sets down two alternative although substantially similar formats for the balance sheet, subject, of course to the overriding "true and fair view" requirement. The corresponding amounts for the previous financial year must always be given. Paragraphs 26–37 of this Act's schedule sets out matters about which information must be given in or in notes supplementing the balance sheet regarding, for example, share capital and debentures (*e.g.* authorised capital, aggregate of each class of shares allotted, redeemable shares, details of shares allotments made and of debentures issued during the financial year), fixed assets (*e.g.* acquisitions, disposals and transfers during the year, cumulative amount of provisions and provisions and adjustments made during the year), financial assets and investments held as current assets, reserves and provisions, provision for taxation, details of indebtedness, guarantees and other financial commitments.

8–53 There are various rules and principles in the 1986 Act regarding many of these items and the balance sheet. Amounts representing assets and liabilities must not be set off against each other or vice versa. Research costs, preliminary expenses and the expenses of and commission on any issue of shares or of debentures may not be treated as an asset. The accounting principles in section 5 relative to the balance sheet are that the company shall be presumed to be carrying on business as a going concern and, in determining the aggregate amount of any item, the amount of each individual asset or liability that falls to be taken into account should be taken separately. The proper approach to depreciation is dealt with in some detail in Parts II and III of the Act's schedule.

8–54 The abridged balance sheet which small private companies[100]

---

95 See generally, Brennan and Pierce, *op. cit.*, Chaps. 14–22.

96 See below, paras 14–39-40 and Brennan and Pierce, *op. cit.*, Chaps. 29–32.

97 See below, para. 14–80.

98 S.I. No. 294 of 1992 European Communities (Credit Institutions: Accounts) Regulations 1992.

99 S.I. No. 23 of 1996 European Communities (Insurance Undertakings: Accounts) Regulations 1996.

100 As defined above, n. 79: see s.10(1).

may have must contain details of the following: fixed assets (stating intangible, tangible and financial assets,) current assets (stating stock, debtors, investments and cash), creditors (stating amounts falling due within one year and amounts failing due later than that), profit and loss account provisions for liabilities and charges, reserves (revaluation and other) and capital, including called up share capital and share premium account. These companies are also exempted from including in their balance sheet most of the notes required by the Act's schedule; they are the notes regarding debentures issued during the year, reserves and provisions, guarantees and other financial commitments, aggregate amount of loans made to assist persons to buy the company's own shares and the aggregate amount recommended for distribution by way of dividend.

8–55 Medium-sized private companies[101] must provide far more informative balance sheets but need not put in separate figures for the following items: goodwill, land and buildings, plant and machinery, fixtures, fittings, tools and equipment and payments on account and assets in course of construction, shares in group companies, loans to group companies, shares in related companies, loans to related companies, own shares, amounts owed by group companies, amounts owed by related companies, prepayments and accrued income, debenture loans, bank loans and overdrafts, amounts owed to group companies, amounts owed to related companies, other creditors including tax and social welfare, and accruals and deferred income.

Required Disclosures

8–56 In addition to the 1986 Act, there are various other statutory provisions which require particular matters to be disclosed in the accounts. Some aspects of these are dealt with more extensively in the discussion of the subject matters to which they refer.

Directors' Remuneration

8–57 Section 191 of the 1963 Act sets out information regarding directors' remuneration which must be disclosed in the annual accounts or in a statement annexed to them. There must be disclosed the aggregate amounts of emoluments, pensions and "golden handshakes" paid to directors and *de facto* directors of the company and of any of its subsidiaries. Emoluments here are principally directors' fees and salaries; they are defined to include percentages, contributions by the company to a pension scheme for directors, expense allowances that are charged

---

[101] As defined above, n. 81: s.11(2).

to income tax, and an estimate of the value of any taxable fringe benefits. The pensions that must be recorded include pensions in respect of present and past services as a director, and paid to or receivable by a director or his nominee or dependant or other person connected with him. But no separate entry need be made for a pension where the contribution by the company under it is substantially adequate to maintain the scheme. Compensation for loss of office in this context includes sums paid as consideration for or in connection with retirement from office.[102]

8–58 What the accounts must show is the aggregate amounts paid under each of these three headings, including sums paid by the company's subsidiaries and by any other person. It is the amounts receivable in respect of the financial year in question that must be shown, whenever paid. In the case of sums not so receivable, the sums paid during the financial year must be shown; expenses charged to tax after the end of the relevant year must be shown in the first set of accounts in which it is practicable to do so. The accounts must distinguish between payments made in respect of services rendered or holding office as a director and in respect of other services and offices. The entry for "golden handshakes" must distinguish between those paid by the company and its subsidiaries and those paid by any other person.

Directors' Contracts, Loans, Transactions, etc.

8–59 Sections 41–43 of the 1990 Act replace the provisions in the 1963 Act requiring disclosure of all loans made to directors. They cast the net far wider to cover an extensive range of transactions with the company in which any director, including any shadow director, has a financial interest. Particulars regarding the principal terms of these various arrangements, as well as the aggregate amounts outstanding, must be contained either in the accounts or in notes to them. Where this information is not so disclosed, the auditors' report on the company's accounts is required to state that information.[103] Arrangements and transactions with the company of comparatively modest value need not be so disclosed;[104] special provisions are made for licensed banks disclosing information about these matters.[105] The information to be disclosed is set out in section 42 of the 1990 Act.

---

[102] s. 191(4); *cf.* s.189(3); see above, paras 5–71 *et seq.*
[103] 1990 Act, s.46.
[104] *ibid.*, s.45.
[105] *ibid.*, ss. 43(5), 44.

Directors' and Secretary's Interest in Shares

8–60 As is explained later, whenever a director acquires or disposes of a beneficial interest in his company's shares, he is required to notify the company of that fact.[106] A notifiable interest for this purpose is defined very widely and includes any such interest held by his spouse or any minor child of the director.[107] Section 63 of the 1990 Act requires specified details of those interests to be disclosed in notes to the annual accounts or in the directors' annual report and similar details of interests held by the company's secretary.

Directors' Report

8–61 The directors are required to make a report "on the state of the company's affairs" and those of any subsidiaries, which must be laid before the company's annual general meeting and circulated to every member and debenture-holder.[108] This must state what dividend it is recommended to pay and how much it is proposed to carry to reserves.[109] Where it is necessary to understand fully the company's affairs, the report must deal with any changes during the financial year in the nature of the company's business or in the classes of business it does. It must also contain a list, stating the name, place of incorporation and nature of the business of all the company's subsidiaries and affiliates under the 1986 Act. The following additional information must be provided, regarding the company and any of its subsidiaries,[110] namely, a fair review of how the business developed over the year; particulars of any important events occurring since the end of the year which affect the company or its subsidiaries; an indication of likely future developments in the business; an indication of activities in the field of research and development. Where during the year the company carried out various kinds of transactions in its own shares, relevant details must be given.[111] The report must also contain an evaluation of the extent to which the policy set out in the company's "safety statement", under the Safety, Health and Welfare at Work Act 1989, has been fulfilled during the year covered by the report .[112]

Auditors' Report

8–62 As was explained earlier, a company's accounts must be audited

---

[106] See below, paras 9–82 *et seq*.
[107] 1990 Act, ss. 54, 55.
[108] 1963 Act, ss. 158, 159; see generally, Brennan & Pierce, *op. cit.*, Chap. 4.
[109] *ibid.*, s.158(1).
[110] 1986 Act, s.13.
[111] *ibid.*, s.14.
[112] Safety, Health and Welfare at Work Act 1989, s.12(6).

every year by a qualified auditor, who then makes a report on them.[113] The auditors' primary obligation, as set out in section 193(1) of the 1990 Act, is to "make a report to the members on the accounts examined by them, and on every balance sheet and profit and loss account, and all group accounts, laid before the company in general meeting. . . ." A Bill was published in 1999 under which small companies need not have their accounts audited or a consequent auditors' report.

8–63 Their report must be read at the annual general meeting and be open to inspection by any member.[114] What this report must now contain is set out in section 193(4) of the 1990 Act as follows:

i. Whether the [auditors] have obtained all the information and explanations which, to the best of their knowledge and belief, are necessary for the purposes of their audit,

ii. Whether, in their opinion, proper books of account have been kept by the company,

iii. Whether, in their opinion, proper returns adequate for their audit have been received from branches of the company not visited by them,

iv. Whether the company's balance sheet and (unless it is framed as a consolidated profit and loss account) profit and loss account are in agreement will the company's books of account and returns,

v. Whether. in their opinion, the company's balance sheet and profit and loss account and (if it is a holding company submitting group accounts) the group's accounts have been properly prepared in accordance with the provisions of the Companies Acts and gave a true and fair view –
   (a) in the case of the balance sheet, of the state of the company's affairs at the end of its financial year,
   (b) in the case of the profit and loss account (if it is not framed as a consolidated profit and loss account), of the company's profit and loss for its financial year,
   (c) in the case of group accounts submitted by a holding company, of the state of affairs and profit or loss of the company and its subsidiaries dealt with thereby, so far as concerns members of the company.

vi. Whether, in their opinion, there existed at the balance sheet date what is described as a "capital haemorrhage" situation, which re-

---

[113] See generally, Brennan and Pierce, *op. cit.*, Chap. 6.
[114] 1963 Act, ss. 148, 159.

quired that an extraordinary meeting of the company be convened.[115]

vii. Where the accounts do not contain the required details of loans and comparable transactions with any of the directors, details of those matters.[116] The reports must also express an opinion as to whether the information it contains is consistent with the company's accounts for that year.[117]

THE ANNUAL RETURN

8–64 Requirements regarding a company's annual return are contained principally in sections 125–129 of the 1963 Act and section 7 of the 1986 Act. An annual return must be made each year by every company to the registrar of companies whether the company is registered or, since 1990, unregistered. Companies that do not make annual returns for two consecutive years risk being stuck off the register of companies. In the case of companies having a share capital, the return must be made within 60 days of the annual general meeting being held. Its contents and format are set out in the Fifth Schedule to the 1963 Act. Before 1986 private companies, regardless of their size, did not have to file any annual accounts or annual reports along with the annual return. Since then, small limited companies are exempted only from filing a profit and loss account and the directors' report, and are allowed to file an abridged balance sheet, leaving out certain notes.[118] But they must file a copy of the entire auditors' report.

Contents

8–65 The information that must be provided in the annual return[119] is the address of the company's registered office; a summary indicating which of its shares have and have not been issued for cash, together with some other details about sums paid and due on those shares, particulars of its total indebtedness in respect of all charges on its property that must be registered; a list of its members' names, showing what shares they hold; particulars about its directors and secretary, including all *de facto* directors and shadow directors; the location of its registers of members and of debenture-holders where not kept at the registered office.

---

[115] See above, para. 7–08.
[116] 1990 Act, s.46.3.
[117] 1986 Act, s.15.
[118] 1986 Act, ss. 10(2), 12.
[119] 1963 Act, s.125 and Fifth schedule.

Annexed Documents

8–66 Companies must annex to their annual return certified copies of the balance sheet and profit and loss account laid before their previous annual general meeting and of the accompanying directors' and auditors' reports.[120] Every copy of the annexed accounts and reports must be certified by one of the company's directors and also its secretary to be a true copy of that document laid before the annual general meeting.[121] Where any of those documents are in a language other than English or Irish, certified translations into one of those languages must be provided.

8–67 Where the exemptions for small or medium-sized private companies were availed of, the accounts must contain a statement by the directors and a special report of the auditors to that effect.[122] The directors' statement must appear immediately above the signatures to the balance sheet and say which of the exemptions is being availed of. Before doing this they should have a written report of the auditors saying that the accounts were properly prepared and expressing the opinion that the directors are entitled to file those accounts. A copy of this report must be filed with the accounts.

8–68 But not all companies must annex all the above documents. Small private companies need not file their profit and loss account nor their directors' report.[123] Banks' and similar companies' annexed accounts need only comply with the 1963 Act's Sixth schedule.[124] Authorised insurance companies are exempted from annexing any documents to the return,[125] as are certain non-profit companies[126] and also the subsidiary of any company or body formed and registered in an E.C. Member State if it satisfies the conditions laid down in section 17 of the 1986 Act.[127]

COMPULSORY DISCLOSURE OF INFORMATION

8–68 A number of the matters that must be disclosed by companies

---

120 1963 Act, s.128.
121 See notes to 1963 Act, Fifth schedule.
122 1986 Act, s.18.
123 *ibid.*, s.10(2).
124 *ibid.*, s.7(1)(a)(2).
125 *ibid.*, s.2(3).
126 *ibid.*, s.2(1); see below, para. 14–68.
127 See below, para. 14–90.

either to their members or to the general public, have already been dealt with in some detail above, for instance, notices of general meetings and of resolutions to be proposed at them; the information to be made available to individual directors and to the auditors; filing with the registrar of companies the address of the registered office, copies of non-ordinary resolutions passed at general meetings, the names of and details concerning company officers and the annual return. Other major matters that must be so registered, that are considered separately later, include prospectuses, returns of allotments, details of any non-cash consideration that shares have been issued for, special rights attached to shares, details of any "organs" authorised to bind the company, charges on company property and the appointment of a receiver or manager, of an examiner or of a liquidator.

Disclosure to Members and Creditors

8–70 Regardless of whether or not they are entitled to notice of the annual general meeting, every member of and debenture-holder in a company must be forwarded a copy of the accounts and reports that must be presented to each A.G.M.,[128] *i.e.*, balance sheet, profit and loss account and group accounts, and directors' and auditors' reports. They are entitled without charge to be furnished with copies of these documents on demand.[129] Every member and creditor is entitled to inspect the company's register of members and debenture-holders,[130] copies of any charges that have to be registered and that are kept at the company's registered office,[131] and the register of directors', secretaries' and their families' holdings of shares in the company.[132] Every member must be given access to the minutes of general meetings[133] and to the book of declarations by directors of their interests in contracts made by the company.[134]

The *Iris Oifigiúil*

8–71 The *Iris Oifigiúil* is the official Government periodical, resembling the *London Gazette in* England and the *Journal Officiel* in France. Notification in the *Iris Oifigiúil* has become prominent in consequence of the E.C. Directives on company law, although it already existed in

---

[128] 1963 Act, s.159.
[129] *ibid.*, s.159(4).
[130] *ibid.*, ss. 92, 119.
[131] *ibid.*, s.110.
[132] 1990 Act, s.60(8).
[133] 1963 Act, s.146.
[134] *ibid.*, s.194(5).

respect of appointing a receiver[135] and commencement of a winding-up.[136] Notices must be published in the *Iris*, within six weeks of the delivery to the registrar of companies or of the issue by him, of any of the following documents:[137] the certificate of incorporation, the memorandum and articles of association and any alterations thereto, any change of directors, any return regarding the register of directors, details concerning any "organ" authorised to bind the company, the annual return, address of the registered office, a copy of a winding up order and any subsequent order dissolving the company. The civil sanction for non-publication in the *Iris Oifigiúil* of any of these notices is that the document in question 4may not be relied upon by the company as against any other person unless the company proves that such person had knowledge of [it]."[138] The following matters must also be published in the *Iris Oifigiúil* within six weeks of delivery to the registrar, but there is no civil sanction for default:[139] the statutory declaration made before a p.l.c. is permitted to do business, a copy of a resolution dealing with authority to issue further shares or waiving members' pre-emption rights, an expert's valuation of non-cash assets received by a p.l.c. in return for an allotment of its shares, any statement concerning shareholders' special rights, any notification of the redemption of preference shares, a copy of any resolution to reduce share capital, a copy of any resolution or agreement that states or varies any "class rights" and certain matters regarding an examination under the Companies (Amendment) Act 1990.

Other Forms of Publicity

8–72 Every company's name must be displayed legibly and conspicuously outside of its registered office and every other place it carries on business.[140] Its name must be mentioned in a legible manner on all its business letters, notices, cheques, invoices, receipts and the like.[141] The following must be stated in every company's "letters and order forms": where it is registered and its registration number, the address of its registered office, details regarding its directors, and the fact that it is being wound up if that is the case, and any references made there to its share capital must be to its paid up share capital.[142] On payment of a

---

[135] 1963 Act, s.107.
[136] *ibid.*, ss. 227, 252.
[137] S.I. No. 163 of 1973.
[138] *ibid.*, reg. 10. *cf. Official Custodian for Charities v. Parway Estates Development Ltd.* [1985] Ch. 151.
[139] 1983 Act, s.55.
[140] 1963 Act, s.114.
[141] *ibid.*
[142] S.I. No. 163 of 1973, reg.9.

small sum, any person may inspect a company's register of members and debenture-holders, except when they are closed, and may require that copies be made of those registers.[143]

8–73 Companies that are listed on the Stock Exchange are required by the "Yellow Book" to provide the Exchange with information on various matters. Indeed, much of the listing agreement comprises of an itemisation of information that must be supplied to shareholders, the Exchange and the general public. This book's very first clause on disclosure stipulates that "[g]enerally and apart from compliance with all specific requirements which follow", it is agreed to "keep the Stock Exchange informed by means of notifications . . . of any information necessary to enable the shareholders and the public to appraise the position of the company and to avoid the establishment of a false market in its securities." One reason why some major companies decline to seek a quotation on the Exchange is to avoid its extensive disclosure obligations.

[143] 1963 Act, ss. 92, 119.

9

Members' Status and Rights

9–01 The rights and obligations of company members or shareholders are defined principally by their company's memorandum and articles of association and by the Companies Acts. Occasionally those may be supplemented by a separate shareholders' agreement. Among the principal rights of members are to obtain specific information concerning the company's affairs, to be paid a dividend when one is duly declared, to vote at meetings and to transfer their shares. Where one class of members are given preferential rights with regard to these matters, they are called preference shareholders. The process of becoming a member of a company and of title to shares and other proprietary interests in them requires consideration of shares as items of personal property. One of the features of the 1990 Act is the introduction of machinery whereby the true ownership of shares can be ascertained.

THE NATURE OF SHARES

9–02 Section 79 of the 1963 Act defines the "nature of shares" as personal property which are inherently transferable:

> "The shares or other interest of any member in a company shall be personal estate, transferable in manner provided by the articles of the company, and shall not be of the nature of real estate."[1]

A share is a chose in action and is not a "good" within the meaning of the Sale of Goods Acts.[2] Membership of a company, or holding a share in a company, represents a complex of liabilities to and interests in the company, the classic definition of a share being that of Farwell J.:

> "A share is the interest of a shareholder in the company measured by a sum of money, for the purpose of liability in the first place, and of interest in the second, but also consisting of a series of mutual covenants en-

---

[1] See generally Rice, "The Legal Nature of a Share" (1957) 21 Conv. 433 and Granthan, 'The Doctrinal Basis of the Rights of Company Shareholders' [1998] Can. L.J. 554.

[2] *Lee & Co. (Dublin) Ltd. v. Egan (Wholesale) Ltd.*, Kenny J., December 18, 1979.

> tered into by all the shareholders *inter se* in accordance with [s.25 of the 1963 Act]. The contract contained in the articles of association is one of the original incidents of the share."[3]

Kenny J. adopted and amplified on this definition in a case concerning the valuation of shares for tax purposes:

> "No shareholder has a right to any specific portion of the company's property, and save by, and to the extent of, his voting power at a general meeting of the Company, cannot curtail the free and proper disposition of it. He is entitled to a share of the Company's capital and profits, the former . . . being measured by a sum of money which is taken as the standard for the ascertainment of his share of the profits. If the Company disposes of its assets, or if the latter be realised in a liquidation, he has a right to a proportion of the amount received after the discharge of the Company's debts and liabilities. In acquiring these rights — that is, in becoming a member of the Company — he is deemed to have simultaneously entered into a contract under seal to conform to the regulations contained in the articles of association. . . . Whatever obligations are contained in those articles, he accepts the ownership of the shares and the position of a member of the Company, bound and controlled by them. He cannot divorce his money interest, whatever it may amount to, from these obligations. They are inseparable incidents attached to his rights, and the idea of a share cannot, in my judgment, be complete without their inclusion."[4]

9–03 As well as having various entitlements and obligations under the company's own regulations, shareholders now enjoy an extensive range of rights under the Companies Acts 1963–1999. A share, therefore, is more completely described as the interest of a person in a company, that interest being comprised of rights and of obligations which are defined by the Companies Acts and by the memorandum and articles of association. The precise extent of a shareholder's interest in the company is determined by the par value of the shares and the number of shares he possesses; occasionally, the amount actually paid up on the shares may be the determinative measure. Generally, the amount of any dividends being paid and any return of capital being made is measured by reference to the par value of the shares. Such voting rights as may exist, by contrast, are not normally fixed by reference to either the par or paid up value of the shares.

---

3 *Borland's Trustee v. Steel Brothers* [1901] 1 Ch. 279 at 288. *cf.* somewhat different definitions of a "share" for tax purposes, *e.g.* Capital Acquisitions Tax Act 1976, s.2(1) and Capital Gains Tax Act 1975, s.2(1).

4 *Attorney General v. Jameson* [1904] 2 I.R. 644 at 669–670.

9–04 Ownership of one or more shares does not give the member any proprietary rights in the underlying assets of the company. By virtue of the separate legal personality principle, it was held in the *Macaura* case[5] that even the sole beneficial shareholder of a "one person" company does not even have an insurable interest in the assets of his company.[6]

9–05 A member of or shareholder in an unlimited company is personally liable for the company's debts on it becoming insolvent. In the case of a limited company, the shareholder's liability is only in respect of the amount remaining unpaid on the shares.[7] Although the Companies Acts allow for alteration of the memorandum and articles of association, section 27 of the 1963 Act stipulates that a member's financial obligations to his company may not be increased unilaterally in this way. Subject to any written agreement to the contrary,

> "No member of the company shall be bound by an alteration made . . . after the date on which he became a member, if and so far as the alteration requires him to take or subscribe for more shares than the number held by him . . . or in any way increases his liability . . . to contribute to the share capital of, or otherwise to pay money to, the company."

This provision occasionally gives rise to difficulties in companies that are primarily co-operative ventures.[8]

BECOMING A MEMBER

9–06 There are three major ways in which a person can become a member of a company, or, for short, become a shareholder. The original subscribers to the company's memorandum of association become shareholders as soon as the company is registered.[9] Persons who agree to become members and whose names are registered as such also become shareholders.[10] Thirdly, the successors in title of the original members and of those to whom shares were allotted become shareholders on their being registered as members;[11] *i.e.* persons who agreed to acquire the subscribers' or the allottees' shares, and persons to whom

---

5 *Macaura v. Northern Assurance Co.* [1925] A.C. 619; see above, para. 3–14.
6 *cf. Kerry Co-Op Creameries Ltd. v. An Bord Bainne* [1990] I.L.R.M. 664 at 715.
7 1963 Act, s.207(1)(d), (e).
8 See below, paras 14–61 *et seq.*
9 1963 Act, s.31(1). *cf. Baythurst Holdings Ltd. v. I.R.C.* [1971] 1 W.L.R. 1333 at 1355–1356.
10 *ibid.*, s.31(2). *cf. Re Nuneaton Borough Association F.C.* [1989] B.C.L.C. 454.
11 *Re Baku Consolidated Oilfields Ltd.* [1994] 1 B.C.L.C. 173.

those shares passed by operation of law, like personal representatives on death, trustees in bankruptcy, etc. The mechanisms by which shares may be transferred or transmitted are summarised separately below, as is the question of restrictions imposed by the articles of association on the free transferability of shares.[12]

Restrictions on Membership

9–07 Aliens, bankrupts, lunatics, minors, and entities with a legal personality of their own are not prevented by law from holding shares in companies registered in Ireland. But the acquisition of shares by a minor may be repudiated by him or by the company on it learning that its member is not *sui juris*.[13] A company's own regulations may exclude certain individuals or categories of persons from membership; although it could be argued that exclusion on the grounds of religion, sex, marital status and the like violates the Constitution. Subject to certain exceptions, any purported acquisition by a limited company of its own shares or of shares in its holding company is void.[14] Special provision is made for shares that a company possesses in its holding company and for its own shares held by and on behalf of a p.l.c.[15]

The Register of Members

9–08 Every company must keep a register of its members.[16] Entry of a person's name in this register is a precondition of becoming a member or a shareholder.[17] Where a company does not register as a member the name of someone who subscribed to its memorandum of association, it has been held that once the company itself is registered the subscribers become the holders of whatever number of shares they subscribed for.[18] Except where the general law so requires or its own regulations authorise it to do so, a company cannot refuse to register as a member a person who has properly acquired shares in it.[19] Often the real ownership of shares is disguised by having them registered in the name of nominees — frequently in the name of special nominee companies that financial institutions establish for this purpose. Article 7 of Table A authorises the company to require that information be

---

[12] below, paras 9.63 *et seq* and paras 9–32 *et seq*.
[13] *cf. Cork & Bandon Railway Co. v. Cazenove* (1847) 10 Q.B.D. 935.
[14] 1983 Act, s.41 and 1963 Act, s.32; See above, paras 7–46 *et seq*.
[15] 1963 Act, s.32 and 1983 Act, s.43.
[16] 1963 Act, s.116.
[17] *cf. Re Baku Consolidated Oilfields Ltd.* [1994] 1 B.C.L.C. 173 concerning who a liquidator should treat as a member.
[18] *Evan's Case* (1867) L.R. 2 Ch. 427.
[19] *Tangney v. Clarence Hotels Co.* [1933] I.R. 51.

furnished to it as to the beneficial ownership of shares in it. Before 1990 there was no requirement in the Companies Acts to record separately the names of those who hold substantial interests in a company's voting shares, or for ascertaining who in fact owns shares that are registered in the names of nominees. These matters are now dealt with in detail in Part IV of the 1990 Act (sections 53-106), which is headed "Disclosure of Interests in Shares".[20] Reference has already been made to the separate register that must be kept of shares held by or for a company's directors and secretaries, and their immediate families.[21]

9–09 Sections 116–124 of the 1963 Act[22] contain various provisions regarding the register of members. It must contain every member's name, address, the amount and the numbers of shares held, the amounts paid up on the shares, and the date on which each became and ceased to be a member. The contents of the register are not absolutely conclusive; they are only prima facie evidence of what it contains.[23] Persons who wish to have their names removed from the register because, for instance, they are no longer members or they never agreed to take shares in the company, or the agreement they made was void (*e.g.* for misrepresentation), may either bring an action for rescission or apply under section 122 of the 1963 Act to have the register rectified. On such an application, the court is empowered to decide questions concerning title to the shares in question and to award compensation for any loss sustained by a party. Not only can any member examine the register of members but it is a public document that must be left open to inspection by everybody.[24]

INCIDENTS OF MEMBERSHIP

9–10 Shareholders have a general right against those who control their company to have it run in accordance with its regulations and the Companies Acts (such as to notices of meetings, copies of the annual accounts, pre-emption in respect of additional shares being issued, etc.); also that majorities do not unfairly discriminate against minorities[25] and that the majority do not "defraud" the company.[26] Shareholders ordinarily have five vital contractual rights against the company,

---

[20] See below, paras 9–86 *et seq*.
[21] See above, paras 5–182 *et seq*.
[22] As amended by 1982 Act, s.20.
[23] 1963 Act, s.124.
[24] *ibid*., s.119.
[25] See below, paras 10–23 *et seq*.
[26] See below, paras 10–44 *et seq*.

namely, to transfer their shares, to vote in general meeting, to a dividend when declared, to a return of their capital on a winding up, if the company is solvent, and to a share in any surplus that may exist then. A company's regulations may give particular classes of shareholders, such as those with preference shares or indeed named individuals, "class" or "special personal" rights.

The Memorandum and Articles of Association

9–11 In determining an individual shareholder's rights and obligations *vis-à-vis* the company under its own regulations, the following four principles apply (although on occasion these are subject to certain qualifications and exceptions). They will be referred to as the "construction", "exhaustiveness", "equality" and "nominalist" principles.

Interpretation of Regulations

9–12 The extent of a member's or class or members' rights and obligations is primarily a question of the interpretation of the company's memorandum and articles of association, any resolutions passed under the articles and the terms on which the shares in question were issued. Members' rights "must depend on the terms of the instrument which contains the bargain that they have made with the company and each other".[27] That the answer to most disputes about shareholders' rights is to be found in the correct construction of the company's regulations was emphasised in *Cork Electric Supply Co. v. Concannon*,[28] where Kennedy C.J. warned against relying too much on reported decisions on similar questions. One set of articles "cannot [be] construe[d] by the construction applied by some court to another set of articles (save, or course, as to any principle or rule of construction of general application authoritatively declared for the purpose of such construction)".[29] However, FitzGibbon J. observed that "If a particular article, clause, or expression has received a judicial interpretation, and has been subsequently adopted as precedent in the formation of other companies, it is better, in a doubtful question of construction, to adhere to previous decisions rather than upon a nice balance of opinion to disaffirm a construction in reliance upon which large amounts of capital may have been invested."[30] The general principles regarding the construction of contracts apply to interpreting companies' memoranda and articles of association, which are a statutory contract between the

---

27 *Scottish Insurance Corp. v. Wilson & Clyde Coal Co.* [1949] A.C. 462 at 488.
28 [1932] I.R. 314.
29 *ibid.* at 328.
30 *ibid.* at 333.

members, subject to some qualifications. Terms may be implied into them by way of purely constructional implication but not otherwise.

9–13 Although the memorandum of association is the dominant instrument and must prevail where there is any conflict, reference may be made to the articles to explain ambiguities in the memorandum or to supplement it on matters about which it is silent.[31] Where there is inconsistency between provisions in the articles, the following two principles of interpretation were stated by Gavan Duffy J. in *Re Imperial Hotel (Cork) Ltd.*[32] Where an "earlier clause is followed by a later clause which destroys altogether the obligation created by the earlier clause, the later clause is to be rejected as repugnant and the earlier clause prevails."[33] And a "clause embodying a declaration of rights for a class of preferred members must, on a conflict of language, prevail . . . over administrative provisions of an intrinsically ancillary and subordinate character."[34]

9–14 Whatever provisions are contained in the company's regulations regarding a particular kind of right are deemed to be exhaustive, *i.e.* as regards any one of the major rights that are defined in the regulations, shareholders are entitled to nothing more than what is expressly provided for. For instance, where one class of shares is described as being entitled to a 10 per cent dividend, their holders have no right to be paid dividends over and above that amount.

9–15 Where, however, the regulations are silent as to any of the usual rights, then all shareholders possess those rights in an equal measure. Thus, where nothing is said about voting or about dividend entitlements, every shareholder has the same rights to vote and to dividends.

9–16 Finally, there is the nominalist principle, by which is meant that, in the absence of some contrary provision in the regulations, for most purposes the measure of members' rights is the nominal value of their shares and not the amount paid up on them or the price paid for them. Thus, where the right to dividends is stated in percentage terms (*e.g.* dividend of 12 per cent), this means 12 per cent of the share's nominal or par value.[35] Similarly, the measure of the member's right to share in a surplus that is left over in a winding up, after all debts have been

---

[31] *e.g. Re Bansha Woollen Mills Co.* (1887) 21 L.R. Ir. 181.
[32] [1950] I.R. 115.
[33] *ibid.* at 119, quoting *Forbes v. Gitt* [1922] 1 A.C. 256 at 259.
[34] *ibid.*
[35] *Oakbank Oil Co. v. Crum* (1882) 8 App. Cas. 65; but *cf.* Table A, art. 120.

paid and provision is made to repay the subscribed capital, is the share's nominal value;[36] although unpaid amounts may have to be paid up before holders of partly paid shares can participate in the surplus.[37]

Enforcing the Regulations

9–17 According to section 25 of the 1963 Act, a company's memorandum and articles of association are the equivalent of a contract made under seal between the company and all its members and between the members *inter se*. Accordingly, where either the company or any member contravenes those regulations, the company and at times the other members are entitled to redress for breach of contract. However, the courts do not enforce every one of those regulations in this manner; there are several kinds of articles which will only be enforced in limited circumstances.[38] For instance, a shareholder cannot always sue for damages because the company acted *ultra vires*, several procedural requirements in the regulations may be held to be matters not directly concerning individual shareholders and it is only rights conferred on them *qua* shareholders which they can enforce in this manner. It is convenient to deal with these complications and with the more general question of minority shareholders' rights in the next chapter and to confine the discussion here to the nature and extent of the principal rights which shareholders enjoy.

Evidence of Members' Rights and Obligations

9–18 Since the memorandum and articles of association and any amendments made to them must be registered in the registry of companies,[39] the incidents of membership as recorded in them are matters of public notice. However, incidents can be attached to shares by virtue of an ordinary resolution of the company or otherwise. Section 5 of the 1982 Act requires every company to have forwarded to the registry of companies a return stating any rights or restrictions attaching to their shares that have not previously been registered; but no sanction for contravening this requirement is stipulated. Section 5 furthermore requires all resolutions varying any of these incidents to be forwarded to the registry of companies within 15 days of their being passed. Finally, where shares are allotted with rights attaching to them that are not stated in the company's regulations or in a resolution that must be

---

36 *Birch v. Cropper* (1889) 14 App. Cas. 525.
37 *Re Newtownards Gas Co.* (1885) 15 L.R. Ir. 51.
38 See below, paras 10–20 *et seq.*
39 1963 Act, ss. 17, 143.

registered, section 39 of the 1983 Act requires particulars of those rights to be delivered to the registrar of companies within one month of the allotment. This section also requires that particulars of any variation of those rights be registered and, as well, particulars of any name or designation assigned to the shares. The articles of association of listed companies must state how their various classes of shares rank for distribution; any non-voting or limited or restrictive voting shares must be described in the articles as such.[40]

Information Concerning the Company

9–19 The terms under which shares were issued may stipulate that those shareholders are entitled to certain information concerning the company's affairs; the terms may even go so far as to give a representative of those shareholders a seat on the board of directors. The company's articles of association may also provide for the disclosure of information. However, Table A is remarkably undemanding in this regard; its only purely informational requirements are for circulating notices of general meetings and of resolutions to be considered at them and for circulating, to those entitled to receive them, copies of the annual accounts and the directors' and the auditors' reports. Article 127 of Table A authorises the directors to determine the circumstances under which members may inspect the company's books and records but adds that members shall have no right to inspect those documents "except as conferred by statute or authorised by the directors or by the company in general meeting." The main items of information which the Companies Acts require to be circulated to shareholders are notices of all general meetings and of all resolutions which will be passed at those meetings, the annual accounts, together with accompanying auditors' report and directors' report.[41]

9–20 Exceptionally, the failure to provide information over and above that required in the legislation may amount to "oppression" under section 205 of the 1963 Act. In *Re Clubman Shirts Ltd.*,[42] where the company was in serious financial difficulties and was threatened with receivership and liquidation, the directors transferred its business to another company under a scheme whereby the transferor's shareholders received no payment. For a number of years the directors had refused to hold annual general meetings or to present annual accounts or file an annual return. Nor would they give the petitioner, who held 20 per cent of the equity, full details about the transfer of the undertak-

---

[40] Yellow Book, Chap. 13, Appendix I.
[41] See above, paras 8–38 *et seq*.
[42] [1983] I.L.R.M. 323.

ing. O'Hanlon J. characterised most of their conduct as "negligence, carelessness [and] irregularity" rather than oppression. But he found that, despite the position in "strict law", a minority shareholder ought ordinarily to he provided with adequate information about such a vital matter as disposal of the undertaking and that, accordingly, the petitioner had been a victim of oppression. It was held in England that minority shareholders were wrongfully oppressed where the company had not filed annual accounts for several years and no general meeting had been held for years.[43] They were thereby deprived of "their right to know and consider the state of the company and its directorships and to ask questions of its directors. . ."[44]

Voting

9–21 Another of the most important rights that a shareholder possesses is to vote in general meetings. When and in what ways shareholders are entitled to vote turns on the first three principles referred to above. Nominalism applies to voting in the sense that, in the absence of some contrary stipulation, the amount paid up on or paid for shares does not affect the value of the vote they carry.[45] In the past, the presumption was that every shareholder had one vote regardless of the number of shares they held.[46] Now, under section 134(e) of the 1963 Act, one vote attaches to every share or to each £10 stock unless the regulations provide otherwise. The law governing the convening and conduct of general meetings and reaching decisions by resolutions has been dealt with in Chapter 4 above.

Voting Inequalities

9–22 It is entirely a matter for the shareholders or members to determine the actual voting system within their company. Article 63 of Table A provides that every member at the general meeting has one vote on a show of hands and, when a poll is taken, one vote per share; but this is subject to any special voting rights or restrictions attached to any class or classes of shares that were issued. Where it is sought to allocate control in a company in a way other than that reflected by the actual amount shareholders have invested in it, *i.e.* other than the "one share one vote" system, a device commonly used is to create different kinds of voting shares. For instance, the shares may be divided into

---

[43] *Re a Company, ex p. Shooter* [1990] B.C.L.C. 384.
[44] *ibid.* at 393.
[45] *cf. Re Wakefield Rolling Stock Co.* [1892] 3 Ch.D. 165.
[46] cf. *Kinsella v. Alliance & Dublin Consumers Gas Co.*, Barron J., October 5, 1982, Cases, p. 168.

separate classes, like "ordinary" and "deferred" shares, or "A" and "B" shares, with one category carrying greater voting rights per share than the other. Alternatively, on certain issues, such as the removal of directors, one group of shares may carry more votes than the others. Or there may be a basic "one share one vote" system but with no individual shareholder entitled to cast more than a specified number of votes regardless of how many shares they possess; which is the system of voting in Alliance & Dublin Consumers Gas Co., said to have been introduced at the instigation of Daniel O'Connell to ensure that the company would not be taken over by large financial interests. There are companies with some classes of shares that have no voting rights whatsoever but non-voting shares are discouraged by the Stock Exchange. Article 2 of Table A empowers companies subject to it to issue shares "with such preferred, deferred or other special rights or restrictions, . . . in regard to . . . voting . . . as the company may from time to time by ordinary resolution determine."

9–23 The freedom of companies to devise whatever voting scheme suits them best was affirmed in *Bushell v. Faith*.[47] There the articles of association provided that, on any proposal to remove him from office, a director shall have three votes for each share that he holds. It was argued that this contravened section 182 of the 1963 Act, under which any director can be removed from office by ordinary resolution "notwithstanding anything in the articles . . . " But that contention was rejected on the grounds that the legislature "has never sought to fetter the right of the company to issue a share with such [voting] rights or restrictions as it may think fit. There is no fetter which compels the company to make the voting rights or restrictions of general application and . . . such rights or restrictions can be attached to special circumstances and to particular types of resolution."[48]

Imposed Equalities

9–24 Where, however, it is proposed to make an arrangement or reconstruction under section 201 of the 1963 Act,[49] the matter cannot he resolved in accordance with any special voting system the company adopted. Instead, the proposal must have been accepted by at least 75 per cent in nominal value of the class or classes affected and who vote before it can become binding on that class and the company. Somewhat similarly, for a "take-out merger" under section 204 of the 1963

---

[47] [1970] A.C. 1099.
[48] *ibid*. at 1109.
[49] See below, paras 11–53 *et seq*.

Act to take place,[50] the acquiring company must have bought at least 80 per cent in value of the shares affected. And rights given to minority shareholders to apply to the court to veto certain fundamental structural changes in the company are expressed in terms of a minority who hold a stipulated percentage in value of the issued share capital, and not in terms of a percentage of votes.

Dividends

9–25 Where a company's business is profitable, the shareholders will expect to be rewarded by being paid dividends, which cannot be paid out of a company's capital or if it is insolvent.[51] Application of the "construction", "exhaustiveness", "equality" and "nominalist" principles to dividend rights has given rise to considerable litigation in the context of preference shares, as is explained below. Although the presumption is that dividend rights are based on the nominal amounts as opposed to the amounts called up or in fact paid up,[52] article 120 of Table A provides that dividends are to be calculated on the amounts paid up or credited as paid up. The question of the financial circumstances in which dividends may not be paid has been dealt with in Chapter 7, regarding distributions from capital and not from available profits. Article 118 Table A reiterates the 1983 Act's requirements, that no dividend shall be paid "otherwise than out of profits".

9–26 In companies that are subject to Table A, the decision on dividends is split between the directors and the members in general meeting. Before any dividend can be declared, Article 116 requires that it be recommended by the board. But it is for the general meeting to decide whether any dividend should be paid, provided that the amount does not exceed that recommended by the board.[53] Special classes of shareholders, like those owning preference shares, may be entitled to be paid in priority to other classes.[54] Under Table A, the directors have authority to pay such interim dividend "as appear to [them] to be justified by" the company's profits.[55] They, moreover, are given a wide discretion to carry forward any profits "which they think it prudent not to divide";[56] and they are empowered "as they think proper" to place profits in reserves and either to invest those funds or use them in the company's business.

---

[50] See below, paras 12–38 *et seq.*
[51] See above, paras 7–25 *et seq.*
[52] *Oakbank Oil Co. v. Crum* (1882) 8 App. Cas. 65.
[53] *cf. Scott v. Scott* [1943] 1 All E.R. 582.
[54] See below, para. 9–47.
[55] Art. 117.
[56] Art. 119.

Declining to Declare a Dividend

9–27 In the case of large companies with many shareholders and where the directors tend to have a considerable degree of autonomy, the likelihood of their control over dividends being abused must be set alongside economic considerations that deter abuse. For instance, the take-over bid can be a response to a pattern of either unduly miserly or excessively generous distributions. But where small companies are concerned, it is not unusual for the majority shareholders to occupy all the seats on the board, to pay themselves lavish, though not unlawfully excessive, directors' fees and never recommend a dividend; in consequence the minority shareholders may be discriminated against in fact. While such conduct might be a breach of directors' fiduciary duties, in the absence of other aggravating factors it is unlikely to amount to an unlawful interference with minority shareholders' rights. What tends to prevent the courts from intervening in such matters is that a decision against the company may in effect require the judge to determine its dividend policy, a task which he would be reluctant, and may be ill-equipped, to undertake. Exceptionally, however, the failure to declare dividends where there are more than ample funds to cover any distribution may constitute "oppression" under section 205 of the 1963 Act.[57]

9–28 For instance in *Re Sam Weller & Sons Ltd.*,[58] the company was a prosperous family business. The two petitioners held about 15 per cent of the shares in it but then inherited shares, taking their stake up to 42.5 per cent. The company's net assets were worth approximately £500,000 and half of that was held in cash. For the previous 37 years the company always paid the same dividend, which at the relevant time was covered 14 times by earned profits. There was no indication that dividends would be increased. These proceedings were an application to strike out a petition for oppression, on the grounds that, on the evidence, the case could not possibly succeed. But it was held that there can exist circumstances where no dividend or a derisory dividend is paid for a long period, without any reasonable business justification, that a court would be justified in making an order under section 205. Whether those circumstances existed in this case was to be determined at the trial of the action. There is a famous American case of 80 years ago involving the Ford Motor Co.,[59] where minority shareholders, the Dodge brothers, obtained an order from a Michigan court that the company pay $U.S.19,000,000 in dividends. Non-payment of divi-

---

[57] See below, paras 10–74 *et seq.*
[58] [1990] 1 Ch. 683.
[59] *Dodge v. Ford Motor Co.* 170 N.W. 668 (1919).

dends in exceptional circumstances might even justify winding up the company on just and equitable grounds.

A Debt

9–29 Unless there is a stipulation to the contrary in the company's regulations, dividends must be paid in cash.[60] Table A authorises payment of dividends by cheque.[61] It was held in *Re Drogheda Steampacket Co.*[62] that a duly declared dividend is a speciality debt and therefore may be recovered from the company after more than six years have elapsed. This was reiterated by Kenny J. in *Re Belfast Empire Theatre of Varieties,*[63] where it was held that the appropriate period under the Statute of Limitations, 1957, in which dividends declared can be recovered from the company, is twelve years. However, the English Chancery Division has concluded that the debt is a simple contract debt and, therefore, becomes statute-barred after six years.[64] Table A empowers the company to deduct from the dividends payable any sums immediately due to it in respect of the share, such as unpaid calls.[65]

Distributing Specie

9–30 Table A also permits distributions *in specie* by way of dividend,[66] in particular, paid up shares and debentures of any other company; but this provision has not yet been the subject of judicial interpretation. The reference there to "specific assets" and to securities of "any other" company means that the article does not authorise a company to distribute its own shares by way of dividend — what are called "scrip" or "stock" dividends. Yet many companies today have special articles giving themselves such authority — which often take the form of giving the shareholders an option of taking their dividends either in money or in additional equity in the company.

Transfer of Shares

9–31 One of the great advantages of the registered company as a vehicle for transacting business, or indeed for achieving other co-operative objectives, is that members can transfer their interests in the company without disrupting the entire enterprise.[67] The inherent trans-

---

[60] *Wood v. Odessa Waterworks Co.* (1889) 42 Ch. D. 636.
[61] Art. 123.
[62] [1903] 1 I.R. 512.
[63] [1963] I.R. 41.
[64] *Re Compania de Electriciadad de la Provincia de Buenos Aires Ltd.* [1980] Ch. 146.
[65] Art. 121.
[66] Art. 122.
[67] The actual mechanics of transferring shares is dealt with below, at paras 9–63 *et seq*.

ferability of a member's interest in a company is proclaimed in section 79 of the 1963 Act. How far-reaching this right to transfer is can be gathered from *Re Discoverers Finance Corp.*[68] Fearing that the company was in difficulties and that he might be obliged to pay further calls on his shares, the owner of 2,000 shares of £1 par, on which 30 pence each had been paid up, sold them for £5 in all to a journeyman tanner from Germany. The consideration was never paid nor even asked for. It was held that, provided the company's regulations did not place a restriction on the free transferability of the shares and that the sale in fact was genuine, the seller ceased to be a member of the company once the share transfer was registered. He, therefore, was no longer liable for calls on those shares. The fundamental principle is that

> "in the absence of restrictions in the articles the shareholder had by virtue of (s.79 of the 1963 Act) the right to transfer his shares without the consent of any body to any transferee, even though he be a man of straw, provided it is a bona fide transaction in the sense that it is an out-and-out disposal of the property without retaining any interest in the shares — that the transferor bona fide divests himself of all benefits. . . .
>
> It was the policy of the [Companies Acts] to give a right of free disposition, leaving it to the regulations of the company to impose such restrictions upon its exercise as might be desired. In the absence of restrictions it is competent to a transferor, notwithstanding that the company is in extremes, to compel registration of a transfer to a transferee notwithstanding that the latter is a person not competent to meet the unpaid liability upon the shares. Even if the transfer be executed for the express purpose of relieving the transferor from liability, the directors cannot upon that ground refuse to register it. . ."[69]

Restrictions on Transfers

9–32 Members' freedom to transfer their shares may be restricted or conditioned by the company's own regulations; every private company's regulations are required to impose some constraint on the transferability of its shares.[70] There is a great variety of restrictions, for instance, that the transferee must be an existing member of the company or that he must be a close relative of the transferor. One common form is a pre-emption requirement: that existing members, or sometimes directors, be given the first refusal before the shares are otherwise disposed of. Some pre-emption clauses that are often used lay down quite complicated procedures which must be followed before

---

[68] [1910] 1 Ch. 312, *Lindlar's* case.
[69] *ibid*. at 316, 317.
[70] 1963 Act, s.33(1)(a).

the shares can become freely transferable. Article 24 of Table A empowers the directors to block the transfer of partly paid shares to any person they "do not approve" of; the obvious example being someone not able to pay up the calls when made on the shares. The directors are also empowered to block a transfer of shares over which the company has a lien; where the transfer would prejudice the company's status in the State; where it would imperil any tax concession or rebate coming to the company and, fourthly, where the transfer would require the company to pay any additional stamp or other duty on a conveyance of property to the company.

9–33 The form of restriction contained in clause 3 of Part II of Table A is perhaps as extensive as could be formulated. According to it:

> "the directors may, in their absolute discretion, and without assigning any reason therefor, decline to register any transfer of any share, whether or not it is a fully paid share."

Clause 3, accompanied by a pre-emption requirement, often features in the very same set of articles of private companies. A good argument could be made that, in the light of the Constitution's protection for private property,[71] a restriction on the right to transfer shares must not be unreasonable, notably that transferees should not be excluded on grounds of their sex, race or religious beliefs. In the United States all restrictions on the transferability of shares are required to be reasonable because they are restraints on the alienation of property rights.[72] How the Irish courts should approach these clauses does not appear to have obtained extensive judicial analysis since 1943 and such constitutional consideration as may exist were not canvassed then.

Judicial Review of Refusal to Register Share Transfers

9–34 The principles applied when construing clauses restricting share transfers may be summarised as follows. First, a formal decision to refuse registration must be made. If the transferee is not notified of the refusal after a reasonable time has passed, then, unless there are special circumstances, the right of veto will be deemed to have lapsed.[73] Ordinarily, two months will be regarded as a reasonable time because section 84 of the 1963 Act requires transferees to be informed within that time that their applications have been refused. Special circum-

---

[71] Art. 40, 1, 2 and 3.

[72] See generally, Andre, "Restrictions on the Transfer of Shares: A Search for a Public Policy" (1979) 53 Tulane L. Rev. 776.

[73] *Re Swaledale Cleaners Ltd.* [1968] 1 W.L.R. 432; *Re New Cedos Engineering Co.* [1994] 1 B.C.L.C. 797; *cf. Popely v. Planarrive* [1997] 1 B.C.L.C. 8.

stances may warrant either extending or indeed contracting this period. Where the board are deadlocked, then it cannot resolve to refuse registration and the transfer accordingly can go ahead. But that is not the case where the articles state that the shares shall not be transferable except with the approval of the directors, the members or whoever. Whether the "reasonable time" rule referred to above applies in these latter circumstances has not been determined, but the usual rationale for that rule would not seem to have any application here, *i.e.* that the inherent right to transfer can be blocked by the directors' power of veto but all powers lapse after a reasonable time.

9–35 Second, where the clause in question possesses more than one potential meaning, then the narrowest construction will be adopted.[74] For instance, in *Tangney v. Clarence Hotels Co.*,[75] the clause empowered the directors to refuse to register a transfer to any person who, in their opinion, was not desirable to admit into membership. Johnston J. held that the directors had no power to refuse registration where the transferee already held some shares in the company. However, the courts will not indulge in excesses of literalism in order to defeat the obvious purpose behind a clause. Indeed in *Re Dublin North City Milling Co.*,[76] where the clause required that the transferee "is approved of by the board", Meredith M.R. held that the mere fact that the transferee of shares was already a member of the company did not oblige the directors to approve the transfer to him.[77]

9–36 Third, where the directors possess a discretion to veto a transfer, the governing principles are those set down in *Re Smith & Fawcett Ltd.*:

> "they must exercise their discretion bona fide in what they consider — not what a court may consider — is in the interests of the company, and not for any collateral purpose. They must have regard to those considerations, and those considerations only, which the articles on their true construction permit them to take into consideration... Where articles are framed with some... limitation on the discretionary power of refusal ... if the directors go outside the matters which the articles say are to be the matters and the only matters to which they are to have regard, [they] will have exceeded their powers."[78]

---

[74] *e.g. Re New Cedos Engineering Co.* [1994] 1 B.C.L.C. 797; *Stothers v. William Stewart (Holdings) Ltd.* [1994] 2 B.C.L.C. 266.

[75] [1933] I.R. 51.

[76] [1909] 1 I.R. 179.

[77] *cf. Re Bede Steam Shipping Co.* [1917] Ch. 123.

[78] [1942] 1 Ch. 304 at 306, 307.

In practice, it is difficult to have set aside an exercise of the directors' discretionary power of veto.[79] Directors are not obliged to give reasons and the plaintiff may not simply allege but must show that the directors were acting for an improper purpose.

9–37 As was explained in *Re Dublin North City Milling Co.*, the disappointed transferee "must allege and prove some indirect motive on the part of the directors in refusing his application [and] the law allows the directors to hold their tongues. It allows them to say that everything was done honestly and bona fide in the interests of their company; [the court has] no power to make them say more".[80] This leads to the situation where, as Black J. put it in *Re Hafner*, "[h]edged round with the privilege of remaining mute and the prima facie presumption of rectitude, the astutely silent director who wishes to exercise this power illegitimately may well consider himself all but invulnerable. No need to speak and no unfavourable inference from reticence — that is the settled rule."[81] In *Re Smith & Fawcett Ltd.*,[82] the company was founded by two persons on a 50/50 basis and, when one of them died, he bequeathed his shares to his two children. The directors refused to register the transfers of his shares, although the survivor shareholder offered to register half of them if he were allowed to purchase the other half at a price to be fixed by himself. It was argued that the true reason for not registering the share transfers was so that the surviving member could acquire those shares for himself at an under-value. It was held that insufficient evidence had been brought forward to show that the directors had abused their power of veto.

9–38 Where, however, it is demonstrated that the directors acted for some improper motive then the court will inquire carefully into the real reasons. *Re Hafner*[83] is an excellent example of the mute directors' defence of presumed rectitude being overcome. It concerned a small but very profitable family company, the regulations of which contained a clause— similar to Article 3 of Part II of Table A. The plaintiff inherited some shares in the company, but the directors refused to register him as a member, without assigning any reasons. However, it was shown in evidence that, by 1939 standards, one director was to be paid the "exorbitant" sum of £7,000 a year, another was given the "commercially fantastic" service contract of £3,000 a year for a term of 20

[79] See *Charles Forte Investments Ltd. v. Amanda* [1964] 1 Ch. 240 and authorities cited there, and *Popely v. Planarrive Ltd.* [1997] 1 B.C.L.C. 8.
[80] [1909] I.R. 179 at 183 and 184.
[81] [1943] I.R. 426 at 440.
[82] [1942] 1 Ch. 304.
[83] [1943] I.R. 426.

years and, if the company was wound up before that term expired, he was to be entitled to half that sum for the unexpired residue of the term. In the light of these facts, Black J. felt constrained to conclude that one reason for refusing to admit the plaintiff into membership was to prevent those payments from being questioned and indeed challenged in court. Accordingly, "[o]nce an illegitimate motive for such a decision is [shown], the normal legal presumption that they acted legitimately must go by the board and [the court] is no longer bound to ignore their silence, or to refuse to draw any inference from it."[84] He found that in the circumstances the directors had acted improperly in excluding the plaintiff.

9–39 It is only persons who have been registered as members of the company who can commence proceedings for oppression under section 205 of the 1963 Act.[85] Accordingly, the transferee of shares whose registration is being blocked cannot avail of this mode of redress. An exception to this is made by section 205(6) for a deceased member's personal representative or any person beneficially interested in his shares by virtue of his will or intestacy. Accordingly, if the circumstances in *Re Hafner* occurred today, the plaintiff there could have petitioned for appropriate redress under section 205 and almost certainly would have succeeded — his interest in being registered as a member being disregarded for no apparently good reason. Where the transferor of shares is alive and the company refuses to register his transferee, the oppression remedy is open. But it remains to be seen whether, when a veto is challenged in section 205 proceedings, the courts will be less indulgent of the directors' standing on their privilege of mute presumed rectitude.

Pre-emption Clauses

9–40 Most private companies also stipulate for some kind of pre-emption arrangement before shares can be transferred, especially where the transferee is a complete outsider. The precise form of pre-emption used here can vary enormously. Most often they provide that, where a member wishes to transfer his shares, he should thereupon notify the company secretary, who will notify the directors or the other members, as the case may be. If any of these wish to purchase the shares, he should so notify the secretary, who then will arrange for the shares to be valued in accordance with a prescribed formula or by an arbitrator or a valuer, or in some other manner as provided for. The intending

---

[84] [1943] I.R. 426 at 444.
[85] See below, para. 10–74.

transferor may then either be obliged to sell the shares at that price or remain a member. Given the statutory presumption of transferability, provisions of this nature are construed strictly in favour of the intending transferor. For instance, the frequently-used triggering formula, "wishes to transfer his shares", has been interpreted as meaning taking decisive steps to transfer legal title to them. Transfers of a beneficial interest in the shares, even where obligations are also assumed to transfer the legal interest at some later stage, normally will not suffice for these purposes.[86] Of course, the article in question might very well expressly deem a transfer of a beneficial interest as sufficient to get the pre-emption machinery going.

9–41 Except where the article clearly states otherwise, the initial notification of an intention to transfer is construed as a notice to treat and not an offer for sale.[87] Therefore, if a would-be purchaser wants to buy the shares, he must make an offer for them. Where this is the case, the proposing vendor can change his mind, for instance, because he is dissatisfied with the price at which the shares were valued. The extent to which any value reached for the shares can be challenged in court depends on the mode of valuation used. Most often, that is by the company's auditors acting as experts and not as arbitrators.[88]

9–42 Where pre-emption exists, its requirements must be complied with before the member becomes free to transfer his shares. In *Re Hafner*,[89] the company's articles provided for pre-emption as well as a discretionary veto on share transfers. The defendants there also contended that, because the shares there had not been put into pre-emption, the plaintiff could not be registered as a member. Even though they had improperly blocked registration of a transfer of the shares to him, they sought to prevent him from becoming a member simply by claiming his shares under the pre-emption clause. Under the relevant articles there, no member could dispose of his shares "without first offering them to the directors . . . who shall have the first option of purchasing same . . ." But the Supreme Court held that, having attempted to block the transfer under the discretionary clause, the directors had thereby waived their rights to pre-emption.

---

86 *Safeguard Industrial Investments Ltd. v. National Westminster Bank* [1982] 1 W.L.R. 589; *Theakston v. London Trust p.1.c.* [1984] B.C.L.C. 390; *Re Macro (Ipswich) Ltd.* [1994] 2 B.C.L.C. 354 at 401–402.

87 *Tett v. Phoenix Pty. & Investment Go.* [1986] B.C.L.C. 149.

88 *cf. Burgess v. Purchase & Sons (Farms) Ltd.* [1983] Ch. 216.

89 [1943] I.R. 426.

Return of Capital and Share in the Surplus

9–43 Where a company is being wound up and all its creditors are paid off, the shareholders then become entitled to be repaid their investment from the company's remaining assets.[90] And where there are still funds left over after repaying the shareholders, they are entitled to divide that surplus between themselves. The claims of shareholders *inter se* to priority in return of capital on a winding up have been the subject of little litigation, presumably because this matter tends to be provided for unambiguously in companies' regulations. Where no express provision is made, application of the "equality" and "nominalist" principles does not give rise to serious difficulties.[91] But division of the surplus left over after all the claims against the company are satisfied is the subject of an extensive case law.[92]

9–44 A cause of particular difficulty with the surplus is the relevance of how it could have been disposed of prior to liquidation. Assume that there are just ordinary and preference shares, and that all outstanding preference dividends have been paid. Before liquidation, what can be done with any surplus? Unless there are regulations to the contrary, the ordinary shareholders may pay themselves a dividend out of it. Therefore, the argument goes, where this is the case the equality principle should not apply in a liquidation to deprive the ordinary shareholders of what hitherto was theirs, albeit contingently. If, on the other hand, the surplus was capitalised, in the sense of not being available for paying dividends, then the ordinary shareholders no longer have a special claim on it and, therefore, it is said, the equality principle should come into play in the liquidation. Two complications cloud this argument. Often it can be difficult to determine whether funds were capitalised and, even where the intention to capitalise is uncontrovertable, the funds may not have been spent on capital items when the company goes into liquidation. Furthermore, since the matter ultimately is one of construction, meaning must be given to stipulations in the regulations that deal with these matters though these be in ambiguous terms. All of the leading cases on the controversial surplus question have concerned preference shares.

---

[90] 1963 Act, s.275(1)(b) (as amended by 1990 Act, s.132).

[91] *cf. Re Wakefield Rolling Steel Co.* [1892] 3 Ch. D. 165.

[92] See generally, B.H. McPherson, *The Law of Company Liquidation* (3rd ed., 1987), Chap. 13.

PREFERENCE SHARES

9–45 Preference shares are shares that carry prior or preferential rights over other shares.[93] The preferential rights are usually as regards dividends and return of capital, *i.e.* usually the preference shareholders must be paid a dividend or repaid their investment, or both as the case may be, before any such payment can be made to the other shareholders. In the past, preference shares were popular with investors because they guaranteed a degree of income and capital security but in recent years inflation has eroded their value. Although they are equity and not debt, companies tend to regard preference shares as a form of borrowing, in that they provide a source of capital on which the company is expected to pay a fixed percentage dividend every year. The advantage to a company of these shares is that they enable it more easily to gear its capital structure. Usually, there is no absolute obligation to pay a dividend on them every year or to repay them by a fixed date, nor is there any question of the company putting up security to obtain the funds. But dividends cannot be set off against profits for taxation purposes.

9–46 The exact rights and liabilities of preference shareholders, like those of other members, are set out in the memorandum and articles of association, resolutions passed and the terms on which the shares were issued. Although Table A envisages creating a class of share with certain preferential rights, it does not contain provisions dealing specifically with preference shares. A preference shareholder's liability is simply to pay any unpaid amounts on his shares when called upon to do so. In determining his rights, the "construction", "exhaustiveness", "equality" and "nominalist" principles referred to above apply. For pragmatic reasons, however, there have been some deviations from exhaustiveness and equality in several circumstances. It is almost unheard of for companies' regulations to contain special provisions about the transferability of their preference shares. As regards voting rights, companies' regulations usually give preference shareholders a vote in general meeting only when their dividends are in arrears or where it is proposed to alter their rights as a class.

Dividends

9–47 Where the company's regulations give one class of shares preferential rights regarding dividends, then those are their entire income

[93] See generally, Picketing, "The Problems of the Preference Share" (1963) 26 Mod. L. Rev. 499 and Rice, "Capital Rights of Preference Shares" (1962) 26 Conv. 115.

rights; there is "something so definitely pointed to as to suggest that it contains the whole of what [they are] to look to from the company".[94] If those members are to be paid a fixed preferential dividend, then they have no entitlement to participate any further in the profits unless expressly enabled to do so. Any claim they may have to equal participation with the other members is derogated from by the exhaustive statement of their entitlement to the company's profits.[95]

Participation

9–48 Occasionally, preference shares carry participating dividend rights. That is to say, over and above their basic (usually fixed) dividend entitlement, they may be given some right to participate with other shareholders in the remaining profits for distribution. At times, companies' regulations stipulate that their preference shareholders' dividend rights are not just cumulative, in the sense described below, but that a dividend shall be payable on those shares every year — or perhaps every year in which profits are earned or every year when there are profits available for distribution.[96] Any such obligation must be clearly provided for in the regulations; ambiguities tend to be read in favour of the directors' and members' discretion as to what should be done with the profits.[97] In *Re Lafayette Ltd.*[98] the company's regulations stated that the preference shareholders shall be entitled to a six per cent "cumulative preferential dividend for each year . . . out of the subsequent profits of the company." Kingsmill Moore J. held that the preference shareholders, therefore, became entitled to a dividend in every year in which there were "business profits" and that this right was not contingent on any dividend being declared; the articles give them "a right to their dividend, irrespective of any declaration, and, again without any declaration, automatically charge arrears of preference dividend on any future profits".[99]

Cumulation

9–49 Because entitlement to a dividend is usually contingent on one being declared in general meeting and on the directors' recommendation, the "exhaustiveness" principle has been qualified somewhat in respect of preferential dividend rights. Unless the company's regula-

---

[94] *Will v. United Lankat Plantation Co.* [1914] A.C. 11 at 17 and 18.

[95] *ibid.*

[96] *e.g. Staples v. Eastman Photographic Materials Co.* [1896] 2 Ch.303 and *Evling v. Israel & Oppenbeimer* [1918] 1 Ch. 101. In *Re Bradford Investments Ltd.* [1991] B.C.L.C. 224: articles deemed dividend payable even if no available profits.

[97] *Re Buck* (deceased) [1964] V.R. 284.

[98] [1950] I.R. 100.

[99] *ibid.* at 112.

tions provide otherwise, preference shareholders have no right to be paid a dividend in any year. It has been said that if it were otherwise it "might enable the preference shareholders to ruin the company, and would certainly lead to great inconvenience in enabling them to compel the payment out of the last penny without carrying forward any balance."[100] Yet this state of affairs can work unfairly against preference shareholders, who most likely acquire their shares in anticipation of receiving dividends at least in years when the company is making good profits; for over a number of years the company could retain all profits earned and then in one year declare a single (usually fixed) preference dividend together with a bumper dividend for the ordinary shareholders. On account of this, preference dividends tend to be presumed to be cumulative, *i.e.* in the absence of contrary provision, where a preference dividend has not been declared in any year or years, then all arrears of undeclared preference dividends for those years must be paid before any other class of shareholder may get a dividend. Thus, if there are 12 per cent preference shares and no dividend has been paid on them between 1996 and 1999, and in 2000 the company proposes to pay dividends on its ordinary shares, then the preference shareholders must be paid their 2000 dividend and the outstanding dividends for each of the years 1996–1999 before a distribution can be made to the ordinary shareholders.

9–50 The presumption that preference dividends are cumulative is traced to *Webb v. Earle*.[101] There, ordinary shareholders sought a declaration of invalidity against decisions by directors, in years where no dividends were paid, to place in a special reserve sums representing preference dividends to be paid when the funds became available. It was held that "there is nothing to prevent [the directors] from going to the profits of a subsequent period when they are sufficient to make up" preference dividends that had not been paid.[102] The case does not say in so many words that preference dividends are presumed to be cumulative but, if that were not so, the directors would not have the power to set sums by in order to pay arrears of dividends on them. However, authority supporting presumed cumulation is not very weighty[103] and that presumption might be rejected by an Irish court in favour of exhaustiveness.

---

[100] *Bond v. Barrow Haematite Steel Co.* [1902] 1 Ch. 353 at 362.

[101] (1875) L.R. 20 Eq. 556.

[102] *ibid.* at 561, following another "no reason why not" case, *Henry v. Great Northern Railway Co.* (1857) 1 De G. & J. 606.

[103] *Partick, Hillhead & Maryhill Gas Co. v. Taylor* (1888) 15 R. 711; *Ferguson & Forrester Ltd. v. Buchanan* [1902] S.C. 154; *cf. JJ. Thornycroft & Co. v. Thornycroft* (1927) 44 T.L.R. 9.

Winding Up

9–51 Where a company has not paid a preference dividend for a number of years and then goes into liquidation, the question arises of whether the preference shareholders have a claim against the company for those dividends it passed or could not have paid. Generally, once a winding up commences no claims to undeclared dividends can arise.[104] But where, as in *Re Lafayette Ltd.*,[105] the company's regulations treat dividend expectations as if they were declared, they then become a debt of the company from the time they were deemed to have been declared. Those sums are in the understandably "peculiar position of not being payable *pari passu* with the liabilities generally, because [they are] a deferred debt, not payable in competition with those of creditors who are not members of the company . . .[106] In recent years the English courts have tended to strain the meaning of companies' regulations in order to conclude that preference shareholders were granted a right in a winding up to have arrears of dividends paid to them.[107]

Return of Capital and the Surplus

9–52 It is usual when issuing preference shares to attach to them priority in respect of repayment of capital but to exclude them from participating in any surplus that may remain in a winding up after all classes of shareholders are paid off. Under the "exhaustiveness" principle, whatever the company's regulations say about preference shareholders' right to a return of capital and to any surplus, respectively, is a complete statement of their rights in these regards. Under the "equality" principle, where the regulations do not deal with these matters then the ordinary and preference shareholders have equal rights to a repayment and to share in any surplus. And where preference shares participate in the surplus, the measure of their rights is their nominal amounts and not the amounts paid up on them.[108] Beyond this, the legal position in Ireland is somewhat unsettled, the central question being whether or to what extent our courts will follow the prevailing orthodoxy in Britain.

The Surplus

9–53 The area of greatest controversy has been preference sharehold-

---

[104] *Re Crichton's Oil Co.* [1901] 2 Ch. 184.
[105] [1950] I.R. 100.
[106] *Re Imperial Hotel (Cork) Ltd.* [1950] I.R. 115 at 119.
[107] *E.g. Re F. de Jong & Co.* [1946] 1 Ch. 211 and *Re E.W. Savory Ltd.* [1951] 2 All E.R. 1036.
[108] *Birch v. Cropper* (1889) 14 App. Cas. 525.

ers' claims to participate in a surplus where the regulations do not address the question directly. At one time it was accepted that, by virtue of a combination of the exhaustiveness and the equality principles, those preference shareholders were entitled to participate rateably in the surplus. This view was endorsed in 1932 in *Cork Electric Supply Co. v. Concannon*[109] and also in 1946 by the Canadian Supreme Court in *International Power Co. v. McMaster University*.[110] However, when in 1949 the matter came before the Law Lords in *Scottish Insurance Corp. v. Wilsons & Clyde Coal Co.*,[111] by a majority they reached the contrary conclusion. It remains to be seen which analysis will recommend itself to the present Supreme Court. There are weighty logical and practical arguments for both points of view.

9–54 In the *Wilsons & Clyde Coal Co.* case a large capital profit was made by the defendant company when its major assets, coal mines, were nationalised in return for cash. It then proposed to repay its preference shareholders under section 72 of the 1963 Act, following which it intended to distribute the sizeable surplus to its ordinary shareholders. Predictably, the preference shareholders opposed this scheme on the grounds *inter alia* that they had a legal right to a share in the surplus.[112] Under the company's regulations, the preference shareholders had priority as to repayment of capital in a winding up but nothing at all was said about which group was to get any surplus or whether it should be shared. Other regulations deemed relevant were to the effect that the board could create a reserve fund for repaying the preference shares and that the company might convert any surplus funds it had into capital and distribute it among the ordinary shareholders, for instance by issuing bonus shares. Lord Morton of Henryton, in his dissent, emphasised the underlying equality principle; he found in the company's regulations "not a word which raises the implication that [the preference holders] are to be excluded from the ordinary right, as corporators, to share equally with other corporators in a winding up on this portion of "the property of the company' "; he reiterated the principle that "the considerations affecting capital and dividend are entirely different"; he concluded that the case law as it stood indicated that the surplus had to be shared between the two classes.[113] The kernel of the contrary, and successful, argument was that a surplus represents retained profits that the ordinary shareholders, had they chosen

---

[109] [1932] I.R. 314.
[110] (1946) 2 D.L.R. 81.
[111] [1949] A.C. 462.
[112] See below, paras 11–44 *et seq*. on general fairness considerations.
[113] [1949] A.C. 462 at 501 and 506.

to do so, could have appropriated to themselves in the form of dividends or bonus shares. It would therefore, be unjust and indeed illogical if the claims they had over those funds were defeated by the event of a liquidation. Repayment of capital and participation in any surplus are not distinct matters; the central question is what rights to "company property" arise in a winding up. If a company's regulations are silent on any aspect of this matter, then the equality principle comes into play. But where the regulations address either repayment of capital or the surplus, or both, those provisions are an exhaustive recitation of the preference shareholders' entitlement to both.[114] This analysis, it was said, is consistent with the business world's perception of the preference shareholder's position.

9–55 In the earlier *Cork Electric Co.* case,[115] which arose out of very similar facts, a unanimous Supreme Court adopted the same reasoning as in Lord Morton's dissent. There the company, that ran trains in Cork and supplied the city with electricity, was expropriated under the Electricity Supply Act, 1927. The central issue was how should the compensation paid for the undertaking be divided among the ordinary and the preference shareholders. Under the company's regulations, the preference shareholders were entitled to a 5 per cent cumulative preference dividend per annum and, in a winding up, "to priority in payment of the capital over the ordinary shares." According to Kennedy C.J.:

> "Preference shareholders are holders of shares in the capital of a company in the same way as ordinary shareholders are holders of shares in its capital. Both classes of shareholders are equally members of the Company. Their respective positions are differentiated only to the extent to which the rights and privileges attaching to their respective shares are qualified contractually by the Memorandum and Articles of Association of the Company. 1 turn, therefore, to the Memorandum and Articles of Association of the plaintiff company to ascertain whether the right of the preference shareholder to participate in surplus assets on a winding up of the company has been abrogated, cut down, or qualified in any way. There is no such specific provision, and we have to look for a limitation by implication. Upon the construction of the Articles of Association before us it is to be observed that, while as regards participation in profits, the words of exclusion "but to no further dividend" were carefully inserted, no such limitation was added to the immediately following clause as to priority in payment of capital. Moreover, I can find no grounds for cutting down the word 'shareholders' . . . or the words 'member of the Company for the time being' in [the articles] to ordinary shareholders

114 *cf. Re Isle of Thanet Electricity Supply Co.* [1950] Ch. 161.
115 [1932] I.R. 314.

> only . . . I must say that there is not, so far as I know, any rule of law or construction requiring a Court of construction to find a logical consistency between the rights of preference shareholders while a company is a going concern and their rights on a winding-up. It is difficult to know what is meant precisely by 'logical consistency' in this connection, but, as I understand it, it is quite foreign to the great diversity of bargains which may lawfully be made in these business contracts."[116]

That the numerous Companies Acts passed since this case was decided never sought to interfere with the principle as stated here suggests that it would still be followed today.

Sharing the Surplus

9–56 Where both ordinary and preference shareholders are entitled to share in the surplus, the question then arises of whether a distinction should be drawn between the part of the surplus that remains or was available for distribution as dividends and that which has been capitalised. Where the regulations are silent about rights to the surplus, the practice would appear to be that all classes share in the capitalised amounts but only the ordinary shareholders are entitled to participate in the sums that were not capitalised. For example, in *Re Marshall Bros., Belfast, Ltd.*[117] where the surplus comprised *inter alia* of a profit on the sale of the undertaking, which was treated as a capitalised amount, and tax refunds held in "special reserve", which was treated as uncapitalised, the former was divided among all the shareholders whereas the latter went to the ordinary shareholders only. Yet difficulties can arise in determining whether particular reserves were, or were intended to be, capitalised. Article 119 of Table A does not differentiate between the two kinds of reserves; and in the *Wilsons & Clyde Coal Co.* case reference was made to the unlikelihood of investors "intend[ing] a bargain which would involve an investigation of an artificial and elaborate character into the nature and origin of surplus assets."[118] Indeed, it is doubtful whether *Re Marshall Brothers* would be followed today in the light of the *Dimbula Valley Tea* case.[119]

9–57 Where it is expressly provided that the two or more classes are to share in the surplus, how exactly this is to be distributed turns on how the regulations in their entirety are construed. It would appear

---

116 [1932] I.R. 314 at 327, 329. In *Re Northern Engineering Industries p.l.c.* [1994] 2 B.C.L.C. 704 a "class rights" clause in the articles of association prevented the repayment of preference shareholders without their consent; see below, paras 11–21 *et seq.*

117 [1956] N.I. 78.

118 [1949] A.C. 462 at 489.

119 below, para. 9–57.

that there is no presumption against the parties having intended to distinguish between capitalised and uncapitalised funds. In *Dimbula Valley (Ceylon) Tea Co. v. Laurie*,[120] preference shareholders were entitled to a cumulative preference dividend, to priority in the return of capital and any arrears of dividend, and to participate in "any further surplus assets" rateably with other shareholders. The company's regulations stated that, subject to any preferential rights, profits remaining after placing sums in reserve "shall be divisible among the members"; and the company could capitalise sums standing in any "reserve fund" and any "undivided profits". One question was whether the preference shareholders could participate rateably in the entire surplus or only in such part of it as could not have been paid as dividends on the ordinary shares. Buckley J. acknowledged the ordinary shareholders' power to defeat any preference shareholders' expectation of sharing in undistributed profits by, on the one hand, declaring a dividend from the profits and, on the other, where profits could not be so distributed, to capitalise them and issue the ordinary shareholders with further equity representing the capitalised amount. This, however, it was said, is not necessarily inconsistent with the preference shareholders on a winding up having a right to participate in retained earnings. It was concluded that, in the absence of clear contrary indications, "the right of the ordinary shareholders to the exclusive enjoyment of accumulated profits . . . depends on appropriate resolutions being passed before liquidation begins, and that in default of appropriate resolutions such accumulated profits will form part of the fund of assets distributable" between all members rateably on a winding up. In order to reach this conclusion and to distinguish pre-1900 authority[121] on the matter, the judge fastened on the terminology of the company's dividends regulation, where it was said that profits were "divisible among" the members once preference dividends were met and subject to sums being placed in reserve. This, it was said, meant not that those profits "belonged to" the ordinary shareholders, but merely that such profits could be divided among them by a decision of the general meeting before a winding up commenced. Yet an Irish court might choose to follow *Re Bridgewater Navigation Co.*,[122] where 70 years earlier the English Court of Appeal reached the opposite conclusion when construing somewhat similar articles.

---

[120] [1961] Ch. 353.
[121] *Re Bridgewater Navigation Co.* [1891] 2 Ch. 326.
[122] *ibid.*

PROPERTY RIGHTS IN SHARES

9–58 Questions about becoming a shareholder and title to shares are more appropriately considered as aspects of personal property law.[123] A share is classified as a chose in action, as contrasted with a tangible thing, and rights regarding the ownership of shares follow the same general principles as for other choses in action. Unlike bills of exchange, cheques and the like, registered shares are not negotiable instruments. As with other forms of property, a person's title to shares may be complete legal ownership of them, or joint ownership, or ownership in common[124] or beneficial ownership, for instance, the *cestui* of a trust.[125] Several important matters regarding title to shares and the transfer of ownership of them are laid down in the Companies Acts; these are usually supplemented by provisions in each company's articles of association. As was explained above, a person is a member of or shareholder in a company when his name is entered in the register of members.

Share Certificates

9–59 Companies, as a general rule, issue share certificates to their members, which state how many shares the person has registered in his name and how much is paid up on them. Since 1996, however, it has been possible to use computer-based evidence of title.[126] Article 8 of Table A requires the company, within two months of registering a person as a member or receiving an instrument of transfer, to send the transferee a sealed share certificate.[127] These certificates are not documents of title to the shares in question; they are only prima facie evidence of their contents.[128] However, a company is estopped from denying the correctness of statements made in its share certificates to any persons who have altered their position in reliance on a certificate. As Lord Herchell L.C. explained in *Balkis Consolidated Co. v. Tomkinson*,

> "an estoppel might arise where a certificate was issued stating that the person named on it was the registered holder of certain shares in the company. . . . [T]he giving of the certificate amount[s] to a statement by the company, intended by them to be acted upon by the purchasers of shares in the market, that the persons certified as the holders were enti-

---

123 See generally, A.P. Bell, *Modern Law of Personal Property* (1989).
124 *e.g. O'Connell v. Harrison* [1927] I.R. 330.
125 *e.g. Rearden v. Provincial Bank of Ireland* [1896] 1 I.R. 532.
126 Companies Act, 1990 (Uncertified Securities) Regulations 1996, (S.I. No. 68 of 1996).
127 See also 1963 Act, s.86 and 1977 Act, s.5(2).
128 1963 Act, s.87 and 1977 Act, s.5.

> tled to the shares; and that the purchasers having acted on that statement by the company, they were estopped from denying its truth and liable to pay as damages the value of the shares. . . . [I]f the company have been deceived and the statement is not true, they may have been guilty of negligence, but they and no one else had power to inquire into the matter."[129]

There, without their owner's authority, the company was deceived into registering a transfer of his shares and issued a new share certificate to the purported transferee. When the full facts came to light, by virtue of the *nemo dat quod non habet* principle, that "transferee" never acquired title to those shares. It was held that nevertheless he was entitled to be compensated by the company for the loss he thereby suffered, on the basis of estoppel.[130] This principle can also apply to statements on share certificates about how much has been paid up on the shares in question.[131] Of course, circumstances can arise where this estoppel will not operate.

9–60 In *Ruben v. Great Fingall Consolidated*[132] it was held that a company is never estopped by a forged certificate, *i.e.* one issued without the company's authority. However, in the light of subsequent developments in the law of agency, the fact that an instrument issued in a company's name is a forgery does not always deprive it of legal effect.[133]

Certification of Transfers

9–61 Certifying transfers is the practice that arises where, say, A sells 100 shares, which are the subject of the one share certificate, and B buys, say, 60 of them and C buys the remainder. Because A's share certificate cannot be given to both buyers, the practice is for it to be sent to the company, which then certifies that it has been received; the buyers then pay against delivery of the certified transfers. A certification given by a duly authorised officer of the company estops it from denying the truth of the essential facts stated on it. The 1963 Act provides, however, that certification is a representation to anyone acting on the faith of it that the transferor has a prima facie title to the shares in question but it is not a representation that he has any title to them.[134]

---

[129] [1893] A.C. 396 at 403–404, referring to decision in *Re Bahia etc. Railway Co.* (1868) 3 Q.B. 584.
[130] See also *Dixon v. Kennaway & Co.* [1900] 1 Ch. 833.
[131] *Bloomenthal v. Ford* [1897] A.C. 156.
[132] [1906] A.C. 439.
[133] See below, para. 13–42.
[134] 1963 Act, s.85.

Share Warrants

9–62 Very exceptionally, in place of share certificates, fully paid up shareholders in p.l.c.s may be issued with share warrants to bearer.[135] Shares represented by such warrants may be transferred by delivery and provision is usually made for detaching coupons from the warrants in order to claim future dividends. However, Central Bank permission is required before an Irish company can issue share warrants.[136] There is no provision for warrants in Table A.

Transfer and Transmission of Shares

9–63 The ownership of shares changes hands by them either being transferred under a proper instrument of transfer or by vesting in another person by operation of law, the name of the new owner being entered in the register of members.[137] Shareholders have a statutory right to transfer their shares subject to any restrictions in the company's regulations,[138] such as those set out in article 24 of Table A and in article 3 of Part 11 of those model articles. Apart from those restrictions, tranferees under a valid instrument of transfer are entitled to be registered as members.[139] Specific performance can be ordered of an agreement to transfer shares.

9–64 By transmission of shares is meant the title changing hands by operation of law, as by vesting in the deceased member's personal representative or, if a bankrupt member, in the Official Assignee or the trustee in bankruptcy. A personal representative or the Assignee may be registered as a member, without an instrument of transfer being executed, but the company will satisfy itself of their right to be entered on the register. However, a power in the company's articles to veto share transfers or giving pre-emption rights may prevent their names being registered as members.[140]

9–65 A company may register a transfer of its shares only on it receiving a proper instrument of transfer.[141] The standard form for transferring fully paid up transferable shares in most limited companies is set out in the First Schedule to the Stock Transfer Act, 1963, as amended

---

[135] 1963 Act, s.88.
[136] Exchange Control Act 1954, s.10.
[137] *Re Baku Consolidated Oilfields Ltd.* [1994] 1 B.C.L.C. 173.
[138] 1963 Act, s.79.
[139] *Tangney v. Clarence Hotels Co.* [1933] I.R. 51.
[140] *Re Hafner* [1943] I.R. 426.
[141] 1963 Act, ss. 81, 82.

in 1996.[142] This stock transfer form must be executed only by the transferor and need not be attested. It must show particulars of the consideration, the description and number or amount of the shares, the transferor's full name, and the transferee's name and address. However, the company may accept transfers in another form if that form was common or usual before 1963 and it is a form that the company has authorised, provided that it is executed by the transferor and contains the above-mentioned information.

9–66 In order to facilitate the transfer of shares in publicly-quoted companies a broker's transfer form for stock exchange transactions that involve transfers to a number of transferees is set out in the Stock Transfer Act's second schedule. Transactions on the London Stock Exchange are now generally carried out by computer, what is known as the CREST system. It was to accommodate this and equivalent systems that regulations were passed in 1996 making it possible to transfer title to shares by way of computer operations, without any need for the usual written instrument.[143]

9–67 Where a person contracts to sell shares to another, in the absence of any stipulation to the contrary, the transferor impliedly undertakes to do nothing to prevent or delay registration of the transferee. But there is no implied term that the transferee will be registered. Thus, in *Casey v. Bentley*,[144] the plaintiff executed a transfer of shares to the defendant as member. It was held that, since purchasers who are refused registration in those circumstances cannot rescind their contracts,[145] neither could the vendor there rescind. Once the contract to transfer is entered into, the transferor holds the shares as trustee for the transferee.[146] Until the purchase price is fully paid, the vendor remaining on the registrar remains free to vote in respect of the shares without reference to the purchaser's wishes.[147]

9–68 In the *Egan (Wholesale) Ltd.* cases[148] the company's articles of association gave existing members a pre-emptive right to buy shares which any other member sought to sell. The co-defendant, who was

---

[142] Stock Transfer (Forms) Regulations 1996 (S.I. No. 263 of 1996).

[143] Companies Act, 1990 (Uncertified Securities) Regulations 1996 (S.I. No. 68 of 1996).

[144] [1902] 1 I.R. 376. *cf. Rackham v. Peek Foods Ltd.* [1990] B.C.L.C. 895.

[145] *London Founders' Association v. Clarke* (1888) 20 Q.B.D. 576.

[146] *Hardoon v. Belilios* [1901] A.C. 118.

[147] *Musselwhite v. Musselwhite & Sons Ltd.* [1962] Ch. 964.

[148] *Lee & Co. (Dublin) Ltd. v. Egan (Wholesale) Ltd.*, Kenny J., April 27, 1978; May 23, 1978; December 18, 1979.

the company's principal shareholder, agreed in substance to sell all the company's issued shares to the plaintiff, although he did not have the other shareholders' authority to do this. Kenny J. held that the co-defendant could be enjoined to take such steps as were possible to ensure that the shares he owned be transferred to the plaintiff. Additionally, damages should be paid where the articles' pre-emption clause prevented that transfer from taking place. It was held, furthermore, that it would be an unlawful abuse of power for the co-defendant to use his 75 per cent shareholding to amend or rescind the articles' pre-emption requirement. Damages were also awarded for breach of the agreement to transfer what were the other members' shares.

Charges on Shares

9–69 Shares are often given by their owners as security for obligations they have assumed.[149] A legal mortgage of shares involves the mortgagee's name being entered as a member of the company in respect of those shares. The mortgagor's right to redeem would then be contained in a separate document. On default, the mortgagee has an implied power to sell the shares. A disadvantage for the creditor with a legal mortgage is that he can be made liable for any unpaid calls on the shares he holds.

9–70 For this reason, assignments of shares as security usually take the form of an equitable charge, such as an express agreement to mortgage the shares, a deposit of the shares, a purported transfer which is not in a registrable form or a registrable transfer which was never registered. By far the commonest form of security with shares is the deposit of the share certificate with the creditor. In the past, those transactions were regarded as pledges, not mortgages.[150] This attitude led to debtors depositing a written memorandum declaring that the deposit was by way of a mortgage. Eventually in 1901 it was decided that where a share certificate is deposited as security, but without any transfer form or memorandum, an equitable mortgage is created and the creditor then holding the share certificate is entitled, on default, to foreclose.[151] Later, in similar circumstances, it was held that the depositee of the shares had an implied power of sale; that the deposit is "a transaction of mortgage and not . . . of pledge" and, where no express power to sell was given, the law "implies a right in the mort-

---

[149] See generally, M. Forde, *Commercial Law* (2nd ed., 1997), pp. 245–247.
[150] *cf. Re Butler* [1900] 2 I.R. 153.
[151] *Harrold v. Plenty* [1901] 2 Ch. 314.

gagee to sell after giving reasonable notice."[152] Of course, if the depositee does not have a signed transfer form, he will not be able to exercise that right without a court order, for the company will not recognise his beneficial ownership of the shares. Against that, if the depositee is given such a form there is always the danger that, dishonestly and in breach of his contract, he will dispose of the shares entirely.[153] There are several leading cases which deal with the question of who is the "reputed owner" of shares which have been charged in this manner, for the purpose of bankruptcy law,[154] but the reputed ownership rule was repealed in 1988.[155]

Shares Held in Trust

9–71 When someone other than the true or beneficial owner of shares is registered as the shareholder, he holds those shares as trustee for their owner; for instance, for someone who has agreed to buy and has paid for the shares,[156] or who has not yet paid for them,[157] a transferor of the shares who has not yet been paid for them,[158] a person in whose favour the shares have been charged, a mortgagor of shares who has an equity of redemption, as well as the *cestui* of a trust. The reciprocal rights and duties of the registered owner and the beneficial owner are governed by the law of trusts.[159] A registered owner must comply with the terms of whatever arrangement under which he holds the shares for another and must not exercise his membership rights, such as to vote, for his own personal gain to the detriment of the beneficial owner.

9–72 Normally, the company itself will not be party to any trust arrangement affecting its shares. And Company Law attempts to insulate the company from those arrangements so that, insofar as the company is concerned, the registered owner and nobody else has all the rights attaching to the shares. According to section 123 of the 1963 Act, no notice of any trust may be entered in the register of members or be receivable by the company; so that a beneficiary who is not registered as the holder of shares has no direct connection with, or rights in, the company. Article 7 of Table A goes further by providing that, ex-

---

152 *Stubbs v. Slater* [1910] 1 Ch. 632 at 639.
153 *cf. Waterhouse v. Bank of Ireland* (1891) 29 L.R. Ir. 3 84.
154 *Re McClement* [1960] I.R. 141; *Re Morrissey* [1961] I.R. 442.
155 Bankruptcy Act 1988.
156 *e.g. Lyle & Scott v. Scott's Trustee* [1959] A.C. 763.
157 *e.g. Musselwhite v. C.H. Musselwhite & Son Ltd.* [1962] Ch. 964.
158 *cf. Langen & Wind Ltd. v. Bell* [1972] 2 W.L.R. 170.
159 *e.g. International Credit & Investment Co. v. Adham* [1994] 1 B.C.L.C. 66. See generally, R. Keane, *Equity and the Law of Trusts in the Republic of Ireland* (1988), Pt II and H. Delaney, *Equity and the Law of Trust in Ireland* (1996), Chaps 3–12.

cept where required by law, no person shall be recognised by the company as holding any share on trust and that the company shall not be bound by any equitable or analogous interest in its shares. The purpose behind these provisions was explained as to

> "spare the company of the responsibility of attending to any trusts or equities whatever attached to their shares, so that they might safely and securely deal with the person who is registered owner, and with him alone, recognising no other person and no different right; freeing them . . . from all embarrassing enquiries into conflicting claims as to shares, transfers, calls, dividends, right to vote, and the like; and enabling them to treat the registered shareholder as owner of the shares for all purposes, without regard to contract as between himself and third persons."[160]

9–73 However, some potentially drastic implications of those two provisions were rejected in *Rearden v. Provincial Bank,*[161] where it was held that, if a company's duly authorised agent actually knows of some equitable interest held in its shares, then it is not always exonerated by section 123 or article 7 from liability it otherwise might incur for ignoring facts of which it was aware. There, the trustee of shares in a bank was registered as their owner and the bank knew full well that he held those shares in trust. When he failed to pay his own debts to the bank, it claimed a lien over those shares, contending that the articles' lien clause entitled it to override the *cestui's* interest in shares. This view was rejected on the grounds that "[t] he mere fact of notice does not convert the company into trustees for the persons of whose beneficial interest they have notice; but if, having that notice, they advance money to the trustee on the security of the trust property, their conduct is not protected by [section 123] and they participate in a breach of trust."[162] As for the common form article, it "applies to the company qua company, in respect of matters arising between the company and its members, as such; [but] it has no application to the acts of the company in its trading character, such as lending money upon security, [and] as a lender of money, upon the security of its own shares, the company is bound by the same equities as if it were advancing money upon the security of the shares of any other company."[163]

9–74 Additionally, a beneficial owner can obtain orders against the trustee and indeed the company in order to protect his interest in the

---

160 *Rearden v. Provincial Bank of Ireland* [1896] 1 I.R. at 567.
161 [1896] 1 I.R. 532.
162 *ibid.* at 578, following *Bradford Banking Co. v. Briggs* (1886) 12 App. Cas. 29.
163 *ibid.* at 583.

shares where that interest may be prejudiced. The effect of article 7 is not that the company shall never be affected by a trust or that no trust shall be created on any share, but that the company is not to be affected by any notice of a trust. Thus, in *McGrattan v. McGrattan*,[164] in breach of trust the registered owner of shares voted for a members' resolution that seriously prejudiced their beneficial owner. It was the votes attaching to those shares which were decisive in carrying the resolution. Kelly L.J. held that the resolution was thereby invalid.

9–75 Where there is an agreement to sell shares but the vendor has not yet been paid, he remains free to exercise his voting rights in the company whatever way he wishes and regardless of the intending purchaser's wishes, except perhaps where voting a particular way would damage the very subject matter of the purcase.[165] Even then, while the intending vendor may be restrained by an injunction or have damages awarded against him, it would seem that the court will not direct him to vote in accordance with the purchaser's desires.[166]

The Company's Lien on its Shares

9–76 A lien is a security interest; it is a right that a person in possession of something of value has over the thing, in respect of obligations owed by its owner, and he is entitled to retain possession of that thing until the owner's obligation has been discharged. A company has no inherent lien over or right to forfeit its own shares.[167] However, most articles of association grant companies these rights in particular circumstances. Private companies, by their regulations, may give themselves a lien over their own shares, whether partly paid or fully paid, in respect of any sums owed to them by their shareholders.[168] In *Allen v. Gold Reefs of West Africa Ltd.*[169] which is the leading authority on altering the articles of association, and where the broad equitable criterion of "good faith" was articulated, it was held that a company may alter its articles to acquire for itself a lien over its own shares, even if they are fully paid, together with the right to forfeit them. By virtue of section 44 of the 1983 Act, however, any lien or charge held by a p.l.c. over its own shares is void except for a charge on partly paid shares for

---

164 [1985] N.I. 28.

165 *Musselwhite v. C.H. Musselwhite & Son Ltd.* [1962] Ch. 954 and *JRRT (Investments) Ltd. v. Hoycraft* [1993] B.C.L.C. 401.

166 *Michaels v. Horley House (Marlybone) Ltd.* [1997] 2 B.C.L.C. 166 at 178–170; affirmed on other grounds [1999] 1 B.C.L.C. 670.

167 *Re Kingston Yacht Club* (1888) 21 L.R. Ir. 199.

168 *Re Balgooley Distillery Co.* (1886) 17 L.R. 239. *cf. Champagne Perrier-Jouet v. Finch & Co.* [1982] 1 W.L.R. 1359.

169 [1900] 1 Ch. 656.

amounts payable on them, or a charge that existed when the company re-registered as a p.l.c., or a charge by a money-lending company arising out of its ordinary business transactions.

9–77 Article 11 of Table A gives the company a "first and paramount" lien on every share that is not fully paid in respect of sums due on those shares and in respect of all other debts owed to the company by any shareholder or his estate. This lien extends to dividends payable on the shares in question but does not extend to fully paid shares. The directors may exempt any shareholder from a lien. The Table A scheme gives the directors a power of sale under this lien, which may be exercised provided that the shareholder in default is given at least 14 days notice of the fact. A matter of frequent dispute is the priority between the company's lien and other persons' claims to the shares, for instance a chargee who has notified the company that he has a security interest in those shares.

Forfeiture of Shares

9–78 Forfeiture means exercising a right to deprive a person of ownership of something; the person entitled to forfeit becomes its owner instead. It is often provided in leases, for instance, that the tenancy shall be forfeited on the occurrence of certain events. Article 35 of Table A authorises the directors to forfeit shares for non-payment of calls. Before they can do this, the directors must notify the shareholder in question,[170] requiring payment of the amount due and stating that, if it is not paid, the shares are liable to be forfeited. Because of its drastic implications, the courts construe the power to forfeit strictly.[171]

9–79 Not alone must every prescribed detail be followed scrupulously but *mala fides* or abusive exercise by the directors of their fiduciary power will cause the forfeiture to be struck down. Provided, however, that the power was properly exercised, a court will not award relief against forfeiture. Once the power to forfeit is exercised, the shareholder ceases to be a member of the company and, therefore, prima facie any liability by him to the company on the shares is extinguished. Under article 37 of Table A, however, the ex-member remains liable for all unpaid amounts on the shares due to the company at the date the forfeiture took place; this liability ceases when those sums are paid up either by him or by whoever the shares were re-issued to. A right of forfeiture that was exercised in fact to relieve a shareholder of liability

---

[170] *cf. Parkstone Ltd. v. Gulf Guarantee Bank* [1990] B.C.L.C. 850.
[171] *Ward v. Dublin North City Milling Co.* [1919] 1 I.R. 5.

to the company is ineffective.[172] Article 38 of Table A provides for executing a statutory declaration about forfeiture that enables the company to give whoever the shares are re-issued to a good title that cannot be impeached because the forfeiture was irregular.

ASCERTAINING BENEFICIAL INTERESTS IN SHARES

9–80 Frequently the registered owner of shares is not their full beneficial owner. For a variety of reasons, the real owner of shares will choose to have them registered in some other person's name — be it a member of his family, some other company which he controls or a nominee company which is actually in the business of holding shares on behalf of others. Many of the major banks have nominee companies for this very purpose. The reason for the real owner keeping his name off the share register may be simply to hide from the company the extent of his interest in it or to hide from others — be they his family, or the Revenue or regulatory authorities — what his assets are. However, the public authorities or the company or its other members have a distinct interest in ascertaining who the true beneficial owner of shares is, for instance, to monitor insider trading, fraud, tax evasion or building up by stealth a controlling interest in the company. In several parts of the tax legislation transactions involving companies are deemed to be transactions with their beneficial shareholders, for instance, dispositions by or to private companies for the purpose of capital acquisition tax.[173]

9–81 Before 1990 the legislature hardly addressed the question of the anonymity of share-holdings — apart from restricting the use of bearer shares, which are common in many Continental European countries and are the reason why companies there are referred to as *societes anonymes*. However, there is Article 7 of the Table A, dealing with notice of shares being held in trust, which adds that "this shall not preclude the company from requiring the members or a transferee of shares to furnish the company with information as to the beneficial ownership of any share where such information is reasonably required by the company". There does not appear to be any case law on this clause. The question of beneficial ownership is now dealt with in several ways in Part IV of the 1990 Act (sections 53-106), which is headed "Disclo-

[172] *Re London & County Assur. Co. ex p. Jones* (1858) 27 L.J. Ch. 666.
[173] Capital Acquisitions Tax Act 1976, s.34.

sure of Interest in Shares". Several of these provisions also apply to debentures.

Share Dealings by Directors, Secretaries and their Families

9–82 Shareholders have a particular interest in knowing the extent, if any, of the directors' holdings of shares in the company and of any dealings in those shares. Section 53 of the 1990 Act requires every director and secretary of a company to notify the company promptly on every occasion where he acquired or disposed of an "interest" in the company's shares. A similar notice must be given when the interest is acquired or disposed of by the director's or secretary's spouse or minor child; for this purpose, these family interests are deemed to be interests of the director or secretary.[174] The company must also be notified where those persons have an interest in debentures of the company. Shadow directors are also bound by this duty.[175] Generally, notice must be given to the company within five days of the transaction in question occurring or of the matter first coming to the director's notice.[176]

9–83 What constitutes an "Interest" in securities for these purposes is defined in sections 54 and 55 of the 1990 Act:

i. Being a beneficiary of a trust where the company's securities form any of the trust assets. However, excluded are any discretionary interest, an interest in reversion or remainder or an interest as a bare trustee. Excluded also is a life interest under an irrevocable settlement provided the settlor has no interest at all in the income or property of the settlement.
ii. Entering into a contract to purchase the securities.
iii. Being entitled to exercise or to control the exercise of any right arising from holding the securities, for instance, to vote in general meetings or to receive distributions. But this does not include acting as a proxy at any meeting or as some company's representative at a meeting.
iv. Being entitled to call for the delivery of securities or to acquire an interest in them; also being obliged to take an interest in them.
v. Having an indirect interest through a substantial stake in a company which is interested in the securities. That stake arises where the director controls more than one-third of the votes in that company or its directors are accustomed to act in accordance with his instructions. The same applies where the securities are held by another company still in which a company controlled by the director has a substantial stake as described here.

---

174 s.64.
175 s.53(9).
176 s.56.

Where persons have a joint interest, each of them is deemed to have that interest in the securities. In determining if an interest in securities exists, any restriction or restraint on the right to exercise that interest must be disregarded.[177] As well as the excluded trust and settlement interests, the Act also excludes an interest held by a stockbroker as security for transactions on a recognised stock exchange, an interest in a scheme made under the Charities Act, 1961, and the holding of units in several kinds of unit trust.

9–84 When giving the company notice of acquiring or disposing of an interest in securities, information must also be given about the price or other consideration at which that interest changed hands.[178] Where an agent has been authorised to acquire or dispose of any interest in securities, the principal must ensure that he is notified immediately by his agent of any acquisition or disposal made. Provision is made for the company keeping a register of interests which are notified in this manner.[179] Where the securities in question are dealt on a recognised stock exchange, any notification the company gets under this Part must be forwarded by the company to the exchange authorities.[180]

Order for Disclosure of Interests in Shares of Private Companies

9–85 The "disclosure order" provisions of sections 97–104 of the 1990 Act apply to several types of incorporated bodies but not p.l.c.s — principally, to private companies. These enable any person with a "financial interest" in the company to apply to the court for an order compelling the disclosure of information about share holdings in the company. Those eligible to apply for such orders are any member, contributory, creditor, employee, co-adventurer, examiner, lessor, lessee, licensor, licensee, liquidator or receiver of the company or of a "related company".[181] Notice of an intention to apply for a disclosure order must be given to the company and to the person to whom it is intended to direct the order. The application must be supported by such evidence as the court may require and the court may require the applicant to provide security for costs. In order to obtain an order under this Part, the applicant must demonstrate that his "financial interest" will be prejudiced by non-disclosure of the information being sought and, additionally, that it is "just and equitable" to make the order.[182]

---

177 s.54(2).
178 s.57.
179 ss. 60–62.
180 s.65.
181 s.98(2), (6).
182 s.98(5).

9–86 A disclosure order may be directed at a person whom the court believes to have had an "interest" in the shares or debentures during a specified period.[183] An order may also be directed at any person whom the court believes to possess information or to be able to acquire information about persons interested in a company's securities. What is an interest in shares for these purposes is the same as for notifying directors' dealings in securities,[184] except that it does not extend to an indirect interest via a substantial stake in another company and section 78(1)(d)–(g) excludes certain interests, most notably an interest held by way of security only for a transaction entered into in the ordinary course of business. What can be ordered to be disclosed includes one's present or past interest in the company's voting shares, any other interest held in the company's securities during the time of having an interest in its voting shares and, where an interest has ceased, particulars about the person who immediately thereafter acquired that interest.[185] The court is given a wide discretion to limit the scope of any disclosure order, to rescind or vary it and to grant persons relief from its application.[186] The registrar of companies, the company and others affected by a disclosure order must be duly notified of its having been made.[187] Unless the court otherwise directs, information provided to it in consequence of a disclosure order will be passed on to the applicant.[188]

9–87 Non-compliance with a disclosure order results in the shares and debentures, which are the subject of the inquiry, being virtually taken off the person in breach.[189] He cannot enforce by action or legal proceedings, whether directly or indirectly, any right or interest of any kind whatsoever in respect of those shares. For instance, if he had contracted to buy or to sell them, he cannot enforce performance of that contract.

Investigation into Interests in Shares of p.l.c.s

9–88 Sections 81–85 of the 1990 Act enable a p.l.c. to ascertain who has an interest in its own shares without the necessity of obtaining a court order. Furthermore, at least ten per cent of those who hold voting shares in a p.l.c. can require it to investigate the beneficial owner-

---

[183] s.98(1).
[184] above, para. 9.83.
[185] s.100.
[186] s.101
[187] s.102.
[188] s.103.
[189] s.104.

ship of its shares, as provided for here.[190] This is done by the company notifying any person whom it has reasonable cause to believe to have held an interest in its voting shares at any time during the preceding three years.[191] That person is required to confirm whether or not he had an interest in those shares and to give further particulars if required to so do. What constitutes an "interest" for these purposes is the same as for private company disclosure orders[192] but also includes an interest held by the person's spouse or minor child and an interest held directly or indirectly through having a substantial stake in another company or companies.

9–89 If the person does not give the required information, an application can be made to the court to virtually freeze the shares, as provided for in section 16 of the 1990 Act.[193] For so long as the shares are restricted under this section, they cannot be transferred, they cannot be voted, no dividend or other distribution can be made in respect of them nor can any "rights" issue be made in respect of them.[194] However, a person aggrieved may apply to the court to lift the "freeze" in an appropriate case.[195] Information about interests in its shares which a company acquires under this procedure must be recorded separately in the register kept for this purpose.[196]

Acquiring Interest in More than 5 per cent of the Shares in a p.l.c.

9–90 Where any person acquires an interest in more than 5 per cent of the voting shares in a p.l.c., sections 67–72 of the 1990 Act require them to notify the company of that fact within ten days of making the acquisition. The percentage figure here can be altered by the Minister. An "interest" in shares for these purposes is the same as for investigations by p.l.c.s as described above.[197]

9–91 Sections 73–76 of the 1990 Act deal with what are often described as "concert parties", where people have agreed to act in concert when acquiring shares in a company — usually to avoid detection before eventually launching a take-over bid. These provisions can apply even if their agreement was not strictly legally binding. Each party is re-

---

[190] s.83.
[191] s.81.
[192] above, para. 9.86.
[193] s.85.
[194] *cf. Re Lonrho plc. (No. 2)* [1990] 1 Ch. 695.
[195] *cf. Re Geers Gross plc.* [1987] 1 W.L.R. 1649.
[196] s.82.
[197] above, para. 9–88.

quired to notify the other of every interest he has in the company's shares, apart from those subject to the agreement. Each party is deemed to be interested in all of the shares which are subject to the agreement as well as any other shares he may be interested in.

Large Interests in Quoted Shares

9–92 Where a person acquires specified interests in shares which are quoted on the Dublin Stock Exchange, section 91 of the 1990 Act requires him to notify the Exchange authorities of that fact.[198] The relevant interests for this purpose are 10 per cent, 25 per cent, 50 per cent and 75 per cent. Those authorities must also be notified where the person disposed of an interest in shares, bringing his beneficial stake below any of those percentage figures.

[198] *cf.* E.C. Directive [1988] O.J. L348/62.

10

Minority Shareholder Protection

10–01 Often differences will arise between shareholders about their company's affairs. One of the fundamental principles of company law is majority rule: that it is for the majority of members with voting rights to decide most matters concerning the company and that certain fundamental matters should be resolved by super-majorities (usually either a special resolution or decision of three-quarters in value of the shareholders). Consequently, the dissatisfied shareholder or shareholders who cannot persuade the majority to come around to their point of view will often have to choose between having their preferences ignored or selling out their shares. In companies whose shares are quoted on the Stock Exchange, the threat by disgruntled members to dispose of a large block of shares may persuade the majority to make their peace with the minority. In private companies, on the other hand, restrictions in the articles of association on the transferability of shares may render a minority stake virtually unsaleable.

10–02 Judges have always been somewhat hesitant about adjudicating on inter-shareholder disputes.[1] Many of the matters that give rise to conflict between shareholders concern essentially business judgments, like hiring and firing employees, expanding or contracting particular lines of activity, paying dividends or placing profits in reserve. If such matters were readily reviewable by the courts, then the spectre of judges "taking on the management of every playhouse and brewhouse" in the country[2] would be realised. Lawyers do not possess any special competence in business matters and legal procedures are far too expensive and cumbersome processes for resolving differences of policy between shareholders. There nevertheless are several grounds on which the courts will intervene on the minority shareholder's behalf and, since the enactment of section 205 of the 1963 Act on

---

1 See generally, Wedderburn, "Shareholders' Rights and the Rule in *Foss v. Harbottle*" (1957) 17 Cam. L. J. 194 and 18 (1958) Cam. L. J. 93.

2 *Carlen v. Drury* (1812) 1 V. & B. 154 at 158.

"oppression", the basis for judicial intervention and the remedies available have been radically expanded.

10–03 The law here (apart from section 205) is often analysed and explained with reference to a case decided some 160 years ago with a Dickensian-sounding name, *Foss v. Harbottle*,[3] and the so-called exceptions to it. This case tends to be cited for the preposition that, if some wrong has allegedly been committed in the course of a company's affairs, it is the company in its corporate capacity which should seek redress and not any of its shareholders. The acknowledged "exceptions", where a shareholder is permitted to bring proceedings, are usually classified under four heads:

(1) where the act complained of is illegal or *ultra vires*;

(2) where the requirement of a "special majority" or procedure has been ignored;

(3) where the plaintiff's own "personal and individual" rights have been invaded

(4) where those who control the company committed a "fraud on the minority".[4]

To those grounds must now be added "oppression" under section 205 of the 1963 Act and the petition under section 213(f) to have the company wound up on "just and equitable" grounds.

ANTI-INTERVENTIONISM

10–04 The hands-off stance taken by courts in the past to many inter-shareholder disputes is founded on three broad doctrines, each of which is a manifestation of an underlying majority rule principle.

Injury to the Corporation

10–05 Judicial abstentionism is most commonly associated with the leading case of *Foss v. Harbottle*[5] and the injury to the corporation principle derived from it. By this is meant that where, as a consequence of some unlawful act, the company suffers a loss, it is for the company itself and not individual shareholders to sue the wrongdoer because in law the company is a separate legal person. In *Foss* a group of share-

---

[3] (1843) 2 Hare 461.
[4] *Edwards v. Halliwell* [1950] 2 All E.R. 1064 at 1067 (summarised).
[5] (1843) 2 Hare 461.

holders sued promoters and directors alleging fraud: that the defendants had arranged to sell their own properties to the company at exorbitant prices. It was held that the immediate victim of the alleged wrong was the corporation and" [I]t [is] not . . . a matter of course for any individual members of a corporation . . . to assume to themselves the right of suing in the name of the corporation."[6] What the plaintiff ought to have done was call an extraordinary general meeting at which the majority could have voted to avoid those voidable contracts or take other appropriate action.

Mere Irregularity

10–06 Next there is what may be termed the mere irregularity principle: that if the company or those acting for it do something which, though unlawful, could be "cured" and rendered lawful by the shareholders ratifying it in general meeting, then the illegal act is a mere irregularity out of which aggrieved individual shareholders do not have a right of action. The most far-reaching example is *MacDougall v. Gardiner*,[7] where the plaintiff, who suspected that the defendant directors were implicated with the promoters in fraudulent transactions involving the company's property, convened an extraordinary general meeting to consider the matter, and obtained proxies representing almost half of the company's voting capital. But the directors and their supporters, including the chairman, prevented a poll from taking place.[8] A claim against the directors brought in the name of the plaintiff, the company and all the shareholders other than the directors, was rejected on the grounds that what was alleged was a mere irregularity which was within the power of the majority shareholders to ratify; therefore, any legal claim against those responsible for the alleged fraud ought to be brought by the company rather than by individual shareholders. Mellish L.J., whose judgment is generally referred to, stated that, since it is common for irregularities to occur in companies, if there were no principle deterring resultant shareholder suits, the courts would be flooded by actions brought by one or other "cantakerous member" or "member who loves litigation". Accordingly, he concluded, a shareholder has no personal right of action

> "if the thing complained of is a thing which in substance the majority of the company are entitled to do, or if something has been done irregularly which the majority of the company are entitled to do regularly, or if

---

6 *ibid.* at 490. Followed most recently in *Stein v. Blake (No. 2)* [1998] 1 B.C.L.C. 573 and *Crindle Investments v. Wymes*, Supreme Court, March 5, 1998.

7 (1875) 1 Ch.D. 13.

8 This would not be permissible today: 1963 Act, s.137.

> something has been done illegally which the majority of the company are entitled to do legally . . . If the matter is of that nature, the majority are the only persons who can complain that a thing which they are entitled to do has been done irregularly."[9]

Modern statements of the so-called rule in *Foss v. Harbottle* usually add this irregularity principle to that of injury to the corporation.

Voting Property

10–07 Thirdly, there is what may be referred to as the voting property principle: that, save in exceptional circumstances, a shareholder's vote in general meeting cannot be impeached merely because he voted for self-serving reasons. This "novel" point was decided in *North-West Transportation Co. v. Beatty*,[10] where minority shareholders sued their company and five ex-directors in an action to have set aside the sale to the company of a substantial asset by one of those directors, who was also its largest shareholder. It was contended that the common law rule, under which contracts with directors are rendered enforceable when ratified by the company in general meeting, ought not apply where the director, who makes the contract, votes his own shares and that vote is decisive in carrying the ratifying resolution. In the interests of legal certainty, the Privy Council rejected the view that the validity of resolutions might turn on the motives or circumstances of individuals voting for them. Instead, in matters such as this "a pure question of policy . . . the voice of the majority ought to prevail; [and] to reject the votes of the [majority] would be to give effect to the views of the minority, and to disregard those of the majority".[11]

10–8 Had the central themes of these cases gone unqualified, investors would have scant legal protection against fellow-shareholders taking unfair advantage of the company or running it in an irregular fashion and to their own personal advantage. Such a state of affairs would turn a system of majority rule into a tyranny of the majority. It, therefore, was necessary to find some compromise: one that discouraged unnecessary litigation of intra-corporate disputes but which nonetheless did not permit grave injustices to go unremedied. In *Moylan v. Irish Whiting Manufacturers Ltd.*,[12] Hamilton J. said that, having regard to the provisions of the Constitution, an exception must be made to the anti-intervention principle "when the justice of the case demands it."

---

[9] *ibid.* at 25. *cf. Cotter v. National Union of Seamen* [1929] 2 Ch. 58.

[10] (1887) 12 App. Cas. 589.

[11] *ibid.* at 601. See also *Burland v. Earle* [1902] A.C. 83 and an extreme example, *Northern Counties Securities Ltd. v. Jackson & Steeple Ltd.* [1974] 1 W.L.R. 1133, above, para. 3–17.

[12] Hamilton P., April 14, 1980.

Ratifying Officers' Wrongs

10–09 Many of the instances where minority shareholders seek redress involve breaches of directors' duties which, where those directors and their allies own a majority of the voting shares, are most unlikely to give rise to a claim by the company against them. If their wrong is to be remedied, that can only be done by permitting individual shareholders to bring a claim. Accordingly, especially in "close companies", for practical purposes the whole question of enforcing the directors' duties of care and fiduciary duties is inextricable from the rights of minority shareholders under the "exceptions" to *Foss v. Harbottle*. As was explained when dealing with directors' duties, a general resolution purporting to ratify a breach of directors' duty does not legally prevent the company from later claiming damages from the errant director, because any effective release of the director's liability must be supported by consideration.[13] But there are certain kinds of officers' wrongs which are capable of being ratified by a majority of the members. In those conflict of interest situations, where the mode of redress is for the company to avoid contractual obligations, a members' resolution adopting the contract may debar the company from later seeking to rescind the contract. Similarly, where some of the directors' powers are used for an improper purpose, at least as regards "insiders" the company is not bound by what the directors have done. But a members' resolution approving what the directors did may operate to bind the company. Where, however, the directors acted unlawfully, contravened the memorandum or articles of association, discriminated unfairly against the minority or defrauded the company in an equitable sense, the purported ratification of their wrong will be ineffective unless perhaps done by the entire membership of the company.[14]

ILLEGALITY

10–10 Where the company has contravened the Companies Acts, the section in question may give the aggrieved shareholder a right to civil redress. If the breach is made a criminal offence, then it depends on the nature of the legislative requirement and the surrounding circumstances whether a civil right of action also arises.[15] Many transactions

---

[13] See above, paras 5–175 *et seq*.

[14] *cf*. analysis of *Re Greendale Developments Ltd*. [1998] 1 I.R. 8, above, paras. 3–77 *et seq*. on capacity of unanimous consent to *ultra vires* acts; also Whincop, 'Of Fault and Default: Contractarianism as a Theory of Anglo-Australian Law' 21 Melbourne U.L. Rev. 187 (1997).

[15] See above, paras 1–58 *et seq*

entered into by a company which contravene these Acts are deemed to be *ultra vires* and, accordingly, unenforceable.[16]

10–11 A rare example of unlawful activities outside of the Companies Acts giving rise to questions of shareholders' actions is *Cockburn v. Newbridge Sanitary Steam Laundry Co.*[17] The company had a contract to do certain work for the armed forces for £3,000 but payment was made to the defendant director, who handed only £1,000 over to the company. When the plaintiff brought suit in his own and other shareholders' names against the director and company to recover the difference, the first and unsuccessful line of defence was the *Foss v. Harbottle*[18] injury to the corporation principle, *i.e.* since it was only the company that was wronged, the plaintiff had no cause of action. Another defence was that much of the missing £2,000 had been paid in bribes and these payments had the tacit consent of the company's shareholders. Even if this was so, the Irish Court of Appeal held that the company would still have been acting illegally (breaking the Prevention of Corruption Acts) and in those circumstances *ultra vires*:

> "The whole matter is tainted with criminality. The real agreement which it is suggested the directors did make in this case would have been an agreement, if made, so tainted with crime and so subversive of public policy as to be illegal in itself. It would, accordingly, have been quite beyond the powers of the company to have entered into it, nor could any memorandum or articles have given it power; it would be equally wrong for the company to ratify it."[19]

10–12 But not every unlawful act done by a company is *ultra vires* in the sense that any shareholder is entitled to have its continuation enjoined. As was said in the *Newbridge Laundry* case, " [I]llegality and *ultra vires* are not interchangeable terms", though it was added there that "it is difficult, if not impossible, to conceive a case in which a company can do an illegal act, the illegality arising from public policy, and act within its powers."[20]

---

16 *e.g. Exchange Banking Co., Flitcroft's Case* (1882) 21 Ch.D. 519 (dividend from capital).
17 [1915] 1 I.R. 237.
18 (1843) 2 Hare 461.
19 [1915] 1 I.R. 237 at 255.
20 *ibid.* at 254. *cf. Gall v. Exxon Corp.*, 418 F. Supp. 508 (S.D.N.Y. 1976) and *Auerbach v. Bennett*, 47 N.Y. 2d 619, 393 N.E. 2d 994 (1979).

BREACH OF THE MEMORANDUM OR ARTICLES OF ASSOCIATION

10–13 Section 25 of the 1963 Act provides that:

> "The memorandum and articles [of association] shall, when registered, bind the company and the members thereof to the same extent as if they respectively had been signed and sealed by each member, and contained covenants by each member to observe all the provisions of the memorandum and of the articles."

Many shareholder-company and inter-shareholder claims, therefore, are for breach of what is referred to as the section 25 contract, *i.e.* the contract contained in the memorandum and articles of association.[21] As the cases on pre-emption clauses illustrate,[22] individual members can sue other members for breach of any obligation the members assumed to each other in this contract. The company can enforce some provisions of this contract against individual members.[23] And subject to some exceptions, any member can require the company to abide by the terms of this contract.

Ultra vires

10–14 Section 8(2) of the 1963 Act provides that any member or debenture-holder may bring an action to enjoin a company from "doing any act or thing which [it] has no power to do"; in other words, to prevent it from acting *ultra vires*. The core meaning of *ultra vires* is acting contrary to or beyond the company's objects or capacity. Violations of at least some duties imposed by the Companies Acts have also been characterised as *ultra vires*, such as a company purchasing its own shares[24] or making other unauthorised distributions from capital.[25] Even some breaches of the general law can be *ultra vires*, as the *Newbridge Laundry* case[26] illustrates. At times, however, the term *ultra vires* is used to signify excessive generosity, especially commercially sterile payments to persons who have no legal status in the company's power structure, for instance, lavish *ex gratia* redundancy payments made by a company immediately before it is to be wound up.[27] On other occa-

---

[21] See generally, Goldberg, "The Enforcement of Outsider Rights Under s.20(1) of the Companies Act, 1948" (1972) 35 Mod. L. Rev. 362; Gregory, "The Section 20 Contract" (1981) 44 Mod. L. Rev. 526 and Drury "The Relative Nature of a Shareholder's Right to Enforce the Company Contract" (1986) 45 Cam. L.J. 219.
[22] *e.g. Rayfield v. Hands* [1960] 1 Ch. 1.
[23] *e.g. Peninsular Co. v. Fleming* (1872) 27 L.T. 93.
[24] See above, paras 7.40 *et seq.*
[25] See above, paras 7.25 *et seq.*
[26] [1915] 1 I.R. 255.
[27] *e.g. Parke v. Daily News Ltd.* [1962] Ch. 927; see above, para. 3–74.

sions those who benefit from the company's largesse may be directors who *de facto* or *de jure* control the general meeting and thereby are in a position to ensure that any breach of their fiduciary duties is ratified. In such instances, it has been held, a shareholder cannot sue for breach of the "section 25 contract" as such but, in appropriate circumstances, may bring a derivative suit on the company's behalf and against its controllers charging them with equitable fraud.[28]

10–15 In what circumstances will the courts deny a member injunctive redress against *ultra vires* conduct has not been considered by the courts. That the remedy is no longer based solely on the ordinary equitable jurisdiction, but is conferred without qualification by section 8(2) of the Act, suggests that it is only in the most exceptional of circumstances that redress might be denied. Where a shareholder sued seeking to have an *ultra vires* transaction set aside, he was permitted also to seek recovery of money or property which the company had wrongfully paid or transferred away.[29] However, where the plaintiff brings a so-called derivative action, seeking damages for the loss *ultra vires* activities caused the company, it would seem that the case might not be allowed to proceed where a substantial number of completely independent shareholders are against the case being heard, on account of the damage that the litigation might visit on the company.[30]

Allocation of Powers

10–16 Where the board of directors acts within its exclusive competence, as defined in the company's regulations, then the generally superior organ, the general meeting, is not entitled to issue legally binding instructions to them.[31] Whether or in what circumstances the general meeting is entitled to veto board decisions is not entirely clear, in particular board decisions made under the broad authority in Article 80 of Table A to "manage . . . [t]he business of the company" and that concern strategic matters that will have a major impact on the company's development. Where decision-making power over certain matters is allocated by the company's regulations to a named shareholder or narrow group of shareholders, the member or members in question may prevent the company's other organs from acting contrary to his or their properly expressed decisions. In *Quin & Axtens Ltd. v. Salmon*,[32]

---

[28] As is explained below, paras 10.44 *et seq*.
[29] *Simpson v. Westminster Palace Hotels Co.* (1860) 10 H.L. Cas. 712.
[30] *Smith v. Croft (No.2)* [1988] 1 Ch. 114; see below, paras 10–65 *et seq*.
[31] *Automatic Self-Cleansing Filter Syndicate Co. v. Cunninghame* [1906] 2 Ch. 4; see above, para. 4.50.
[32] [1909] 1 Ch. 311, affirmed [1909] A.C. 442.

the articles of association gave each of two named managing directors, who as well were the company's principal shareholders, what in effect was a veto over major property transactions envisaged by the company. Against the objections of one of them, the board and then the general meeting resolved to enter into such a transaction. It was held that the company should be enjoined from acting on that resolution because it in effect sought to alter the articles without going through the requisite procedures; "these resolutions are absolutely inconsistent with [the] article[s]; in truth this is an attempt to alter the terms of the [section 25] contract between the parties by a simple resolution instead of by a special resolution."[33] If a company's regulations purported to authorise a particular shareholder to issue instructions to the board or the general meeting, the court presumably would compel the organ in question to act in accordance with those instructions, or would at least declare invalid resolutions that are inconsistent with those instructions.

Procedures at Meetings

10–17 Where a company's regulations set down the procedures to be followed in order to pass an ordinary or a special resolution, as a general rule any shareholder can enjoin the majority from acting on a decision reached by the members that is not consistent with those procedures.[34] A shareholder may stop the holding of a general meeting called at great haste so as to prevent him from voting at it.[35] There are numerous reported instances of resolutions being held invalid because the shareholders were given misleading or inadequate information about what it was they were being asked to vote on.[36] Although in *MacDougall v. Gardiner*[37] the court refused to intervene against a breach of the regulations about calling a poll, that decision must be regarded as very exceptional and may be explained by the particular facts of the case.

10–18 There are also numerous reported instances that deal with what procedures should be followed at company board meetings, but few of these are actions brought by minority shareholders as such against the company or its directors. Often contravention of board procedures is pleaded by a shareholder as a defence to an action by the company for forfeiture of shares, or is pleaded by the company itself (usually

[33] [1909] 1 Ch. 311 at 319, affirmed [1909] A.C. 442.
[34] *e.g. Pender v. Lusbington* (1877) 6 Ch.D.70; see above, para. 4–32.
[35] *e.g. Cannon v. Trask* (1875) L.R. 20 Eq. 669.
[36] *e.g. Kaye v. Croydon Tramways Co.* [1896] 1 Ch. 358; see above, para. 4–19.
[37] (1875) 1 Ch.D. 13; see above, para. 10–06.

unsuccessfully) in order to disclaim liability on a contract supposedly made by the board. In *Browne v. La Trinidad*[38] it was held that a shareholder ordinarily has no cause of action merely because there was a breach of the procedures set down in the company's regulations for board meetings. The plaintiff shareholder and director sought to restrain the holding of a general meeting, which was to consider a resolution proposing that he be removed from the board, on the grounds that the board meeting that purported to convene the general meeting had not been properly constituted; inadequate notice of it had been given to the plaintiff. Accepting for the purposes of the argument that the board meeting had been improperly held and, strictly speaking, was incompetent to act, the court concluded that the notice of the general meeting nevertheless was legally effective: "if there was an irregularity at the board meeting it was not such an irregularity as to vitiate the action of the board, and even if there had been an irregularity in the constitution of the board, it would not have deprived the general body of shareholders of the power of acting, when the notice was issued by the directors as such, and was signed in the usual way . . . as required in the articles . . ."[39]

10–19 The difficult question, of course, is how one is to determine which board improprieties are and are not ratifiable by a simple majority of the shareholders who vote. In the *Browne* case it was emphasised that the plaintiff, who was aware of the irregularity, did not protest to his fellow directors until the very last minute and that to uphold his application in those circumstances " [w]ould be paralysing the whole course of business of these companies."[40] This suggests that the outcome depends on the circumstances of each case, especially whether the plaintiff stands to suffer irreparable harm if the court does not rule in his favour. Many of the cases in this area are applications for interlocutory injunctions, where the balance of convenience is always an important consideration, and undertakings are often extracted from the defendants to preserve the status quo.[41]

Substantive Entitlements

10–20 Many actions brought by shareholders against their companies are to recover something of tangible economic benefit, to which they claim to be entitled under the memorandum or articles of association. Thus, once a dividend is declared every member may claim his

---

[38] (1887) 37 Ch.D. l.
[39] *ibid.* at 10. See too, *Bentley Stevens v. Jones* [1974] 1 W.L.R. 638.
[40] *ibid.* at 17.
[41] *e.g. Harben v. Phillips* (1883) 23 Ch. D. 14 at 42.

proportionate share as a simple contract debt.[42] Where the regulations grant members a right of pre-emption, any member entitled to additional shares can insist on that provision being complied with.[43] The same applies to undertakings in the regulations that a transfer of shares in the stipulated circumstances will be registered[44] and, apparently, to provisions that members shall not sell their shares at more than a stipulated price.[45]

10–21 A source of considerable dispute has been what may be called the individualised substantive right, *i.e.* where a named shareholder is described in the company's regulations as being entitled to something of value from it. For instance, that Ms X shall be the company's advertising manager at a certain remuneration, or shall be paid a special dividend each year in recognition of unique services to the company, or shall be entitled to buy a fixed proportion of the company's output at a favourable price. The conventional wisdom is that these rights will not be enforced against companies. But it has never been satisfactorily explained why this should be so. In some of the authorities relied on to support the non-enforceability of individualised rights, the article relied upon by its very terms did not purport to confer the right being claimed.[46] In others, such as in *Eley v. Positive Government Security Life Assurance Co.*,[47] the plaintiff was not an original party to the contract. There, one provision in the articles of a newly-formed company was that the plaintiff should be its solicitor for life. On a case stated by the arbitrator, the court held, for reasons that are far from clear, that the plaintiff was not entitled to enforce that clause. Although the plaintiff had not been a subscriber to the memorandum and articles of association, he still acquired shares in the company not long after it was incorporated. Whether this analysis would be applied to clauses designating a member to be a director of the company on certain terms is questionable, especially where he was appointed to the office and the company then seeks to contravene the articles.

10–22 The most recent exposition of the so-called outsider rights controversy in companies' regulations is *Beattie v. Beattie*,[48] where it was held that only those provisions in a company's regulations "as apply

---

42 *Re Drogheda Steampacket Co.* [1903] 1 I.R. 512; see above, para. 9–29.
43 *Rayfield v. Hands* [1960] 1 Ch. 1.
44 *Tangney v. Clarence Hotel Co.* [1933] I.R. 51; see above, para. 9–35.
45 *Heron International Ltd. v. Grade* [19831 B.C.L.C. 244.
46 *e.g. Pritchard's Case* (1873) 8 Ch. App. 956.
47 (1876) 1 Ex. D. 88.
48 [19381 1 Ch. 708. See also *Hickman v. Romney Marsh Sheep Breeders Association* [1915] 1 Ch. 881.

to the relationship of the members in their capacity as members" are rendered enforceable by section 25 of the 1963 Act. There, one of the company's regulations provided that, whenever "any . . . dispute shall arise between any members of the company, or between the company or any member or members", it shall be referred to arbitration. The plaintiff sought to bring a derivative suit (*i.e.* sue on the company's behalf) against the company's chairman and managing director, who was also a shareholder, for breach of the fiduciary duty not to enrich himself unjustly at the company's expense. The central issue was whether, in virtue of section 25, the above regulation amounted to a contract between the parties to submit that dispute to arbitration. Accepting the members'/outsiders' rights dichotomy, it was concluded that there was no binding agreement to arbitrate this dispute because section 25 does not give contractual force to an article as between the company and its directors as such.

UNFAIR DISCRIMINATION

10–23 One of the so-called exceptions to what *Foss v. Harbottle*[49] is supposed to stand for is where there has been a "fraud on a minority". That particular concept subsumes two completely distinct situations. One, being dealt with here, is where the majority shareholders directly discriminate against the minority in a wholly unacceptable matter; the other situation, directly defrauding the company, is considered separately below.

10–24 The common law tradition has been one that regards rights, and especially property rights, in absolute terms. That is to say, if a person has a right to something, he may exercise that right regardless of whether he is being inspired by selfish, petty, spiteful or anti-social motives.[50] Because a share in a company is essentially a property right, the view used to be that a shareholder could exercise his right to vote those shares for any reason whatsoever. But the common law does not adopt an unqualifiedly absolutist stance to legal rights[51] and equity, which is relevant to much inter-shareholder litigation, is far from being absolutist.[52] Some of the most important rights that shareholders possess are based on contract, namely, the memorandum and articles of association. But it is now accepted that rights arising out of con-

---

[49] (1843) 2 Hare 461.
[50] *Bradford Corp. v. Pickles* [1895] A.C. 587.
[51] *e.g. Quinn v. Leatham* [1901] A.C. 495.
[52] *cf. Snell's Principles of Equity* (29th ed., 1990).

tracts that form the basis of a continuing and active relationship are subject to a good faith qualification.[53] Put negatively, rights arising from such contracts must not be exercised in bad faith. Other shareholder rights are founded on statute, like the right by special resolution to alter the articles of association. But discretions conferred by statute on subordinate representative bodies must not be exercised unreasonably or for an improper purpose.[54]

Benefiting the Company as a Whole

10–25 In *Allen v. Gold Reefs of West Africa*[55] where the company's regulations were amended to enable it to forfeit shares for non-payment of calls, it was held that the right by special resolution to alter the memorandum or articles of association is subject to a broad equitable criterion of good faith. Not alone must the requisite majority give its approval, but the alteration must be adopted "bona fide for the benefit of the company as a whole".[56] Accordingly, amendments made simply to give the majority a significant advantage over the minority will be set aside. However, precise criteria for ascertaining what is for the benefit of the company have not been articulated by the courts, other than that the company in this context "does not . . . mean the company as a commercial entity, distinct from the corporators: it means the corporators as a general body. That is to say, the case may be taken of an individual hypothetical member and it may be asked whether what is proposed is, in the honest opinion of those who voted in its favour, for that person's benefit."[57]

10–26 A number of criticisms may be levelled against this standard for judging special resolutions. Its application often depends on the individual judge's intuition: what the judge believes the hypothetical member would have voted for. If it were applied literally, this test would impose an unduly high standard on shareholders: that they must never canvass their own individual interests or, at least, an individual interest not shared by the other members. Furthermore, in companies that are comprised of two rival shareholders or factions, ascertaining what in the hypothetical member's view would be in the company's interest is virtually an impossible task. While in companies with diverse groups of shareholders (such as pensioners, financial institutions,

---

[53] *Secretary of State for Employment v. A.S.L.E.F. (No.2)* [1972] 2 Q.B. 456. *cf.* Goetz & Scott, "Principles of Relational Contracts" (1981) 67 Virginia L. Rev. 1089.
[54] *Listowel U.D.C. v. McDonagh* [1968] I.R. 312.
[55] [1900] 1 Ch. 656; see below, paras 11–05—11–06.
[56] *ibid.* at 671.
[57] *Greenhalgh v. Arderne Cinemas Ltd.* [1951] 1 Ch. 286 at 291

private speculators, professional managers, the firm's major suppliers or customers, competing enterprises, aliens, those who are pro-or anti-Apartheid, or the bomb, or whatever), determining what is the company's own interests becomes almost as difficult as discovering the national interest in large modern states. The entire matter becomes even more confusing if majorities must take some account of employee interests and the interests of creditors. Even if some agreement can be reached on what in fact "benefit [s] the company as a whole", ascertaining what motivated a collective decision, be it legislation or a local government regulation, or a resolution passed by shareholders in general meeting, is no easy task.

Non-Discrimination

10–27 An alternative criterion, therefore, has been suggested, that of non-discrimination.[58] It was held in *Greenhalgh v. Arderne Cinemas Ltd.*,[59] that a majority decision "would be liable to be impeached if the effect of it were to discriminate between the majority shareholders and the minority shareholders, so as to give the former an advantage of which the latter were deprived . . . "[60] In favour of this test, it is said, that it is "not necessary to require that persons . . . should, so to speak, dissociate themselves altogether from their own prospects and consider whether what is thought to be for the benefit of the company as a going concern."[61] Equality, or non-discrimination, is a fundamental principle of most modern systems of public law and, given the similarities between public law and this part of company law, non-discrimination has much to recommend it as the appropriate standard here. Indeed, it is incorporated into the E.C. Second Directive, where it is stipulated that "[f]or the purposes of the implementation of this Directive, the laws of the Member States shall ensure equal treatment to all shareholders who are in the same position."[62] Perhaps the reason why non-discrimination has not taken hold in English company law is that, until recently, English public law has eschewed equality as a basic norm.[63]

10–28 Although the criterion of non-discrimination is no panacea for resolving all inter-shareholder disputes, if taken seriously it can be a useful analytical tool and may indeed help to explain the outcomes of

---

58 See generally, B. Cheffins, *Company Law: Theory, Structure and Operation* (1997), pp. 472–495.
59 [1951] 1 Ch. 286.
60 *ibid.* at 291.
61 *ibid.*
62 Art. 42.
63 *e.g. Theodore v. Duncan* [1919] A.C. 696 and *Short v. Poole Corp.* [1926] Ch. 66.

cases that tend to confound some commentators. It does not require identical treatment for all shareholders of the same class in every conceivable circumstance; such a requirement would paralyse the flexibility needed in the governance of companies, just as much as it would frustrate sensible public administration. Where, however, a shareholders' resolution would adversely affect a minority to a significant extent, it should be evaluated carefully in order to see if indeed it is unfairly discriminatory. If the contested decision is aimed against a single member, then it is the equivalent of a Bill of Attainder and would be struck down unless there are overwhelming justifications for it. If the impugned decision does not simply degrade the economic value of a minority's shares but encroaches directly on some fundamental interest of the shareholder, such as to vote in general meeting or to veto vital decisions, or to designate certain persons as directors, it would require weighty justifications to be upheld. Where the decision does not directly take away or cut down a shareholder's right but only adversely affects it by impact, it is easier to justify than direct discrimination.

10–29 In *Greenhalgh v. Arderne Cinemas Ltd.*[64] it was held that, in the circumstances, the plaintiff had not made out a case of unlawful discrimination. This case was part of a series of litigation between persons with interests in the defendant company, a private company the regulations of which restricted the transferability of its shares in one of the usual ways: no shares could be transferred to outsiders unless they were first offered to and refused by existing members, and the directors could decline to register any share transfer. Principally, to enable a controlling director to sell his shares to an outsider, the company resolved to alter these provisions by adding that, with the sanction of an ordinary resolution in general meeting, any member could transfer his shares to any named outsider. This amendment was contested by the plaintiff, a minority shareholder. The governing principle, said the Court of Appeal, is that a shareholder has no right to expect that a company's articles will remain unaltered, provided that any alteration is passed bona fide or does not unfairly discriminate. The Court accepted that the amendment in question would work very much to the majority's advantage; if they found an outsider buyer they had it in their hands to ensure that their shares could be transferred. Whereas a minority holder would be faced with both losing in general meeting any proposal to transfer his stake and, additionally, having any purported transfer blocked by the board. Because, however, the alteration was merely a relaxation of the very stringent restrictions on transfer-

---

[64] [1951] 1 Ch. 286.

ring shares, and the directors in any event could always refuse to register a transfer, it was held that the plaintiff was not unlawfully discriminated against.[65]

10–30 Some commentators have criticised this conclusion, contending that it is difficult to conceive of a clearer case of discrimination. The late Professor Gower asked "if discrimination is the true test, why was [this] resolution upheld . . . ?"[66] The result of the resolution was that a majority would always be in a position to sell to an outsider whereas the minority would not. Is this not discrimination? But the test propounded by Lord Evershed M.R. was not the simple but impractical one of non-discrimination *per se*. Rather, it was "discrimination as falls within the scope of the principle as [was] stated", namely, that shareholders should not be treated differently in a way that "give[s] the [majority] an advantage of which the [minority] were deprived."[67] Some points can be made in support of the outcome in *Greenhalgh*. Given the scorn that courts in the past have poured on equality as a norm in company law, it was a dramatic breakthrough to suggest that Lindley M.R.'s hallowed "bona fide in the interests of the company as a whole" test is better expressed as a proscription against unfair discrimination. Secondly, it would appear that the plaintiff in *Greenhalgh* would not have incurred an immediate financial loss if the proposed resolution was passed and acted upon; it seems that the outsider was prepared to pay a fair price for all the company's shares. Finally, the discrimination against the plaintiff was at most indirect and by impact, thereby being easier to justify in the egalitarian calculus. Could it be said that the advantage taken by the majority in *Greenhalgh* was acquired unfairly at the plaintiff's expense? Granted, the minority there lost a right to acquire shares in the company before they could be transferred to an outsider. But the resolution deprived every shareholder of that right; and in the light of what was happening in that company at the time, it is fantasy to assume that the majority might have turned around and offered their shares to the plaintiff. In the jargon of U.S company law, the impugned transaction did not cause the minority to be "frozen in" to the company; they were always frozen in until the directors consented to their disposing of their shares, and the proposed resolution did not alter that fact.

---

65 *cf. Lee & Co. (Dublin) Ltd. v. Egan (Wholesale) Ltd.*, Kenny J., May 23, 1979.
66 *Principles of Company Law* (4th ed., 1979), p. 627.
67 [1951] 1 Ch. 286 at 292 and 291.

Ordinary Resolutions and Non-Discrimination

10–31 While differences of opinion exist about the relative merits of these two criteria and about their application in particular instances, it is settled law that in principle special resolutions will be set aside on the grounds that they were passed not for the company's benefit or that they discriminate unfairly against the minority.[68] But will ordinary resolutions passed in general meeting be set aside on similar grounds? Most commentators contend that they will not; that the majority rule principle applies without qualification to ordinary resolutions. The cases, however, suggest otherwise and support the proposition that, in certain exceptional circumstances, the court will intervene against ordinary resolutions that discriminate unfairly against the minority. As is explained in Chapter 15, because of the special character of closely-held companies, or "quasi-partnerships" as they are often called, a court will much more readily block discriminatory action by majorities in such companies than it would in the case of companies with numerous members and the shares of which have a ready market.

10–32 The principle considered below of "fraud on the company" (that serious breaches of directors' duties may not be ratified by those directors voting *qua* shareholders in general meeting) could be regarded as an illustration of an overriding standard of non-discrimination against minorities. Another example is *Alexander v. Automatic Telephone Co.*,[69] where the plaintiffs, minority shareholders, sued the majority and directors for having allotted shares to themselves without any calls being made on them, while the plaintiffs had to pay up nearly two-thirds of the nominal amounts of their own shares. In other words, the directors practically bootstrapped themselves into control of the company. Even though it was stipulated in the company's articles of association that the directors may differentiate between shareholders as regards the amounts and the times of calls,[70] it was held that the directors/shareholders had acted wrongfully here. Stress was placed on the fact that the company was newly-formed and the defendants were all subscribers to its memorandum of association; that they had allotted to themselves about two-thirds of the issued shares and, in not making calls on themselves, they paid nothing in respect of their own shares. Most significant of all, the minority had not been fully appraised of the fact that the defendants "had so managed matters as to place themselves in a better position as regards payment than the other share-

---

[68] *e.g.* the expulsion cases, below at paras 10–37 *et seq.*
[69] [1900] 2 Ch. 56.
[70] *e.g.* Table A art. 20.

holders. . . "[71] Judgment was given for the plaintiffs on the grounds that the defendants, "threw upon other shareholders a burden which they did not share themselves", and the relevant article of association did not "justify them in making a difference in their own favour without disclosing the fact to the [others] and obtaining their consent . . . "[72] In other words, the defendants acquired for themselves full control of a potentially profitable concern without paying hardly a penny for it. To compound this, they hid from the plaintiffs the fact that they had obtained their shares in that manner, while at the same time the plaintiffs' funds were being used to finance the entire undertaking. Furthermore, the defendants could have paid to themselves the bulk of the company's profits by way of dividends, thereby possibly financing the calls that ultimately would be made on them, because dividend rights, as a general rule, are based on the nominal value of the shares.[73]

Wrongful Rights Issues

10–33 As was explained in the chapter on directors, it is a breach of fiduciary duty for them to issue shares in the company for an improper purpose, in particular where the object is to convert an existing majority stake in the company into a minority holding[74] or to thwart the present majority from accepting a take-over bid about to be made for the company.[75] As has also been explained, exercises of the power to issue new shares is now considerably curtailed by sections 21 and 23 of the 1983 Act.[76] In none of the leading cases has a plaintiff been prevented from bringing his action against a "wrongful rights issue" on the grounds that the breach of duty is one which the majority could ratify by way of ordinary resolution. Indeed, it would be most undesirable if the matter could be rectified in that manner by the newly-created majority. In *Nash v. Lancegaye Safety Glass (Ireland) Ltd.*,[77] Dixon J. came down squarely in favour of the personal action and rejected the contention that only the company could be a plaintiff in these situations, stating that:

---

[71] [1900] 2 Ch. 56 at 64.
[72] [1900] 2 Ch. 56 at 66.
[73] *Oakbank Oil Co. v. Crum* (1882) 8 App. Cas. 65. Of course the articles of association may provide for paying dividends on the called up share capital only or otherwise, *e.g.* art. 120 of Table A.
[74] *e.g. Nash v. Lancegaye Safety Glass (Ireland) Ltd.* 92 I.L.T.R. 11 (1958); see above, para. 5–120.
[75] *e.g. Howard Smith Ltd. v. Ampol Petroleum Co.* [1974] A.C. 821; see above, para. 5–121.
[76] See above, paras 6–25 and 6–29.
[77] (1958) 92 I.L.T.R. 11.

> "*Foss v. Harbottle* . . . and the cases which have followed and applied it, were concerned with wrongs alleged to be done to the company as a whole and in respect of which it was, therefore, for the company as such to complain or not. In the present case, particular wrong has been done to individual shareholders, including the plaintiff, by lack of good faith on the part of the directors in the purported exercise of their discretionary powers."[78]

10–34 Even where the share issue is approved by a majority of the members, circumstances can arise where it would be declared invalid on the grounds that it unfairly discriminated against a shareholder. An excellent example is *Clemens v. Clemens Brothers Ltd.*,[79] concerning a small family company, or close company, with only two shareholders — the plaintiff who held 45 per cent of the voting shares and her aunt who held the remaining 55 per cent. Resolutions were passed in general meeting to issue additional shares in the company to the aunt and her associates. The effect of implementing these would have been to dilute the plaintiff's stake to just less than 25 per cent of the voting shares, and thereby deprive her of the power to block alterations to the company's regulations. Among the relevant facts were that the plaintiff was not a director whereas the aunt and her associates were on the board; for some years no dividends were paid; directors' generous emoluments exceeded the substantial profits the company made; the company did not obviously need further capital; and the aunt declined to give any evidence. Emphasising the difficulty of formulating hard-and-fast rules for such cases, Foster J. concluded his judgment by saying that "it would be unwise to try to produce a principle, since the circumstances of each case are infinitely varied", other than that majority shareholders' rights are "subject to equitable considerations which may make it unjust . . . to exercise [them] in a particular way."[80] The outcome can be explained under the non-discrimination principle in that the impugned resolutions did not merely degrade the value of the plaintiff's holding but directly deprived her of a fundamental interest, namely, her power to veto any proposed alterations to the company's regulations. This right is so fundamental that its violation by the directors cannot ordinarily be rectified by a majority of the shareholders approving what was done.[81]

Expelling Members

10–35 One form of inter-shareholder controversy that has been the

---

78 (1958) 92 I.L.T.R. 11 at 25.
79 [1976] 2 All E.R. 268.
80 *ibid.* at 282.
81 *Residue Treatment & Trading Co. v. Southern Resources Ltd.* (1988) 6 A.C.L.C. 1160.

subject of some litigation is an attempt by the majority to expropriate individual members' shares; in other words, to expel individuals from the company. For instance, members may owe money to the company and it may claim a lien on shares and seek to forfeit them[82] rather than go through the usual and more cumbersome processes for recovering the amount due. Or members may be acting so much against the company's interests that most other shareholders may desire to exclude them entirely from the company. An example might be a company that prospers on a reputation for being anti-alcohol or anti-tobacco, but one of its prominent shareholders becomes addicted to the bottle or the pipe and, if this became public knowledge, the business would be adversely affected. One case on this question involved the National Association for Mental Health, a non-profit company limited by guarantee and without a share capital, that sought to expel Scientologists from its ranks.[83]

10–36 The commonest method of excluding unwanted members is by way of a resolution under an expulsion power contained in the articles of association; where the company has a share capital, this would take the form of a compulsory transfer of the member's shares to other members, usually at a fair price. Expulsion may in principle also be brought about by other and more complex devices, such as by repaying a shareholder his investment under the procedures set out in sections 72-77 of the 1963 Act;[84] making a take-over bid for the company and then expropriating a minority of not more than 20 per cent under the "take-out" power in section 204 of the 1963 Act;[85] buying out dissidents in the context of a reconstruction under section 260 of the 1963 Act,[86] or of an arrangement under section 201 of that Act.[87] However, resort to these powers of fundamentally changing the nature of the company is cumbersome and expensive, and the court possesses a wide discretion to prevent them from being used simply to expel unwanted shareholders. The following questions arise in respect of expulsion clauses in a company's own regulations.

Adopting Expulsion Articles

10–37 As regards their inherent validity, these provisions must not bring about an impermissible "distribution" within the meaning of the

---

[82] Table A, art. 35.
[83] *Gaiman v. National Association for Mental Health* [1971] Ch. 317.
[84] See below, paras 11–35 *et seq*.
[85] *cf. Re Bugle Press Ltd.* [1961] Ch. 270; see below, para. 12–43.
[86] *e.g. Castello v. London General Omnibus Co.* (1912) 107 L.T. 576; see post, para. 12–49.
[87] *e.g. Re National Bank Ltd.* [1966] 1 W.L.R. 819; see below, paras 12–45—12–46.

1983 Act, or constitute a prohibited acquisition of the company's own shares as contemplated by that Act.[88] It has been held that a power compulsorily to transfer a member's shares in the event of his becoming bankrupt is not repugnant to the bankruptcy law, at least where the transfer is at a fair price;[89] but a clause forfeiting the shares of any member who should commence litigation or threaten to sue the company or its directors was held invalid as an infringement of shareholders' legal rights.[90] An expulsion provision that sought to discriminate on grounds such as sex, race, religion or politics might possibly be unlawful in the light of the Constitution's equality and other guarantees. The fact that the regulation permits expropriation for less than fair value does not of itself render the power invalid.

10–38 The circumstances in which it is permissible to alter the articles of association in order to incorporate an expulsion or expropriation power in them was the subject of a number of decisions in 1919 and 1920, and in a 1994 decision from Australia.[91] In *Sidebottom v. Kershaw, Leese & Co.*[92] a private company passed a special resolution introducing a new article, under which the directors were empowered to compel any member who carried on a business that competed directly with the company to transfer his shares to another member for a fair price. It was said that the test of validity — whether the clause was adopted bona fide for the company's benefit— ultimately comes down to a narrow question of fact. The court found that an objectively reasonable view might he taken that it could be very much in the interests of a company to expel members that compete with it. Emphasis was placed on the shareholder's position as an insider to obtain behind-the-scenes information about the company's activities; though one doubts whether minority shareholders could get their hands on vital information about the company's trading plans, especially in those pre-Fourth Directive days. Indeed, the argument could be made that it potentially damages the company to expel a competitor in that pique may then induce him to step up the competition.

10–39 A most important aspect of the case was that it was admitted that what induced the company there to adopt the expulsion power was that one member, not the plaintiff, was known to the directors to be in a competing business. This, it was held, did not invalidate the resolution. Two judges confined their observations to the narrow is-

---

[88] See *Hopkinson v. Mortimer, Harley & Co.* [1917] 1 Ch. 646.
[89] *Borland's Trustee v. Steel Brothers & Co.* [1901] 1 Ch. 279.
[90] *Hope v. International Financial Soc.* (1876) 4 Ch.D. 327.
[91] *Gambotto v. W.C.P. Ltd.* (1994) 182 C.L.R. 432.
[92] [1920] 1 Ch. 154.

sue: the resolution "was directed against every competing person, and Mr. B was only the occasion of [its] passing";[93] and "the fact that Mr. B was in their minds when they proposed this alteration does not in the least prevent it from still being passed bona fide for the benefit of the company."[94] Eve J. ventured a more general proposition, namely:

> "where it is established that an alteration is adopted for the particular purpose of getting rid of an individual shareholder, the circumstance may furnish evidence of mala fide; but I demur altogether to the suggestion that it constitutes mala fides . . ." [95]

10–40 In other words, if there are indications that the purpose is to exclude a member because the majority simply desire a greater stake in the company for themselves, then the majority would need to produce highly convincing evidence of benefit to the company's business for the alteration to be upheld. Thus in the earlier *Brown v. British Abrasive Wheel Co.*[96] case, when the 90 per cent majority failed to persuade the minority to sell out to them at par, they amended the articles by introducing an expulsion power. The majority wished to pump additional capital into the company but did not want to share with the minority the benefits that might flow from the company's finances improving. It was held that expelling shareholders in those circumstances could not be for the company's benefit; it was merely a device enabling a majority "on failing to purchase the shares of a minority by agreement, [to] take power to do so compulsorily."[97]

10–41 A wholly discretionary authority to expropriate, somewhat along the lines of that in Part II of Table A restricting the transferability of shares at the directors' absolute discretion,[98] may be introduced into the articles only where it is demonstrably for the company's benefit that it possesses such "blunderbuss" powers, which in practice is rarely if ever. As Peterson J. observed in the *Dafen Tinplate* case:

> "It may be for the benefit of the majority of the shareholders to acquire the shares of the minority, but how can it be said to be for the benefit of the company that any shareholder, against whom no charge of acting to the detriment of the company can be urged, and who is in every respect a desirable member of the company, and for whose expropriation there

---

93 [1920] 1 Ch. 154 at 167.
94 *ibid.* at 172.
95 *ibid.* at 173. The Australian High Court in *Gambotto v. W.P.C. Ltd.* (1994) 182 C.L.R. 432 said that this was not a sufficiently exacting test.
96 [1919] 1 Ch. 290.
97 *ibid.* at 295–296.
98 Cf. above, paras 9–32 *et seq.*

> is no reason except the will of the majority, should be forced to transfer his shares to the majority or to anyone else? . . .
>
> To say that such an unrestricted and unlimited power of expropriation is for the benefit of the company appears to me to be confusing the interests of the majority with the benefit of the company as a whole."[99]

There the defendant company was formed by a number of tinplate manufacturers to supply them with steel bars, and an understanding existed, though without legal obligation, that each member would take its supplies of steel from the company. Having done that for a number of years, the plaintiff transferred its custom to a subsidiary it set up. This caused the defendant to amend its articles by including a power enabling the majority of shareholders to resolve that any member's shares be transferred to another at a fair price. It was held that the virtually unbounded discretion this power purported to give was fatal to its validity; by its terms, it went further than striking at members who reneged on the original and perhaps vital understanding, and purported to authorise expulsion of any shareholder at the majority's will and pleasure.

The Decision to Expel

10–42 As compared with the question of the board refusing to register transfers of shares, there is scant authority on trading and commercial companies invoking the expulsion power.[100] Where that power is conferred on the directors, they must exercise it in accordance with the fiduciary standards of bona fides and proper purpose. But where the power is formulated in wholly discretionary terms, it has not been settled on what grounds exercises of it will be impeached. In the only reported Irish case on the matter, *Walsh v. Cassidy,*[101] the "family" company's regulations authorised directors to expropriate any member who is "employed in the company in any capacity [and who] ceases to be so employed by [it]." It is implicit in Kingsmill Moore J.'s judgment that such a power should be construed as narrowly as is reasonably possible. He suggested that the clause there might not authorise expelling a member who acquired shares for full value and who subsequently took up some employment in the company. But he emphasised that an expulsion falling four square within the clause's terms would not be set aside merely because it would result in considerable hardship. On the other hand, "fraudulent" exercises of the power would be restrained.

---

[99] [1920] 2 Ch. at 141.

[100] *cf. Gaiman v. National Association for Mental Health* [1971] Ch. 317, concerning expulsions from a non-profit company.

[101] [1951] 1 Ir. Jur. Rep. 47. See also, *Wong Kim Fatt v. Leang & Son* [1975] 1 Malaya L.J. 20.

10–43 The only reported case in which exercise of an expulsion power by the members in general meeting appears to have been considered is *Phillips v. Manufacturers' Securities Ltd.*,[102] which concerned a non-profit federation, or trade union, of bedstead manufacturers. In a move to assert its authority and even though its shares were worth around £1.00 each, it was resolved to transfer the plaintiff's shares to other members on a pro rata basis for 1/- per share. There was a power in the articles whereby the members "may, by resolution ... determine that the shares of any member shall ... be offered for sale ... to the other members" at a price of not less than one shilling. There was no evidence supporting an allegation of fraud and the contention that the resolution should be struck down because it was motivated by "malicious intention" was rejected with a reference to *Bradford Corp. v. Pickles*.[103] The matter was treated as essentially one of construction of the articles; what happened there fell squarely within their terms; and the evidence indicated that the majority believed, and reasonably believed, that the resolution was in furtherance of the objects of the company and therefore for its benefit.

FRAUD ON THE COMPANY AND THE "DERIVATIVE" CLAIM

10–44 The true exception to what actually was decided in *Foss v. Harbottle*[104] is that part of the "fraud on a minority" rubric which involves the majority shareholders directly defrauding or damaging the company itself, and only indirectly prejudicing the minority — as contrasted with directly disadvantaging the minority shareholders themselves. In *Foss*, the complaint was that the directors and promoters practically "looted" the company by causing it to buy property from them at extravagant prices. Because that loss fell directly on the company and only indirectly on the plaintiff, it was held that ordinarily the company was the proper plaintiff. More recently in *O'Neill v. Ryan*,[105] the plaintiff sued several other shareholders in his company alleging that they had contravened Articles 85 and 86 of the E.E.C. Treaty (the competition rules) and thereby damaged the company. Again, since the immediate victim of their alleged wrongdoing was the company and not the plaintiff, he could not bring that action.[106] Where, however, it can be demonstrated that those who control the company are inflicting losses on it and, because of their control, the company will

[102] (1917) 116 L.T. 290.
[103] [1895] A.C. 587.
[104] (1843) 2 Hare 401; see above, para. 10–05.
[105] [1990] 2 I.R. 200.
[106] Distinguished in *Murray v. Times Newspapers Ltd.* [1997] 3 I.R. 97.

not bring proceedings against them, then the courts permit an individual shareholder to bring proceedings on behalf of the company. If that were not allowed, there would be no effective mechanism for protecting the company from the depredations of its controllers. Thus the term "fraud on a minority"; in this context it forms the basis for giving *locus standi* to aggrieved minority shareholders. Proceedings under this heading are often described as "derivative" actions; the plaintiff derives his entitlement to sue from the virtual helplessness of the company to protect itself against its very controllers. Accordingly, a court will not entertain a claim of this nature where it is being prosecuted for some ulterior motive, especially where there is an alternative remedy.[107] Nor does a shareholders' action of this nature lie when the company is in liquidation.[108]

10–45 A difficulty with describing the law as it stands under this heading is that, until the *O'Neill* case, there were no major Irish cases of derivative claims where the present legal position is expounded in any comprehensive fashion. Such a claim was also made in the *Crindle Investments* case[109] but, as in the circumstances the claim being made was so plainly misconceived, the Supreme Court's judgement does not analyse the law in detail. On the other hand, within the past 15 years the topic has been the subject of substantial litigation in England, which has yielded judgments showing formidable erudition and sophistication, most notably in the *Newman Industries Ltd. (No.2)* case[110] and in *Smith v. Croft (No. 2)*.[111] However, what was decided in these cases has not received universal acclaim and the judges have been criticised for placing unnecessary obstacles in the path of aggrieved minority shareholders. The question then arises of the extent to which the Irish courts would be guided by these decisions, not all of which have gone against plaintiffs. The *Newman Industries Ltd. (No.2)* case was hardly decided when it was rejected in Australia.[112] Perhaps partly because of the complications raised by these cases, almost all plaintiffs who might bring a derivative claim would be advised to proceed instead under section 205 of the 1963 Act for redress against oppression or disregarded interests.[113] If, however, the English practice is followed, of often giving

---

[107] *Barrett v. Duckett* [1995] 1 B.C.L.C. 243.
[108] *Fargo Ltd. v. Godfroy* [1986] B.C.L.C. 370.
[109] *Crindle Investments v. Wymes*, Supreme Court, March 5, 1998).
[110] *Prudential Assurance Co. v. Newman Industries Ltd. (No.2)* [1982] Ch.204; see below, para. 10–53.
[111] [1988] 1 Ch. 114; see below, paras 10–64—10–67.
[112] *Hurley v. B.G.H. Nominees Property Ltd.* (1982) 6 A.C.L.R. 791.
[113] See below, paras 10–74 *et seq*.

plaintiffs an indemnity against costs in derivative claims,[114] there are bound to be occasions where this procedure is more attractive.[115]

Fraud

10–46 What exactly amounts to "fraud" for these purposes has never received a comprehensive judicial definition but signifies the methods of taking unfair advantage of a company which can be remedied at the instigation of any aggrieved shareholder. With the general trend towards higher standards of conduct in companies' affairs, the ambit of fraud here continues to expand. Megarry J. observed in one instance that "[I]t does not seem to have yet become very clear exactly what the word 'fraud' means in this context; but I think it is plainly wider than fraud at common law in the sense of *Derry v. Peek* . . . [It] seems to be being used as comprising . . . fraud in the wider equitable sense of that term, as in the equitable concept of fraud on a power".[116] A blatant example of fraud on the company is the first reported derivative suit, *Atwool v. Merryweather*,[117] which concerned a sale by promoters and directors of over-valued property to their company.[118] When other shareholders discovered what really had occurred they sought to sue on behalf of the company, but their action was adjourned pending consideration of the matter in general meeting. At the meeting a motion to discontinue the action and to refer it instead to arbitration was carried by a narrow majority, the defendants voting their own shares together with proxies that they controlled. Because of the nature of the fraud and the way shareholder approval had been obtained, the court allowed the action to proceed.[119] At the other end of the spectrum are instances such as "where the majority think that one of themselves is the best person to be managing director and proceed to appoint that person managing director at a remuneration [that is not] excessive or grossly unfair"; this is not "appropriat[ing] to themselves the assets of the company"[120] and it cannot give rise to an action by a minority shareholder. In *Palvides v. Jensen*,[121] where it was alleged that the board agreed

---

[114] See below, paras 10–70 *et seq*.

[115] See generally, Wedderburn, above, para. 10–01, n. 1, Sullivan, "Restating the Scope of the Derivative Action" (1985) 44 Cam. L.J. 236; Beck, "The Shareholders' Derivative Action" (1974) 52 Can. Bar Rev. 159 and Sealy, "The Rule in Foss v. Harbottle in Australia" (1989) 10 Co. Law. 52.

[116] *Eastmanco (Kilner House) Ltd. v. Greater London Council* [1982] 1 W.L.R. 2 at 12.

[117] (1868) L.R. 5 Eq. 464n.

[118] This particular problem is now covered by special statutory provisions, notably1983 Act, ss. 30, 32 and 1990 Act, s.29.

[119] See also, *Menier v. Hooper's Telegraph Works* (1874) L.R. 9 Ch. App. 350.

[120] *Foster v. Foster* [1916] 1 Ch. 532 at 549. See also, *Normandy v. Ind. Coope & Co.* [1908] 1 Ch. 84.

to the sale of one of the company's properties for significantly less than its market value, it was held that an individual shareholder could not institute proceedings against the directors for being negligent.

10–47 The difficult question has been the drawing of the boundary between what constitutes mere breach of controllers' and directors' duties on the one hand and, on the other hand, improper conduct that entitles any individual shareholder to initiate proceedings against the wrongdoers. In the past and perhaps even still today the boundary was defined by reference to certain kinds of wrongs which are inherently ratifiable by a majority of the members, including the alleged wrongdoers. They could ratify directors' negligence and the making of "incidental" secret profits from their position provided they acted bona fides. But misappropriation of the company's property and also mala fides exercises of directors powers could only be sanctioned by the votes of shareholders who were entirely independent of the wrongdoers. However, the cases do not wholeheartedly support this analysis, the suitability of which in any event is questionable. Two main situations call for special consideration.

Corporate Opportunity

10–48 Directors owe a fiduciary duty to their company not to divert corporate opportunities to their own ends and they must account to the company for any personal profit they make from such opportunities.[122] Depending on the circumstances, moreover, a company in general meeting cannot exonerate directors from this obligation. The classic instance is *Cook v. Deeks*[123] which, it will be remembered, concerned highly lucrative construction contracts that the defendant directors diverted to their own benefit. One of their defences was that the company in general meeting had passed resolutions renouncing any legal claims it might have had against them. But those resolutions were passed with the votes of the defendants *qua* shareholders. It was held that to allow the defendants to retain the profits they made in the circumstance "would be to allow a majority to oppress the minority". *North-West Transportation Co.*[124] was distinguished on the grounds that it concerned a sale of directors' (and majority shareholders') own property to the company and not, as in the instant case, property which "belonged in equity to the company".

---

121 [1956] Ch. 565.
122 See above, paras 5–129 *et seq*.
123 [1916] 1 A.C. 554.
124 (1887) 12 App. Cas. 589; see above, para. 10–07.

10–49 Contrast with *Cook v. Deeks* the other leading case, *Regal (Hastings) Ltd. v. Gulliver,*[125] which concerned directors who pumped their own funds into their company's subsidiary, to enable it to acquire some cinemas, and who made a sizeable profit on this investment when the entire group company was taken over shortly afterwards. Even though they acted in good faith, they had broken their fiduciary duty to the company and, therefore, had to account for the profits they made. But Lord Russell observed that the defendants there "could, had they wished, have protected themselves [from liability] by a resolution (either antecedent or subsequent) of the Regal shareholders in general meeting" ratifying the entire transaction.[126]

10–50 There are three grounds on which the outcome in *Cook v. Deeks* and Lord Russell's suggestion in *Regal (Hastings)* have been distinguished, viz. control, property and motive. Although it would appear that the defendant directors in *Regal (Hastings)* were also its controlling shareholders, Lord Russell may have been speaking as if they were not the controllers, or as if their action would most likely have obtained the support of the independent shareholders at the time the entire transaction was decided upon. Assuming that the defendants in *Regal (Hastings)* had control, it has been said that the construction contracts in *Cook v. Deeks* were company property whereas the investment opportunity in *Regal (Hastings)* was not its property. Thirdly, in *Cook v. Deeks* there was bad faith which did not exist in *Regal (Hastings)*. The problem with the "property" explanation is that it can be used in virtually every case to rationalise why a party wins in one instance and loses in another: he wins because in that instance his property was being interfered with. The difficulty with motive is that often it is not easy to show that a group of persons, such as shareholders when voting, reached a decision for mala fide reasons.

Interest in Contract

10–51 *North-West Transportation Co. v. Beatty*[127] is often cited in support of the proposition that, where a company enters into a contract in which a director has a financial interest, then, provided the director complies with the letter of the articles of association and the Companies Acts, he may vote his shares on the proposed resolution to ratify the contract; he may do so even where he is the majority shareholder. It is nevertheless significant that the Privy Council examined the details and circumstances of the contract there, and concluded that its

[125] [1967] 2 A.C. 134; see above, para. 5–131.
[126] *ibid.* at 150.
[127] (1887) 12 App. Cas. 589; see above, para. 10–07.

terms were not unduly unfair on the company.[128] Additionally, the issue before the meeting there was whether to adopt the contract — not whether to bring proceedings against the controller to recover an excessive profit he made from the contract. It therefore would appear that where directors/controllers deal with their companies and thereby make an excessive profit for themselves, but the minority interests object and demand that the transaction be rescinded or the gain be repaid to the company, it is fraud for those directors, voting *qua* shareholders, to block proposals made in general meeting that the company should sue them for compensation.

10–52 A more recent instance of such a claim is *Daniels v. Daniels*,[129] which was an application to strike out a statement of claim as disclosing no real cause of action. Minority shareholders sued a director and controlling shareholder who had bought property from the company for significantly less than its current value. But the statement of claim accused him of gross negligence and not fraud. The contention that, since fraud was not pleaded, there could be no cause of action was rejected on the grounds that:

> "If minority shareholders can sue if there is fraud, [there is] no reason why they cannot sue where the action of the majority and the directors, though without fraud, confers some benefit on those directors and majority shareholders themselves. It would seem to me quite monstrous, particularly as fraud is so hard to plead and difficult to prove, if the confines of the exception to *Foss v. Harbottle* were drawn so narrowly that directors would make a profit out of their negligence."[130]

The full implications of this decision remain to be seen. At one extreme it could signify that a case should not be prevented from going to trial simply because it does not allege fraud or does not fall within one of the other established exceptions to *Foss v. Harbottle*. At the other, it may mark a stage in the evolution of a rule that shareholders have a right of action in respect of all forms of self-dealing negligence committed by the directors and majority shareholders, *i.e.* out of bad business judgments that nevertheless leave the majority financially better off to a significant extent.

Act, Motive or Circumstance?

10–53 The question has been posed whether the answer lies not in classifying into fixed legal categories the kinds of wrongs majorities

---

[128] See also, *Burland v. Earle* [1902] A.C. 83.
[129] [1978] Ch. 406.
[130] *ibid.* at 414.

may and may not cure by ratification but more in considering the circumstances in which and methods by which directors and controllers prevent the company from taking action against themselves in respect of their wrongs. The traditional view has been that, although there is some uncertainty about precisely what amounts to defrauding the company, nevertheless the "fraud lies rather in the nature of the transaction than in the motives of the majority".[131] But this analysis is not universally accepted and was rejected by Vinelott J. in *Prudential Insurance Co. v. Newman Industries Ltd. (No.2).*[132] The proper approach to such matters, he asserted, is that "fraud lies in [the majority's] use of their voting powers, not in the character of the act or transaction giving rise to the cause of action. [The question is not what is the] category of acts or transactions which are incapable of being authorised or ratified by the majority in general meeting."[133] In his view, the fraud exception to *Foss v. Harbottle* applies even:

> "where there is [no] conscious and deliberate wrongdoing on the part of the directors who are alleged to be liable to the company for breach of their fiduciary duty or improper retention or appropriation of property or advantages belonging to the company, [such as where] it is alleged that the directors though "acting in the belief that they are doing nothing wrong" are guilty of a breach of duty to the company (including their duty to exercise proper care) and as a result of that breach obtain some benefit."[134]

The Court of Appeal declined to comment on this analysis other than to express dissatisfaction with a broad and "[im]practical" test, of "whenever the justice of the case so requires",[135] to determine when shareholders can bring suit.

10–54 Since the question is not settled by authority, the merits of Vinelott J.'s approach must be assessed. According to him, virtually every breach by controllers-directors of their fiduciary duties, other than ones from which they obtain no significant financial advantage at the company's expense (such as mere negligence), can be the subject of a derivative shareholders' claim unless it is shown that the independent shareholders, being properly informed, voted or would vote to ratify the breach of duty. His analysis has been criticised as conflicting with the understanding that a share is the property of its holder and can be voted as he wishes in general meeting. But if a share is that kind of

---

[131] Wedderburn (1958) 17 Cam. L.J. 93 at p.96.
[132] [1981] 1 Ch. 257.
[133] *ibid.* at 307.
[134] *ibid.* at 312.
[135] [1982] 1 Ch. 204 at 221.

property, how is it that a special resolution will be struck down if it is shown that it was not passed for the benefit of the company as a whole? The principal criticism of Vinelott J.'s approach is its impracticability-that it would introduce "great confusion . . . into the affairs of joint stock companies . . . "[136] Against this, it is unjust if controllers-directors, acting in breach of their fiduciary duties to their company, are allowed to make large profits for themselves and at their company's expense. This is especially so in companies whose shares cannot be transferred without the directors' consent (*i.e.* most private companies) or whose shares do not have a ready market, in that the minority do not even have the option of cutting their losses by selling off their somewhat devalued investment.

Procedural Matters

10–55 In choosing between the various grounds for and methods of judicial intervention on behalf of aggrieved shareholders, some vital and mainly procedural questions arise.

Personal and Representative Actions, and the Derivative Suit

10–56 A crucial difference exists between the "personal" and the "representative" claims, on the one hand, and "the derivative suit" on the other. A personal claim is simply one based on a duty owed directly to the plaintiff *qua* shareholder, arising either from the "section 25 contract" or from a statutory duty that gives a private right of action. Frequently, the personal action is brought in a "representative" form, *i.e.* the individual plaintiff sues on behalf of himself/herself and other shareholders in the same position against individual defendants (usually directors) and the company.[137] A derivative suit, by contrast, is brought where the company itself has been wronged but, because the defendants control the company, the only way in which the wrong can be remedied is to allow any member to bring suit on the company's behalf. The practice grew up of minority shareholders being permitted to bring an action in their own names, although in truth on the company's behalf. The form of action is "AB (a minority shareholder) on behalf of himself and all other shareholders in the company" against the alleged fraudsters and the company.[138]

---

136 *North West Transportation Co.* case (1877) 12 App. Cas. at p. 600.

137 *e.g. Prudential Assurance Co. v. Newman Industries Ltd.* [1981] 1 Ch. 229. See also, *Irish Shipping Ltd. v. Commercial Union Assurance Co., p.l.c.* [1991] 2 Q.B. 206.

138 *cf.* Ord. 15 r. 12A in the English Rules of the Supreme Court, discussed in *Cooke v. Cooke* [1997] 2 B.C.L.C. 28.

10–57 In those instances where the immediate victim of the wrong complained of is the company rather than the shareholders themselves, those shareholders stand to lose considerably in that the value of their investment can decline by an amount related to what was taken from the company. Be that as it may, it was held on appeal in *Prudential Assurance Co. v. Newman Industries Ltd. (No.2)*[139] that where the gravamen of the complaint is financial loss inflicted on the company, then the only form of shareholders' action open is the derivative suit, where the fact of control by the alleged fraudsters and a good prima facie case must be established before the action will be allowed to proceed. There, B and L, the personal defendants, were the two senior directors of Newman, a company with a Stock Exchange quotation. Through a series of manipulations they persuaded Newman to purchase at an over-valued price a "package" of assets and liabilities of and shares in TPG Co., a near-insolvent company in which they both had a large personal financial stake. B and L's status in Newman practically ensured that any plausible business proposition they supported would be accepted by the board and, by use of some deception, they secured the directors' agreement to buy without TPG being independently valued. On account of the cross-holdings of shares, it was necessary under the Stock Exchange rules for the purchase to be approved by the Newman shareholders. A "tricky and misleading" circular drafted by B and L helped to win the members' consent, though only by a small majority. It would appear that by the time proceedings were launched the contract could not have been rescinded since the acquisition had been completed and third party interests would have been adversely affected. Prudential, which was a minority shareholder, instituted personal claims for breach of the directors' fiduciary duty and conspiracy; a representative claim for the same and for a declaration that the circular was misleading and tricky; and a derivative claim for breach of the directors' fiduciary duty to the company. At the trial, Vinelott J. held that there was a good cause of action on the personal and representative claims for damages and a declaration. Newman had been induced by fraud to approve the agreement; the fraud caused a reduction in net profits, which inevitably led to a fall in its share price; and therefore the plaintiffs as shareholders suffered loss. Most argument turned on the second question: whether on these facts Prudential could pursue the derivative claim.

10–58 Perhaps the most significant feature of the Court of Appeal's decision is that, in instances such as this, there is no basis whatsoever for the personal or representative claims, since it cannot be said that

---

[139] [1982] 1 Ch. 204.

any of the plaintiff's rights *qua* member were infringed. Here the core allegation was of defrauding the company and, ever since *Foss v. Harbottle*,[140] it has been for the company itself to seek redress for an injury done to it, though in appropriate circumstances a derivative claim by a minority shareholder on the company's behalf might be allowed. This, it was said:

> "is not merely a tiresome procedural obstacle placed in the path of a shareholder by a legalistic judiciary. The rule is a consequence of the fact that a corporation is a separate legal entity. Other consequences are limited liability and limited rights. The company is liable for its contracts and torts; the shareholder has no such liability. The company acquires causes of action for breaches of contract and for torts which damage the company. No cause of action vests in the shareholder. When the shareholder acquires a share he accepts the fact that the value of his investment follows the fortune of the company and that he can only exercise his influence over the fortunes of the company by the exercise of his voting rights in general meeting. The law confers on him the right to ensure that the company observes the limitations of its memorandum of association and the right to ensure that other shareholders observe the rule, imposed on them by the articles of association."[141]

Inevitably, difficulties arise in the in-between situations where it cannot fairly be said that the corporate coffers were looted, but neither was there a violation of clear "personal" rights under the Companies Acts or the memorandum or articles of association.[142]

The Prima Facie Case

10–59 No dispute will be allowed to proceed to a full trial where the originating summons or petition does not state a case that requires answering. That is to say, on the application of the defendant, the court is empowered to strike out the claim and dismiss the action summarily on the grounds that the statement of claim "discloses no reasonable cause of action".[143] In such an application the court does not look at the evidence, not even at affidavit evidence. If, taking the facts as alleged by the plaintiff to be true, it is clear that the action could not succeed, it must be dismissed. For instance, in *Palvides v. Jensen*,[144] a claim against directors-controllers for damages on the grounds of grossly negligent management was dismissed because the facts as alleged in the statement of claim made it "impossible to see how the . . .

---

[140] (1843) 2 Hare 461; see above, para. 10–05.
[141] [1982] 1 Ch. 204 at 224.
[142] *cf. Gordon v. Elliman*, 306 N.Y. 456 (1954).
[143] Many of the recent cases on statutory "oppression" take this form.
[144] [1956] Ch. 565.

action can be maintained".[145] In the derivative suit the principal questions are whether the defendants "control" the company and have they "defrauded" it. However, what constitutes fraud in these circumstance may very well turn on how the defendants have used or are likely to use their voting powers and influence within the company. On account of special features of the derivative suit, a plaintiff may be required to make out a prima facie case before a full trial can take place.

Control

10–60 Those who bring the derivative suit must allege and show that the defendants control the company,[146] which is the justification for not leaving it to the company to obtain redress for the wrong done to it. Thus in *Atwool v. Merryweather*,[147] the defendants virtually bribed other shareholders for their support and manipulated the proxy machinery in their own favour. The fact of control must be alleged and proved. The English courts used to take a somewhat over-legalistic approach, requiring that the defendants control at least a majority of the voting shares; though it was admitted that a court would "in certain cases go behind the apparent ownership of shares in order to discover whether a company is in fact controlled by wrongdoers-as, for instance . . . where the shares are held by mere nominees, bound to vote as the owners required them to vote."[148]

10–61 Deciding, though incorrectly as it transpired, that the derivative claim should be heard, the central issue in *Newman Industries Ltd. (No. 2)*[149] at first instance become whether the defendants there had sufficient control of the company. A somewhat novel test was propounded by Vinelott, J., namely:

> "whether it can be demonstrated that the defendants, even if they do not directly or indirectly own a majority of the voting shares, are in a position to influence decisively any general meeting consideration of any resolution that they should or should not be proceeded against. From the evidence there, he found that "there was no way in which [the minority shareholder] could have ensured that the question whether proceedings should be brought by [the company] would be fairly put to the shareholders or even that a full investigation would be made into the transaction [in question]. In those circumstances [the minority share-

[145] [1956] Ch. 565 at 576. See also *Heyting v. Dupont* [1964] 1 W.L.R. 843.
[146] *Re Downs Wine Bar Ltd.* [1990] B.C.L.C. 839.
[147] (1867) L.R. 5 Eq. 464.
[148] *Palvides v. Jensen* [1956] Ch. 565 at 577.
[149] [1981] 1 Ch. 257.

> holder] has shown that the interests of justice do require that a minority action should be permitted."[150]

Given its decision on the appropriate nature of the claim, the Court of Appeal declined to "decide [or] express any concluded view on . . . the scope of the exception to the rule in *Foss v. Harbottle*", apart from voicing disapproval of such a wide and "[im]practical" an exception as "whether the justice of the case so requires.[151]

"Fraud"

10–62 Those who institute a derivative suit must allege and show, secondly, that the controllers committed a fraud on the company[152] — fraud in this context bearing the wide equitable connotation. If "fraud lies in the nature of the transaction being impugned",[153] then it should be possible to ascertain from the statement of claim whether there was at least some case to answer. In *Newman Industries Ltd. (No. 2)*, however, Vinelott J. propounded a contrary approach that, not alone conflicts with this practical pigeon-holding concept of fraud, but raises again in a slightly different guise the question of control, namely, is it because of the defendants' dominant position in the company that a resolution to proceed against them was or would be rejected in general meeting?[154]

10–63 The Court of Appeal would neither endorse nor condemn this approach. Instead, it ruled that an action of this nature should not go to a full-blown trial merely because the appropriate kind of fraud is alleged. The judge here is confronted with a dilemma:

> "For at the time of the application the existence of the fraud is unproved. . . . If on such an application, the plaintiff can require the court to assume as a fact every allegation in the statement of claim . . . the plaintiff will frequently be able to outmanoeuvre the primary purpose of the rule in *Foss v. Harbottle* [which is to avoid unnecessary litigation] by alleging fraud and "control" by the fraudster. If on the other hand the plaintiff has to prove fraud and "control" before he can establish his title to prosecute his action, then the action may need to be fought to a conclusion before the court can decide whether or not the plaintiff should be permitted to prosecute it. In the latter case the purpose of the rule in *Foss v. Harbottle* disappears."[155]

---

[150] [1981] 1 Ch. 257 at 327.
[151] [1982] 1 Ch. 204 at 221.
[152] *Re Downs Wine Bar Ltd.* [1990] B.C.L.C. 839.
[153] Wedderburn (1958) 17 Cam. L.J. at p.96.
[154] See above, para. 10–60.
[155] [1982] 1 Ch. 204 at 219.

Consequently, the plaintiff should be in position to make out a *prima facie* case before the action will be allowed to go to trial:

> "he ought at least to be required before proceeding with his action to establish a prima facie case (i) that the company is entitled to the relief claimed and (ii) that the action falls within the proper boundaries of the exception to the rule in *Foss v. Harbottle* (which does not include whenever the justice of the case so requires court intervention)."[156]

It remains to be seen whether the Irish courts would want the judge to speculate, on perhaps the flimiest of evidence, where control lies and on the likelihood of the company having being wronged by its controllers before allowing aggrieved shareholders to proceed with their case.

10–64 In order to answer both of these questions, especially if abuse of voting power is the criterion of fraud, it may be necessary to convene a general meeting to vote on the impugned transaction. In *Newman Industries Ltd. (No. 2)* the Court of Appeal stressed the advisability "for the judge trying the preliminary issue to grant a sufficient adjournment to enable a meeting of the shareholders to be convened by the board, so that he can reach a conclusion in the light of the conduct of, and proceedings at, that meeting."[157] For instance, armed with adequate information, independent shareholders may in the event approve of the transaction or reach some compromise with the named defendants. Or the issue may be put to a vote where all the defendants, standing on their "property" rights, vote to absolve themselves from liability to the company and virtually all the other shareholders vote against them, which usually would justify letting the matter go to a full trial.

Independent Shareholders Opposing Litigation

10–65 Even where the requisite elements of control and fraud exist, a shareholder's action on behalf of the company may be blocked if a sufficient number of entirely independent members of the company do not want his action to proceed. So it was held in *Smith v. Croft (No. 2)*.[158] The plaintiffs, who held approximately 14.5 per cent of the company's capital, sought to bring a derivative claim alleging fraud on the company on several grounds. The defendants, who held 62.5 per cent of the shares, were the company's executive director, its chairman and non-executive director, and companies associated with them. A substantial shareholder, which was not directly involved in the dispute, was a trust but the company chairman was the trust's nominee on the

---

156 [1982] 1 Ch. 204 at 221–222.
157 *ibid.* at 222.
158 [1988] 1 Ch. 114.

board. The allegations made by the plaintiffs were that the executive directors were paid excessive remuneration, that they dishonestly caused the company to make substantial payments to other companies which they controlled, that they caused it to make payments of what were really gifts to themselves and that they used the company's money to enable another company to buy shares in it. Thus, the allegations were of breach of fiduciary duty, *ultra vires* and illegality. However, the trust, which held 20 per cent of the shares, and a handful of other shareholders were opposed to pursuing the claim in the courts. The preliminary question of whether the action should be allowed to go ahead was argued for fifteen days before Knox J., who ordered that it should be struck out.

10–66 The net issue was had the plaintiffs "establish[ed] a prima facie case (i) that the company is entitled to the relief claimed and (ii) that the action falls within the proper boundaries of the exceptions to the rule in *Foss v. Harbottle*."[159] It was found that a prima facie case had been made out only in respect of one head of the claim, namely, financing the purchase of the company's shares. While the various other payments that were challenged may have been an abuse of the directors' powers, they could not be regarded as *ultra vires* the company in the sense of beyond its corporate capacity. With regard to the claim in respect of unlawfully financing the purchase of its own shares, which by definition is *ultra vires*,[160] it was held that the fact that the majority has caused the company to act *ultra vires* and to its detriment does not invariably entitle any minority shareholder to bring proceedings in the company's name to recover what the company may have lost. As was emphasised by the Court of Appeal in the *Newman Industries Ltd. (No.2)* case,[161] the right to recover loss caused to the company is the company's right of action and not a right personal to any of its shareholders. Because loss to the company might often go uncompensated, the courts have permitted individual shareholders to bring claims on behalf of their company against the wrong-doing controllers. But this procedural device to assist the company does not entitle a shareholder to bring suit in all conceivable circumstances. If there is some valid reason why the company should not bring the claim then the shareholder will not be permitted to sue on the company's behalf. One such reason is where a majority of the independent shareholders are opposed to the proceedings on the grounds that, in the end, a trial of the action may cause the company far more damage than good. This prin-

[159] *Newman Industries Ltd.* case [1982] Ch. at 221.
[160] *Re M.J. Cummins Ltd.* [1939] I.R. 60; see above, para. 7–60.
[161] [1982] 1 Ch. 204.

ciple, it was held, applies as much to actions to recover loss resulting from *ultra vires* acts as it applies to other forms of "fraud" on the company.

10–67 Focus on the question of control in this context is more complex than determining who has voting control of the company. Rather, the question is — has the company been improperly prevented from suing the alleged wrongdoers. It is being so prevented where the overwhelming majority of the other shareholders want the claims to be pursued but the wrongdoers out-vote them on the proposal to bring proceedings. On the other hand, the company is not being improperly prevented from bringing the claim if a substantial group of independent shareholders have concluded that legal proceedings will indeed damage the company. As Knox J. explained:

> "Ultimately the question which has to be answered in order to determine whether the rule in *Foss v. Harbottle* applies to prevent a minority shareholder seeking relief as plaintiff for the benefit of the company is: Is the plaintiff being prevented improperly from bringing those proceedings on behalf of the company? If it is an expression of the corporate will of the company by an appropriate independent organ that is preventing the plaintiff from prosecuting the action he is not improperly but properly prevented and so the answer to the question is No. The appropriate independent organ will vary according to the constitution of the company concerned and the identity of the defendants who will in most cases be disqualified from participating by voting in expressing the corporate will."[162]

Discovery

10–68 Fraud will be alleged in the statement of claim only where the party is confident that fraud can be established, which explains the preparedness of judges to allow a case to go to trial once that allegation is made. But often aggrieved shareholders may not be in possession of sufficient facts to be sure that their suspicions of fraudulent conduct will be confirmed at the trial. Thus the judge is confronted with another dilemma: to strike out the action, because fraud as such is not alleged[163] or to allow it to go ahead in the expectation that malpractices will be unearthed in the course of discovery and trial. As was pointed out in *Daniels v. Daniels*, "the plaintiffs do not really know what happened; all they know is what is set out in the statement of claim. There has been a sale at an undervalue and the defendant (director) has made a substantial profit. . . ."[164]

---

[162] [1988] 1 Ch. 114 at 185.
[163] *e.g. Re Downs Wine Bar Ltd.* [1990] B.C.L.C. 839.
[164] [1978] Ch. at p. 409.

10–69 Where the facts are in dispute then discovery can be a crucial matter. Seeing copies of all the relevant documents in the company's and the majority's possession should be sufficient in many instances to tell a shareholder whether claims against those controlling the company will succeed. Responding to requests for discovery, however, can be a cumbersome and expensive process. And when deliberations about business policy must be revealed, there is a risk of confidential information not directly relevant to the claim getting into the wrong hands. Thus the real question in *Daniels v. Daniels* was whether, in the light of the allegations made, discovery ought to be ordered. And the central flaw in Vinelott J.'s conduct of *Newman Industries Ltd. (No. 2)* was that he allowed discovery to go ahead and an entire trial to take place without first considering whether the plaintiffs had adduced sufficient evidence to warrant discovery being ordered and having the company's managers defend their actions in court.

Costs

10–70 In derivative suits costs present two sets of problems. In the first place, to what extent do the ordinary rules about costs prevent deserving cases from getting a hearing in court? Any consideration of costs in civil litigation must now be made in the light of *Airey v. Ireland,*[165] a decision of the European Court of Human Rights, where it was held that the right under Article 6(1) of the European Convention on Human Rights of access to the court for a determination of one's "civil rights and obligations" includes a right to legal aid in appropriate circumstances. The right to private property guaranteed by the Convention's First Protocol and by the Constitution have been interpreted expansively. It nevertheless is unlikely that, in the foreseeable future, this right will be interpreted as entitling plaintiffs in derivative suits to legal aid. The English Court of Appeal in *Wallersteiner v. Moir (No.2)*[166] refused to allow derivative claims to go ahead on a contingency fee basis, *i.e.* on an arrangement with the plaintiff's legal advisers that they would be remunerated only in the event of his case eventually succeeding. Contingency fee arrangements traditionally have been regarded as contrary to public policy.

10–71 But it was held in *Wallersteiner* that the court can order the company to indemnify the nominal plaintiffs' costs down to judgment, *i.e.* that they should be reimbursed their taxed costs by the company whether or not they succeed in the claim. This is because they do not stand to gain directly if they win; any damages that are awarded go to

---

[165] (1979) 2 E.H.R.R. 305.
[166] [1975] Q.B. 373.

the company itself, which is the real plaintiff. All that the minority shareholders gain is that judgment against the defendants may cause the value of their shares to appreciate. Thus the necessity to remove financial deterrents against shareholders bringing derivative suits. In order to get an indemnity from the company for costs, it must be shown that bringing action in the circumstances "was a reasonable and prudent course to take in the interests of the company".[167] And the indemnity will extend to costs down to the judgment "if it would have been reasonable for an independent board exercising the standard of care which a prudent businessman would exercise in his own affairs" to continue the action to that stage.[168] Consequently, plaintiffs who are either impecunious or do not wish to jeopardise their own resources will have to make out a fair prima facie case at the outset, which often will require discovery and may need convening a general meeting of the company.

10–72 In *Smith v. Croft*[169] the indemnity in this context was described as a mechanism for ensuring that the minority shareholders "should not be prevented from pursuing an obviously just cause through lack of funds, for fear that he may, for some reason, fail at the end of the day and be at risk as to costs which he cannot possibly pay.[170] On the other hand, giving the indemnity could result in injustice if the plaintiff's case ultimately fails because the company and other defendants, who prove to be completely blameless, nevertheless are burdened with the plaintiff's costs. The test of whether a plaintiff should get an indemnity is whether "an independent board of directors exercising the standard of care which prudent businessmen would exercise in their own affairs [would] consider that [the company] ought to bring the action."[171] In answering this question, particular weight will be given to the views of any major independent shareholder, *i.e.* a shareholder who is neither in the plaintiff's nor in the defendant's camp. In this case, there was such a shareholder who opposed the plaintiff's action on the grounds that pursuing it would cause the company to lose its extremely valuable directors, who had built up a highly profitable business for the company. In the light of the allegations made against those directors and the independent shareholder's view, Walton J. concluded that this action should not be allowed to proceed and refused to give the indemnity being sought.

---

[167] [1975] Q.B. 373 at 392.
[168] *ibid.* at 404.
[169] [1986] 1 W.L.R. 580.
[170] *ibid.* at 597.
[171] *ibid.* at 590. See also *Jaybird Group Ltd. v. Greenwood* [1986] B.C.L.C. 319 and *Re A Company (No. 005136 of 1986)* [1987] B.C.L.C. 82.

OPPRESSION AND DISREGARD OF INTERESTS

10–73 When the Companies Act, 1948, was being drawn up in Britain, it was felt that the law as it stood at the time did not afford minority shareholders adequate protection against abuse of power by majorities. The various grounds considered above (*i.e.* breach of contract, fraud and bad faith) were regarded as insufficiently demanding and, it should be remembered, the *Greenhalgh*[172] anti-discrimination principle had not yet been articulated by the courts. One remedy against certain abuses did exist, namely, having the company wound up on "just and equitable grounds".[173] But few aggrieved shareholders would want to see the entire enterprise being brought to an end and sold off and the courts were most reluctant to invoke that drastic power against tyrannical majorities. This state of affairs led to the enactment of section 210 of the 1948 Act, which was a novel provision empowering the court, in instances where it found that a minority was "oppressed", to order that appropriate remedial measures be taken. It is no exaggeration to say that this provision was revolutionary; it sat alongside the existing statutory and common law rules regarding inter-shareholder relations as a new form of equity jurisdiction based on the somewhat vague concept of oppressive conduct.[174] A close analogy is the Unfair Dismissals Act, 1977, which complements much of traditional employment law with an overriding standard of "fairness in the circumstances". Perhaps because it could range so widely and in sense wreak havoc on the established company law, the British courts used to interpret section 210 in a very restrictive fashion.[175] But for that approach, instances like *Clemens v. Clemens Brothers Ltd.*[176] probably would have been brought under section 210 rather than under the common law. Criticism of the excessive caution with which this provision was being applied in Britain eventually led to its being replaced by section 75 of the Companies Act, 1981, which is now section 459 of the Companies Act, 1985, as amended in 1989.[177]

---

[172] *Greenhalgh v. Arderne Cinemas Ltd.* [1951] 1 Ch. 286; see above, para. 10–29.

[173] 1963 Act, s.213(f); see below, paras 10–89 *et seq*.

[174] The history is summarised in *Re BSB Holdings Ltd. (No.2)* [1996] 1 B.C.L.C. 155 at 234–250.

[175] See Rajak, "The Oppression of Minority Shareholders" (1972) 35 Mod. L. Rev. 156.

[176] [1976] 2 All E.R. 268; see above, para. 10–34.

[177] See generally, E. Boros, *Minority Shareholders' Remedies* (1995); R. Hollington, *Minority Shareholders' Rights*, (1990); Prentice, "The Theory of the Firm: Minority Shareholder Oppression: Section 459-461 of the Companies Act, 1985" (1988) 8 Oxf. J.L. Stud. 55 and Hannigan, "Section 459 of the Companies Act, 1985 — A Code of Conduct for the Quasi-Partnerships?" [1988] Ll. Mar. Comm. L.Q. 60.

10–74 Section 205 of the 1963 Act, which was inspired by the British section 210, authorises the court to intervene against the oppression of shareholders:

> "Any member of a company who complains that the affairs of the company are being conducted or that the powers of the directors of the company are being exercised in a manner oppressive to him or any of the members (including himself), or in disregard of his or their interests as members, may apply to the court for an order under this section."

Where the court is "of the opinion" that oppression as thus defined has taken place, it is empowered to make orders of various kinds.[178] A shareholder may also apply to have the company wound up compulsorily because oppression as defined above has taken place.[179] Claims concerning typical minority shareholder complaints tend more and more to be brought under section 205 of the 1963 Act. Its attractions for plaintiffs are obvious. The substantive criteria to be applied are very broad, provision is made for hearing all or part of the proceedings *in camera* and the court has an extensive choice over which remedy should be awarded. Against these, however, section 205 remains very much unexplored territory. The other modes of redress provide greater predictability of outcome, which in turn enhances the prospect of a satisfactory settlement before the costs and inconveniences of a trial are incurred. And in *Re R. Ltd.*,[180] the Supreme Court held that only in the most exceptional cases should the court agree to hear the proceedings *in camera*.[181]

10–75 Because of some differences in terminology between the substantive and the remedial provisions of the British Acts and section 205 of the 1963 Act, the British decisions (especially those rejecting applications under section 210 of the 1948 Act) are not reliable indicators of exactly what the position is in Ireland. But the more recent decisions in Britain show a far less restrictive attitude to what amounts to oppression and most likely would be followed by an Irish court. Over the last ten years a very substantial body of case law has accumulated there,[182] which constraints of space render it impossible to consider in any detail here. Almost all of these cases have concerned small family companies or incorporated so-called "quasi partnerships", where the

---

178 s.205(3); see below, para. 10–85.
179 1963 Act, s.213(g); see below, para. 10–87.
180 [1989] I.R. 126.
181 Followed in *Irish Press p.l.c. v. Ingersoll Irish Publications Ltd (No. 1)* [1994] 1 I.R. 176.
182 See above, n. 174 and n. 177.

complaining minority either could not have disposed of his shares or, even if they were disposable legally, there was no market for them.

10–76 Applications under section 205 are often used as mere leverage to obtain better bargaining positions and, unless carefully controlled, can themselves become a medium of oppression.[183] For the threat of such proceedings by a dissident shareholder in a small company can be used to bring pressure on a majority to accept the price he demands for his shares. Often the dispute is really only about the price to be paid for shares and the petition is used as a powerful negotiating tactic. At least in England pending the hearing, the company has to apply to the court for the validation of dispositions and the practice of banks, on being appraised of the position, is to freeze the company's bank accounts on the grounds that the court may very well order that the company be wound up, which would be deemed to have commenced on the day the petition was presented. In the case of small companies the burden of legal costs and expenditure of management time in defending these petitions can be crippling. Additionally, where the dispute results from a breakdown of relations between the shareholders, where it is better that one or some leave the company entirely and the dispute is really one about the price to be paid for the shares, a strong case can be made that the expensive section 205 procedure should not be used where the company's own articles of association contain a satisfactory and fair mechanism for dealing with the sale of the shares.[184] However, in *Re Murray Consultants Ltd.*,[185] the Supreme Court refused to dismiss, as an abuse of the process, a section 205 claim where the respondents (majority shareholders) offered to buy out the petitioner's shares at a price to be determined independently. O'Flaherty J. there dissented, observing that "while undoubtedly the citizen is entitled to full and free access to the courts, nonetheless, the courts have an obligation too, to provide for exit mechanisms from litigation so that people are not put to the burden of paying costs and expenses which are totally disproportionate to the end to be achieved."[186] Although Murphy J., for the majority, was sympathetic to this view, he concluded that once a *prima facie* case of oppression is stated in the pleadings, the case should not be struck out, reflecting the greater reluctance of Irish courts generally to strike out actions *in limine*.

---

183 *cf.* remarks of Hoffman J. in *Re A Company* [1986] B.C.L.C. 362 at 367; English Law Commission's paper, *Shareholders' Remedies* (1996).

184 *Re A Company (No. 004377 of 1986)* [1987] 1 W.L.R. 102 at 110; *Re a Company (No. 00330 of 1991) ex p. Holden* [1991] B.C.L.C. 597.

185 [1997] 3 I.R. 23, *sub. nom. Horgan v. Murray.*

186 *ibid.* at 30.

Locus Standi

10–77 Only a "member" can apply for an order under section 205 or petition for a winding up order under section 213 (g) on the basis of oppression. Ordinarily, a majority shareholder cannot seek relief under section 205 because his control of the company should empower him to rectify whatever loss he may be suffering.[187] The question arises whether persons other than those whose names are on the register of members can be members for the purposes of these provisions — such as transferees of shares whom the directors refuse to register as members. Gannon J. has held in an *ex tempore* judgment that, subject to the exceptions explained below, the petitioner must be on the register of members.[188] It appears that former members of the company lack *locus standi,* even where they complain about what was done when they were members. Section 205(6) provides that, where a member dies, an application for relief may be made by his personal representative and also by trustees of or any person beneficially interested in his shares under a will or intestacy. Accordingly, persons like the plaintiff in *Re Hafner*[189] could now complain, under section 205, that the refusal to register them as shareholders amounts to oppression. But this extended definition does not encompass the Official Assignee or a trustee in bankruptcy, or a receiver appointed over the shares.

Where the gravamen of the complaint would entitle a plaintiff to proceed with the case if he brought a "derivative suit", it remains to be seen whether a court would allow a petitioner under section 205 an indemnity in respect of his costs?[190]

Focus of Complaint

10–78 The focus of the complaint must be either the exercise of the directors' powers or the conduct of the company's affairs. For instance, it was held not to cover the sale of shares in a football club's holding company rather than offering them first to the aggrieved minority shareholder.[191] In what perhaps is the leading British case, *Scottish Co-op Wholesale Society v. Meyer,*[192] it was held that studied inaction by the majority directors, who were in a position of conflict of interests and when the company was facing financial disaster, can be caught by sec-

---

[187] *Re Baltic Estate Ltd. (No. 2)* [1993] B.C.L.C. 503.

[188] *O'Tuama v. Allied Metropole Hotel Ltd* December 19, 1988, noted [1989] in Ir. L. Gaz. 195 (McCann).

[189] [1943] I.R. 426; see above, para. 9–37.

[190] *cf. Wallersteiner v. Moir (No. 2)* [1975] Q.B. 373; above, para. 10–71.

[191] *Re Leeds United Holdings p.l.c.* [1996] 2 B.C.L.C. 503.

[192] [1959] A.C. 324; see below, para. 14–45.

tion 205.[193] As for the "affairs of the company are being conducted", it used to be the view that use of the term "are being" in this context means that the complaint must be against some course of conduct rather than a single act, and that the conduct objected to must be taking place up to the time the application was made.[194] But in *Re Westwinds Holding Co.*[195] it was held that a single instance can come within the terms of section 205. Additionally, the fact that a complaint would have succeeded if it were brought under the general common law grounds, such as in a "derivative" claim, does not preclude consideration of it under section 205.

Oppressive or Disregarding Interests

10–79 What must be shown is that the directors' actions or the company's activities are either "oppressive to" the applicant or "disregard . . . his or their interests" as members. It should be noted that the term used is not contravening "rights" of a member but impairing "interests" as such, which broadens the inquiry considerably. What precisely is meant by an interest in this context has not been defined, but the recent cases tend to treat it as some form of "legitimate expectation", arising from membership, that certain action either will be taken or will not be taken.[196] Although section 205 may not provide a forum for resolving disputes between the company and a member-director or member-creditor, regarding claims *qua* director or creditor, circumstances can arise where those very claims are a part of their interests as members. For instance, in *Re Murph's Restaurants Ltd. (No. 2)*[197] where three shareholders started up a company on the clear understanding that each of them were to participate equally in its management and profits, there was oppression where one of them, for no good reason, was dismissed from the board and from employment with the company. There, the excluded member's legitimate expectations to be involved in running the business and participating in profits via directors' remuneration was held to be unfairly frustrated.[198]

10–80 The word oppression has been defined as "burdensome, harsh

---

[193] *cf. Nicholas v. Soundcraft Electronics Ltd.* [1993] B.C.L.C. 360.
[194] *Re Jermyn St. Turkish Baths Ltd.* [1971] 1 W.L.R. 1042.
[195] Kenny J., May 21, 1974.
[196] cf. *Re Astec* (BSR) p.l.c. [1998] 2 B.C.L.C. 556 at 584—590.
[197] Gannon J., July 31, 1979, Cases p. 476; see below paras 10–96—10–97.
[198] Similarly, *Re Ghyll Beck Driving Range Ltd.* [1993] B.C.L.C. 1126; *R. & H. Electrical Ltd. v. Hayden Bill Electrical Ltd.* [1995] 2 B.C.L.C. and *Quinlan v. Essex Hinge Co.* [1996] 2 B.C.L.C. 417; *cf. Re Tottenham Hotspur p.l.c.* [1994] 1 B.C.L.C. 655.

and wrongful";[199] it is something akin to unconscionable. Disregarding interests must involve doing so most unfairly or without justification, which is much the same thing. An almost intolerable situation would arise if perfectly reasonable and understandable disregard of interests fell foul of section 205. However, unlike the comparable present British provisions, section 205 is not expressly conditioned on the conduct in question being "unfairly prejudicial". Accordingly, circumstances might arise where the petitioner is not being distinctly prejudiced but, nevertheless, his interests are being disregarded to such extent as warrants redress under section 205. In nearly all cases, however, the court would insist on the petitioner's position being unfairly prejudiced. Even in Britain, it is not essential to demonstrate that the directors' or the company's intention was to oppress or to prejudice; the test is an objective one. In applications under section 205 the court has insisted on "looking at the business realities of the situation" as opposed to the "narrow legalistic view".[200] Whether a petitioner has made out grounds for court intervention depends very much on the circumstances of the case.

10–81 As was said in *Re Sam Weller & Sons Ltd.*,[201] regarding section 459 of the English 1985 Act,

> "The word 'interests' is wider than a term such as 'rights' and its presence as part of the test . . . suggests that Parliament recognised that members may have different interests, even if their rights as members are the same. Further, the adverb 'unfairly' introduces the wide concept of fairness in relation to the prejudice of the interest of some part of the members that must be established . . . [I]t is possible that even if all the members are prejudiced by the conduct complained of, the interests of some only may be unfairly prejudiced . . .
>
> [T]he wording of the section imports an objective test. One simply looks to see whether the manner in which the affairs of the company have been conducted can be described as 'unfairly prejudicial to the interests of some part of the members'. That . . . requires an objective assessment of the quality of the conduct. Thus, conduct which is 'unfairly prejudicial' to the petitioner's interests, even if not intended to be so, may nevertheless come within the section."[202]

This case was an application to strike out a claim of oppression on the grounds that the facts alleged did not disclose any cause of action under this heading. The petitioners, who held a substantial majority stake

---

199 *Scottish Co-op Case* [1959] A.C. at 24; but "wrongful" does not mean unlawful in itself apart entirely from s.205.
200 *ibid.* at 343.
201 [1990] 1 Ch. 683.
202 *ibid.* at 690.

in a prosperous family company, alleged oppression principally because for many years past a derisory dividend was paid, even though the company had abundant reserves and cash to pay much higher dividends. The company would not disclose what remuneration its directors were being paid and it refused to register transfers of shares which the petitioners had inherited, thereby locking them into the company. It was held that, in appropriate circumstances, these facts could amount to oppression or unfairly prejudicial conduct. Section 205 is applicable to cases of serious mis-management, as compared with differences of view about the appropriate commercial desision.[203] But it does not provide redress where the majority keep the company in business when it had substantial assets but was trading poorly and perhaps a reasonable board of directors would have wound up the company and distribute its assets.[204] The courts do not second guess management by judging the business merits of a particular decision with the benefit of hindsight.

10–82 Perhaps the most far-reaching of the Irish cases is *Re Williams Group Tullamore Ltd.*[205] which illustrates the liberal interpretation given to section 205. The case concerned a major and very successful private company, the share structure of which had been reorganised in the 1970s to take into account the different forms of family involvement in the company. Because only some members of the family were involved in the management, it was decided to create and to issue to those members preference shares, which were to carry non-cumulative dividend rights of 8 per cent, be entitled to priority when repaying capital on a liquidation and, most significantly, carried the sole right to attend and to vote at general meetings. For as long as these shares were in existence the ordinary shareholders could not participate in the company's general meetings. The focus of the petition was a decision by the company (in effect made by the preference shareholders only) to pay a very substantial dividend (£267,080 in aggregate) of £1 per share to every one of the company's shareholders. This course of conduct was adopted because it was felt that, on account of the huge inflation since the capital reorganisation, the preference shareholders, who managed the company so successfully, ought in all fairness to be paid something more than their fixed 8 per cent per annum. Because almost certainly there would be considerable objection if all of the funds available for distribution were paid to the preference shareholders only, it was decided that the money should be paid to every shareholder on a pro

[203] *Re Macro (Ispwich) Ltd.* [1994] 2 B.C.L.C. 354.
[204] *Re Saul D. Harrison & Sons p.l.c.* [1995] 1 B.C.L.C. 14.
[205] [1985] I.R. 613.

rata basis. Some ordinary shareholders claimed that even this scheme disregarded their interests as members.

10–83 Barrington J. found that the share structure as established in the 1970s was one that contemplated "that the ordinary shareholders would take the greater risks and would, in the event of the company being successful, reap the greater rewards."[206] The money it was proposed to pay the preference shareholders could have been used, for example, to reduce borrowings or for some other purpose of which the ordinary shareholders approved. If the proposed distribution would give the company a distinct advantage, for instance regarding taxation, a court might take a different view of it. But it was held that the only real beneficiaries of the scheme proposed here were the preference shareholders. Consequently, it was "contrary to the interests of the ordinary shareholders", it disregarded their interests and, if the company persisted in implementing the scheme, it would be oppressive to them. The argument does not seem to have been made that it was within the preference shareholders' power not to pay any dividends whatsoever to the ordinary shareholders and that the latter could not change the company's articles of association in order to deprive the former of that power — presumably because it is likely that such action of itself would be regarded as oppressive in the circumstances. The facts of the other leading Irish cases on this section, the *Murph's Restaurants* case,[207] the *Greenore Trading* case[208] and the *Clubman Shirts* case[209] and of the seminal *Scottish Co-op* case,[210] are considered briefly elsewhere.

10–84 The boundaries of section 205 are not confined to what may be called the matters of constitutional propriety. Arrangements or understandings between parties, albeit not incorporated in the memorandum or articles of association, ordinarily will be upheld, in the sense that a remedy will be provided where those arrangements are flouted without good justification. The central question is the fairness and reasonableness of the impugned conduct in all the circumstances of the case. For instance, while ordinarily courts will not interfere with decisions regarding the payment of dividends or making a rights issue, provided the legislation and the articles are complied with, exceptional circumstances. however, may warrant judicial intervention.[211] Many

---

206 [1985] I.R. 613 at 621.

207 See below, paras 10–96—10-97.

208 *Re Greenore Trading Co.* [1980] I.L.R.M. 94; see above, para. 7–90.

209 *Re Clubman Shirts Ltd.* [1983] I.L.R.M. 323; see above, para. 9–20.

210 [1959] A.C. 324; see below, para. 14–45.

211 *e.g. Re Sam Weller & Sons Ltd.* [1990] 1 Ch. 682 (dividends); *Re A Company, ex p. Harries* [1989] B.C.L.C. 383 (share allotment).

of the reported cases involve excluding the petitioner from managing the company.[212] So far, there has been no leading case where use of the veto that boards of private companies commonly have over the transfer of shares has been held to be oppressive or unfair.[213] It is not necessary to establish a good case that the conduct complained of adversely affected the value of the petitioner's shares. In some cases the relationship between the members of what in effect is an incorporated partnership will simply break down, without any one really being at fault. An inevitable result may be that it is in the interests of all involved that one or more of the members should sever their relationships at a fair price rather than allow matters to continue, probably leading eventually to the company being wound up on just and equitable grounds.

Remedies

10–82 The remedies available under section 205(3) when the court is of the opinion that the petitioner was oppressed are

> "with a view to bringing an end to the matters complained of, [to] make such order as it thinks fit, whether directing or prohibiting any act or cancelling or varying any transaction or for regulating the conduct of the company's affairs in future, or for the purchase of the shares of any members . . ."

In many instances the court orders that the oppressed member's shares be bought out, either by the oppressors or by the company, at a fair price. At times, as in *Re Greenore Trading Co.*,[214] an element is built into the price to compensate for losses that the oppressed member previously suffered. Indeed, the court could even order the oppressors to sell their shares to those who were being oppressed; but an order of this nature would be made only in very unusual circumstances.[215] The court even has power to order a person who is no longer a member of the company to purchase the petitioner's shares.[216] But it has no jurisdiction to award damages or compensation *per se*.[217]

---

[212] *e.g.* the *Murph's Restaurants* case, below, paras 10–94—10–95, *R.A. Noble (Clothing) Ltd.* [1983] B.C.L.C. 273; *Re A Company (No. 004377 of 1986)* [1987] 1 W.L.R. 102; *Re A Company ex p. Schwarcz* [1989] B.C.L.C. 427; *Re Elgindata Ltd.* [1991] B.C.L.C. at 1006–1008.

[213] *cf. Thomas v. H.W. Thomas Ltd.* [1984] 1 N.Z.L.R. 686.

[214] [1980] I.L.R.M. 94.

[215] *Vujnovich v. Vujnovich* [1988] 2 N.Z.L.R. 129 at 152. *cf. Re a Company (No. 00789 of 1987) ex p. Shooter (No.2)* [1991] B.C.L.R. 267 and *Re Brentfield Squash Racquettes Club Ltd.* [1996] 2 B.C.L.C. 184.

[216] *Re A Company (No. 005287 of 1985)* [1986] 1 W.L.R. 281; *Re Little Olympian Each-Ways Ltd.* [1994] 2 B.C.L.C. 420.

[217] *Irish Press p.l.c. v. Ingersoll Publications Ltd.* [1995] 2 I.R. 175.

The Purchase Price

10–86 Where a minority stake in a private company is being sold the shares are usually valued at a discount in the sense that, *pro rata*, a substantially higher price would be paid for shares comprising a majority holding.[218] A very important matter, therefore, is whether, when ordering that the petitioner's shares be purchased and they are a minority holding, there should be a discount for that reason? Alternatively, if the majority shareholders are ordered to sell their shares to the petitioner, should the majority be paid the premium they almost certainly would obtain in a free sale on the open market? In *Re Bird Precision Bellows Ltd.*[219] it was held that it depends on the entire circumstances of a case whether or not the minority shareholding should be made subject to a discount. The court rejected the contention that, when the court orders the purchase of shares, the price must be the normal market price as determined by ordinary valuation principles. According to Oliver L.J., "the whole framework of the section . . . is to confer on the court a very wide discretion to do what is fair and equitable in all the circumstances of the case, in order to put right and cure for the future the unfair prejudice which the petitioner has suffered at the hands of the other shareholders."[220] These views were endorsed by O'Hanlon J. in *Re Clubman Shirts Ltd.*[221] where the company's shares were first valued by an accountant who had been appointed by the court for that purpose.

Winding Up

10–87 Section 213 (g) of the 1963 Act empowers the court to wind up a company where a winding up petition was presented and the court is satisfied that the petitioner was oppressed or his interests as a member were disregarded. Where an aggrieved shareholder chooses this drastic mode of redress, he usually will seek to have the company also wound up on "just and equitable grounds", as explained next below. However, where a member seeks a winding up order under section 213(g) on account of oppression, even though he establishes his case the court may dismiss the petition if it concludes that seeking another remedy under section 205 is a more appropriate solution in the cir-

---

[218] *Dean v. Prince* [1954] Ch. 409; *Re Castleburn Ltd.* [1991] B.C.L.C. 89.

[219] [1986] 1 Ch. 658.

[220] *ibid.* at 669. *cf. Re Elgindata Ltd.* [1991] B.C.L.C. at 1006–1008 and *Re A Company (no. 00709 of 1992)* [1997] 2 B.C.L.C. 739.

[221] [1991] I.L.R.M. 43.

cumstances.[222] It therefore would be only in the most serious cases of oppression that the company will be wound up. For instance, in *Re Murph's Restaurants (No.2) Ltd.*,[223] it was held that, because of the total breakdown in the relationship between the three original partners, any attempt to remedy their dispute under section 205 would have been inappropriate.

Interim Relief

10–88 Section 205 contains no express authority to grant interim relief. It has been held in England that interim relief cannot be given because, under the relevant section there, the court must "be satisfied" that there was oppression before it can make any order.[224] Under section 205(3) of the 1963 Act, the prerequisite is that the court "is of the opinion" that there was oppression or disregard of interests, which may distinguish that case. In any event, interlocutory injunctions preserving the status quo can be obtained in an appropriate case.[225] And if the aggrieved shareholder chooses the winding up option, a provisional liquidator will be appointed in an appropriate case.[226]

WINDING UP ON JUST AND EQUITABLE GROUNDS

10–89 Ever since 1848, the courts have been empowered to order that a company be wound up on "just and equitable grounds".[227] For many years the courts adopted a restrictive interpretation of what is now section 213(f) of the 1963 Act. But in *Re Newbridge Steam Laundry Ltd.*[228] it was held that the phrase just and equitable "ought not to be construed in this restrictive way, but that in all cases which cannot be brought under the preceding clauses [of section 213], but where, having regard to the established principles of courts of equity, justice and equity require a company to be wound up, an order for its winding up ought to be made."[229] That case was the sequel to the *Cockburn* case,[230] where it was held that the managing director of the same company had acted unlawfully in taking £3,000 for laundry work done by the

---

[222] Proviso to s.213(g).
[223] Gannon J., July 31, 1971, Cases p. 476; see below paras 10–96—10–97..
[224] *Re A Company (No. 004175 of 1986)* [1987] 1 W.L.R. 585.
[225] *e.g. McGilligan v. O'Grady* [1999] 1 I.L.R.M. 303, but such an order was refused in *Feighery v. Feighery*, Laffoy J., February 25, 1998.
[226] 1963 Act, s.226; see below, para. 18–33.
[227] Companies Act 1848, s.5(8).
[228] [1917] 1 I.R. 67.
[229] *ibid.* at 90.
[230] *Cockburn v. Newbridge Steam Laundry Co.* [1915] 1 I.R. 237; see above, para. 5–125.

company for the military authorities but paying only £1,000 of that over to the company.

10–90 Although the court has a broad discretion to order that a company be wound up under section 213(f), it is far from a completely free discretion; its exercise must be founded on reasoning which can be examined and justified. The principal factor limiting the availability of this ground for winding up is the existence of an alternative mode of liquidation in the form of voluntary winding up.[231] Whether or not the company should go into liquidation has always been treated as a matter of domestic policy which the members are entitled to determine, but it is not sufficient to show that a simple majority of members favour liquidation (unless the company is insolvent). Otherwise a resolution for voluntary winding up must be passed by a majority of threequarters of those entitled to vote,[232] and it follows that an order for compulsory winding up will only be made where the circumstances are so exceptional as to justify the court in disregarding that statutory requirement. Analysis of the authorities suggests that there are only five situations in which those circumstances exist; these are as follows:

(1) where the company was fraudulent in its inception;[233]

(2) where it becomes impossible for the company to achieve its main objects;[234]

(3) where the company is unable to carry on business, for instance because there is complete deadlock between the members;[235]

(4) where control or management of the company's affairs is characterised by fraud, misconduct, or oppression; and

(5) where the company is substantially a domestic company, in the nature of a partnership, whose members are unable to co-operate in the conduct of its affairs.

10–91 Because of its drastic consequences, a compulsory winding up is a significant deterrent against majorities over-reaching themselves. Yet the winding up procedure itself is slow and expensive, and the aggrieved shareholder may ultimately get far less than his shares are

---

[231] See below, paras 18–03—18-08.
[232] 1963 Act, s.251.
[233] *cf. Princess of Reuss v. Bos* (1871) L.R. 5 H.L. 176.
[234] *Re German Date Coffe Co.* (1882) 20 Ch.D. 169. *cf. Re Dublin & Eastern Regional Tourism Organisation Ltd.* [1990] 1 I.R. 579.
[235] *e.g. Re Yenidie Tobacco Co.* [1916] 2 Ch. 426; *Re Vehicle Buildings & Insulations Ltd.* [1986] I.L.R.M. 239.

really worth when the company's business is disposed of in a forced sale. Indeed, up to 1990 there was the danger of the liquidator disposing of the undertaking at a bargain price to the oppressors themselves.[236]

Fraud and Misconduct

10–92 That the winding up jurisdiction will be invoked against truly oppressive, as compared with manifestly unlawful, conduct was confirmed in *Loch v. John Blackwood Ltd.*[237] This was a private family company and its managing director held the majority of the shares. The minority petitioned to have it wound up, claiming that the directors never held general meetings nor submitted annual accounts, that they never recommended dividends and, by keeping the petitioners in ignorance, hoped to acquire their shares for a small consideration. It was held that, if these claims could be substantiated, the court would have jurisdiction to order that the company be wound up. The basis of the law was summed by Lord Shaw:

> "It is undoubtedly true that at the foundation of applications for winding up on the 'just and equitable' rule, there must lie a justifiable lack of confidence in the conduct and management of the company's affairs. But this lack of confidence must be grounded on conduct of the directors, not in regard to their private life or affairs, but in regard to the company's business. Furthermore, the lack of confidence must spring not from dissatisfaction at being outvoted on the business affairs or on what is called the domestic policy, of the company. On the other hand, wherever the lack of confidence is rested on a lack of probity in the conduct of the company's affairs, then the former is justified by the latter and it is, under the statute, just and equitable that the company be wound up."[238]

The *Newbridge Laundry* case[239] was one of the earliest applications of this principle, involving breach of directors' duties and fraud on the company. But where the focus of dispute may be described as "domestic policy", it must be demonstrated that the directors' powers have been exercised in a flagrantly improper manner before winding up will be directed; for instance, in the matters concerning the registration of share transfers,[240] the declaration of dividends and placing profits in reserve. The precise boundaries of the "misconduct-oppression" heading remain to be determined.

---

[236] 1990 Act, s.124, amending 1963 Act, s.231.
[237] [1924] A.C. 783.
[238] *ibid.* at 788.
[239] [1917] 1 I.R. 67.
[240] *Charles Forte Investment Ltd. v. Amanda* [1964] Ch. 240.

Partnership Analogy

10–93 Special considerations arise, however, where the company is what may be described as an incorporated partnership.[241] By that is meant where a relatively small number of persons form a company with the understanding that there will be a close personal business relationship between them, often involving equal participation in the management and profits of the business, and where the articles made it difficult for any of them to freely dispose of his shareholding. Generally, a winding up order will be made if a shareholder demonstrates that the company has disregarded his rights and legitimate expectations, even where the company acts entirely consistently with the legislation and its own articles of association.

10–94 The leading authority, where the criteria under which the court will wind up ordinary partnerships[242] was applied to registered companies, is *Re Westbourne Galleries Ltd.*[243] The petitioner and his partner for many years incorporated their business, each holding equal shares. When the partner brought his son into the business, the petitioner became a minority shareholder. Both were executive directors. Substantial profits were earned, all of which were distributed by way of directors' remuneration; dividends were never paid. Having acted on that basis for ten years, a disagreement arose between the petitioner and the other two members and directors. As a result, they removed him from the company's board and dismissed him from his employment with the company. It was held that, in these circumstances, he was entitled to an order that the company be wound up.

10–95 Three major principles were laid down or confirmed there. This section is not confined to circumstances that affect the petitioner *qua* member; while the petitioner must be a member, there "is no reason for preventing him from relying upon any circumstances of justice or equity which affect him in his relations with the company, or . . . with the other shareholders."[244] Therefore, prejudicing the petitioner *qua* director or creditor or employee of the company is not by definition excluded from consideration under section 213(f). Secondly, the fact that what is being complained of is perfectly consistent with the company's own regulations does not invariably justify it; "[a]cts which,

---

[241] See generally, Prentice, "Winding Up on the just and Equitable Ground: the Partnership Analogy" (1973) 89 L.Q.R. 107 and Chesterman, "The just and Equitable Winding Up of Small Private Companies" (1973) 36 Mod. L. Rev. 129.
[242] Partnership Act 1890, s.35(f).
[243] [1973] A.C. 360.
[244] *ibid.* at 375.

in law, are a valid exercise of powers conferred by the articles may nevertheless be entirely outside what can fairly by regarded as having been in the contemplation of the parties when they became members of the company; and in such cases the fact that what had been done is not in excess of powers will not necessarily be an answer to a claim for winding up."[245] Finally, as for the criterion against which cases under section 213(f) are to be judged, Lord Wilberforce's words defy paraphrase:

> "The foundation . . . lies in the words 'just and equitable' . . . [These] are a recognition of the fact that a limited company is more than a mere legal entity, with a personality in law of its own: that there is room in company law for recognition of the fact that behind it, or amongst it, there are individuals, with rights, expectations and obligations inter se which are not necessarily submerged in the company structure. That structure is defined by the Companies Act and by the articles of association by which shareholders agree to be bound. In most companies and in most contexts, this definition is sufficient and exhaustive, equally so whether the company is large or small. The just and equitable provision does . . . not entitle one party to disregard the obligation he assumed by entering a company, nor the court to dispense him from it. It does, as equity always does, enable the court to subject the exercise of legal rights to equitable considerations; considerations, that is, of a personal character arising between one individual and another, which may make it unjust, or inequitable, to insist on legal rights, or to exercise them in a particular way.
>
> It would be impossible, and wholly undesirable, to define the circumstances in which these considerations may arise. Certainly the fact that a company is a small one, or a private company, is not enough. There are very many of these where the association is a purely commercial one, of which it can safely be said that the basis of association is adequately and exhaustively laid down in the articles. The superimposition of equitable considerations requires something more, which typically may include one, or probably more, of the following elements: (i) an association formed or continued on the basis of a personal relationship, involving mutual confidence-this element will often be found where a pre-existing partnership has been converted into a limited company; (ii) an agreement, or understanding, that all, or some (for there may be sleeping members), of the shareholders shall participate in the conduct of the business; (iii) restriction upon the transfer of the members' interest in the company-so that if confidence is lost, or one member is removed from management, he cannot take out his stake and go elsewhere."[246]

---

[245] [1973] A.C. 360 at 378.

[246] [1973] A.C. 360 at 377. The various matters referred to here must be alleged in the petition: *Re a Company (No. 00314 of 1989), ex p. Estate Acquisition & Development Ltd.* [1991] B.C.L.C. 154.

10–96 Accordingly, circumstances which would not justify winding up a non-"domestic" company may warrant intervention in the affairs of an incorporated partnership. Questions arising in companies with a significant number of members, which are subject to the majority rule principle, therefore assume a different aspect in incorporated partnerships, where the aggrieved member cannot easily exit from the company, especially when he is dependent on it for his livelihood.[247] An extreme example is *Re Murph's Restaurants Ltd. (No.2)*[248] concerning a successful restaurant enterprise which had grown very rapidly, and had three shareholders who were also its directors, BS., K. and M. The latter two were brothers and had worked full-time for the company since its foundation in 1972, whereas BS., the petitioner, in 1977 gave up a promising career in the computer business in order to work for the company full-time. No annual meetings were ever held, no annual accounts were prepared, and board meetings were most informal. Dividends and directors fees as such were never paid. Instead, drawings were made by the directors against projected earnings; there was an informal arrangement by which each could take about £200 a month "slush money" from cash, and on various occasions sums were transferred into accounts in building societies in the names of one or other of the directors. Special care was taken to ensure that each shared these disbursements equally. In 1977 they agreed to enter the property market, and they bid, unsuccessfully, for a hotel. But in the following year K. and M. bought that property on their own behalf. In the meantime, BS. had gone to Cork to run the very successful branch there. In early 1979 K. and M. agreed that BS. should be removed from the board and be no longer employed by the company. While BS.'s management of the Cork branch was criticised by K. and M., it was the profits from it that, in the form of a loan from the company, financed K. and M.'s hotel purchase; and BS. did not agree with various aspects of the loan.

10–97 Gannon J. characterised the entire enterprise as one where BS., K. and M. "were equal partners in a joint venture, and the company was no more than a vehicle to secure a limited liability for possible losses and to provide a means of earning and distributing profits to their best advantage with minimum disclosure." The "strict equity" of their participation in the profits of a company that was run in such an informal and irregular nature "was achieved, and could be achieved, only by a relationship of mutual confidence and trust and active open participation in the management and conduct of the affairs of the com-

---

[247] *Tay Bok Choon v. Tahanson Sein. Bhd.* [1987] 1 W.L.R. 413; *cf. Re Burgess Homes Ltd.* [1987] 1 N.Z.L.R. 513.

[248] Gannon J., July 31, 1979; Cases p. 476.

pany . . . " The evidence showed that "[w]hatever cause of complaint or fault K. and M. may have found in BS. it did not relate to the talents or qualifications which he had shown, and must have been known to them to have had, at a time when he was induced to join with them in a venture of strictly drawn equality." Therefore, K. and M.'s attempt to treat BS. as a mere employee and to exclude him from further participation in the company, as well as being "entirely irregular", was "a deliberate and calculated repudiation by both of them of that relationship of equality, mutuality, trust and confidence between the three of them which constituted the very essence of the existence of the company. The action of K. and M . . . deprived BS. of a livelihood, and not simply of an investment, which he was induced by their representations to take and in so doing to abandon to his irretrievable loss a [promising] career . . . " Not alone was the petitioner unlawfully oppressed but he was entitled to an order that the company be wound up.

Oppression and the relationship with section 205

10–98 The Companies Acts contain no provision to the effect that, even though the basis for a winding up order under section 213(f) has been established, the court should not liquidate the company if some other remedy is available to the petitioners and they are being unreasonable in not pursuing that other remedy.[249] On account of the discretionary nature of the jurisdiction here, a court might nevertheless refuse to order a winding up in those circumstances. However, a strong case could be made against that view, based on the absence of express provision to this end, combined with the choice which section 213(g) gives the court in an application to have the company wound up for oppression or disregard of the petitioner's interests.

[249] *e.g.* s.125(2) of the U.K. Companies Act 1985; *Re A Company (No. 002567 of 1982)* [1983] 1 W.L.R. 927. *cf. Virdi v. Abbey Leisure Ltd.* [1990] B.C.L.C. 342.

11

Fundamental Structural Changes

11–01 The system laid down in the Companies Acts for the governance of companies can be divided into four distinct tiers. The board, which ordinarily runs the business, is subject to the *de facto* control of a simple majority of the shareholders, who have the power to remove directors by an ordinary resolution.[1] Most provisions of a company's regulations can be altered by special majorities of the members in that the articles of association can be changed by special resolution.[2] But certain vital changes in the nature of companies cannot be made unless they are approved of by super-majorities of the members and either are not vetoed by or are endorsed by the court: notably, altering the objects clause, reducing or repaying capital, varying class rights and making an arrangement under section 201 of the 1963 Act. In dealing with most of these matters, the Companies Acts override or modify any special voting rights and disabilities that may exist under the company's own regulations and wholly or partly enfranchise shareholders to the extent of their shares' nominal values. Thus, a section 201 arrangement must be approved by a majority representing 75 per cent in value of those members of each class affected by it who vote on the proposal.[3] Similarly, the holders of not less than 15 per cent in nominal value of the company's issued share capital or any class of shares or debentures may apply to the court to veto a change in the company's objects.[4] And the holders of not less than 10 per cent of the issued shares of the class in question can apply to the court to have an agreed variation of class rights blocked.[5] The Companies Acts also empower the court, when approving some of these changes, to order appraisal for dissenting shareholders, *i.e.* order that their shares be bought out at an

---

1 1963 Act, s.182; see below, paras 5–38 *et seq*.
2 *ibid.*, s.15; see below, paras 11–05 *et seq*.
3 *ibid.*, s.201(3).
4 *ibid.*, s.10(3).
5 *ibid.*, s.78(1) and 1983 Act, s.38(2).

objectively determined price.[6] The fourth tier in the statutory system of governance is provided for in sections 9 and 28 of the 1963 Act, which permits matters to be "entrenched" in the memorandum of association so that they can be altered only in some special way, or indeed, be unalterable.

CONSTITUTIONAL CHANGES: ALTERING THE MEMORANDUM AND ARTICLES OF ASSOCIATION

11–02 A company's constitution or regulations, *i.e.* its memorandum and articles of association, may be altered by its members. The Companies Acts forbid inclusion of certain provisions in a company's regulations — such as clauses purporting to exonerate directors from liability for egregious breaches of duty to the company.[7] In addition, the power given by sections 9 and 15 of the 1963 Act to alter the memorandum and articles of association is subject to the broad equitable constraint, that it must not be exercised *mala fide* or in an unfairly discriminatory manner.

Memorandum of Association

11–03 It is stipulated in section 9 of the 1963 Act that the memorandum of association can be changed. This power to amend is put negatively; the memorandum "may not [be] alter[ed] . . . except in the cases, in the mode and to the extent for which express provision is made" in the Acts. Thus, in order to reduce share capital in any way, the articles must permit this and there must be a special resolution authorising the reduction, which must be confirmed by the court.[8] The objects clause may be changed by special resolution but dissenters, if they make up at least 15 per cent of the shareholders or of any "class" of shareholder, or of debenture-holders, may apply to the court to have any such change cancelled.[9]

11–04 Where there is a provision in the memorandum that could lawfully be contained in the articles, it can be altered by special resolution in the absence of a stipulation to the contrary or interference with "class rights", or increasing a member's liability as a shareholder.[10] But an

---

[6] 1963 Act, s.10(6) (change of objects), s.203(1)(e) (arrangements under s.201), s.260(3) (restructuring under s.260) and 1983 Act, s.15(7) (going private).

[7] 1963 Act, s.200; see above, paras 5–171 *et seq.*

[8] *ibid.*, ss.72-77; see below, paras 11–34 *et seq.*

[9] *ibid.*, s.10; see below, paras 11–13 *et seq.*

[10] *ibid.*, s.28(1), (3)

application can be made to the court to cancel any such change and the procedure for dealing with objections of this nature is the same as for contesting resolutions changing the objects clause.[11] Any proposed change of this nature in the memorandum is not permitted to take effect until it has been confirmed by the court.[12] Special provision is made for "entrenched" clauses[13] and for "class rights"[14] in the memorandum.

Articles of Association

11–05 Any clause that could lawfully have been contained in the original articles may subsequently be inserted in them by amendment. A company's power to change its articles by special resolution is stated in the most unequivocal terms in section 15 of the 1963 Act. The scope of this power is well illustrated by *Allen* v. *Gold Reefs of West Africa Ltd.*,[15] where the company sought to change its articles so as to enable it in effect to confiscate the shares of any member indebted to it. It was held that, once the requisite majority is not acting in bad faith, even an alteration as drastic as this is permissible. The circumstances in which a special resolution to alter the articles will be declared to be invalid are considered in Chapter 10 under the heading "breach of faith and unfair discrimination".[16]

11–06 Where the amendment sets up a conflict between the interests of the company as a commercial entity and the objecting shareholder, the primary test of validity is that used in the *Allen* case, *i.e.* whether it was adopted "bona fide for the benefit of the company as a whole".[17] It is for the objector to demonstrate that those who voted for the change were motivated by some improper purpose. Since, however, *mala fides* can be very difficult to prove, in an appropriate case bad faith may be inferred from the nature of the change being made and the surrounding circumstances, as is exemplified in two of the "expulsion" cases.[18] As was observed in a case concerning altering a clause that affected the tenure of directors, "[t]he alteration may be so oppressive as to cast suspicion on the honesty of the persons responsible for it, or so extravagant that no reasonable man could really consider it for the ben-

---

[11] 1963 Act, s.28(3) and see below, para. 11–15.
[12] *ibid.*, s.28(2).
[13] *ibid.*, ss. 28(3), 10(3)–(10).
[14] See below, para. 11–12 *et seq.*
[15] [1900] Ch. 656.
[16] See above, paras 10–23 *et seq.* See generally, Rixon, "Competing Interests and Conflicting Principles: An Examination of the Power of Alteration of Articles of Association" (1986) 49 Mod. L. Rev. 446.
[17] *Gold Reefs* case [1900] 1 Ch. 656 at 671.
[18] *e.g. Dafen Tinplate Co. v. Llanelly Steel Co.* [1920] 2 Ch. 124; see above, para. 10–41.

efit of the company."[19] Where the change being made affects the rights and liabilities of the shareholders *inter se*, the primary test of validity is that of unfair discrimination articulated in *Greenhalgh* v. *Arderne Cinemas Ltd.*,[20] *i.e.* did it "discriminate between the majority shareholders and the minority shareholders, so as to give to the former an advantage of which the latter were deprived?"[21] For instance, in one Australian case[22] a change which curtailed the voting rights of one group of members was condemned on those grounds. More recently a change which would allow 90 per cent of the shareholders to forcibly buy out the minority was also condemned on similar grounds.[23]

11–07 Where objectors under section 205 of the 1963 Act, seek to challenge an alteration claiming that it is oppressive or it unfairly prejudices them, presumably the same general approach is followed as in *Allen* and in *Greenhalgh*. It is possible, however, that some changes which would pass the tests laid down in those cases might still be regarded as amounting to oppression, given the petitioner's exceptional circumstances. But it would not follow that the change is unlawful. If it was passed bona fide for the company's benefit and does not unfairly discriminate, most likely the new article would be allowed to stand, subject to special arrangements being made to redress any prejudice which would have fallen on the section 205 petitioner.

Agreement Not to Alter the Regulations

11–08 Leaving aside where the clause being changed is entrenched in the company's memorandum of association or that change abrogates class rights, to what extent is a company's statutory discretion to amend its articles in any way mandatory and incapable of being contracted out of? A variant of this question called for decision in *Russell* v. *Northern Bank Development Corp.*,[24] which concerned the statutory discretion to increase a company's capital in whatever manner is envisaged by the articles of association. Following the reconstruction of their businesses, the four managers/shareholders of the company entered into a shareholders' agreement that forbade any increase in capital without the assent of all of them. When three of them, notwith- standing, proposed a resolution to have the capital increased, the plaintiff sought an injunction restraining them. Insofar as that agreement was a contract

---

[19] *Shuttleworth v. Cox Brothers & Co. (Maidenhead)* [1927] 2 K.B. 9 at 18.
[20] [1951] Ch. 286; see above, paras 10–29 *et seq*.
[21] *ibid.* at 291.
[22] *Peters' American Delicacy Co. v. Heath* (1938–9) 61 C.L.R. 512.
[23] *Gambotto v. WCP Ltd.* (1994) 182 C.L.R. 432.
[24] [1992] 1 W.L.R. 588.

between the four individuals, it was held that it simply created personal obligations between them "dehors the . . . or collateral to" the company's articles, "neither in substitution for nor in conflict with" them.[25] Accordingly, any effort by some of those four to increase the share capital would be a breach of contract on their part. The same logic would apply to a stipulation in a shareholders' agreement not to change the articles of association. It is debatable, however, whether the court would enjoin breach of contract between the company itself and a third party not to affect such a charge.[26] But it has been held that damages can be awarded against a company which acts on such a charge being made, contrary to what it had agreed with a third party.[27]

11–09 In the *Russell* case, somewhat unusually the company itself also was a party to the shareholders' agreement. Insofar as that agreement purported to prevent the company from exercising its statutory discretions, it was held that "such an undertaking [was] as obnoxious as if it had been contained in the articles of association and therefore is unenforceable."[28] Whether this statement was part of the *ratio decidendi* or was *obiter* has been questioned[29] and the assertion that a stipulation of that nature is entirely void and without legal effect has been the subject of critism.[30] It has been pointed out that the position is complex and depends *inter alia* on whether the stipulation in the contract had the assent of all the members at the time and what the company was to receive in return for it.

11–10 The picture regarding contracts of this nature was explained in the *Cumbrian Newspapers Ltd.* case as follows:

> "Firstly. . . a company cannot, by contract, deprive its members of their rights to alter the articles by special resolution.
>
> Secondly, if a company does contract that its articles will not be altered, none the less its members are entitled to requisition a meeting and pass a special resolution altering the articles.
>
> Thirdly, if the articles are validly altered, the company cannot be prevented from acting on the altered articles, even though so to act may involve it in breach of contract. . . .

---

25 [1992] 1 W.L.R. 588 at 593.

26 *cf. Punt v. Symons & Co.* [1903] 2 Ch. 506 and *British Murac Syndicate Ltd. v. Alperton Rubber Co.* [1915] 2 Ch. 186.

27 *Southern Foundries (1926) Ltd. v. Shirlaw* [1940] A.C. 701.

28 [1992] 1 W.L.R. 588 at 594.

29 Davonport, "What did *Russell v. Northern Bank Developments Corp. Ltd.* Decide?" (1993) 109 L.Q.R. 553.

30 Ferran, "The Decision of the House of Lords in *Russell v. Northern Bank Development Corp. Ltd.*" (1994) 53 Cam. L.J. 343.

Fourthly, where a company has contracted that its articles will not be altered, [there is] no reason why it should not, in a suitable case, be injuncted from [itselfl initiating the calling of a general meeting with a view to alteration of the articles."[31]

Entrenchment

11–11 The 1963 Act provides for entrenching provisions in the regulations against alteration. The power to change the articles of association is "subject to . . . the conditions contained in the memorandum"[32] and, as has been pointed out, the memorandum of association itself may be altered only in the ways permitted by that Act.[33] In order to entrench some clause, all that is necessary is to put it into the memorandum with the stipulation that it may not be altered or may be altered only in some particular way.[34] It would appear that the original memorandum, once registered, cannot subsequently be amended to entrench some clause; although a not implausible argument could be made against such a view.[35] Some uncertainties about the impact of attempted entrenchments of "class rights" are resolved by sections 38 and 39 of the 1983 Act, which are considered separately below.

CHANGING THE NATURE OF THE BUSINESS

11–12 The management or the shareholders may wish to change the nature of their company's business or alter drastically the way it conducts its existing business. For instance, the proposal may be that a tailoring company becomes a candlestick-maker, that a construction firm goes into property development, that a trading concern should possess its own financial arm etc. Or it may be proposed that the company sell off a major asset; for example, that in order to raise funds, a retailing company sells the freehold of all its stores to some financial institution and then leases them back, or that the stores be sold off to the parent company's shareholders under the aegis of a separate company.

---

[31] *Cumbrian Newspapers Group Ltd. v. Cumberland & Westmorland Herald Newspaper & Printing Co.* [1987] Ch. 1 at 24.
[32] 1963 Act, s.9.
[33] *ibid.*, s.28(3).
[34] *ibid.*
[35] Based on s.28(1) of the 1963 Act.

Altering the Objects

11–13 The change envisaged may be so drastic that it is necessary for the company to amend its objects clause. From 1862 onwards companies' objects clauses were immutable. It was to enable such changes to be made that the Companies (Memorandum of Association) Act, 1890, was enacted, which enumerated what kinds of alterations would be permissible and required confirmation by the courts of all proposed changes.[36] The position is now governed by section 10 of the 1963 Act, which simply provides that, subject to various procedures being satisfied, a company by special resolution may "alter the provisions of its memorandum by abandoning, restricting or amending any existing object or by adopting a new object . . ." A company, therefore, may take any object with which it originally could have been incorporated and may abandon all or any of its existing objects. The informal unanimous agreement by all of a company's members to a course of conduct that otherwise would be *ultra vires* can be equivalent to a special resolution sanctioning a change in the objects to permit that conduct.[37]

11–14 In *Northern Bank Finance Corp.* v. *Quinn*[38] it was held that the objects cannot be changed with retroactive effect. When the second defendant, a company, realised that the guarantee it had given for a bank loan to the first defendant might be *ultra vires*, it sought to alter its objects so as to enlarge its legal capacity retroactively. It was contended that, by providing that any duly made alteration of the objects "shall be as valid as if originally contained" in the memorandum of association, section 10 of the 1963 Act allows such changes to be made. Keane J., however, took the view that this meant only that it is not necessary to go through all the formalities of drawing up a new memorandum. He moreover pointed to "strange" consequences if companies could retrospectively deprive themselves of certain objects;[39] although this point is not convincing against retroactively extending objects, especially in the light of section 10's machinery for dealing with objections to proposed changes.

11–15 Not alone must the alteration of the objects clause have been approved by a special resolution, but a minority of 15 per cent in value of the shareholders, or of any class of shareholders, within 21 days

---

[36] Similarly s.5 of the British Companies Act 1948; see Davies, "Alteration of a Company's Objects Clause and the Ultra Vires Rule" (1984) 90 L.Q.R. 79.

[37] *Re Home Trust Ltd.* [1991] B.C.L.C. 705; in 1991 the British Companies Acts adopted a procedure similar to s.10 of the 1963 Act.

[38] [1979] I.L.R.M. 221; see above, paras 3–66 *et seq.*

[39] *ibid.* at 230.

may apply to the court to veto any such change. A similar application may be made by 15 per cent of the holders of debentures who are entitled to object to alterations of the objects clause.[40] The section does not say by what criteria the court is to evaluate alterations and objections to them. Presumably, it would veto proposals that in the circumstances are oppressive or unduly discriminatory, or that go against some accommodation the shareholders previously had reached between themselves. It was suggested in *Re Munster & Leinster Bank Ltd.*,[41] which was decided under the 1890 Act, that questions of general public interest ought not to be the court's concern in these applications. There some shareholders, who in fact were speaking for the Incorporated Law Society and the Southern Law Association, sought to prevent approval being given to a proposed change in the bank's objects that would allow it to act as a professional trustee. It was said that this would damage the solicitors' profession; that as a precedent this could lead to an undesirable concentration of trustee business in banks; and that it was likely to lead to an interruption of the friendly relations existing between the legal profession and the court. It was held that these matters were not relevant to the question, which was whether the proposed change would benefit the bank and its shareholders; it was found that it would.[42]

11–16 That the court possesses a wide discretion in this area is underlined by the power it has to make appropriate orders. It may cancel the alteration or confirm it, or confirm it only partly or on such terms as it thinks fit. One such term is that the dissidents' interests be bought out and the court may give directions and make orders to render any such arrangement effective.

Strategic Matters — Expansion and Contraction

11–17 Even where the proposed change of direction or method of doing business does not require altering the objects clause, there are a number of ways in which the members can decisively influence the outcome. Where it is necessary to increase the authorised share capital to finance expansion, then the memorandum of association must be amended to permit the increase.[43] In companies with articles like clause 44 of Table A this requires only an ordinary resolution. Where it is

---

[40] s.10(3)(b), (7).
[41] [1907] 1 I.R. 237.
[42] See also, *Re Ulster Marine Insurance Co.* (1891) 27 L.R. Ir. 487; *Re Marcus Ward & Co.* [1897] 1 I.R. 435; *Re Cork Employers' Federation* [1921] 1 I.R. 69.
[43] 1963 Act, s.68(1)(a).

proposed to issue additional shares then sections 21 and 23 of the 1983 Act's provisions on authority and pre-emption must be satisfied, as must any special requirements in the company's own regulations regarding share issues.

11–18 Issuing a new class of shares carrying preferential rights in respect of dividends, capital or voting does not normally amount to a variation of existing shareholders' class rights and, therefore, does not require separate class approval. In *Andrews* v. *Gas Meter Co.,*[44] previous authority to the effect that issuing new shares with preferential rights is unlawfully discriminatory was rejected, on the grounds that companies' memoranda of association do not imply an overriding stipulation that all groups of shareholders be treated equally at all times. The governing principles have been expressed as follows:

> "While the memorandum must state the amount of capital, divided into shares of a certain fixed amount, provision as to the character of the shares and rights to be attached to them is more properly made by the articles of association, which may be altered from time to time by special resolution of the company. If equality of the shareholders is expressly provided in the memorandum, that cannot be modified by the articles of association. If nothing is said in the memorandum, the articles of association may provide for the issue of the authorised capital in the form of preference shares; if the articles do not so provide, or do provide for equality *inter socios,* the power to issue preference shares may be obtained by alteration of the articles. If the memorandum prescribes the classes of shares into which the capital is to be divided and the rights to be attached to such shares respectively, the company has no power to alter that provision by special resolution."[45]

These principles, however, must now be read in the light of recent developments in the law regarding minority shareholders' protection, most notably section 205 of the 1963 Act.

11–19 How the board takes what has been called major strategic decisions, or indeed every day business decisions, can always be regulated by an appropriate change in the articles of association. Whether the general meeting by ordinary resolution can veto strategic decisions remains an open question. As has been pointed out above, *Automatic Self-Cleansing Filter Syndicate Co.* v. *Cunninghame*[46] can be distinguished on a number of grounds and, it in any event, did not deal with resolutions in the negative. It was held in *Re Clubman Shirts Ltd.*[47] that refusal

---

[44] [1897] 1 Ch. 361.
[45] *Campbell v. Rofe* [1933] A.C. 91 at 98.
[46] [1906] 2 Ch. 34; see above, para. 4–50.
[47] [1983] I.L.R.M. 323; see above, para. 9–20.

to divulge to a major minority shareholder details concerning drastic changes in the nature of the company, in appropriate circumstances, can amount to oppression under section 205 of the 1963 Act.

VARIATION OF CLASS RIGHTS

11–20 Where there is more than one category of shares in a company, like ordinary and preference shares, it is said that there are different classes of shares. The special rights attaching to these classes are termed "class rights". Whereas a company may alter its articles of association by a special resolution of the entire company, as a general rule class rights may be taken away or cut down only with the consent of that particular class.[48] Questions regarding class rights arise especially when a company is contemplating restructuring its capital, by raising further equity or debt, or repaying some categories of shares. If what is proposed is an infringement of one group's class rights — such as taking away the preference shareholders' voting rights entirely or in particular circumstances, or cutting their dividend entitlement, or depriving them of their claim to any surplus — then as a rule this proposal must obtain the class's approval before it can be put into effect.

"Class Rights"

11–21 There is no comprehensive definition of what a class of shareholders is or of what class rights are. Generally, the absence of precision on these matters is of little practical consequence; it will be clear that in a particular company there are, say, ordinary, preference and deferred shares, *i.e.* three classes, and their respective rights regarding voting, dividends, repayment of capital and to any surplus would be class rights. Bowen L.J. once announced a somewhat vague definition of class, namely, "those persons whose rights are not so dissimilar as to make it impossible for them to consult together with a view to their common interest."[49] There are three possible answers to the question of what are class rights: (1) all rights that attach to a class of shares; (2) those rights that distinguish a class from other classes; or (3) those central and fundamental rights that attach to a class, such as to vote, to dividends and to repayment of capital and a share in any surplus, as

---

[48] See generally, Rice, "Class Rights and Their Variation in Company Law" [1958] J. Bus. L. 29; Rice, "Problems on the Variation of Shareholders' Class Rights" (1958) 22 Conv. 126; Baxt, "The Variation of Class Rights" (1968) 41 Australian L.J. 490; Reynolds, "Shareholders' Class Rights: A New Approach [1996] J. Bus. L. 554.

[49] *Sovereign Life Assurance Co. v. Dodd* [1892] 2 Q.B. 573 at 583.

opposed to more peripheral rights. Any right *vis-à-vis* the company given to a group of shareholders is most likely to be a class right if it is described in the company's regulations as such. Rights of this nature contained in a separate shareholders' agreement and not in the memorandum or articles of association are also treated as class rights.[50]

11–22 It may be that the best approach is to focus on a particular right under the company's regulations and, if it can be regarded as a class right, then the shares to which it attaches are a class, at least for the purposes of that right. This analysis was adopted in one of the few decisions that addresses the question, *Greenhalgh* v. *Arderne Cinemas Ltd.*[51] The company's share capital was comprised of ten shillings and two shillings ordinary shares that were identical in all respects except for the different nominal values. It was proposed to sub-divide each ten shillings share into five two shillings shares, the consequences of which would be to dilute considerably the existing two shillings shares' voting power. Vaisey J. concluded that the two kinds of ordinary shares formed one class, but was disposed to think that in any question which arose as to voting rights or anything of that kind the ten shillings shares formed a different class from the two shillings shares.

11–23 This matter was considered again in *Cumbrian Newspapers Group Ltd.* v. *Cumberland & Westmoreland Herald Newspaper & Printing Co. Ltd.*[52] Two newspaper companies decided to forge closer links, in the course of which the plaintiff acquired slightly more than 10 per cent of the shares in the defendant company and the defendant altered its articles of association in such a way as would enable the plaintiff to block any attempt to take over the defendant. The altered articles provided that the plaintiff company had rights in respect of unissued shares of the defendant, rights to override the directors' veto on registering transfers of shares, rights of pre-emption over other shares and the right, so long as it held 10 per cent of the company's shares, to appoint a director to the defendant company's board. The articles also contained a class rights variation clause along the lines of clause 3 of Table A. The defendant company now proposed to alter its articles once more so as to cancel all of the above special rights of the plaintiff. If those rights were indeed class rights then the proposed alteration could not be made without the plaintiff's consent, which was not forthcoming.

11–24 In reaching a conclusion, Scott J. found some guidance in sec-

---

[50] *Harman v. BML Group Ltd.* [1994] 2 B.C.L.C. 674.
[51] [1945] 2 All E.R. 719, affirmed [1946] 1 All E.R. 512.
[52] [1987] Ch. 1.

tion 38 of the 1983 Act, which he described as "intended to provide a comprehensive code setting out the manner in which" class rights may be varied. Those rights and benefits that articles of association may confer can be divided into three main categories. One is where the rights and benefits are annexed to particular shares only; they are class rights. But the entitlements in this case were not attached to any specific share or shares held by the plaintiff; the articles simply described the plaintiff as having the above mentioned rights, which would enable it to block a take-over bid. Section 38(1) of the 1983 Act might seem not to embrace entitlements of this nature, because it speaks of "rights attached to any class of shares" when the company's shares are divided into "different classes". It was held, however, that these two phrases have the same meaning and embrace entitlements as just described where they are conferred on a shareholder *qua* member of the company. According to Scott J.:

> "if specific rights are given to certain members in their capacity as members or shareholders, then those members become a class. The shares those members hold for the time being, and without which they would not be members of the class, would represent . . . a "class of shares" for the purpose of section 38 . . . The share capital of a company is . . . divided into shares of different classes, if shareholders, qua shareholders, enjoy different rights."[53]

Therefore, the special entitlements that the articles of association conferred on the plaintiff constituted it a class of shareholder for the purpose of the rights and, accordingly, those rights could not be changed without its consent. On the other hand, where the right in question was not conferred on the individual *qua* shareholder but in some other capacity it is not a class right. It will depend on the entire circumstances of the case what capacity the articles purported to confer the right in question.

"Variation" or "Abrogation" of Rights

11–25 As a general rule, class rights may not be "varied or abrogated" without the consent of that class. Probably in the interests of allowing companies a degree of freedom to alter their capital structures, the courts have adopted a very narrow concept of what constitutes variation or abrogation in this context, so as to place many proposed increases in, and reductions of, capital outside the veto power of classes. In particular, where a company has excess funds and wishes to repay its preference shareholders, by way of reducing the preference capital, those members' class rights have not been varied or abrogated. Instead,

---

[53] [1987] Ch. 1 at 22.

their right to be repaid their capital in a winding up before any of the other shareholders can get repaid has been given effect to.[54] But this is not the case where the company's articles provide otherwise[55] nor where the preference shareholders are entitled to a share in any surplus which might arise in a winding up.[56] The view appears to be that, unless the proposal involves a literal and direct alteration of a class right, it does not constitute a "variation" of the right, even though in consequence the right is reduced in its relative effect or value. What seems to matter is the form and not the substance of what is done. This approach has been criticised for being unduly narrow and legalistic. In any event, it may be virtually redundant today in the light of modern developments in minority shareholders' rights. That is to say, changes which do not amount to varying class rights may still be challenged under section 205 of the 1963 Act on the grounds of oppression.

11–26 In *White* v. *Bristol Aeroplane Ltd.*[57] for example, the company's capital was comprised of £600,000 preference shares and £3,000,000 ordinary shares. It was proposed to increase the capital by issuing £660,000 new cumulative preference shares and £1,000,000 new ordinary shares and that the entirety of the new issues would be distributed among the existing ordinary shareholders. The actual impact of this scheme on the existing preference shareholders' voting strength would be significant; even within their own class they would become outnumbered by the existing ordinary shareholders who would get new preference shares. Yet it was held that their class rights were not varied. A distinction was drawn between "an affecting of the rights and an affecting of the enjoyment of the rights, or of the stockholders' capacity to turn them to account";[58] between, for instance, a direct reduction in the actual weight of a share's vote or a deprivation of the vote over a particular issue, and something that indirectly dilutes the significance of the class' voting power. For there to be a variation, the right must be "varied as a matter of law" and not just "affected as a matter of business".[59] The following are examples drawn from cases on voting and on dividend rights.

---

[54] *House of Fraser p.l.c. v. ACGE Investments Ltd.* [1987] 2 W.L.R. 1083.
[55] *Re Northern Engineering Industries p.l.c.* [1994] 2 B.C.L.C. 704.
[56] *Cork Electric Supply Co. v. Concannon* [1932] I.R. 314; see above, para. 9–55.
[57] [1953] 1 Ch. 65.
[58] *ibid.* at 74.
[59] *ibid.* at 80.

11–27 The *Bristol Aeroplane* case demonstrates that it is possible by "upstream conversion" to undermine a class's voting rights. An almost identical earlier instance is the *Arderne Cinemas* case[60] referred to above, where the company had ten shillings and two shillings ordinary shares, and where it was proposed to sub-divide the ten shillings shares into five two shillings shares. The consequences of this would be to swamp the existing two shillings shares' voting power. Assuming that the voting rights there were class rights, it was held that those were not varied because "[t]he only right of voting which is attached . . . to the [two shillings] shares . . . is the right to have one vote per share pari passu with the other ordinary shares . . . for the time being issued [and] that right has not been taken away."[61]

11–28 In *Re Mackenzie & Co.*[62] the company had 5,000 4 per cent £1 preference shares and 1,500 £1 ordinary shares. A scheme to reduce capital under the predecessor of section 72 of the 1963 Act was drawn up, in which the par value of each share would be reduced by 25p, and a further 15p per share would be returned to each shareholder. The effect of this was to reduce significantly the existing preference shareholders' income per share while making no difference to the ordinary shareholders' expectations about income. It was held that the former's right to dividends was not thereby varied, since they remained entitled to a 4 per cent cumulative preference dividend on the nominal amount of their shares. The "Australian Pound" cases[63] are striking examples of a dilution of a class' dividend expectations without it infringing their actual rights to a dividend.

Power to Vary or Abrogate

11–29 Most companies' regulations contain authority to vary or abrogate class rights — but it is usually contingent on the class giving its consent by a special resolution of the class. Table A has a class rights variation clause to this effect.[64] Table A furthermore stipulates, principally to set aside any doubts, that two major kinds of change in capital structure shall not *ipso facto* be deemed to vary class rights in the absence of some provision to the contrary. These are the issue of additional shares ranking *pari passu* with the existing ones, and the issue of new shares carrying preferential rights as regards voting, dividend,

---

60 [1945] 3 All E.R. 719, affirmed [1946] 1 All E.R. 512.
61 [1946] 1 All E.R. at 516.
62 [1916] 2 Ch. 450.
63 Most notably, *Adelaide Electric Supply Co. v. Prudential Assurance Co.* [1934] A.C. 122; see below, para. 14–95.
64 Reg. 3.

return of capital "or otherwise".[65] A number of major questions regarding a company's power to vary class rights that were the subject of some controversy have now been resolved by section 38 of the 1983 Act, although that Act does not define what precisely is meant by the central concern of that section, namely, "shares of different classes", "rights attached to a class of shares" and "variation of class rights".

11–30 The basic rule is that if, as usually is the case, the class rights attach otherwise than by way of the memorandum of association (such as by the articles or by the shares' terms of issue), any variation procedure contained in the articles must be followed.[66] But if the class rights attach by way of the memorandum, then they can only be varied either in accordance with the procedure set down in the memorandum itself or a procedure that was in the articles from the time the company was originally incorporated.[67] If there is neither procedure, then class rights set out in the memorandum may be varied only with the consent of every member.[68]

11–31 One matter of dispute was whether class rights could be varied where a company's regulations contains no express authority to vary them. It is now provided that, where those rights attach otherwise than by the memorandum of association, they may be varied only by way of a special resolution of the class meeting separately or by written consent of at least three-quarters in nominal value of that class.[69]

11–32 Another disputed issue was whether a class rights variation clause in the articles of association could itself be altered by a special resolution of the company. The cases that deal with section 15 of the 1963 Act suggest that the answer is yes; but if this were so, it would defeat the entire logic underlying special protection for class rights. It is now provided that any alteration of the variation clause shall be treated as if it too were a variation of class rights.[70]

11–33 There then was the question of authority to vary class rights in the course of capital reductions under section 72 of the 1963 Act. In one case[71] it was said that a court may permit class rights to be varied in

---

[65] Art.4 and *e.g. Bristol Aeroplane* and *Arderne Cinemas* cases, above.
[66] s.38(4)(b).
[67] s.38(4)(a).
[68] s.38(5).
[69] s.38(2).
[70] s.38(7).
[71] *Re Holders Investments Trust* [1971] 1 W.L.R. 583. *cf.* Telfer & Mitchell, "Reduction of Capital and the Rights of Minority Shareholders" (1981) 55 Australian L.J. 249.

this way even though the requisite consents under the class rights variations clause in the articles were not obtained. Some argue that this analysis is wrong and is not consistent with prior authority. A provision in the articles of association may be construed as conferring a class right not to be repaid capital without the consent of the class.[72] In any event, it is now provided that the variation may take place only with the approval of three-quarters in nominal value of the class or by a special resolution of the class and, moreover, any additional requirements that are contained in the regulations must be complied with.[73] This is the case even if the variation of rights clause in the articles lays down less stringent requirements. A similar rule exists for variations that ensue from giving, changing, revoking or renewing authority under section 20 of the 1983 Act for the directors to allot additional securities.

Contesting the Change

11–34 Where a proposed variation of class rights obtains the requisite approval of the class affected, under the rights variation clause, dissenting shareholders representing at least 10 per cent in value of the class are empowered by section 78 of the 1963 Act to apply to the court to stop the proposal being put into effect. The criterion against which the court will evaluate any such application is whether, "having regard to all the circumstances of the case . . . the variation would unfairly prejudice the shareholders of the class represented by" the objector. That the change prejudices only the minority who are objecting most likely is not enough to have it condemned under this procedure. There is no reason, however, why any member of the company could not, under section 205 of the 1963 Act, challenge an agreed variation on the grounds that, in all the circumstances, he is being oppressed or his interests were disregarded.

CAPITAL REDUCTION AND REPAYMENT

11–35 While it is a fundamental principle of company law that contributed capital must be "maintained" in the company, sound business reasons may nevertheless exist for distributing part of the capital to the shareholders or otherwise reducing capital. For instance, the company may have far more funds in its coffers than it needs to finance its business and, therefore, may prefer that the money be re-

---

[72] *Re Northern Engineering Industries p.l.c.* [1994] 2 B.C.L.C. 704.
[73] s.38(3).

turned to the individual shareholders.[74] Or it may not need any additional capital and, accordingly, may wish to cancel the unpaid amounts on its shares.[75] Or trading losses may have been incurred to such extent that the figure in the balance sheet for the capital no longer represents the true position and, therefore, it is sought to write off the losses.[76] Or an individual member or group of members may want to realise their investment and the only practical way that this can be done is for the company to repay the capital they contributed.[77] A frequent reason since 1983 is to enable a company, which has accumulated past losses, to pay dividends from current profits, because the Act of that year makes the company's capital and undistributable reserves a factor in determining whether dividends may be paid.[78] Section 9 of the Companies Act of 1867 first responded to these needs; sections 72-77 of the 1963 Act now set out the machinery whereby, subject to confirmation by the court, a limited company may reduce or repay its capital "in any way".[79] Since 1991, capital also can be repaid by the company purchasing its own shares in accordance with Part XI of the Companies Act 1990.

11–36 In a number of leading cases decided around the turn of this century, the House of Lords placed great emphasis on the generality of what now are sections 72–77 of the 1963 Act. Provided that the statutory procedures are satisfied, it is for the company itself "to determine the extent, the mode, and the incidence of the reduction, and the application or disposition of any capital moneys which the proposed reduction may set free."[80] It is "no part of the business of a court of justice to determine the wisdom of a course adopted by a company in the management of its own affairs"; restrictions will not readily be implied into the "perfectly general" power to reduce capital because that would "lead to inconvenience and expense and hamper and embarrass companies in the conduct of their domestic affairs".[81] While the court retains a discretion to veto any proposed capital reduction,

> "if the parties to the transaction come to the conclusion that the bargain is a fair one, why should the court say that there is a preference on the one side or on the other? If there is nothing unfair or inequitable in the

---

[74] *e.g. Cork Electric Supply Co. v. Concannon* [1932] I.R. 314.
[75] *e.g. Re Northern Bank Ltd.* [1963] N.I. 90.
[76] *e.g. Bannatyne v. Direct Spanish Telegraph Co.* (1886) 34 Ch.D. 287.
[77] *e.g. British & American Trustee & Finance Corp. v. Couper* [1894] A.C. 399.
[78] *e.g. Re Jupiter House Investments (Cambridge) Ltd.* [1985] 1 W.L.R. 975; *Re Grosvenor Press p.l.c.* [1985] 1 W.L.R. 980.
[79] s.72(2).
[80] above, n. 77, at 411–412.
[81] *Poole v. National Bank of China* [1907] A.C. 229 at 236 and 237.

> transaction, . . . there is [no] objection to allowing a company . . . to extinguish some of its shares without dealing in the same manner with all other shares of the same class. There may be no real inequality in the treatment of a class of shareholders although they are not paid in the same coin or in coins of the same denomination."[92]

Thus there is no absolute requirement of formal or even of substantive equality for shareholders of the same class on a partial distribution of capital.

11–37 Assuming that the proper procedures were followed and the creditors' interests are sufficiently safeguarded, there are four broad grounds on which the court will refuse to sanction a proposed reduction, namely, infringements of class rights, discrimination, disproportionality and the public interest. Confirmation by the court may be granted "on such terms and conditions as it thinks fit."[83] In particular, it may order the company to add the words "and reduced" to its name, and to publish the reasons for the reduction and such other relevant information as directed. Every reducing resolution must be registered with the registrar of companies before it can become effective.[84]

Procedures

11–38 A number of procedural steps are laid down in sections 72-77. There must be separate authority in the articles of association to make the kind of reduction in question; clause 46 of Table A gives extensive authority for this purpose. The proposal to make the reduction must be approved by a special resolution of the company.[85] Where what is being proposed is to extinguish liability in respect of unpaid capital, or to actually refund capital, or whenever the court so directs, then every creditor is entitled to object. In these cases the proposal will not be sanctioned unless every creditor consents or is paid off, or their debts are adequately secured.[86] But in "special circumstances" the court may waive this requirement as regards a class or classes of creditors.[87] Where the capital reduction is sought on the grounds that the company has suffered a serious loss of capital, the loss must be permanent and not temporary.[88] However, the court has a discretion to order a duly sanc-

---

[82] See above, n. 77 at 415–416.
[83] 1963 Act, s.74(1).
[84] s.75.
[85] *cf. Re Barry Artist Ltd.* [1985] 1 W.L.R. 1305 on "informal" resolutions and *Re Meuxs Brewery Co.* [1919] 1 Ch. 28 on full disclosure in this context.
[86] ss. 73(2), 74(1).
[87] s.73(3); *e.g. Re Northern Bank Ltd.* [1963] N.I. 90 and *Re Ransomes p.l.c.* [1999] 1 B.C.L.C. 775.
[88] See cases cited above, n. 78.

tioned capital reduction where the loss may prove to be temporary, on condition that the company gives appropriate undertakings.[89] In England an application to reduce capital was heard which had the unanimous support of the shareholders but no special resolution as such was passed.[90] However, the judge there ruled that henceforth the company must go through the formalities of passing a resolution for this purpose.

Disclosure

11–39 Where the notice convening the meeting or any accompanying circular contains some inaccuracy, that often is fatal to the outcome. The question is whether the shareholders or creditors, as the case may be, had been given a fair warning of exactly what was to be considered at the meeting. Exceptionally, however, it can be established that an inaccuracy would not have influenced the minds of reasonable shareholders or creditors.[91] Even where the information provided to the members is correct at the time the notices were sent but circumstances changed between then and when the meeting was held, that is often fatal. The principle is that "material representations must not only be accurate when made but must remain the whole story when they come to be acted upon."[92]

Impact on Class Rights and Discrimination

11–40 As was explained above,[93] for nearly a hundred years the courts have adopted a markedly restrictive approach to what are "class rights" and what constitutes a "variation" of such rights, as is illustrated in the context of capital reductions by In *re Mackenzie & Co.*[94] and the *Wilsons & Clyde Coal* case.[95] Even where a capital reduction did amount to variation or abrogation of those rights, there was some authority that it was not absolutely essential to have separate class approval for the reduction to go ahead,[96] although opinions were divided on this

---

[89] *ibid.*

[90] *Re Barry Artist Ltd.* [1985] 1 W.L.R. 1305.

[91] *Re European Home Products p.l.c.* [1988] B.C.L.C. 690; *Re Heron International N.V.* [1994] 1 B.C.L.C. 667.

[92] *Re Minister Assets p.l.c.* [1985] B.C.L.C. 200 at 201. See also *Re Jessel Trust p.l.c.* [1985] B.C.L.C. 119; *Re M.B. Group p.l.c.* [1989] B.C.L.C. 672 and *Re Ransomes p.l.c.* [1999] 1 B.C.L.C. 775.

[93] above, paras 11–20 *et seq.*

[94] [1916] 2 Ch. 450. See also *Bannatyne v. Direct Spanish Telegraph Co.* (1886) 34 Ch.D. 287.

[95] [1949] A.C. 462; see above, para. 9–54. See also *Re William Jones & Sons Ltd.* [1969] 1 W.L.R. 146.

[96] *Re Holders Investments Trust* [1971] 1 W.L.R. 583.

matter.[97] Another source of confusion was the status of class rights in the absence of a variation clause along the lines of clause 3 of Table A. These questions are now resolved by section 39(3) of the 1983 Act: class rights may not be varied in a capital reduction without the requisite class approval.[98]

11–41 It is not forbidden to repay only one class of shareholders. That the class which it is intended to repay could not get as favourable a return on their funds if invested elsewhere does not *ipso facto* prevent a company from paying them off.[99] That one class has a prior right to be repaid its capital in a winding up does not of itself entitle that class to be paid off before other classes when the company proposes to repay part of the capital.[100] Nor is it forbidden to pay off a discrete group of shareholders in one class, or even one individual member. But it has been held that, where preference shareholders have priority as regards repayment of capital, then prima facie it is unfair to repay all, or a considerable proportion of, the ordinary shares without paying anything off on the preference shares.[101] Indeed, any scheme that does not provide for uniform treatment of shareholders whose rights are similar will be carefully scrutinised by the court.[102]

11–42 Where the entire membership of the class that votes for a reduction is split into factions, with one group in a position of significant conflict of interests, in that it uniquely suits them for other reasons that the reduction goes ahead, then the court would tend to refuse confirmation. There is a theoretical difficulty in that shares are property rights and the classic view has been that every member is entitled to canvass his own selfish interests when voting in general meeting. However, majorities are not permitted to discriminate unfairly against minorities; especially when making major decisions about the company's structure, members are required to cast their votes for the benefit of the company as a whole.[103] An alternative ground for refusing to sanction a proposed reduction that is tainted by a significant conflict of interests is to conclude that it affects not just one but two classes of shareholders, namely, those in the position of conflict and the other

---

97 See Telfer & Mitchell (1981) 55 Australian L.J. 249.

98 See above, para. 11–33.

99 *Re Chatterly Whitfield Collieries Ltd.* [1948] 2 All E.R. 593.

100 *Re Fowlers Vacola Manufacturing Co.* [1966] V.R. 97 and *Re Ransomes p.l.c.* [1999] 1 B.C.L.C. 775.

101 *e.g. British & American Trustee* case [1894] A.C. 399 and *Re Thomas de la Rue & Co.* [1911] 2 Ch. 361.

102 *ibid.*

103 *British American Nickel Corp. v. O'Brien Ltd.* [1927] A.C. 369.

shareholders, and if the latter have not given their approval the requisite authority of a class affected was not obtained.[104] In any event, the court's veto power here is entirely discretionary.

11–43 A classic example of unfair discrimination is *Re Holders Investment Trust Ltd.*[105] The company had an issued share capital comprised of ordinary shares and 5 per cent cumulative preference shares which were to be redeemed in 1971. It was proposed in 1970 that the preference shares should be repaid then by their holders being allotted the same nominal amounts of 6 per cent unsecured loan stock 1985–1990. This was approved by a special resolution of the company and by a special resolution of the preference shareholders meeting as a separate class. Of the latter, approximately 3 per cent did not vote and 7 per cent opposed the proposal; but the remaining 90 per cent which voted for it were trustees who also held over 50 per cent of the equity. From the evidence it was clear that the trustees were influenced solely by the benefit of the trust as a whole, which in the circumstances meant what was most advantageous to the equity. According to Megarry J.,

> "the question [is] whether the supporting trustees voted for the reduction in the bona fide belief that they were acting in the interests of the general body of members of [the preference shareholders. There is] no evidence that the trustees ever applied their minds to what, under company law, was the right question, or that they ever had the bona fide belief that is requisite for an effectual sanction of the reduction."[106]

Therefore the necessary class approval was not given.

Fairness — Proportionality

11–44 The court attempts to ensure that the very terms of the proposed reduction are not unjust as between shareholders. To this end, it has been guided by two prima facie principles. Where there is no preference as to a return of capital in a winding up, a reduction should fall rateably on all classes of shares.[107] Where there is a preference as to capital, any losses should be borne by those who have a last claim on the assets in a winding up.[108] But the circumstances of the case may warrant departure from these guidelines. In the end, it is the broad criterion of "fairness, reasonableness and equity" that applies.[109] Con-

---

[104] cf. *Re Hellenic & General Trust Ltd.* [1978] 1 W.L.R. 123; below, para. 11–59.
[105] [1971] 1 W.L.R. 583.
[106] *ibid.* at 589.
[107] *Re Barrow Haematite Steel Co.* (1888) 39 Ch.D. 582.
[108] *Re Floating Dock Co. of St. Thomas* [1895] 1 Ch. 691.
[109] *Wilsons & Clyde Coal* case [1949] A.C. 462 at 462. See, *e.g. Re Quebrada Rail etc. Co.* (1889) 40 Ch.D. 363 and *Re Showell's Brewery Co.* (1914) 30 T.L.R. 428.

firmation will be refused where one class or group, or individual, is being asked to bear a disproportionate sacrifice in the light of what advantages others derive from the reduction. The courts, nevertheless, have shown considerable reluctance to reject as unfair compromises that were reached by at least a three-quarters majority of the membership. As one judge explained, when proposed reductions have "been considered, first of all by a committee consisting of businessmen chosen by the shareholders themselves, and that they have subsequently been sanctioned by large majorities at the various meetings of shareholders which have been held, it would require a very strong case to induce [a] Court to interfere."[110] The perspective from which the court views such proposals is the "common sense man-of-the-world point of view."[111] An analysis of the cases led one commentator to conclude that "in practice the reduction will always be confirmed in the absence of the very strongest evidence that it is inequitable. So long as the petitioners can give some semblance of reasonableness to their argument, the presumption in their favour is almost irrebuttable."[112] Because of the discretionary nature of the jurisdiction, the cases cannot be treated as precedents on the matter, but the following themes can be derived from some of the leading cases.

11–45 There are numerous reported instances of preference shareholders as a class being repaid in cash. In the *Wilsons & Clyde Coal Co.* case[113] and its companion case, *Re Chatterley-Whitfield Collieries Ltd.*,[114] it was contended that, even if the repayments there did not vary class rights, they nevertheless were unfair in the circumstances. In the *Chatterley-Whitfield* case the court sanctioned the repayment by a cash-bloated company of its six per cent preference shares, at a time when interest rates were at an historic low, because:

> "A company which has issued preference shares carrying a high rate of dividend and finds its business so curtailed that it has capital surplus to its requirements and sees the likelihood, or at any rate the possibility, that its preference capital will not . . . earn its keep, would be guilty of financial ineptitude if it did not take steps to reduce its capital by paying off preference capital so far as the law allowed it to do so. That is mere commonplace in company finance. . . . The position of the company itself as an economic entity must be considered, and nothing can be more destructive of a company's financial equilibrium than to have to carry the

---

[110] *Re Welsback Incandescent Gas Light Co.* [1904] 1 Ch. 87 at 101.
[111] *Re Old Silkstone Colleries Ltd.* [1954] 1 Ch. 169 at 189.
[112] Rice, "Capital Reduction and its Effect on Class Rights" (1959) 23 Conv. 244 at 258.
[113] [1949] A.C. 462.
[114] [1948] 2 All E.R. 593.

> burden of a high rate of dividend which it cannot earn. In a company so situated, the ordinary shareholders will be unfairly treated *vis-à-vis* the preference shareholders, and the company may well fall into the situation when its preference dividends will begin to fall into irretrievable arrears. It is a fallacy to suppose that because ordinary shareholders will benefit, the transaction ought to be vetoed as being unfair to the preference shareholders."[115]

11–46 In *Wilsons & Clyde Coal Co.* counsel for the preference shareholders emphasised that 45 per cent of that class actively opposed the proposed reduction; that the ratio between ordinary and preference shares was 13–1; that unlike in *Chatterley-Whitfield*, the company proposed to go into liquidation shortly afterwards, so that there was no question of the business carrying a continuing burden of relatively high dividend payments; that the proposed repayment of preference shares was designed "not in the interests of the company but "solely in order that the ordinary stockholders may eventually appropriate 13/13ths of the surplus assets instead of 12/13ths".[116] Perhaps acting on the then prevailing public policy of post-war reconstruction, the Law Lords held that the scheme was not unfair. Contrast a very similar case that was decided four years later,[117] where confirmation was refused because the proposed scheme was inconsistent with representations that had been made to the preference shareholders and that they had acted upon; the scheme "Involve[d] a volte-face of which these . . . stockholders can legitimately complain as amounting to a breach of faith."[118]

11–47 Where capital is being repaid otherwise than in cash, it is not essential that there be an exact correspondence between the amount of capital paid off and the value of the assets used to pay it off, because in many cases it is impossible to make any exact valuation of such assets.[119] But in the face of objections by shareholders, the court will attempt to ensure that the consideration is, at least, not disproportionately inadequate. To this end, account is taken of the proportions of the group in question voting for and against the proposal and also valuers' evidence. Thus in the case arising out of I.C.I.'s major capital reconstruction in the mid-1930s,[120] where *inter alia* deferred shareholders were repaid with four ordinary shares for every deferred share, and where

---

115 [1948] 2 All E.R. 593 at 595–596.
116 Lord Morton dissenting, [1949] A.C. 462 at 508.
117 *Re Old Silkstone Colleries Ltd.* [1954] 1 Ch. 169.
118 *ibid.* at p. 199. See also, *Re W. Jones & Sons Ltd.* [1969] 1 W.L.R. 146 and *Re Saltdean Estate Co.* [1968] 1 W.L.R. 188.
119 *Ex. p. Westburn Sugar Refineries Ltd.* [1951] A.C. 625 at 632–633.
120 *Carruth v. I.C.I. Ltd.* [1973] A.C. 707.

only one of the deferred shareholders lodged objections, it was held that "interpreting the scheme in its business sense . . . the fair equivalent" was given.[121] By contrast, in *Re Holders Investment Trust Ltd.*, it was concluded that, in particular, the substitution of a one point increase in guaranteed income for a twenty years postponement of the repayment date in the circumstances fell "substantially below the threshold of anything that can justly be called fair."[122]

Public Interest

11–48 What precisely the public interest is in this context has never been clearly articulated and there is no major reported instance of a scheme that satisfied the other criteria being vetoed because of its effects on the general or the investing public. One instance where the public interest was raised is *Ex parte Westburn Sugar Refineries Ltd.*[123] A scheme was devised in order to evade a feared nationalisation of the company's principal assets, sugar refineries. The proposal, which had the shareholders' unanimous consent, was that the assets should be returned to the members *in specie*. It was held that the ulterior object was no reason for the court to block the scheme — that "the contingency of nationalisation has [no] relevance to the public policy that the [court] should support."[124]

Reducing the Share Premium Account

11–49 Section 62 of the 1963 Act provides that the procedure outlined above applies where a company wants to reduce its share premium account in any manner other than that allowed by this section, most notably by funding an issue of bonus shares. In recent years there have been numerous court applications to reduce share premiums, principally it would appear because of S.S.A.P. No. 22's treatment of what it calls "goodwill". That goodwill can be written off over time against profits or, alternatively, against reserves in the premium account in order to create a capital reserve which, on consolidation into group accounts, can be used to eliminate so-called goodwill. So far the Irish courts do not appear to have adopted any set practice for these applications but the practice in England is as follows.

11–50 Normally, the special resolution would provide that the capi-

---

[121] [1973] A.C. 707 at 751. See also, *Poole v. National Bank of China Ltd.* [1907] A.C. 229.

[122] [1971] 1 W.L.R. 583 at 590.

[123] [1951] A.C. 625.

[124] *ibid.* at 635; *cf. Re Data Homes Property Ltd* [1972] 2 N.S.W.L.R. 22 where a scheme devised for tax-avoidance purposes was rejected.

tal or share premium, as it stands when the resolution is passed, shall be reduced by the specified amount. However, it is permissible to resolve that capital will be reduced in some way after it has been increased, *i.e.* a resolution to take effect after the contingency of an increase in capital has occurred. Because the actual reduction of capital does not take effect until the resolution is duly registered, the court will confirm a contingent resolution in those terms, provided that contingency occurs before the date of the court hearing.[125] The criteria against which resolutions to reduce the share premium are judged are whether proposals were properly explained to the shareholders,[126] whether the creditors' position is adequately safeguarded, whether the shareholders are treated equitably and the reduction is for some discernible purpose.[127]

SCHEMES OF ARRANGEMENT AND RECONSTRUCTION

11–51 At times it may be necessary to alter a company's capital structure somewhat more drastically than can be done under sections 66–78 of the 1963 Act. Most typically, the company may be in financial difficulties and seeks either to eliminate one or more category of preferred or deferred shares that prevent it from raising further capital, or to persuade creditors to exchange some or all of their claims against the company for shares in it or for less demanding obligations. Reconstructions of this latter kind are very common in times of economic recession. The leading Irish case on these matters, *Re John Power & Sons Ltd.*,[128] concerned a distillery company that was established in 1921 with a capital of 400,000 ordinary shares of £1 par and 400,000 preference shares of £1 par, which were entitled inter alia to a cumulative preference dividend of 8 per cent per annum. The company's profits continually and drastically fell during its first ten years' existence, until the directors concluded that there was no prospect of it ever earning sufficient to meet the preference dividend each year and at the same time set aside sums for depreciation. They, therefore, proposed that the nominal value of the ordinary shares be reduced to 50 pence a share and that each preference share be exchanged for a redeemable loan carrying interest at 5 per cent per annum. Often the schemes are much

---

[125] *Re Tip-Europe Ltd.* [1988] B.C.L.C. 231.
[126] *Re European Home Products p.l.c.* [1988] B.C.L.C. 690.
[127] *Re Thorn E.M.I. p.l.c.* [1989] B.C.L.C. 612; *Re Ratners Group p.l.c.* [1988] B.C.L.C. 685.
[128] [1934] I.R. 412. Another excellent example is *Re Van Dyk Models Ltd* (1966) 100 I.L.T.R. 177.

more elaborate — such as that adopted in 1982 for the T.M.G. group and in 1984 for Pye (Ireland) Ltd., and, at the transnational level, that adopted in 1981 to rescue the Massey-Ferguson group.

11–52 Where the company is in such serious difficulties that it is insolvent, it most likely will resort instead to the court protection and examination system under the Companies (Amendment) Act, 1990.[129] But if the company is not heavily insolvent and there is no immediate danger of its creditors seeking to enforce their security or levy execution on the company's assets or seek to have it wound up, section 201 may be a preferable option. For this procedure will not give the impression that the company is in severe difficulties, it does not involve a third party coming in and examining the company's entire affairs and making a detailed report on them to the court, and there is not as much running back and forth to the court involved. This procedure can be much less expensive for the company and its creditors. On the other hand, if there is one class of creditors who will not agree to a scheme or compromise which is acceptable to all the others, section 201 may be impracticable because, for that scheme to be adopted, the dissenting class must be paid off in full.[130]

11–53 Drastic capital reorganisation may be brought about with the approval of the court under sections 201-203 of the 1963 Act. These originated in the Joint Stock Companies Arrangement Act 1870, affecting creditors only, and in 1900 was extended to schemes for altering the rights of shareholders. This procedure is used occasionally to engineer take-over bids — usually where the bidder cannot succeed under the ordinary rules.[131] Arrangement in this context is defined as including "a reorganisation of the share capital", but it has been held that the term is of very wide import and extends to practically anything that colloquially could be called an arrangement involving a company other than something that is *ultra vires* the company or that must be done under some special statutory procedure.[132] These sections confer on majorities in companies one of the most extensive of powers to bind minorities. Indeed, they might give rise to constitutional difficulties but for the broad supervisory power exercised by the court. Bowen L.J. explained their outer limits as follows:

> "The object . . . is not confiscation. It is not that one person should be a victim, and that the rest of the body should feast upon his rights. Its

[129] See generally, M. Forde, *The Law of Company Insolvency* (1993) Pt II.
[130] *Re Pye (Ireland) Ltd.*, Costello J., November 12, 1984.
[131] *e.g. Re Savoy Hotel Co.* [1981] 1 Ch. 351 (unsuccessfully).
[132] *Re Guardian Assurance Co.* [1917] 1 Ch. 431.

> object is to enable compromises to be made which are for the common benefit of the creditors as creditors [or shareholders as shareholders], or the common benefit of some class . . . as such."[133]

Procedures

11–54 If a compromise or arrangement between shareholders or creditors, or between any class of them, is proposed, an application may be made to the court to stay or restrain all further proceedings against the company.[134] A company in financial difficulties thereby can continue in business in the expectation that some arrangement will be made with its creditors. When the arrangement has been negotiated, an application will be made to the court to summon meetings of each class of shareholder and creditor affected. To determine who the various classes of shareholders are, the classic definition of a class in this context is that of Bowen L.J., namely, "those persons whose rights are not so dissimilar as to make it impossible for them to consult together with a view to their common interests".[135] How the creditors are to be divided up is also based on this criterion. If the terms of the proposed scheme are such that they would not be sanctioned by the court, if eventually put before it, the court will not even take the first step of summoning class meetings.[136]

11–55 In order to obtain sanction from the court, the scheme must be supported by at least threequarters in value of each class affected by it who vote, either in person or by proxy.[137] Unlike in capital reductions under section 72, therefore, a special resolution of the company as a whole or a special resolution of those in each class who vote is not enough. The Act sets out formalities that must be satisfied when the scheme is being considered by creditors.[138] In deciding whether to sanction a proposed scheme, the court must satisfy itself that the above procedures were followed and, in addition, that "the proposal is such that an intelligent and honest man, a member of the class concerned and acting in respect of his interest, might reasonably approve."[139] Once the requisite majority of each class votes for the scheme, which obtains court approval, it binds all the members of the class and the company.[140]

---

[133] *Re Alabama etc. Railway Co.* [1891] 1 Ch. 213 at 243. *cf. Bramelid & Malmstrom v. Sweden, Eur. Comm. H.R.*, October 12, 1982, 5 E.H.R.R. 249; above, para. 1–37.

[134] s.201(2).

[135] *Soverign Life Assurance Co. v. Dodd* [1892] 2 QB. 573 at 583.

[136] *Re El Pollo (N.Z.) Ltd.* [1990] 1 N.Z.L.R. 356.

[137] s.201(2).

[138] s.202.

[139] *Re Dorman Long & Co.* [1934] 1 Ch. 635 at 657.

[140] s.201(3); or if the company is being wound up it binds the liquidator and the contributories.

The court, however, is empowered to order that provision be made for persons who dissent from what their class agreed to.[141] The scheme takes effect once a copy of the court's sanction is delivered to the registrar of companies.[142]

11–56 Where the scheme sanctioned is for a "reconstruction" of one or more companies or an "amalgamation" of two or more companies, and involves the transfer of property or of the undertaking between companies, the court possesses extensive powers to make orders that facilitate making the scheme effective.[143] The orders it can make are itemised and include the transfer of the transferor company's assets or liabilities, allocating shares or debentures in the transferee company, and dissolving a transferor company without winding it up. Property in this context is defined as including "property, rights and powers of every description", and liabilities as including duties; but it has been held that the court does not have the power to order the transfer of rights and duties under an employment contract.[144]

Disclosure

11–57 Details of the proposed arrangement and an adequate explanation of its effect must be circulated to all members of the classes who would be affected. That information must include a statement of any material interest the directors possess, whether as directors or as creditors or otherwise, and of any material interest of the trustees for the debenture-holders.[145] Where the nature of that interest has changed following the dispatch of the notices, the court will not approve the scheme unless it is satisfied that no reasonable shareholder would have changed his decision as to how to act on the scheme if he had been aware of the change of circumstances. Where the change occurred before the meetings were held, there is a particularly strong onus on those supporting the scheme to prove that "knowledge of the undisclosed change in the material interests of a director of the company could not have influenced the minds of reasonable shareholders . . ."[146] As in the case of reductions of capital, inaccurate information supplied to the class meetings will usually cause the scheme to be rejected by the court.[147]

---

141 s.203(1)(e).
142 s.201(5).
143 s.203.
144 *Noakes v. Doncaster Arnalg. Colleries Co.* [1940] A.C. 1014.
145 s.202(1).
146 *Re Jessell Trust Ltd.* [1985] B.C.L.C. 119 at 126.
147 *ibid.* See also, *Re M.B. Group p.l.c.* [1989] B.C.L.C. 672 and *Re Minister Assets*

11–58 In a case concerning a take-over in the form of an arrangement of the old National Bank,[148] it was held that it was not necessary to disclose to the shareholders the worth of the Bank's secret reserves. The reason given was that "to say that full disclosure must be made of all material facts begs the question of the nature of the scheme which is being proposed. The extent of the disclosure required must depend on the nature of the scheme. Here the scheme is one which is based on the withholding of exempt information. [And since] the scheme is fair [there is] no reason why [the court] should not sanction it."[149] While there may be a case for banks having hidden reserves, it is difficult to justify withholding from shareholders information about a bank's actual worth when they are asked to vote on an arrangement to have it taken over. The need for complete disclosure is underlined by the events surrounding the take-over bids made for the Royal Bank of Scotland in 1981. There, the directors sought to persuade shareholders to accept an agreed bid, but another bidder then came on the scene to offer a much higher price.

Impact on Class Rights and Discrimination

11–59 The rules in section 38(2)-(5) of the 1983 Act on varying class rights do not affect the court's power under section 201 to sanction schemes of arrangement.[150] However, any scheme that would vary class rights must have the support of three-quarters in value of that class which voted. The courts, moreover, have adopted a somewhat expansive view of what is a "class" in this context. Whether a group of shareholders constitutes a class depends on the nature of the proposed scheme and the circumstances of the case. Where a group of shareholders that ordinarily would be regarded as a class are divided, and one faction is in a position of significant conflict of interests, the courts may treat them as separate classes. In *Re Hellenic & General Trust Ltd.*[151] an arrangement was proposed whereby all of the company's existing shares would be cancelled, new shares in it would be issued to a merchant bank that owned the company's 53 per cent majority shareholder (MIT), and the remaining shareholders would be paid off in cash. The proposal was approved by 84 per cent of the members in value; one member, a foreign bank with 14 per cent of the shares, voted against. That bank contended that the requisite class majority had not been

p.l.c. [1985] B.C.L.C. 200, where sufficient information was held to have been provided.

148 *Re National Bank Ltd.* [1966] 1 W.L.R. 819.

149 *ibid.* at 829.

150 1983 Act, s.38(10).

151 [1976] 1 W.L.R. 123.

obtained because MIT had a major conflict of interests, in that the object of the scheme was that its parent company should acquire all the shares in the investment trust. It was held that in the circumstances there were two classes — MIT and the other shareholders — and, since three-fourths of the latter did not endorse the scheme, it could not go ahead. According to Templeman J., the merchant bank "are purchasers making an offer. When the vendors meet to discuss and vote whether or not to accept the offer, it is incongruous that the loudest voice in theory and the most significant vote in practice should come from the wholly owned subsidiary of the purchaser. No one can be both a vendor and a purchaser and, . . . for the purpose of the class meeting [here], MIT were in the camp of the purchaser."[152]

Fairness — Proportionality

11–60 In the same way as it deals with reductions of capital, the court will not sanction an arrangement where the terms are unfair or disproportionate. Perhaps the best statement of the governing principle is that of Bowen L.J.:

> "a compromise or arrangement which has to be sanctioned by the court must be reasonable, and no arrangement or compromise can be said to be reasonable in which you can get nothing and give up everything. A reasonable compromise must be a compromise which can, by reasonable people conversant with the subject, be regarded as beneficial to those on both sides who are making it. Now, 1 have no doubt at all that it would be improper for the Court to allow an arrangement to be forced on any class.., if the arrangement cannot reasonably be supposed by sensible business people to be for the benefit of that class as such. . ."[153]

Whether or not the exchange of old for new interests in, or claims against, the company is adequate turns on the circumstances of the case, account being taken of objective valuations, of the proportions of the class concerned that voted in support of and against the proposal, and any sizeable though not fatal conflict of interests in the class. In *Re John Power & Sons Ltd.*,[154] for instance, the proposal to replace 8 per cent cumulative preference shares with an equal amount of 5 per cent redeemable debentures had the support of nine-tenths of the preference shareholders and three-quarters of them did not own ordinary shares. The court rejected the suggestion that debt ought never to be simply substituted for equity in these schemes; it accepted that, in the circumstances, the proposed scheme there was fair.

---

[152] [1976] 1 W.L.R. 123 at 126.
[153] *Re Alabama etc. Railway Co.* [1891] 1 Ch. 213 at 243.
[154] [1943] I.R. 412; above, para. 11–51.

11–61 Some judges are of the view that, where in reality there is no *quid pro quo* worth speaking of, then the proposal does not even qualify as a compromise or arrangement under the sections; that a member "whose rights are expropriated without any compensating advantage is not . . . having his rights rearranged in any legitimate sense of that expression."[155] Although in the past courts have leaned in favour of sanctioning any compromise where adequate information was provided and where there was no wholly unacceptable conflict of interests, on the grounds that the statutory majorities are themselves the best judges of whether a scheme is a reasonable one for their class, there are indications that judges today assess these schemes more critically.[156]

Public Interest

11–62 The authorities do not refer to the public interest as a matter that should be taken into account here. An Australian court has invoked commercial morality as a reason for not allowing companies to use the equivalent of section 201 to obtain large tax windfalls by acquiring "loss" companies that in fact, though not legally, were insolvent.[157]

SECTION 260 MERGER/RESTRUCTURING

11–63 An alternative method of bringing about major changes in a company's capital structure or constitution is what may be called a merger/restructuring under section 260 of the 1963 Act, originally section 161 of the 1862 Act. There is no definition of the kinds of schemes that fall within this section. It can be used, for example, to bring about a straightforward merger, to segregate liquid assets from the rest of the business or for other purposes. However, something that is *ultra vires* the company or that must be done under some special statutory procedure cannot be accomplished under this power. Nor can class rights be varied without the requisite class approval.[158] Creditors' rights cannot be adversely affected by any such scheme.[159] The principal ad-

---

155 *Re N.F.U. Development Trust Ltd.* [1972] 1 W.L.R. 1548 at 1555.

156 *e.g. ibid.* and *Re Hellenic & General Trust Ltd.* [1976] 1 W.L.R. 123.

157 *Re Brian Cassidy Electrical Industries Property Ltd.* (1984) 9 A.C.L.R. 140.

158 *Griffith v. Paget* (1877) 5 Ch.D. 894; *Re Sandwell Park Colliery Co.* [1914] 1 Ch. 589. See generally, Rice, "Safeguards Against Class Oppression Under Section 287 of the Companies Act 1948" (1958) 22 Conv. 435.

159 If the company is insolvent, the committee of inspection or the court must consent.

vantage for companies in proceeding under section 260 is that a mere special resolution of the company as a whole suffices to initiate the scheme and there is no requirement of court approval.[160] On the other hand, this procedure requires that dissenters be bought off in cash and that the company be wound up.

Procedure

11–64 Section 260 was designed principally to enable one company to absorb another. Where it is sought by this method to change a company's constitution or rearrange its capital structure, a new company, which need not be registered under the 1963–1990 Acts, is created with the desired regulations or structure. The old company then resolves to be wound up voluntarily, and authorises the liquidator to transfer the undertaking to the new company in return for stock, shares, debentures and other interests in the new company. These securities are then distributed to the old company's shareholders in accordance with their capital rights in it. The old company then goes into liquidation. Thus, when the smoke clears the old company has been transformed into one with a different constitution or capital structure. Where a company is already in voluntary liquidation, these transactions can be carried out at any time.

Dissent

11–65 Because a scheme under section 260 cannot adversely affect class rights or creditors' rights, it is not necessary that its adoption should be approved by the court. Shareholders who dissent from the special resolution adopting such a scheme are entitled to be bought out if the liquidator decides to go ahead with the scheme. Where the price cannot be agreed upon, it must be fixed by independent arbitration.[161] Notice of such dissent must be left with the liquidator within seven days of the special resolution being passed.[162] It, however, has been held that a dissenter is not entitled to examine the company's books or the directors in an attempt to show the value of the shares;[163] although these decisions might now fall foul of the Constitution.[164]

---

[160] But *cf.* s.260(7).

[161] s.260(6) incorporates the arbitration procedure of the Companies Clauses Consolidation Act 1845.

[162] *cf. Braily v. Rhodesia Consolidated* [1910] 2 Ch. 95.

[163] *Re Glamorganshire Banking Co., Morgan's Case* (1884) 28 Ch.D. 620; *Re British Building Stone Co.* [1908] 2 Ch. 450.

[164] *cf. Bramelid & Malmstrom v. Sweden*, 5 E.H.R.R. 249.

11–66 A device once used to deprive dissident shareholders of their full right of appraisal — having a provision in the company's regulations whereby it was sought to contract out of the statutory requirements — was permitted in some circumstances until it was condemned in a number of cases, culminating in *Bisgood* v. *Henderson's Transvaal Estates Ltd.*[165] There, one of the company's objects was said to be to sell all its property or the undertaking and to distribute the proceeds among the shareholders in *specie*. It was resolved that the entire undertaking be sold to a new company, that the first company be wound up and that the partly paid shares received in the sale be distributed among its members on a pro rata basis. But instead of being paid cash immediately, dissenters were to receive the proceeds from the sale of those shares in the new company that they would not take up. It was contended that what was happening was merely carrying out one of the company's objects. Buckely L.J., however, held that any such object was invalid because objects under the Companies Acts can have "no relation to acts to be done after the corporate life has come to an end" and cannot "define. . . the distribution of the assets after the corporate life is over."[166] Although a company's regulations may within limits provide how its assets are to be dealt with following liquidation, they cannot provide that a shareholder "shall not enjoy the rights and immunities which the statute gives him",[167] such as to appraisal. Furthermore, the proposals contravened section 27 of the 1963 Act because they sought to "impose upon [each] member the alternative of accepting liability for a larger sum or of being dispossessed of his status as a shareholder upon terms which he is not bound to accept. . ."[168]

RE-REGISTRATION

11–67 Occasionally it is sought to transform a private company into a public company or a public company into a private one, or that a limited company become unlimited, or vice versa. The 1983 Act obliged existing public companies with limited liability either to become p.l.c.s or else re-register under some other form.

Becoming a p.l.c.

11–68 The public limited company, or p.l.c., was inaugurated by the

165 [1908] Ch. 749.
166 *ibid.* at 757–758.
167 *ibid.* at 758.
168 *ibid.* at 759.

1983 Act and its principal features have already been described.[169] An old public limited company is defined by that Act as a company that, when the Act came into force, was a public company with limited liability and having a share capital;[170] in other words, a limited company the articles of which did not satisfy section 33 of the 1963 Act. Section 12 of the 1983 Act sets out the procedures whereby those companies became p.l.c.s. If at any time after January, 13 1985, an old public company has not applied to be re-registered as a p.l.c. or under some other form, the company and any officer in default commit an offence;[171] and if an application to re-register is made but the requirements for the change in status have not been satisfied by January 13, 1986, the company and any officer in default also commit an offence.[172]

11–69 The procedure for a private company becoming a p.l.c. is set out in sections 9 and 10 of the 1983 Act. Briefly, a special resolution to this effect, and appropriately altering the company's memorandum and articles of association, must be passed. A statutory declaration, together with various documents, such as the amended regulations, a balance sheet and an auditors' statement and report, must be delivered to the registrar of companies. Conditions regarding capital for public limited companies must be satisfied. The directors must resolve that the company's memorandum of association be appropriately altered and that the company be re-registered as a p.l.c.; and there must be given to the registrar of companies a copy of the changed memorandum and a statutory declaration that the allotted share capital is not less than £30,000; that a quarter of the nominal amount, together with any premium, was paid up on those shares; where the consideration for any shares allotted was performing work or services, that due performance was already made; and where such consideration was some other undertaking, that it either has been discharged or that there is a contract to have it performed within five years. Additionally, the company must be financially healthy in that its net assets must exceed the aggregate of its called up share capital and its undistributed reserves.[173] There must be a written statement from the company's auditors to this effect, supported by a balance sheet dated within seven months of the application to re-register and an unqualified report of the auditors in relation to the balance sheet. The statutory declaration to be filed must say that, in the meantime, the net assets have not fallen below the called up capital and undistributable reserves and also that

---

[169] See above, paras 2–09—2–10.
[170] s.12(1).
[171] s.13.
[172] s.16.
[173] s.9(3)(b) and (e)(ii).

the above minimum conditions have been met and the special resolution was passed.

11–70 The ways in which unlimited companies and joint stock companies can register as p.l.c.s are set out respectively in sections 11 and 18 of the 1983 Act. In the case of unlimited companies seeking transformation, the procedure just described for private companies becoming p.l.c.s must be followed, but the special resolution to change the company's share capital will be that the members' liability is limited by shares, and make other appropriate changes to the company's regulations.

Going Private

11–71 Section 33 of the 1963 Act defines a private company as one the regulations of which place a ceiling of fifty on its membership, restricts the right to transfer its shares and forbids invitations to the public to subscribe for its securities. Section 14 of the 1983 Act sets out the procedures for p.l.c.s to "go private". Briefly, a special resolution must be passed taking all reference to being a p.l.c. out of the memorandum of association and altering the articles so as to bring them into line with section 33 of the 1963 Act; and an application to re-register, together with a copy of the company's amended regulations, must be delivered to the registrar of companies. However, shareholders who object to this change of status can apply to the court to cancel or vary the special resolution;[174] the court has an extensive discretion in dealing with such applications and may make such relevant orders as it thinks fit, including appraisal of dissident members' shares.

Going Limited

11–72 Machinery to enable unlimited companies to transform themselves into organisations with limited liability was first introduced following the celebrated City of Glasgow bank crash,[175] and shortly afterwards was availed of by many banks to protect their shareholders from financial disaster.[176] This matter is now governed by section 53 of the 1983 Act. Briefly, a special resolution must be passed, altering the company's regulations in the appropriate places, and an application to re-register, together with a copy of the amended regulations, must be made to the registrar of companies. If, however, the company is wound up within three years of its going unlimited, any past member who

---

[174] s.15.
[175] *cf. Houldsworth v. City of Glasgow Bank* (1880) 5 App. Cas. 317.
[176] *cf.* Bank of Ireland Act 1935 (private), s.2.

was a member when it re-registered can be held liable to contribute to the company's assets in respect of obligations incurred before that time.[177]

Going Unlimited

11–73 There are certain advantages that accrue from unlimited liability status[178] and section 52 of the 1983 Act sets out the procedure whereby limited companies can go unlimited. Every member of the company must agree to this change of status. Briefly, there must be delivered to the registrar of companies the prescribed form of assent by or on behalf of all the members, a statutory declaration that the entire membership assented, and a copy of the appropriately changed memorandum and articles of association.

---

177 1983 Act, s.53(7).

178 See above, para. 2–04.

12

Take-Overs and Mergers

12–01 By take-overs and mergers[1] is meant where one company (or exceptionally an individual) acquires control of another company or where both companies amalgamate. There are no general definitions for these terms in the Companies Acts.[2] Transactions of this nature can be brought about in significantly different ways. For instance, one company may simply sell its entire undertaking to another — either for cash[3] or for securities in that other company. Section 260 of the 1963 Act provides a convenient mechanism where it is sought to sell the undertaking for shares in the acquiring company and then distribute those securities to the seller's own shareholders.[4] The procedure under section 201 of the 1963 Act for arrangements can be used in order to take over or merge with another company.[5] But the most common method today is where one company simply acquires most or all of the shares in another company, so that the latter becomes a subsidiary of the former.

12–02 Under this method, where B Co. (call it the "bidder") wishes to take over or merge with T Co. (call it the "target"), B Co. will make an offer to T Co.'s shareholders to buy their shares in T Co.. The consideration offered may be cash or a new issue of B Co.'s own shares, or some combination or permutation of B Co.'s own shares, cash and debt. Where all or most of the consideration being offered is shares in the bidder, then the target's shareholders are being asked to exchange their shares in T Co. for those in B Co.; if they accept, depending on the relative sizes of the companies, they may end up owning a significant stake in B Co. It is usual where the target's shares are widely dispersed to make the offer conditional on a certain proportion of its shareholders accepting — either 50 or 75 or 80 per cent. The bidder, therefore,

---

1 See generally, *Weingberg and Blank on Takeovers and Mergers* (5th ed., 1989) and G. Steadman, *Takeovers* (1993).

2 *cf.* 1983 Act, s.30(4).

3 *e.g. Hutton v. West Cork Railway* (1883) 23 Ch.D. 654.

4 See above, paras 11–63 *et seq*.

5 *e.g. Re National Bank Ltd.* [1966] 1 W.L.R. 819; below, paras 12–45—12–46.

does not have to acquire any of those shares unless there were sufficient acceptances as will guarantee the degree of control he wants.

12–03 Take-overs and mergers almost invariably involve major changes in the acquired company and often in the buyer itself and, accordingly, may be resisted strenuously by some shareholders in those companies. At times, shareholders and managements can make sizeable profits out of these transactions. Take-over bids for companies whose shares are traded on the Stock Exchange occasionally become bitter battles between rival managements, and even attract extensive press coverage. Formerly, take-overs in Irish-quoted companies were regulated by the London-based Panel on Take-Overs and Mergers in accordance with the Stock Exchange's City Code on Take-Overs and Mergers (the "City Code") and Rules Governing the Substantial Acquisition of Shares. That function is now being carried out by the panel established under the Irish Takeover Panel Act 1997.

12–04 Take-overs and mergers involving large firms, whether or not they are quoted on a stock exchange, are also subject to the Mergers, Take-Overs and Monopolies (Control) Acts 1978–1996, which are designed to prevent the undue concentration of economic power by way of monopoly and the like.[6]

12–05 An E.C. Council Directive on mergers[7] was implemented in 1987;[8] not alone does it apply only to p.l.c.s but the transaction affected must be a transfer of assets for securities, similar to that envisaged by section 260 of the 1963 Act. There is a draft Tenth Directive on cross-border mergers of p.l.c.s,[9] which was first published in 1985, and also a draft Thirteenth Directive on take-overs[10] which was published in 1989 but neither of these has been finally adopted by the Council.

AUTHORITY AND DISCLOSURE

12–06 Where a company is required to alter its objects clause in order lawfully to engage in some new form of activity, it must also extend its objects where it intends to merge completely with another concern that

---

[6] See generally, M. Forde, *Commercial Law* (2nd ed., 1997), pp. 415–416 and I. Maher, *Competition Law* (1999), Chap. 5..

[7] [1978] O.J. L295/36.

[8] European Communities (Mergers and Divisions of Companies) Regulations 1989.

[9] [1985] O.J. C23/11.

[10] [1989] O.J. C24/8; see generally, Woulters, "Towards A Level Playing field for Takeovers in the European Community?" (1993) 30 C.M.L. Rev. 267.

is already empowered to engage in that activity. Thus in *Hennessy v. National Agricultural & Industrial Development Association*,[11] an agreed amalgamation between the two defendant non-profit companies was held to be invalid because *inter alia* their combined activities would be *ultra vires* the first defendant. Presumably, if a company acquired all or virtually all the shares in another that carried on a completely different business, the newly-acquired business would have to fall within the purchaser's objects. But it is not clear and there is no leading authority on the question of whether acquisition of, say, 50 per cent or 75 per cent of the shares in another company would be treated as carrying on that company's business for the purpose of *vires* considerations.

12–07 An argument can be made that a majority of the shareholders in a company with a regulation along the lines of clause 80 of Table A are entitled by ordinary resolution to veto a drastic "strategic" decision by the directors to take over or merge with another company. At least, *Automatic Self-Cleansing Filter Syndicate v. Cunninghame*[12] does not preclude this view and there are weighty practical arguments in its favour. Where a take-over requires alteration of the bidder's objects clause or is carried out under sections 260 or 201 of the 1963 Act, then the requisite shareholder approval must be obtained. Where all or some of the consideration being offered by the bidder is its own shares, the requirement of shareholders' prior authority in section 20 of the 1983 Act has to be satisfied. But in those circumstances the bidder does not have to issue a prospectus that complies with the 1963 Act's requirements.[13] And a p.l.c. bidder need not follow the independent valuation and reporting requirements set down in section 30 of the 1983 Act if the transaction is an "arrangement" or a "merger" as defined there.[14] Sections 186–189 of the 1963 Act require that details of "golden handshakes" given in the context of take-overs and mergers be disclosed. Shareholders in mergers subject to the E.C. Third Directive must be provided with a detailed directors' report and an independent experts' report on the proposals.[15]

12–08 The courts have always insisted that information provided by directors to shareholders, with a view to obtaining the latters' approval for a take-over or merger, or their consent to measures taken to resist a bid, should not be misleading.[16] Resolutions passed on foot of mis-

---

11 [1947] I.R. 159; see below, para. 14–67.
12 [1906] 2 Ch. 34; see above, para. 4–49.
13 See above, para. 6–85.
14 1983 Act, s.30(2)–(4).
15 S.I. No. 137 of 1987; see below, para. 12–51.
16 *e.g. Goldex Mines Ltd. v. Revill* (1974) 54 D.L.R. (3d) 672, noted in (1976) 39 Mod.

leading information will be declared invalid, as may agreements entered into that were connected with such resolutions. For instance, in *Kaye v. Croydon Tramways Co.*,[17] where payments made by the acquiring company to the defendant's directors were not disclosed, a declaration was given that the agreement to sell the defendant's undertaking and the special resolution purporting to authorise that sale were held to be void and unenforceable, resulting in an injunction restraining the agreement from being carried out.

12–09 If some material misrepresentation is made to the target company's shareholders and they act on it to their detriment, they may have a claim for deceit or for negligent misrepresentation under the general law of contract and tort.[18] Not infrequently where successful bidders discover that they have acquired a "pig in a poke", they sue the target company's auditors, seeking damages for negligence.[19]

12–10 While directors owe a fiduciary duty to their company, ordinarily they have no such duty to the company's shareholders, even when a take-over is taking place. Their position *vis-à-vis* the members has been summed up as follows: There is:

> "no good reason why it should be supposed that directors are, in general, under a fiduciary duty to shareholders, and in particular current shareholders with respect to the disposal of their shares in the most advantageous way... If on the other hand directors take it on themselves to give advice to current shareholders, . . . they have a duty to advise in good faith and not fraudulently, and not to mislead, whether deliberately or carelessly. [This is] a potential liability arising out of their words or actions which can be based on ordinary principles of law."[20]

12–11 In one exceptional instance, the target's managing director, who was also the purchaser of its shares, was held responsible in damages to the sellers for not disclosing the extent of the profit he stood to make from the acquisition. That was *Coleman v. Myers*,[21] a somewhat compli-

---

L. Rev. 331 and *Winthrop Investments Ltd. v. Winn Ltd.* [1975] 2 N.S.W.L.R. 666, noted in (1977) 40 Mod. L. Rev. 587.

[17] [1898] 1 Ch. 358.

[18] *e.g. Northern Bank Finance Corp. v. Charlton* [1979] I.R. 149 (deceit) and *Securities Trust Ltd. v. Hugh Moore & Alexander Ltd.* [1964] I.R. 417 (negligence).

[19] *e.g. Morgan Crucible Co. p.l.c. v. Hill Samuel & Co. Ltd.* [1991] Ch. 295, *James McNaughton Paper Group Ltd. v. Hicks Anderson & Co.* [1991] 2 Q.B. 113 and *Galoo v. Bright Grahame Murray* [1994] 1 W.L.R. 1360. See above, paras 18–31 *et seq.*

[20] *Dawson International p.l.c. v. Coats Patons p.l.c.* [1989] B.C.L.C. 233 at 243–244; appeal in [1990] B.C.L.C. 560. See also *Re A Company* [1986] B.C.L.C. 382.

[21] [1977] 2 N.Z.L.R. 225.

cated case concerning the take-over of a "close" company. The plaintiffs, who had been minority shareholders, sold their shares to the defendant, its managing director, which enabled him to secure control of the company. He knew that the company's assets were worth far more than their stated value in the accounts and, on buying the shares, he had some of the assets sold off and the proceeds distributed as dividends (going principally to himself). It was concluded that the defendant owed a fiduciary duty of the utmost good faith not alone to the company but to the shareholders in the special circumstances of the case — which were the closely-held nature of the company, the degree of confidence that existed between the parties and the extent to which the plaintiffs depended on the defendant for information, the extent of the defendant's personal interest in the transaction and its very significance. Analogy was drawn with contract cases where bargains made are stuck down on account of undue influence and inequality of bargaining power.[22] Although there is nothing inherently wrong in directors making a profit when dealing directly with shareholders,[23] where their relations with shareholders are sufficiently intense to assume a fiduciary character the directors must "disclose material matters [of] which [they] know or have reason to believe that the shareholders whom they are trying to persuade to sell are or may be inadequately informed."[24] The defendant had not done this and, in any event, it was found that he had been guilty of fraudulent misrepresentation in having deliberately misrepresented his intentions and the value of the company's assets. As for the appropriate remedy, one judge favoured rescission in the form of an order that a fairer transaction be renegotiated. But the majority opted for damages (and not just equitable compensation) on the grounds that rescission was not commercially practicable there.

FINANCING AND SECTION 60

12–12 Where the acquisition (be it of shares in the target or the target's assets) is for cash, then if the acquiring company does not possess sufficient funds it must borrow the money or else raise further capital by issuing and allotting additional shares. The whole question of issuing new shares has already been considered in detail. It has been held that where the bidder issued its own shares to pay for the target and the value of what is acquired exceeds those shares' nominal value, the

---

[22] *e.g. Lloyds Bank v. Bundy* [1975] Q.B. 326.
[23] *Percival v. Wright* [1902] 2 Ch. 421; see above, para. 5–151.
[24] [1977] 2 N.Z.L.R. at p.333. See *Chez Nico Restaurants Ltd.* [1992] B.C.L.C. 192 at 208.

shares have been issued at a premium.[25] That premium must be placed in the share premium account and used only in the manner permitted by section 62 of the 1963 Act.

12–13 One aspect of financing take-overs that gives rise to considerable difficulties is when an acquirer, with little resources of its own, believes or knows that the company being bought is worth considerably more than the going price. In order to make the acquisition, the buyer may borrow the necessary funds and, when the take-over has been completed, assets in the acquired company may be sold off at a high profit and the proceeds of the sale then used to pay off the acquiring company's borrowings. Self-financing mergers of this variety may fall foul of the prohibition of section 60 of the 1963 Act against companies financing the acquisition of their own shares.[26] For instance, in *Heald* v *O'Connor*[27] the plaintiff agreed to sell to the defendant all the shares in a company and, as well, to lend him the money to make the purchase. Since the defendant could not provide adequate security of his own for the loan, it was agreed that the loan should be secured by a charge on the company's assets. This was held to fall within the statutory prohibition and the charge and the personal guarantee given on it by the defendant were held to be void and unenforceable.[28]

12–14 Not every "self-financing" merger is caught by section 60, however; much depends on the circumstances of each case. Thus in *Re Wellington Publishing Co.*,[29] which was described as a decision which will delight asset strippers, a company obtained approximately $NZ 3,000,000 bridging finance in order to take over another. Once the merger was completed, the acquired company's assets were revalued and were shown to be worth far more than their stated worth. In anticipation of the profit that would be made when those assets were realised, a dividend of about $NZ 3,000,000 was declared.[30] It was held that the potentially expansive scope of section 60 must be confined by its *raison d'etre*, which it was said was to protect creditors and minority shareholders. Since, in the circumstances there, the creditors' interests were not jeopardised by the transaction and there were no minority

---

[25] *Henry Head & Co. v. Ropner Holdings Ltd.* [1952] Ch. 124.
[26] See above, paras 7–62 *et seq.*
[27] [1971] 1 W.L.R. 497.
[28] *cf. McCormick v. Cameo Investments Ltd*, McWilliam J., October 27, 1978, Cases p. 564.
[29] [1973] 1 N.Z.L.R. 133, noted in (1974) 90 L.Q.R. 452. See also *Rossfield Group Ltd. v. Austral Group Ltd.* (1980) 5 A.C.L.R. 290.
[30] It is not now possible to pay a dividend from unrealised profits; see above, para. 7–34.

shareholders, all the acquired company's members having accepted the offer, the dividend was held not to constitute financial assistance within the prohibition. While it may be debated whether an Irish court would follow this functional approach to section 60 or this particular version of functionalism, it is provided in section 60(12) that the section does not prohibit the payment of a dividend "properly declared" by the company. It is most likely that properly declared here means declared in compliance with the procedures set down in the articles of association and the statutory provisions on capital maintenance. As *Coleman v. Myers*[31] demonstrates, in exceptional circumstances "self-financing" take-overs can fall foul of general equitable principles.

DEFENCES AGAINST TAKE-OVER BIDS

12–15 In the usual take-over bid by offering to buy the target company's shares, it is for the target's shareholders to decide for themselves whether or not to accept the bid. The fact that they may make handsome profits if they accept, or indeed that all or some of them may incur significant losses if the bid does not succeed, ordinarily has no legal bearing on their decision. It is quite common for boards of directors to resist bids being made for their companies. Opposition may be based simply on the threat to the directors' own position on the target's board. Or they may believe that the price being offered is too low and that resistance is in the shareholders' interest, in that the bidder will be induced to offer more, or indeed that other more generous bidders may be attracted. Or the directors may be of the view that the bidder would damage the company because it has no experience or has a bad record in that business, or that it is an "asset stripper". Or they may prefer that, if control is to pass out of the existing shareholders' hands, it should go to one favoured company (a "White Knight") and not to another.

12–16 Where there is opposition to a bid, various defensive strategies present themselves, which *Weinberg & Blank*[32] divide into two categories. Before a bid is made or is imminent, voting agreements may be concluded between shareholders; interlocking shareholdings may be established between a number of companies; the company's capital structure may be altered by introducing weighted or non-voting shares, or a category of shares entitled to acquire additional equity; the company may dispose of a key asset that is attracting bidders; a block of

---

[31] [1977] 2 N.Z.L.R. 225.

[32] *Takeovers and Mergers* (1989) Chap. 7.

shares may be issued to some outsider who would favour the status quo; or a defensive merger may be concluded with some "White Knight". Measures that may be adopted against a particular bid include refusal by the board to register transfers of the company's shares; purchases in the market of the company's shares by the directors and their associates; increasing the dividend; a "bonus" share issue or a reconstruction of capital to improve gearing; and disclosure of favourable information about the company's prospects or of unfavourable information about the bidder.

Fiduciary Principles and Minority Rights

12–17 The directors' ability to oppose take-over bids is constrained by their fiduciary duties to their company. In determining the legality of defensive measures, the proper approach is that set out by Lord Wilberforce in the *Ampol Petroleum Ltd.* case,namely:

> "to start with a consideration of the power whose exercise is in question. . . . Having ascertained, on a fair view, the nature of this power, and having defined as can best be done in the light of modern conditions the, or some, limits within which it may be exercised, it is then necessary for the court, if a particular exercise of it is challenged, to examine the substantial purpose for which it is exercised, and to reach a conclusion whether that purpose was proper or not. In doing so it will necessarily give credit to the bona fide opinion of the directors, if such is found to exist, and will respect their judgment as to matters of management; having done this, the ultimate conclusion has to be as to the side of a fairly broad line on which the case falls."[33]

12–18 Assuming that by adopting certain defensive measures the directors break their fiduciary duties, an individual shareholder at least in some circumstances can bring suit to have those measures enjoined.[34] But in all the principal authorities where such shareholder claims (either "personal" or "derivative") succeeded the defendant directors who controlled the companies' boards held only a minority of the shares. This was so even in *Clark v. Workman*,[35] where, on the casting vote of the chairman who had promised full support for the bidders, the board resolved that any transfers of shares to the bidding syndicate should be registered. Although part of Ross J.'s judgment there suggests that defensive action by directors who were also the majority shareholders would be enjoined,[36] any such injunction would be futile because, if

---

[33] *Howard Smith Ltd. v. Ampol Petroleum Ltd.* [1974] A.C. 821 at 835.
[34] *e.g.* the *Ampol Petroleum* case, above and *Hogg v. Cramphorn* [1967] Ch. 254.
[35] [1920] 1 I.R. 108; see above, para. 5–117.
[36] *ibid.* at 112–113.

the majority resist the bid, then there is no way in which it can succeed. In *Bamford v. Bamford*,[37] which concerned a "wrongful rights issue", it was held that at least some unlawful defensive measures by directors could be cured by ratification in general meeting. It would seem that this curing power may be exercised *ex ante, i.e.* before the breaches of duty actually take place.[38]

Refusal to Register Transfers

12–19 Whether directors exceed or abuse the powers they possess over registering transfers of shares depends on the circumstances of the case and on the very nature and scope of the power in question. Thus, in the *Alliance & Dublin Gas Co.* case,[39] it was intimated that directors must not obstruct registration of transfers with a view to influencing shareholders' decisions on an offer for the company or for its shares.[40] On the other hand, it would appear that directors of private companies almost have an "absolute discretion" to decline to register transfers when the articles of association incorporate clause 3 of Part 11 of Table A.[41]

Issuing and Allotting Additional Shares

12–20 Use by directors of their power to issue and allot additional shares in the company in an attempt to defeat a take-over bid may, in the circumstances, amount to a breach of their fiduciary duties. Examples include *Hogg v. Cramphorn Ltd.*,[42] where the "primary object" of creating a trust for the employees and lending it money, so that it could subscribe for a large block of shares in the company, was to resist a bid; and *Howard Smith Ltd. v. Ampol Petroleum Ltd.*,[43] where the "substantial purpose" of allotting further equity to a "White Knight" company was to prevent the plaintiff's bid from succeeding. Steps like these are prohibited by the Take-over Panel's principles unless they have the prior approval of shareholders in general meeting; without that authority, the directors must not, once they believe that a *bona fide* bid might be imminent, issue shares, grant options in respect of unissued shares or create or issue securities that carry conversion rights into the

---

37 [1970] Ch. 212.

38 *Winthrop Investments Ltd. v. Winns* [1975] 2 N.S.W.L.R. 666, noted in (1977) 40 Mod. L. Rev. 587.

39 *Kinsella v. Alliance & Dublin Consumers Gas Co.*, Barron J., October 5, 1982; Cases p. 168.

40 See too, *Australian Metropolitan Life Assurance Co. v. Ure* (1923) 33 C.L.R. 199.

41 See above, para. 9.32.

42 [1967] Ch. 254; see above, para. 5–121.

43 [1974] A.C. 821; see above, para. 5–121.

company's shares. Such steps will become rare in the light of the 1983 Act's authority and pre-emption provisions, but they can still occur. The board's authority under section 20 to allot shares may be general and may last for up to five years; section 23 exempts from the pre-emption requirement inter alia private companies whose regulations exclude it and, also, where the consideration for the shares is wholly or partly otherwise than in cash[44] and where the issue is in pursuance of an employees' share scheme.[45]

12–21 It may be that a major reason, but not the only reason, for issuing the shares was other than to thwart the wishes of a majority by blocking a bid. For instance, the target company may genuinely have needed additional capital or a particular asset, or the services of another company, while the directors at the same time may desire to defeat a bid being made for their company. In the *Ampol Petroleum Ltd.* case it was emphasised that the courts will not become entangled in the commercial merits of those decisions; that "such a matter as the raising of finance is one of management within the responsibility of the directors [and] it would be wrong for the court to substitute its opinion for that of the management, or indeed to question the correctness of the management's decision, on such a question, if bona fide arrived at."[46] The legal position where it is established that a significant though not the "primary purpose" was to prevent a bid from succeeding is subject to somewhat conflicting authority.

12–22 In *Nash v. Lancegaye Safety Glass (Ireland) Ltd.*,[47] which was not a take-over case but concerned an attempt by those who controlled 49 per cent of the shares to acquire overall control of the company, Dixon J. held that the existence of an improper motive was fatal to the allotment. However, in an Australian case[48] where the contested allotment did not turn a minority into a majority, but diluted a 19 per cent stake in the company that otherwise would have prevented the bid from succeeding, it was said that the criterion of validity is the "but for" test: would the allotment not have been made but for the improper purpose? Whereas in another Australian case[49] and in a Canadian case[50] it was said that, if the allotment is made to raise funds or to acquire some other business advantage, and at the same time the directors

---

[44] *cf. Teck Corp. v. Millar* (1973) 33 D.L.R. (3d) 288; below, para. 12–23.
[45] *cf. Hogg v. Crampborn Ltd.* [1967] Ch. 254.
[46] [1974] A.C. 821 at 832.
[47] 92 I.L.T.R. 11 (1958); see above, para. 5–120.
[48] *Winthrop Investments Ltd. v. Winns* [1975] 2 N.Z.W.L.R. 666.
[49] *Harlowe's Nominees Ltd. v. Woodside (Lakes Entrance) Oil Co.* (1968) 121 C.L.R. 483.
[50] *Teck Corp.* case, above, n. 46.

would like to see a take-over bid defeated or one bidder succeed rather than another, the net question becomes whether in fact the directors acted to promote the company's interests. According to the Australian High Court in the *Harlowe's Nomines* case, in those circumstances:

> "the ultimate question must always be whether in truth the [new] issue was made honestly in the interests of the company. Directors . . . may be concerned with a wide range of practical considerations, and their judgment, if exercised in good faith and not for irrelevant purposes, is not open to review in the courts."[51]

But this formula virtually denies the existence of an irrelevant purpose, which is the cause of the entire difficulty. Furthermore, if the test is the directors' *bona fide* belief then, in the absence of damning written evidence and assuming that the directors are convincing witnesses, it would be virtually impossible to prevent, under some plausible pretext, an allotment being made to advance the directors' own interests.

12–23 The most recent major reported decision on the matter is the Canadian *Teck Corp.* case,[52] concerning a small mining company with several properties that were ripe for development. Its directors were convinced that the business would be best served if a long term development contract was concluded with one major mining group. In the meantime the plaintiff had been buying shares in Teck on the Stock Market, with a view to a take-over, and had secured just over a 50 per cent stake in it. Fully conscious of this, Teck's directors concluded a development contract with the other company, part of which involved allotting shares to it and the consequence of which was to dilute the plaintiffs stake in Teck. It was held that, just as directors today are no longer absolutely prohibited from taking some account of employees' interests or of the consequence of the company's actions in the general community, so too they might concern themselves with the company being infiltrated by persons or groups who they *bona fide* consider not to be desirable in the best interests of the company. It was concluded from the evidence that the directors were not seeking merely to retain control for themselves, that throughout they believed that the development contract was in the company's best interests, and that the mines would not be developed efficiently and profitably for the benefit of the shareholders if the plaintiff had obtained control. The share allotment therefore was upheld.

12–24 One can only speculate whether an Irish judge would reach the same conclusion. A vital matter that does not appear to have been

---

[51] above, n. 49 at 493.
[52] above, n. 44.

canvassed in *Teck Corp.*, but which may call for evaluation in the courts, is the function of take-overs generally from an economic perspective and the insights economic analysis can contribute to formulating the appropriate rule. Although it did not call for decision in the *Ampol Petroleum Ltd.* case, some disapproval was expressed there with the view that "the absence of any element of self-interest is enough to make an issue valid", while at the same time the outcome in the *Teck Corp.* case was described in *Ampol Petroleum Ltd.* as being "in line with" existing authority.

Lock-Out Arrangements

12–25 By a lock-out arrangement is meant some understanding or agreement between the target company or its directors and the bidder that the latter will be favourably treated if there are competing bids. Where such an arrangement has been made without the approval of the shareholders, the question arises whether the directors have unlawfully fettered their discretion. That question was answered in the affirmative in *Clark v. Workman*,[53] where the chairman of a Belfast-based shipbuilding company had promised the chairman of a British-based syndicate that he would use his best endeavours to see that they would get control of the company. A board resolution to approve all share transfers that may be made to that consortium, passed with his casting vote, was held to be invalid; he had "fettered himself . . . and had disqualified himself from acting *bona fide* in the interests of the company he was leaving."[54]

12–26 The issue in *Dawson International Ltd. v. Coats Paton p.l.c.*[55] was whether fiduciary principles provided a defence to a claim for damages for breach of a lock-out arrangement. There had been negotiations about the plaintiff company taking over the defendant and both made a joint press announcement that the defendant's directors would recommend the bid. It was contended that, in addition, both companies had agreed that the defendant would not co-operate with any rival bidder. When the plaintiff's bid did not succeed, it claimed damages for breach of contract, and an application was made to have the action dismissed *in limine* as disclosing no cause of action. At the hearing, the plaintiff conceded that such contract as it may have had with the target company was subject to fiduciary principles in that, if circumstances altered materially, the target's directors were entitled to put their shareholders interests foremost and refuse to implement the agreement. It

---

[53] [1990] 1 I.R. 107.
[54] *ibid.* at 117–118.
[55] [1989] B.C.L.C. 233, affirmed [1990] B.C.L.C. 560.

was held that there was a stateable case on the pleadings of breach of contract but there seems to be no reported decision on the ultimate outcome. In an earlier similar instance,[56] Vinelott J. dismissed the disappointed bidder's claim because, in the circumstances, the directors properly recommended a rival's bid, notwithstanding previous undertakings they had given to the plaintiff.

12–27 A variant of the lock-out arrangement is where the directors themselves own the majority of the company's shares and they side with one rather than with another bidder. While the directors *qua* shareholders would then be in a position to give their preferred bidder voting control of the company, that bidder most likely will want to acquire almost all if not all of the issued shares, in order to avoid possible difficulties with minority shareholders. That was the position in *Re a Company*[57] where, in addition, the bidder for a private company who was preferred by the directors was another company that they controlled. However, a rival bidder offered a better price. The issue to be decided was whether the directors acted properly in sending a circular to the shareholders advising them, notwithstanding, to accept their company's bid and not that of the rival, because its bid could not possibly succeed in the circumstances, since the directors would never accept its offer. It was held that, providing the circular was not misleading, no breach of fiduciary duty would be committed.[58]

PROFITEERING BY DIRECTORS AND BY SHAREHOLDERS

12–28 Management and shareholders engage in take-overs and mergers almost invariably to make a profit. In the typical take-over by acquiring the target company's shares, the buyer will believe that it can run that company more efficiently than it is being managed at present and that its real worth is not fully reflected in its existing share price; its shareholders will be tempted to sell out because the price being offered exceeds the then going rate for their shares. Both companies' management may also stand to gain; for instance, positions in a merged and much larger entity may carry greater prestige and be more lucrative. Moreover, both sets of directors may be tempted to chase quick profits by "insider trading" before the envisaged merger becomes public knowledge. Also, the target's directors may negotiate "golden hand-

---

56 *John Crowther Group p.l.c. v. Carpets International p.l.c.* [1990] B.C.L.C. 460.
57 [1986] B.C.L.C. 382.
58 A more complex variant of the situation here, involving a quoted company, is *Heron International Ltd. v. Grade* [1983] B.C.L.C. 244.

shakes" and "golden umbrellas" for themselves. The Take-over Panel's principles, which apply to quoted companies, subject profiteering by the target's shareholders in take-overs to the equality principle and either forbid, or require extensive prior disclosure of profiteering by directors. Subject to a number of exceptions, however, the general law tolerates profiteering by sections of the shareholders and the management.

Fiduciary Principles and Minority Rights

12–29 Not alone must company directors not enrich themselves at their company's expense but they must not place themselves in a position where their own private interests and those of the company conflict. It will depend on the circumstances of each case whether or not these duties were complied with. Is it permissible, for example, for directors to recommend acceptance of a take-over bid in the knowledge, not disclosed to shareholders, that the acquiring company will give them places on its board, or that they will be allowed to retain their seats on the target company's board? Assuming that this is a breach of fiduciary duty, what is the appropriate remedy: resignation from the directorship or handing up the directors' fees? There are no authorities squarely on those questions.

12–30 The fact that directors' duties are owed to their companies rather than to the shareholders individually gives rise to an anomalous situation where the target company's officers made a profit from their position. Those with the greatest reason to feel aggrieved by such practices are the target's old shareholders; they may feel that they were, so to speak, sold down the river so that the directors could make large profits for themselves. In very exceptional circumstances, like in *Coleman v. Myers*,[59] the directors will be fiduciaries for those shareholders as well, who therefore may have a remedy. Usually, however, fiduciary duties are owed to the company only but, when the bid succeeds, the company would have new owners who may have collaborated with the errant directors, and the company may choose not to pursue the matter.[60] This dilemma cannot be resolved satisfactorily by placing profiteering by directors on the same level as "defrauding" the company, because any redress obtained in a derivative action would be in favour of the target and not its aggrieved shareholders. Additionally, most if not all of those aggrieved would have disposed of their shares so that they would not possess the essential qualifications to institute a

[59] [1977] 2 N.Z.L.R. 225; above, para. 12–11.
[60] The converse occurred in *Regal (Hastings) Ltd. v. Gulliver* [1967] 2 A.C. 134n.

derivative suit or make an application under section 205 of the 1963 Act for "oppression".

"Golden Handshakes" and "Golden Umbrellas"

12–31 A company that acquires another may wish to remove all or some of the latter's directors. Assuming that the acquirer controls at least 50 per cent of the voting shares, it can remove the directors by an ordinary resolution, subject to whatever rights to compensation as exist under their service contracts.[61] Often, however, the acquirer may choose to pay those directors *ex gratia* sums on their retirement, for instance, in order to win their support for a take-over bid or simply to avoid the embarrassment of having to put down removal resolutions for the general meeting. Where a "golden handshake" of this nature has a bearing on any resolution being proposed in general meeting, full disclosure must be made to the shareholders;[62] a resolution passed without such disclosure being made is invalid. Section 186 of the 1963 Act requires that the details of any payment made to directors and *de facto* directors by way of compensation for loss of office, or as consideration for or in connection with retirement from office, as defined in it, be disclosed to the members and approved by them in general meeting.

12–32 Sections 187 and 188 of the 1963 Act apply this disclosure and shareholder approval rule to two kinds of take-over or merger. One is where the payment is made in connection with the transfer of all or part of the company's undertaking to another. Any such payment that is not approved in general meeting is deemed to be received by the director in trust for the company. Section 188 deals with the usual kind of take-over: where an offer to buy their shares is made to all the shareholders, or an offer is made with a view to the target becoming a subsidiary company, or with a view to the offeror obtaining control of at least one-third of the voting rights, or an offer that is conditional on acceptance to a given extent. The particulars of a payment proposed to be made to a director in any of these circumstances must accompany the notice of the offer sent to the shareholders and those shareholders must approve of the payment in a meeting summoned for that purpose.[63] Otherwise, the director is deemed to have received the funds in trust for those who sold their shares in consequence of the offer.

12–33 Sections 186–188's requirements do not apply to any *bona fide*

---

[61] 1963 Act, s.182; see above, para. 5–45 *et seq.*

[62] *Kaye v. Croydon Tramways Co.* [1898] 1 Ch. 358; see above, para. 4–19.

[63] *cf.* subs.(4) and (5).

payment by way of damages for breach of contract or by way of pension in respect of past services Although the compensation paid to the retiring managing director in *Taupo Totara Timber Co. v. Rowe*[64] was held to fall outside of the New Zealand version of these rules, most likely those payments come within sections 186-188. The requirements in sections 187 and 188 are supplemented by general fiduciary standards; they do not prejudice the operation of any rule of law concerning disclosure or accountability.[65] Those sections, moreover, are supplemented by a number of deeming provisions designed to prevent their evasion. Two kinds of payment are deemed to be subject to the disclosure and shareholder approval rule. One is the difference between the price paid to a director for shares in the company and the amount that other like shareholders could have obtained at the same time, or any valuable consideration given to such director in connection with the transfer of assets or of shares.[66] Another kind of payment deemed to fall within those requirements, unless the contrary is shown, is a payment made in pursuance of any "arrangement" that was made within one year before or two years after the time of the offer, or the transferee was privy to that arrangement.[67]

12–34 The term "golden umbrella" signifies service contracts made with company directors where the remuneration is significantly high and that are for long periods. Often those arrangements serve the purpose of deterring shareholders from removing directors, in that the amount of damages payable for breach would be prohibitively high. Such contracts are entered into especially with a view to the existing membership changing in a take-over. As was explained when considering directors' remuneration generally, service contracts of longer than five years duration must now be approved by the shareholders.[68] Assuming the company's regulations permit the board to decide on service contracts for less than that duration, the question will be whether the directors used their powers for an extraneous purpose. Assuming that directors break their fiduciary duties in entering into "golden umbrella" contracts, it would appear that any damages paid subsequently for breach of those contracts must be disclosed as a "golden handshake", on the grounds that it is not a "*bona fide* payment by way of damages" as envisaged by section 189(13) of the 1963 Act.

---

64 [1978] A.C. 537; see above, paras 5–61 and 5–73.
65 s.189(4).
66 s.189(2).
67 s.189(1).
68 1990 Act s.28; see above, para. 5–35.

Price Discrimination

12–35 By "price discrimination" is meant charging different prices for what is essentially the same product or service. As far as the general law is concerned, where there are no exceptional circumstances,[69] every shareholder is entitled to have the best terms that he can get for his shares. In particular, a person with a controlling or a key block of shares may accept more than what the others obtained for their shares. Although majorities in companies must not discriminate unfairly at the expense of minorities, it would appear that it is permissible to obtain a premium for the controlling shares.[70] Any premium obtained by directors for their shares in the context of a take-over must be disclosed to and approved by the shareholders,[71] but this is not the case where they retain their office as directors of the company.

Insider Trading

12–36 Insider trading or dealing is a notorious source of easy profits when a take over bid is being mounted. Before 1991 the legal remedies against that practice were very deficient but the matter is now governed by Part V of the 1990 Act and several other provisions of that Act regarding directors and other insiders dealing in their company's shares.[72]

REMOVING DISSIDENTS

12–37 A company that is seeking to take over another may succeed in acquiring the vast majority of the shares in the target but there may remain a minority who refuse to sell out their shares at the price being offered; or indeed that minority may be so opposed to the bid that they refuse to sell out at almost any price. Section 204 of the 1963 Act, first introduced by section 8 of the 1959 Act, which is sometimes referred to as the "take-out merger" provision, was enacted to enable bidders who acquire the bulk of the target's shares to compel the remaining shareholders to sell out to them. It also enables a minority that originally refused to accept the bid to change their minds and insist that the partially successful bidder buys them out. Where a bidder does not satisfy the requirements laid down in section 204 for take-

---

69 *e.g. Heron International Ltd. v. Grade* [1983] B.C.L.C. 244.

70 *cf. Perlman v. Feldmann*, 219 F 2d 173 (1955). See generally, Boyle, "The Sale of Controlling Shares" (1964) 13 Intl. & Comp. L.Q. 185.

71 1963 Act, s.189(2).

72 See above, para. 5–155 *et seq.*

outs, it may nevertheless in exceptional circumstance be permitted to achieve the same result through the section 201 mechanism for arrangements or through the section 260 procedure for restructuring.

Section 204 "Take-Out"

12–38 Subject to what is said below, where at least 80 per cent of the target's shareholders accept a full take-over bid, section 204 of the 1963 Act authorises the bidder to expropriate the remaining 20 per cent or less on the same terms as the others got. This power of expropriation could possibly fall foul of the Constitution's private property guarantees, although, in view of the requirement of equal treatment and the provision for judicial supervision, it would most likely be sustained against such a challenge. In *Bramelid and Malmstrom v. Sweden*[73] the European Commission of Human Rights ruled that a somewhat similar provision in Swedish law did not contravene the property rights guaranteed in the First Protocol of the European Convention on Human Rights. However, the critical proportion in the Swedish law there, and also in the present British legislation[74] is 90 per cent of the target's shares, whereas under Irish law it is only 80 per cent. Because of the drastic powers given by the section, it is strictly construed by the courts.[75]

Procedure

12–39 For a bidder to be entitled to take out the dissident shareholders, the following must be satisfied. There must have been an offer or arrangement made by one company to acquire ownership of all the shares in another, and at least 80 per cent in value of the latter's shareholders must have accepted or endorsed this offer. Where, however, the bidder at the outset was the beneficial owner[76] of at least 20 per cent in value of the target's shares, the offer or arrangement must be accepted by three-quarters in number of the shareholders as well. Where the offer is being made for a particular class or classes of shares, then these requirements apply to each class in question. Within 6 months of the bid being published, the bidder may notify the dissenting minority of its intention to acquire their shares. When one month of giving that notice expires, provided that the court does not intervene, the bidder becomes entitled to acquire the dissidents' shares on the same terms as

---

[73] 5 E.H.R.R. 249.
[74] Companies Act 1985, ss. 428–430.
[75] *e.g. Blue Metal Industries Ltd. v. Dilley* [1970] A.C. 827, holding that it does not apply to "consortium" bids, and *Re Chez Nico Restaurants Ltd.* [1992] B.C.L.C. 192, holding that it does not apply to non-binding offers or to offers to treat.
[76] *cf.* s.204(3).

it offered the accepting shareholders.[77] The bidder may then send the target company instruments of transfer, together with payment for those shares, and the target is obliged to register the shares in the name of whoever is designated as transferee. Any sums that the target company receives in payment for the dissidents' shares must be held in a separate bank account in trust for them.

12–40 When a bidder acquires 80 per cent of the target's shares in the manner described above but chooses to leave the minority hold on to their shares, section 204(4) provides an appraisal machinery whereby the minority can change their minds and insist on the bidder buying them out on the same terms as were offered to the accepting shareholders.[78]

Challenging the Take-Out

12–41 Section 204(1) allows any dissenting shareholder who is notified of the intention to expropriate in this manner to apply to the court, which "if it thinks fit [may] order otherwise". It has been held that this gives the court a discretion to veto a take-out when in the circumstances it is particularly unjust, even if all the section's procedural requirements have been satisfied." Where the entire transaction is at arm's length then the burden of proof is on the dissident. Where those who held the bulk of the shares have accepted the bid, it is a heavy burden to overcome, for the court naturally starts with the assumption that the other shareholders are likely to know where their own interests lie as well as the objector. In an appropriate case, however, for instance where the directors advised acceptance of the bid on the strength of advice they got from independent experts, the court will order discovery of documents in the possession of either or both companies.[79] Circumstances can arise where the dissidents have been left in the dark about major features of the bid, that the target's own directors are obliged to provide them with "full particulars of the transaction, its purpose, the method of carrying it out and its consequences."[80]

12–42 If the transaction is not at arm's length, like where the bidder already has a large stake in the target's shares, then the burden of proof is reversed. In those circumstances, it is for the bidder to satisfy the

---

[77] *Re Simo Securities Trust Ltd.* [1971] 1 W.L.R. 1455.

[78] *McCormick v. Cameo Investments Ltd*, McWilliam J., October 27, 1978; Cases p. 564.

[79] *Re Lifecare International Ltd.* [1990] B.C.L.C. 222.

[80] *Securities Trust Ltd. v. Associated Properties Ltd.*, McWilliam J., November 19, 1980; Cases p. 552.

court that the price being offered is fair.[81] This may require the bidder to disclose information about valuations and related matters to the dissidents. In *Re Chez Nico Restaurants Ltd.*,[82] although section 204 was held not to apply because the offer made was one to receive offers of shares rather than of acceptance (*i.e.* a notice to treat), it was stated that court approval would not have been given if the matter had come within section 204. This was because those seeking control were directors and substantial shareholders already in the "target" company, which was quoted, but all the information that the City Code required to disclose was not made available to the other shareholders. Since the transaction there was covered by the City Code, Browne Wilkinson V.C. found it unnecessary to decide whether, under the general law, directors seeking to acquire control of a company must make full disclosure of all relevant facts to the other shareholders.

12–43 Even where exception cannot be taken to the price, the court may veto the take-out where the expropriation power is being abused, for instance, where the target's directors had misled some of its shareholders into accepting the offer[83] or where a majority in the target are merely seeking to expel unwanted shareholders from the company. Thus in *Re Bugle Press Ltd.*,[84] two shareholders tried to use the take-out machinery to rid themselves of the remaining shareholder and thereby acquire complete control of the company. The two, who held 4,500 shares each, formed the bidder company and it then made an offer for all the shares in the target. Predictably, this was accepted by the two but was rejected by the third shareholder, who held 1,000 shares. Since its offer had secured 90 per cent acceptance, the bidder sought to acquire those 1,000 shares under the British equivalent of section 204 (which does not have the proviso about acceptance by three-quarters in number in these circumstances). Given the actual background to the bid, the court enjoined the "barefaced attempt simply to expel" a shareholder from the company, stating that:

> "the section has been used not for the purpose of any scheme or contract properly so called or contemplated by the section but for the quite different purpose of enabling majority shareholders to expropriate or evict the minority and that . . . is something for the purposes of which prima facie, the court ought not to allow the section to be invoked — unless at any rate it were shown that there was some good reason in the interests of the company for so doing, for example, that the minority shareholder

[81] *Re Bugle Press Ltd.* [1961] 1 Ch. 270; below, para. 12–43.
[82] [1992] B.C.L.C. 192.
[83] *Gething v. Kilner* [1972] 1 W.L.R. 337.
[84] [1961] 1 Ch. 270.

was in some way acting in a manner destructive or highly damaging to the interests of the company from some motives entirely of his own."[85]

Section 201 Arrangement

12–44 Provided that 75 per cent in value of each class affected, who vote, agree and that the court consents, companies may bring about drastic changes in their constitutions or capital structures under sections 201–204 of the 1963 Act.[86] While this procedure is usually resorted to so that companies in financial difficulties can reorganise their balance sheets, it can also be used in order to take over another company. Before any such scheme can take effect, it must be one to which the company is a party.[87] On one occasion of great significance in Irish financial history it was permitted to be used to remove dissident shareholders who objected to a take-over bid and who most likely could not have been taken out under the section 204 procedure.

12–45 This was in *Re National Bank Ltd.*,[88] which concerned the former National Bank, a mainly Irish bank that was founded by Daniel O'Connell but was registered as a company in England, and had its headquarters and some other offices there. An elaborate scheme was devised to enable the Bank of Ireland and a Scottish Bank to take over National. In brief, National's Irish business was to be transferred to a company, N.B.I., in return for shares in it; those shares would then be sold to the Bank of Ireland in return for cash and renounceable loan stock, which would be distributed *pro rata* to National's members once the scheme was approved of by special resolution.[89] Although the scheme was supported by a 90 per cent majority at a general meeting held in London, this represented only 61 per cent of National's entire shareholders. Since 72 per cent of its shareholders had Irish addresses, many of them being small shareholders living in rural Ireland, and because opposition to the entire arrangement appears to have been badly organised, it could be argued that approximately 35 per cent of National's shareholders did not support the proposals.

12–46 Two grounds were put forward in opposing the petition requesting that the court sanction the scheme. It was said that National's secret reserves should have been disclosed to the members, the implication being that those reserves were worth a considerable amount

---

[85] [1961] 1 Ch. 270 at 287.
[86] See above, paras 11–51 *et seq*.
[87] *Re Savoy Hotel Ltd.* [1981] 1 Ch. 351.
[88] [1966] 1 W.L.R. 819.
[89] *cf.* National Bank Transfer Act 1966.

and that therefore the purchase price for National's shares was insufficient. But accountants' reports approved the price in question; and in any event, it was held, the Companies Acts did not oblige banks to disclose "secret" reserves.[90] The second objection was that use should not be made of section 201 to acquire full control of another company by way of take-over in circumstances where the bidder could not take out dissidents under section 204. Plowman J's somewhat cryptic answer was that:

> "It seems to me to involve imposing a limitation or qualification either on the generality of the word "arrangement" in section 201 or else on the discretion of the court under that section. The legislature has not seen fit to impose any such limitation in terms and I see no reason for implying any. Moreover, the two sections, section 201 and section 204, involve quite different considerations and different approaches. Under section 201 an arrangement can only be sanctioned if the question of its fairness has first of all been submitted to the court. Under section 204 on the other hand, the matter may never come to the court at all. If it does come to the court then the onus is cast on the dissenting minority to demonstrate the unfairness of the scheme. There are, therefore, good reasons for requiring a smaller majority in favour of a scheme under section 201 than the majority which is required under section 204 if the minority is to be expropriated."[91]

12–47 In the subsequent and very similar *Re Hellenic & General Investment Trust* case,[92] which involved the most blatant conflict of interests and some unfairness, although the price paid was not objectionable, undercutting the requirements of section 204 was one of the reasons why the court refused approval for the arrangement there that envisaged expelling the minority.

Section 260 Restructuring

12–48 An alternative strategy for removing dissidents in a take-over is for the majority to get the company to sell its undertaking or principal assets to themselves; they then put the company into liquidation in which they recover much of the purchase price they paid. But it is highly unlikely that the court would give its consent under section 10 of the 1963 Act to a change of objects that is designed to facilitate such a manoeuvre. However, section 260 of the 1963 Act provides a mechanism whereby the company can sell the undertaking without running into

---

[90] 1963 Act, 6th Sched., pt III; this is no longer the position – see below, para. 14–67.
[91] [1966] 1 W.L.R. 819 at 829–830.
[92] [1976] 1 W.L.R. 123; see above, para. 11–59.

this obstacle. The company can resolve to go into voluntary liquidation; then require the liquidator to transfer the undertaking to another company in return for cash and securities in the transferee, which will then be distributed among the transferee's members; and the transferor will be wound up.[93]

12–49 A rare reported instance of this procedure being used to remove dissidents arose out of measures adopted to reorganise privately-owned public transport in London early in this century. In *Castello v. London General Omnibus Co.*,[94] 95 per cent of a company's equity was owned by the defendant, which sought to acquire the remaining 5 per cent. To this end, a scheme was drawn up under which the defendant would form a new company, the first company would then be put into liquidation and the new company would buy the entire undertaking in return for paying off debentures, repaying the preference shareholders and paying enough cash to distribute £275 per share among the former's £100 ordinary shareholders. Once approved by a special resolution, a section 260 scheme is binding on the company's members; though members who dissent are entitled to have their shares bought out for cash at a price fixed by arbitration. The minority sought an injunction against implementing these proposals, contending that they were entitled to continue to participate in the company's prosperity, such as by coming into the new company on a *pro rata* basis, and that it was improper for the purchaser to in effect set the price for the exchange. Since "there [was] no pretence of fraud [or] bad faith" and the price was shown to be fair, the court declined to intervene, citing the *North-West Transportation* case.[95] The court conceded that "it may well be that the [majority] will get an advantage from the opportunity to invest in the new company which possibly the plaintiff . . . will not have."[96] This outcome, however, was justified on the grounds that it "is not an inequality produced by these resolutions. As to the effect of these resolutions it appears . . . to be an effect produced by the [parties] unequal position";[97] and in any event, it was concluded, the majority acted not in bad faith but merely in their own interests. It is doubtful if a court today would make the same decision.

---

[93] See above, paras 11–63 *et seq*.
[94] (1912) 107 L.T. at 576.
[95] (1887) 12 App. Cas. 589; see above, para. 10–07.
[96] (1912) 107 L.T. at 581.
[97] *ibid*.

THE E.C. DIRECTIVES

12–50 One of the aspects of Company Law which has become the subject of E.C. intervention is take-overs and mergers, either directly, like under the Third and Sixth Directives on Company Law,[98] or indirectly through the Insider Trading Directive.[99] Under the proposed 13th Directive[100] there will be standardised rules governing the timetable for offers, the content of offer and defence documents, the obligation on all bidders who acquire a specified percentage of the shares (33⅓ per cent) to make a bid for the remaining shares, the prohibition of certain kinds of "poison pills" designed to frustrate bids and the independent supervision of the entire take-over process.

12–51 The European Communities (Merger and Divisions) of Companies Regulations 1987[101] gave effect to the Third and Sixth Directives. These Regulations' requirements apply only to p.l.c.s and to certain unregistered companies which are subject to section 377 of the 1963 Act. Even with regard to all of these companies, its provisions do not apply to the commonest form of take-over, *i.e.* the bidder acquiring most or all of the shares in the target company. They apply only to two forms of merger. One is a merger by acquisition, which means where the bidder acquires all the target's assets and liabilities in return for shares in the bidder, with or without a cash payment, and it is envisaged that the target will shortly afterwards be wound up; for instance, a take-over using section 260 of the 1963 Act. The other is an essentially similar operation except that the bidder forms a new company which acquires the target and the latter is then wound up; again, the procedure under section 260 of the 1963 Act. Briefly, what the Regulations call for in either of these circumstances is that, where a merger is proposed, the directors of both merging companies draw up draft terms for a merger setting out various relevant matters and the directors of each company must draw up separate written reports on those draft terms, which explain them and discuss their implications for the company and its shareholders. A report on the draft terms must also be made by an independent person, who must give an opinion on *inter alia* whether the proposed terms are fair and reasonable. If either or both companies' last annual accounts are more than six months out of date, an accounting statement in the format of the balance sheet must

---

98 [1978] O.J. L295/36 and [1982] O.J. L378/47, implemented by S.I. No. 137 of 1987.

99 [1989] O.J. L334/30; see above, paras 5–150 *et seq.*

100 Doc. XV/63/87 rev. 1.

101 S.I. No. 137 of 1987.

be drawn up for the company. Copies of these documents must be sent to the registrar of companies and also be made available for inspection by shareholders at both companies' own registered offices.

12–52 Before the merger can take place, the proposed terms must be approved by special resolutions of both companies' shareholders. Provision is made for acquiring the shares owned by dissenting shareholders and for protecting the interests of any creditors who object to the merger. Ultimately, the merger must be confirmed by order of the court, which is empowered to make various ancillary orders.

REGULATORY MACHINERY

12–53 In many countries the entire process of take-overs is regulated by independent administrative agencies which are given extensive powers to ensure that the contestants observe fair play. The oldest, the most well known and perhaps the most powerful of these is the U.S. Securities and Exchange Commission.[102] Since its inception in **19..**, the Australian Securities Commission has been extremely active in supervising take-overs and mergers.[103] A body somewhat along the same lines is envisaged by the proposed E.C. Thirteenth Directive,[104] although it remains to be seen the extent to which the apparatus eventually agreed on is required to be a direct arm of the State. Before 1997, take-overs of quoted Irish companies were subject to what is known as the City Code on Take-Overs and Mergers and the Rules Governing the Substantial Acquisition of Shares. Compliance with these rules was supervised by the Panel on Take-Overs and Mergers, the decisions of which could be appealed to an Appeal Committee. That Panel and Committee are in effect a United Kingdom administrative agency and are based in London.[105] The extent of their authority over events occurring in Ireland and whether their activities can be made subject to judicial review in this country raised serious questions of the conflict of laws and of constitutional law.

12–54 Enactment of the Irish Takeover Panel Act 1997 has rendered these very interesting questions largely academic because it establishes

---

102 See generally, L. Loss and J. Seligman, *Securities Regulation* (3rd ed., 1988–90).

103 See generally, H. Ford et al., *Principles of Corporations Law* (9th ed., 1999), Chap. 23 and I. Renard and J. Santanaria, *Takeovers and Reconstructions in Australia* (1990, looseleaf).

104 above, n. 100.

105 An excellent account of the regime in the U.K. is in P. Davies, *Gower's Principles of Modern Company Law* (6th ed., 1997) at 772–805.

an indigenous regulatory agency resembling somewhat the United States S.E.C. and the Australian A.S.C. A Panel has been established under this Act, the principal function of which is to monitor bids for quoted companies in order to ensure that competitions for corporate control are carried out fairly and that shareholders' interests are not prejudiced. This panel has published rules regarding how take-overs should and should not be carried out and is empowered to apply to the High Court for orders securing compliance with those rules. Decisions of and directions given by the Panel can be challenged in the courts through the judicial review procedure and persons disciplined by the Panel have a right of appeal to the High Court.

12–55 The substantive rules governing take-overs and mergers are the principles contained in the schedule to the 1997 Act, which are elaborated on in regulations that were promulgated in 1997. Their content closely resembles the previous regime administered from London. The fundamental principles, scheduled to the 1997 Act, are as follows:

1. All shareholders of the same class of the offeree shall be treated similarly by an offeror.
2. Where information is tendered by the offeror or offeree or their respective advisers to shareholders of the offeree in the course of any offer it shall be made available equally to all of the shareholders who may accept the offer.
3. No offer shall be made and no announcement of a proposed offer shall be made save after careful and responsible consideration of the matter by the offeror and any advisers of the offeror and only if the offeror and any advisers of the offeror are satisfied that the offeror will be able to implement the offer if it is accepted.
4. Shareholders to whom an offer is made shall be entitled to receive such information and advice as will enable them to make an informed decision on the offer. For that purpose the information and advice should be accurate and adequate and be furnished to the shareholders in a timely fashion.
5. It is the duty of all parties to a takeover or other relevant transaction to prevent the creation of a false market in any of the securities of the offeror or offeree and to refrain from any statement or conduct which could mislead shareholders or the market.
6. It is the duty of the directors of an offeree when an offer is made or when they have reason to believe that the making of an offer is imminent to refrain from doing anything as respects the conduct of the affairs of the offeree which might frustrate that offer or de-

prive shareholders of the opportunity of considering the merits of the offer, except upon the authority of those shareholders given in general meeting.

7. Directors of the offeree shall give careful consideration before they enter into any commitment with an offeror (or any other person) which would restrict their freedom to advise shareholders of the offeree in the future.

8. The directors of the offeree and (if it is a company) of the offeror owe a duty to the offeree and the offeror respectively and to the respective shareholders of those companies to act in disregard to personal interest when giving advice and furnishing information in relation to the offer; in discharging that duty the said directors shall be bound to consider the interests of the shareholders as a whole.

9. Rights of control must be exercised in good faith and the oppression of a minority is not acceptable in any circumstances.

10. Where an acquisition of securities is contemplated as a result of which a person may incur an obligation to make an offer, he or she must, before making the acquisition, ensure that he or she can and will continue to be able to implement such an offer.

11. An offeree ought not to be disrupted in the conduct of its affairs beyond a reasonable time by an offer for its securities.

12. A substantial acquisition of securities (whether such acquisition is to be effected by one transaction or a series of transactions) shall take place only at an acceptable speed and shall be subject to adequate and timely disclosure.

13

Company Contracts

13–01 The vast majority of companies are formed with a view to their doing business with persons other than their principal shareholders or directors, *i.e.* with "outsiders". A major problem, therefore, is when or in what circumstances contracts and engagements with outsiders, which are purported to be entered into by or on behalf of companies, are legally binding on them.[1] Since companies by their very nature can act only through individuals, or agents, it must first be established that the person negotiating the transaction in question is authorised by the company to do so. The transaction may even be *ultra vires,* or the company's regulations may place other restrictions on that agent's power to act. Subject to what is said below, since companies' memoranda and articles of association are public documents, outsiders dealing with companies are deemed to know the contents of those documents; accordingly, they have "constructive notice" of companies' objects and any other restrictions that those documents impose on company agents' authority.[2] In the past, companies would not be bound by contracts made on their behalf but contrary to such restrictions. Nor would companies be held to contracts made for them before they were incorporated. Nor could companies ratify either *ultra vires* or pre-incorporation contracts. Doing business with companies, therefore, presented special risks, in that contracts and other undertakings entered into with them could transpire not to be legally binding on them.

13–02 These very questions were the subject of the E.C.'s First Directive on Company Law.[3] According to the central part of this Directive's preamble:

> "Whereas the basic documents of the company should be disclosed in order that third parties may be able to ascertain their contents and other information concerning the company, especially particulars of the persons who are authorised to bind the company; Whereas the protection of third parties must be ensured by provisions which restrict to the greatest

---

1 See generally, A.G. Guest (ed.), *Chitty on Contracts* (27th ed., 1994), Chap. 9.
2 *Ernest v. Nicholls* (1857) 6 H.L. Cas. 401.
3 O.J. L65/41 (1968-special ed.).

> possible extent the grounds on which obligations entered into in the name of the company are not valid . . ."

Most of the matters that the First Directive, and indeed the Second Directive, call to be disclosed were in fact covered by the 1963 Act's disclosure requirements. Two of the principal legal traps, into which persons, doing business with companies, could fall were removed by sections 37 and 8(1) of the 1963 Act that deal with pre-incorporation agreements and *ultra vires* engagements, respectively. Statutory Instrument no. 163 of 1973 deals with another of these traps.

13–03 Account ought to be taken of the terms and background of E.C. Directives in construing legislation enacted in order to implement their terms into national law.[4] In one English case regarding pre-incorporation agreements, for example, the Court of Appeal examined carefully the relevant parts of the First Directive and indeed its background in French Law.[5] However, sections 37 and 8(1) of the 1963 Act were enacted in anticipation of the First Directive, which was not cast in its final form until 1968. There are significant differences in terminology between key phrases in the Directive and in these sections, notably in respect of the degree of knowledge a third party dealing with the company must possess in order to attract certain legal consequences. Section 37(2) uses the term "express agreement to the contrary"; section 8(1) talks of being "actually aware" that the company lacks the requisite capacity. The need for consistency in commercial law and practice would suggest that, where possible, account should be taken of the E.C. measure when interpreting these sections.

FORMALITIES

13–04 Being entirely artificial persons in law, formerly companies could not make written contracts otherwise than under seal; having a seal was one of Blackstone's attributes of corporate personality.[6] This is no longer the case. Under the heading "Contracts, Deeds and Powers of Attorney", sections 38 and 39 of the 1963 Act set down rules as to the minimum formalities for companies making contracts and issuing bills of exchange and promissory notes. The contracts rule is simply that the same formalities are required as if the transaction in question was one between individuals; there are no peremptory special requirements for companies regarding seals, counter-signatures and the like.

---

[4] *Murphy v. Bord Telecom Eireann* [1989] I.L.R.M. 53.

[5] *Phonogram Ltd. v. Lane* [1982] 1 Q.B. 938; below, para. 13–10.

[6] See above, para. 3–03.

Thus a company must use a seal or writing, or provide evidence in writing, as the case may be, only where those forms are demanded by the general law.[7] There are special statutory provisions regarding executing deeds and transacting other business abroad.[8]

Company Seal

13–05 Every company is required to have a seal with its name engraved on it;[9] it is usual for the seal to be put under the control of the directors or a committee of them.[10] Transactions that still need a seal for their execution include conveyances of property,[11] granting a power of attorney and issuing certificates of title to shares. Although debentures are usually issued under seal, it is not necessary that they take this form;[12] all that is required is some written instrument which is capable of being registered as a company charge and that satisfies section 38 of the 1963 Act. In *Re A Debtor's Summons*[13] it was held that a legal assignment by a company of debts must be sealed because that transaction was not a "contract" within the previous version of section 38. Kennedy C.J. there could "not (though Parliament might if it intended so to do) stretch the denotation of the ordinary word 'contract' to include within it 'an absolute assignment', nor of the expression 'party to be charged therewith' to include a simple assignor of a piece of property or right."[14] Perhaps the assignment of chattels or of choses in action by way of security might be treated differently but, in the light of this decision, the prudent course is to execute the debenture under seal.

Bills of Exchange and Cheques

13–06 Any person duly authorised may make, accept or endorse a bill or note for or on behalf of the company.[15] Company officers should make sure when signing cheques, bills and the like that the company's name is clearly and correctly stated, and that it is stipulated that they are signing on its behalf; otherwise, they can incur personal liability on the instrument. Section 26 of the Bills of Exchange Act 1882 provides that

---

[7] *E.g. UBAF Ltd. v. European American Banking Corp.* [1984] 1 Q.B. 713.
[8] 1963 Act, ss. 40, 41.
[9] *ibid.*, s.114(1)(b).
[10] *e.g.* Table A, art. 115.
[11] *Catley Farms Ltd. v. A.N.Z Banking Group* [1982] 1 N.Z.L.R. 430 at 437.
[12] *Re Fireproof Doors Ltd.* [1916] 2 Ch. 142 and *Haddow Nominees Ltd. v. Rarawa Farms Ltd.* [1981] 2 N.Z.L.R. 16.
[13] [1929] I.R. 139.
[14] *ibid.* at 145–146.
[15] 1963 Act, s.39.

> "Where a person signs a bill as drawer, endorser or acceptor, and adds words to his signature, indicating that he signs for or on behalf of a principal, or in a representative character, he is not personally liable thereon; but the mere addition to his signature of words describing him as an agent, or as filling a representative character, does not exempt him from personal liability."[16]

As has been explained earlier,[17] under section 114(4) of the 1963 Act, any director who is responsible for issuing or signing any bill or cheque wherein the company is not properly described may be held personally liable on it.

PRE-INCORPORATION AGREEMENTS

13–07 Before a company is incorporated, it is common for promoters to enter into various arrangements on its behalf, like hiring staff and purchasing stocks. In the *Salomon & Co.* case,[18] for instance, the plaintiff had made a preliminary agreement with a trustee for the future company setting out the generous terms on which the company, when incorporated, would acquire the plaintiff's business. It is a general principle of contract law that a contract cannot be made on behalf of a non-existent principal, and any such contract purported to have been made cannot subsequently be given legal effect by a principal coming into being and ratifying it.[19] Therefore, pre-incorporation contracts made on behalf of companies could not bind them on their incorporation,[20] nor could they be ratified by the company.[21] In the past, the way legal effect was given to those contracts was for the company, on becoming incorporated, to enter formally into new contracts similar to the pre-incorporation engagements.

13–08 Persons dealing with embryo and newly-formed companies used to fall into the trap of discovering that their only security was a pre-incorporation agreement that was not enforceable against the company. They nevertheless might have a claim against the person who purported to make the contract for the company. There were no hard and fast rules as to when the so-called agent could be held

---

16 *cf. Bondina Ltd. v. Rollaway Shower Blinds Ltd.* [1986] 1 W.L.R. 517.
17 See above, para. 5–166.
18 [1897] A.C. 22.
19 See generally, F.M.B. Reynolds, *Bowstead on Agency* (16th ed., 1996), pp. 609 *et seq*.
20 *Kelner v. Baxter* (1866) L.R. 2 C.P. 174; *Rover International Ltd. v. Canon Film Sales Ltd.* [1987] B.C.L.C. 540.
21 *Re Empress Engineering Co.* (1880) 16 Ch.D. 125.

personally responsible to the outsider, or when the agent could enforce the contract in his own name against the outsider.[22] In *Kelner v. Baxter*[23] it was suggested that, in the absence of adequate indications by them to the contrary, the actual signatories are personally liable "where a contract is signed by one who professes to be signing 'as agent', but who has no principal existing at the time, and the contract would be altogether inoperative unless binding upon the the person who signed it, he is bound thereby."[24] There, the defendants, who were to be directors of a company in the process of formation, agreed to purchase stock that was offered to them, "on behalf of the proposed . . . company"; they signed the stock list with their names "on behalf of the" company. In the light of the above principle, it was held that they were personally liable on the contract and that the rider to their signature 'operate[d] no more than if a person should contract for a quantity of corn "on behalf of my horses'."[25] But in a later instance it was in effect held that the agent's right to sue on, and incur liability under, the contract could be excluded where the contract purports to be made by the (non-existent) company itself rather than by somebody on its behalf.[26] A New Zealand judge sought to explain the cases in this area by saying that "there is, or should be, a presumption of personal liability so long as a presently binding contract is intended", but that "the result of each case will depend on its particular facts."[27] The uncertain status of pre-incorporation contracts was a subject of considerable criticism in company law circles.[28]

Binding the Company

13–09 The principle that pre-incorporation contracts are incapable of being ratified by the company was reversed by section 37(1) of the 1963 Act. Thenceforth, a company could ratify any contract or other transaction made on its behalf or purportedly by it prior to its incorporation. The effect of the ratification is to subject the company to all the liabilities and confer on it all the rights arising from the transaction as if the company had existed at the time the transaction

---

22 See generally, Gross, "Pre-Incorporation Contracts" (1971) 87 L.Q.R. 367.
23 (1866) L.R. 2 C.P. 174.
24 *ibid.* at 183.
25 *ibid.* at 185.
26 *Newborne v. Sensolid (Great Britain) Ltd.* [1954] 1 Q.B. 45; see also *Cotronic (UK) Ltd. v. Dezonie* [1991] B.C.L.C. 721
27 *Marblestone Industries Ltd. v. Fairchild* [1975] 1 N.Z.L.R. 529, at p. 542. See also, *Elders Pastoral Ltd. v. Gibbs* [1988] 1 N.Z.L.R. 596.
28 *cf. Inver Resources Ltd. v. Limerick Corp.* [1987] I.R. 159; the non-existence of an applicant for planning permission does not render the application itself a nullity and the decision to grant permission is not thereby invalid.

had been concluded.[29] It was held in the *HKN Invest* case[30] that a company, even in liquidation, can ratify a pre-incorporation contract even though a breach of its terms has occurred. Ratification there meant that "as a matter of law the contracts will have existed from their date of execution — it will not affect the rights of either party arising from the manner in which the contract has or has not been performed since then."[31] Ratification need not comply with any particular formalities.[32]

The "Agent's" Position

13–10 One objective of the E.C. First Directive was to cut through the uncertainty surrounding *Kelner v. Baxter*[33] and later cases, and establish a clear principle that, where there is no agreement to the contrary, persons who contract on behalf of an unincorporated company are fully liable on the contract until the company becomes a party to it.[34] This very principle is set out in section 37(2) of the 1963 Act. Up to the time the company ratifies the contract, the persons who purported to act for or on behalf of the company are personally bound by and are entitled to the full benefit of the transaction. But their personal liability and benefit can be excluded by "express agreement to the contrary". The understanding negating the so-called agent's personal liability or entitlement under the contract, therefore, cannot arise by implication from the circumstances. In *Phonogram Ltd. v. Lane*,[35] which concerned the similar though not identical provisions of the British law, it was said that any purported exclusion of the agent's personal liability must be clear and unambiguous; that "where a person purports to contract on behalf of a company not yet formed, then however he expresses his signature he himself is personally liable on the contract . . . unless there is a clear exclusion of personal liability . . . "[36]

Transitional Agreements

13–11 A person may have been dealing with a partnership which, unknown to him, is converted into a registered company with the same name as that used by the partners. Any contracts made for the company before it is actually registered are governed by the principles set

---

[29] *cf. State (Finglas Industries Estates Ltd.) v. Dublin County Council*, McMahon J., July 10, 1981.

[30] *HK Invest OY v. Incotrade PVT Ltd.* [1993] 3 I.R. 152.

[31] *ibid.* at 161.

[32] See generally, *Bowstead on Agency*, above, n. 19, at pp. 61 *et seq.*

[33] (1866) L.R. 2 C.P. 174.

[34] Art. 7.

[35] [1982] 1 Q.B. 938.

[36] *ibid.* at 944. See generally, Green, "Security of Transaction After Phonogram" (1984) 47 Mod. L. Rev. 671.

out above. As for post-registration contracts, it depends on the intentions of the parties whether the company is liable or liability can be imposed on the former partners.[37] For instance in *Smallman Ltd. v. O'Moore*,[38] the partners publicised to some extent the conversion of their business but the plaintiff continued supplying goods to the business without knowing about the change. It was held that the parties were not *ad idem*, the plaintiff believing he was dealing with partners but the defendants dealing on behalf of their new company. However, the company had to pay for whatever goods it had accepted and used. Neither fraud nor estoppel were pleaded here. In the case of contracts made by a company which is in the process of changing its name — made in the new name but before the certificate of incorporation in that name has been issued — the company is liable on those contracts. An individual acting for the company in such a case is not personally liable as in the case of pre-incorporation contracts.[39]

Pre-Trading Certificate Contracts

13–12 A public company that has issued a prospectus inviting subscriptions for its shares is not permitted to commence business or to borrow until certain formalities have been complied with. Section 115(4) of the 1963 Act stipulates that any contracts made or ratified by a company before it becomes entitled to do business are "provisional only" and do not bind the company until it has satisfied the above formalities. On the other hand, section 6 of the 1983 Act, which forbids a p.l.c. from doing business until it is issued with an appropriate certificate, states that contravention of this requirement does not invalidate any contracts that the company has concluded.

CAPACITY AND ULTRA VIRES ENGAGEMENTS

13–13 The general scope and effect of the *ultra vires* doctrine has already been explained.[40] A company acts *ultra vires* when it enters into some transaction that falls outside of its objects or is otherwise prohibited by the Companies Acts. In the *Rolled Steel Products Ltd.* case,[41] it was stressed that *ultra vires* should not be confused with excess of au-

---

[37] *Pitner Ligking Co. v. Geddis* [1912] 2 I.R. 163.

[38] [1959] I.R. 220.

[39] *Osbkosb B'Gosb Inc. v. Dan Marbel Inc. Ltd.* [1989] 1 C.M.L.R. 94 and *Badgerbill Properties Ltd. v. Cottrell* [1991] B.C.L.C. 805.

[40] See above, paras 3–60 *et seq.*

[41] *Rolled Steel Products (Holdings) Ltd. v. British Steel Corp.* [1986] 1 Ch. 246; see above, paras 3–71—3–72.

thority; the former concerns the very capacity of the company to enter into transactions, the latter concerns whether those who concluded the transaction were duly authorised to do so by the company. The fact that the directors entered into a transaction for an improper purpose does not *ipso facto* render it *ultra vires*. It was held in the *Ashbury Railway Carriage Co.* case,[42] that *ultra vires* transactions are void and cannot be ratified by the company on whose behalf they are entered into. But this principle often operated most unfairly against persons dealing with companies in the utmost good faith. Whether this principle against ratification remains the law today is debateable because, under the 1963 Act, it became possible for the members to change their company's objects.[43]

13–14 There are numerous instances of company liquidators successfully invoking *ultra vires* to defeat claims by small traders against companies that were engaged in some business not referred to in their objects clause. For example, in *Re Jon Beauforte (London) Ltd.*,[44] without changing its objects clause, a company that had been incorporated to make women's dresses, embarked on the business of household furnishing. This latter business proved to be a failure and the company was forced into liquidation. It was held that the debts it had incurred in the course of its furnishing business were *ultra vires* and that even its supplier of coke, which could equally have been consumed in the original business as in the latter business, could not recover sums owing to it. It is somewhat unrealistic to expect small traders to check a company's objects clause every time they intend to sell something to it. Indeed, persons who examine objects clauses at times come away with the mistaken impression that the transaction in question is not *ultra vires*. An intelligent individual seeing the objects clause in the *Ashbury Railway Carriage Co.* case could quite easily have come to the conclusion that the company there was authorised to engage in general contracting works like constructing railways. Nor could the objects clause in *Northern Bank Finance Corp. v. Quinn*[45] be described as unambiguous.

13–15 Another objective of the E.C. First Directive was to protect persons dealing with companies from being caught in the *ultra vires* trap. This Directive stipulates that:

---

[42] *Ashbury Railway Carriage & Iron Co. v. Riche* (1875) L.R. 7 H.L. 653; see above, para. 3–62.
[43] s. 10; see above, paras 11–13 *et seq*.
[44] [1953] 1 Ch. 131.
[45] [1979] I.L.R.M. 221; below, para. 13–20.

> "Acts done by the organs of a company shall be binding upon it even if those acts are not within the objects of the company . . . However, Member States may provide that the company shall not be bound where such acts are outside the objects of the company, if it proves that the third party knew that the act was outside those objects or could not in view of the circumstances have been unaware of it; disclosure of the statutes shall not of itself be sufficient proof thereof."[46]

Section 8(1) of the 1963 Act is almost identically worded:

> "Any act or thing done by a company which if the company had been empowered to do the same would have been lawfully and effectively done, shall, notwithstanding that the company had no power to do such act or thing, be effective in favour of any person relying on such act or thing who is not shown to have been actually aware, at the time when he so relied thereon, that such act or thing was not within the powers of the company. . . "

This section has been supplemented by reg. 6 of the European Communities (Companies) Regulations 1973,[47] which may encapsule *ultra vires* transactions as well as transactions which otherwise are beyond an authority given in the memorandum or articles of association; reg. 6 is widely accepted as applying to traditional *ultra vires* as well. But if it does, it does not give persons dealing with companies any greater protection than arising from section 8(1) of the 1963 Act.

Binding the Company

13–16 The following questions arise in considering the extent to which, by virtue of section 8(1), *ultra vires* contracts and transactions are made legally effective.

Parties Affected

13–17 Section 8(1) does not merely enable outsiders to sue companies on what heretofore were *ultra vires* acts. "Any person" is entitled to the benefit of section 8(1). Thus, in principle, even "insiders", such as the principal shareholders and directors, may be able to sue on such acts, and so may the company itself; but provided that the *scienter* requirement, explained below, is satisfied.

Things Affected

13–18 Section 8(1) does not speak of contracts or transactions but of "[a]ny act or thing done" by a company. Accordingly, even non-con-

---

[46] Art. 9(1).

[47] S.I. No. 163 of 1973, discussed below at paras 13–56 *et seq*.

tractual engagements fall within its scope, like gifts and promises of gifts that are completely "sterile", and torts and other breaches of legal duties committed in the course of *ultra vires* activities.

Scienter

13–19 Section 8(1) renders legally effective the act or thing done by the company provided that the person in question "is not shown to have been actually aware, at the time when he so relied thereon", that it was *ultra vires*. That is to say, if it is proved that the person in fact knew that the contract or act in question was *ultra vires*, then section 8(1) will not render that transaction effective. The E.C. formulation of this *scienter* requirement is phrased more flexibly; it speaks of a person who "could not in view of all the circumstances have been unaware of" the engagement falling outside the objects clause; reg. 6 of the 1973 Regulations referred to above speaks of a person "dealing ... in good faith" with a company. The question therefore has arisen whether the term "actually aware" extends beyond proved knowledge of *ultra vires*, *i.e.* beyond unequivocal recognition that the company had no legal capacity to do what it was purporting to do.

13–20 In *Northern Bank Finance Corp. v. Quinn*[48] the bank loaned the defendant money, taking as security a guarantee given by his unlimited investment company. Since that guarantee transpired to be *ultra vires*,[49] the bank sought to rely on section 8(1) to validate the guarantee. But it was argued that, in the circumstances, the bank should have known the guarantee was *ultra vires* and, consequently, it had no rights under the section. While there was no convincing proof that the bank's solicitor saw the company's objects, it was held that in the light of the normal practice "the probabilities are" that he did read the memorandum but mistakenly concluded that the guarantee was *intra vires*. Thus, he was "aware of the contents of the objects clause".[50] But was he "actually aware" that the company was exceeding its powers? Keane J. held that he was, reasoning that

> " the section was designed to ensure that . . . persons who had entered into transactions in good faith with the company without ever reading the memorandum and accordingly with no actual knowledge that the transaction was *ultra vires* were not to suffer. I can see no reason in logic or justice why the legislature should have intended to afford the same protection to persons who had actually read the memorandum and simply failed to appreciate the lack of vires.

---

[48] [1979] I.L.R.M. 221.

[49] See above, para. 3–66.

[50] At p. 15.

> [W]here a party is shown to have been actually aware of the contents of the memorandum but failed to appreciate that the company were not empowered thereby to enter into the transaction in issue, section 8(1) has no application."[51]

Perhaps a more convincing way of coming to this conclusion might be to place emphasis on the Directive's "could not in view of all the circumstances have been unaware" formula.[52]Accordingly, knowledge of the actual contents of the memorandum is treated as knowing what the company's objects are. It remains to be seen whether this principle equally applies to the legally unsophisticated person who may have seen the memorandum and the objects clause but did not appreciate their full significance. Another matter to be resolved is the position of the party who deliberately refrains from reading the memorandum which has been made available for his perusal.

13–21 One would have hoped that the Supreme Court would have clarified the position in *Re Frederick Inns Ltd.*[53] but, instead, its decision introduces considerable confusion in the matter. Under threat of being wound up by the Revenue, a group of companies made a settlement of outstanding tax liabilities. This involved some companies in the group, which were insolvent, making payments in respect of the liabilities of other group companies. Lardner J. held that those payments were *ultra vires* and would be so even if the companies were not insolvent. Because, from the information at the Revenue's disposal, it should have known that those paying companies were insolvent, the judge held that the Revenue was sufficiently aware that the payments it received were *ultra vires;* the Revenue knew of those companies' precarious financial circumstances and must be presumed to know the law, that one company in a group cannot gratuitously alienate its property for the benefit of another group company. On appeal, however, Blaney J. for the Court found that (subject to what is said below) the Revenue could rely on section 8(1) because the tax official there "seems generally to have been of the belief that he was dealing with a group of companies and that the payment was being made by some of the companies within the group on behalf of the entire group."[54] Apart from

---

[51] [1979] I.L.R.M. at p. 229.

[52] *cf. International Sales Agencies Ltd. v. Marcus* [1982] 3 All E.R. 551. The company in the *Northern Bank* case was unlimited and the Directive therefore would not have applied to it. Notwithstanding, that is no reason for not construing s.8(1) of the Act along the lines of the Directive because s.8(1) does not differentiate between limited and unlimited companies.

[53] [1994] I.L.R.M. 382.

[54] *ibid.* at 395.

this bald assertion, there is no reasoning nor analysis of any kind to support the conclusion.

13–22 In principle, "insiders" and possibly the company itself can rely on section 8(1). But this is subject to the proviso that they are not "actually aware" that the act in question is *ultra vires*. If "actually aware" is interpreted in the light of the Directive, then it would be only in the most exceptional circumstances that insiders can avail of the section. The company itself would have to be treated as being "actually aware" of what its own objects are.

Extent of Validation

13–23 Section 8(1) saves from invalidity engagements and the like that in the past would be *ultra vires* because they fell outside the company's objects. Whether it goes further and validates other company transactions, like arrangements that contravene provisions of the Companies Acts, is an open question; probably not. It is clear that the First Directive envisages only *ultra vires* in the traditional sense of outside the objects; the parallel provisions in the British law have been said to give relief only against "the old *ultra vires* doctrine."[55]

13–24 However, the Supreme Court's decision in *Re Frederick Inns Ltd.*[56] introduces further confusion here. Having held that the Revenue there did not have the requisite *scienter* ("actually aware") to be precluded from relying on section 8(1), the court went to find that, by paying the Revenue, the companies' directors had been in breach of their fiduciary duty to the general creditors. Accordingly, Blayney J. concluded, those payments were not "lawfully and effectively done", which took them outside section 8(1) entirely. The view that company directors owe fiduciary duties to the general creditors is not accepted in any comparable common law jurisdiction and the cases relied on by Blayney J. do not support the proposition.[57] But even if there were such a duty and it was broken, that can have nothing to do with *ultra vires*, which concerns the intrinsic capacity of companies to conclude transactions, as opposed to whether directors are abusing their powers. Accepting that the gratuitous payments there were *ultra vires* (the companies making them were insolvent)[58] but that the Revenue were not

---

[55] See above, n. 52 at p. 559.
[56] [1994] 1 I.L.R.M. 387.
[57] See below, paras 16–06 *et seq*.
[58] Gratuitous alienations to group companies (guaranteeing loans to them) were held to be *intra vires* in *Re P.M.P.A. Garage (Long Mile) Ltd.* [1992] 1 I.R. 315, although it would seem that the guarantor companies there were insolvent at

"actually aware" of that infirmity, then it must follow that the Revenue was entitled to rely on section 8(1) regardless of what was deemed to be the directors' breaches of duties. Of course, it does not automatically follow that contracts made in such circumstances bind the company if, under the general law of agency, the other party (the Revenue here) has notice of directors' breaches of duty that would render the payments voidable at the company's instigation. In such a case, the company would be entitled to recover the money for the benefit of its general creditors, including the Revenue. If section 8(1) did not exist at all and the companies were entitled to invoke the *ultra vires* "trap", the position would be similar to that in the controversial "interest swaps" cases in England.[59] The payments to the Revenue would have been made under a void or voidable contract and the paying companies would be entitled to demand restitution. Such monies as were received would be shared among the general creditors, including the Revenue. But none of these subtleties troubled the Supreme Court, which adopted the quite novel proposition that directors of insolvent companies hold assets in trust for the general creditors;[60] accordingly, the Revenue held the money it got under a resulting trust for those creditors[61] and was not even entitled to set-off that money against legitimate Revenue claims.[62]

Officer Liability

13–25 Any company that suffers loss in consequence of section 8(1) validating an *ultra vires* transaction is empowered to claim compensation against any director or officer who was "responsible" for actually concluding the transaction in question. It is not clear whether liability under this is founded on negligence principles or is strict or absolute. But under section 319 of the 1963 Act the court possesses a discretion to exonerate the officer from liability in appropriate circumstances.

---

the time. *cf.* the Supreme Court's decision in *Re Greendale Developments Ltd. (No.2)* [1998] 1 I.R. 8 discussed above, paras 3–77 *et seq.*, holding gratuitous alienations by solvent companies *ultra vires.*

59 *Westdeutsche Landesbank Girozentrale v. Islington L.B.C.* [1994] 4 All E.R. 890, aff'd [1994] 1 W.L.R. 938 (C.A.) and [1996] A.C. 669 (H.L.).

60 The eccentricity of this holding is explained in Fealy, "The Role of Equity in the Winding Up of a Company", [1995] D.U.L.J. 18.

61 *cf. Re Polly Peck International p.l.c.* (Times L.R., May 1998).

62 The lengthy quotation at [1994] 1 I.L.R.M. 400 from Mr Robb's book on the nature of set-off has no real bearing on the issue to be decided; if there could not be a set-off, little purpose is served in elaborating on what a set-off generally achieves.

Restitution and *Ultra Vires* Transactions

13–26 Apart entirely from section 8(1) of the 1963 Act, *ultra vires* transactions are not wholly legally ineffective, for they can give rise to restitutionary obligations.[63] Companies ordinarily will not be permitted to enforce contracts which are *ultra vires* their own objects. Although there are various *obiter dicta* to the contrary,[64] the non-enforceability view was endorsed in *Cabaret Holdings Ltd. v. Meeanee Sports and Rodeo Club Inc.*[65] In pursuance of an agreement, the plaintiff paid expenses incurred by the defendant company and subsequently sued the defendant to recover those sums. The agreement and the payment made under it were *ultra vires* the defendant and, accordingly, the defence was that as a result the money could not be recovered. It was held that once the agreement is *ultra vires* it cannot be enforced by either party; that

> "It is not possible for a company or incorporated society to sue upon a contract into which it has no power to enter. To say that a corporation is not barred from recovery because a transaction is *ultra vires* is one thing. To say that it may sue upon a contract which never came into existence is a wholly different thing. That conclusion may occasion some regret but we regard it in the present state of the law as inevitable."[66]

13–27 In recent years, however, there have been dramatic developments in the law of restitution that, in consequence, protects companies or their creditors from suffering undue loss where they were parties to *ultra vires* transactions. Even prior to these developments, the courts were inclined to order restitution in certain discrete cases. Thus, in *Re Lough Neagh Ship Co., ex p. Workman*[67] a company that failed to raise the necessary capital to pay for a ship that was being built for it borrowed the funds from the plaintiff and paid the builder. Even though this loan was outside the company's borrowing powers, it was said in the first place that "the fact that the [loan] was really an advance of capital not in existence seems. . . to distinguish the case from" other instances where *ultra vires* loans were held not be recoverable.[68] In any event, it was held, the plaintiff was entitled to be subrogated for the shipbuilder. According to Porter, M.R., this

> "is the case of a person interested in the affairs of the company, discharging with the privity and consent of the company, a liability of the latter

---

[63] See generally, R. Goff & G. Jones, *The Law of Restitution* (5th ed., 1998), pp. 441–448.
[64] *e.g. Bell Houses Ltd. v. City Wall Properties Ltd.* [1986] 2 Q.B. 657 at 694.
[65] [1982] 1 N.Z.L.R. 673.
[66] *ibid.* at 676.
[67] [1895] I.R. 533.
[68] *ibid.* at 539.

> by payment. This has the effect of placing the person making the payment in the position in which the creditor stood before he was paid off. [Therefore] the claimants became equitable assignees of [the ship-builder's] rights, including the right to sue the company; and on that ground are . . . entitled to sustain [their] claim. There has in the result been no real borrowing by the company at all. . . . It is simply a change of creditor, not a new debt."[69]

Where money borrowed can be traced, the lender would be entitled to a tracing order.[70] In *Flood v. Irish Provident Assurance Co.*[71] it was held that premiums paid to an insurance company on *ultra vires* policies were recoverable as money paid without consideration.

13–28 More recently in the *Westdeutsche Landesbank case*[72] concerning the controversial "interest swaps" in Britain, where many local authorities got money from banks under agreements which, it transpired, were beyond those bodies' legal capacities, it was held that those banks were entitled to reclaim the money along with simple interest. This claim was not based on there being some resulting trust or on some implied contract but was found to be a personal action for money had and received by virtue of there being a failure of consideration. The outcome there was anticipated in *Re P.M.P.A. Garage (Longmile) Ltd. (No. 2),*[73] where an industrial and provident society had lent money to several related companies but those loans were *ultra vires* the society, being contrary to the Industrial and Provident Societies Act 1893.[74] Following an extensive survey of the case law in several countries, Murphy J. concluded that the party who has obtained goods or money under an *ultra vires* transaction can be compelled to return the property. While accepting the general proposition that a body corporate cannot enforce a contract which it never had the capacity to make, the judge observed that no court would permit the manifest injustice of a party retaining money or goods he got under a contract which, inadvertently, was *ultra vires*. Of course, if the society there had been a registered company, the contract would not have been unenforcible by virtue of section 8(1)

---

[69] [1895] I.R. 533 at 540, relying on *Blackburn & District Building Society* v. *Cunliffe Brooks & Co.* (1885) 29 Ch.D. 902 and *Re Cork & Youghal Railway Co.* (1869) 4 Ch. App. 748. See also *Re Ulster Railway Co. v. Bambridge etc. Railway Co.* [1868] Ir. 2 Eq. 190 and *Re Bagnalstown & Wexford Railway Co.* (1870) 6 Ir. Eq. 505.

[70] *cf. Re Diplock* [1948] Ch. 465 and *Shanaban Stamp Auctions Ltd. v. Farrelly* [1962] I.R. 386.

[71] (1912) 46 I.L.T.R. 214, [1912] 2 Ch. 597, n. 16.

[72] *Westdeutsche Landesbank Girozentrale v. Islington L.B.C.* [1994] 4 All E.R. 890, affirmed [1994] 1 W.L.R. 938 (C.A.) and [1996] A.C. 669 (H.L.).

[73] [1992] 1 I.R. 332.

[74] *Re P.M.P.A. Garage (Longmile) Ltd.* [1992] 1 I.R. 315.

of the 1963 Act unless the other parties were "actually aware" of the infirmity.

AGENCY AND UNAUTHORISED TRANSACTIONS

13–29 Pre-incorporation and *ultra vires* considerations aside, there remains the question of in what circumstances engagements purportedly assumed on behalf of companies bind them; in other words, when is a person empowered to act as a company's agent. Two related matters arise here. One concerns the existence of authority to act on behalf of a company and the scope or range of that authority. The other asks the same question from a negative perspective, namely, whether any restriction exists on the authority of a person prima facie empowered to bind the company. For instance, managing directors generally have very extensive authority; but a particular company's regulations may considerably constrict its managing director's powers, like, for example, requiring board or even general meeting approval before certain kinds of transactions can be entered into by him.

13–30 It is usual to analyse questions of authority to bind companies in terms of agency law: whether the company empowered the person in question to act for it, either actually authorised the controverted transaction or clothed the person in question with apparent authority to enter into it, and whether any apparent authority was cut down by the company's regulations. Yet in the most authoritative case in the entire area, *Mahony v. East Holyford Mining Co.*,[75] the House of Lords appears to have approached the issue from a comparative negligence perspective. There a group of fraudsters formed a company ostensibly to work a mine in Co. Tipperary and, by issuing a prospectus, persuaded numerous members of the public to invest in it. But instead of spending investors' funds on mining equipment and the like, the fraudsters withdrew it from the company's bank account for their own use. They misled the company's bank into believing that they were authorised to draw cheques on behalf of the company. When what transpired was discovered, the question became who should bear the loss of the fraud: the investors or the bank that, without actual authority to do so, handed over the funds to the fraudsters.

13–31 It was held that the party that had been the more careless must bear the loss. This comparative negligence theme is most pronounced in Lord Hatherley's speech:

---

[75] (1875) L.R. 7 H.L. 869.

> "A banker dealing with a company must he taken to be acquainted with the manner in which, under the articles of association, the moneys of the company may be drawn out of his bank for the purposes of the company...
>
> But, after that, when there are persons conducting the affairs of the company in a manner which appear to be perfectly consonant with the articles of association, then those so dealing with them, externally, are not to be affected by any irregularities which may take place in the internal management of the company...
>
> Now, if the question came to be which of two innocent parties (as it is said) was to suffer loss, I apprehend, my Lords, that in point of law what must be considered in cases of that kind is this: which of the two parties was bound to do, or to avoid, any act by which the loss has been sustained. It think there can be no doubt that in this case the shareholders of the company were the persons who were bound to see that nobody usurped or assumed the office of director unduly.
>
> On the other hand, on the part of the bankers, I see no possible mode by which they might have pursued their inquiries in the manner contended for at the Bar without requiring all the minute books of the company to be produced to them, and without conducting a detailed investigation into all the transactions of the company as to the appointment of directors and the like — a duty they were not called upon to perform."[76]

The same result could be reached using agency principles as follows. By their inaction, the investors led the bank to believe that the fraudsters had authority to draw funds from the company's account and the bank acted in good faith on the basis of that holding-out.

The Kinds of Authority

13–32 There are three major categories of agency.[77] An agent can be someone with "actual authority" to conclude the transaction question; he was in fact given full authority to do so. Or he may have "usual" or "ostensible" authority, by which is meant the scope of authority persons holding certain positions usually or ordinarily possess.[78] For instance, in the context of purchases and sales of property, solicitors, estate agents and auctioneers all have varying degrees of usual authority to act for their clients. In the absence of notice of any restrictions on an agent's powers, a principal is bound by everything an agent does within his usual authority, even if the agent in fact is not authorised to act in certain ways. The third type, "holding-out", is where a principal leads someone to believe that a person has authority to enter into certain

---

[76] (1875) L.R. 7 H.L. 869 at 894, 897 and 898.

[77] See generally, F.M.B. Reynolds, *Bowstead on Agency* (16th ed., 1996).

[78] See *ibid.* at 108–119.

transactions although in fact that authority does not exist.[79] In the case of companies, there is also section 178 of the 1963 Act, under which the acts of a director are rendered valid "notwithstanding any defect which may afterwards be discovered in his appointment or qualification." But in *Morris v. Kanssen*[80] that section's scope was confined narrowly to mere slips and irregularities in appointments. Companies generally follow the Table A model, under which there is to be a board of directors empowered to "manage . . . the business of the company", and which allows for the appointment of a managing director and the delegation of some board functions to management committees.

Actual Authority

13–33 Whether a person has actual authority to act for a company in a certain way is primarily a question of fact. For instance, in *Freeman & Lockyer v. Buckhurst Park Properties (Mangal) Ltd.*[81] one K, a director of a small property development company, instructed the plaintiffs to do certain work for it. In its defence to a claim for fees for that work, the company contended that K was not authorised to enter into such contracts and that he was not its managing director. It was not essential that there was a formal board resolution recorded in the minutes for him to have been authorised to act in that capacity, but there had to have been a communication to him of the directors' consent that he so act. In the event, it was held that there was insufficient evidence to support a conclusion of actual appointment to that office.[82]

Usual Authority

13–34 Company boards have usual authority to enter into virtually all kinds of business engagements on the company's behalf. So too have managing directors, although there is no modern case law which defines the extent of their usual authority. But ordinary directors have practically no usual authority to bind the company.

13–35 In the past, company secretaries were deemed to have very limited usual authority, but in recent years the scope of their implied powers has been expanded. As one judge put it:

> "times have changed. A company secretary is a much more important person nowadays. . . . He is an officer of the company with extensive duties and responsibilities. This appears not only in the modem Compa-

---

[79] See *ibid.* at 284.
[80] [1946] A.C. 459; see above, para. 5–11.
[81] [1964] 2 Q.B. 480.
[82] *ibid.* at 501–502. *cf. Kilgobbin Mink & Stud Farms Ltd. v. National Credit Co.* [1980] I.R. 175.

> nies Acts, but also by the role which he plays in the day-to-day business of companies. He is no longer a mere clerk. He regularly makes representations on behalf of the company and enters contracts on its behalf which come within the day-to-day running of the company's business. So much so that he may be regarded as held out as having authority to do such things on behalf of the company. He is certainly entitled to sign contracts connected with the administrative side of a company's affairs, such as employing staff, and ordering cars and so forth. All such matters now come within the ostensible authority of a company secretary."[83]

13–36 In quite a number of cases the alleged agent was the company chairman.[84] The difficulty with the chair's usual authority is that there are contrasting perceptions of the chair's role. Generally, its occupants are regarded as having no special functions apart from presiding over directors' meetings. But there is a breed of company chairman that has far more in common with managing directors.

Holding-Out

13–37 A person or persons may be held-out as authorised to act for a principal in certain ways, in which case the principal is bound by whatever was done within the scope of that holding-out, provided the agent was held out by somebody duly authorised to do so. The requirements for an effective holding-out were put as follows by Diplock L.J. in the *Freeman & Lockyer* case:

> "It must be shown: (1) that a representation that the agent had authority to enter on behalf of the company into a contract of the kind sought to be enforced was made to the contractor; (2) that such representation was made by a person or persons who had "actual" authority to manage the business of the company either generally or in respect of those matters to which the contract relates; (3) that he (the contractor) was induced by such representation to enter into the contract, that is, that he in fact relied on it; . . ."[85]

The holding-out must have been by the principal or by someone who was duly authorised by him to do so; a holding-out by the agent himself is meaningless.[86]

---

[83] *Panorama Developments (Guilford) Ltd. v. Fidelis Furnishing Fabrics Ltd.* [1971] 2 QB. 711 at 716–717.

[84] *e.g. Hely Hutchinson v. Braybead Ltd.* [1968] 1 Q.B. 549; below, para. 13.38.

[85] [1964] 2 Q.B. 480 at 506. See *Ebeed v. Soplex Wholesale Supplies Ltd.* [1985] B.C.L.C. 404.

[86] *Savill v. Chase Holdings (Wellington) Ltd.* [1989] 1 N.Z.L.R. 257; *Armagod v. Mundogas (The Ocean Frost)* [1986] A.C. 717.

[87] (1875) L.R. 7 H.L. 869, above, para. 13–30.

13–38 Most of the major authorities on company agency concern holding-out. As was indicated above, the *Mahony* case[87] can be explained on the grounds that the duped investors, by their inaction, held the fraudsters out to the bank as possessing authority to draw company funds from its bank accounts; the fraudsters were a *de facto* board of directors. In the *Freeman & Lockyer* case even though K may not have been appointed managing director, the evidence clearly showed that, with the board's approval, he used to act in that capacity and the articles of association allowed for one member of the board to be appointed to that office. It was held that he therefore had been held-out to the plaintiffs as being authorised to act as managing director; the board by its conduct "represented that he had authority to enter into contracts of a kind which a managing director or an executive director responsible for finding a purchaser would in the normal course be authorised to enter into on behalf of the company."[88]

13–39 Instances of company chairmen being held-out as having extensive authority to bind their companies include *Hely-Hutchinson v. Braybead Ltd.*,[89] the facts of which are somewhat complex. Briefly, the defendant's chairman, R, was also its chief financial executive; and with its board's acquiescence he used to act as *de facto* managing director. The defendant had a stake in another company, in which the plaintiff was a major shareholder. There had been some discussions about the defendant putting further funds into that company. Immediately following a board meeting and in an office adjacent to the defendant's board room, R and the plaintiff agreed that, if the plaintiff lent money to that other company, the defendant would guarantee the loan. But later when the guarantee was called upon, the defendant denied R's authority to give it. It was held that in the circumstances R did have ostensible authority in this regard, and indeed the Court of Appeal judges were prepared, if necessary, to accept that he had actual authority to give it. This decision has been criticised for employing different concepts of agency from those used here, thereby engendering confusion. In particular, there is the belief that R had actual authority. Since the defendant's board never in fact empowered him to negotiate the guarantee, he did not have actual authority. Since he was not in fact a managing director, concluding transactions of that nature fell outside his usual authority. Therefore, if there was any authority it must have been based on a holding-out.[90]

---

[88] [1964] 2 Q.B. 480 at 509. Other instances of directors being held out as having somewhat extensive authority are *Houghton & Co. v. Northard, Lowe & Wills* [1928] A.C. 1 and *Rama Corp. v. Proved Tin & General Investments Ltd.* [1952] 2 QB. 147.

[89] [1968] 1 Q.B. 549.

[90] Other instances involving company chairmen include *British Thomson-Houston*

The Positive Constructive Notice "Heresy"

13–40 Something must be said of a doctrine that had some popularity around the 1930s but which is wrong, it being a simplistic perversion of *Turquand's* "excusing" rule,[91] which is explained below. The doctrine's thrust, inherent potential for mischief, and eventual partial discrediting is well illustrated by reference to *Kreditbank Cassel G.m.b.H. v. Schenkers*.[92] It was sought to make a company liable on a bill of exchange issued in its name by its branch manager, who had neither actual nor usual authority to do so. The company's articles of association contained a regulation empowering the board to delegate *inter alia* the authority to draw bills. It was contended that the articles therefore operated as a kind of holding-out; that, because the power here could have been delegated to the branch manager, he therefore could bind the company. That is to say, the articles operate as a positive, or power-conferring, constructive notice. Carried, one hesitates to say, to its logical extreme, this means that, where a company's regulations allow for certain corporate powers to be delegated, then virtually anybody is deemed to have been authorised to bind the company in respect of those powers.

13–41 This view did not find full acceptance in *Kreditbank*. In the first place, it was said, the doctrine could not clothe impostors with power to bind the company; where the purported agent answers the description "messenger or office boy", that of itself "would take the case out of the category of persons who would ordinarily be entrusted with the power. . . . and would further carry with it notice of irregularity according to business usage."[93] In other words, whatever power-conferring capacity a power of delegation in the articles had, it cannot clothe persons with authority in excess of their usual authority. Therefore, it was held, since the branch manager's usual authority had not been shown to include power to draw bills of exchange on the company's behalf, the company was not liable on the bills in question. In the later *Freeman & Lockyer* case it was stressed that "constructive notice is not a positive doctrine. . . . It does not entitle [a contractor] to say that he relied on some unusual provision in the constitution of the corporation. . . "[94]

Co. v. Federated European Bank [1932] 2 K.B. 176 and *Kilgobbin Mink* case, above, n. 8. In *First Energy (UK) Ltd. v. Hungarian International Bank Ltd.* [1993] B.C.L.C. 1408, a senior manager of a bank's branch was held to have been held out as being authorised to make the contract in question.

[91] See below, para. 13–47.

[92] [1927] 1 K.B. 826.

[93] [1926] 2 K.B. 450 at 460.

[94] [1964] 2 Q.B. 480 at 504.

The Forgery "Heresy"

13–42 *Kreditbank Cassell G.m.b.H. v. Schenkers* lends some support to the view that a forgery uttered in a company's name can never bind it unless, in the circumstances, "the person setting up the forgery [is] estopped from doing so."[95] The authority cited for this proposition is *Ruben v. Great Fingall Consolidated.*[96] But the basis for *Ruben* (that a company cannot be held liable for something done in its name by one of its servants to line his own pockets, because the servant was acting outside the scope of his employment) was subsequently rejected in *Lloyd v. Grace, Smith & Co.*[97] Moreover, the *Mahony* case[98] concerned forgeries on two levels, namely a letter to the bank stating, wholly incorrectly, that the fraudsters were authorised to withdraw sums from the company's account, and later fraudulently uttered withdrawal demands. Nevertheless, the judges in *Kreditbank* declined to depart from *Ruben*. While this view has obtained the uncritical approval of some authors, such as the editors of *Palmer,*[99] others, like *Gower,*[100] excoriate it. It is difficult to see any logical reason why, in principle, a forgery uttered by some company agent acting within his usual or held-out authority should not bind the company where the contracting party was acting in good faith and was not put "on inquiry" about possible irregularities. Recently the Australian High Court roundly rejected the heresy.[101]

Limitations on Agents' Powers

13–43 Ordinarily, a principal is bound by whatever its agent does within the agent's actual, usual or held-out authority. Sometimes, however, agents will be denied actual authority to bind a company in a manner that falls within their usual or held-out authority. This restriction on agents' powers may be based either on the Companies Acts or on the company's own regulations; in the latter case, however, the company may be bound by a contract made in breach of its own articles, depending on the circumstances.

Statutory Restrictions

13–44 Statutory restrictions on a company's contracting power tend

---

95 [1926] 2 K.B. 826 at 835.
96 [1906] A.C. 439.
97 [1911] 2 K.B. 489.
98 (1875) L.R. 7 H.L. 869; above, para. 13–30.
99 para. 21–16. *Palmer's Company Law* (24th ed., 1987).
100 *Principles of Company Law* (6th ed., 1997), p. 228.
101 *Northside Developments Property Ltd. v. Registrar General* (1990) 64 A.L.J.R. 427 at 443.

to fall into three major categories. One is where the Act states that non-compliance with its provisions does not invalidate the contract in question, as is done by section 6(8) of the 1983 Act, concerning p.l.c.'s pre-trading certificate contracts, and section 178 of the 1963 Act that purports to validate things done by directors who subsequently are found to have been defectively appointed.[102] Another is where the Act stipulates the sanction for non-compliance with the section in question, as in section 115 of the 1963 Act on the "provisional" nature of pre-trading certificate contracts made by public companies that have offered their securities to the public. The third is where the provision is silent as to what happens when its requirements are broken. A court in the first place will have to decide whether such a provision is mandatory or merely directory. And if it is mandatory, it must then be determined whether the impunged transaction is void or voidable, or *ultra vires*, or whatever. There are no major modern Irish or British authorities squarely on these matters in the company law context.

Restrictions in the Company's Own Regulations — Negative Constructive Notice

13–45 A company agent's powers to bind it may be restricted by the terms of the company's memorandum or articles of association, the contents of which everyone is deemed to have knowledge of as public documents.[103] If by its own regulations a company is flatly prohibited from entering into certain transactions, then, subject to S. I. No. 163 of 1973[104] it is not bound by any such transaction concluded by an agent otherwise authorised to act for it. One fundamental condition of a company being bound by what is done on its behalf is that "under its memorandum or articles of association the company was not deprived of the capacity to either enter into a contract of the kind sought to be enforced or to delegate authority to enter into a contract of that kind to the agent."[105]

13–46 The same principle has been held to apply where the company is permitted to enter into the transaction in question provided the members approve of it by special resolution. In *Irvine v. Union Bank of Australia*,[106] the company's regulations restricted the board's borrowing powers except where extended by a special resolution. It was held that the bank could not recover a loan that the company, in excess of these

---

[102] In the context of public corporations law, see *North West Leicestershire District Council v. East Midlands Housing Association* [1981] 1 W.L.R. 396.

[103] *Ernest v. Nicholls* (1867) 6 H.L. Cas. 401.

[104] See below, paras 13–56 *et seq*.

[105] *Freeman & Lockyer* case [1964] 2 Q.B. at 506.

[106] (1887) 2 App. Cas. 366.

powers, had obtained from it. By way of explanation, the Privy Council said that:

> "the bank would have seen that by the articles of association, the directors were expressly restricted from borrowing beyond a certain amount, and they must have known that if the general powers vested in the directors . . . had been extended or enlarged by a resolution of a general meeting of the shareholders. . . a copy of that resolution ought, in regular course, to have been forwarded to the Registrar of joint Stock Companies, . . . and would have been found amongst his records."[107]

In other words, special resolutions, like the memorandum and articles of association, are public documents. Persons have "constructive notice" of any restrictions on contracting capacity contained in companies' regulations. But it is unlikely that this doctrine applies to the contents of each and every company document that is public in the sense that it must be registered in the registry of companies.[108]

Turquand's Case and the "Internal Management" Rule

13–47 The invalidating effect of restrictions in the company's regulations, which has parallels with the old *ultra vires*: rule, is subject to two major qualifications. One is referred to as the "internal management" rule or as the "excusing rule" in *Turquand's* case. According to this and subject to the exceptions to it set out below, if a company's regulations prohibit certain forms of transactions unless specified internal formalities (other than special resolutions) have been complied with, an outsider dealing with the company is not obliged to ensure that those formalities in fact were satisfied. Thus in *Royal British Bank v. Turquand*,[109] under the company's articles the directors were allowed to borrow on bond only if the general meeting by ordinary resolution approved. In an action to recover borrowings the company had made without that approval, it was held that the breach of the company's regulations did not provide it with a defence. A distinction is drawn between what may be called a flat prohibition and a conditional prohibition. Where, for example, borrowings are simply forbidden or borrowing in excess of a certain amount are flatly proscribed, a company therefore does not possess the authority to borrow, or to borrow more than that sum; (excess) borrowings cannot be recovered from it.[110] But it is different where the restriction is couched in terms of a prohibition unless certain formalities are first satisfied. Here, the outsider is enti-

---

[107] (1887) 2 App. Cas. 366 at 379–380.

[108] See generally, W. Gough, *Company Charges* (2nd ed., 1996), Chap. 23.

[109] (1856) 6 E. & B. 327.

[110] Subject, of course, to rights of subrogation; *cf. B. Liggett (Liverpool) Ltd. v. Bardays Bank* [1928] 1 K.B. 48 with *Re Cleadon Trust* [1939] Ch. 332.

tled to assume that those formalities were met; he is under no duty to satisfy himself that every detail of the company's internal management was properly executed. As the judge in *Turquand* explained,

> "the parties dealing with [registered companies] are bound to read the [memorandum and articles of association]. But they are not bound to do more. The party here, on reading the [articles], would find, not a prohibition from borrowing but a permission to do so on certain conditions. Finding that the authority might be made complete by a resolution, he would have the right to infer the fact of a resolution authorising that which on the face of the document appeared to be legitimately done."[111]

13–48 *The Rule Applied* Another example of this excusing rule in operation is the *Rudry Merthyr Steam Co.* case.[112] There the company's articles of association empowered the directors to determine the number of their quorum, which by a board resolution they fixed at three. At a board meeting that only two directors attended it was decided to affix the company's seal to a mortgage, which was done by the secretary in the two directors' presence. In an action on the mortgage, it was held that the irregularity of its execution did not invalidate it against the company because

> "If a person looked at the deed and looked at the articles he would not see anything irregular at all; he would be at liberty to infer, and any one in the ordinary course of business would infer, that if the directors had appointed a quorum they appointed the two who signed that deed. But supposing that three were wanted, he is not bound to go and look at the directors' minutes; he has no right to look at them except as a matter of bargain. The directors' minutes, unless he knows what they are, do not affect him at all. There is nothing irregular on the face of the deed even taken with the articles — there is nothing illegal in it."[113]

13–49 *The "On Inquiry" Exception* *Turquand's* excusing rule is subject to its own qualifications and exceptions, however. One has already been mentioned: where passing a special resolution is required to permit the transaction, then outsiders are deemed to have notice that it was not passed.[114] Nor does the excusing rule operate where the person dealing with the company was put on inquiry about a probable irregularity. That is to say, if a person was in a situation where his

---

[111] (1856) 6 E. & B. 327 at 332.
[112] *County of Gloucester Bank v. Rudry Merthyr Steam & House Coal Colliery Co.* [1895] 1 Ch. 629.
[113] *ibid.* at 636, considered in *Ulster Investment Bank Ltd. v. Euro Estates Ltd.* [1982] I.L.R.M. 57 and *Cox v. Dublin Distillery Co. (No. 2)* [1915] 1 I.R. 345. See also *Re Bank of Syria* [1900] 2 Ch. 272.
[114] *Irvine* case, above, n. 106.

suspicions should have been aroused, then he should have inquired further into the alleged agent's authority. As one judge explained, the excusing rule "proceeds on the assumption that certain acts have been regularly done" but "If there are circumstances which debar [a] person from relying on the prima facie presumption. . . . he cannot claim the benefit of the rule."[115] When these circumstances arise depend on the facts of the case.

13–50 There are countless instances of circumstances not putting the contracting party on inquiry. Thus in *Mahony's* case[116] it was concluded that the bank there had done everything that could reasonably have been expected of it and there was nothing unusual about what the self-styled directors were doing which should have put it on notice. In *U.I.B. Ltd. v. Euro Estates Ltd.*,[117] the quorum for the plaintiffs directors' meetings was fixed at one "A" and one "B" director. Twelve months before the resolution in question was voted on, the two directors present, two "B" directors, had been issued with all the "B" shares; and the defendant bank had been provided with information to this effect. Carroll J. held that this did not put the bank on inquiry:

> "[B]ecause such an agreement was made in August 1973 does not fix some one in June 1974 with a notice that the shareholding had not changed. Alternatively, there was nothing to prevent the W ordinary shareholders agreeing that either [W director] would become an W Director. There was no particular shareholding qualification required for directors in the articles."[118]

13–51 Numerous examples also exist of where the party contracting with the company was deemed to be on inquiry. In *A.L. Underwood Ltd. v. Bank of Liverpool*[119] the principal shareholder and sole director of a company endorsed in that capacity cheques payable to the company and then lodged them in his own personal bank account. The defendant bank knew that he had recently converted his own business into a company but did not know that the company's bank account was with another bank. It nevertheless was held that the circumstances of a company's agent paying company cheques into his own account were so exceptional as to put the bank on inquiry; what occurred there was something unusual which ought to have attracted the attention of the bank employees.

---

[115] *Liggett* case [1928] 1 K.B. at 57.
[116] (1875) L.R. 7 H.L. 869; above, para. 13–30.
[117] [1982] I.L.R.M. 57.
[118] *ibid.* at 66.
[119] [1924] 1 K.B. 775.

13–52 Many of the cases of irregularity concern contracts made by an inquorate board of directors, for instance *Rolled Steel Products (Holdings) Ltd. v. British Steel Corp.*[120] One S. controlled a company which owed a very substantial sum of money to British Steel's predecessor in title and which was secured by his personal guarantee. S. was also a director and major shareholder of Rolled Steel. British Steel doubted S.'s financial ability to honour his guarantee and persuaded him to have that guarantee substituted by one from Rolled Steel. A board meeting of Rolled Steel's two directors then took place, which gave the new guarantee. Because S. did not declare his financial interest in the agreement, under the company's articles, he could not be counted in the quorum or vote.[121] Accordingly, the guarantee was not granted in accordance with the articles and would not bind the company if the person to whom it was given knew of that irregularity or should have made full enquiries. It was held that since British Steel were sufficiently aware of the likely irregularity they could not avail of the "indoor management" plea.[122]

13–53 A more recent example of the nature of the transaction in question putting a party on notice is *Northside Developments Property Ltd. v. Registrar General,*[123] concerning a guarantee given by the company. The guarantee was to secure the liabilities of several companies not directly connected with Northside but which were controlled by a man who was one of Northside's three directors. When executing the guarantee certain formalities regarding affixing the company seal had not been scrupulously complied with. The court refused to enforce the guarantee; to enforce it, said one judge, would be to "furnish a charter for dealings between the fraudulent officials of companies and supine financiers."[124] The implications of this case for cross-guarantees within a group of related companies will require consideration.

13–54 *"Insiders" and "On Inquiry"* The exception to the excusing rule for "insiders" dealing with their companies is merely a special application of the "on inquiry" exception. Insiders, such as directors, are in a position to know and ought to know whether the necessary internal formalities were complied with. As was said in *Morris v. Kanssen,*[125] a director or *de facto* director cannot presume in his own favour that things

---

[120] [1986] 1 Ch. 246.
[121] See above, paras 5–139 *et seq*.
[122] [1986] 1 Ch. 246 at 282-286. *cf. Cowan de Groot Properties Ltd. v. Eagle Trust p.l.c.* [1991] B.C.L.C. 1045 at 1113–1117.
[123] (1990) 64 A.L.J.R. 427.
[124] *ibid.* at 445.
[125] [1946] A.C. 459.

done are rightly done if inquiry that he ought to make would tell him that they were wrongly done. It is

> "the duty of directors, and equally those who purport to act as directors to look after the affairs of the company, to see that it acts within its powers and that its transactions are regular and orderly. To admit in their favour a presumption that that is rightly done which they have themselves wrongly done is to encourage ignorance and condone dereliction from duty. . . His duty as director is to know; his interest when he invokes the rule is to disclaim knowledge. Such a conflict can be resolved in only one way."[126]

For instance, in *Cox v. Dublin City Distillery Co. (No.2),*[127] the company's regulations fixed the quorum of directors at two and provided that no director should vote on any matter in which he was individually interested. At a series of board meetings the directors resolved to issue debentures as security for advances made by themselves to the company. It accordingly was held that the resolutions were invalid and that the debentures were void. On the other hand, debentures issued at that same time to outsiders were held to be valid despite the irregularities in the board resolutions authorising them.

13–55 It depends on the circumstances whether non-directors, such as persons in senior managerial positions and majority shareholders, can be characterised as *de facto* directors to render them "insiders" for the purpose of these rules. Indeed in *Hely-Hutchinson v. Brayhead Ltd.,*[128] the background to which is summarised above, a duly appointed director was held not to be an insider for these very purposes. The plaintiff there sought to recover on a guarantee given by the defendant company's chairman and *de facto* managing director on its behalf. At the relevant time the plaintiff had a seat on the defendant's board. His claim nevertheless was upheld by the Court of Appeal on the grounds that there was actual authority in this instance. The trial judge upheld his claim on the grounds that the insider exception applies only where the director deals with the company *qua* director; but this is a travesty of the underlying rationale propounded in *Morris v. Kanssen*. What the case therefore suggests is that exceptional situations can arise where insiders will not be assumed to know that company agents acted without proper authority.

---

[126] [1946] A.C. 459 475–476.
[127] [1916] 1 I.R. 345.
[128] [1968] 1 Q.B. 549.

13–56 *"Organs" and S.I. No. 163 of 1973* Article 9(2) of the E.C. First Directive[129] calls for the repeal of the negative constructive notice rule, *i.e.* that a company is not bound where the person or body that concluded the transaction on its behalf was forbidden to do so by the company's memorandum or articles of association:

> "The limits on the powers of the organs of the company, arising under the statute or from a decision of the competent organs, may never be relied on as against third parties, even if they have been disclosed."[130]

This objective was already partly achieved by the excusing rule in *Turquand's* case. In response to the First Directive, Statutory Instrument No. 163 of 1973 was adopted, regulation 6 of which stipulates that:

> "(1) In favour of a person dealing with a company in good faith, any transaction entered into by any organ of the company, being its board of directors or any person registered under these regulations as a person authorised to bind the company, shall be deemed to be within the capacity of the company and any limitation of the powers of that board or person, whether imposed by the memorandum or articles of association or otherwise, may not be relied upon as against any person so dealing with the company.
>
> (2) Any such person shall be presumed to have acted in good faith unless the contrary is proved."

Companies can register persons as organs authorised to bind them by delivering to the registrar of companies a notice of who those persons are; it would appear that no Irish company has yet done this. For the vast majority of companies, therefore, this regulation only applies to transactions entered into by their boards of directors. This regulation may also validate *ultra vires* transactions within its scope but section 8(1) of the 1963 Act is more extensive in that regard. The regulation's effects are as follows.

13–57 *Scope of Regulation 6* A company that wants to claim the benefit of a forbidden transaction made by its agent cannot invoke this regulation in order to render that transaction effective. Only a person "dealing with" a company can claim under regulation 6. But transactions made with "insiders", like directors and sometimes majority shareholders, are not of necessity excluded.

13–58 Two major questions arise concerning the types of arrangement that are made binding by the regulation. An argument could be made

---

[129] [1968] O.J. L65/41 (1968-special ed.).
[130] Art. 9(2).

that use of the terms "dealing" and "transaction" means that only arrangements that are of some economic benefit to the company are covered by it; that "sterile" arrangements like gifts are not. Against this view stand the words of the Directive itself, which do not in terms confine its scope to enforceable contracts. The other question is what precisely is meant by "entered into by [the] board of directors"? Undoubtedly, it embraces transactions that the board formally approved of in advance or by subsequent ratification. And it most likely extends to transactions that the board subsequently acquiesced in. But the terms "entered into by" would appear to exclude what is done by any officer, such as a managing director, within their usual authority, or what is done by a person held out by the board to have authority to act in a particular way. If, however, subsequent acquiescence falls within these terms, it is hard to see why transactions within usual and held out authority should then be excluded. In *Re Frederick Inns Ltd.*[131] the Supreme Court held that regulation 6 did not apply to the substantial payments made to the Revenue by insolvent companies because there was noting on affidavit before the Court to show that the transactions had been entered into by the directors.[132] It should be noted that the formulation used in the parallel British provision is transaction "decided on by the directors".[133] Companies are also bound by the acts of persons they have registered as authorised to act for them, as envisaged by these regulations. It is common practice in Germany to specially register who a company's "organs" are.

13–59 Unlike section 8(1) of the 1963 Act, the Statutory Instrument does not state in positive terms what effect it has on transactions that fall within its terms. All it says is that "any limitations on the powers of that board or person . . . may not be relied upon" to upset the transaction.

13–60 *The "Good Faith" Exception* Whereas section 8(1) of the 1963 Act introduced a *scienter* requirement where the E.C. Directive did not insist on one, although one was made optional, the statutory instrument imposes a good faith standard where the Directive is silent about *scienter*. The person dealing with the company must have been acting in "good faith". It remains to be seen whether this deviation is within the choice of form and methods of implementation allowed by Article

---

131 [1994] 1 I.L.R.M. 387.

132 Blaney J. at 394–395 provides no guidance as to what this phrase in the regulation means. It is hard to believe such large payments to the Revenue had been made without the approval of the directors.

133 Companies Act 1985, s.35.

189 of the Rome Treaty. Presumably good faith in this context will be given essentially the same meaning as "on inquiry" is in general agency law, of which cases such as *Morris v. Kanssen,*[134] *Underwood Ltd. v. Bank of Liverpool,*[135] and *Liggett (Liverpool) Ltd. v. Barclays Bank*[136] are examples. In *International Factors Ltd. v. Steeve Construction Ltd.*[137] Gibson L.J. defined "good faith" in the parallel Northern Irish provision, as "actual knowledge" that the transaction was not duly authorised or "that the person dealing with the company could not have been unaware" of that, which "amounts to a deliberate closing of one's mind to circumstances which would have pointed towards the conclusion" of absence of authority.[138] It depends on all the circumstances of the case whether the other party to the transaction lacked "good faith" in this sense.

13–61 A crucially important matter is that S.I. No. 163 of 1973 provides that a person "shall be presumed to have acted in good faith until the contrary is proved". If the *Rolled Steel Products Ltd.* case[139] had to be decided under this provision, it is most likely that the defendants would be regarded as not possessing good faith; they were aware of the plaintiff's directors' substantial financial interest in the transaction in question and they had originally proposed that his own personal guarantee should be substituted by a guarantee from the plaintiff company. On the other hand in the *International Factors Ltd.* case[140] and in *T.C.B. Ltd. v. Gray*[141] it was held that, in the circumstances, the plaintiffs there had acted in good faith. The presumption of good faith furthermore suggests that somebody who, *Northern Bank v. Quinn*[142]-style, read the company's regulations but who reasonably and honestly failed to appreciate that they proscribed the kind of transaction in question, was not acting without good faith.

---

134 [1946] A.C. 459.
135 [1924] 1 K.B. 775.
136 [19281] 1 K.B. 48.
137 [1984] N.I. 245.
138 [1984] N.I. 245 at 249.
139 [1986] 1 Ch. 246.
140 [1984] N.I. 245.
141 [1986] 1 Ch. 621.
142 See above, para. 13–20.

14

Distinctive Types of Company

14–01 The essential features of the principal kinds of registered company, namely limited and unlimited companies, private and public companies, p.l.c.s, have already been described. Registered companies, moreover, may possess certain unique characteristics that are not necessarily legal but which influence, and at times shape, how the law treats them. Among the most distinctive kinds of companies are closely-held companies, companies that form part of a group enterprise, foreign-based companies and companies that form part of a multinational group of companies, banking and insurance companies, non-profit companies and co-operatives.

CLOSELY-HELD COMPANIES

14–02 A "closely-held", or "close", company is a company the shares of which are owned mainly by one person or by a closely knit group, like the members of a family or a few partners. The vast majority of companies that are registered under the Companies Acts are closely-held in this sense, being either so-called "one-person" companies, family firms or partnerships that have taken the corporate form. While most of these companies are small concerns, some of Ireland's largest enterprises remain closely-held. In many Continental European countries there are separate legislative provisions for close companies, which in France are known as S.A.R.L.*s (Societe a responsabilite limitee)*[1] and in Germany as GMbHs (*Gessellschaft mit beschrankter Haftung*).[2] Various American States have included in their companies statutes special chapters on close corporations.[3] In Ireland and Britain, however, there are no special rules governing this type of company, other than provisions

---

1 See generally, von Sernberg, "The Close Corporation's Counterparts in France, Germany and the United Kingdom" (1982) 5 Hastings Int'l & Comp. L.Q. 291.

2 *ibid.* and law of July 4, 1980 on the "one person" company.

3 See generally, H. Henn & J. Alexander, *Laws of Corporations* (1983), Chap. 10; Kariala, "A Second Look at Special Close Corporation Legislation" (1980) 53 Texas L. Rev. 1207 and Mitchell, "Close Corporations Reconsidered" (1989) 63 Tulane L. Rev. 1143.

on taxation. However, a strong argument could be made for similar measures in this country, which would free very many small concerns from the shackles and red tape now imposed by complex companies legislation. The 1989 E.C. Directive on one-person companies[4] was implemented by the European Communities (Single Member Private Limited Companies) Regulations, 1994,[5] but these have not made any profound changes to the existing system.

14–03 A close company will almost invariably be registered as a private company, principally so that it does not have to disclose to the public extensive information about its financial affairs. Part 13 of the Taxes Consolidation Act 1997, contains special rules regarding the taxation of "close companies".[6]

Minimum Numbers

14–04 Until the "single member" company was made possible in 1994,[7] every private company had to have at least two members[8] but every company is still required to have at least two directors.[9] Prior to 1994, in "one-person" companies, one individual would hold all but one of the issued shares and the remaining share would be held by a "dummy" shareholder — who might be the principal shareholder's spouse, child, solicitor or accountant. This, of course, still remains to case unless the company is actually incorporated or re-registers as a single-member company under the 1994 Regulations.

14–05 The Companies Acts do not say what happens when there is only one or no director. But where a company's membership falls below the legal minimum, the court will entertain a petition to have it wound up compulsorily.[10] And if a private company with only one member (other than a duly registered "single member" company) continues doing business for more than six months, he becomes personally liable for all debts that the company contracted during that time.[11] Section 135 of the 1963 Act, which empowers the court to order that a general meeting be held and in the manner directed by it, also author-

---

4 (1989) O.J. L395/40.
5 S.I. No. 225 of 1994.
6 See generally, P. Moore & F. Brennan, *Corporation Tax* (9th ed., 1997), Chap. 8 and M. Feeney, *Corporation Tax* (1997), Chap. 9.
7 above, n. 5.
8 1963 Act, s.36.
9 *ibid.*, s.174.
10 *ibid.*, s.213(d).
11 *ibid.*, s.36; *e.g. Nisbet v. Shepherd* [1994] 1 B.C.L.C. 300.

ises the court to direct that one member present, either in person or by proxy, shall constitute the meeting.[12]

Internal Regulations and Governance

14–06 A close company's articles of association will usually include Part II of Table A, which contains rules on such matters as refusal to register transfers of shares in the company,[13] calling general meetings at short notice,[14] the quorum for general meetings,[15] informally adopted resolutions,[16] directors voting on matters in which they have a financial interest etc.[17] A close company's regulations may contain special clauses that deal with particular concerns of the members; some of these clauses may even he entrenched in the memorandum of association.[18] Perhaps the commonest special clause is a pre-emption provision, whereby existing members or directors are given a first option on shares in the company which any member wishes to dispose of.[19] Examples of special clauses from the leading cases include *Bushell v. Faith*,[20] where the directors were given weighted votes on any proposed resolution to remove them, thereby rendering them virtually irremovable; the *Quin & Axtens* case,[21] where each of two joint managing directors was given a veto over major transactions in property by the company; the *Lee's Air Farming*[22] case, where the principal shareholder was designated the company's governing director for life with authority to do everything that is not by law required to be done in general meeting; and *Beattie v. Beattie Ltd.*,[23] where it was provided that all internal disputes should be submitted to arbitration. Often, however, instead of putting special clauses in the articles of association, they will form part of a collateral shareholders' agreement, which takes precedence over the articles.

14–07 Closely-held companies are frequently run on a very informal basis. Indeed, many of them never even make up annual accounts, have annual general meetings, or file an annual return or other documents

---

[12] *e.g. Noel Tedman's Holdings Property Ltd.* [1967] Q'd L.R. 561, where the sole two directors and members had been killed in a road accident.
[13] Art. 3; see above, paras 9–32 *et seq.*
[14] Art. 4; see above, para. 4–06.
[15] Art. 5; see above, para. 4–24.
[16] Art. 6; see above, para. 4–42.
[17] Art. 7; see above, para. 5–139 *et seq.*
[18] 1963 Act, s.28.
[19] See above, paras 9–40 *et seq.*
[20] [1970] A.C. 1099; see above, para. 5–41.
[21] [1909] A.C. 442; see above, para. 10–16.
[22] [1961] A.C. 12; see above, para. 3–13.
[23] [1938] Ch. 708; see above, para. 10–22.

with the registrar of companies. Under Part II of Table A, the quorum for general meetings (other than for "one-person" companies within the 1994 Regulations) is two members present either in person or by proxy when the meeting "proceeds to business".[24] It is not necessary to actually hold formal general meetings in order to pass resolutions; a resolution in writing signed by all the members entitled to attend the meeting and vote is "valid and effective for all purposes" as a duly passed resolution, provided that section 141 of the 1963 Act on notices was satisfied.[25] *Cane v. Jones*[26] goes even further than this and makes fully effective any unanimous agreement of all the members who, acting together, can do anything which is *intra vires* the company, such as alter the articles of association. And where all of the members assent to a course of conduct that would be *ultra vires* in the conventional sense, that conduct will be regarded as *intra vires*.[27]

14–08 Complex voting systems are features that occur principally in closely-held companies; their function is to ensure that a majority of the members do not out-vote a minority on all questions or on certain issues that are of particular concern to the minority. Thus, the regulations may adopt the common law rule of one member — one vote; or the shares may be divided into two or more classes with different voting strengths; or some members may be given weighted votes on particular issues. There may even be entirely separate contracts in which shareholders undertake either to vote or not to vote, or not to vote in a particular way.

14–09 On account of their small membership and especially where they are owned by two individuals or two families, or where some shareholders possess extensive veto powers, close companies are often deadlocked. Sometimes the company's regulations will contain a mechanism for untying deadlocks, for instance, that the matter in dispute be referred to arbitration or that the dissenting members shall be bought out under certain conditions. Where deadlock persists the court may order that the company be wound up on just and equitable grounds.

Shareholders' Agreements

14–10 Members of close companies at times conclude shareholders' agreements between themselves, which are entirely separate from the

---

[24] Art. 5; *cf. Re London Flats Ltd.* [1969] 1 W.L.R. 711.
[25] Table A, pt II, art. 6.
[26] [1980] 1 W.L.R. 1451; see above, para. 4–41.
[27] *Re Home Treat Ltd.* [1991] B.C.L.C. 705.

memorandum and articles of association but which purport to regulate in some detail how aspects of their company's affairs are to be run. One rarely encounters agreements of this nature where a company has many members because multiplicity of parties can make these agreements cumbersome. These agreements are often made at the time when the company is set up and are designed to ensure, from the very outset, that the various understandings reached by the individuals concerned are fully implemented, thereby avoiding disputes and divisions. A common form is a voting or "pooling" agreement, whereby the members agree either to vote or not to vote in a particular way or under particular circumstances.[28] But these agreements may range far wider and deal with matters like issuing new shares, declaring dividends, borrowing, disposal or acquisition of major assets, composition of the board and the remuneration of directors. There are specialist precedent books on drafting shareholders' agreements.[29] Unlike the articles of association, these agreements need not be disclosed to the public through the registry of companies.

14–11 There is no provision in the Companies Acts expressly recognising these agreements. At one time voting agreements were regarded as contrary to public policy and not enforceable, but that is no longer the case. However, such agreements are strictly interpreted, with the presumption favouring freedom to vote.[30] There also were reservations about agreements that operated to fetter the discretion of the directors but, provided that all the present members of a company are party to them, those agreements are not fundamentally objectionable.[31] Reservations also existed about agreements that purported to prevent the company in question (and not just its directors) from exercising a discretion which the Companies Acts granted the company as such, for instance, to amend the articles of association or to increase the share capital. Those doubts were laid to rest by the House of Lords in 1992, at least insofar as rights and obligations between the members *inter se* are concerned.

14–12 That was in *Russell v. Northern Bank Development Corp.*,[32] where the four founding members of a company had separately agreed be-

---

[28] *E.g. Greenwell v. Porter* [1902] 1 Ch. 530; *Puddepath v. Leith* [1916] 1 Ch. 200. See generally, Kruger, "Pooling Agreement under English Company Law" (1978) 94 L.Q.R. 557.

[29] G. Steadman & J. Jones, *Shareholders' Agreements* (1986) contains a variety of precedents, as does *Longman's Practical Commercial Precedents* (loose leaf). Vol. I.

[30] *E.g. Greenhalgh v. Mallard* [1943] 2 All E.R. 234.

[31] *Fulham F.C. Ltd. v. Cabra Estates Ltd.* [1994] 1 B.C.L.C. 363.

[32] [1992] 1 W.L.R. 588.

tween themselves that no additional shares would be issued without all of them consenting. This was held to be a valid and enforceable contract, even though its effect was to veto the discretion contained in section 68(1)(a) of the 1963 Act; the agreement was "purely personal to the shareholders who executed it and [did] not purport to bind future shareholders".[33] However, the company there was also a party to that agreement but it was held that, *qua* the company, the agreement was void and created no legally binding obligations, although there is speculation that this finding is *obiter* because it is not fully consistent with earlier cases.[34] The courts there "severed" this part from the remainder of the agreement, which it enforced by giving a declaration that any attempt to issue additional shares would be a breach of the inter-shareholder part of the agreement. It remains debatable whether any such attempted breach would be enjoined or whether, in view of section 68(1)(a)'s discretionary authority, the breach would be remediable only in damages.

Management

14–13 A closely-held company's most distinctive feature is the overlap between its membership and management; usually the company's principal shareholders are also its directors. Moreover, these companies often possess other devices that give groups of shareholders or individuals extensive control over the board of directors. Part II of Table A allows any director, with the board's approval, to appoint an alternate or substitute who shall be entitled to notices of board meetings and to attend and vote at them.[35] The informal way that many close companies are run is also reflected in their management, where persons may be acting as directors, or as the managing director, without ever having formally been appointed to those offices. However, the company will be held to contracts made by a *de facto* board of directors or a *de facto* managing director. Many of the Companies Acts' provisions imposing duties on directors extend to *de facto* directors.[36]

Fiduciary Duties

14–14 There is some support for the view that the rules regarding fiduciaries' conflicts of interests and abuse of powers should be relaxed somewhat in the case of those who direct close companies. Many of those directors are not full-time executives and may have other business interests, even in related businesses, so that a company may fre-

[33] [1992] 1 W.L.R. 588 at 594.
[34] See above, para. 11–09.
[35] Art. 9.
[36] *Re Lo Line Electric Motors Ltd.* [1988] Ch. 477.

quently have to enter into contracts in which its directors have a personal interest. It is for this reason that article 7 of Part II of Table A allows directors to vote in respect of such contracts, and to be counted in the quorum present at the board meeting. They nevertheless must declare their interests and satisfy the requirements of the interests in contracts book.[37] Article 8 of Part II allows directors to secure some personal advantage from their position where the company owns some shares in another, by permitting them to exercise the votes on those shares "in such manner and in all respects as they think fit" and, in particular, for resolutions appointing them or any of them to remunerated offices in that other company.

14–15 The British courts have taken a categorical approach to corporate opportunities,[38] in that directors are not allowed to exploit opportunities for themselves, even where that action would enure to the company's advantage or where in fact the company could not have exploited the opportunity itself. Some commentators have condemned this approach for being unrealistic and inefficient when applied to close companies.[39] It may ignore a tacit understanding between those involved in such companies that the directors should have some freedom to engage in other businesses; and prohibiting part-time directors from getting personally involved in projects that the company itself cannot finance or otherwise cannot exploit might result in that project never getting under way or a valuable director resigning. Against that, if the company's incapacity to exploit the opportunity is a defence, this could easily induce self-serving directors not to try their best for the company. In *Queensland Mines v. Hudson*[40] the Privy Council upheld the incapacity defence in the special circumstances of that case. The company was formed to exploit mining licences that it expected to obtain. It had two shareholders, F with 51 per cent of the shares, who was to finance the undertaking, and A who possessed the "know how". When Hudson, the company's managing director, was engaged in difficult negotiations to obtain the licences, F was forced into liquidation, which then left the company without working capital. Hudson thereupon took the licence in his own name, resigned from the managing directorship (but not from the board), formed a company to exploit the properties and, after years of strenuous endeavour, made a sizeable profit from them. Shortly after he obtained the licences, he provided the board with a full account of what he had done and, having consid-

[37] 1963 Act, s.194.
[38] See above, paras 5–129 *et seq*.
[39] *cf.* Brudney and Clarke, "A New Look at Corporate Opportunities" (1981) 94 Harv L. Rev. 9981981.
[40] (1978) 52 A.L.R. 399; note in (1979) 42 Mod. L. Rev. 711.

ered the matter, the board agreed that he should be permitted to "go it alone". It was held that, having obtained the board's informed consent, he need not reimburse the company for the profits he had made.

Remuneration

14–16 There are a number of instances of generous directors' remuneration paid to company controllers or their dependents being held invalid as *ultra vires*. In *Re Halt Garage (1964) Ltd.*,[41] where the insolvent company's only two shareholders and directors were Mr C and his wife, and the articles of association empowered the general meeting to pay directors' remuneration, the test of *vires* propounded was two-fold. One is the financial state of the company at the time: were the payments made from earned or retained profits, or did they come from contributed capital? If in fact they came from capital, there then arises the motive for payment: were the payments really directors' remuneration or were they gratuitous distributions to a shareholder out of capital, dressed up as remuneration? In the event, it was concluded that the payments made to Mr C were valid but part of the sums paid to his since-deceased wife were *ultra vires* on the above test.

14–17 The facts as stated in that much criticised case dealing with pensions for ex-directors' dependents, *Re Lee, Behrens & Co.*,[42] do not tell us who held the shares in the company at the time the impugned covenant for a £500 per annum annuity was entered into in favour of the deceased ex-managing director's widow. It would appear that she was an outsider, *i.e.* did not possess a significant or possibly any shareholding in the company. In any event, the issue there was not *ultra vires* in the sense presently understood, being beyond the very capacity of the company. Because the company's shareholders there never gave their approval for the covenant entered into by their board, the issue was simply whether that contract exceeded the directors' powers. In *Re W. & M. Roith Ltd.*[43] the pension in dispute was agreed between the company and its ailing managing director, who owned two-thirds of the shares, many of the other shares being held by his relatives. Because, however, the articles of association there expressly authorised paying pensions to directors' widows, the tests of reasonably incidental to carrying on the company's business and bona fides and to promote the prosperity of the company were of no relevance to the question of *vires*. Insofar as the issue there may have been *ultra*

---

[41] [1982] 3 All E.R. 1016; see above, paras 5–56 *et seq*.
[42] [1932] 2 Ch. 46; see above, para. 5–69.
[43] [1967] 1 W.L.R. 432; see above, para. 5–70.

vires, the proper test in this case should have been the disguised repayment of capital criterion announced in the *Halt Garage* case.

Distributions

14–18 In the case of solvent companies, any substantial distribution of surplus assets to their members is unlawful where one or more of the members object to such unnecessary benevolence.[44] Where the company is insolvent, then any such distribution would contravene the 1983 Act's provisions against paying dividends from capital[45] and in any event is *ultra vires*.[46] Where, however, the company is solvent and all of the members assent to the distribution, the legal position is unclear in view of the Supreme Court's decision in *Re Greendale Developments Ltd. (No. 2)*[47] In that case, the legal issue was not dealt with by the trial judge and was decided by the Supreme Court *de novo*, without affording the defendant a proper opportunity to argue the point.[48]

14–19 *Greendale* concerned a small property development company which had a paid up share capital of £18 and three shareholders, two of whom were also its directors. Substantial payments were made by the company to one director; the cheques were countersigned by the other director and the third shareholder (the recipient's wife) assented to the money being so paid. Later the company was would up on "just and equitable" grounds because of a dispute between the two directors. The Court accepted for the purposes of the case that the company was solvent at the relevant time and there was no suggestion that the payments had been made for some unlawful purpose, such as tax evasion, nor that they had rendered the company insolvent. No consideration was given by the Court to whether the contents of the company's memorandum of association might be relevant to the issue,[49] being whether those payments were *ultra vires*.

14–20 Giving judgment, Keane J. (Blaney and Murphy J.J. concurring) held that they were *ultra vires*. He relied principally on the famous dictum of Bowen L.J. in the *West Cork Railway* case,[50] but of course the benevolence at issue there was a directors' proposal to pay themselves

---

44 *e.g. Cook v. Deeks* [1916] 1 A.C. 554.
45 *Aveling Barford Ltd. v. Perion Ltd.* [1989] B.C.L.C. 626.
46 *Re George Newman & Co.* [1895] 1 Ch. 174.
47 [1998] 1 I.R. 8.
48 See above, paras 3–37 *et seq*.
49 They were of profound significance, because they expressly authorised paying "gratuities" to directors and their dependants and also the distribution of company assets to members.
50 *Hutton v. West Cork Railway Co.* [1883] 23 Ch.D 654; see above, para. 5–74.

gratuities which was being challenged by a minority shareholder;[51] similarly with the *Daily News* case,[52] which Keane J. cited "to the same effect". Further, in both of these cases, the payments were intended to be made at a time when the companies had ceased trading entirely and all that was left was to wind them up. Keane J. cited "to the same effect" the *Lee Behrens* case, [53] but the issue there concerned the powers of the directors only, and further the company was insolvent at the time.[54] Keane J. finally cites "to the same effect" *Roper v. Ward*,[55] but the point in that case has no bearing whatsoever on the matter in dispute. None of the matters referred to earlier in the general discussion of *ultra vires*[56] were considered by the Court, which seems to render the entire decision *per incuriam*.

14–21 Keane J. distinguished *S. M. Barker Ltd.*[57] on the grounds that the shareholders' assent given there was encapsulated in a formal resolution, whereas the assent of the members in *Greendale* had been informal. However, in the similar *Buchanan* case,[58] involving substantial distributions of surplus assets in order to avoid paying tax in Scotland, the informality of the members' assent was not considered relevant by Kingsmill Moore J.; what was decisive there was that the purpose being served was unlawful and the company was left spectacularly insolvent. Why the formality of passing a resolution would have made the difference is not explained.[59] Keane J. described the *Barker* case as authority for the proposition that "shareholders in a company cannot be made amenable under misfeasance proceedings for profits made

---

[51] Bowen L.J. emphasised at p. 671 that "the money which is going to be spent is not the money of the majority" and that a majority resolution on how it should be spent cannot bind objecting shareholders. Bowen and Cotton L.J.J. declared the payments *ultra vires* because s.12 of the private Act of Parliament applicable there (42 and 43 Vict., c. clxxxvii) circumscribed what the company could do with its assets when its business had ceased and they were to be transferred over to the acquiring company.

[52] *Parke v. Daily News* [1962] Ch. 927; see above, para. 3–74..

[53] *Re Lee Behrens & Co.* [1932] 2 Ch. 46; see above, para. 5–69.

[54] Five years after the managing director died, the board agreed to pay an annuity of £500 per annum to his widow for life; three years later, the company was wound up as insolvent. Because the shareholders had never sanctioned this agreement, the only issue was whether it was within the directors' powers; it had nothing to do with *ultra vires* in the sense of the inherent capacity of the company to make the payments.

[55] [1981] I.L.R.M. 408.

[56] Especially the *Rolled Steel* case [1986] Ch. 246; see above, paras 3–72—3–73.

[57] [1950] I.R. 123.

[58] *Peter Buchanan Ltd. v. McVey* [1954] I.R. 89, discussed below, para. 14–22.

[59] Hoffman J. did not regard the lack of formality as decisive in *Re Bradford Investments p.l.c. (No. 2)* [1991] B.C.L.C. 688 at 704.

by them, not in their capacity as directors of the company, but as shareholders."[60] What exactly is contemplated by these two "capacitities" is not elaborated on; again in the *Buchanan* case, no such distinction was drawn. Once all of the shareholders approved the transaction in question and the company is solvent, there does not seem to be any practical grounds for differentiating between those capacities, assuming such difference indeed exists. Further, it was held in the *Home Treat* case[61] that, where a company does something that would be *ultra vires*, it is not to be treated as *ultra vires* where all of its members informally assented to it. Keane J. makes no reference to this case, nor even more surprisingly to the *Rolled Steel Products* case,[62] which is the leading modern authority on the law of *ultra vires* and emphasises the distinction between the intrinsic capacity of a company and abuse of powers that profit-orientated companies possess, such as to make distributions of surplus assets to their members in such manner as they choose.

14–22 The facts in *Greendale* resemble those in the *Buchanan* case, except that the £300,000 which was distributed (in 1943) there to the company's principal shareholder was through a device to evade tax and which rendered the company insolvent. Granted, a clause in the memorandum of association there expressly authorised distributions from the company's assets, except from paid up capital; but so did *Greendale's* memorandum and further Table A, which applied in *Greendale*, contained an equivalent stipulation, thereby making it clear that the company was empowered to make any other kind of distribution. The company in the *Buchanan* case, with £100 paid capital, made enormous profits in whiskey-dealing during the War. When punitive taxes were imposed on those transactions, the owner of all but one of its shares decided to take almost all of those profits out of the company and transfer the money to Ireland, in the belief that the Scottish Revenue could not then recover what was due to them. His scheme was devised to keep the Revenue in the dark about disposals of the company's stocks and, when most of them were sold, drew a cheque for £200,000 on the company's account, payable to another Bank but for his own benefit. When all of the stocks were sold, his co-shareholder and director who remained in Scotland filled in several signed blank cheques for about £100,000, payable to a man in Dublin, who was a nominee of her co-shareholder and director. Subsequently, the company was wound up and the Scots liquidator brought proceedings to have those disbursements recovered, arguing that they were *ultra vires*. He succeeded on

---

[60] [1998] 1 I.R. at 24.
[61] *Re Home Treat Ltd.* [1991] B.C.L.C. 705.
[62] *Rolled Steel Products (Holdings) Ltd. v. British Steel Corp.* [1986] Ch. 246.

that point, not because the payments had never been sanctioned by a formal resolution, nor because the recipient got the money *qua* shareholder rather than *qua* director, but because the underlying purpose was unlawful and the transaction left the company unable to pay off its only creditor, the Revenue, which had raised an assessment for £370,000.

Minority Shareholder Protection

14–23 A court is more likely to intervene against majority action that approximates to fraud on the company by its controllers or unfair discrimination against the minority[63] where the company concerned is closely-held. This tendency has not been formally stated in any of the leading cases but it rests on a number of practical and legal considerations. If the company's shares are traded on the Stock Exchange, the view may be taken that in the marginal case the shareholder should look to the Exchange's own disciplinary mechanisms for redress; the outcome in the *Newman Industries Ltd. (No.2)* case[64] would seem to support this analysis. Where the company's shares are freely transferable, especially if they have a ready market, the view may be taken that in the marginal case the dissatisfied shareholder always has the option of selling out, thereby cutting his losses. It may also be the case that there is far less likelihood of shareholders in widely-held companies forming grand coalitions with a view to unfairly discriminating against the minority. And where those coalitions are formed, there probably would be unambiguous evidence of their true objectives.

14–24 Majorities in close companies, by contrast, cannot be disciplined by the Stock Exchange or by the capital markets. Because of restrictions on the transferability of shares, often along the lines of article 3 of Part II of Table A,[65] aggrieved minorities in close companies may not be able to avail of the exit option. Where this is so, their funds would then be locked into a company, the governance of which they are profoundly dissatisfied with. In close companies, moreover, coalitions against minorities can be formed relatively easily and without formalities, so that it may be very difficult to prove the majority's actual improper motives. Indeed in *Clemens v. Clemens Bros. Ltd.*[66] there were only two shareholders in the company and the majority shareholder declined to testify at the trial. That close companies have a greater propensity to treat minority shareholders in unacceptably unfair ways

---

[63] See above, Chap. 10.
[64] [1982] 1 Ch. 204.
[65] See above, para. 9–33.
[66] [1976] 2 All E.R. 268; see above, para. 10–34.

would appear to be borne out by the reported cases on "oppression" and on winding up on "just and equitable grounds",[67] virtually all of which involve such companies.

14–25 It was stressed, however, in *Re Westbourne Galleries Ltd.*[68] that the fact that a company is a small private company is not enough to warrant judicial intervention on behalf of dissatisfied minority shareholders. The House of Lords there also cautioned against undue emphasis on the analogy with partnership law; that:

> "To refer, as so many of the cases do, to "quasi-partnerships" or "in substance partnerships" may be convenient but may also be confusing. It may be convenient because it is the law of partnership which has developed the conceptions of probity, good faith and mutual confidence, and the remedies where these are absent, which become relevant once [certain other] factors are found to exist . . . And in many, but not necessarily all, cases there has been a pre-existing partnership the obligations of which it is reasonable to suppose continue to underlie the new company structure. But the expressions may be confusing if they obscure, or deny, the fact that the parties (possibly former partners) are now co-members in a company, who have accepted, in law, new obligations. A company, however small, however domestic, is a company not a partnership or even a quasi-partnership and it is through the just and equitable clause that obligations, common to partnership relations, may come in."[69]

14–26 While these remarks were addressed specifically to petitions for winding up on "just and equitable" grounds, they are also relevant where oppression is alleged and ought indeed to be taken into account in the personal action claiming unfair discrimination. Notable examples of this latter category of case include *Clemens Bros. Ltd.*,[70] which concerned a blatant "freeze in", and *Coleman v. Meyers*,[71] a blatant "squeeze out" case where the managing director and chairman used inside information about the company's affairs to buy out the minority shareholders for much less than their shares were really worth. It was held in *Coleman* that, in the light of the family character of the company and the way the defendant went about the takeover and persuaded the plaintiffs to sell him their shares, he owed a fiduciary duty not alone to the company but to the minority shareholders as well. This is not to say that all action taken by majorities in close companies

---

[67] See above, paras 10–73 *et seq*.
[68] [1973] A.C. 360; see above, paras 10–94—10-95.
[69] [1973] A.C. 360 at 379–380. See generally, Rider, "Partnership Law and its Impact on Domestic Companies" (1979) 38 Cam. L. J. 148.
[70] [1976] 2 All E.R. 268.
[71] [1977] 2 N.Z.L.R. 255; see above, para. 12–11.

that disadvantages the minority will be held to be unlawful. The classic instance of somewhat unfair action by the majority being upheld is *Greenhalgh v. Arderne Cinemas Ltd.*,[72] where the gravamen of the plaintiff's case was that he had been "frozen in" to the company.

Company Contracts

14–27 Close companies often enter into engagements simply to facilitate their shareholders and the question accordingly arises whether those transactions are *ultra vires* or were duly authorised under the articles of association. For instance, in *Northern Bank Finance Corp. v. Quinn*,[73] the defendant company, which was the first defendant's private and unlimited investment vehicle, gave security for a loan to him. The objects clause most strongly relied upon in support of the security was one under which the company was to "do and carry out all such other things as may be deemed by the company to be incidental and conducive to the attainment of the above objects or any of them or calculated to enhance the value of or render profitable any of the company's properties or rights." It was held that the security fell outside this clause because that security's "sole object . . . was to facilitate the borrowing by Mr Quinn. . . . Only the bank and Mr Quinn could possibly derive any benefit from this transaction; the company could derive no benefit from the advancing of money to Mr Quinn. The secur[ity, therefore,] could not properly be regarded as being fairly incidental to the objects expressly authorised by" the above clause."[74] The *Rolled Steel Products Ltd.* case[75] illustrates how easily contracts made by closely-held companies can contravene the requirements of their internal regulations.

Piercing the Veil and Creditor Protection

14–28 That a company is owned almost entirely by one individual does not warrant the court disregarding its incorporation, whether it be to hold the owner liable for the company's obligations or to confer on the owner rights accruing to the company. Instances like *Salomon v. Salomon & Co.*,[76] *Macaura v. Northern Assurance Co.*[77] and other cases that are considered in Chapter 3 illustrate the legal significance of individuals running their businesses as registered companies. Indeed, those individuals can be convicted of stealing from their own "one

---

[72] [1951] Ch. 286; see above, para. 10–29.
[73] [1979] I.L.R.M. 221; see above, para. 3–66.
[74] *ibid.* at 226.
[75] [1986] Ch. 246; see above, para. 13–52.
[76] [1897] A.C. 22; see above, paras 3–09—3–10.
[77] [1925] A.C. 619; see above, para. 3–14.

person" companies.[78] Courts nevertheless disregard the incorporation of one kind of closely-held company, the wholly owned subsidiary, where it is merely its parent's *alter ego*;[79] but there are no leading examples of "one-person" companies being treated similarly.

14–29 Where a limited company is wound up and cannot pay its creditors in full, then various kinds of fraud affecting the company raise special problems for the liquidator by virtue of the company's closely-held nature. If the company was managed negligently and, consequently, would have a right of action against its directors, that right is lost if its shareholders assented to or ratified the negligent acts. In the complicated *Multinational Gas* case,[80] which concerned a company that was owned by three giant oil companies, at those shareholders' behest the nominee directors made some financially disastrous negligent decisions. The company was wound up insolvent, owing enormous debts, and the liquidator sought to have its three owners made responsible for those debts. His claim against them was rejected by a divided court on the grounds that the company was a separate legal entity; that it was not its owners' agent; that its owners owed it no duty of care and owed no such duty to its creditors. Whatever claim the company might have had against its directors for negligence was lost because they were carrying out its owners' wishes. One judge, however, suggested that the result would be different if the enormous damage to the company was plain before the owners endorsed the directors' wrongs.[81] Another judge suggested that the owners would be held liable if the directors' wrongs constituted statutory misfeasance.[82] According to the dissenting judge, the company had a cause of action in negligence against its directors and this was an asset that could only be gratuitously released for the company's benefit.[83] An important argument that does not appear to have been made in this case is that the justifications for limited liability in the *Salomon & Co.*-type situation does not obtain here because the owners of the insolvent company here were organisations that themselves possessed limited liability; that the company's real

---

78 *Attorney General's Reference (No. 2 of 1982)* [1984] 2 W.L.R. 453. See generally, Sullivan, "Company Controllers, Company Cheques and Theft" [1983] Crim. L. Rev. 512.

79 *Power Supermarkets Ltd. v. Crumlin Investments Ltd,* Costello J., June 22, 1981; Cases p. 78.

80 *Multinational Gas & Petrochemical Co. v. Multinational Gas & Petrochemical Services Ltd.* [1983] 1 Ch. 258.

81 Lawton J, *ibid.* at 571.

82 Dillon J., *ibid.* at 587.

83 May J., *ibid.* at 579–580.

owners were seeking to shield themselves from personal liability by an elaborate tier of limited companies.[84]

14–30 Where the wrong done to the company is an unratifiable fraud on the company then, by definition, the liquidator can press the company's claim against the fraudsters. But the authorities (apart from *Greendale*), most of which are cited in *Multinational Gas*,[85] tell us that the shareholders of a solvent company, acting unanimously, can do anything that is not *ultra vires* the company; of course, since 1963, all the shareholders are able to alter the objects clause without the need for court approval. It, therefore, follows that, subject possibly to the *ultra vires* principle, all of the shareholders can ratify frauds on the company that are not ratifiable by a simple majority. This happens frequently in "one person" companies; the owners take or, as is sometime put, give themselves presents of, company property. But according to Gavan Duffy P. in *Re S. M. Barker Ltd.*,[86] it is not officer misfeasance where the directors, who are also all of the shareholders, help themselves to company property, so long as the company is not thereby rendered insolvent. This state of affairs, however, does not leave creditors of companies that were looted by their owners without redress.

14–31 To begin with, there is the *ultra vires* principle, which will catch straightforward fraud and the owners who were aware of the fraud would not be protected by section 8(1) of the 1963 Act. However, some forms of what might be regarded as looting may be expressly authorised by the company's regulations, like paying lavish directors' remuneration or even appropriating company property for its owners' benefit, *i.e.* distributions of surplus assets to them. Secondly, Gavan Duffy P. did not question *Re George Newman & Co.*,[87] where it was said that insolvent companies have no right to give their directors presents out of their capital or borrowings. Indeed, Lawton L.J. in *Multinational Gas* ventured that, if it becomes clear that the directors' negligence will bankrupt the company, then the shareholders, even acting unanimously, cannot exonerate those directors from liability by ratifying their wrongs.[88] Thirdly, as *Re Halt Garages (1964) Ltd.*[89] illustrates, there is the principle against repaying shareholders their capital and such payments will not be permitted even if they are disguised as directors' remuneration. Fourthly, if the looting takes the form of repaying money

---

84 See below, para. 14–54.
85 [1983] 1 Ch. 258.
86 [1950] I.R. 123; see below, para. 18–70.
87 [1895] 1 Ch. 674; see below, para. 18–71.
88 [1983] 1 Ch. at p. 288.
89 [1982] 3 All E.R. 1016; see above, paras 5–62 *et seq.*

lent to the company by its owners, this might constitute a fraudulent preference under section 286 of the 1963 Act.[90] Fifthly, if the owners abstract assets from the company in order to prevent it from paying a particular debt, the creditor may have a direct right of action against them for the tort of inducing breach of contract.[91] Finally, all of what is said above must now be read in the light of the Supreme Court's decision in *Re Greendale Developments Ltd.*,[92] discussed earlier. In order to be valid and *intra vires*, it seems that there must be a formal resolution of all of the shareholders of a solvent company sanctioning a substantial distribution by it to one or more of them; their informal assent to such a distribution does not prevent it from being *ultra vires*. It remains to be seen if *Greendale* may be overruled or may be distinguished almost out of existence.[93]

GROUP ENTERPRISES

14–32 Many businesses are run in the form of groups of companies. At the centre, typically, is the parent or controlling company. If the parent is a private company it may be registered without limited liability, either for reasons of taxation or to avoid having to make certain disclosures to the public about its affairs. Various parts of the business may be operated by subsidiary companies, the shares in which are owned either entirely or mainly by the parent company. Other aspects of the business may be run by affiliate companies in which wholly separate interests have a sizeable stake. If the business extends to different parts of the world then it may be described as a multinational enterprise.

14–33 The Companies Acts contain a number of rules for group enterprises;[94] a prominent feature of many parts of the 1990 Act is the

---

[90] See below, paras 18–40 *et seq.*

[91] *Einborn v. Westmount Investments Ltd.* (1969) 6 D.L.R. (3d) 71, note in (1970) 33 Mod. L. Rev. 309.

[92] [1998] 1 I.R. 8. See above, paras 14–19 *et seq.*

[93] The same may be said of another recent Supreme Court decision on major points in company law where Blaney J. presided, *Re Frederick Inns Ltd.* [1994] 1 I.L.R.M. 387; discussed below, para. 16–08.

[94] See generally, C. Schmitthoff and F. Woolidge, *Groups of Companies* (1991); Austin, "Corporate Groups" in *Corporate Personality in the 20th Century* (C. Rickett and R. Grantham eds., 1998) and Yeung, "Corporate Groups: Legal Aspects of the Management Dilemma" [1997] Ll. M.L.Q. 208. *cf. The Encylopaedic Works* by P. Blumberg — *The Law of Corporate Groups — Procedural Law* (1983), *Bankruptcy Law* (1985), *Substantive Law* (1987) and *Statutory Law* (1989), on the U.S. law and practice. Also, Hofstetter, "Parent Responsibility for Subsidiary Corporations; Evaluating European Trends" (1990) 39 Int'l & Comp. L.Q. 576.

extent to which it provides for group transactions and relationships. There is an E.C. Seventh Directive on consolidated accounts[95] and at present the Commission is working on draft legislation to regulate other aspects of groups' activities.[96] Sections 410–429 of the Taxes Consolidation Act 1997 provide for various tax reliefs for associated companies and for companies within groups.[97]

Subsidiary, Related and Associated Companies

14–34 The principal legal relationship within a group of companies is that between the holding or parent company and its subsidiary company or companies. Most of the rules considered here were adopted with this relationship in mind. However, there are certain rules which cast the net far wider and bring in other companies with some lesser connection with the company in question.

"Holding"/"Subsidiary" Company

14–35 A company is another's (*i.e.* holding company's or parent company's) subsidiary for the purposes of the Companies Acts if it satisfies any of three criteria set out in section 155 of the 1963 Act.[98] One is based on owning a majority of the company's shares, namely where one company or its nominee holds more than half in nominal value of the other's voting shares or, alternatively, more than half in nominal value of the other's "equity share capital". Shares held in a fiduciary capacity, shares held under the provisions of a debenture or under a trust deed securing a debenture, and shares held by a money-lending company as security for loans made in the ordinary course of business are excluded for the purposes of this computation.[99] Another criterion is based on ability to control the company's directors, namely where one company is a member of the other and controls the composition of the board. By control is meant where one company has the unrestricted power to appoint or remove all or at least a majority of the other's directors.[100] A holding company-subsidiary relationship arises, thirdly, where one company is a subsidiary of the other's subsidiary. How-

---

95 [1983] O.J. L193/1; below, paras 14–39—14–40.

96 See generally, Bohshoff & Budde, "Company Groups — The E.E.C. Proposals", (1984) 6 Comp. Bus. & Capital Mkts. L. Rev. 163; Derom, "The E.E.C. Approaches to Group of Companies" (1976) 16 Virginia J. Int'l L. 565.

97 See generally, P. Moore and F. Brennan, *Corporation Tax* (9th ed., 1997) and M. Feeney, Corporation Tax (1997), Chap. 7.

98 *cf. Michaels v. Harley House (Marlybone) Ltd.* [1999] 1 B.C.L.C. 670 concerning a slightly different definition in the U.K. Landlord and Tenant Acts.

99 1963 Act, s.155(3).

100 *cf. ibid.*, s.155(2).

ever, arrangements can easily be made whereby one company effectively owns and controls another without there being a holding company-subsidiary relationship as therein defined.[101]

"Related" Company

14–36 Several provisions are made with reference to what are called "related companies", notably, the extension of an inspection under Part II of the 1990 Act to such companies,[102] the extension of an examination under the Companies (Amendments) Act 1990, to such companies,[103] the obligation to contribute towards the liabilities of an insolvent company,[104] and the pooling of assets of those companies when insolvent.[105] By "related" here is meant, in addition to parent and subsidiary companies,

— where more than half the nominal value of the company's equity share capital is held by the other company and by companies related to that other company (whether directly or indirectly, but not in a fiduciary capacity); or

— where more than half of the nominal value of the equity share capital of each of them is held by members of the other (whether directly or indirectly, other than in a fiduciary capacity); or

— where that other company or a company or companies related to that other company, or that other company together with a company or companies related to it, are entitled to exercise or control the exercise of more than one half of the voting power at any general meeting of the company; or

— where the businesses of the companies have been so carried on that the separate business of each company, or a substantial part thereof, is not readily identifiable; or

— there is another company to which both companies are related.[106]

14–37 A very different definition is used for determining if companies are related for the purpose of disclosure in the annual accounts. Companies are then presumed to be related where one holds more than 20 per cent of the voting shares in the other.[107]

---

[101] See generally, Picketing, "Shareholders' Voting Rights and Company Control" (1965) 81 L.Q.R. 248 at 263–267.
[102] s.9.
[103] s.4
[104] 1990 Act, s.140; see below, para. 18–72.
[105] *ibid.*, s.141.
[106] 1990 Act, s.140(5).
[107] 1986 Act, sched., para. 73.

"Associated" and "Connected" Companies

14–38 The Companies Acts occasionally use the terms affiliate or associate company, which connote companies in which another has a sizeable equity stake, whether directly or indirectly, but are not subsidiaries within the section 155 definition explained above. Thus, for purposes of the annual accounts, holding 20 per cent of the voting shares or of the allotted shares renders one company another's "associated company".[108] For the purposes of section 16 of the Redundancy Payments Act 1967, concerning the re-engagement of an employee by an "associate company", this term signifies holding and subsidiary companies, as defined by section 155 of the 1963 Act, and also two or more companies which are subsidiaries of a third company. This concept also appears in the regulatory legislation, for instance in section 17 of the Central Bank Act 1971, as amended in 1989, which enables persons authorised by the Central Bank to inspect all books and records of an "associated enterprise", *i.e.* a business which is associated with a licensed bank in the manner defined there. A similar provision exists in section 16 of the Insurance Act 1989, for what are described there as any "connected body". Under section 432 of the Taxes Consolidation Act 1997, an "associated company" is defined as any company which controls or is under the control of another, or companies under the control of the same person; what constitutes "control" for this and other purposes is defined extensively.[109] For the purposes of the Irish Takeover Panel Act 1997, control means directly or indirectly holding 30 per cent of the voting rights in the company.[110]

Group Accounts

14–39 Holding companies must ensure that their financial year coincides with that of their subsidiaries, except where there are good reasons for not doing so.[111] Where those years do not coincide, an explanation must be given by way of a note to the company's or the group's accounts."[112] Holding companies are required by section 150 of the 1963 Act to lay group or consolidated accounts before their annual general meetings. A private holding company, however, need not do this provided that it makes available on request to every member a copy of each subsidiary's balance sheet, documents that must be an-

---

[108] 1986 Act, s.16(1)(b).

[109] ss. 432(2)–(6) and s.11; see also Capital Acquisitions Tax Act 1976, s.16(4). See generally, M. Feeney, *Corporation Tax* (1997), pp. 19–33.

[110] s.1(1) of the Act. *cf. Bermuda Cable Vision Ltd. v. Colica Trust Co.* [1998] 1 B.C.L.C. 1 on meaning of "control" in Bermuda.

[111] 1963 Act, s.153.

[112] 1986 Act, sched., para. 55.

nexed thereto and the directors' and auditors' reports.[113] Group accounts are not required where the company in question is another Irish company's wholly owned subsidiary.[114] Nor need group accounts deal with a subsidiary where the parent company's directors are of the opinion that, in view of the insignificant amounts involved and disproportionate expense, such accounts would be impractical or of no real value to members, or the results would be misleading.[115] But where a subsidiary's accounts are not incorporated into the group accounts any member of the holding company is entitled to be furnished with a copy of that subsidiary's balance sheet, annexes and directors' and auditors' reports.[116] An explanation must be given by way of a note to the group accounts why the accounts of any subsidiary have not been incorporated into them.[117]

14–40 Group accounts are defined as a consolidated balance sheet and a consolidated profit and loss account, both of which deal with the state of affairs of the parent and of its subsidiaries.[118] Those accounts may take a different form where the directors are of the opinion that another form would present a better picture of the group's affairs.[119] As with a company's own accounts, the over-riding requirement is that the group accounts give a "true and fair" view of the group's situation. Subject to this, group accounts must comply with the requirements of the 1986 Act and its schedules and, in particular, with the European Communities (Companies: Group Accounts) Regulations, 1992,[120] which gives effect to the E.C. Directive on consolidated group accounts.[121]

Holding Shares in Parent Company

14–41 Subject to a very limited number of exceptions, section 32 of the 1963 Act forbids a subsidiary company from acquiring or holding shares in its own parent company. Any such purported shareholding

---

113 1963 Act, s.154.
114 1963 Act, s.150(2)(a).
115 *ibid.*, s.150(2)(b).
116 *ibid.*, s.150(3).
117 1986 Act, sched., para. 54(2)(a).
118 1963 Act, s.151.
119 *ibid.*, s.151(2).
120 S.I. No. 201 of 1992; see generally, N. Brennan and A. Pierce, *Irish Company Accounts* (1996), Pt 6.
121 [1983] O.J. L193/1; see generally, Petite, "The Conditions for Consolidation Under the Seventh Company Law Directive" (1984) 21 Comm. Mkt. L. Rev. 81 and Cooke, "The Seventh Directive — An Accountant's Perspective", [1984] Eur. L. Rev. 143.

is declared void. The main exception here is where, before it became a subsidiary company, that company already held shares in what was to become its parent company;[122] for instance, it held extensive investments and was then taken over by one of the companies in which it held shares. No provision was made for dealing with the situation where, by accident or oversight, shares in the parent became registered in the subsidiary's name. But that lacuna is now rectified by section 89 of the 1963 Act, as amended in 1990,[123] which gives the court a discretion to declare that an invalid acquisition of shares shall be deemed valid in circumstances where it is just and equitable to do so.[124]

14–42 Section 224 of the 1990 Act permits subsidiary companies to acquire shares in their holding companies, subject to the safeguards laid down there. Before that acquisition can be made, the relevant contracts must have been authorised in advance by resolutions of both the subsidiary company and the holding company. The same general principles apply to these resolutions as apply where the company wishes to purchase its own shares.[125] For instance, if it is an "off market" purchase, there must be a special resolution authorising the transaction and the parent company's votes must not have been the decisive ones in carrying that proposal. And a copy of the proposed contract must have been available for inspection by the members for at least three weeks before the resolution was passed. The consideration for this acquisition must come from profits of the subsidiary which are available for distribution as profits. In order to fill some gaps in the statutory scheme, in 1997 the definition of a p.l.c.'s subsidiary for this purpose was extended and changes were made to section 224.[126]

14–43 When the shares are purchased, a form of capitalised reserve in the subsidiary is then created, in that any profits it possesses for distribution must be reduced by an amount equal to the purchase price for so long as the subsidiary holds those shares.[127] No voting rights can be exercised on those shares.[128] But there is no prohibition on dividends being paid to the subsidiary. These shares must not be shown in the consolidated accounts as an asset but disclosure must be made in the notes to the accounts of those shares' par value and the cost of

---

[122] s.32(4).
[123] s.227. *cf. Acatos & Hutchenson p.l.c. v. Watson* [1995] 1 B.C.L.C. 218.
[124] In *Re Sugar Distributors Ltd.* [1995] 2 I.R. 194 such a declaration was refused.
[125] See above, paras 7–49 *et seq.*
[126] European Communities (Public Limited Companies Subsidiaries) Regulations 1997 (S.I. No. 67 of 1997).
[127] s.224(2)(b)(i).
[128] 1963 Act, s.32(6) and 1990 Act, s.224(2)(b)(3).

aquiring them. A special return must be made to the registrar of companies within 28 days of the purchase.[129] If, within six months after the acquisition, the subsidiary is wound up and is insolvent, the directors can be made liable to pay it the price it paid for its holding company's shares.[130]

Minority Shareholder Protection

14–44 A major dilemma that confronts holding or parent companies is how to deal with a subsidiary in which independent shareholders have a significant stake. Especially when the subsidiary is an integral part of the parent's general business, the natural tendency is for the parent to make use of the subsidiary for the benefit of the entire enterprise and not just for the subsidiary alone. This practice raises the threshold question about directors' duties.[131] Do a subsidiary's directors, who are appointed by its parent and who put the advantage of the group enterprise before benefit to the subsidiary, violate their fiduciary duties? It would appear that they do,[132] although the question does not appear to have received exhaustive judicial consideration in this context.[133] If a breach of fiduciary duty of this nature occurs, when is it ratifiable by the majority shareholders and when does it amount to a fraud on the company or unfair discrimination against the minority? The standards discussed in Chapter 10 above apply in these circumstances, although application of those standards to parent-subsidiary relations might give rise to special difficulties. Indeed, what often happens where conflicts of interest look likely is for the parent to buy out the minority shareholders at an attractive price in order to obtain a free hand in running the entire enterprise.

14–45 The leading early case on statutory oppression, *Scottish Co-op Wholesale Soc. v. Meyer*,[134] is a text book example of the parent unfairly exploiting its subsidiary to the detriment of the latter's minority shareholders. There the parent, having failed to buy out the minority at a relatively low price, in effect ran down the subsidiary's business and removed the minority shareholders from their offices as the subsidiary's principal executives. The parent's main defence was that the cir-

---

[129] 1990 Act, s.226.
[130] *ibid.*, s.225.
[131] See generally, Yeung, "Corporate Groups: Legal Aspects of the Management Dilemma", [1997] Lloyds Maritime L.Q. 208.
[132] *Boulting v. A.C.T.A.T.* [1963] 2 Q.B. 606 at 627; *Lonrho Ltd. v. Shell Petroleum Co. (No. 2)* [1982] A.C. 173.
[133] *cf. Lindgren v. L. & P. Estates Ltd.* [1968] 1 Ch. 572 for the converse question.
[134] [1959] A.C. 324.

cumstances — the parent refused to furnish the subsidiary with raw materials for its product and the parent's nominee directors on the subsidiary's board never took steps to reverse the company's decline — did not satisfy even the objective requirements for oppression in what is section 205 of the 1963 Act. The Law Lords' answer to this was that:

> "all the evidence [shows no] trace that the [nominees] regarded themselves as owing any duty to the company of which they were directors. They were nominees of the [parent] and, if the [parent] doomed the company to destruction, it was not for them to put out a saving hand. Rather, they were to join in that work . . . That is how they conducted the affairs of the company and it is impossible to suppose that that was not part of the deliberate policy of the [parent] . . . It is not possible to separate the transactions of the [parent] from those of the company. Every step taken by the latter was determined by the policy of the former . . . It is just because the [parent] could not only use the ordinary and legitimate weapons of commercial warfare but could also control from within the operations of the company that it is illegitimate to regard the conduct of the company's affairs as a matter for which the [parent] had no responsibility."[135]

14–46 Parent companies, therefore, must not take undue advantage of subsidiaries in their business dealings with them. As it was put in the *Scottish Co-op* case:

> "whenever a subsidiary is formed as in this case with an independent minority of shareholders, the parent company must if it is engaged in the same class of business, accept as a result of having formed such a subsidiary an obligation so to conduct what are in a sense its own affairs as to deal fairly with its subsidiary. [In other words,] conducting what are in a sense its own affairs may amount to misconducting the affairs of the subsidiary."[136]

Company Contracts

14–47 Transactions entered into by companies that are members of a group occasionally give rise to special problems of capacity and authority, although those difficulties may be resolved by section 8(1) of the 1963 Act[137] and S.I. No. 163 of 1973.[138] Where the company enters into a transaction not for its own benefit but instead to facilitate one of its associated companies in the group or the group as a whole, then the transaction may be *ultra vires*. In *Charterbridge Corp. v. Lloyds Bank*[139]

---

[135] [1959] A.C. 324 at 341.
[136] *ibid.* at 362. *cf. Nicholas v. Soundcraft Electronics Ltd.* [1993] B.C.L.C. 360.
[137] See above, paras 13–15 *et seq.*
[138] See above, paras 13–56 *et seq.*
[139] [1970] Ch. 62.

the legal position was summarised as follows:

> "Each company in the group is a separate legal entity and the directors of a particular company are not entitled to sacrifice the interest of that company. This becomes apparent when one considers the case where the particular company has separate creditors. The proper test [in such circumstances] must be whether an intelligent and honest man in the position of a director of the company concerned, could, in the whole of the existing circumstances, have reasonably believed that the transactions were for the benefit of the company."[140]

14–48 Benefiting an associated company or the entire group will often enure to the advantage of the company in question. The *Charterbridge Corp.* case, for instance, concerned a large group of companies in the property development business. For each site being developed, a separate company would be incorporated; the parent's function was to acquire sites, provide common office and financial services, and supervise the various associated companies' activities. The bank obtained security for the parent's overdraft, which included a deposit by the plaintiff associate company of title deeds to its property. Later, the associate sought a declaration that the security was *ultra vires*. Among the associate's objects was one enabling it to "secure or guarantee . . . the performance and discharge of any . . . obligation . . . [of the company] or any other person or corporation with whom or which [the company] has dealings or having a business or undertaking in which [the company] is concerned or interested whether directly or indirectly." It was held, firstly, that giving the security here fell four square within the terms of these objects and, therefore, was binding on the company regardless of bringing it any financial benefit. But in any event, it would have been disastrous for the company if its parent collapsed and, accordingly, it was very much to its advantage to assist the parent financially. This case also suggests that where the lender has knowledge of the group's affairs and knows that, when agreeing to put up the security, the subsidiary looked to the group's benefit rather than to its own advantage, that should not be treated as if the lender was "actually aware" that the transaction was *ultra vires*.[141]

Piercing the Veil and Creditor Protection

14–49 The whole question of disregarding the fact of incorporation — of what is often referred to as piercing the corporate veil — has

---

[140] [1970] Ch. 62 at 74.

[141] Similarly, *Re PMPA Garage (Longmile) Ltd.* [1992] 1 I.R. 315; compare *Re Frederick Inns Ltd.* [1994] 1 I.L.R.M. 387, where the group companies in question were insolvent at the time.

already been discussed in Chapter 3,[142] where many of the leading examples of where the court either did or did not pierce the veil involve group enterprises are given. There is no hard and fast rule for groups for these purposes. While generally the courts will not pierce the veil, occasions arise where they will do so; perhaps the best reported example in recent years is *Munton Bros. Ltd. v. Secretary of State,*[143] where the wholly-owned subsidiary had no independent commercial existence of its own whatsoever. Gibson J. held that the subsidiary was a mere agent or *alter ego* of the parent and that, in any event, the unique circumstances there in all fairness warranted lifting the veil. That case can be contrasted with *State (McInerney) Ltd. v. Dublin County Council,*[144] concerning a planning application, where Carroll J. stressed that "the corporate veil is not a device to be raised or lowered at the option of the parent company or group."[145]

14–50 On a number of occasions the courts have by-passed the separate corporate existence in order that a company obtain a benefit that otherwise it would have been denied. Thus in one instance, *Smith, Stone & Knight Ltd. v. Birmingham Corp.,*[146] a company acquired a partnership, which it registered as a subsidiary company, and then carried on the partnership business through the subsidiary. When the local authority compulsorily acquired the subsidiary's business premises, the parent sought compensation in respect of removal and disturbance. Its claim succeeded on the grounds that, because of the way the subsidiary was run, it ought to be treated as the parent's agent or *alter ego*. Criteria were set out there for determining when a subsidiary is its parent's agent, namely:

> "were the profits treated as profits of the . . . parent company? Secondly, were the persons conducting the business appointed by the parent company? Thirdly, was the [parent] the head and brain of the trading venture? Fourthly, did the [parent] govern the adventure, decide what should

---

142 above, paras 3–19. *et seq.* See generally, Rixon, "Lifting the Veil Between Holding and Subsidiary Companies" (1986) 102 L.Q.R. 415; Landers, "A Unified Approach to Parent, Subsidiary and Affiliate Questions in Bankruptcy" (1975) 42 U. Chicago L. Rev. 589; Posner, "The Legal Rights of Creditors of Affiliated Corporations: An Economic Approach" (1976) 43 U. Chicago L. Rev. 449 and Landers, "Another Word on Parents, Subsidiaries and Affiliates in Bankruptcy" (1976) 43 U. Chicago L. Rev. 527.

143 [1983] N.I. 369; see above, para. 3–25.

144 [1985] I.R. 1.

145 *ibid.* at 7. *cf. Lac Minerals Ltd. v. Chevron Minerals Corp.* [1995] 1 I.L.R.M. 161; *Allied Irish Coal Suppliers Ltd. v. Powell Duffryn International Fuels Ltd.* [1998] 2 I.R. 519 and *National Dock Labour Board v. Pinn & Wheeler Ltd.* [1989] B.C.L.C. 647.

146 [1939] 4 All E.R. 116.

> be done and what capital should be embarked on the venture? Fifthly, did the [parent] make the profits by its skill and direction? Sixthly, was the [parent] in effectual and constant control?"[147]

In a later and somewhat similar case it was observed that there is "a general tendency to ignore the separate legal entities of various companies within a group, and to look instead at the economic entity of the whole group. This is especially the case when a parent company owns all the shares of the subsidiaries, so much that it can control every movement of the subsidiaries."[148] But these remarks exaggerate somewhat the legal position.

Separate Personality

14–51 The distinct legal personality of a holding company and each of its subsidaries, even wholly-owned subsidiaries, was emphasised in *Re Frederick Inns Ltd.*[149] That concerned the winding up of a group of companies, several of which were heavily indebted to the Revenue. Before those companies were wound up, the group made a settlement with the Revenue; several of them would sell property they owned and pay the proceeds of the sale to the Revenue, who then appropriated that money towards the tax liabilities of the group. Because this settlement was made against the Revenue's threat to wind up all the companies, it would not have been struck down as a fraudulent preference. But the payments by some of the companies, not indebted to the Revenue, of the tax liabilities of their related companies was held in the circumstances to be unlawful and that the money must be returned to the liquidator. This was because the Revenue received that money in the full knowledge of the entire circumstances and, furthermore, it is a fundamental principle that companies which are insolvent should not in effect make presents of their own assets. That the payments were in respect of the liabilities of other companies in the group did not alter that position. According to Lardner J.,

> "this principle [of separate legal personality] and the statutory rules of company law in which the principle is implicit apply to the relationship between holding companies and subsidiaries and to transactions between them and third parties. The assets of such companies are treated as owned by them legally and beneficially as distinct legal entitles. And except were circumstances enable a court to discover an agency or trustee relationship between them, a holding company is not treated as the owner of its

---

[147] [1939] 4 All E.R. 116 at 121.
[148] *D.H.N. Food Distributors Ltd. v. Borough of Tower Hamlets* [1976] 1 W.L.R. 852 at 860.
[149] [1994] 1 I.L.R.M. 582.

> subsidiaries' assets. And the liabilities of companies which are members of the same group are those of the individual companies which incur them. There is no common group liability for the obligations of individual members of the group imposed by law. The principle is reflected in many aspects of company law . . . Taxing statutes also recognise the principle that each company is a separate legal entity, to the extent that they do not tax a holding company and its subsidiaries as if it were one."[150]

14–52 In another recent instance where this entire matter was examined most thoroughly, *Adams v. Cape Industries p.l.c.*,[151] the issue was whether a judgment obtained in Texas should be enforced in England against a company registered in England and which was never physically present in Texas. It was argued that the company should be deemed to have been present there because it had a wholly-owned subsidiary which carried on the American side of its business there. Because, in the circumstances, the group were one highly integrated economic unit, it was contended that the subsidiary's presence was the equivalent of the parent's presence. That view was rejected. Even if economically they were the one entity, the court was concerned not with economics but with law. Most of the authorities tending to favour the one-unit contention can be explained by reference to particular terms of the Act or the contract under consideration at the time. Slade L.J. summed up the law as follows:

> "There is no general principle that all companies in a group of companies are to be regarded as one. On the contrary, the fundamental principle is that each company in a group of companies (a relatively modern concept) is a separate legal entity possessed of separate legal rights and liabilities . . . [Slave in cases which turn on the wording of particular statutes or contracts, the court is not free to disregard [that] principle merely because it considers that justice so requires . . . If a company chooses to arrange the affairs of its group in such a way that the business carried on in a particular foreign country is the business of its subsidiary and not of its own, it is . . . entitled to do so . . . [T]he court is [not] entitled to lift the corporate veil as against a [holding] company which is the member of a corporate group merely because the corporate structure has been used so as to ensure that the legal liability (if any) in respect of particular future activities of the group (and correspondingly the risk of enforcement of that liability) will fall on another member of the group rather than the [parent] company."[152]

---

[150] [1991] I.L.R.M. 582 at 587–588, upheld [1994] 1 I.L.R.M. 387 at 395. But *cf. Re PMPA Garage (Longmile) Ltd.* [1992] 1 I.R. 315, upholding guarantees given for the debts of associated companies.

[151] [1990] 1 Ch. 433.

[152] *ibid.* at 532, 536—537 and 544. See also *Re Polly Peck International p.l.c. (No. 3)* [1996] B.C.L.C. 428.

14–53 Ordinarily, a parent company has no right of action in damages in respect of a loss suffered by its subsidiary; it is for the latter alone to prosecute such claim as it may have. However, where the parent company contracts with a third part to render some service to its subsidiary or to otherwise deal with it, and that third party breaches the contract, the parent is entitled to damages for such foreseeable loss as it has suffered in consequence of that breach. Thus in the *George Fischer* case,[153] there was a holding company and several operating subsidiaries, one of which carried out the sales function. The holding company contracted with the defendant to install equipment at the sales subsidiary, but that equipment was defective, leading to losses in group sales and increased operating costs. The parent company was held entitled to recover substantial damages. Circumstances even can arise where a parent company may have a right of action in negligence for what a third party has done in respect of its subsidiary. This was held to be the case in *Barings plc v. Coopers & Lybrand*,[154] where it was held that auditors of the now defunct plaintiff bank's Singapore subsidiary, who failed to detect the defalcations occurring there, owed a duty of care to the parent in London as well as to the subsidiary; on the facts, there was sufficient "proximity" between the parent and that auditors to found a duty of care. There is "no legal principle that a holding company is unable to recover damages for loss in the value of its subsidiaries, resulting directly from a breach of duty to it, as distinct from a duty owed (or not owed as the case may be) to the subsidiaries.[155]

Limited Liability

14–54 There is no major reported instance in these islands of a parent being held liable for its insolvent subsidiary's debts on the grounds that it controlled the subsidiary. In the absence of fraud or wholly exceptional circumstances, the principle in *Salomon & Co.*[156] would insulate the parent from liability. It could be argued that the justifications for limited liability do not obtain in these circumstances;[157] for instance, that limited liability was designed to insulate individual investors and not organisations that already possess limited liability. It could also be contended that, when the subsidiary is being run as an arm of the group enterprise, then loans advanced to it by the parent or by another subsidiary should not be treated as debts that must be preferred over outside unsecured creditors, on the grounds that those advances are more

---

[153] *George Fischer (Great Britain) Ltd. v. Multi Construction Ltd.* [1995] 1 B.C.L.C. 260.
[154] [1997] 1 B.C.L.C. 427.
[155] *ibid.* at 435.
[156] [1897] A.C. 22.
[157] See Landers' articles in 42 and 43 U. Chicago L. Rev. (1975-76), above, n. 142.

akin to equity investment. This is because funds placed by a parent in its subsidiary are made over in the expectation of enhancing the entire group's profit and, accordingly, are more in the nature of equity than debt. The fact that the subsidiary was left seriously under-capitalised and was never given the opportunity to grow into an independently profitable unit might give credence to such arguments in an appropriate case.

Statutory Exceptions to the Principle

14–55 Several tax cases which would appear to disregard separate incorporation can be explained by reference to the statutory provisions in question there. To an extent, arguments for treating companies in a group as one unit were accepted by the Oireachtas in some provisions to the 1990 Act dealing with winding up insolvent companies. Thus misfeasance proceedings, under section 298 of the 1963 Act, may be brought not only against various officers of the insolvent company but also against any director of its holding company who is guilty of misfeasance in relation to it.[158] Where a parent or other "related" company was very closely involved in managing the insolvent company or led its creditors to believe that its liabilities would be covered, section 140 of the 1990 Act authorises the court to order payment by the related company of a contribution towards the liabilities of the insolvent company.[159] In *Re Bray Travel Ltd.*,[160] where a whole number of inextricably connected companies were being wound up, the Supreme Court ordered that they all could be wound up as if they were a single entity. Section 141 of the 1990 Act puts that decision on a firm statutory basis, enabling related companies' assets to he pooled and that they be wound up together where that is just and equitable to do so.[161]

14–56 In *Re Goodman International Ltd.*,[162] the court was asked to confirm a very elaborate scheme, drawn up under the Companies (Amendments) Act 1990, for dealing with the debts of many companies in the Goodman group of companies, over which an examiner had been appointed in 1990.[163] It was proposed that the same scheme should bind all the companies in the group, even though many of them had different creditors and some had different shareholders. It was argued that, since the 1990 Act makes no express provision for a composite across-the-board scheme, it was necessary to draw up separate schemes for

---

158 1990 Act, s.148; see below, paras 18–66 *et seq*.
159 See below, para. 18–72.
160 Supreme Court, July 13, 1981.
161 *cf. Re Dalkoff & King Holdings Ltd.* [1991] 2 N.Z.L.R. 296.
162 Hamilton P., January 28, 1991.
163 On this legislation generally, see below, Chap. 17.

each related company. It was pointed out that the "examiner" Act, which originally was part of the Companies Act 1990, did not contain a provision similar to section 141 of the latter Act, authorising across-the-board liquidations; that this absence from the "examiner" Act was highly significant. That contention was rejected by Hamilton R, on the grounds that the "very purposes of the Act . . . would be nullified if the Examiner were not entitled to take into account the position with regard to each and every one of the related companies and to formulate a scheme . . . which would deal with the overall picture".[164] Certainly this hastily enacted measure, which contains a lengthy section on related companies, could be criticised for not making express provision for group schemes and there was much substance in the argument that the Oireachtas had considered the entire question of group schemes but decided that the position in each company should be dealt with individually.[165] Against that, however, the Supreme Court had ordered a group solution in *Re Bray Travel Ltd.*, where too there was no express statutory authority for not treating each group company individually. Although in that case the group companies never kept any separate accounts or books, thereby rendering it practically impossible for a liquidator to wind them up on an individual basis.

Fraud

14–57 The corporate veil, whether between individuals and their companies or between parent and subsidiary companies, will be lifted in instances of fraud.[166] One explanation for the *Bray Travel Ltd.*[167] decision may be that the absence of any separate books and records and other circumstances disclosed to the court there strongly suggested that there had been fraud in connection with those companies. Kenny J. referred to the company's property having been sold at a "gross under-value". Ordinarily, when deciding to disregard the separate corporate existence on the grounds of fraud, the motive for establishing the subsidiary calls for consideration. In the *Cape Industries* case,[168] it was held that the objective of minimising the parent's exposure to legal liability could not be a fraudulent motive for this purpose. There does not appear to be any reported cases where liability was imposed on a parent company because it established a subsidiary company for fraudulent reasons.

---

164 At p.16.
165 *cf. McDonald v. Australian Guarabovee Corp. (No.2) Ltd.* [1990] 1 N.Z.L.R. 227.
166 See above, paras 3–22 and 3–28; *e.g. Re A Company Ltd.* [1985] B.C.L.C. 333 and *Re H.* [1996] 2 B.C.L.C. 500.
167 Supreme Court, July 13, 1981.
168 [1990] 1 Ch. 433.

Agency

14–58 On at least one occasion, the *Munton Bros.* case,[169] it was held that a wholly-owned subsidiary was its parent company's agent. But the mere fact that their businesses are very closely integrated is not enough to establish agency; the subsidiary has to have practically no independent commercial existence of its own. In the *Cape Industries* case the court examined carefully the internal arrangements of the group there and concluded that the subsidiary had a business of its own and was not simply its parent's *alter ego*.[170]

Justice

14–59 In the *Cape Industries* case, the court rejected the view that it is "free to disregard the principle of *Salomon v. Salomon* merely because it considers that justice so requires".[171] However, in *Re Bray Travel Ltd.*, the Supreme Court endorsed the view that:

> "a court may, if the justice of the case so requires, treat two or more related companies as a single entity so that the business notionally carried on by one will be regarded as the business of the group, or another member of the group, if this conforms to the economic and commercial realities of the situation".[172]

Justice was also invoked in the *Munton Bros.* case for reaching the conclusion there that the holding company should receive compensation for the loss of its subsidiary's business.[173]

14–60 The actual justice of the holding in *Re Bray Travel Ltd.* was that separate records were never kept for the different companies and, accordingly, it was practically impossible to carry out separate liquidations of them. A similar instance, although not involving liquidations, is *Power Supermarkets Ltd. v. Crumlin Investments Ltd.*[174] There the first defendant, a company that later was acquired by the Dunnes Stores group, leased a unit in a shopping centre to the plaintiff. In the lease the defendant covenanted not to allow any extra-large supermarket to be operated in the centre; not to "grant a lease for or to sell or permit or suffer the sale by any of its tenants or . . . any sub or

---

169 [1983] N.I. 369.

170 Similarly in *Stewarts Supermarkets Ltd. v. Secretary of State* [1982] N.I. 286, *Woolfson v. Strathclyde Regional Council* (1978) S.C. 90, *Dimbleby & Son Ltd. v. National Union of Journalists* [1984] 1 W.L.R. 427 and *Re Polly Peck International p.l.c. (No.3)* [1996] 1 B.C.L.C. 428.

171 [1990] 1 Ch. 433 at 537.

172 Quoting Costello J. in *Power Supermarket* case, below, para. 14–60.

173 [1983] N.I. 369 at 380–381.

174 Costello J., June 22, 1981; Cases p. 78.

under tenants" of groceries in a unit greater than 3,000 square feet. Subsequently, the group decided to open a 3,000 square feet-plus supermarket in the unit. To that end, it incorporated a new company, the second defendant, and the first defendant conveyed to it the fee simple in the unit. All the evidence showed that the Dunnes companies involved were merely vehicles for carrying out the wishes of the controlling family and that their wishes prevailed in respect of each company in the group. The first defendant was the wholly-owned subsidiary of Cornellscourt Shopping Centre Ltd., which was a wholly-owned subsidiary of Dunnes Holding Co., which was an unlimited company whose shareholders were trustees of a discretionary trust for the Dunne family. Through another chain of subsidiaries, the second defendant's ownership could be traced back to Dunnes Holding Co. Since the time they were incorporated, there had been no meetings as such of either defendants' shareholders or board of directors. Instead, they were managed and controlled by members of the Dunne family meeting informally. Costello J. instanced the conveyance of the unit to highlight the reality of the relationship between the companies. The consideration was only £100, it contained none of the usual easements and it was not registered. In the light of all this, he said, it would be "very hard to find a clearer case . . . for the application of [the] principle" that the corporate veil should be set aside "if the justice of the case so requires.[175]

NON-PROFIT COMPANIES AND CO-OPERATIVES

14–61 There are numerous organisations that are formed for purposes other than engaging in business, to the ultimate financial benefit of their members, but which nevertheless are registered as companies under the Companies Acts. While many sporting, charitable, political, social, cultural, professional and analogous organisations take some other legal form (such as mere associations or unincorporated companies[176] and friendly societies), quite a number of these non-profit bodies are registered companies. Examples from the reported cases include the Dublin Gas Co. Employees' Social and Sports Club[177] the Liverpool and District Hospital for Diseases of the Heart,[178] the New Zealand Netherlands Society "Oranje",[179] the Ulster Society for the

---

[175] At pp. 8 , 9.
[176] See generally, D. Lloyd, *The Law of Unincorporated Associations* (1938).
[177] *Roper v. Ward* [1981] I.L.R.M. 408.
[178] *Liverpool & District Hospital for Diseases of the Heart v. Attorney General* [1981] 1 Ch. 193.
[179] *New Zealand Netherlands Society "Oranje" v. Kuys* [1973] 1 W.L.R. 1126.

Prevention of Cruelty to Animals,[180] the Cyclists' Touring Club[181] and the Secular Society.[182]

14–62 These organisations fall into four major categories, although there can be significant overlapping between them.[183] The majority of them are donative bodies, *i.e.* most of their income is in the form of grants or donations; often they have charitable objects.[184] But others are commercial, *i.e.* their main income is from selling goods or (usually) services, for instance private hospitals and the Automobile Association. Many of these organisations are mutual, *i.e.* they are controlled by those persons who consume whatever product or service they provide. But others are entrepreneurial in the sense that they, either by law or in fact, are controlled by a self-perpetuating directorate. One form of non-profit company that should become more prevalent in the future is the condominium. It is a housing estate or block of flats, where titles to all the houses or flats are vested in the company and each house or flat-owner possesses a transferable share in the company that represents his interest in the unit. A category of non-profit company that is referred to in section 128(4)(c) of the 1963 Act is one without a share capital, has charitable objects and is "under the control of a religion recognised by the State under Article 44 of the Constitution, and which exercises its functions in accordance with the laws, canons and ordinances of the religion concerned."

14–63 What are commonly referred to as co-operatives are a variant of non-profit institutions. As a rule, co-operatives are commercial. But they tend to do business principally with their members, they try to limit the price they charge for whatever they sell and, even if they distribute some of their earned surplus to their members, their principal objective is not to earn high profits so that big dividends can be paid. Co-operatives in this sense are usually registered under either the Industrial and Provident Societies Acts 1893–1978,[185] or the Companies Acts. Special legislation exists for two kinds of co-operatives, namely building societies and credit unions;[186] although one Irish building so-

---

[180] *Re Ulster Society for Prevention of Cruelty to Animals* [1936] N.I. 97.

[181] *Cyclists' Touring Club v. Hopkinson* [1910] 1 Ch. 179.

[182] *Bowman v. Secular Society Ltd.* [1917] A.C. 406.

[183] See generally, Hannsmann, "The Role of Nonprofit Enterprise" (1980) 89 Yale L.J. 835.

[184] See generally, Warburton, "Charitable Companies" [1984] Conv. 112 and Warburton, "Charity Corporations: The Framework for the Future", [1990] Conv. 95.

[185] *cf. Kerry Co-Operative Creameries Ltd. v. An Bord Bainne Co-Operative Ltd.* [1990] I.L.R.M. 664.

[186] Building Societies Act 1989, and Credit Union Act 1966, as amended.

ciety was a registered company and its shares were listed on the Stock Exchange until it was taken over in 1984.

14–64 Some provisions in the Companies Acts were designed specifically with non-profit and co-operative companies in mind. These organisations also get special treatment in the tax laws[187] and, until 1982, were excluded from the reach of the Trade Disputes Act 1906.[188] Leaving aside questions of statutory construction, these companies occasionally pose special problems in the case law. In *Gaiman v. National Association for Mental Health,*[189] for example, extensive consideration was given to the extent to which the principles of natural justice obtain in guarantee companies, in particular as regards expulsions from membership. Matters that call for further clarification include remuneration paid to the directors of such companies[190] and those directors' fiduciary duties.[191]

Guarantee Companies

14–65 Non-profit companies are usually registered as companies limited by guarantee.[192] That is to say, in a winding up the members will be held liable for the company's unpaid debts to the extent that they undertook, or guaranteed, to be so liable.[193] A guarantee company's articles of association must state the number of members with which it proposes to be registered.[194] The company cannot use the sum guaranteed as security for current expenses.[195] Guarantee companies generally do not possess a share capital, although companies the membership of which is based on shareholdings and which also are limited by guarantee do exist.[196] Table C of the 1963 Act's First Schedule sets out a model memorandum of association and articles of association for guarantee companies without a share capital; Table D sets out model regu-

---

187 *e.g.* Finance Act 1979, s.50 (stamp duty), Capital Gains Tax Act 1975, s.22; Capital Acquisitions Tax Act 1976, s.54; Value Added Tax Acts 1972–78, 1st schedule (esp. paras v-vii, xxii and xxiii). *cf. Customs & Excise Commissioners v. Bell Concord Education Trust Ltd.* [1990] 1 Q.B. 905 and *Royal British Legion v. Commissioners of Valuation* [1979] N.I. 138.

188 *Smith v. Beirne* (1955) 89 I.L.T.R. 24.

189 [1971] 1 Ch. 317.

190 *cf. Cyclists Touring Club v. Hopkinson* [1910] 1 Ch. 179.

191 *cf. New Zealand Netherlands Society "Oranje" v. Kuys* [1973] 1 W.L.R. 1126.

192 See generally, Rice, "Companies Limited by Guarabovee — A New Look" [1964] 28 Conv. 214.

193 1963 Act, ss. 5(2)(b), 6(3) and 207(1)(e).

194 *ibid.*, s.12(2).

195 *Re Irish Industrial & Agricultural Fair, Cork* (1933) 67 I.L.T.R. 175.

196 *e.g. Re Performing Right Society Ltd.* [1978] 1 W.L.R. 1197. *cf. Re Parnell G.A.A. Club Ltd.* [1984] I.L.R.M. 246.

lations for such companies with a share capital. Section 7 of the 1983 Act forbids p.l.c.s henceforth to adopt the latter hybrid form.

Omitting "Limited" from Name

14–66 Section 24 of the 1963 Act provides for a mechanism whereby the Minister can permit limited liability non-profit companies to omit the term "limited" from their names. In order to be allowed to do this, they must satisfy the Minister that their objects are to promote commerce, art, science, religion, charity or any other useful object; that they intend to apply their profits or any other income in promoting those objects; and that they prohibit paying any dividend to their members. Paying a retirement gratuity to a company's salaried officer who also is one of its members does not contravene the proscription against paying dividends to members.[197] The Minister may impose conditions on companies wishing to avail of this facility and may direct that those conditions be incorporated in the companies own regulations.

14–67 In *Hennessy v. National Agricultural etc. Assn.*,[198] a company that held such a licence purported to merge with another company that possessed very different objects and that did not hold such a licence. Although its governing body was advised that the scheme for amalgamation was unlawful, the company nevertheless sought Ministerial consent to make the necessary changes in its regulations. They were informed that the Minister "as at present advised . . . will be prepared to sanction the proposed alterations . . . " It was held that the amendments made in pursuance of this authority were wholly invalid. According to Overend J., "until the Minister had given his definite and final approval, the company's power to alter its articles did not come into existence . . . Any amendments purporting to have been made without such previous approval were null and void. Being nullities, they are incapable of being made effective or binding ex post facto, by sanction of the Minister, by ratification by the [company], or in any other way."[199]

Annual Accounts and Return

14–68 The 1986 Act, which gives effect to the E.C.'s Fourth Directive, does not apply to non-profit companies as defined in section 2(1) of that Act. These are any company "not trading for the acquisition of gain by the members"; a company with no share capital and which

---

[197] *Cyclists' Touring Club v. Hopkinson* [1910] 1 Ch. 179.
[198] [1947] I.R. 159.
[199] *ibid.* at 191. *cf. Ulster Society for Prevention of Cruelty to Animals* [1936] N.I. 97.

was formed with a charitable object, is controlled by any of several religious and exercises it functions in accordance with the rules of that religion; and a charitable company without share capital in respect of which an order has been made by the Commissioners of Charitable Donations and Bequests. Instead, the accounts of these bodies need comply with the 1963 Act's Sixth Schedule. These companies need not annex to their annual return a profit and loss account or balance sheet nor any report of their auditors or directors.[200]

Altering Members' Liability

14–69 The basis on which co-operatives do business with their members is often set out in the articles of association, which can give rise to various related questions. The statutory right of companies to amend their regulations cannot be surrendered or waived by contract with the members or even with outsiders.[201] Subject to what in said below, therefore, a co-operative can alter those provisions in its regulations concerning how it is to do business and in effect unilaterally alter its trading arrangements. It would appear, however, that the courts will enjoin it from acting on the basis of its new arrangements where they are inconsistent with separate contractual stipulations.[202] Moreover, section 27 of the 1963 Act provides that no member shall be bound by an alteration to the company's regulations made after becoming a member that requires taking any additional shares, or "in any way increases his liability" to the company, "or otherwise to pay money to [it]." Thus, for instance,[203] where a dairy co-op's regulations required each member to hold three shares for every 250 pounds of butterfat they supplied, the court enjoined an otherwise proper alteration of this to a requirement of holding one share for every 60 pounds of butterfat supplied. In another instance,[204] under a dairy co-op's regulations any member who did not supply the co-op with the entirety of their milk output could be fined £1.00 for every cow he owned. It was held that this was an unreasonable restraint of trade and also contravened section 27 of the 1963 Act, which forbids a company by its regulations to "impose upon its members any pecuniary obligation over and above their statutory obligation to pay up the amount of their shares [, and n]o distinction can be made . . . between an obligation to provide the company with money and an obligation to provide it with money's worth".[205]

---

[200] 1963 Act, s.128(4), (5).
[201] See above, paras 11–08 *et seq*.
[202] *British Murac Syndicate Ltd. v. Alperton Rubber Co.* [1915] 2 Ch. 186.
[203] *Macdonald v. Normandy Co-Operative etc.* [1923] N.Z.L.R. 122.
[204] *Shalfoon v. Cheddar Valley Co-Operative etc.* [1924] N.Z.L.R. 561.
[205] *ibid*. at 577.

14–70 However, section 27(2) of the 1963 Act acknowledges that members can agree in writing to increase their pecuniary obligations to the company, and that the terms of such agreement may be incorporated in the company's regulations. In those circumstances, the company's right to exact additional sums from members arises out of the separate contract.[206] That contract can take the form of agreeing that the company may change its regulations to exact contributions from the members; the scope of this levying power depends on the construction of that contract.[207]

14–71 In *Hennessy v. National Agricultural & Industrial Development Assn.*[208] one feature of a purported merger between two non-profit guarantee companies was that one of them should alter its memorandum of association to exclude some of its members and, in consequence, to vary the liability of its guarantors. Overend J. held that this scheme was unlawful. In his words, "[I]f, in a company limited by guarantee, the guarantors are discharged from liability to any appreciable extent, is not the effect upon the creditors of the company precisely the same as the effect of paying back capital to the shareholders . . . ? Furthermore, is not the effect on the guarantors who remain to increase their liability?"[209] Other arrangements between non-profit limited companies and their members that at first sight look unexceptional can fall foul of the rules against distributions from capital, as the arrangements for granting long leases to the condominium owners in *Jenkins v. Harbour View Courts Ltd.*[210] illustrates. McCarthy J.'s reasoning was that "[t]he prohibition against a return of capital blocks any return whatever the form, whether it be by a payment of money, by a transfer of assets in specie, or in any other way, unless [sections 72–76 of the 1963 Act] have been observed . . . [It] can [not] really be contested that a grant of a leasehold interest in favour of shareholders for no consideration other than the payment of moneys subscribed for shares, or for a consideration so inadequate that it is plain that the substance of the transaction is a return of part of the capital of the company to shareholders, amounts to a prohibited return of capital."[211]

---

[206] [1924] N.Z.L.R. 561 at 574–575.
[207] *Black, White & Grey Cabs Ltd. v. Reid* [1980] 1 N.Z.L.R. 40.
[208] [1947] I.R. 159.
[209] *ibid.* at 191.
[210] [1966] N.Z.L.R. 13; see above, para. 7–28.
[211] *ibid.* at 27, 28.

FINANCIAL COMPANIES

14–72 By financial companies is meant companies whose principal business is performing financial services of one kind or another, for instance banks, insurance companies and investment companies. Some of the activities of these companies are subject to special rules which do not apply to companies generally. This is primarily because the financial services sector is a comparatively highly-regulated industry. The main objective of regulating this sector is to ensure that the financial companies do not become insolvent, which could easily trigger off a series of business collapses and indeed a very serious slump in the entire economy. To that end the Central Bank, the Minister for Finance and the Minister for Enterprise are given extensive regulatory authority over many financial companies, the nature of which is explained in detail elsewhere. To the extent that these requirements involve matters of strict company law, they include the following.

Banks

14–73 Banks are regulated by the Central Bank Acts 1942–1998.[212] All the main banks in the State are registered companies. The Bank of Ireland, which is a chartered corporation established in 1782 under an Act of Parliament of that year,[213] has registered under Part IX of the 1963 Act. On several occasions the Bank of Ireland's charter has been amended by legislation.[214] Trustee savings banks are established under special legislation for that purpose.[215]

14–74 Before a company the objects of which include banking will even be registered, the Central Bank must have indicated to the Registrar of Companies its willingness to grant that body a banking licence.[216] By virtue of Central Bank guidelines, banks must have a very substantial minimum capital before they will be issued with a banking licence and the Central Bank has very wide powers to intervene in their affairs should doubts arise about their solvency. The Central Bank can veto the appointment of an auditor of a licensed bank[217] and bank auditors are obliged to supply the Central Bank with information regarding their

---

[212] See generally, M. Forde, *Commercial Law* (1997), pp. 451–461 and J. Breslin, *Banking Law in the Republic of Ireland* (1998), Chaps. 2–8.

[213] 21 & 22 Geo. III, c. 16.

[214] *e.g.* Bank of Ireland Acts (private) of 1929 and 1935 and Central Bank Act 1971, s.51.

[215] Trustee Savings Banks Act 1989.

[216] Central Bank Act 1971, s.15.

[217] Central Bank Act 1989, s.46.

company in the circumstances specified in section 47 of the Central Bank Act 1989.

14–75 Most of the provisions of the 1986 Act, which incorporates the E.C. Fourth Directive, do not apply to banks and other financial institutions. Those excluded by section 2(2) of that Act are licensed banks; certified trustee savings banks; companies engaging solely in the business of hire purchase or credit sale with goods which the company owns; companies engaged in the business of accepting deposits or other repayable funds or granting credit for their own account; the Agricultural Credit Corp. p.l.c. and the Industrial Credit Corp. p.l.c. But section 7 (annexing documents to the annual return) and sections 13–16 (information to be included in directors' reports, consistency of that report with audited accounts and information regarding subsidiary and associate companies) apply to these otherwise exempted companies. Bank accounts must comply with an E.U. Directive on accounts,[218] which was implemented in 1992.[219] Banks must file annual returns which include copies of the audited profit and loss account and balance sheet and the directors' and auditors' reports.[220] In the case of banks which were registered since August 1879, the accounts must be signed by the secretary and by at least three directors.[221]

14–76 Where a licensed bank or any of its subsidiary companies enters into a loan or other regulated credit transaction or arrangement with one of the bank's directors,[222] the rules regarding disclosure of information relating to those transactions are set down in sections 44 and 45 of the 1990 Act. In several of the provisions regarding financial transactions by companies, a complete or partial exception is made for transactions entered into by companies whose ordinary businesses includes money lending, in the ordinary course of that company's business; for example, section 60(13)(a) of the 1963 Act, regarding companies financing the purchase of their own shares. Sometimes the transaction is required to be on no better terms than would be offered to persons of similar standing to the person in question; for instance section 37 of the 1990 Act, regarding making loans and the like to a company's officers. The winding up of banks is governed by Chap. IV (sections 48–52) of the Central Bank Act 1989.

---

[218] [1986] O.J. L37211.
[219] European Communities (Credit Institutions: Accounts) Regulations 1992.
[220] 1986 Act, s.7(a)(ii).
[221] 1963 Act, s.156(2).
[222] Of the nature described above, paras 5–79 *et seq*.

Insurers

14–77 The affairs of insurance companies are regulated principally by the Insurance Act 1989, and by several regulations implementing E.C. Directives on that topic.[223] A minimum capital of £500,000 is prescribed before a company will be authorised to transact insurance business.[224] The Minister may veto the appointment of any director, chief executive or authorised agent of an insurer if he is not suitably qualified.[225] Section 35 of the 1989 Act obliges insurers' auditors to disclose specific information about the company to the Minister for Enterprise, along the same lines as the disclosure requirement for bank auditors. Most provisions of the 1986 Act regarding companies' accounts do not apply to authorised insurance companies;[226] instead, their accounts are regulated principally by a statutory instrument[227] issued on foot of a 1991 E.C. Directive on insurance.[228] But sections 13–16 of that Act apply to insurers as well as to banking and other companies. Certain other exceptions are made to the Companies Acts in respect of the insurance companies. For instance, in determining what are realised profits for the purposes of ascertaining whether or how much a dividend may be paid, section 48 of the 1983 Act lays down a special rule for assurance companies.

14–78 Special provision is made in section 13 of the Assurance Companies Act 1909, and in section 38 of the Insurance Act 1989 to facilitate amalgamations and transfers of insurance business. Provision is made in the Insurance (No. 2) Act 1983, for the High Court, on the Minister's application, to appoint an administrator to take control and manage the affairs of non-life insurers which are insolvent or in comparable difficulties. The winding up of insurers is governed by Part IV (sections 44–47) of the Insurance Act 1936, and sections 30-32 of the Insurance Act 1989.

Investment Companies

14–79 An investment company is a company which simply holds investments in other companies on behalf of its members; the composition of these investments may change from time to time but the company does not engage in any other activities. Part XIII of the 1990

---

[223] See generally, M. Forde, *Commercial Law* (1997), pp. 467–474 and N. Legh-Jones *et al.*, *MacGillivray on Insurance Law* (9th ed., 1997), Chap. 34.
[224] Insurance Act 1989, s.23.
[225] *ibid.*, s.20.
[226] 1986 Act, s.2(3).
[227] European Communities (Insurance Undertakings: Accounts) Regulations 1996.
[228] Directive 91/674, [1991] O.J. L374.

Act treats investment companies, as defined there, very differently in many respects from other companies. In order to come within this Part, the company must possess two main characteristics. Its sole and exclusive object must be stated as

> "the collective investment of its funds in properties — meaning real or personal property of any kind, (including securities) — with the aim of spreading investment risk and giving members of the company the benefit of the results of the management of its funds."[229]

Additionally, under its regulations, the actual value of its paid up share capital must always be equal to its net assets and the company must always be authorised to purchase its members' shares on request by them. What the Oireachtas had in mind, therefore, is an incorporated form of unit trust. However, these provisions do not apply to what are known in short as "UCITS" as provided for in accordance with an E.C. Directive of 1985.[230] There is a different definition of an investment company for the purposes of the 1983 Act's rules regarding dividends and distributions.[231]

14–80 Among the main features of the unit trust-type investment company, as defined in section 253 of the 1990 Act, are the following. The share capital need not possess a nominal value and the amount of its authorised capital can vary with its issued share capital. It shall be entitled to purchase its own fully paid up shares in accordance with its articles of association, without creating any corresponding reserve fund. An investment company cannot commence business without being so authorised by the Central Bank and the Bank is given extensive powers to regulate the affairs of these companies, for instance, regarding minimum paid up capital, investment policy and information disseminated. Section 260 of the 1990 Act exempts them from many provisions of the Companies Acts, 1963-1990. The Minister is empowered to make regulations to give full effect to all of the above provisions.

14–81 The definition of an investment company for the purposes of section 47 of the 1983 Act is not as restrictive. It is a p.l.c. the business of which:

> "consists of investing its funds mainly in securities, with the aim of spreading investment risk and giving members of the company the benefit of the results of the management of its funds."

Additionally, none of its holdings of securities should exceed 15 per

---

[229] 1990 Act, s.253.
[230] [1985] O.J. L375/3.
[231] 1983 Act, s.47(3), (4).

cent of the value of its entire investments, its own regulations must forbid it from distributing any capital profits, most of its investment income must be distributed every year in dividends and it must have notified the registrar of companies of its intention to carry on business as an investment company. That section deals with where these companies may make distributions from accumulated realised revenue profits. The accounts of these companies must comply with Part VI of the Schedule to the 1986 Act.[232]

UNREGISTERED COMPANIES

14–82 There are a handful of companies which carry on some trade or business but which were never registered under the Companies Acts, 1963-1999, or their predecessors. They are companies which instead were established by a royal charter or by letters patent. Despite the origins of these bodies, several provisions of the Companies Acts are made applicable to them, principally by section 377 of the 1963 Act. For these purposes an unregistered company is defined as a "body corporate incorporated in and having a principal place of business in the State", other than four categories of corporation. Those excluded are any body corporate incorporated by or registered under a public general statute, for instance many of the State-owned commercial bodies; any body exempted for the time being by the Minister; any non-profit body in the sense that it was not formed to carry on business with a view to making gains or it is prohibited from distributing its assets among its members in any event. Application of the prescribed provisions to unregistered bodies does not affect their charter or other constituting instrument except insofar as they are not consistent with the legislation thereby applied.

14–83 Every unregistered company as defined above must deliver to the registrar of companies a copy of its charter or other constituting instrument.[233] In June 1999 the following bodies were registered in this manner; the Bank of Ireland, the Dublin Corn Exchange Building Company, the Waterford City Gas Company and the Dundalk Gas Company. Those provisions which have been made applicable to the unregistered companies are set out in the 1990 Act's schedule. They are a more extensive list of provisions than one might have expected; for instance almost all of the 1990 Act is rendered applicable to them.[234]

---

[232] See definition in schedule, para. 58.
[233] 1963 Act, s.377(6).
[234] s.250 and schedule.

14–84 Should any of these companies choose to register under the Companies Acts, the procedure to be followed is laid down in Part IX (sections 328–343) of the 1963 Act. Whilst the kind of company which can register in this manner is defined much wider than in section 377 of the 1963 Act, not all section 377 companies may so register. In particular, unless it is a "joint stock company", a company with limited liability imposed by statute or by letters patent cannot register under Part IX. Accordingly, it would seem that the Bank of Ireland could convert itself into a registered company should its members choose to do so.

14–85 Part X of the 1963 Act empowers the court to wind up unregistered companies. Unregistered companies for the purposes of winding up under this procedure covers a very wide spectrum of associations and companies, including certified trustee savings banks, but excludes associations not formed abroad and which have less than eight members. What Part X envisages principally is foreign-registered companies as well as unregistered companies as defined by section 377 of the 1963 Act. The circumstances in which the High Court would order the winding up of a company which was established under some special Act is a complicated matter.[235]

FOREIGN COMPANIES

14–86 There are numerous companies registered abroad that do business in Ireland — either directly through an establishment they have here, through local agents or through subsidiaries that are registered here. That most Irish of companies and proprietor of the St James' Gate brewery, Arthur Guinness, Son & Co. (Dublin) Ltd., is a wholly-owned subsidiary of Guinness p.l.c., which is registered in England and the shares of which are listed on the Stock Exchange. Irish registered companies also do business abroad in one guise or another. What are commonly referred to as multinational enterprises have become a very significant feature of economic life over the last three decades or so.[236] There is no received legal definition for multinationals, but a useful one is a cluster of companies registered in different countries that are tied together by ties of common ownership and respond to a common management strategy. Many of the firms that have been attracted to

---

[235] *cf. Re Portstewart Tramway Co., ex p. O'Neill* [1896] 1 I.R. 265 and *Re Commercial Buildings Co. of Dublin* [1938] I.R. 477.

[236] See generally, C.D. Wallace, *Legal Control of Multinational Enterprises* (2nd ed., 1990).

Ireland by the Industrial Development Authority's assistance schemes are components of multinationals.

14–87 Except where it is otherwise so provided, the word company in the Companies Acts means company registered in Ireland. Accordingly, it has been held, the prohibitions against a subsidiary company financing the purchase of shares in its parent company does not apply to foreign-registered subsidiaries.[237]

The External Register and Other Statutory Provisions

14–88 Part XI of the 1963 Act (sections 351–360) requires every company incorporated outside the State, that establishes a place of business in the State, to make up annual accounts and to deliver certain particulars about themselves to the registrar of companies. Irish companies that set up business in the United Kingdom must comply with similar requirements there. By establishing a place of business is meant more than just carrying on business; it connotes having a specified or identifiable place from which it does business with some regularity.[238] It is not sufficient that the foreign company acts through some local agent or through an Irish subsidiary or affiliate. What must be given to the registrar of companies are a certified copy of the company's regulations; a list of its directors and secretaries; the address of the company's principal place of business in the State; and the name and address of some person resident in Ireland who has authority to accept service of process on the company. The provisions in the 1963 Act regarding the prosecution of officers apply as much to foreign companies with a place of business here as they apply to Irish-registered companies.[239]

14–89 Except where they would be private companies if they were registered here, these foreign companies are subject to requirements regarding annual accounts.[240] In every year they must make out a balance sheet, a profit and loss account and, if a holding company, group accounts; and copies of these accounts must be delivered to the registrar of companies. These accounts must comply with the 1986 Act's requirements. Private companies are exempted from the requirements.

14–90 Section 17 of the 1986 Act exempts Irish subsidiaries of companies registered within the E.C. from the obligation to annex a profit and loss account and balance sheet to their annual return, provided

---

[237] *Arab Bank p.l.c. v. Merchantile Holdings Ltd.* [1992] 1 B.C.L.C. 330.
[238] *Deverall v. Grant Advertising Inc.* [1955] Ch. 11; *Re Oriel Ltd.* [1986] 1 W.L.R. 180.
[239] 1963 Act, s.382(7).
[240] *ibid.*, s.354.

certain conditions are met. The company must be a private company or be either a subsidiary of an E.C. registered company or be a body which would be a subsidiary if its parent organisation were a company. In order to obtain the exemption, the following conditions must be met. Every shareholder must have agreed in that year that the company should not file that information; the parent must have irrevocably guaranteed its liabilities for that year and the previous year; the company's annual accounts must have been consolidated in the group accounts; confirmation of the above matters in writing must be annexed to the annual return; the parent body's accounts must have been drawn up, so far as is possible, in accordance with the E.C. Fourth Directive and the group accounts must be annexed to the annual return.

14–91 Part XII (sections 361-367) of the 1963 Act modifies somewhat the rules regarding prospectuses when issued in connection with an offer of shares in any company that is registered abroad. Provision is made for Irish-registered companies empowering persons to execute deeds for them abroad, for having an official seal for use abroad and for registering charges on property that is located abroad.[241] The 1963 Act's rules regarding registering company charges apply to charges made by foreign companies established here on property located here, and also to judgment mortgages affecting such property and receivers of that property.[242] The High Court can enforce any order connected with winding up a company that is made by a court in any country recognised for these purposes by the Minister;[243] and the court's power to order that a company be wound up extends to foreign companies.[244] A certificate by a person purporting to be a registrar of companies in a foreign country recognised for these purposes by the Minister is prima facie evidence of incorporation there.[245]

14–92 Several provisions of the 1990 Act apply to the foreign companies which have a place of business in Ireland and are registered under Part XI, notably section 29 concerning substantial property transactions involving directors, and Part VII concerning disqualifications and restrictions on directors. Other provisions of that Act apply to compa-

---

[241] 1963 Act, ss. 40, 41, 99(3)–(5).

[242] *ibid.*, s.111. *cf. N.V. Slavenburg Bank v. Intercontinental National Resources Ltd.* [1980] 1 W.L.R. 1076.

[243] *ibid.*, s.250 and S.I. No. 42 of 1964. *cf.* M. Forde, *Bankruptcy Law in Ireland* (1990), pp. 186–190 and *Boyd v. Lee Guinness Ltd.* [1963] N.I. 49.

[244] *ibid.*, s.345(7). *cf. Re Portarlington Electric Light & Power Co.* [1922] 1 I.R. 100; *Re A Company* (00359 of 1987) [1987] 3 W.L.R. 339 and *International Westminster Bank v. Okeanos Maritime Corp.* [1987] B.C.L.C. 450.

[245] 1963 Act, s.389 and S.I. No. 42 of 1964 Companies (Recognition of Companies) Regulation.

nies which have carried on a business here, notably several of the rules concerning court-appointed inspectors (sections 8–11, 13, 18, and 22), the Minister's power to direct that certain books and documents be delivered up (section 19(1)(e)). Securities issued by foreign companies come within the insider dealing restrictions in Part V of 1990 Act. An examiner cannot be appointed over foreign-registered companies even though they may be related to an Irish company which is under examination.

14–93 A company that ceases to have a business place in the State should forthwith notify the registrar of companies to that effect.[246] The company can still be served with a process for two years following that notification if addressed to the person who was last designated to accept service for the company and left at his address.[247] In an appropriate case, however, the court may put a stay on the action on the grounds that some foreign court is a more appropriate forum to hear the claim.[248]

Internal Affairs

14–94 A company's internal affairs (*i.e.* relations between the company and its members and directors) are governed in the main by the law of the State in which the company is registered, what is called the company's personal law;[249] although the dividing line between internal and external affairs is not always clear. The personal law has been held to govern questions such as the incidents of the company's status (*e.g.* amalgamation, succession, capital reduction or increase),[250] the dividend rights of the different classes[251] and the validity of directors' appointments.[252] However, the company may decide that at least some aspects of its internal affairs shall be subject to some other legal system.

14–95 For instance, in *Adelaide Electric Supply Co. v. Prudential Assurance Co.*[253] the company was registered in England, but all its business

---

246 1963 Act, s.357.
247 *ibid.*, s.356(3); *cf. Rome v. Punjab National Bank (No. 2)* [1989] 1 W.L.R. 1211.
248 *e.g. Cleveland Museum of Art v. Capricorn Art International S.A.* [1990] B.C.L.C. 546.
249 See generally, W. Binchy, *Irish Conflicts of Law* (1988), Chap. 26 and L. Collins (ed.), *Dicey & Morris on the Conflict of Laws* (11th ed., 1987), Chap. 31.
250 *National Bank of Greece v. Metliss* [1958] A.C. 509.
251 *Spiller v. Turner* [1897] 1 Ch. 91.
252 *Banco de Bilbao v. Sancha* [1938] 2 K.B. 176.
253 [1934] A.C. 122. See generally, F.A. Mann, *The Legal Aspects of Money* (3rd ed., 1992), pp. 239–246.

was carried on in Australia, where many of its shareholders resided and where it kept a branch register of members. In order to avoid double taxation of its dividends, it resolved in 1921 that thenceforth its dividends should be declared and paid only in Australia. When later the value of the Australian pound fell below that of the English pound sterling, the question arose of whether dividends payable on its five per cent and 6.5 per cent preference shares were payable in English or in Australian currency. Because the company was registered in England, any repayment of capital or distribution in a winding up would have to be made in English currency. But it is an established rule in the conflict of laws that, whatever law governs a contract as a whole, the performance of any particular obligation is subject to the law of the place where it is to be performed; as regards paying money, a stipulation to pay a sum in a designated place means to pay in the currency of that place.[254] Accordingly, it was held, the effect of the 1921 resolution was to authorise payment of the dividends in Australian currency. And because the preference shareholders did not object in 1921 to the proposed change, which was made to benefit the entire company and which would have been most advantageous to the preference shareholders if exchange rates had moved in the other direction, the resolution could not be regarded as unlawfully discriminatory or oppressive, or as violating their class rights.

14–96 Regarding the jurisdiction of the Irish and other E.C. State courts to determine disputes relating to companies' internal affairs, Article 16(2) of the 1968 Brussels Convention on Jurisdiction etc.[255] provides that the courts where the company has its "seat" have exclusive jurisdiction over the following matters: proceedings "which have as their object the validity of the constitution, the nullity or dissolution of companies . . . , or the decisions of their organs . . . " Accordingly, it has been held that a dispute between a company and some of its directors, concerning the validity of the exercise of their powers, can only be heard in the courts where the company has its headquarters.[256] The word "object" above means the subject matter of the claim as contrasted with its underlying purpose.

Company Contracts

14–97 Transactions between foreign and multinational companies and

---

[254] Case *de Mixte Moneys* (1604) Davis's Rep. (Ireland) 18.

[255] Jurisdiction of Courts and Enforcement of Judgments (European Communities) Act 1988.

[256] *Newtherapeutics Ltd. v. Katz* [1990] B.C.L.C. 700. *cf. Re Fagan's Bookshop p.l.c.* [1992] B.C.L.C. concerning Art. 16(3) of this Convention.

outsiders are governed by the normal conflict of laws rules, just as if the company were an individual. Thus in one well known instance in 1959,[257] where an English company entered into a contract in Germany that would have been *ultra vires* under English law, the German Supreme Court, applying German law (the *lex loci contractus*), held that the contract was binding on the company. One reason for adopting the E.C. First Directive on company law was to protect outsiders in one country from the adverse consequences of *ultra vires* and related rules in other countries.

[257] December 17, 1959, BGHZ 367.

15

Company Employees

15–01 While the main concern of company law is regulating relations between investors and between shareholders and management, the Companies Acts also contain provisions on dealings between companies and others who have interests in them, most notably creditors. In the past, relations between companies and their employees were regarded as the concern of labour law, the most significant exception being that employees possess certain preferential rights *qua* creditors in a winding up.[1] More recently, there has been a trend towards inserting into companies' legislation far-reaching provisions that acknowledge the employees' interest in and claims against their incorporated employer.[2] Two arguments can be made for granting employees rights against the company for which they work. If employees are given a greater stake in and say in the running of the business, it is very likely that they will work more enthusiastically and be more sympathetic to management's dilemmas. Put simply, greater employee involvement in the company improves productivity. Secondly, in the light of the extensive contribution that employees make to the commercial success of companies and because employees are so dependent economically on their companies, employees deserve greater rights *vis-à-vis* those companies.

15–02 At one time, the principal technique used to accommodate employee interests was to grant workers and their representatives greater negotiating power in their dealings with companies. To this end, the Industrial Relations Act, 1990, makes lawful strikes and peaceful picketing in the context of a trade dispute and confers extensive immunities from suit on trade unions.[3] Legislation granting employees directly enforceable rights used to be confined to the most vulner-

---

1 1963 Act, s.285; see below, paras 18–101 *et seq*.

2 See generally, B. Cheffins, *Company Law: Theory, Structure and Operation* (1997), Chap. 12; Wedderburn, "Companies and Employees: Common Law or Social Dimension?" (1993) L.Q.R. 220 (1993); and Xuerb, "The Juridification of Industrial Relation through Company Law Reform" 51 Mod. L. Rev. 156 (1988).

3 See generally, M. Forde, *Industrial Relations Law* (1991).

able classes of workers (*e.g.* children and women) and to particularly dangerous or outrageous work practices (*e.g.* the Factories Acts and the Truck Acts). Especially since the 1960s, however, numerous measures have been enacted that give extensive rights to most categories of workers, such as the Redundancy Payments Acts 1976–1979, the Unfair Dismissals Act 1977, and the Employment Equality Act 1998.[4] Over and above these, legislation dealing with companies as such rather than *qua* employers contain provisions specific to employee relations, although Irish law in this regard is far behind that of most other Western European countries.

ENTITLEMENT TO ACCOMMODATE EMPLOYEE INTERESTS

15–03 Without authority in the memorandum and articles of association to do so, formerly major decisions within companies could not be made with the primary object of furthering employees' interests, unless of course all of the members were in agreement. The law identified companies almost exclusively with their shareholders. Directors must exercise their powers 'bona fide in what they consider . . . is in the interests of the company';[5] special resolutions of shareholders, or any class of shareholders, are unlawful where they are not adopted 'bona fide for the benefit of the company as a whole'.[6] And by the company as a whole was meant the shareholders in general or the hypothetical average shareholder. Ambiguous though these formulae may be, it was not permissible to place employees' interests before those of the shareholders. The classic instance is *Parke* v. *Daily News Ltd.*,[7] where a proposal by a newspaper company, that had sold off its assets, to distribute most of the proceeds among its employees as *ex gratia* redundancy pay, was challenged by a minority shareholder and was enjoined because such massive benevolence was *ultra vires* the company; although the case might more appropriately be regarded as one of fraud on a minority than *ultra vires* as presently understood.

15–04 The position has been changed somewhat by section 52 of the 1990 Act, according to which:

> "the matters to which directors of a company are to have regard in the performance of their functions shall include the interests of the company's employees in general, as well as the interests of its members."

---

4 See generally, M. Forde, *Employment Law* (1991), Chap. 8.
5 See above, paras 5–110 *et seq*.
6 See above, paras 10–25 *et seq*.
7 [1962] 1 Ch. 927; see above, para. 3–74.

But this does not entirely reverse the position under the *Daily News* case. It deals only with the position of the directors and not alone allows them to take account of employees' interests but actually requires them to do so. However, section 52(2) adds that this obligation is owed only to the company and that the employees do not have a right of action to enforce compliance with its requirements. Where the benevolence towards employees would be *ultra vires* or unfairly discriminates against minority shareholders, it is not validated by section 52, in the sense that an objecting shareholder is entitled to have the proposed action blocked and, possibly, to recover extravagant payments that were made. Section 52 nevertheless is likely to have an indirect influence as indicating a general legislative policy in favour of upholding measures adopted by companies for the benefit of their employees.

15–05 Even in the past devoting company resources to employees was permissible where that was incidental to and within the general scope of the company's business. As Bowen L.J. put it in *Hutton v. West Cork Railway Co.*,[8] which also involved a minority shareholder challenge to company benevolence:

> "Most businesses require liberal dealings. The test . . . is . . . whether [the transaction is] done bona fide [and] is done within the ordinary scope of the company's business and whether it is reasonably incidental to the carrying on of the company's business for the company's benefit. Take this sort of instance. A railway company, or the directors of the company, might send down all the porters at a railway station to have tea in the country at the expense of the company. Why should they not? It is for the directors to judge, provided it is a matter which is reasonably incidental to the carrying on of the business of the company, and a company which always treated its employees with Draconian severity, and never allowed them a single inch more that the strict letter of the bond, would soon find itself deserted — at all events unless labour was very much more easy to obtain in the market than it often is. The law does not say that there are to be no cakes and ale, but there are to be no cakes and ale except such as are required for the benefit of the company."[9]

DISCLOSURE AND CONSULTATION

15–06 Some of the recently-enacted labour laws require companies to disclose certain facts about their activities to their employees' representatives and to consult with those representatives, notably where

---

8 (1883) 23 Ch.D. 645.
9 *ibid*. at 672–673.

collective redundancies are envisaged,[10] where it is proposed to transfer all or part of the business to some other company,[11] and in what may be described as community-wide multinational enterprises.[12] These requirements were enacted in order to give effect to E.C. Directives made under the Rome Treaty's approximation of laws powers. Limited companies must include in their annual accounts details of staff costs (*i.e.* wages and salaries, pensions and social security costs), together with the average number of persons employed during the financial year broken down by categories of activity.[13] Every employee has *locus standi* to apply for a "disclosure order" under section 98 of the 1990 Act, to ascertain who really owns the shares in his employer-company. Every directors' annual report to the shareholders must contain an evaluation of the extent to which the policies set out in the company's "safety statement" have been fulfilled during the year covered by the report.[14]

FINANCIAL PARTICIPATION — WORKER/SHAREHOLDERS

15–07 Some companies encourage and even help their employees to acquire shares in them. The view is that, by having a financial stake in the firm and being entitled to participate in its distributed profits, employees will more readily identify with the company and indeed become participants in a form of economic democracy. On the other hand, there is a danger that workers who invest most of their savings in their employer's business will lose everything if it falls; Marxists would tend to condemn schemes to distribute shares to employees as the carrots of class collaboration. It is for companies themselves to decide whether and on what terms shares should be offered to employees. There is no legal obligation on companies to allot shares to their employees as exists, for example, in France.[15] Part 17 of the Taxes Consolidation Act 1997 provides a variety of tax incentives for schemes facilitating employees to purchase shares in their company.[16] One of the matters that the Pensions Board no doubt will regulate in due course is 'self-invest-

---

[10] Protection of Employment Act 1977.

[11] European Communities (Safeguarding of Employers Rights on Transfer of Undertakings) Regulations 1980 (S.I. No. 306 of 1980).

[12] Transnational Information and Consultation of Employees Act 1996.

[13] 1986 Act, sched., para. 42.

[14] Safety, Health and Welfare at Work Act 1989, s.12(6).

[15] Law No. 80–834 of October 24, 1980.

[16] See generally, N. Judge, *Irish Income Tax*, Pt 16.1.

ment' by occupational pension schemes, *i.e.* the fund investing heavily in the employing enterprise.[17]

15–08 The prohibition in section 60 of the 1963 Act against companies financing the purchase of their own shares does not apply in two related circumstances. One is where a private company loans money to any of its bona fide employees to enable them to acquire for themselves shares in it or in its holding company.[18] The other is where a private company provides money under a scheme whereby its shares are to be held by or on behalf of its employees, or former employees or employees of its subsidiaries.[19] Loans under the former cannot be made to directors who are also employees; but the scheme under the latter can include salaried directors. Public limited companies (*i.e.* p.l.c.s) can also give financial assistance for these two purposes, provided the funds come out of profits available for distribution or the company's net assets are not thereby reduced.[20]

15–09 Exception is made to the 1983 Act's authority and pre-emption requirements[21] in respect of employee share schemes. These are defined as "any scheme for the time being in force, in accordance with which a company encourages or facilitates the holding of shares or debentures in the company or its holding company by or for the benefit of employees or former employees of the company or of any subsidiary",[22] including salaried directors. The requirement of shareholders' prior authority does not apply to shares being allotted in pursuance of such a scheme.[23] Shares being allotted in connection with such a scheme need not be offered on a pre-emptive basis and employees offered shares under a scheme are not prevented by the 1983 Act from renouncing or assigning the offer even to persons who are outside of the scheme.[24] P.l.c.s are forbidden to allot shares under such schemes where less than one-quarter of the shares' nominal value has not been paid up on them.[25] A p.l.c. may not allot shares in exchange for any service contract.[26]

---

17 *cf. Cowan v. Scargill* [1985] Ch. 270.
18 s.60(13)(b).
19 s.60(13)(c); *cf. Hogg v. Crampborn Ltd.* [1967] Ch. 254.
20 s.60(1513), inserted by 1983 Act, sched., para. 10.
21 See above, paras 6–25 and 6–29.
22 1983 Act, s.2(1).
23 s.20(10)(a).
24 s.23(13)(b), (6).
25 s.28(4).
26 s.26(2).

CO-DETERMINATION — WORKER/DIRECTORS

15–10 The laws of many Western European States oblige companies to place representatives of their workers on their boards of directors, of which the West German *Mitbestimmung* system is perhaps the best known.[27] There is considerable variety among the different national schemes in respect of, for instance, the degree of compulsion to have workers' directors, the level in the company at which such directors act, the methods of selecting those directors and the weight and scope of those directors' power to make decisions. In Britain the report of a committee of inquiry, known as the Bullock Report,[28] recommended in 1977 that a particular method of what it termed industrial democracy should be adopted there, but little has been done to implement its suggestions. The Worker Participation (State Enterprises) Act 1977 inaugurated a system of employee directors in the principal State-owned industrial and commercial enterprises. In the 1980 discussion paper, Worker Participation,[29] the Minister for Labour called for consideration by employer and worker interests of the best approach to introducing employee representation at board level, but it would appear that the matter does not fire enthusiasm in trade union or employer circles.

15–11 Much of the impetus for worker directors has come from the E.C., and in particular from the proposed Fifth Directive on companies' structures which calls for worker participation on company boards. The scheme as originally envisaged was somewhat like that pertaining in West Germany. It, however, has attracted powerful opposition, especially from U.S.-based multinational enterprises and the Conservative government in Britain. In May 1982 the European Parliament endorsed the Guerstin Report, which drastically amended the original scheme by giving E.C. Members numerous options as to what particular method they should adopt.[30] It remains to be seen what permutation the Council of Ministers eventually adopts, or indeed whether the entire endeavour will be abandoned. Any system of worker directors that is imposed on companies will require significant changes in

---

[27] See generally, Vagts, "Reforming of 'Modern' Corporation: Perspectives from the German" (1966) 80 Harv. L. Rev. 23.

[28] Camd. 6706; see Prentice. "Employee Participation in Corporate Government" (1978) 56 Can. Bar Rev. 277.

[29] Prl. 8803.

[30] [1983] O.J. C240/2, [1984] 2 C.M.L.R. 680. See generally, Dine, "Implications for the United Kingdom of the E.C. Fifth Directive" (1989) 38 Int'l & Comp. L.Q. 547 and Du Plessis & Dine, "The Faith of the Draft Fifth Directive on Company Law" [1997] J.B.L. 23.

the law on shareholders' rights and directors' duties; for instance, regarding the appointment and removal of directors, what matters remain with the shareholders' exclusive discretion and the extent to which employees' interests can be given precedence over those of the shareholders.

16

Creditors and Security

16–01 While shareholders' entitlements and protection are the predominant concern of company law, a major secondary theme is protecting those who give credit to companies.[1] Because the debtor is the corporation itself and not its shareholders, and since the vast majority of companies possess limited liability, it is inevitable that there are special rules for companies' debts. Before addressing these in detail, it is useful to consider in brief some of the major principles of company law that protect creditors' interests.

16–02 First and foremost are the various requirements to disclose information — be it to the registrar of companies, in the *Iris Oifigiúil*, in newspapers and otherwise. In particular, every creditor is entitled to examine the company's book of registrable charges;[2] every debenture-holder must be sent a copy of the annual profit and loss account, balance sheet and group accounts, and the directors' and auditors' reports;[3] where an insolvent company is being wound up and a meeting of its creditors is being convened, a notice of the meeting must be inserted in at least two local daily newspapers;[4] the appointment of a receiver over the company's assets and of an examiner into the company's affairs must also be notified in that manner.[5]

16–03 The principles of capital integrity — of minimum amounts, anti-watering and maintenance of capital — are designed primarily to protect creditors. As the preamble to the E.C. Second Directive[6] puts it, "provisions should be adopted for maintaining the capital, which constitutes the creditors' security . . . " In special circumstances and express statutory authority aside, a court might "pierce the veil" of an

---

1 See generally, B. Cheffins, *Company Law: Theory, Structure and Operation* (1997), Chap. 11.
2 1963 Act, s.110.
3 *ibid.*, s.159.
4 *ibid.*, s.266(2); for voluntary winding ups, *ibid.*, s.263.
5 1963 Act, s.107 and Companies (Amendment) Act 1990, s.12(2).
6 [1977] O.J. L26/1.

undercapitalised company; under-capitalisation is a significant feature in most actions under section 297A of the 1963 Act for fraudulent trading and even more so for reckless trading.[7]

16–04 Not alone must creditors give their consent to fundamental changes in the company's capital structure that directly affect their rights, but they have power to veto some other major changes that concern them indirectly. Every debenture-holder may apply to restrain a company from acting *ultra vires*.[8] And the holders of at least 15 per cent of debentures that were, or form part of a series that were, issued before April 1964, and are secured by a floating charge, may apply to the court to block a proposed alteration of the objects clause.[9]

16–05 There are a number of statutory provisions that deal with discrimination between creditors, *i.e.* giving one creditor or one class of creditors advantage over others. Certain categories of creditors are entitled to be paid off in a winding up before other unsecured creditors: principally, the State in a number of its manifestations and company employees.[10] On the other hand, paying some creditors before others might amount to a fraudulent preference under section 286 of the 1963 Act.[11] A floating charge granted within twelve months of an insolvent company being wound up may be invalid under section 288 of that Act.[12]

DIRECTORS' DUTIES TO CREDITORS

16–06 Since company directors' duties are owed to the company itself and not to its shareholders, it would seem to follow that directors owe no general duty of care or fiduciary duty to their company's creditors. As Lord Lowry observed in the *Kuwait Asia Bank* case, as a general principle "a director does not by reason only of his position as director owe any duty to creditors or to trustees for creditors of the company".[13] This point was emphasised more recently in the *Yukong Line* case, where it was stated that:

---

[7] See below, paras 18–51 *et seq.* and paras 18–58 *et seq.*

[8] 1963 Act, s.8(2).

[9] *ibid.*, s.10(3), (7).

[10] *ibid.*, s.285; see below, paras 18–96 *et seq.*

[11] See below, paras 18–40 *et seq.*

[12] See below, paras 18–46 *et seq.*

[13] *Kuwait Asia Bank v. National Mutual Life Nominees* [1991] 1 A.C. 187 at 217. See generally, Prentice, "Creditors' Interests and Director's Duties" (1990) 10 Oxf J.L.S. 265 and Riley, "Directors' Duties and the Interests of Creditors" (1990) 10 Co. Law 87.

> "[W]here a director or a person having the management of an insolvent company acts in breach of his duty to the company by causing assets of the company to be transferred in disregard of the interests of its creditor or creditors, ... he is answerable through the scheme which Parliament has provided. . . . [H]e does not owe a direct fiduciary duty towards an individual creditor, nor is an individual creditor entitled to sue for breach of the fiduciary duty owed by the director to the company."[14]

Any legal obligations directors may have to creditors would seem to arise either from specific contracts with them, such as personal guarantees, and from provisions in the Companies Acts. An extra-contractual duty in tort may arise in very exceptional circumstances. Lord Lowry qualified the above statement by observing that "although directors are not liable as such to the creditors of the company, a director may by agreement or representation assume a special duty to a creditor of the company. A director [for instance] may accept or assume a duty of care in supplying information to a creditor analogous to [that] described . . . in *Hedley Byrne* . . . "[15]

16–07 In an Australian case concerning an insolvent company in liquidation, Barwick C.J. went so far as to "emphasis[e] that the directors of a company in discharging their duty to the company must take account of the interests of its shareholders and its creditors. Any failure by the directors to take into account the interests of creditors will have adverse consequences for the company as well as for them."[16] There, a transaction that was entered into in total disregard of the interests of the company and its creditors, that seriously prejudiced the unsecured creditors, was held to constitute misfeasance within the meaning of what is section 298 of the 1963 Act. The usual mode for creditors obtaining redress against directors' wrongs is the liquidator's claim for misfeasance under section 298 when the company is being wound up.[17]

16–08 It is not entirely clear whether the orthodox view, described above, remains the law in Ireland, or whether directors of insolvent companies owe some general fiduciary duty or duty of care to the creditors. For the Supreme Court's decision in *Re Frederick Inns Ltd.*[18] suggests that there is such a duty, although the court there did not so hold. The rather confused judgment given by Blayney J. has been the subject

---

[14] *Yukong Line Ltd v. Rendsburg Investment Corp.* [1998] 1 W.L.R. 294 at 312.
[15] [1991] 1 A.C. at 219.
[16] *Walker v. Wimborne* (1976) 50 A.L.J.R. 446 at 449. In the same vein, *West Mercia Safetywear Ltd v. Dodd* [1988] B.C.L.C. 250 and *Nicholson v. Permakraft (NZ) Ltd* [1985] 1 N.Z.L.R. 242.
[17] See below, paras 18–66 *et seq.*
[18] [1994] 1 I.L.R.M. 387; for details, see above, para. 14–51.

of compelling critical commentary, particularly its assertion that the assets of an insolvent company are held by the directors in some form of trust for its creditors.[19] In any event, in *Jones v. Gunn*[20] McGuinness J. felt bound by Blayney J.'s analysis to hold that, entirely separate from the statutory framework for winding up companies, directors of insolvent companies owe a fiduciary duty to their creditors. Whether this decision will hold on appeal is anybody's guess; it does not reflect the law as it is understood in all other comparable common law jurisdictions that have companies legislation similar to that in Ireland. What probably will happen is that the *Frederick Inns* case will be "distinguished" on grounds that are far from being convincing, with the result that the legal position will become even more confusing still. From the law report of the *Jones* case, it seems that most of the material relevant to the argument that there is no such fiduciary duty was not brought to the attention of the trial judge.

FIXED AND FLOATING CHARGES

16–09 Usually debtors will be required to provide security for loans made and other forms of substantial credit afforded to them, for instance by having the loan guaranteed by a person of substance, by giving the lender a mortgage or charge over property or by permitting the lender to retain possession of property or of title documents to property. Lenders of substantial sums to companies often require personal guarantees from the directors or the shareholders; often companies in a group will be required to provide cross-guarantees for loans to associated companies. Companies frequently give charges over all or part of their assets to secure repayment of money they borrowed or some other obligation they incurred, like under guarantees. Provided the charge is *intra vires* and was duly authorised by the company's management, it binds the company; questions of *ultra vires* and of agency are analysed in Chapter 15.

Charges

16–10 The law regarding charges generally is adequately treated elsewhere[21] but the following elementary propositions deserve reiteration.

---

[19] Fealy, "The Role of Equity in the Winding Up of a Company" (1995) 17 D.U.L.J. 18.

[20] [1997] 3 I.R. 1.

[21] See generally, M. Forde, *Commercial Law* (2nd ed., 1997), Chap.5; E.I. Sykes, *The Law of Securities* (5th ed., 1993); E.L.G. Tyler, Fisher & Lightwood's *Law of Mortgage* (10th ed., 1988); W.J. Gough, *Company Charges* (2nd ed., 1996) and J. Breslin, *Banking Law in the Republic of Ireland* (1998), Chaps 24–41.

There is no statutory definition for the term charge but, in the context of debtor/creditor relations, the term connotes some proprietary interest in assets which is transferred by their owner to another in order to secure the performance of a legal obligation. Mortgages, either legal or equitable, of land are charges; charges can also be given over chattels and over choses in action. Most company charges are not outright mortgages in that, unlike a mortgage, they do not involve the transfer of title in the security to the chargee, subject to an equity of redemption. Instead, the chargee obtains certain rights in respect of the charged assets which may be pursued in the event of default.[22] A charge is to be contrasted with a sale and with the creation of a lien. In a sale, the owner of property transfers the entire ownership of it to another, who then is completely free to deal with the property in any way he wishes.[23] A proper retention of title arrangement is not strictly a security by way of charge but is an outright sale of the goods, albeit subject to title in them remaining in the seller for the time being.[24] A lien means having possession of someone else's property coupled with the right to retain that property until its owner pays whatever he owes the lien-holder.[25] But the lien-holder acquires no proprietary interest in the property; he frequently gets possession of title documents relating to the property but nevertheless is not free to deal with the property in any way he wishes.

16–11 There are two principal categories of company charge, the fixed charge and the floating charge. The former is a charge on a specific identifiable item of property, like on land or buildings appropriately described, or on designated items of plant, machinery, motor vehicles, inventory, shares, insurance policies and items of industrial and intellectual property. Apart from the registration requirements, as described below, there are no significantly special company law rules governing fixed charges.

Floating Charges

16–12 A floating charge, by contrast, is a charge on a designated category or categories of assets but their actual constituent elements are continually changing.[26] For instance, a floating charge can be given

---

[22] Those remedies principally being obtaining an order for sale and the appointment of a receiver; see Breslin, above, Chaps 40, 41.

[23] *cf. Welsh Development Agency v. Export Finance Co. Ltd* [19921 B.C.L.C. 148.

[24] See post paras 18–82 *et seq*.

[25] Certain kinds of non-possessory equitable interests in property are also referred to, somewhat confusingly, as "liens".

[26] See generally, W.J. Gough, *Company Charges* (2nd ed., 1996), Pt II (Chaps 5–12), Gough, "The Floating Charge: Traditional Themes and New Directions" in *Equity*

over a company's stock in trade, raw materials and debtors, and, although these items are subject to the charge, the company is permitted to use and even dispose of them in the ordinary course of its business and replace them with new stock, machinery and the like. The great advantage of the floating charge over a specific security is that the company which grants a floating charge remains relatively free to deal with the charged assets until it defaults and a receiver is appointed or some other crystallising event occurs.

16–13 Floating charges, therefore, are a convenient way of obtaining finance for companies with an appreciable portion of current assets in their balance sheets. Lenders, on the other hand, are not as enthusiastic about floating charges because of the freedom that the company may have to dispose of the charged assets; also because these charges rank in priority after any fixed charges, and after the State's and company employees' statutorily preferred debts;[27] because a company's most valuable current assets may be subject to retention of title clauses;[28] and especially in recessionary times, current assets may not obtain anything like their book value in a sale when the lender seeks to enforce the security. Moreover, a floating charge given within twelve months of the company being wound up is invalid if the company was insolvent at the time the charge was created.[29] Another disadvantage of the floating charge was the "reputed ownership" rule in bankruptcy[30] and the provisions of the Bills of Sale Acts,[31] but these do not apply to charges given by registered companies.[32]

16–14 It is only in the past hundred years or so that it has been possible to grant a floating charge. Previously it was believed that charges on future property and charges on choses in action, like book debts, could not be given. But in 1862 it was held that a contract to grant a charge on future property, be it real or personal property, would be enforced in equity and that the party who agreed to grant the charge held the property as trustee for the chargee.[33] Then in 1888 it was held that an assignment of future choses in action was enforceable in equity

---

and Commercial Relationships (P.D. Finn ed., 1987), Chap. 9; R.M. Goode, *Legal Problems of Credit and Security* (2nd ed., 1988); Ferran, "Floating Charges — the Nature of the Security" (1988) 47 Cam. L. J. 213 and Pennington, "The Genesis of the Floating Charge" (1960) 23 Mod. L. Rev. 630.

27 1963 Act, s.285(7)(b).

28 See below, para. 18–82.

29 1963 Act, s.288.

30 See M. Forde, *Bankruptcy Law in Ireland* (1990), p. 74.

31 See generally, M. Forde, *Commercial Law* (2nd ed., 1997), pp. 225–230.

32 *Re Royal Marine Hotel Co.* [1895] 1 I.R. 368.

33 *Holroyd v. Marshall* (1862) 10 H.L.C. 191.

in the same manner.[34] These decisions enabled the Chancery court in a series of leading cases to give full effect to floating charges. Most of these authorities are set out in *Re Dublin Drapery Co. Ltd.*,[35] where a floating charge over the business of what was to become Clery's department store in O'Connell St., Dublin, was upheld. But the Scottish and the American courts never recognised the floating charge; it only became possible to grant such charges in Scotland and in the United States following adoption of the Companies (Floating Charges) (Scotland) Act 1961, and Article 9 of the Uniform Commercial Code, respectively.

16–15 There is no statutory definition for the term floating charge and, while judges often describe the main attributes of these charges, there is no exhaustive judicial definition of the term. The lack of a comprehensive definition, like the lack of definitions for some other key legal concepts, was explained by Hoffman J. as resulting from the fact that:

> "A floating charge [is] not susceptible of being defined by the enumeration of an exhaustive set of necessary and sufficient conditions. All that can be done is to enumerate its standard characteristics. It does not follow that the absence of one or more of those features or the presence of others will prevent the charge from being categorised as "floating"; there are bound to be penumbral cases in which it may be difficult to say whether the degree of deviation from the standard case is enough to make it inappropriate to use such a term."[36]

16–16 Bearing these observations in mind, floating charges possess three basic features, namely,

1. Until they "crystallise", the charge does not fasten or attach to any specific property of the company but, instead, floats over whatever category of assets are charged;
2. Until crystallisation, the company is able to transfer the charged assets, whether by way of sale or as security, so as to confer on a third party a good title against the creditor who is secured by the charge;
3. In the event of the charge crystallising, as when the company defaults and a receiver is appointed, the charge then ceases to float and becomes converted into a specific charge over the category of

---

[34] *Tailby v. Official Receiver* (1888) 13 H.L.C. 523.
[35] (1884) 13 L.R. Ir. 174; the very terms of the charge there are reproduced below, at para. 16–96.
[36] *Re Brightlife Ltd* [1987] 2 W.L.R. 197 at 205.

assets in question, and in all respects takes on the attributes of a specific charge over those assets and any future assets of that category which the company acquires.

16–17 Floating charges have been described on various occasions as follows and these descriptions are often analysed in order to determine if a particular charge is indeed a floating charge and also to ascertain the precise incidents of these charges. In *Re Old Bushmills Distillery Co. Ltd. ex P. Brett*, Walker L.J. observed that:

> "It is involved in such a charge that the company shall continue as a going concern and the debenture-holder has no power to interfere till his charge becomes payable. He can claim no account of mesne profits or challenge any authorised dealing by the company with its property or business. The directors, as masters, carry on meantime the business for which the company was incorporated according to its constitution, and remain clothed with the power of doing all things necessary for carrying on that business, including the meeting of special emergencies. Assets may be withdrawn by sale, and the proceeds then takes their place, or other assets may be substituted or additional assets added by trading; but the floating security follows the concern, reduced or added to, through every form of its trading existence, which existence continues as if the debentures were not there till the floating charge becomes a fixed one. Till then, to use the words of one learned judge, 'the charge is dormant'."[37]

According to Lord MacNaghten in *Government Stock etc. Co. Ltd. v. Manila Railway Co.*,

> "A floating security is an equitable charge on the assets for the time being of a going concern. It attaches to the subject charged in the varying condition in which it happens to from time to time. It is of the essence of such a charge that it remains dormant until the undertaking charged ceases to be going concern, or until the person in whose favour the charge is created intervenes. His right to intervene may of course be suspended by agreement. But if there is no agreement for suspension, he may exercise his right whenever he pleases after default."[38]

In *Illingworth v. Houldsworth* the same judge said that:

> "I should have thought there was not much difficulty in defining what a floating charge is in contrast to what is called a specific charge. A specific charge, I think, is one that without more fastens on ascertained and definite property or property capable of being ascertained and defined; a floating charge, on the other hand, is ambulatory and shifting in its nature, hovering over and so to speak floating with the property which it is intended to affect until some event occurs or some act is done which

---

[37] [1897] 1 I.R. 488 at 508.
[38] [1897] A.C. 81 at 86.

causes it to settle and fasten on the subject of the charge within its reach and grasp."[39]

16–18 A particularly helpful description or test is that of Romer L.J. in *Re Yorkshire Woolcombers' Association*:

> "I certainly do not intend to attempt to give an exact definition of the term 'floating charge', nor am I prepared to say that there will not be a floating charge . . . which does not contain all the three characteristics that I am about to mention, but I certainly think that if a charge has the[se] three characteristics,— it is a floating charge.
>
> (1) If it is a charge on a class of assets of a company present and future;
>
> (2) if that class is one which in the ordinary course of the business of the company, would be changing from time to time; and
>
> (3) if you find that by the charge it is contemplated that, until some future step is taken by or on behalf of those interested in the charge, the company may carry on its business in the ordinary way as far as concerns the particular class of assets I am dealing with."[40]

16–19 Many legal questions that floating charges give rise to may be resolved by reference to Buckley, L.J.'s description of them in *Evans v. Rival Granite Quarries Ltd.*:

> "A floating security is not a future security; it is a present security, which presently affects all the assets of the company expressed to be included in it. On the other hand, it is not a specific security; the holder cannot affirm that the assets are specifically mortgaged to him. The assets are mortgaged in such a way that the mortgagor can deal with them without the concurrence of the mortgagee. A floating security is not a specific mortgage of the assets, plus a licence to the mortgagor to dispose of them in the course of his business, but is a floating mortgage applying to every item comprised in the security, but not specifically affecting any item until some event occurs or some act on the part of the mortgagee is done which causes it to crystallise into a fixed security . . . [I]t is a mortgage presently affecting all the items expressed to he included in it, but not specifically affecting any item till the happening of the event which causes the security to crystallise as regards all the items. This crystallisation may be brought about in various ways."[41]

16–20 Professor Pennington summed up the nature of a floating charge thus:

> "[A] floating charge today occupies a position midway between the tra-

---

39 [1904] A.C. 355 at 358.
40 [1903] 2 Ch. 284 at 295.
41 [1910] 2 K.B. 979 at 999.

ditional mortgage and the Roman hypotheca. Unlike the traditional mortgage, it is not a specific charge on the assets of the company at the date of its creation and on the assets later added thereto, subject to a licence of somewhat indeterminate extent for the company to dispose of such assets. On the other hand, unlike the Roman hypotheca, a floating charge does not merely create a right to take possession of assets which are ascertained on the occurrence of a specified future event. In practice, however, the difference between the floating charge and hypotheca are minute, and probably amount to no more than that a debenture holder secured by a floating charge has an immediate proprietary interest in the property owned by the company from time to time, whereas the rights of a lender secured by an hypotheca are basically contractual, and although he may recover possession of the property subject to the hypotheca, he will acquire a proprietary interest therein only by foreclosing."[42]

16–21 Companies often give a floating charge over the entire assets of their business — usually described in the charging instrument as a charge on "the undertaking", although it is not essential to use that very term. The charge in *Re Dublin Drapery Co. Ltd.*,[43] for instance, was on "the undertaking, stock in trade, lands, premises, works, plant property and effects (both present and future) of the said company". At times the charge may only be on particular categories of property or on one category of property, for instance, all present and future book debts, all assets located abroad, all trading assets, etc. Charging instruments frequently confer a specific charge on certain designated property and at the same time give a floating charge over the remainder of the company's assets. As soon as a company gives a floating charge a present security comes into existence, but the chargee does not obtain equitable title in the assets which are charged until crystallisation occurs. Yet it would seem that the chargee possesses some kind of equitable interest in the assets prior to crystallisation in that there are remedies available to him which cannot ordinarily be invoked by mere creditors.

Fixed or Floating Charge?

16–22 A charge must be either specific or floating. The existence of one excludes the other; a floating charge is the very antithesis of a fixed charge. A matter that therefore frequently arises is whether the charge in question is a specific or a floating security. When drafting the instrument of charge, the parties may not have addressed themselves to

---

[42] (1960) 23 Mod. L. Rev. 630 at 646.
[43] (1884) 13 L.R. Ir. 174.

this particular matter and the terms of the charge may be unintentionally ambiguous. In recent years, attempts are made to have a specific security which nevertheless possesses some of the flexibility associated with floating charges, most notably the fixed charge on future book debts. Whether a charge is a fixed or a floating one depends, not on how it describes itself, but on its substance; whether it possesses the characteristics of a floating charge set out above. Whether it possesses those features turns on the intention of the parties: was the charge intended to be a specific security or was it intended that the company could freely deal with the charged assets until some crystallising event occurred? Jessel M.R. once emphasised that the court's function in instances such as this is to ascertain the parties' intentions:

> "The real question we have to decide is on the meaning of a written instrument, which . . . might have been better drawn. [That] question . . . must be decided, like all other questions of the kind, having regard to the surrounding circumstances under which the instrument was executed, and especially the respective positions of the parties who were the contracting parties, to carry out whose agreement that instrument was executed."[44]

Charge on Future Property

16–23 As was explained above, charges can be given over future property because, once property as described in the charge is acquired, equity will compel the mortgagor to assign that property to the chargee. Such charges are usually floating charges but are not necessarily so; it is possible to have a fixed charge on future assets. Indeed, in *Holroyd v. Marshall*[45] which was decided almost ten years before floating charges obtained general judicial recognition, it was assumed that the charge on new machinery given there was a fixed charge. It is also possible to have a floating charge over a class of present assets only, although a charge so limited is most unusual. In each case it will depend on the parties' intentions, as evidenced by the terms of the charging instrument and the surrounding circumstances, whether the security is indeed a fixed or a floating security. Since fixed assets, like land, plant, machinery and equipment, tend to be retained by the companies throughout their useful life, a charge over them is as compatible with being a fixed charge as being a floating charge.[46] Since current assets, like stock in trade, raw materials and book debts, generally tend to be turned over in the course of the business, a charge on them is more compatible with being a floating charge. But current assets can be the

---

[44] *Re Florence Land & Public Works Co.* (1878) 10 Ch. 530 at 537.
[45] (1862) 10 H.L.C. 191.
[46] *cf. Welch v. Bowmaker (Ireland) Ltd* [1980] I.R. 251, below, para. 16–33.

subject of a fixed charge where that is the parties' unequivocal intention as set out in the debenture.[47]

Charge on the Undertaking

16–24 Where the charge is on all the company's property then the inference is that it is a floating charge. As was explained in the *Florence Land Co.* case, where the entire undertaking is charged, it is

> "inconsistent to suppose that the moment you executed a bond or debenture you paralysed the entire company and prevented it carrying on its business, for if you read the words to mean a specific charge on the property of the company, then, of course, no practical use could be made of the money borrowed . . . [I]t would be an extravagant result . . . if the company is formed to build and to let and mortgage its property, you can neither lease nor mortgage without the assent of every individual bond or debenture holder . . . But if you read it as making a charge only to this extent, subject to the powers of directors whilst they are carrying on the business, then if they make default in payment of the principal or interest a creditor can apply . . . for a receiver and stop them from going on; but subject to that they carry on their business as usual . . . That appears . . . to be a rational view."[48]

That case concerned a company that was formed to invest in and to develop land, which issued a series of debentures that were secured by "all the [company's] estate, property and effects". In the absence of language indicating clearly an intention to give a fixed or a floating charge, it therefore was reasonable to assume that the parties intended to have a floating charge, because a fixed charge on all the company's assets would prevent it from doing any business.

Fixed Charge on Book Debts

16–25 In 1888 it was held that a charge could be given on future book debts.[49] By its very nature such a charge is a floating charge because the company would use the funds it collects from its debtors in order to finance continued trading. In *Re Lakeglen Construction Ltd.*, Costello

---

[47] Recent cases on the fixed/floating charge characterisation concerning chattels include *Re Coslett Contractors Ltd* [1998] 2 W.L.R. 131 and *Re G.R Tunbridge Ltd* [1995] 1 B.C.L.C. 34 (held to be floating charges); *cf. Re Cimex Tissues Ltd* [1995] 1 B.C.L.C. 409. Cases concerning choses in action, other than book debts, include *Royal Trust Bank* v. *National Westminster Bank* [1996] 2 B.C.L.C. 682 (rentals on hiring agreements), *Re Atlantic Medical Ltd* [1993] B.C.L.C. 386 (rentals on hiring agreements) and *Re CCG International Enterprises Ltd* [1993] B.C.L.C. 1428 (insurance policies).

[48] (1878) 10 Ch. 530 at 541.

[49] *Tailby v. Official Receiver* (1888) 13 H.L.C. 523.

J. observed that "[w]hen a company charges all its book debts and when it is specifically permitted to continue trading, . . . such a charge should not be construed in a restrictive sense unless there is some other provision in the debenture or some fact in the surrounding circumstances which would call for a contrary interpretation."[50] There an "absolute charge" on book debts was held to be a floating charge.[51]

16–26 At times, sophisticated creditors try to structure their charges on book debts as fixed charges and, thereby, hope to get the enhanced priority of the specific security over statutory preferential debts and floating charges, and to prevent the security from being held invalid as a final 12 months floating charge.[52] In *Siebe Gorman & Co. v. Barclays Bank*,[53] Slade J. held that it was possible, by appropriate drafting, to give a fixed charge on future book debts and that the charge there was a specific security. A similar agreement was considered in *Re Keenan Brothers Ltd.*,[54] where the company gave its bankers a charge on all its book debts and other debts, present and future, which was described in the charging instrument as a "fixed charge". This instrument went on to stipulate that the company shall pay all money it received by way of book debts into a specified account with the bank; the company could not, without the bank's written consent, make any withdrawal from that account or direct any payment from it; if called upon to do so by the bank, the company would execute a legal assignment of its debts to the bank. It was also provided that, at the company's request, the bank in its discretion could permit the transfer of funds from that special account to the company's trading account. Keane J. accepted that it is possible to create a fixed charge on book debts but held that, in the circumstances here, the charge was not a fixed one, principally because what the bank had sought to do was "to create a hybrid form of charge which incorporates all the advantages of a floating charge with none of the statutory limitations on its operation",[55] such as the provisions of sections 288 and 285(7) of the 1963 Act. The parties' real intention was to enable the company to collect the book debts, lodge them to its bank account and use them in the business in the ordinary way. This construction of the charge was overruled by the Supreme Court, which held that the parties had succeeded here in creating a

---

[50] *Kelly v. McMahon* [1980] I.R. 347 at 355.

[51] Similarly, *Re Brightlife Ltd* [1987] Ch. 200, *Re Pearl Maintenance Services Ltd* [1995] 1 B.C.L.C. 449 and *Re Westmaze Ltd* (*Times L.R.*, July 15, 1998).

[52] See generally, Pearce, "Fixed Charges Over Book Debts" (1987) J. Bus. L. 18 and McCormack, "Fixed Charges on Future Book Debts" (1987) 8 Co. Law. 3.

[53] [1979] 2 Ll.L.R. 142.

[54] [1985] I.R. 401.

[55] [1985] I.R. 401 at 415.

charge which possessed none of the typical characteristics of a floating charge.

16–27 As Henchy J. put it, because the book debts received were "relegated into a special account" and were then "virtually frozen and rendered unusable" by the company, save with the bank's written prior consent, this "restricted use permitted to the company of the assets charged was incompatible with the essence of a floating charge."[56] McCarthy J. concluded that "it is because it was described as a specific or fixed charge and was intended to be such, that the requirement of a special bank account was necessary: if it were a floating charge payment into such an account would be entirely inappropriate and, indeed, would conflict with the ambulatory nature of the floating charge . . . "[57] Although it was "somewhat hybrid in form", it nevertheless was a specific charge on present and future book debts. Referring to what may be termed the policy objection to essentially hybrid charges, McCarthy J. observed that "[i]f the borrower, the company, is driven to such financial straits that it is prepared to effect an immediate charge upon its book debts, the existence of which charge is [by registration], in effect, published to the commercial and financial world, I do not accept that an elaborate system set up to enable the company to benefit by the collection of such debts detracts from its qualifying as a specific or fixed charge."[58]

16–28 The reasoning there was dramatically extended in *Re Wogans (Drogheda) Ltd.*,[59] which concerned a debenture that gave a most extensive range of securities to a non-clearing bank, including what purported to be a fixed charge on debts and other forms of income. It was stipulated that the company could get in its debts and realise them in the ordinary course of its business, but could not factor or similarly deal with those debts. It was further stipulated that the bank could designate a bank account at any time into which those funds must then be paid, but no such account had actually been designated in the intervening 12 months; all moneys received were paid into the company's account with its clearing bank, over which the secured creditor bank had no control other than via a general floating charge. Denham J. held that, accordingly, since the company was being permitted to use those debts in the ordinary course of its business, pending a special account being designated by the secured bank, the presumption was that it is a

---

[56] [1985] I.R. 401 at 419.
[57] *ibid.* at 424.
[58] *ibid.* Followed in *Re A.H. Masser Ltd* [1986] I.R. 455 and in *Jackson v. Lombard & Ulster Banking Ltd* [1992] 1 I.R. 94.
[59] [1993] 1 I.R. 157.

floating charge; this was fortified by the third requirement in the classic *Woolcombers* test[60] of a floating charge, namely is it contemplated that, until some future step is taken, the company could continue using the assets in question for its business. That view was rejected on appeal. According to Finlay C.J.:

> "If a lender, having availed of a debenture in these terms as a concession delays the designation of a bank account or suspends for some period the operation of direct control over the bank account into which the proceeds of book debts is paid, thus permitting the company issuing the debenture to carry on trading in a more normal fashion than strict compliance with the terms of a fixed charge would permit, there does not appear to be any principle of law or of justice which would deprive such a lender of the rights agreed by the debtor company of a fixed charge over the assets, whereas, a lender with a more draconian approach to the rights which were granted to it by a debenture would be in a more advantageous position."[61]

It, therefore, would seem that in Ireland one can have a fixed charge over assets even though the company is permitted to use them up without restriction in the course of its business for a prolonged period. It is not explained in the judgment how this paradoxical state of affairs is reconciled with the *Woolcombers* test and the received view of floating charges.[62] It seems that in Ireland a fixed charge exists once the creditor is legally in a position to bring about a state of affairs which will authorise him to control the use of the assets, even though he is presently not exercising that control. In other words, a charge which enables the creditor to crystallise it at any time and for any reason may be a fixed charge.

16–29 Following the above reasoning, a fixed charge has been created but, as a concession, the chargee is permitting the company, nonetheless, to deal with the charged property for the time being as if it were a floating charge. Up to now, that kind of arrangement would generally be regarded as a floating charge incorporating an automatic crystallisation clause. Now apparently, under Irish law, it is a fixed charge, even it seems when the chargee's concession to deal with the property lasts for years. If this analysis is indeed correct, then the floating charge is practically defunct and changes in the Companies Acts, to deal with preferential debts, can be anticipated.

---

[60] Above, para. 16–18.
[61] At pp.15–16.
[62] Especially, Pennington, "Fixed Charge over Future Assets of a Company" (1985) 6 Co. Law. 9 at 18–21.

16–30 Following entirely different reasoning, the Court of Appeal in England has held that an appropriately drafted debenture can give a fixed charge over a company's book debts.[63] However, that view has been criticised by several eminent commentators on the subject[64] and has been disregarded by the Court of Appeal on occasion.[65] Curiously, the question of whether it is ever possible to create a fixed charge over book debts, other than in favour of the company's own clearing bankers using the *Keenan Brothers* device, has not been considered by the House of Lords. Ireland's highest court reconsidered the *Wogans* case in *Re Holdair Ltd.*,[66] which concerned an almost identically worded debenture. Blayney J. "distinguished" *Wogans* on grounds that are not easy to fathom;[67] if the court there had followed *Wogans*, as Costello P. had done at first instance, a large construction company would have been forced into liquidation, leading to widespread job losses and other losses. Accordingly, it is far from clear whether the reasoning in *Wogans* would be followed today, *i.e.* that a fixed charge may, on sufferance, be permitted to operate temporarily as a floating charge and yet remain a fixed charge; this unique Celtic hybrid might be described as a "shifting charge" or a "transmuting charge". Nor can one confidently predict whether the courts here will follow the reasoning in the English Court of Appeal — and which division of that court — on whether it is possible for creditors other than the company's own clearing bank ever to get a fixed charge over its own book debts.[68]

Fixed Charge on Other Current Assets

16–31 Following the reasoning in *Re Wogans (Drogbeda) Ltd.*,[69] it now appears that one can also have a fixed "transmuting" charge on a company's other current assets, such as stock in trade, raw materials and the like, if it is structured as follows. The debenture describes that charge as a fixed charge; it adds that, nevertheless, the company can continue

---

[63] *Re New Bullas Trading Ltd* [1994] 1 B.C.L.C. 485, overruling Knox J. [1993] B.C.L.C. 1389.

[64] Goode, "Charges Over Book Debts: A Missed Opportunity" (1994) 110 L.Q.R. 592; R. Goode, *Commercial Law* (2nd ed., 1995), pp. 667 (n. 127) and 738 (n. 35) and Fealy, "Fixed Charges Over Book Debts: A Loosening of the Reins" [1993] I.L.T. 133. The contrary view is argued persuasively in Berg, "Charges Over Book Debts: A Reply" [1995] J. Bus. L. 433.

[65] *e.g. Royal Trust Bank v. National Westminster Bank* [1996] 2 B.C.L.C. 682 (see note in (1997) 113 L.Q.R. 562) and *Re Westmaze Ltd Times L.R.*, July 15, 1998 (see note in 115 L.Q.R. 14 (1999).

[66] [1994] 1 I.R. 416.

[67] *ibid.* at 448.

[68] The author was junior counsel for the examiner in *Wogans'* case, which may colour the views expressed here.

[69] Above, n.59.

dealing with those items in the ordinary course of its business; but the creditor is also authorised, at any time, to designate some person who will have full authority to take control of those assets and to determine how they will be disposed of. Hitherto that would be regarded as a floating charge subject to an automatic crystallisation clause.[70]

Composite Charges

16–32 Security documents frequently stipulate that they create both fixed charges and floating charges over various categories of assets; the question then arises of which kind of charge is a particular category of assets subject to. The answer lies in the parties' intentions with respect to those assets. Where the assets in question are of a kind that tend to get turned over in the course of the business the presumption is that they are subject to a floating charge; where the assets are fixed in nature, the presumption is in favour of a specific charge. The parties' characterisation of the charge as falling into one category or another is an important indication of their real intentions but is not determinative. For instance in *Re Armagh Shoes Ltd.*,[71] the company had already given its bank a fixed charge over its land and buildings and a floating charge over the entire undertaking, when it executed a further charge in the bank's favour. This was expressed as a "fixed charge [on] all receivables, debts, plant, machinery, fixtures, fittings and ancillary equipment now or at any time hereinafter belonging to the mortgagor." Despite the express characterisation as a fixed charge and the existence of the earlier floating charge on these items, Hutton J. held that the parties created a floating charge, because the parties must have intended that the company could continue dealing with the charged items in the course of its business.

16–33 A more difficult case was *Welch v. Bowmaker (Ireland) Ltd.*,[72] which concerned the status of a charge over one parcel of land. Under a debenture, the company gave an undesignated charge on its "undertaking and all its property and assets, present and future . . . for the time being"; at the same time it gave a specific charge over three identified properties it owned. But it also owned a fourth property and the question was whether, under the undesignated charge, that property was the subject of a fixed charge. Overruling Costello J., a divided Supreme Court held that it was only a floating charge, on the basis of the principle of construction *generalia specialibus non derogant*; it was fair to infer from the express references to the other properties as being sub-

---

[70] *e.g. Re Cosslett Contractors Ltd* [1998] 2 W.L.R. 131.
[71] [1982] N.I. 59.
[72] [1980] I.R. 251.

ject to a fixed charge that the fourth property was not to be so charged. Kenny J., dissenting, was persuaded by the fact that this property was owned by the company when the charge was given and it "certainly was not a class of asset which would be changing from time to time."[73]

Restrictions on Dealing with the Charged Assets

16–34 A person who has given a specific charge over assets is not allowed to sell or otherwise to dispose of them without the chargee's consent; he may not deal with those assets as if the charge does not exist. But the floating charge's most distinctive feature is that the assets charged can continue to be used in the company's business. Although it is implicit that the company is not to do anything with the charged assets other than in the ordinary course of business, absent explicit restrictions on particular transactions, the courts take an expansive view of what constitutes dealings in the ordinary course of business. Because certain transactions with those assets could very well render the charge worthless, or at least take from its value, it is common for instruments creating these charges to forbid certain kinds of prejudicial dealings with the assets,[74] for instance, granting a fixed charge over some of them. Occasionally, the restrictions on use can be so extensive that the charge cannot truly be regarded as a floating charge.

Ordinary Course of Business

16–35 In *Re Old Bushmills Distillery Co. ex p. Brett*[75] Lord Ashbourne C. observed that the courts are "anxious to uphold all reasonable bona fide transactions (in the charged property) that are entered into for the purpose of keeping up the business of a company and saving it from collapse or paralysis . . . "[76] Curiously, most of the Irish cases on this matter concern distillery companies dealing with stocks of whiskey that were subject to floating charges.[77] Dealing in the ordinary course of business includes selling some of the charged assets, leasing them on hire purchase,[78] a sale and a lease back of the assets[79] and giving a specific charge over the assets in priority to the floating charge.[80]

---

73 [1980] I.R. 251 at 258.
74 See generally, Gough, *Company Charges*, Chaps 9, 10.
75 [1897] 1 I.R. 488.
76 *ibid.* at 495.
77 *ibid. Re Bushmills Distillery Co., ex p. Brydon* [1896] 1 I.R. 301, *Cox v. Dublin Distillery Co.* [1906] 1 I.R. 446 and *Coveney v. Persse* [1910] 1 I.R. 194.
78 *Dempsey v. Traders Finance Corp. Ltd* [1933] N.Z.L.R. 1258.
79 *Paintin & Nottingham Ltd v. Miller, Gale & Winter* [1971] N.Z.L.R. 164 at 168–169.
80 *Wheatly v. Silkstone & Haigh Moor Coal Co.* (1885) 29 Ch.D. 715.

16–36 It depends on the circumstances whether a sale of the undertaking itself constitutes a transaction in the ordinary course of business. It undoubtedly is not so where the sale is with a view to ceasing doing business entirely.[81] But in *Re Borax Co.*,[82] where the company agreed to sell all its property and assets, except for certain investments, in return for securities in the purchaser company, it was held that the company there had not in fact stopped business or ceased to be a going concern. And in *Re H.H. Vivian & Co.*[83] it was held that it is not inconsistent with the general terms of a floating charge for a company with businesses being carried on at several branches to dispose of all the assets of one of those branches. Presumably an *ultra vires* transaction or a fraudulent transaction would not be regarded as within the ordinary course of business.

Restrictive Clauses

16–37 A great variety of specific prohibitions on dealings with the charged property can be imagined; by far the most common restriction is on creating any mortgage or charge on the assets in question ranking in priority to or *pari passu* with the floating charge. The four major Irish cases on these clauses[84] concerned such restrictions and whether what the distillery companies had done there contravened those prohibitions. These clauses are strictly construed.[85] Prohibitions against creating any charge ranging in priority to or *pari passu* with the floating charge do not forbid persons from acquiring liens that rank in priority to the charge, like a solicitors' lien, a sub-contractors' statutory lien or, indeed, a general lien under contract.[86] As was explained in *Brunton v. Electrical Engineering Corp.*,[87] where it was held that the charged assets could become subject to a solicitors' lien, these prohibitions do not apply to "a mortgage or charge given by the general law, and arising through the company carrying on its business in the ordinary course. So long as the company are acting to the ordinary course of business and not so as to give their [chargee] any advantage by their own direct act, but are merely allowing him, in the ordinary course of business, to acquire that lien which the law gives him. . . . they are not creating a mortgage or charge in his favour."[88]

---

[81] *Hubbuck v. Helms* (1887) 56 L.J.Ch. 536.
[82] [1901] 1 Ch. 326.
[83] [1900] 2 Ch. 654.
[84] Above, n. 77.
[85] Above, n. 76.
[86] *cf. George Baker (Transport) Ltd v. Eynon* [1974] 1 W.L.R. 462.
[87] [1892] 1 Ch. 434.
[88] *ibid.* at 411.

16–38 In one of the *Old Bushmills Distillery Co.* cases,[89] the company gave a charge on the undertaking, subject to a restrictive clause. But then, in order to raise additional funds, the company agreed that a syndicate, who comprised some of its creditors, should buy quantities of whiskey from it at specified prices and that, under the syndicate's direction, the money should be applied to satisfy the company's trade debts and other pressing liabilities. It was held that the transactions under this agreement were genuine sales of assets and were not charges forbidden by the restrictive clause. FitzGibbon L.J. observed there that "a financing motive, and even a financing disposal of the money received, will not deprive a transaction of its character as a dealing in the course of business."[90] In another of the *Old Bushmills* cases,[91] the company applied to a financier to accept a bill against its whiskey and the transaction was carried out by what purported to be a sale of the whiskey to him, subject to the company's right to repurchase it. The bill was discounted at a bank and the whiskey was then transferred into the bank's name in the company's books and also at the bonded warehouse. It was held that the entire transaction there was a sham sale and that, accordingly, it was a transaction that contravened the express prohibition contained in the debenture. In FitzGibbon L.J.'s words, the Bank "was throughout a mortgagee and a mortgagee only and never bought any whiskey. The company transferred the whiskey and purported to sell it to people who [were] only trustees for the company, holding upon trust to mortgage to the bank . . . , but themselves standing in a fiduciary relation to the company, which made it impossible for them to claim to be out and out purchasers. The whole transaction was a colourable sale, and an evasion, for a real purpose of giving a security to the bank, leaving an equity of redemption still in the company."[92] In *Cox v. Dublin City Distillery Co.*[93] it was held that pledging whiskey to the bank, by delivering to it the bonders' warrants for the whiskey along with the invoices, breached the prohibition in the debenture against granting other charges.

16–39 In *Coveney v. Persee Ltd.*,[94] the company originally purported to sell whiskey together with an undertaking to repurchase it. But on taking legal advice that this arrangement could very well contravene the debenture's prohibition against granting other charges, the company amended the agreement. All references to pledges and to redemp-

---

89 *Ex p. Brett* [1897] 1 I.R. 488.
90 *ibid.* at 504.
91 *Ex. p. Brydon* [1896] 1 I.R. 301.
92 His account of the case given in *Ex. p. Brett* [1897] 1 I.R. 488 at 505.
93 [1906] 1 I.R. 446.
94 [1910] 1 I.R. 194.

tion were struck out, and it was made clear that the whiskey was to be the buyer's property but that the company had an option to repurchase the whiskey after four years. It was held that transactions under this agreement were sales, not mortgages or pledges that the debenture proscribed, and were made in the ordinary course of business. According to Palles C.B.:

> "I hold, not that the form only of the transaction was changed, its substance remaining the same — but that the substance was changed, that the real transaction was that which was represented by the documents . . . The presence or absence of reciprocal rights is the determining element in ascertaining whether the document evidences a sale or a pledge. It is too much to ask us to hold that in a honest commercial transaction, in which the parties were at arms' length, the stipulation upon which, to their knowledge, the validity of the transaction depended is to be abrogated with the view of avoiding the transaction."[95]

16–40 Persons who subsequently acquire an interest in the charged assets, who know that a restrictive clause in respect of them was breached by the company granting that interest, cannot have priority over the chargee.[96] What constitutes notice in this context is dealt with later.[97] Provided he has no knowledge of the restriction on granting other charges, that restriction does not operate against any subsequent equitable mortgagee who gets possession of the title documents to the property in question.[98] Nor does the restriction stand in the way of creating a specific charge over property subsequently acquired when that charge arose out of the very acquisition. This is because the equitable rights arising from the contract of purchase make the charge attach to the property before the legal ownership vests in the company and, consequently, the charge has priority over the equity created by the restriction. Thus, the restriction does not override the charge that the vendor of after-acquired property gets to secure the purchase money, nor a charge to secure an advance by a third party of part of the purchase money.

Crystallisation of Floating Charges

16–41 By a floating charge crystallising[99] is meant that the charge, so to speak, ceases to float over the assets in question and is converted into a fixed charge (or specific security) over those assets described as

---

95 [1910] 1 I.R. 194 at 214.
96 See generally, Farrar, "Floating Charges and Priorities" (1974) 38 Conv. 315.
97 Below, para. 18–109.
98 *Re Castell & Brown Ltd* [1898] 1 Ch. 315.
99 See generally, Gough, *Company Charges*, Chaps 8, 11.

security that the company then possessed or subsequently acquires. After crystallisation, the company is no longer free to deal with those assets in the course of its business and the holder of the charge becomes entitled to have those assets sold off in order to be reimbursed from their proceeds.[100] But until crystallisation occurs, the debenture-holder is not entitled to intervene unless the company jeopardises the security, does some act which is *ultra vires* its memorandum of association or has ceased to be a going concern. Where a floating charge crystallises before a receiver is appointed or before a winding up commences, the chargee obtains priority over the statutorily preferred creditors (*e.g.* the Revenue and the employees) since his charge has become a fixed charge.[101] Because of the important consequences of crystallisation, it is vital to know what brings it about and precisely when it occurs.

Crystallising Events

16–42 Crystallisation occurs once a company goes into liquidation, even where it is being wound up merely to restructure its capital.[102] A compulsory winding up is deemed to have commenced when the petition was presented[103] and a voluntary winding up begins once the members' resolution to wind up is passed.[104] Provision is made in the 1963 Act for notifying the registrar of companies and publicising the fact of a winding up having commenced.[105]

16–43 Crystallisation also occurs when a receiver is appointed under the charge.[106] But taking preliminary steps to have a receiver appointed does not of itself cause crystallisation. Appointment of a receiver is required to be publicised in several ways.[107]

16–44 Crystallisation occurs as well when, under a power in the charge, the debenture-holder intervenes and takes possession of the assets, at least where doing so causes the company to cease to carry on business as a going concern.[108]

---

[100] *e.g. Re ELS Ltd* [1994] 1 B.C.L.C. 743.
[101] *Re Brightlife Ltd* [1987] 2 W.L.R. 197.
[102] *Re Crampton & Co. Ltd* [1914] 1 Ch. 954.
[103] 1963 Act, s.220(2).
[104] 1963 Act, s.220(1).
[105] 1963 Act, ss. 221, 227, 252.
[106] *Taunton v. Sheriff of Warwickshire* [1895] 2 Ch. 319.
[107] 1963 Act, ss. 107, 319(1)(a), 317.
[108] *Biggerstaff v. Rowatt's Wharf Ltd* [1896] 2 Ch. 93 at 105–106.

16–45 As for whether the company itself ceasing to carry on business brings about crystallisation, prior to 1985 there was no authority squarely on the point.[109] There is a 40 years old decision of Lavery J., *Halpin v. Cremin*,[110] where it was assumed that the business ceasing did not have a crystallising effect. But this matter does not appear to have been considered thoroughly there and most likely the case would not be followed today. There also were several dicta that those circumstances constituted a crystallising event and it is settled that ceasing to do business is a ground for having a receiver appointed. One reason for not regarding ending the business as invariably a crystallising event is that trading can cease without the debenture-holder or third parties ever being aware of that fact; crystallisation in those circumstances could give rise to unfair consequences. However, in *Re Woodroffes (Musical Instruments) Ltd.*[111] it was held that crystallisation occurs once the company ceases to carry on its business. According to Nourse J., that result:

> "is in accordance with the essential nature of a floating charge. The thinking behind the creation of such charges has always been a recognition that a fixed charge on the whole undertaking and assets of the company would paralyse it and prevent it from carrying on its business . . . On the other hand, it is a mistake to think that the chargee has no remedy while the charge is still floating. He can always intervene and obtain an injunction to prevent the company from dealing with its assets otherwise than in the ordinary course of its business . . . A cessation of the business necessarily puts an end to the company's dealings with its assets. That which kept the (floating) charge hovering has now been released and . . . causes it to settle and fasten on the subject of the charge." [112]

Automatic Crystallisation Clauses

16–46 An automatic crystallisation clause is a provision in a debenture stipulating that, on any designated event occurring, a floating charge shall crystallise into a specific security.[113] For instance, the debenture in the *Re Woodroffes* case stated that the debenture-holders might at any time, by giving notice to the company, convert their floating charge into a fixed charge. Nourse J. observed that clauses of that nature are widely regarded as undesirable because they purport to bring about crystallisation, often without those doing business with

---

[109] See H. Picarda, *The Law Relating to Receivers and Managers* (1984), pp.16–18.
[110] [1954] I.R. 19.
[111] [1986] 1 Ch. 366
[112] *ibid.* at 377–378.
[113] See generally, Boyle, "The Validity of Automatic Crystallisation Clauses" [1979] J. Bus. L. 231.

the company being aware of what is happening and, indeed, some clauses could commence crystallisation without even the debtor company itself knowing that the charge had ceased to float over its assets. In Britain the Cork Committee concluded that "[t]he practical consequences of automatic crystallisation of a floating charge without liquidation or receivership lead us to the conclusion that there is no place for it in a modern insolvency law. There are strong policy arguments against it; there is no need for it; the debenture-holder is sufficiently protected if he has the right to take steps to crystallise his security by appointing a receiver".[114]

16–47 But it was held in *Re Brightlife Ltd.*[115] that these clauses are permissible and effective, at least where the designated crystallising event involves delivering a notice to the debtor company. In this case, Hoffman J. rejected the arguments usually made against automatic crystallisation, while conceding that there were some persuasive practical commercial objections to those clauses. A floating charge is a purely contractual arrangement between debtor and creditor; "the rights and duties which the law may or may not categorise as a floating charge are wholly derived from the agreement of the parties, supplemented by the terms implied by law".[116] That charges crystallise when a winding up commences, when a receiver is appointed and when the company ceases to do business is an implied term of security agreements. But there is no rule preventing the parties from stipulating that one or more of these events shall not cause crystallisation. Hoffman J. observed that "the commercial inconvenience of automatic crystallisation gives rise to a strong presumption that it was not intended by the parties. Very clear language will be required. But that does not mean that it is excluded by a rule of law."[117] According to the clause being considered in that case, crystallisation was to occur when the debenture-holder notified the company that the floating charge was to convert into a fixed charge as regards any of the assets specified in the notice and which the debenture-holder considered to be in jeopardy. In was held that delivering a notice in those terms crystallised the charge as regards the designated assets.

16–48 The New Zealand Supreme Court has upheld an automatic crystallisation clause that has another significant effect on priorities too. In *Re Manurewa Transport Ltd.*,[118] one clause in the debenture was

[114] *Report – Insolvency Law and Practice* (Cmnd. 8588, 1982) para. 1579.
[115] [1987] 2 W.L.R. 197.
[116] *ibid.* at 205.
[117] *ibid.* at 204.
[118] [1971] N.Z.L.R. 909.

that the charge shall crystallise "once the company mortgages, charges or encumbers or attempts to mortgage, charge or encumber" any of the charged assets. It was held that, once the company attempted to charge any of those assets, the charge consequently crystallised. This was because "a floating charge is not a word of art, it is a description for a type of security contained in a document which may provide a variety of circumstances whereupon crystallisation takes place."[119] In other words, a floating charge is not some special kind of proprietary interest but is merely a security all the incidents of which are stipulated by the parties; it is entirely for the company and the chargee to define their security's ambit and characteristics. On the basis of this reasoning, Hoffman J. in *Re Permanent (Houses) Holdings Ltd.*[120] held that designating default in payment of a loan can be made a crystallising event:

> "The particular attraction to creditors of an 'attempted charge' stipulation is that generally, persons who obtain a specific charge over assets, that were subject to a restriction on creating such charges, have priority over the floating chargee. But if the earlier charge crystallised when the company attempted to grant the specific charge, the earlier charge then would have priority — provided the later one is an equitable charge and subject to principles of estoppel."

Effects of Crystallisation

16–49 Once the floating charge crystallises, the property covered by it immediately passes to the chargee.[121] In *Re Tullow Engineering Holdings Ltd.*,[122] it was held that where the company had given a third party an option to purchase property and a floating charge over that property crystallises, the option then lapses. That option was to purchase certain shares held by the company. According to Blayney J.:

> "The effect of the crystallisation . . . was that there was an immediate equitable assignment of the shares to the debenture-holders so that in equity they became the owners of the shares. [The Company] was divested of its ownership in favour of the debenture-holders. Accordingly, it no longer had the capacity to enter into a contract to sell the shares in pursuance of the option which it granted. Its ownership had been terminated and its irrevocable offer to sell became a dead letter. No longer having the ownership of the shares, it could not contract to sell them. The only person who could do that was the receiver under the powers

---

[119] [1971] N.Z.L.R. 909 at 917.
[120] [1988] B.C.L.C. 563.
[121] *e.g. Re ELS Ltd* [1994] 1 B.C.L.C. 743.
[122] [1990] I.R. 452.

given in the debenture. And the purported exercise of the option did not alter the position."[123]

However, it does not seem to have been argued there that the principle stated in *Dempsy v. Bank of Ireland*[124] should have applied, *i.e.* that a liquidator cannot take a better title to the assets than the company itself had. Accordingly, it could be contended, since the company's title to the shares was subject to an option, the receiver's title remained subject to that clause.[125]

Decrystallisation or Refloating

16–50 It has never been established conclusively whether a floating charge which has crystallised can afterwards lose its specific character and, so to speak, float again over what charged assets as remain. Decrystallisation in this sense is possible so long as the debenture-holder is in a position to deal directly with the company. If a winding up has commenced, the liquidator takes control of the company and represents all the creditors, thereby rendering decrystallisation impossible. If a receiver is appointed, decrystallisation is possible provided the statutorily-preferred creditors were paid off and either the receiver's task was completed or the receiver was removed under a power of removal contained in the instrument of appointment, thereby freeing the debenture-holder to bargain with the company. It would not be necessary again to register the charge under section 99 of the 1963 Act in order to render it effective against creditors.

REGISTRATION OF CHARGES

16–51 Part IV of the 1963 Act (sections 99–112) establishes a system whereby, in order to be legally effective, most kinds of charges created by companies on their assets must be registered in the registry of companies.[126] The principal purpose of requiring that companies register charges is so that persons dealing with them can determine how much of their assets are mortgaged, or charged, and thereby assess the company's credit-worthiness. Persons dealing with companies are deemed to have notice of the existence of all registered charges but not necessarily of the detailed contents of those securities. The effect of registration under section 99 of the 1963 Act is not to confer title or priority; that registration only protects an existing priority. An unregistered

---

[123] [1990] I.R. 452 at 457.
[124] Supreme Court, December 6, 1985; see below, paras 18–86—18–88.
[125] *cf. Ash & Newman Ltd v. Creative Devices Research Ltd* [1991] B.C.L.C. 403.
[126] See generally, Gough, *Company Charges*, Chaps. 17–36.

charge is not an entire nullity; although it cannot establish rights against other creditors of the company or against the liquidator, it is not invalid and, accordingly, can give rise to certain rights and obligations against the company. For example, non-registration of a charge does not prevent the chargee from appointing a receiver under the charge.[127] As well as the duty to register charges in the companies' office in Parnell Square, Dublin, companies are required by section 109 of the 1963 Act to keep copies in their own registered office of every registrable charge, which can be inspected by any shareholder or creditor of the company.

16–52 The system of registration was established initially by the Companies Act 1900, and applied only to a limited category of charges, which was expanded by the 1907 Act and again by the 1963 Act and by the 1990 Act. The leading case of *Salomon v. Salomon & Co. Ltd.*[128] influenced the establishment of this system. It will be recalled that there Mr Salomon owned a moderately successful business which he had incorporated into a limited company, of which he was the dominant shareholder. Part of the consideration the company gave him to acquire his business was an undertaking to pay him £10,000, which was secured by a floating charge on its property. When the company was wound up and found to be insolvent, the question arose of whether in the circumstances Mr Salomon should be preferred to the unsecured creditors; it was held that he should. But the view was then taken in the commercial world that persons dealing with companies should at least be given the protection of having the essential details of assets charged by companies under a floating charge recorded in the registry of companies and open for inspection by everybody.

16–53 Part IV of the 1963 Act is not the only statutory scheme providing for registration of charges. Schemes have also been established for recording charges given over land[129] for agricultural chattel mortgages,[130] for bills of sale[131] and for charges on ships.[132]

Charges to be Registered

16–54 Perhaps the Companies Acts should require that full details of

---

[127] *Alexander Hull & Co. v. O'Carroll Kent & Co.* (1955) 89 I.L.T.R. 70.
[128] [1897] A.C. 22.
[129] Registration of Title Act 1964, and Registration of Deeds (Ireland) Act 1707; see generally, J.C.W. Wylie, *Irish Land Law* (3rd ed., 1998), Chaps. 21, 22.
[130] Agricultural Credit Act 1978; see generally, M. Forde, *Commercial Law* (2nd ed., 1993), pp. 234–238.
[131] Bills of Sale (Ireland) Acts 1879–1883; see generally, M. Forde, above, n. 21, pp. 225–230.
[132] Mercantile Marine Act 1955, ss. 50–57.

each and every security interest given by a company over its assets should be registered under section 99 of the 1963 Act. If that were so, persons dealing with any company could get a reasonably comprehensive picture of the extent to which its assets are subject to charges and analogous commitments. But the compulsory registration requirements are not that extensive; they apply only to "charges" which have been "created by the company" and which fall under one or more of the categories enumerated in section 99(2) of the Act. It is an offence for a company not to register charges which are so registrable[133] and unregistered charges cannot take priority over other charges and can be disregarded by a liquidator.[134]

Charge

16–55 Section 99's registration requirements apply only to charges. They therefore do not apply to outright assignments of property rights[135] nor to unambiguous retention of title clauses.[136] Nor do they apply to security interests which are not charges. As has already been observed, there is no definition of the term charge in the Companies Acts other than that it includes a mortgage,[137] which may be a legal or an equitable mortgage. A charge other than a mortgage transfers neither the beneficial ownership in the property nor the right to possess the property; it exists independently of ownership and possession but confers an interest in the property which carries with it a right to resort to that property.

16–56 Whether a mortgage or a charge exists in particular circumstances is a matter of law and of construction. Charges arise by virtue of certain relationships and transactions. Whether the oral agreement or an instrument indeed creates a charge, as opposed to an outright assignment or some other transaction, depends on the parties' intentions in the circumstances, as does the question of the scope of any charge which they purport to grant.

According to Murphy J., in an instance where a purported reservation of title clause was held only to create a charge, what matters is the very substance of the transaction:

> "It would be wrong to infer that a particular transaction constituted a mortgage merely because the vendor [of property] structured it in such a

---

[133] 1963 Act, s.100.
[134] *ibid.*, s.99(1).
[135] *e.g. Re George Ingelfield Ltd* [1933] 1 Ch. l. *cf. Welsh Development Agency v. Export Finance Co. Ltd* [1992] B.C.L.C. 148.
[136] *e.g. Re W.J. Hickey Ltd* [1988] I.R. 126; see below, paras 18–82—18–84.
[137] 1963 Act, s.99(10)(a).

> way as to protect his commercial interests. On the other hand, parties cannot escape the inference that a transaction constitutes a mortgage . . . by applying particular labels to the transaction. The rights of the parties and the nature of the transaction in which they are engaged must be determined from a consideration of the document as a whole and the obligations and rights which it imposes on both parties . . . The description may be a material consideration but clearly it cannot be decisive . . . [I]t is the substance of the transaction as ascertained from the words used by the parties and the context in which the document is executed that determines registrability under the Companies Acts."[138]

In order to constitute a charge in equity by deed or writing, it is not necessary that general words of charge should be used. It is sufficient that the court "can gather fairly from the instrument an intention by the parties that the property therein referred to should constitute a security."[139]

16–57 An agreement to create a present equitable interest in property as security is a charge and must be registered.[140] But an agreement to give a security at some future time or in the event of some future event occurring is not a charge.[141] A charge which is later executed in pursuance of that agreement is registrable; such a charge, however, could easily be invalidated as a "fraudulent preference" if the company was wound up and insolvent.[142] The deposit of title deeds with a lender raises a strong implication that a charge has been created over the property to which those deeds relate.[143] In *Re White & Shannon Ltd.*[144] it was held that a new charge was created when the benefit of a debenture was transferred to another creditor and the security was extended to cover all money owing to that creditor as well as to the original debenture-holder.

16–58 While a possessory lien is something distinct from a charge, a contractual lien, *i.e.* a stipulation in a contract giving someone a "lien" over chattels, documents or choses in action, may indeed be a charge. It would seem that where the lien-holder's rights exist only so long as he has possession of the goods, the lien is not a charge, whether his rights arise under the general law or under contract.[145] But it has been

---

138 *Carroll Group Distributors Ltd v. G. & J.F. Bourke Ltd* [1990] 1 I.R. 481 at 486.
139 *Re Inglis Brothers Ltd* [1922] N.Z.L.R. 874 at 878.
140 *Re Jackson & Bassford* [1906] 2 Ch. 467.
141 *Re Gregory Love & Co.* [1916] 1 Ch. 203.
142 *Re Eric Holmes (Property) Ltd* [1965] Ch. 1052.
143 *Pryce v. Bury* (1854) L.R. 16 Eq. 153(n).
144 [1965] N.I. 15.
145 *Waitomo Wools (N.Z.) Ltd v. Nelsons (N.Z.) Ltd* [1974] 1 N.Z.L.R. 484.

held that what is known as the ship-owner's lien on sub-freights is a charge in this context;[146] that lien is a contractual right of the ship-owner to require payment of money owed by the shipper to the charterer and has no connection with actual possession of the shipper's goods. Banks have a general lien over documents they acquire in the course of banking business but, where title deeds are deposited with them as security for a loan, then the bank's rights are in the nature of a charge over the property to which those deeds relate and not merely a lien over those documents.[147] Although equitable liens are charges, they are not registrable under section 99 because they are not created by the company.[148] A pledge is not a charge and, accordingly, is not registrable unless what is given to the creditor is the title documents to the property being pledged.[149] A right of set-off is not a charge for these purposes, although contractual rights to retain funds are not invariably rights of set-off and accordingly can be charges.

Created by the Company

16–59 Section 99's registration requirements apply only to charges "created by" the company. If the charge arises other than by the company's own act, it therefore need not be registered. Thus all security interests arising under the general law escape registration.[150] Accordingly, it is not necessary to decide whether for these purposes those interests are indeed charges or not, for example, legal and equitable liens, the unpaid landlord's common law remedy of distress and creditors' execution rights like *fieri facias,* attachment of debts and appointing a receiver. It would seem that registration of a judgment mortgage under the Judgment Mortgages (Ireland) Act 1850, on company property need not be registered under section 99 of the 1963 Act. So it was held in England with regard to charging orders on land,[151] because companies do not always know that their property has been made the subject of such orders and, therefore, it would be most impracticable and unjust if companies nevertheless were required to register charging orders within 21 days of their being made. If section 99 were intended to apply to judgment mortgages it can hardly be doubted that an express provision would have been made to that effect. However, section 102 of the 1963 Act requires the judgment creditor to give the company a copy of the affidavit registered against the company's land

---

146 *Re Welsh Irish Ferries Ltd* [1986] Ch. 471.
147 *Re Farm Fresh Frozen Foods Ltd* [1980] I.L.R.M. 131.
148 *Bank of Ireland Finance Ltd v. Daly Ltd* [1978] I.R. 79; below, para. 16–60.
149 *Dublin City Distillery Ltd v. Doherty* [1914] A.C. 823.
150 See generally, Gough, *op. cit.*, Chap. 19.
151 *cf. Re Overseas Aviation Engineering (G.B.) Ltd* [1963] 1 Ch. 24 at 47–52.

and, within three days of receiving it, the company must file a copy at the companies' registry. Breach of this obligation is a criminal offence.

16–60 An equitable lien is a right arising from the general law that is based on a certain relationship between the parties but where, unlike in the legal lien, the creditor does not possess the property secured; the most common example being the lien held by unpaid vendors of land in respect of the purchase price of what was their property. In *Bank of Ireland Finance Ltd. v. Daly Ltd.*[152] McMahon J. held that the unpaid vendor of land's lien need not be registered under section 99, following the reasoning of Brightman J. in the earlier case:

> "If such a lien is registrable, the time for registration would expire 21 days after the exchange of contracts for sale, because it is at that date that the lien is created; it is not created on completion because the purchase price is unpaid, but is discharged on completion to the extent that the purchase money is paid. . . . In most cases, the 21 day period would expire well before completion, because contracts for safe of land are not usually completed in three weeks. It would be a profound inconvenience, therefore, if every vendor to a company were compelled as a matter of course to register an unpaid vendor's lien on the exchange of contracts, on the off chance that circumstances might arise in the future which would render it desirable for the vendor to be able to rely on an unpaid vendor's lien . . . [A]n unpaid vendor's lien is the creature of the law; and it does not depend upon contract, but upon the fact that the vendor has a right to specific performance of his contract."[153]

16–61 By contrast, where title deeds are deposited as security for a loan, an equitable charge on those deeds is created. In *Re Farm Fresh Frozen Foods Ltd.*[154] Keane J. held that such charges must be registered under section 99 because they arise from the act of the person depositing the deeds and not merely by operation of law. According to Templeman J. in a similar case:

> "As a general rule a deposit of title deeds to secure a debt creates a charge on the land; it does not make any difference whether the debt is owned by the debtor or whether it is owned by someone else, and the person who deposited the title deeds is in some way acting as a surety. . . . [The deposit of deeds] is a contractual lien [but] is also a contractual charge; true it is that the charge arises by presumption, but it does not arise by operation of law. What the court does is to say: we shall not compel the parties to write down in so many words what the effect of the deposit of

---

[152] [1978] I.R. 79.

[153] *London & Cheshire Insurance Co. Ltd v. Lampgrene Property Co. Ltd* [1971] Ch. 499 at 514.

[154] [1980] I.L.R.M. 141.

> title deeds is; we shall simply assume that when parties contract, and although they probably do not know the consequences, the person who takes the title deeds contracts not only to retain them but also to have an equitable charge on the land. The presumption reads into the contract the charge which is implied. If that is right, the charge was created by the company and is therefore registrable under section 99. No such shorthand appears to be employed in the case of an unpaid vendor's lien, where the parties are directing their minds to something entirely different; but where, as here, there is a security for a loan and unless something is said and done the security consists of a lien and also the charge, then it seems to me that the charge, at any rate for the purposes of section 99, is created by the company and is therefore registerable. If I may turn round the 'inconvenient' argument given (above), far from its being a profound inconvenience if the charge in the present case were registrable, it would be profoundly inconvenient if it were not, because the object of the section is to give information of incumbrances affecting the property of the company, and if the company could deposit title deeds and create a charge without registration the mischief at which the section is aimed could be largely and easily avoided."[155]

The Catalogue of Registrable Charges

16–62 Not every charge created by a company should be registered under section 99 of the 1963 Act. Section 99(2) lists a catalogue of the kinds of charges which ought to be registered. In the original 1900 version, only four of these categories were listed, namely charges for securing an issue of debentures, charges on uncalled capital, company bills of sale and floating charges; two others, were added in 1907, several more were added in 1963 and the list was completed in 1990 with the addition of aircraft. Under an earlier version of the 1990 Act, practically every kind of company charge was to become registrable.[156] That requirement, however, was not implemented. Instead, section 122(b) of the 1990 Act empowers the Minister, by regulation, to add additional categories of charge to these enumerated in section 99(2) of the 1963 Act. This provision also empowers the Minister to delete any of the heads of charge from the list.

16–63 Except for those charges that are expressly mentioned, specific charges over chattels, over choses in action and over other intangibles need not be registered. On the other hand, a particular charge may be registrable under more than one of section 99(2)'s heads, for instance, a charge on book debts is most likely also a floating charge. It is not

---

[155] *Re Wallace & Simmonds (Builders) Ltd* [1974] 1 All E.R. 561 at 573. *cf. Re Moulton Finance Ltd* [1968] 1 Ch. 325.

[156] Companies (Amendment) Bill 1987, s.94 (s.99(5)).

necessary that the company owned the property in question at the time it agreed to give the charge; a charge immediately executed or created over future company property falls within section 99.[157] Such an agreement must be distinguished from an agreement that at some time in the future the company will grant a charge, which is not a creation of a charge. Where the company acquires property which is subject to a charge which is registrable, section 101 of the 1963 Act requires that the charge be registered within 21 days of completion.

16–64 *Land Charge* The requirement that companies separately register every charge they give "on land, wherever situate, or on any interest therein" was adopted in 1907. Even though most land charges will be registered in either the registry of deeds or in the land registry,[158] it presumably was felt that they should also be registered in the companies' registry so that persons can obtain a more comprehensive view of the company's securities. An agreement to create a mortgage or a charge over land is an equitable mortgage and is registrable under the Companies Acts.[159] Any mortgage or charge subsequently created on foot of such an agreement is also registrable; its validity is not affected by that agreement not having been registered.[160] The deposit of title deeds creates an equitable charge and is registrable under the Companies Act.[161] But an unpaid vendor's lien is not so registrable.[162] Where an equitable charge is registered and, under a term of that charge, a legal mortgage is later executed, the latter need not be registered.[163] Section 99 provides that its requirements do not apply to "a charge for any rent or other periodical sum issuing out of land" and, also, that holding debentures which entitle the holder to a charge on land shall not be deemed to be an interest in land.[164]

16–65 Where the property in question is located abroad and the charge is made in this country, the charge must still be registered under section 99, even though further measures may be necessary in order to make the charge fully effective under the *lex situs*.[165] Where the property is located abroad and the *lex situs* requires that the charge be reg-

---

157 *Independent Automatic Sales Ltd v. Knowles & Foster* [1962] 1 W.L.R. 974.
158 See generally, J.C.W. Wylie, *Irish Land Law* (3rd ed., 1998), Chaps. 21, 22.
159 *Re Jackson & Bassford* [1906] 2 Ch. 467.
160 *Re Columbian Fireproofing Co. Ltd* [1910] 2 Ch. 120.
161 *Re Farm Fresh Frozen Foods Ltd* [1980] I.L.R.M. 131.
162 *Bank of Ireland Finance Ltd v. Daly Ltd* [1978] I.R. 79.
163 *Cunard S.S. Co. v. Hopwood* [1908] 2 Ch. 564.
164 s.99(7).
165 s.99(4).

istered in that country, in order to make the charge fully effective there, a certificate saying that the charge was presented for registration there must be lodged with the registry of companies here.[166] There is no express statutory provision about the consequences of contravening either of these requirements.

16–66 *Charge on Ship or Aircraft* In addition to the Mercantile Marine Act 1955's registration requirements,[167] a company charge on a "ship or any share in a ship" should be registered under section 99 of the 1963 Act.[168] The question of what exactly is a ship for these purposes arose in *Re South Coast Boatyard Ltd.*,[169] where it was held that charges on ocean going yachts were not registrable because the term "ship" here envisages vessels of burden as opposed to vessels whose primary function is to go as fast as possible. In 1990 charges on an aircraft or on any share in an aircraft were added to the catalogue.[170]

16–67 *Floating Charge* As has been explained above, a floating charge is a charge which is not specific. Because a company can continue carrying on its business in the ordinary way even though its entire assets may be the subject of a floating charge that can quite easily crystallise, it was essential in order to protect persons dealing with companies to require that these charges be registered. The duty to register every "floating charge on the undertaking or property of the company" includes floating charges over any part of the company's property.[171]

16–68 *Company Bills of Sale* For over a hundred years a special statutory scheme has existed under which bills of sale must be registered but such instruments given by companies are exempt from that scheme.[172] Nevertheless, section 99 of the 1963 Act requires that every charge created by or evidenced by "an instrument which, if executed by an individual, would require registration as a bill of sale" be registered under the Companies Acts.[173] Accordingly, a company's creditors get much the same kind of protection as the Bills of Sale Acts afford an individual's creditors. A bill of sale is not a transaction but is a written document that evidences a particular transaction, namely an as-

---

166 s.99(5).
167 s.50.
168 s.99(2)(h).
169 [1980] I.L.R.M. 186.
170 s.122(a) (amending s.99(2)(h)).
171 *Mercantile Bank of India Ltd v. Chartered Bank of India* [1937] 1 All E.R. 231 at 241.
172 *Re Royal Marine Hotel Co.* [1895] 1 I.R. 368.
173 See generally, Gough, *op. cit.*, Chap. 25.

surance of a legal or an equitable interest in chattels.[174] In the leading case under this heading, *Dublin City Distillery Ltd. v. Doherty*,[175] the company had sought to pledge stocks of whiskey which it had stored in a bonded warehouse as security for a loan, the purported pledge being by way of signed warrants and invoices representing different quantities of whiskey. It was held that these were not effective pledges. Even if they were pledges, it was held that, since they took a documentary form, they were bills of sale and, consequently, they should have been registered under the Companies Act.

16–69 A pledge, a contractual lien and a mortgage where the security-holder takes delivery of the goods are not registrable as bills of sale because proprietary title to the goods passed when possession of them passed to the security-holder. It has been held that a trust receipt is not registrable under these Acts;[176] nor are what are known as letters of lien, or of hypothecation,[177] or unambiguous retention of title clauses[178] so registrable.

16–70 Section 4 of the Bills of Sale (Ireland) Act 1879 exempts certain kinds of instruments from the registration requirement and, consequently, these need not be registered under the Companies Acts either. Most of these exceptions are routine dealings with stock, whether of a mercantile or of a funding nature; in particular, transfers of goods in the ordinary course of business, bills of sale for goods located abroad or at sea, bills of lading, warehouse-keepers' certificates, warrants or orders for the delivery of goods and other documents which are used in the ordinary course of business to prove possession or control of goods, or authorising the possessor to transfer or to receive the goods therein mentioned either by indorsement or by delivery. An instrument that should be registered by an individual as a bill of sale is not registrable under section 99 of the 1963 Act where it does not create a charge on the company's assets.

16–71 *Charge Securing Series of Debentures* Any form of charge given by a company "for the purpose of securing any issue of debentures" should be registered under section 99.[179] An issue of debentures is to

---

[174] The statutory definition is analysed in M. Forde, *Commercial Law* (2nd ed., 1997), pp. 226–229.
[175] [1914] A.C. 823.
[176] *Re David Allester Ltd* [1922] 2 Ch. 211.
[177] *Re Hamilton, Young & Co.* [1905] 2 K.B. 772.
[178] *Re W.J. Hickey Ltd* [1988] I.R. 126.

be distinguished from a single debenture; as is explained below,[180] the former is where several debentures are issued at one time; they are usually issued as part of a series, secured by a trust deed and are transferable as stock. In *Automobile Assn. (Canterbury) Inc. v. Australian Secured Deposits Ltd.*[181] it was held that a single debenture does not fall within this category and, accordingly, is not registrable unless it is caught by any of the other heads in section 99(2). The company there gave a charge over local government stock that it owned. Although that charge was a debenture, it was not a charge to secure an issue of debentures because the term "issue" in this context "must be construed as referring in a collective sense to the aggregate of a number of individual debentures issued by a company".[182] It would seem that the relevant series of debentures, for these purposes, need not be the company's own debentures.

16–72 *Charge on Industrial and Intellectual Property* Charges on "any patent or a licence under a patent, on a trademark or on a copyright or a licence under a copyright" should be registered under section 99 of the 1963 Act. A charge given on a patent should also be registered in the Patents Office in accordance with section 85 of the Patents Act 1992, in that no document which is unregistered will be admitted into evidence to show that the charge exists.

16–73 *Charge on Uncalled Capital and on Unpaid Calls* Charges given on "un-called share capital" and also on "calls made but not paid" are expressly made registrable under section 99.

16–74 *Charge on Goodwill* Goodwill is a somewhat peculiar asset and its actual value as a security is questionable. In any event, company charges on "goodwill" should be registered under section 99.

16–75 *Charge on Book Debts* Section 99 calls for charges on "book debts" to be registered but does not supply a definition for that term.[183] It has been held to mean "all such debts accruing in the ordinary course of a man's trade as are usually entered in trade books (or at least well kept books) but to constitute a book debt it is not necessary that the debt should be entered in a book."[184] Money due to a company otherwise than in the ordinary course of its trade are not book debts and,

---

[179] See generally, Gough, *op. cit.*, Chap. 24.
[180] Above, para. 16–44.
[181] [1973] N.Z.L.R. 417.
[182] *ibid.* at 425.
[183] See generally, Gough, *op. cit.*, Chap. 26.
[184] *Re Brian Tucker Ltd* [1990] 2 I.R. 549.

accordingly, are not registrable under section 99 of the 1963 Act unless that fund is caught by a floating charge or a charge securing an issue of debentures. This is the principal gap in the section 99 scheme, along with specific charges on stocks and shares. For instance, in *Re Brian Tucker Ltd.*[185] a charge given over the proceeds of an insurance policy was held not to be registrable, since that was not a book debt.[186] In *Byrne v. Allied Irish Banks Ltd.*[187] a charge over the actual proceeds of the sale of the company's premises was held not to be registrable for the same reason. In *Re Charge Card Services Ltd.*,[188] where the company entered into a security arrangement regarding its own trading indebtedness, although those sums were book debts, the arrangement was not registrable under section 99 for the simple reason that a charge in favour of a debtor of his own indebtedness to the chargor is conceptually impossible. But this reasoning has since met the disapproval of the House of Lords as, while perhaps logically compelling, being out of line with commercial practice.[189] The original draft of what became the 1990 Act proposed that this category be expanded to "a charge on any debts or other liabilities owing or incurred to the company."[190]

16–76 Section 99(6) provides that the deposit of a negotiable instrument, given to secure payment of book debts, for the purpose of securing an advance shall not be treated as a charge on those debts. Where goods are supplied to a company subject to reservation of title and the supply contract designates the company the supplier's fiduciary agent in respect of the proceeds of sub-sales until the price of the goods is paid, the contract is not registrable under this heading[191]unless all it does is create a charge over these sums.[192]

16–77 *Extending the Catalogue* As has been observed, the original proposals for the 1990 Act would have extended the above catalogue to all charges on funds accruing to the company; they also would have brought within the net any charge "on the company's interests in any stocks, shares or marketable securities."[193] However, a different approach was eventually adopted in section 122(b) of the 1990 Act (sections 99(2A–2Q of the 1963 Act), which enables the Minister, by order,

---

185 *ibid.*, following *Paul & Frank Ltd v. Discount Bank (Overseas) Ltd* [1967] 1 Ch. 348.
186 Similarly, *Jackson v. Lombard & Ulster Banking Ltd* [1992] 1 I.R. 94.
187 [1978] I.R. 446.
188 [1987] Ch. 150. Also *Northern Bank Ltd v. Ross* [1991] B.C.L.C. 504.
189 *Re Bank of Credit & Commerce International S.A. (No. 8)* [1998] A.C. 214.
190 Companies (Amendment) Bill 1987, s.94(5)(e).
191 *Re W.J. Hickey Ltd* [1988] I.R. 126.
192 *Carroll Group Distributors Ltd v. G. & J.F. Bourke Ltd* [1990] 1 I.R. 481.
193 Above, n. 34.

to add new heads of charge to those already enumerated. Presumably, extending the net to all debts and liabilities due to the company might give rise to certain practical difficulties in transactions between financial institutions, that it was thought better to leave the precise delineation of any extension. to a statutory instrument. This may also be the case with rendering charges on securities registrable.

Mechanics of Registration

16–78 Registration is effected by sending in the requisite information in time to the companies' registry.

Who Should Register?

16–79 Within 21 days of the charge being created or the series of debentures being issued, the company should send the requisite particulars and documents to the registrar of companies.[194] Where a charge has not been duly registered, the company and every officer in default can be prosecuted by the registrar and fined up to £500. Because failure to register renders a charge virtually worthless, section 100 of the 1963 Act also provides that any other person "interested therein" may apply to have the charge registered. An interested person, for these purposes, undoubtedly includes the chargee and anybody else with a security interest in the charge; there are no reported authorities on the scope of the term. Where the registration is done by such a person, he is entitled to recover from the company the registration fees.

Time for Registration

16–80 Section 99(1) of the 1963 Act stipulates that the charge must be duly registered "within 21 days after the date of its creation". Thus the relevant details and documents must be presented to the registrar within three weeks of the charge being given. However, section 106 of the Act gives the court a discretion to extend that time.[195]

16–81 The crucial concept for the purposes of timely registration is the date of the charge's "creation".[196] It depends on the parties' intentions and is a question of fact when the charge was actually created. A charge arising under a deed is created at the time the executed deed is

---

[194] s.100.

[195] See below, paras 16–86 *et seq*.

[196] See generally, Gough, *op. cit.*, Chap. 28. The same concept is used in s.288 of the 1963 Act. For invalidating floating charges given by insolvent companies within sux months of their being wound up; see below, paras 18–46 *et seq*.

delivered.[197] Where the company has agreed to give a charge on the occurrence of a particular contingency, the charge is not created until at least the contingency occurred.[198] A simple agreement to give a legal security can constitute creating a charge because the agreement operates immediately in equity as an equitable security; no further steps need be taken to give an effective security. It depends on the circumstances of the case and the parties' intentions whether an agreement to give security in the future creates an equitable charge or whether it was intended that a formal document must be executed at the time envisaged. However, where the agreement created an equitable charge and a formal charge was executed subsequently, the former merges in the latter, and the date of creation then becomes the time the formal charge was given.[199] Where an existing charge is cancelled and it is substituted with a new charge, the latter charge is created at the time it was given — and not as of the date the initial charge was given.[200] Instead of applying to the court for late registration of an unregistered charge, the parties may choose to "re-create" the security in this manner and then register the new charge.

16–82 Where a series of debentures are issued to several debenture-holders, section 92(8) of the 1963 Act stipulates that, in the case of a charge securing such a series, there shall be sufficient registration for the entire series if the required particulars are registered within 21 days after the covering trust deed was executed or, in the absence of such a deed, after the first debenture of the series has been executed. In the case of a charge created abroad over property that is located outside the State, the 21 days runs from the time when, in due course of post and if dispatched with due diligence, the particulars would have arrived in this country.[201]

Particulars to be Registered

16–83 What section 99(1) of the 1963 Act requires to be given to the registrar of companies are the "prescribed particulars of the charge verified in the prescribed manner".[202] While the Act does not specify in terms what these particulars are nor the method of verification, they can be ascertained from section 103 of the Act, which sets out the "fol-

---

197 *Esberger & Sons Ltd v. Capital & Counties Bank* [1913] 2 Ch. 366.
198 *Re Gregory Love & Co.* [1916] 1 Ch. 203.
199 *Re Columbian Fireproofing Co. Ltd* [1910] 2 Ch. 120; *Re Olderfleet Shipbuilding Co. Ltd* [1922] 1 I.R. 26.
200 *Re Cardiff Working Men's Cottage Co.* [1906] 2 Ch. 627 at 630.
201 1963 Act, s.99(3); *cf.* s.101.
202 See generally, Gough, *op. cit.*, Chap. 27.

lowing particulars" which must be entered on the register of charges, namely the date the charge was created by the company,[203] the amount secured by the charge, "short particulars" of the property charged and the persons entitled to the charge. It was proposed in 1987 that the particulars of the amount secured should include "a monetary limit of a fixed and definite sum" on that amount; this was omitted from the 1990 Act. In the case of a charge securing a series of debentures the holders of which rank *pari passu*, section 99(1) requires particulars of the total amounts secured by the whole series, the dates of the authorising resolutions and of the covering deed, if there is one, a "general description" of the property charged and the names of the trustees, if any.

16–84 Under statutory instrument No. 45 of 1964 Companies (Forms) Regulation, the companies' office has issued forms which set out the particulars to be registered, notably form No. 47. In the case of single mortgages and charges, this form is divided into five columns, which are headed as follows:

— Date and description of the instrument creating or evidencing the charge,
— Amount secured by the charge,
— Names, addresses and occupations of the person entitled to the charge,
— Short particulars of the property charged,[204]
— Amount and rate per cent of the commission.

Unlike the parallel provisions in Britain, section 99(1) contains no express obligation to furnish the registrar of companies with the instrument, if any, creating or evidencing the charge. But the form of verification required by the companies office is either being shown the original instrument, getting a certified copy of the instrument or a statement of the particulars verified by the company's seal. Form No. 47 would seem to preclude registration of all charges that are not evidenced in writing.[205] The 1963 Act applies the same registration scheme to charges over property which is located in the State and is owned by foreign-registered companies.[206]

---

203 *cf.* s.103(1)(b)(ii), (iii) for dates where the company acquires charged property and where a judgment mortgage is created.
204 For where all or part of the charged property is substituted by other property, see *Cornbrook Brewery Ltd v. Law Debenture Co. Ltd* [1904] 1 Ch. 103; *Bristol Utd. Breweries Co. v. Abbott* [1908] 1 Ch. 279 and *Cunard S.S. Co. v. Hopwood* [1908] 2 Ch. 564.
205 *cf. Re C.L. Nye Ltd* [1971] Ch. 442.
206 s.111.

16–85 Section 105 of the 1963 Act authorises the registrar of companies to record the fact that a debt has been satisfied, in whole or in part, or that some of the property or undertaking has been released from the charge or no longer belongs to the company. The registrar must be duly satisfied of these circumstances before recording a memorandum of satisfaction and must have notified the chargee or the judgment creditor, as the case may be. But there is no legal obligation on either companies or chargees to notify the registrar that a debt has been satisfied or that the property was released. Consequently, many companies' files give a distorted picture of outstanding charges.

Extending Time for Registration

16–86 Often creditors overlook the fact that their charge should have been registered until perhaps it becomes too late to do so. In much the same way as bills of sale which were not registered in time can be registered out of time, section 106 of the 1963 Act permits the late registration of company charges where the court so directs.[207] Before doing so, the court must be satisfied that the delay "was accidental, or due to inadvertence or to some other sufficient cause, or is not of a nature to prejudice the position of creditors or shareholders of the company . . . " Even where these matters cannot be established, the direction may be given where "on other grounds it is just and equitable to grant relief . . . " Where the court allows late registration of a charge, almost always it will give appropriate directions so that any intervening chargeholders will not thereby be prejudiced. For instance, in *Re O'Carroll Kent Ltd.*,[208] the company agreed to issue a mortgage debenture but, when they presented it to the companies' office, an official there said that it could not be registered; that what was needed was the actual debenture itself. It was ascertained later that this advice was wrong. The company then applied for late registration and was allowed to so do "without prejudice to rights of any parties acquired prior to the actual date the registration was affected."

16–87 When making an application of this nature, the court must be told the reason for the delay; it is not enough simply to say that the applicant acted inadvertently.[209] The court is given a very wide discretion here. Generally, an application will be refused when the company

---

207 See generally Gough, *op. cit.*, Chap. 31 and McCormack, "Extension of Time for Registration of Company Charges" [1986] J. Bus. L. 282.

208 (1955) 89 I.L.T.R. 72.

209 *Re Kris Cruisers Ltd* [1949] 1 Ch. 138.

is in liquidation[210] and even where an insolvent liquidation is imminent and manifestly cannot be avoided.[211] Nevertheless, special circumstances may warrant allowing registration in those cases. That happened in *O'Carroll Kent Ltd.*,[212] where in an earlier proceeding[213] the applicant for the extension got the court to appoint a receiver and manager to protect the assets charged under the debenture. However, Dixon J. added, when granting the extension of time, that if the company were indeed wound up, if the liquidator felt that his interests had been prejudiced by the court's order, he could take appropriate proceedings.

16–88 If late registration was permitted without any proviso, intervening chargees would be very seriously prejudiced. For the charge was always a valid charge, except that it was rendered unenforceable for not being registered. Once it becomes registered, without qualification, its priority position is based on the date the charge was granted. Accordingly, it would rank before subsequent charges which were obtained by persons who were completely unaware of its existence; even if they searched the company's register, no evidence of that charge would be disclosed. Accordingly, where an application for late registration is granted, it almost always is without prejudice to the rights of the parties acquired during the period between when the charge was created by the company and the date of its actual registration. This formula protects all intervening secured creditors.[214]

16–89 It is not regarded as protecting unsecured creditors.[215] However, the actual words used in the common formula do not expressly or by necessary implication confine its scope to secured creditors and an Irish court, in an appropriate case, might interpret it more generously. An obviously deserving case would be an unsecured creditor who gave the company substantial advances because he had consulted its file in the companies' office and learned that there was no charge over its assets. The practice in Australia is for the court to stipulate that unsecured creditors too should not be prejudiced where the circumstances so require.[216]

---

[210] *Re Ashpurton Estates Ltd* [1983] Ch. 110; *Re Farm Fresh Frozen Foods Ltd* [1980] I.L.R.M. 131.
[211] *Re Barrrow Borough Transport Ltd* [1990] 1 Ch. 227; *Re Telomatic Ltd* [1994] 1 B.C.L.C. 90.
[212] 89 I.L.T.R. 72 (1955); also in *Re Braemar Investments Ltd* [1989] 1 Ch. 54.
[213] *Alexander Hull & Co. v. O'Carroll Kent & Co.*, 89 I.L.T.R. 70 (1955).
[214] *cf. Re Fablehill Ltd* [1991] B.C.L.C. 830.
[215] *Watson v. Duff, Morgan & Vermont Holdings Ltd* [1974] 1 W.L.R. 450.
[216] *Re Flinders Trading Co. Property Ltd* (1978) 3 A.C.L.R. 218.

Conclusiveness of Registrar's Certificate

16–90 When a charge is registered, section 104 of the 1963 Act provides that the registrar of companies shall issue a certificate to that effect and that his certificate shall be "conclusive evidence" that the requirements regarding registration were complied with. Once they have this certificate, secured creditors can be confident that their charge cannot be challenged for not being duly registered in time, as required. A vexed question, however, concerns details in the charge which are incorrect, most notably, the date the charge was given. Say the charge was created on January 1 but it was not until February 2 that the chargee addressed his mind to registration. Say that, rather than apply to the court for an extension of time, the chargee substituted January 22 for the creation date and then registers the charge. Does section 104 prevent, say, an intervening chargee or a liquidator from contesting that registration?

16–91 This matter has not yet been dealt with in the Irish courts but it and related questions have given rise to litigation in Britain.[217] The position adopted there is that the courts are bound by the statutory presumption of conclusiveness[218] and proceedings will not be entertained even to have the certificate rectified in an application for judicial review.[219] However, a party who suffers loss on account of the presumption of compliance may have redress under the law of tort. Because of the Constitution, an Irish court might not look so lightly on an "irrebuttable presumption".[220] If the alteration was made deliberately, a creditor who was thereby prejudiced would have a strong case in fraud. If the alteration was purely accidental, that creditor might have a good case in negligence.

DEBENTURES

16–92 Company indebtedness is frequently described with reference to debentures,[221] for instance that a company has issued debentures to a creditor or a creditor holds debentures from a company. Legislation

---

[217] See generally, Gough *op. cit.*, Chap. 29. Prentice, "Defectively Registered Charges" (1970) 34 Conv. 410 and McCormack, "Conclusiveness in the Registration of Company Charge Procedure" (1989) 10 Co. Law. 175.

[218] *Re C.L. Nye Ltd* [1971] 1 Ch. 442; *Exeter Trust Ltd v. Screenways Ltd* [1991] B.C.L.C. 888.

[219] *R. v. Registrar of Companies, ex p. Central Bank of India* [1986] Q.B. 1114.

[220] *cf. State (McEldowney) v. Kelleher* [1983] I.R. 289.

[221] See generally, Gough, *op. cit.*, pp. 645–655.

frequently refers to debentures; thus Part III of the 1963 Act is headed "Share Capital and Debentures" and sections 91-98 of that Act are headed "Special Provisions as to Debentures". In 1934 an Act entitled the Agricultural Co-Operative Societies (Debentures) Act was passed. Several of the statutory provisions which define the term "securities" define it as including debentures and debenture stock.[222] The term debenture signifies an instrument or document creating or acknowledging indebtedness of some permanence. Debentures issued by companies often possess several of the following characteristics: they are one of a series of debentures, they provide for repayment of a principal sum on a named date or on a specified event occurring, they provide for payment of interest on the debt and they contain a charge on the company's property securing the debt. Questions of whether an instrument is a debenture arise in several different contexts, for instance, whether the instrument is exempt from registration under the Bills of Sales Acts[223] whether it must be registered as a charge under section 99 of the 1963 Act,[224] whether a register of the holders of the instruments must be left open to inspection[225] and whether the instrument represents an equity interest or indebtedness for stamp duty or for other taxation purposes.[226] For a comprehensive account of the law regarding debentures, the reader should consult the now 80-years-old Part III of *Palmer's Company Precedents*.[227]

Nature of Debentures

16–93 The term debenture is not a technical one; there is no precise received legal definition of the term. Lindley L.J. once observed that

> "What the correct meaning of 'debenture' is I do not know. I do not find anywhere any precise definition of it. We know that there are various kinds of instruments commonly called debentures. You may have mortgage debentures, which are charges of some kind on property. You may have debentures which are bonds; . . . You may have a debenture which is nothing more than an acknowledgement of indebtedness. And you may have a thing like this, which is something more; it is a statement by two directors that the company will pay a certain sum of money on a given day, and will also pay interest half-yearly at certain times and at a

---

222 *e.g.* Exchange Control Act 1957, s.3 and Central Bank Act 1971, s.2.

223 *e.g. Edmonds v. Blaina Furnaces Co.* (1887) 36 Ch.D. 215; *Levy v. Abercorris Slate and Slab Co.* (1887) 37 Ch.D. 260.

224 See above, para. 16–71.

225 *e.g Lemon v. Austin Friars Investment Trust* [1926] 1 Ch. l.

226 *e.g. British India Steam Navigation Co. v. I.R.C.* (1881) 7 Q.B.D. 165; *I.R.C. v. Pullman Car Co.* [1954] 2 W.L.R. 1029; *Handevel Property Ltd v. Comptroller of Stamps* (1986) 60 A.L.J.R. 40.

227 A. Topham (12th ed., 1920).

> certain place, upon production of certain coupons by the holder of the instrument."[228]

An abundance of judicial dicta exists affirming the impossibility of giving a comprehensive definition of a debenture. According to Chitty, J., "it has no legal definition (but) the term itself imports a debt — an acknowledgement of a debt — and speaking of the numerous and various forms of instruments which have been called debentures without anyone being able to say the term is incorrectly used. . . . generally, if not always, the instrument imports an obligation or covenant to pay".[229] According to Pollock M.R., "whatever the characteristics which you would expect to find or may find in the debentures, the root meaning of the word is "indebtedness"; that it does record an indebtedness".[230] Debentures are often issued as part of a series but single debentures are very common.[231] While debentures are usually secured by a charge, they can be unsecured.[232] Sometimes the term debenture is used colloquially to refer to the security given for the debt evidenced by the debenture. Although the term has an extensive meaning, it does not encompass instruments like bills of exchange or promissory notes,[233] deeds of covenant or several other types of documents in which a company undertakes to pay a sum of money.

16–94 Section 2(1) of the 1963 Act provides a partial definition for the term: "debenture includes debenture stock, bonds and any other securities of a company whether constituting a charge on the assets of the company or not".[234] Debenture stock means a series of debentures that are transferable.[235] Apart entirely from section 2(1), instruments that describe themselves as bonds can be debentures; historically, debentures grew out of bonds. The term securities' ordinarily includes shares as well as other instruments[236] but, in the context of section 2(1) above, debentures cannot include shares. Indeed, the term debenture as used in some parts of the Companies Acts has a more limited meaning than in section 2(1) above; for instance, sections 91–98 of the 1963 Act concerning special provisions as to debentures deal only with debentures that are issued in a series and are registered. Because an instrument describes itself as a debenture, or does not do so, is not conclusive as to

---

228 *British India* case, above, n. 226, at pp.172–173.
229 Above, n. 223, at p. 219.
230 Above, n. 225, at p. 13.
231 *e.g. Knigbtsbridge Estates Trust v. Byrne* [1940] A.C. 613.
232 *e.g. Wyhe v. Carylon* [1922] 1 Ch. 51.
233 See above, n. 225, at p. 20.
234 On the background to this section, see above, n. 231, pp. 619–621.
235 See below, para. 16–99.
236 See above, n. 222.

whether or not it is a debenture; what matters is the substance of the instrument itself. As Chitty J. observed in one instance,

> "In determining what is or is not a debenture . . . I am not bound to hold that the instrument is a debenture because it is called a debenture by the company issuing it, not to hold it is not a debenture because it is not so called by the company. I must look at the substance of the instrument itself, and, without the assistance of any precise legal definition, form the best opinion 1 can whether the instrument (is a debenture)."[237]

Sample Debentures

16–95 Debentures are usually given in the form of sealed instruments and are subject to the same general principles regarding *ultra vires* and agency as other company contracts. Unless the company's articles of association require a seal to be used, it has been held that sealing is not necessary.[238] But there is a later decision of the Irish Supreme Court[239] holding that assignments of debts must be sealed because they are not "ordinary contracts", from which it could be argued that debentures, especially creating a charge on land, must be sealed.

16–96 Perusal of the two sample debentures should convey a better understanding of this topic. In one of the early leading Irish cases on company charges, *Re Dublin Drapery Co. Ltd.*,[240] the debenture there recited as follows:

> "M'SWINEY & COMPANY (Limited).
> "Offices — No. 23, Lower Sackville-street, Dublin.
> "Bankers — The Hibernian Banking Company.
> "Issue of £15,000 in Debentures, ranking equally.
> "No.25. Debenture for £100.
> "M'Swiney & Co. (Limited), in consideration of the sum of the One Hundred Pounds, paid by John Joseph Cox, of 37, Upper Mount-street, in the county of the city of Dublin, hereby covenant with the said John Joseph Cox, his executors, administrators and assigns, to pay the said John Joseph Cox, or to the bearer hereof, on the 31st day of January, 1886, at the registered office or principal office, or the bankers of the Company, the sum of One Hundred Pounds; and also to pay, by way of interest thereon, at the rate of £5 per cent. per annum, to the bearer of every coupon hereto annexed, at the time and place in such coupon mentioned, such sum of money as in such coupon is mentioned. And the said Company do hereby charge with such payments the undertaking, stock-in-trade, lands, premises, works, plant, property and effects (both present and future), of

---

[237] *Edmonds v. Blaina Furnaces Co.* (1887) 36 Ch.D. 215 at 220.
[238] *Re Fireproof Doors Ltd* [1916] 2 Ch. 142.
[239] *Re A Debtor's Summons* [1929] I.R. 139; see above, para. 13–05.
[240] (1884) 13 L.R. Ir. 174.

the said Company, to the intent that this security and the other securities forming part of the above-named issue of £15,000 may rank equally as a first charge upon the said undertaking, stock-in-trade, lands, premises and other property and effects, but so that the same may be a floating security, not hindering any sale, exchange or lease of the said lands or premises, or any of them, or the receipt or payment of any moneys, or any other dealings in the course of the business of the said Company, but attaching to the premises leased, and the proceeds of any sale or exchange, and the lands or other property purchased therewith, or with any moneys of the Company. Provided further, that the bearer of these presents, or of any of the coupons hereto annexed, shall be entitled to the payment of the money intended to be secured by such respective instruments without being affected by any right of set-off, or other right or equity, of the said Company against the original or any intermediate holder of such respective instruments, and that the receipt of the bearer shall be an effectual discharge for such money. And the Company, or persons paying such money, shall not be bound to inquire into the title of the bearer, or to take notice of any trust affecting such money, or be affected by express notice of any trust affecting such money, or be affected by express notice of any equity which may then be subsisting in relation to the title of the bearer, or to the instrument presented for payment, or the money intended to be thereby secured.

"Given under the common seal of the said Company, the 31st day of January, 1876.

"P.J. Plunkett,
Two of the Directors
"Patrick Griffin,".

16–97 The following sample of a much more elaborate debenture is taken from Palmer's *Company Law* (23rd ed., 1982).

The . . . Company Limited
Issue of £100,000 of debentures of £100 each, carrying interest at x per cent per annum,
For valuable consideration already received[241]

DEBENTURE

1. The . . . Company Limited (hereinafter called "the company") will, on the . . . day of . . . . or on such earlier day as the principal moneys hereby secured become payable in accordance with the conditions indorsed hereon, pay to A B of or other the registered holder for the time being hereof, the sum of £100.[242]

[241] Where the instrument is a deed it is not necessary to refer to the consideration for the debenture, although there may be some advantage in referring to it. But the consideration ought to be stated where the instrument is under hand.

[242] Where the loan is temporary, or where it is a bank overdraft, the instrument

Payment of Interest

2. The company will, during the continuance of this security, pay to such registered holder interest thereon at the rate of . . . per cent, per annum by half-yearly payments on the . . . day of . . . and . . . day of . . . in each year, the first of such half-yearly payments or a proportionate part thereof, calculated from the date of issue of this Debenture, to be made on the . . . day of . . . next.[243]

Charges

3. The company hereby charges with such payments its undertaking, and all its property, present and future, including its uncalled capital for the time being.[244]

Reference to indorsed conditions

4. This debenture is issued subject to, and with the benefit of, the conditions indorsed hereon, which shall be deemed to be incorporated herewith.[245]

Sealing

Given under the common seal of the company" this . . . day of . . . Affixed in the presence of . . . . (L.S.)

The conditions within referred to[246]

"Pari passu" clause

1. This debenture is one of a series of 1,000 debentures, each for securing the principal sum of £100 and interest. The debentures of the said series are all to rank *pari passu* in point of charge without any preference or priority one over another[247] and such charge (save as regards the

---

may stipulate that the money shall be repayable on demand in writing, or on the expiry of x days after demand is made in writing.

243 Had the terms said that interest at a certain rate was payable for the duration of the loan, this could be read as interest at that rate until the due payment date and, therefore, damages would be paid for breach of the agreement and those damages would include a reasonable sum for loss of interest payments. *Re Roberts* (1880) 14 Ch.D. 49. Furthermore, where this formula is not used, then if the holder obtained judgment on the debenture the interest would thereupon cease to be payable under it, for the contract would merge in the judgment, which presently carries interest at 8 per cent: *Re European Central Railway Co.* (1876) 4 Ch.D. 33.

244 This creates a good equitable mortgage over the assets charged, although it is not imperative to use the term charge; any cognate expression will suffice.

245 Debentures are usually given under seal, but a seal is not essential: see above, para. 13–05.

246 The conditions will usually be endorsed on the back of the instrument.

247 This places all the debentures in the series on the same level as to security: *cf. Re Smelting Corp.* [1915] 1 Ch. 172. Otherwise the debentures would rank in point of security according to the dates on which they were issued, which would

hereditaments comprised in the trust deed below mentioned) is to be a floating security,[248] but so that the company is not to be at liberty to create any mortgage or charge upon its property or assets or any part thereof so as to rank *pari passu* with or in priority to the debentures of this series except specific charges for securing temporary loans or overdrafts in the ordinary course of business.[249]

Register to be kept

2. A register of the debentures will be kept at the company's registered office wherein there will be entered the names, addresses and descriptions of the registered holders and particulars of the debentures held by them respectively, and such register will at all reasonable times during business hours be open to the inspection of the registered holder hereof, and his legal personal representatives and any person authorised in writing by him or them.[250]

Registered holder only recognised

3. The registered holder, or his legal personal representatives, will be regarded as exclusively entitled to the benefit of this debenture, and all persons may act accordingly; and the company shall not be bound to enter in the register notice of any trust, or, save as herein provided, and except as by some court of competent jurisdiction ordered, to recognise any trust or equity affecting the title to the debenture or the moneys thereby secured, save (as herein provided or) as ordered by a court of competent jurisdiction.[251]

Transfer

4. Every transfer of this debenture must be in writing under the hand of the registered holder or his legal personal representatives.[252] The transfer must be delivered at the registered office of the company (with a fee of 15p) and such evidence of title or identity as the company may reasonably require and thereupon (if this debenture remains registered in the name of the transferor the transferee will be recognised as having become entitled to the benefit of this debenture free from any equities, set-off or cross-claims which, but for this provision, the company would be entitled to set up against the transferor and) the transfer will be regis-

---

render them virtually worthless as security: *Re New Clydach Co.* (1868) L.R. 6 Eq. 514.

248 On floating security, see above, paras 16–12 *et seq*.

249 On the position of later mortgages and charges. see below, paras 18–107 *et seq*.

250 *cf.* 1963 Act, ss. 91, 92 on the duty to keep a register of debenture-holders, and rendering the register available to inspection by any registered debenture-holder or shareholder and by anybody else on the payment of a small fee.

251 This obliges the company to recognise the registered holder exclusively and relieves the company of the obligation to take notice of any trust or equity in the debenture: see below, paras 16–113 *et seq*.

252 On transfers generally. see below, paras 16–111 *et seq*.

tered and a note of such registration will be indorsed hereon. The company shall be entitled to retain the transfer.

Joint holder

5. In the case of joint registered holders, the principal moneys and interest hereby secured shall be deemed to be owing to them on a joint account.

Closing of register

6. No transfer shall be registered during the fourteen days immediately preceding the date by this debenture fixed for payment of interest.[253]

Exclusion of equities

7. The principal moneys and interest hereby secured will be paid (and such moneys are to be transferable free from and) without regard to any equities between the company and the original or any intermediate holder hereof, or any set-off or cross-claim, and the receipt of the registered holder for such principal moneys and interest shall be a good discharge to the company for the same.[254]

Notice by company to pay off

8. The company may at any time give notice in writing to the registered holder hereof, his executors or administrators, of its intention to pay off this debenture, and, upon the expiration of six months from such notice being given, the principal moneys hereby secured shall become payable.[255]

Immediate payment where default as to interest or winding up

9. The principal moneys hereby secured shall immediately become payable:

(a) If the company makes default for a period of six months in the payment of any interest hereby secured, and the registered holder hereof, before such interest is paid, by notice in writing to the company, calls in such principal moneys[256] or

(b) If an order is made or an effective resolution is passed for the winding up of the company; or

(c) If a distress or execution is levied or enforced upon or against any of the chattels or property of the company, and is not paid or discharged within five days; or

---

253 This relieves the company of the considerable administrative inconvenience of having to calculate the interest while transfers are still being registered.

254 This prevents the transferee of a debenture being adversely affected by latent equities that subsisted between the company and a previous debenture holder: see below, para. 16–114.

255 As to the method of giving notice, see clause 13.

256 Accordingly, the creditor can demand repayment of the principal when the interest gets badly in arrears.

(d) If a receiver is appointed of the undertaking of the company or any of its property or assets; or

(e) If the company ceases or threatens to cease to carry on its business.[257]

Automatic Crystallisation where Default[258]

9A. The principal moneys hereby secured shall immediately become due and payable and the charge hereby created shall immediately attach and become affixed:

(a)-(e) as in 9 above

(f) If the company mortgages charges or encumbers or attempts to mortgage charge or encumber any of its property or assets contrary to the provisions of clause 1 hereof without the prior written consent of the registered holder.

Warrant for Interest

10. In respect of each half-year's interest on this debenture a warrant on the company's bankers payable to the order of the registered holder hereof, or, in the case of joint holders, to the order of that one whose name stands first in the register as one of such joint holders, will be sent by post to the registered address of such registered holder, and the company shall not be responsible for any loss in transmission. The payment of the warrant, if purporting to be duly indorsed, shall be a good discharge to the company.

Power to appoint receiver[259]

11. At any time after the principal moneys hereby secured become payable (or after the security constituted by the trust deed below mentioned becomes enforceable) the registered holder of this debenture may from time to time, with the consent in writing of the holders of the majority in value of the outstanding debentures of the same series, appoint by writing any person or persons (approved by the trustees of the said trust deed) to be a receiver or receivers of the property charged by the debentures (and not comprised in such trust deed), and may with the like consent apply to the court to remove any such receiver, and every such appointment or removal shall be as effective as if all the holders of debentures of the same series had concurred therein, and a receiver so appointed shall have power

(1) to take possession of, collect and get in the property charged by the debentures, and for that purpose to take all proceedings in the name of the company or otherwise as may seem expedient;

---

[257] But showing that a company has ceased to do business can be difficult and it can be even more difficult to show that it threatens to stop trading.

[258] It remains to be seen whether the Irish courts would give effect to automatic crystallisation clauses: see above, para. 16–46.

[259] For receivers, see below, paras 16–117 *et seq*.

(2) to carry on or concur in carrying on the business of the company, and for that purpose to raise money on the premises charged in priority to the debentures or otherwise;

(3) to sell or concur in selling all or any of the property charged by the debentures after giving to the company at least seven days' notice of his intention to sell, and to carry any such sale into effect by conveying in the name and on behalf of the company or otherwise;

(4) to make any arrangement or compromise which he or they shall think expedient in the interest of the debenture holders.

A receiver so appointed shall be deemed to be the agent of the company and the company shall be solely responsible for his acts or defaults and for his remuneration.

Trust deed referred to

11A. The holders of the debentures of this issue are and will be entitled *pari passu* to the benefit of, and subject to the provisions contained in, a trust deed dated the .. day of . . . , and made between the company of the one part and .. and . . . of the other part, whereby (certain property) was charged in favour of trustees for securing the payment of the principal moneys and interest payable in respect of the said debentures.[260]

Place of Payment

12. The principal moneys and interest hereby secured will be paid at . . . Bank Limited, No . . . . Street, Dublin, or at the registered office of the company.

Service of notices on holder

13. A notice may be served by the company upon the holder of this debenture by sending it through the post in a prepaid letter addressed to such person at his registered address. Any notice served by post shall be deemed to have been served at the expiration of twenty-four hours after it is posted, and in proving such service it shall be sufficient to prove that the letter containing the notice was properly addressed and put into the post office.

Some Types of Debenture

16–98 Given the very extensive concept of what is a debenture, there are a great variety of kinds of debenture. For instance, a debenture may be a single one or may form part of a series; it may be secured or unsecured; it may be convertible into the company's shares and it may

---

[260] This requirement goes in where there is a trust deed; see below, para. 16–106. Its effect is to render the security subject to the duties in the trust deed and also entitled to the benefit of it.

be irredeemable. The following types of debenture call for some special mention.

Debenture Stock

16–99 Most debentures are instruments given to a single creditor who is owed money by the company.[261] But debentures are popularly regarded as something that are issued in a series of debenture stock and that are transferable in much the same way as shares. Public companies occasionally make prospectus offers to the public to apply for debenture stock, although, like public issues of preference shares, new issues of debentures to the investing public rarely occur these days. A debenture is almost always for a definite or ascertainable sum and can only be transferred in its entirety. But debenture stock is a portion of some large debenture, which can be transferred in fractional amounts and which can be consolidated into larger holdings. With debenture stock, sums are advanced to the company by numerous persons, but those sums comprise a single loan fund, the lenders being issued with stock certificates evidencing the fractional amount of that fund which is theirs. Ordinarily, the company's regulations or the terms of issue will stipulate the basic unit of which the debenture stock may be transferred — units of £1 or of £5, or whatever. Debenture stock is usually constituted by a trust deed which provides for the security and for appointing a trustee to act on the stockholders' behalf.[262] The trustee's principal function is to ensure that the terms of the loan agreement are adhered to by the company and to otherwise safeguard the security. Where debentures are issued in a series ranking *pari passu*, every company is required to keep a register of debenture-holders containing their names and addresses, and stating the amounts held by each of them.[263] This register must be open to inspection by any person. Every charge given by a company over its property to secure any issue of debentures must be registered in the manner set out in sections 99–112 of the 1963 Act.[264]

Perpetual Debentures

16–100 Many debentures stipulate a time within which they must be redeemed. But it has long been customary to issue instruments described as perpetual or irredeemable debentures, which are redeem-

[261] *e.g.* the debenture in *Re Dublin Drapery Co.* (1884) 13 L.R. Ir. 174.
[262] See below, para. 16–106 *et seq*.
[263] 1963 Act, ss. 91, 92.
[264] *cf. Automobile Association (Canterbury Inc.) v. Australian Secured Deposits Ltd* [1973] 1 N.Z.L.R. 417.

able only in the event of the company being wound up or on some other very grave default by the company. Doubts arose whether the prolonged postponement of the right of redemption was a "clog on the equity" of redemption and rendered those instruments ineffective and void.[265] In order to put an end to such doubts, section 94 of the 1963 Act was enacted, according to which:

> "A condition contained in any debentures or in any deed for securing any debentures, whether issued or executed before or after the operative date, shall not be invalid by reason only that the debentures are thereby made irredeemable or redeemable only on the happening of a contingency, however remote, or on the expiration of a period, however long, notwithstanding any rule of law to the contrary."

In *Knightsbridge Estates Trust Ltd. v. Byrne*[266] a company that had mortgaged its land to a single mortgagee with the redemption date postponed to a distant period sought a declaration that, on account of the "clog" doctrine, it should be permitted to redeem the loan at an earlier date. But it was held that the mortgage fell within section 2(1) of the 1963 Act's definition of a debenture and, accordingly, by virtue of section 94 of that Act, its redemption date would not be cut down by a court of equity. Section 94 does not validate a debenture where its terms, other than those relating to the date of maturity, constitute a clog on the equity of redemption.[267]

Convertible Debentures

16–101 A convertible debenture is one that entitles the owner thereof, on or after a certain date or on some contingency occurring, to convert the debenture into shares in the company. Where conversion occurs, the debenture-holder ceases to be a creditor of the company and instead becomes one of its members. Convertible debentures tend to be issued where the company is seeking to raise funds but either cannot or does not wish to issue shares at that particular time. Frequently, the business will be somewhat risky and investors will be reluctant to acquire an equity stake in it until it proves successful, but they may be prepared to lend funds with the option to convert the loan into equity at a later stage. Unlike shares, debentures may be issued at a discount.[268] However, convertible debentures must ensure that the conversion into shares is not at a rate less than the shares' par value.[269] There are de-

---

265 *cf. Snell's Principles of Equity* (28th ed., 1982), pp. 390–394.
266 [1940] A.C. 613.
267 *e.g. Samuel v. Jarrah Timber etc. Ltd* [1904] A.C. 323.
268 *e.g. Re Regent's Canal Ironworks Co.* (1876) 3 Ch.D. 43.
269 *Moseley v. Koftyfontein Mines Ltd* [1904] 2 Ch. 108; *Famatina Development Corp. v. Bury* [1910] A.C. 439.

tailed provisions in the Yellow Book regarding convertible debentures.

Debentures to Bearer

16–102 Usually the principal outstanding and the interest accruing on debentures are payable to the registered holders thereof. But debentures that are payable to bearer can exist,[270] as can debentures with interest coupons that are payable to their bearers. Unless the instrument otherwise provides, a bearer debenture is a negotiable instrument.[271] Those instruments nevertheless are rare because, by virtue of section 10 of the Exchange Control Act 1954, they may only be issued with the Central Bank's permission and the Bank is most reluctant to authorise them.

Interest Payable from Profits

16–103 Usually the interest to be paid to debenture-holders is payable every year as a fixed percentage of the capital sum. But a loan made to the company, the interest which is payable out of profits when earned, has been held to be a debenture. This was in *Lemon* v. *Austin Friars Investment Trust Ltd.*,[272] which concerned a document in which the company acknowledged that it owed a sum of money to the registered holder, described itself as an "income stock certificate", bore a number and was one of a series. The fact that it did not in plain words provide for repayment of the entire loan in specified circumstances did not prevent it from being a debenture; it most likely was an implied term that the money became repayable in the event of the company being wound up. The instrument merely said that the loan was to be repaid from three-quarters of the company's profits as and when profits were earned, which entitled the holder to an enforceable charge on a fractional proportion of the profits when ascertained. It was held that the instrument satisfied "the primary qualification of a debenture . . . namely, that it is an acknowledgement of indebtedness, and the fact that the possibility of payment is limited to three-fourths of the net profits may make the expectation of repayment less than it would otherwise be, but it does not prevent the fact of there being a source from which this recorded indebtedness may be resolved."[273]

---

[270] *e.g. Re Dublin Drapery Co.* (1884) 13 L.R. 1s., 174, and above, para. 16–96.
[271] *Edelstein v. Schuler & Co.* [1902] 2 K.B. 144.
[272] [1926] 1 Ch. 1.
[273] [1926] 1 Ch. 1 at 15.
[274] *e.g. Re Quest Cae Ltd* [1985] B.C.L.C. 266.

Agreement to Secure an Unspecified Amount

16–104 Although debentures usually are issued in respect of a fixed principal sum, at times instruments describing themselves as debentures are issued in respect of unspecified sums, for instance the "all moneys" debenture taken by banks to secure sums advanced by way of overdraft.[274] In *Re White & Shannon Ltd.*[275] the question was raised whether an agreement to secure an unspecified amount can be a debenture, but McVeigh J. would venture no further than observing that "indebtedness in a principal sum is the significant and primary characteristic of a debenture."[276] This question was subsequently answered in the affirmative in England by Lloyd J.,[277] on the grounds that there were no authorities to the effect that those instruments were not debentures, and he would not be the first to so decide.

Agreement to Issue Debentures

16–105 Because equity looks on that as done which ought to be done,[278] an agreement to issue a debenture is a debenture.[279] As one judge put it, "[a]ssuming that there is a clear definite contract to have debentures issued to them in respect of the loan . . . they have as good a claim as any debentures could give them, except that their claim is equitable and not legal."[280] Where such an agreement constitutes a charge securing debentures, particulars of it must be registered at the registry of companies within 21 days of the charge being created;[281] depending on the circumstances, the court may permit an extension of the time for registration.

Trust Deeds

16–106 Where debentures or debenture stock are issued in a series, they are usually secured by a trust deed.[282] These deeds typically convey the charged property to trustees for the debenture-holders, might charge other property and will contain conditions concerning the debenture and the company's property — like covenanting to repay the capital sum and pay the interest, requiring the company to insure and properly maintain the property, specifying the circumstances in which

---

[275] [1965] N.I. 15.
[276] *ibid.* at 20.
[277] *N.V. Slavenburg's Bank v. International Resources Ltd* [1980] 1 W.L.R. 1076.
[278] *Snell's Principles of Equity* (28th ed., 1982), p. 41.
[279] *Levy v. Abercorris State and Slab Co.* (1887) 37 Ch.D. 260.
[280] *Re Queensland Land & Coal Co.* [1894] 3 Ch. 181 at 183–184.
[281] See above, para. 16–52.
[282] See precedent above, para. 16.97, clause 11A.

the security will become enforceable, *e.g.* default, breach of other conditions, winding up, etc., in such circumstances empowering the trustees to appoint a receiver and manager over the property, authorising the trustee to sell the property and to pay off the loan and any outstanding interest with the proceeds, provide for keeping a register of the stock holders, for issuing them with stock certificates, for meetings of the stockholders, etc.

Remuneration

16–107 Provision is usually made in trust deeds for remunerating the trustees. Whether or not trustees are entitled to be paid after the receiver has been appointed depends on the terms of the remuneration clause. As was said in *Re British Consolidation Oil Corp.*, "the real question is what is the true construction of the trust deed."[283] It was held that the remuneration clause in that case was "not one which gives the trustees remuneration only if they can prove that they have done substantial or any work in each year" but was one that, "whether their duties are onerous or light, they are to be entitled to have the stipulated remuneration until the security comes to an end".[284]

Indemnity

16–108 In the past it was a common practice for trust deeds to contain an indemnity clause, but the scope of such provisions are now limited significantly by the 1963 Act. According to section 93 of the Act:

> "any provision contained in a trust deed for securing an issue of debentures, or in any contract with the holders of debentures secured by a trust deed, shall be void in so far as it would have the effect of exempting a trustee thereof from or indemnifying him against liability for breach of trust where he failed to show the degree of care and diligence required of him as trustee, having regard to the provisions of the trust deed conferring on him any powers, authorities or discretions."

This does not preclude every conceivable type of indemnity; trustees may be exonerated from liability for breach of their duties in at least two or possibly three circumstances. A release may be given in respect of a breach that occurred prior to the release. A provision in the deed may enable a majority of at least three-quarters in value of the debenture-holders to give a release in respect of some prior specific breach, or on the trustee dying or ceasing to act.[285] The third case is where the

---

283 [1919] 2 Ch. 81 at 92.
284 *ibid.*
285 1963 Act, s.93(2).

clause was in force on April 1, 1964, and the trustee concerned has remained a trustee of the deed.[286] The benefit of such a clause can be extended to other trustees if a majority or not less than three-quarters in value of the debenture-holders vote to do so.[287]

Majority Clauses

16–109 Trust deeds frequently contain majority clauses, *i.e.* clauses providing that the terms of the trust may be varied or abrogated with the consent of a stipulated majority of the debenture-holders or stock-holders, as the case may be. These clauses give the company and the trustees some flexibility to deal with unforeseen events. As is the case with altering a company's articles of association,[288] the court will not permit the stipulated majority to abuse their power to modify the trust deed's terms. As it was put in *Goodfellow v. Nelson Line (Liverpool) Ltd.*:

> "The powers conferred by the trust deed on a majority of the debenture-holders must, of course be exercised bona fide, and the court can no doubt interfere to prevent unfairness or oppression, but, subject to this, each debenture-holder may vote with regard to his individual interests, though these interests may be peculiar to himself and not shared by the other debenture-holders. . . . [W]here . . . there is, as between different holders, a diversity of interest, it may be necessary or advisable as a matter of business fairness to make special provision for special interests, and . . . there is [no] equity precluding a debenture-holder voting for or against a scheme containing such special provision merely because he is interested thereunder. . . . [H]owever, . . . where there are diverse interests, and none the less where those interests are specially provided for, the court ought to consider carefully the fairness of any scheme by which a majority of debenture-holders seeks to bind a minority."[289]

16–110 A secret bargain by one debenture-holder for special treatment might be considered as grounds for setting aside a majority vote to amend the deed.[290] A modification of the terms that substitutes shares and debentures, even shares and debentures of another company, for the existing debentures is not impermissible.[291] But a majority will never be permitted to sanction a sale by the company of all its assets in order

---

[286] 1963 Act, s.93(3).
[287] *ibid.*, s.93(4).
[288] *Allen v. Gold Reefs of West Africa Co.* [1900] 1 Ch. 656.
[289] [1912] 2 Ch.324, at pp. 333–334, approved in *British America Nickel Corp. v. O'Brien* [1927] A.C. 369. See also *Mercantile Investment etc. Trust Co. v. River Plate etc. Co.* [1894] 1 Ch. 578.
[290] *e.g. British America Nickel Corp. v. O'Brien* [1927] A.C. 369.
[291] *e.g. Re Hutchinson & Son Ltd* (1915) 31 T.L.R. 324.

that the proceeds be divided other than pro rata among the debenture-holders, such as among those holders who are willing to accept the lowest prices for their debentures.[292]

Transfer of Debentures

16–111 The 1963 Act defines company shares as "personal estate, transferable in manner provided by the articles of the company . . . "[293] There is no equivalent definition for debentures, which are contractual rights against a company and the transfer of which, accordingly, is governed by the general principles regarding the assignment of contracts. Section 28(6) of the Supreme Court of Judicature (Ireland) Act 1877 authorises the transfer of debts and other choses in action by writing, provided that the debtor has been duly notified;[294] but any such transfer is subject to existing equities. Debentures payable to bearer are negotiable instruments and, therefore, their ownership changes hands by mere delivery of the document and is not encumbered by any existing equities.[295] Debentures or debenture stock, the holders of which are registered with the company, are transferable in the same way as shares, *i.e.* by executing a proper instrument of transfer or by vesting in another person by operation of law, as on the debenture-holder's death. Unlike the position with shares in a company, there is no statutory right to transfer debentures.

Instrument of Transfer

16–112 A company is not permitted to register the transfer of its debentures unless a properly executed instrument of transfer has been delivered to it.[296] Before 1963 it depended on the company's own regulations and the debentures' terms of issue what that instrument should contain. However, the Stock Transfer Act 1963 introduced a simplified transfer form for all registered securities, which includes debentures, debenture stock, loan stock and bonds. The form of the instrument of transfer is set out in that Act's first schedule; it must be executed by the transferor only and must specify who the transferee is, the consideration and the description and number of the amount of securities in question. Special provision is made in this Act and in the 1977 Act[297] for transfers via the Stock Exchange.

---

[292] *e.g. Re New York Taxi Cab Co.* [1913] 1 Ch. 1.
[293] s.79 and above, para. 9–02.
[294] See generally, A.P. Bell, *Modern Law of Personal Property* (1989), Chap. 15.
[295] See generally, M. Forde, *Commercial Law* (2nd ed., 1997), Chap. 4.
[296] 1963 Act, s.81 (except, of course, where the debentures are payable to bearer).
[297] The Companies (Amendment) Act 1977.

Equities and Trusts

16–113 The power under section 28(6) of the Supreme Court of Judiciature (Ireland) Act 1877, to transfer debts and other choses in action is "subject to all equities which formerly would have been entitled to priority over the right of the assignee." That is to say, the transferee takes the debenture or whatever subject to any defects in the assignor's title and subject to certain claims which the debtor has against the assignor.[298] A transferor cannot confer any greater title than he had himself; the debtor can rely against the transferee in respect of claims arising out of the debenture, whether they arose before or after the notice of the transfer was given, and the debtor may have a claim against the transferee arising out of some other transaction provided that the claim arose before notice of the assignment was given. Thus, the transferee's title to the debenture is subject to any equity, *e.g.* arising from an irregularity or fraud when the debenture was being issued, or some other claim of set-off or cross-claim or other precise equity, available to the company against the original or any previous holder and arising before notice was given of the transfer.[299]

16–114 This "subject to equities" rule greatly restricts the transferability of debentures. However, debentures which are issued in a series usually expressly exclude equities and other personal claims[300] and, accordingly, protect the transferee debenture-holder's interest from being defeated or devalued by some latent equity. For instance, in *Re Goy & Co. Ltd.*,[301] one C, a director of the company and a holder of its debentures, was held guilty of misfeasance and was ordered to compensate the company. As security for a loan, C had transferred his debentures to R. It was contended that the company was entitled to deduct from what it then owed R the amount that C was obliged to pay it, on the grounds that it is "inequitable that a person entitled to a share of a fund should receive anything in respect of that share without paying what he may be bound to contribute to the same fund", and that "the transferee of a chose in action stands in no better position than his transferor".[302] However, the debenture contained a condition excluding equities. It was held that "[t]here is nothing . . . to prevent a debtor from contracting with his creditor that he will not avail himself against

---

298 See above, n. 294, pp. 377–378.

299 *e.g. Athanoeum Life Assurance Society v. Pooley* (1858) 3 De G. & J. 294; *Re Rhodesia Goldfields Ltd* [1910] 1 Ch. 239; *cf. Re Agra and Masterman's Bank* (1879) L.R. 2 Ch. 391.

300 See precedent, above, para. 16–97, para. 7.

301 [1900] 2 Ch. 149.

302 [1900] 2 Ch. 149 at 153–154.

a transferee of any rights which he may possess against the creditor or any assignee of his."[303] Consequently, the company could not enforce against R the equities subsisting between it and C.[304] In one instance which concerned such a clause, Harman J. observed that "any creditor would wish to agree with his debtor that the instruments securing the debt shall be as freely negotiable as possible. So far as the law permits, this debenture is drawn so as to approximate to an negotiable instrument."[305]

16–115 When someone other than the true or beneficial owner of debentures is registered as the debenture-holder, the person registered holds those securities as trustee for their real owner. Most debentures contain a clause along the lines of clause 3 of the sample debenture above[306] relieving the company, so far as is practicable, from the duty to accept notices of trusts or equities. In *Rearden v. Provincial Bank*,[307] which concerned the very similar Article 7 of Table A relieving the company of the duty to accept notice of trusts in its shares, the purpose of those provisions was explained as "to spare the company of the responsibility of attending to any trusts or equities whatever attached to their shares, so that they might safely and securely deal with the person who is the registered owner, and with him alone, recognising no other person and no different right; freeing them . . . from all embarrassing enquiries into conflicting claims as to [securities], transfers, [interests], . . . and the like . . ."[308] But where a company's agents in fact have notice of some equitable interest held in the debentures, the above clause does not relieve it from liability it otherwise would incur for ignoring those facts.[309]

Restriction on Transfers

16–116 Whether or to what extent debentures are freely transferable depends on the terms on which they were issued; restrictions on their transfer along the lines commonly imposed in respect of shares in companies are most exceptional. Under the 1963 Act,[310] however, where a company refuses to register a transfer of debentures, it must notify the

303 [1900] 2 Ch. 149 at 154.
304 *cf. Re Palmer's Decoration and Furnishing Co.* [1904] 2 Ch. 743.
305 *Hilger Analytical Ltd v. Rank Precision Industries Ltd* [1984] B.C.L.C. 301 at 305.
306 Above, para. 16–97. The Companies Acts do not contain a provision for the register of debenture-holders similar to s.123 of the 1963 Act for the register of shareholders.
307 [1896] 1 I.R. 532; see above, para. 9–73.
308 *ibid.* at 567.
309 *e.g.* as occurred in the *Rearden* case.
310 s.84.

transferor of its refusal within two months of the transfer form being lodged. Otherwise, within two months of that being lodged, the company must have ready for delivery the certificate of the debentures or the debenture stock, except where the terms of issue stipulate otherwise. Section 85 of the 1963 Act provides for the certification of transfers of debentures in the same manner as transfers of shares are certified.[311]

RECEIVERS

16–117 One way in which creditors can enforce their security is by having a receiver of the charged assets appointed.[312] Debentures given by companies, especially where they grant a floating charge, often authorise the debenture-holder to appoint a receiver in the event of default and the like.[313] At times receivership is used not simply as a means of reimbursing creditors but more as a device for reorganising insolvent companies, so as to salvage their viable parts for the benefit of those involved.[314] But the legal position of receivers somewhat restricts their effectiveness as company doctors. In recent years investor interests have expressed concern at the undue haste with which some creditors resort to receivership, thereby virtually wrecking inherently sound businesses that are temporarily short of funds; criticism has also been levelled at the way some receivers actually go about their task. Not too long ago the prevailing judicial response to those concerns was summed up by saying that "the moral of the matter is this, if you depend exclusively on borrowed money for the business you propose to carry on, you must at all costs retain the confidence of your lender";[315] but attitudes are beginning to change.

16–118 Part VII (sections 312–323) of the 1963 Act, as amended in 1990, regulates the position of receivers to some extent. However, their status, powers and duties are based primarily on non-statutory sources; the rules have mainly been devised by the courts, applying general contract law and equitable principles to this context.[316] The law regarding company receivers and managers is a complex subject and only a summary outline can be provided here; for detailed treatment the reader

---

[311] Above, para. 9–60.

[312] See generally, M. Forde, *The Law of Company Insolvency* (1993), Pt I and books listed in nn. 317–320.

[313] *e.g.* the sample debenture, above, para. 16–97, clause 11.

[314] Especially when combined with the "hive down" technique.

[315] *Re B. Johnson & Co. (Builders) Ltd* [1955] 1 Ch. 634 at 651.

[316] See Rigby L.J. in *Gaskell v. Gasling* [1896] 1 Q.B. 669 at 691–693.

should consult the standard works of reference, notably O'Donovan,[317] Picarda,[318] Lightman and Moss[319] and Kerr.[320]

Appointing a Receiver

16–119 The court possesses an inherent power to appoint a receiver over charged assets and will do so, for instance, where a winding up of the company commences or where the security is put in jeopardy.[321] By jeopardy is meant a risk of the assets in question being seized or taken to pay claims that are not truly prior to the security-holder's.[322] But the fact that the company at the time is insolvent, or that the security if then realised would not cover the amount of the debt, does not of itself justify appointing a receiver.[323]

16–120 Usually the debenture itself will authorise the creditor to appoint a receiver;[324] then the creditor can designate someone as receiver once the conditions for exercising that power are satisfied, without ever resorting to the court. The vast majority of company receiverships take this form and the designated grounds for making an appointment are almost identical in most debentures. An appointment cannot be made for a reason outside of those grounds. For instance, unless the debenture authorises an appointment because the security is in jeopardy, the creditor cannot appoint a receiver for that reason;[325] instead, he should apply to the court to have one appointed.

16–121 A body corporate cannot be a receiver of company property[326] and it is an offence for an "undischarged bankrupt" to act as one.[327] Since 1991, persons who were closely connected with the company's management have been disqualified from being its receiver; these are anyone who, within 12 months prior to the appointment, was an officer, servant or auditor of the company or of any of its closely-associated companies — including any partner, employee, parent, spouse, brother, sister or child of such person.[328] The court determines the court-

---

317 *Company Receivers and Managers* (1981).
318 *The Law Relating to Receivers and Managers* (2nd ed., 1989).
319 *The Law of Receivers of Companies* (2nd ed., 1994).
320 M. Hunter (ed.), *Kerr on Receivers and Administrators* (17th ed., 1992).
321 See Picarda, above, n. 318, at p. 292. *cf. National Irish Bank Ltd v. Graham* [1994] 1 I.R. 215.
322 *Re New York Taxicab Co.* [1913] 1 Ch. 1.
323 *ibid.*
324 *e.g.* the sample debenture above, para. 16–97, clause 11.
325 *Cryne v. Barclays Bank* [1987] B.C.L.C. 548.
326 1963 Act, s.314.
327 *ibid.*, s.314.
328 1963 Act, s.315(1)(a) (as amended by 1990 Act, s.170).

appointed receiver's remuneration. It is provided by section 318 of the 1963 Act that the company's liquidator, or any of its members or creditors, may apply to the court to fix the remuneration of a receiver appointed under any instrument, notwithstanding that the instrument purports to fix the remuneration. The court may require reimbursal of any excess that was paid over the amount that it fixed.

16–122 A receiver may be removed by the court for "cause shown".[329] Provided he gives one month's notice to the debenture-holder and the company, a receiver appointed under a debenture may resign.[330] A court-appointed receiver may only resign on such terms as the court fixes.[331]

Consequences of Appointment

16–123 Once a receiver is appointed, floating charges crystallise and become fixed.[332] This prevents the company from dealing with the charged assets without the receiver's consent. Appointment of a receiver operates to suspend the company's powers and the directors' authority in relation to the assets covered by the receivership. As one judge put it, "appointment of a receiver and manager over the assets and business of a company does not dissolve or annihilate the company . . . ; but it entirely supercedes the directors in the conduct of its business, deprives it of all power to enter into contracts in relation to that business, or to sell, pledge, or otherwise dispose of the property put into the possession or under the control of the receiver and manager. Its powers in these respects are entirely in abeyance."[333] However, receivership does not wholly disable the company or the directors from acting. The directors retain power, for example, to sue in the company's name provided the receiver is indemnified against the costs.[334] A receiver and manager can not prevent the directors from authorising proceedings against a creditor for breach of contract in wrongfully putting the company into receivership[335] or for otherwise wrongfully causing it to become insolvent.[336]

---

[329] *ibid.*, s.315 (as amended by 1990 Act, s.170).
[330] *ibid.*, s.322C (inserted by 1990 Act, s.177).
[331] *ibid.*
[332] *Taunton v. Sheriff of Warwickshire* [1895] 2 Ch. 319.
[333] *Moss Steamship Co. v. Whinney* [1912] A.C. 254 at 263.
[334] *Newbart Development Ltd v. Co-Operative Commercial Bank* [1978] 1 QB. 814; *Paramount Acceptance Co. v. Souster* [1981] 2 N.Z.L.R. 38. *cf. Tudor Garage Holdings Ltd v. Citibank NA* [1991] B.C.L.C. 1009.
[335] *Newhart Developments* case, above, n. 334.
[336] *Lascomme Ltd v. United Dominions Trust (Ireland) Ltd* [1993] 3 I.R. 412.

16–124 Appointment of a receiver by the court operates to dismiss the company's existing employees,[337] although they may become employed by the receiver. Appointment of a receiver out of court, however, does not of itself automatically terminate employment contracts with the company.[338] There are three qualifications to this principle,[339] namely employment contracts are terminated where appointment of a receiver is accompanied by a sale of the business, where the receiver enters a new agreement with a particular employee that is inconsistent with the old contract, or where continuation in employment of a particular employee would be inconsistent with the receiver and manager's very function. However, the strict contract law position is now modified by the European Communities (Safeguarding Employees' Right on Transfer of Undertaking) Regulations 1980.[340]

Receivers' Powers

16–125 A receiver's function is to do everything necessary to realise the security. Particular powers to this end may be set out in the order of the court, or in the debenture and the instrument, under which he was appointed;[341] for instance, to sue in the company's name or otherwise in order to get in the property charged, to carry on the business and to raise money for that purpose, to realise charged property and execute conveyances in the company's name, and to make such arrangements and compromises as are appropriate. Section 178 of the 1990 Act enables a receiver to bring proceedings to recover assets which were wrongfully taken from the company. Receivers may apply to the court for directions about any aspect of their functions;[342] a similar application may be made by the company's officers or members or employees, or by creditors owed more than £10,000.

16–126 Appointment of a receiver suspends the directors' powers over the assets in question in so far as is necessary for discharging the receiver's functions.[343] But the authority of a receiver appointed over the entire undertaking is not coterminous with that of the directors,[344] his powers are only as extensive as those provided for in the company's regulations regarding giving security and the terms of the appoint-

[337] *Reid v. Explosives Ltd* (1887) 19 Q.B.D. 264.
[338] *Griffiths v. Secretary of State* [1974] 1 Q.B. 468.
[339] See generally, M. Forde, *Employment Law* (1991), Chap. 10.
[340] S.I. No. 306 of 1980; see *ibid.*
[341] *e.g.* in sample debenture, above, para. 16–97, clause 11.
[342] 1963 Act, s.316 (as amended by 1990 Act, s.171).
[343] *Newhart Development* case, above, n. 334.
[344] *ibid.* and *Lascomme Ltd* case, above, n. 336.

ment. Thus, unless the power is expressly granted, a receiver may not use the company's seal.[345] Nor may a receiver petition in the company's name for it to be wound up.[346] If, however, the company is insolvent and a winding up order would protect its assets, the receiver is empowered, by virtue of his duty to protect the security, to petition for a winding up.[347]

16–127 A receiver has authority to dispose of the assets that were charged. In *Industrial Development Authority v. Moran*[348] it was held that, although there was no express power given in the debenture there to use the company's seal, nevertheless by virtue of the Conveyancing Act 1881, the receiver could execute an effective conveyance of the company's property. Kenny J. there observed that, where the receiver is empowered to carry any such sale into effect by deed in the name of and on behalf of the company, the "more usual and better practice is for him to execute the deed of transfer by writing the name of the company and underneath this to write words that indicate that the name of the company has been written by the receiver as attorney of the company under the power of attorney given by the debenture. In addition, he should execute the deed in his own name. In that way he has the best of both worlds".[349]

16–128 A receiver has one quite remarkable power: to, in a sense, frustrate contracts with the company in circumstances where the company itself could not do so. Existing contracts remain binding on the company after a receiver or receiver-manager is appointed. But the receiver is not bound by them and, to an extent, can disregard entirely the company's contractual obligations. This power is particularly useful for what has become known as "hiving down"[350] — which is a method of salvaging the viable parts of the business and disposing of them unencumbered by crippling liabilities. *Airlines Airspares Ltd. v. Handley Page Ltd.*[351] provides an excellent example. An aircraft manufacturer ran into financial difficulties and was put into receivership. It had one aircraft design that, most likely, would be very lucrative. The receiver caused the company to form a subsidiary that would acquire that design; he would then try to sell off the shares in the "clean" sub-

345 *Industrial Development Authority v. Moran* [1978] I.R. 159.
346 *Re Emmadart Ltd* [1979] 1 Ch. 540.
347 *ibid.*
348 [1978] I.R. 159.
349 *ibid.* at 166.
350 See sample "hive down" agreement in M. Forde, *Reorganising Failing Businesses: the Legal Framework* (1991) at pp. 200–213.
351 [1970] 1 Ch. 193.

sidiary with the valuable asset, thereby completing the hiving down. The company had entered an agreement under which the plaintiff was to be paid a commission on the sales of the aircraft in question; the plaintiff accordingly sought an injunction to prevent the receiver from selling the valuable shares in the subsidiary. It was held that the receiver was not bound by this commission agreement and could not be prevented from completing his scheme for disposing of the company's viable parts.

16–129 The extent to which receivers in this way can avoid contracts with the company was stated as follows:

> "[T]he receiver, within limit[s] . . . is in a better position than the company, qua current contracts . . . [O]therwise almost any unsecured creditor would be able to improve his position and prevent the receiver from carrying out, or at any rate carrying out as sensibly and as equitably as possible, the purpose for which he was appointed. . . . It would not be equitable for the receiver to prefer [one contractor] to other unsecured creditors, and it is in the best interests of all such creditors that he should be able to sell that part of [the company's] business which will constitute a viable unit in the way which will secure the highest price. If, in so doing, he does decline to take over [one] contract, he may, of course, render the [company] liable in damages and may also, to some extent, at any rate, damage their reputation as a trustworthy company which can be expected to honour its contracts. This, however . . . he is entitled to do, so long as the realisation of the net assets of the company . . . to the best advantage is not impaired."[352]

But the fact that the company is in receivership provides it with no defence to an action against it for specific performance of a contract.[353]

Receivers' Duties and Liabilities

16–130 Receivers cannot be held liable on contracts existing with the company at the time of their appointment. For instance, in *Ardmore Studios (Ireland) Ltd. v. Lynch*,[354] it was held that a collective agreement that existed between the company and a trade union did not bind the receiver-manager appointed over the company's assets. According to section 316(2) of the 1963 Act, contracts made by receivers in the course of their duties bind them personally unless the contract provides otherwise. But a receiver is entitled to an indemnity out of the company's assets in respect of that liability.

---

[352] [1970] 1 Ch. 193 at 198, 199.
[353] *Freevale Ltd v. Metrostore Holdings Ltd* [1984] 2 W.L.R. 496.
[354] [1965] I.R. 1.

16–131 Section 285 of the 1963 Act enumerates certain "preferential" creditors (the State and company employees) who, in a winding up, must be paid off[355] before the holder of any floating charge can get paid. Section 98 of that Act obliges the receiver, appointed by the holder of a floating charge, to pay those creditors from whatever assets are covered by the charge in priority to any sums due to the chargee.[356] A receiver who does not ensure that the preferential creditors are satisfied will be held responsible to them in damages for breach of statutory duty.[357]

16–132 Receivers appointed by the court are officers of the court and they are not agents or trustees of any person. Receivers appointed by debenture-holders are agents for those who appointed them. However, instruments of appointment frequently designate them as agents of the company, so that the appointing creditor cannot then be held responsible for their wrongs.[358] Receivers are fiduciaries for those who appointed them and owe those persons duties of good faith and to exercise their powers for proper purposes,[359] and also a general duty of care.

16–133 Receivers appointed out of court also owe a duty of care to the company and to whoever guaranteed the debt that gave rise to the receivership, in respect of exercising their powers of sale. In *Standard Chartered Bank Ltd. v. Walker*[360] the position at common law was summarised as follows:

> "The receiver is the agent of the company [and] owes [it] a duty to use reasonable care to obtain the best possible price which the circumstances of the case permit. He owes this duty not only to the company . . . to clear off as much of its indebtedness to the bank as possible, but he also owes a duty to the guarantor because the guarantor is liable only to the same extent as the company. The more the overdraft is reduced, the better for the guarantor. It may be that the receiver can choose the time of sale within a considerable margin, but he should . . . exercise a reasonable degree of care about it . . . .
>
> If it should appear that the . . . receiver [has] not used reasonable care to realise the assets to the best advantage, then the mortgagor, the company, and the guarantor are entitled in equity to an allowance. They

---

355 See below, paras 18–96 *et seq*.

356 *cf. Re H. Williams (Tallaght) Ltd*, [1996] 3 I.R. 531.

357 *I.R.C. v. Goldblatt* [1972] 1 Ch. 498; *Re Christonette International Ltd* [1982] 1 W.L.R. 1245.

358 *cf. W. & L. Crowe Ltd v. E.S.B.*, Costello J., May 9, 1984.

359 *Tse Kwang Lam v. Wong Chit Sen* [1983] 1 W.L.R. 1349.

360 [1982] 1 W.L.R. 1410.

> should be given credit for the amount which the sale should have realised if reasonable care had been used. Their indebtedness is to be reduced accordingly."[361]

This analysis, which no longer represents the law in England,[362] was endorsed by Carroll J. in *McGowan v. Gannon*.[363] It is now complemented by a statutory duty of care; section 316A of the 1963 Act requires a receiver to exercise all reasonable care to obtain the best price reasonably obtainable as at the time of sale.

16–134 Additionally, there are restrictions on receivers selling valuable assets to persons who were officers of the company within the preceding three years.[364]

16–135 As regards care in running the company, at one time the view was that a receiver and manager is under no obligation to carry on the company's business at the expense of the debenture-holders even though discontinuance of the business would be detrimental from the company's point of view.[365] It was held that a receiver and manager, even when designated as the company's agent, is not an "officer" of the company for the purposes of a misfeasance suit under section 298 of the 1963 Act;[366] but section 298 was amended in 1990 to apply to receivers.[367]

16–136 A receiver is not obliged to provide information to the guarantor of the debt or to the other creditors about the proposed selling price of the company's assets.[368] But being the company's designated agent, circumstances can arise where the receiver has an equitable obligation to render it accounts during the receivership.[369] Receivers who encounter evidence of fraud or other criminal offences are required to disclose that evidence to the Director of Public Prosecutions and to cooperate with him in any resulting prosecution he may bring.[370]

---

361 [1982] 1 W.L.R. 1410 at 1415–1416.
362 Since *Downsview Nominees Ltd v. First City Corp. Ltd* [1993] A.C. 295.
363 [1983] I.L.R.M. 516.
364 1963 Act, s.316A(3) (inserted by 1990 Act, s.172).
365 *Kernohan Estates Ltd v. Boyd* [1967] N.I. 27; *Re B. Johnson & Co. (Builders) Ltd* [1955] Ch. 634.
366 *Re B. Johnson & Co.* case, above, n. 365.
367 1990 Act, s.142.
368 *McCowan v. Gannon*, Carroll J., January 25, 1983.
369 *Gomba Holdings Ltd v. Homan* [1986] 1 W.L.R. 1301.
370 1990 Act, s.179.

Publicity and Formalities

16–137 The appointment of a receiver must be publicised in a number of ways. If the receiver is appointed by the holders of a floating charge over all or most of the company's property, the company must be notified immediately.[371] The registrar of companies must also be notified and notices must be published in the *Iris Oifigiúil* and in one local daily newspaper.[372] Every business letter, order for goods or invoice issued by or for a company in receivership must state that fact.[373] The directors and secretary, and such other officers and employees of the company as the receiver directs, must draw up a statement of the company's affairs at the date of the receiver's appointment.[374] This should give particulars of the company's assets, debts and liabilities; names and addresses of creditors, and details about the securities held by them; and such further information as is prescribed. This statement must be given to the receiver; within two months a copy of it, together with the receiver's comments on it, must be sent to the registrar of companies.[375] Copies must also be sent to the company, the trustees of the debenture-holders on whose behalf the receiver was appointed, and to those debenture-holders. At six-monthly intervals from being appointed and within one month after he ceases to act, the receiver must send the registrar of companies an abstract showing the assets of which possession was taken and their estimated value, the proceeds of any assets sold, and receipts obtained and payments made during those periods.[376]

---

371 1963 Act, s.319(1)(a).
372 *ibid.*, s.107.
373 *ibid.*, s.317.
374 *ibid.*, s.320.
375 *ibid.*, s.319(1).
376 *ibid.*, ss. 319(1), 321.

17

Court Protection and Supervised Examination

17–01 The system of temporary protection, investigation and administration of companies' affairs by court-appointed examiners was introduced by the Companies (Amendment) Act 1990.[1] This procedure was part of the more extensive reform of Company Law which had been before the Oireachtas for several years. But the crisis in Iraq in August 1990 and the impact of those events on the Goodman group of companies caused the Oireachtas to be reconvened and the measure to be enacted within a few days. On the evening on which the Bill was signed and became law, the President of the High Court appointed an examiner over many companies of the Goodman group. In June 1999 the Oireachtas was considering proposals to change this Act in several respects – the Companies (Amendment) (No. 2) Bill, 1999.

17–02 What the protection and examination procedure seeks to achieve is to save all or part of the undertaking and to prevent the company from being wound up. This Act is not quite as novel as it may appear at first sight because it extends to companies, within the Companies Act 1963–1990, the kind of protection from creditors which individuals enjoy under Part IV of the Bankruptcy Act 1988, and its predecessor, sections 345–353 of the Bankruptcy (Ireland) Act 1857.[2] The 1990 Act also resembles the court administration procedure with has existed in Britain since 1986[3] and Chapter 11 of the United States Bankruptcy Act,[4] which are aimed at rescuing ailing companies by encouraging a compromise between the claims of the creditors and of the company's owners. Under the 1990 Act, an examiner is appointed by the High Court to look into the company's affairs, to see if there is any real prospect of rescuing the business. Among the effects of such an

---

1 See generally, M. Forde, *The Law of Company Insolvency* (1993).

2 See generally, M. Forde, *Bankruptcy Law in Ireland* (1990), Chap.3.

3 See generally, I. Fletcher *et al., Law and Practice of Corporate Administration* (1994).

4 11 United States Code, ss. 1101–1174 (1988); see generally, Trost, "Business Reorganisations Under Chapter 11" [1980] Ann. Survey of Bankruptcy Law 165.

appointment are to freeze all new litigation involving the company and to prevent creditors, secured as well as unsecured, from levying execution against its assets. If there is a prospect of the company's survival, the examiner reports back to the court and he then seeks to negotiate a compromise between the creditors, the shareholders and the company. When this is voted on by all the parties, the arrangement is brought before the court, which will sanction it if it secured a reasonable degree of support and is "fair and equitable" to the parties and is not "unfairly prejudicial" to any creditor or shareholder.

OBTAINING COURT PROTECTION

17–03 The procedure for having an examiner appointed is by way of a petition for protection to the High Court.[5] Creditors' rights are impaired from the very moment the petition is presented.[6]

Application

17–04 A petition for protection may be presented by any of the following:[7] by any creditor, including any contingent or prospective creditor; by one or more members of the company, provided that they own more than one-tenth of the voting shares in the company; by the company itself and by the company's directors. Where the application is being made by the directors, there must have been agreement among a majority of them to make the application; unanimity among them is not required[8] but a minority of them cannot make an application (unless they own 10 per cent of the voting shares and apply as members). In the case of an application being made by the company, it would seem that there must have been approval by the majority of the company's members with votes; in other words, a decision of the directors is not sufficient to authorise an application in the name of the company.[9] However, since an application can be made by the directors as such, the court may take the view that an application made in the name of the company and sanctioned by the directors is a good application unless there is evidence that the company's members are opposed to the application. In the case of an application by a contingent or prospective creditor, they are required first to provide security for costs.[10]

---

5 See R.S.C. (No. 3) Order, 1991 (S.I. No. 147 of 1991).
6 s.5(1).
7 s.3(1).
8 *Re Equitycorp International p.l.c.* [1989] 1 W.L.R. 1010.
9 *cf. Re Galway & Salthill Tramway Co. Ltd* [1918] 1 I.R. 62.
10 s.3(5).

17–05 When presenting a petition under this Act, the utmost good faith is required; the ex parte application to have an examiner appointed has been described as an *uberrima fides* procedure.[11] Not alone must the petition be factually correct but it ought to give an overall accurate account of the circumstances which give rise to the application. The lack of good faith on the petitioner's part could easily jeopardise ultimate sanction for a scheme of arrangement which might otherwise have secured the court's approval. One of the reasons why proposals, which had been approved by several classes of creditors, were rejected in *Re Wogans (Drogheda) Ltd. (No. 2)*[12] was because the company's initial petition very significantly understated its liabilities; one of its directors knew that large sums were owing to the Revenue but those were not disclosed in the balance sheet put before the Court. Costello J. castigated the petition as an abuse of process by the company and its directors and recommended that, in future, once a discrepancy of that nature is discovered, the examiner should immediately bring the matter to the court's attention. There, when he learned of the discrepancy, the examiner immediately notified the Revenue and set out the true position in his section 15 or "21 day" report.

17–06 A petition must be supported by evidence that the applicant has "good reason for requiring" an examiner to be appointed.[13] Examples of such reasons may include, to prevent a receiver being appointed over the company's assets, to block some other mode of execution being effected or to have litigation stayed. It depends on all the circumstances what kind of evidence the court requires for this purpose. Evidence should also be provided that the company is "likely to be unable to pay its debts",[14] *i.e.* that the company either is, or probably is, insolvent. Indeed, in particular instances, insolvency alone may be sufficient "good reason" for having an examiner appointed. Under the 1999 proposed amendments, instead of this evidence, there must be a detailed report on the company's affairs prepared by an independent accountant.

17–07 Before an examiner will be appointed, the applicant must be qualified to present the petition, the petition and accompanying matters must meet the prescribed requirements, a winding up of the company must not have commenced, the company must not have been in receivership for more than three days continuous before the petition

---

[11] *Re Selukwe Ltd*, Costello J., December 20, 1991; *cf.* s.13 of 1999 Amendment Bill.
[12] Costello J., May 7, 1992.
[13] s.3(3)(b).
[14] s.2(1)(a).

was presented and it must appear to the court that the company is "likely to be unable to pay its debts".[15] By being unlikely to pay its debts is meant[16] that either the company cannot meet its debts as they fall due; or the company's liabilities exceed its assets, both contingent and prospective; or that a form of execution issued against the company was returned unsatisfied in whole or in part; or, finally, a written demand has been left with the company for more than three weeks to pay a debt exceeding £1,000 but the company has not paid, secured or compounded that sum. In other words, the circumstances would warrant it being wound up by the court on the grounds of insolvency. A new indicia of likely insolvency is added by the 1990 Act, that the company has sought from its creditors a significant extension of time to pay its debts.[17]

Interim Examiner

17–08 At times the court will appoint an interim examiner pending the hearing of the petition and any objections that may be raised. It can be helpful that someone is appointed albeit on a temporary basis because some weeks might elapse before the petition is heard. When that hearing takes place the interim appointee may be able to provide the court with a reliable objective assessment of the company's general prospects; he may even have come to the early conclusion that there is no reasonable prospect of survival, thereby rendering further examination unnecessary. However, some judges are reluctant to make interim appointments unless very convincing reasons exist.

Court's Response

17–09 Although the court has a discretion to refuse an application where the above requirements are met, presumably, that power of refusal will be strictly regulated in accordance with relatively well defined principles. However, if protection "would be likely to facilitate the survival of the company, and the whole or any part of its undertaking, as a going concern", the Act creates a form of presumption in favour of appointing an examiner.[18] In England it was held that the word "likely" in a similar context means "a real prospect that . . . the stated purpose may be achieved"; not a more onerous requirement that there must be at least a 50 per cent probability of bringing about the company's survival.[19] A similar approach was endorsed by the

---

[15] s.2(1).
[16] s.2(3).
[17] s.2(4).
[18] s.2(2).
[19] *Re S.C.L. Building Services Ltd* [1990] B.C.I.C. 98.

Supreme Court in *Re Atlantic Magnetics Ltd.*;[20] in that instance, a receiver had already been appointed and it was contended that there was no real prospect of an examination under the 1990 Act proving to be a success. Because the application to appoint an examiner is the first step in a process, which could lead to the company's financial position being carefully scrutinised by the court when a scheme of arrangement has been drawn up, within a relatively short space of time, it would not be appropriate to require a petitioner to prove that the company probably could survive.[21] That probability is something which the court would have to look at in due course during the examination. Perhaps the most significant of the amendments presently before the Oireachtas is that the above criterion will be changed to a requirement that the court be "satisfied that there is a reasonable prospect of the company's survival . . . "

17–10 Ordinarily, the person designated by the petitioner will be appointed as the examiner. Unless a very good explanation is given why he should not be appointed, the court will not appoint the person preferred by other interested parties, even if they are the principal creditors or the main unsecured creditor.[22]

17–11 Where an examiner is appointed, the court may make such other directions as it thinks fit.[23] Directions may concern, for example, the operation of the company's bank account, the conduct and management of its business, the appointment of a committee of inspection and the conditions under which certain powers may be exercised by the examiner. Even where it adjourns the hearing, the court may make such interim orders as it thinks fit in the circumstances; one such order may be restricting the directors' powers.[24] The court can make a protection order over several related companies.[25] In deciding whether to make an order applying to such companies, the criterion is whether that order is "likely to facilitate the survival of the company, or the related company, or both, and the whole or any part of its or their undertaking, as a going concern.[26] In other words, is a consolidated protection and examination likely to salvage one or more of the companies?

---

[20] [1993] 2 I.R. 561.
[21] Similarly, *Re Butler's Engineering Ltd*, Keane J., March 1, 1997.
[22] *Re Wogans (Drogheda) Ltd*, Blayney J., *ex tempore*, January 13, 1992.
[23] s.3(7).
[24] s.3(8).
[25] s.4.
[26] s.4(2).

Consequent Formalities

17–12 Regardless of the outcome of the application, once a petition for protection is presented, the registrar of companies must be notified of that fact within the next three days.[27] Where an examiner is appointed, he is required to fulfil the following formalities. Within three days of his appointment, he must deliver to the registrar of companies a certified copy of the court's order.[28] Within the same period, he must cause to be published in two daily newspapers, circulating where the company's registered office or principal place of business is located, a notice of his appointment and the date that happened; where a date was fixed by the court for considering his report, that date also must be stated.[29] Within 21 days of his appointment, he must cause a similar notice to be placed in *Iris Oifigiúil*.[30] Failure to meet any of these requirements does not invalidate the appointment,[31] although deliberate omission to give the requisite notices may be grounds for the court vacating the protection. Within seven days of the court's order, the directors must make out a sworn statement of affairs of the company and give it to the examiner.[32]

EFFECTS OF PROTECTION

17–13 Once the petition has been presented, the company comes under the court's protection for the prescribed period.[33] The immediate objective and consequence of protection is to provide the company or companies in question with extensive immunity against its creditors and against claims being made against it. By virtue of the 1990 Act, the company becomes legally insulated from a wide range of adverse actions against it.

Shareholders

17–14 Unless the court gives directions otherwise, protection has no immediate effect on the company's members or shareholders. They can continue participating in general meetings and may transfer their shares as if nothing had happened. However, once a company comes

---

27 s.12(1).
28 s.12(3).
29 s.12(2).
30 *ibid.*
31 *cf.* s.12(5).
32 s.14.
33 s.5(1).

into court protection, no orders may be made against it for relief under section 205 of the 1963 Act against "oppression".[34]

Directors

17–15 The same principle applies to the company's directors; subject to the court's directions otherwise, during the protection they can continue to manage the company's business and its affairs. However, from the outset the court may restrict the exercise of any of their powers; as is explained below, the court may order that all or any of the directors' powers be exercisable only by the examiner.[35] Moreover, the examiner is authorised to convene, set the agenda for and to attend board meetings and meetings of the company's members.[36]

Contracts

17–16 Similarly, the advent of protection ordinarily does not affect subsisting contracts with the company, except that goods held under retention of title, a hire purchase agreement, a conditional sale or some other form of bailment cannot be repossessed.[37] As is explained below, however, the company may apply to the court either to affirm or repudiate contracts, other than payment obligations.[38]

Litigation

17–17 Protection insulates the company from fresh litigation unless the court directs otherwise. No proceedings against the company or "in relation to" it may be commenced without the leave of the court and subject to such terms as the court fixes.[39] However, the court readily grants leave to bring proceedings, when sought, although usually putting a stay on any steps following delivery of the statement of claim. As for proceedings already in being relating to the company, the examiner is authorised to apply to the court to have them stayed or for any other order regarding the action.[40] What criteria should guide the court in granting leave or imposing a stay in such cases are not stated.

Company Property

17–18 Unless the court gave directions to the contrary, protection does

---

[34] s.5(1)(g).
[35] s.3(8).
[36] s.7(2), (3).
[37] s.5(2)(e).
[38] s.20.
[39] s.5(3).
[40] *ibid.*

not affect the title to the company's property. There is no express provision whereby title in the property vests in the examiner, although he may be authorised by the court to engage in transactions with that property, even property which is subject to a charge or is held under a hire purchase agreement. But once the company comes under protection, its property cannot be affected in any of the ways described below.

Creditors' Property

17–19 Where property belonging to a creditor is in the company's possession, he may not be able to recover it while the company is under protection. It was observed that the 1990 Act "does not . . . extinguish any entitlement whether of proprietary or contractual rights. It merely restricts to a substantial extent the enforcement of that entitlement while the [protection] remains in force".[41] Where, during the course of the protection, the company makes use of another's property in one way or another, the value of that use becomes an expense of the entire process which, eventually, must be defrayed from the company's own assets.

Creditors' Remedies

17–20 Remedies which the law affords creditors against their debtors' property are drastically curtailed where the debtor is a company and a petition for its protection has been presented. A creditor who resorts to any of these remedies, while a company enjoys the court's protection, commits contempt of court.[42] If he does so deliberately and conscious of the legal implications, he risks a substantial fine and even imprisonment. These restrictions on creditors' remedies can be waived by the examiner but there is no provision, comparable to that in the British legislation, whereby the court may also give leave to realise a security or resort to any of the other remedies.

Repossession

17–21 Goods held under retention of title, a hire purchase or a credit sale agreement or some other form of bailment which can last at least three months, do not belong to the company until they have been paid for. However, once protection commences, no steps may be taken to repossess such goods if they are in the company's possession, except with the examiner's consent.[43]

---

[41] *Re Atlantic Computer Systems p.l.c. (Nos. 1 and 2)* [1990] B.C.L.C. 729 at 741.
[42] *Bristol Airport p.l.c.* v. *Powdrill* [1990] B.C.L.C. 585; *Re Exchange Travel (Holdings) Ltd* [1991] B.C.L.C.728.
[43] s.5(2)(e).

Enforcing Charge

17–22 Unless the examiner consents, no charge over all or part of the company's property can be enforced, in the sense of taking action to realise all or part of the security.[44] Charges so affected include those over the company's effects or income. The term charge here is not defined, which leaves open the question whether the restriction here applies to non-possessory securities, like pledges or liens.[45]

Execution, Attachment, Sequestration and Distress

17–23 The traditional creditors' remedies of execution by the sheriff (or *fieri facias*), sequestration and distress cannot be "put into force" against the company's property without the examiner's consent.[46] The term "put in force" in this context has a precise connotation. In the case of *fi.fa*, execution is enforced only when the sheriff has seized the goods.[47] For all modes of execution, the test is whether proceedings have reached such a stage as the creditor has obtained a charge over the property.[48] However, it would seem to follow from the previously mentioned restriction that, even when a charge has been so obtained, it cannot be realised — unless the two subsections are mutually exclusive.

Set-Off

17–24 Except with the examiner's consent, there cannot be any set-off between the bank accounts a of company which has court protection.[49] Bank accounts here include accounts with the ACC Bank, the Post Office Savings Bank, any certified trustee savings bank, a building society, an industrial and provident society, a friendly society, a unit trust or collective investment scheme, as well as licensed banks. But protection does not affect any set-off which may arise otherwise than between accounts with any of these bodies.

Judgment Mortgage

17–25 There is no express reference in the 1990 Act to registering a

---

44 s.5(2)(d); *cf.* s.14(b)(i) of the 1999 Amendment Bill.

45 The word used in the British Act is "security"; see *British Airport p.l.c.* v. *Powdrill* [1990] Ch. 744 and *Re Sabre International Products Ltd* [1991] B.C.L.C. 470 on liens. *cf. Exchange Travel Agency Ltd* v. *Triton Property Trust p.l.c.* [1991] B.C.L.C. 396: on landlord's right of re-entry a security.

46 s.5(2)(c).

47 *Re London & Devon Biscuits Co.* (1871) 12 Eq. 190.

48 *Crowshaw* v. *Lyndhurst Ship Co.* [1897] 2 Ch. 154.

49 s.5(2)(h); the 1999 Amendment Bill proposes to repeal this subsection.

judgment mortgage against the company's land. Such a measure hardly constitutes "action to realise" the security,[50] which is prohibited without the examiner's consent.

Receiver

17–26 A receiver may not be appointed over the property or undertaking of a company which enjoys court protection.[51] But where a receiver has already been appointed for more than three continuous days, the court cannot then grant the company protection.[52] As for a receiver who has been appointed to all or any part of the company's properties, the court may make such order as it deems fit regarding what he may or should do.[53] In particular, the court may direct that he shall cease to act; that he may act only in respect of certain assets; that he deliver all books and papers and other records regarding the company to the examiner; that he gives the examiner all particulars of his dealings with the company's property or undertaking. In deciding whether to restrict the receiver's activities, the court will have regard to whether that is "likely to facilitate the survival of the company, and the whole or any part of the undertaking, as a going concern."[54]

Winding-Up

17–27 Court protection cannot be obtained where the company has resolved to wind itself up or it has been wound up by the court.[55] But once protection commences, no such resolution can be passed nor proceedings for a winding-up be commenced.[56] Where a winding-up petition has been presented, it was held in England that the court may restrain the advertising of that petition pending the outcome of the examination.[57] Under the 1990 Act, in such cases both petitions should be heard at the one time,[58] except where a provisional liquidator has already been appointed. If there is a provisional liquidator, the court may make such orders as it deems fit regarding what he should or should not do,[59] in particular, that he shall be the examiner as well,

---

[50] s.5(2)(d).
[51] s.5(2)(b).
[52] s.3(6).
[53] s.6(1); *cf.* s.16 of the 1999 Amendment Bill, adding the requirement that the courts is "satisfied that there is a reasonable prospect of survival".
[54] s.6(3).
[55] s.2(1).
[56] s.5(2)(a).
[57] *cf. Re A Company (No. 001992 of 1988)* [1988] B.C.L.C. 9.
[58] s.6(5).
[59] s.6(2).

that he shall cease to act, that he shall deliver papers concerning the company to the examiner and provide particulars regarding his dealings with the company's property. Any direction that he shall cease to act shall be in order to facilitate the company's survival as a going concern.[60]

Sureties, Indemnors and the Like

17–28 So long as the company is under the court's protection, persons who have guaranteed or given indemnities for obligations to be performed by the company are protected against proceedings concerning the company's liabilities and also against modes of enforcing execution against their property in connection with those obligations. The category of persons who are so protected is defined as those who "under any enactment, rule of law or otherwise [are] liable to pay all or any part of the debts of the company."[61]

EXAMINER'S POWERS AND FUNCTIONS

17–29 The examiner's principal functions are two-fold, namely to investigate the affairs of the company and report thereon to the court and, secondly, to seek to put together some scheme or compromise, which will result in the company's survival, and report thereon to the court. In order to facilitate carrying out these tasks, the 1990 Act gives the examiner a wide range of powers.

Directors' and Shareholders' Meetings

17–30 An examiner is entitled to reasonable notice of all meetings of the company's directors and of its shareholders, including a description of the business to be transacted.[62] He, moreover, may convene any such meeting, set the agenda, preside at it, be heard at it, give reports and propose motions.[63]

Powers of Auditors

17–31 Company auditors have an extensive range of powers for obtaining information regarding a company's financial affairs and persons connected with the company are obliged to assist the auditors in

---

[60] s.6(3).
[61] s.6(2).
[62] s.7(2), (3).
[63] *ibid.*

their investigations.[64] All of these rights and powers are conferred on a company's examiner.[65]

Production of Documents and Evidence

17–32 Specific provision is made in section 8 of the 1990 Act to enable the examiner to get documents and evidence concerning the company's affairs. Breach of these requirements can be certified by the examiner and, on the court considering the matter and any witness, can be punished in the same way as a contempt of court.[66] Obligations of this nature are imposed on all officers and agents of the company and certain other persons. Officers and agents for these purposes include those of any "related company", including former officers and agents, and present and past auditors, bankers and solicitors of the company.[67] Regarding former officers and agents, as thus defined, they must produce to the examiner all books and documents concerning the company in their custody or over which they have power. They must attend before the examiner when required to do so, must give him all reasonable assistance in connection with his functions and they may be examined on oath by the examiner, either orally or on written interrogatories. These same obligations apply to any other person who is in possession of any information concerning the company's affairs or who may have such information.[68] Any information covered by legal professional privilege does not have to be disclosed as required here. Provision is made for obtaining details of transactions where any director of the company or "connected person" either has or had a bank account, either in his own name or jointly and either in the State or abroad.[69]

Certifying Liabilities

17–33 When a company obtains court protection, its suppliers, bankers and others may be reluctant to continue dealing with it and extend it credit unless their position is duly safeguarded. If they cease dealing with the company, its business may very well collapse rapidly and there may no longer be any viable trading arrangements to be salvaged through a scheme with the creditors. Section 10 of the 1990 Act goes a long way to meet this situation. Where the examiner is of the view

---

[64] See above, para. 8–27.
[65] s.7(1).
[66] s.8(5); *cf.* s.19 of the 1999 Amendment Bill.
[67] s.8(6).
[68] s.8(2).
[69] s.8(3).

that, unless particular transactions are entered into, the company's survival as a going concern would be seriously prejudiced, he may certify liabilities the company undertakes in respect of those transactions.[70] This applies only to liabilities incurred during the period when he is the examiner and the certification must be made at the time those liabilities were incurred or were to be incurred. The effect of any such certification is to treat those liabilities as an expense of the examination which, under section 29 of the Act, must be paid in full before any other claim against the company may be paid. Those who extend credit to the company and whose entitlements are duly certified are thereby guaranteed payment.

Exercising Directors' Powers

17–34 When an examiner is being appointed, the court may direct that the directors' powers shall be restricted.[71] Additionally, section 9 of the 1990 Act authorises the examiner to apply to the court to take over all or any of the directors' functions and powers, for instance, to borrow money, to manage all or part of the company's business and to bring and defend actions involving the company. Before it can make an order of this nature, the court must have regard to the following matters, although what weight or significance is given to them is not indicated, other than that they must show that it is "just and equitable" to confer the powers being sought on the examiner. Those matters are whether the conduct of the company's affairs are calculated to prejudice the interests of either the company, its employees or its creditors as a whole, or whether the interests of those parties would otherwise be safeguarded. Use of the term "interests" here and not just rights enables the court to consider a wide range of matters. Other matters which the court should take into account include whether a transfer of power to the examiner is expedient for preserving the company's assets, whether the company or its directors support a transfer of powers and "any other matter in relation to the company the court thinks relevant". When due account is to be taken of all of these, the question then is whether it is just and equitable to order a divesting of the directors' powers. Conditions may be imposed on any such order and ancillary orders may be made by the court.

Exercising Liquidators' Powers

17–35 Where the court orders that the examiner may exercise all or

---

[70] *cf. Re Don Bluth Entertainment Ltd* [1994] 3 I.R. 141 and *Re Edenpark Construction Ltd* [1994] 3 I.R. 126.

[71] s.3(8).

part of the directors' powers, it may also confer on him all or part of the powers which can be exercised by a liquidator.[72] Examples include disclaiming onerous property and contracts and bringing misfeasance claims.

Repudiating Contracts

17–36 Generally, company receivers and managers can carry out their functions in disregard of contracts binding the company, other than contracts which can be the subject of an order for specific performance.[73] Where their authority covers the company's entire assets and undertaking, receivers and managers can in effect repudiate contracts, but that action does not relieve the company of the liability to pay damages for breach of the contract. In *Astor Chemicals Ltd. v. Synthetic Technology Ltd.*,[74] it was held that examiners do not have a similar ability to rid the company of its contractual duties, because examiners have a completely different function from that of receivers. A receiver's job is to realise the company's assets for the benefit of one creditor; an examiner's objective when he has been given directors' powers, is to manage the company's affairs for the benefit of all interested parties. Under the 1999 proposed amendments, examiners will be able to repudiate clauses (usually in debentures) prohibiting further borrowing by the company or in creating a change of some kind over all or part of its assets.

17–37 However, section 20 of the 1990 Act gives the company, not the examiner as such, power to repudiate certain contracts, which resembles the power of disclaimer enjoyed by liquidators. Where the examiner is not a party to the company's application, he must be notified of the fact and may appear and be heard on the matter. It is only contracts the performance of which do not involve paying money which can be repudiated; an obligation to pay money cannot be ended in this manner. This power is exercisable only when proposals for a scheme or arrangement "are to be formulated"; the Act does not indicate how far advanced these proposals must be. Where the power is exercised, the other contracting party then stands as an unsecured creditor for the damages which ensue from this breach of contract. Where, in order to facilitate acceptance of proposals for a compromise, it is necessary to quantify the damages which would result from repudiating a contract, the court may hear the matter and determine how much the amount of those damages shall be.

---

[72] s.9(4).
[73] See above, para. 16–128.
[74] [1990] B.C.L.C. 1.

Agreeing Claims

17–38 If he is empowered to do so by the court,[75] either directly or by virtue of obtaining the powers of a liquidator, the examiner can ascertain and agree claims against the company.

Disposing of Charged Property

17–39 Not alone are secured creditors prevented from enforcing their security while a company is under protection,[76] but section 11 of the 1990 Act enables the examiner to dispose of or deal with their security in accordance with the conditions laid down there. Charged property for these purposes includes property which is subject to a floating charge, to a hire purchase or a conditional sale agreement, to retention of title and also any property which is held under a bailment capable of subsisting for more than three months. The criterion of when an examiner is to be permitted by the court to dispose of or to otherwise deal with charged property in this sense is whether doing so "would be likely to facilitate the survival of the whole or any part of the company as a going concern"; the court must be satisfied that this is indeed the case. When considering such applications, "the court has to make a balancing exercise between the prejudice that would be felt if the order is made by the secured creditor, against the prejudice that would be felt by those interested in the promotion of " this criterion.[77]

17–40 However, the examiner cannot thereby interfere with the secured creditors' priority or substantially diminish the value of their security. Where that property is sold, the net proceeds of disposal must be applied towards discharging the sum secured. By the sum secured here is meant not alone the capital sum and outstanding interest but any cost which the security-holder is entitled to add in accordance with the general law and the security instrument.[78] If that sum falls below what would have been realised in a free sale in an open market, the difference between the two prices must be applied by the examiner in discharging the secured debt. If the property is replaced by other property, for instance in a floating charge, any replacement property is subject to the same order of priority.

Recovering Property Fraudulently Disposed Of

17–41 Where the company's property has been fraudulently disposed

---

[75] s.7(7).
[76] s.5(2)(b), (d), (e).
[77] *Re ARV. Aviation Ltd* [1989] B.C.L.C. 664 at 666.
[78] *ibid*. at 669.

of, the examiner can take steps to have it or its worth recovered.[79] Section 139 of the Companies Act 1990, applies where property of the company has been disposed of in a manner which perpetrated a fraud on the company, its creditors or its members; section 139 applies to any type of property and to any mode of disposition. The examiner may apply to the court and, if he shows that a fraudulent disposal has taken place, the court may order that the property be delivered up to him or that a sum be paid to him in respect of the property. An order to that effect will be made if it is "just and equitable" to do so but the court is required to take account of the interests of any bona fide purchaser for value of the property. Under the 1999 proposed amendments, where there is evidence of substantial disappearand of the company's property, without adequate explanation, the court can make directions about investigating the matter.

Preventing "Detriment" to the Company, a Creditor or Member

17–42 Section 7(5) of the 1990 Act gives the examiner an extensive power to take appropriate action to protect the company, any creditor or member from suffering detriment. The full text reads:

> "Where an examiner becomes aware of any actual or proposed act, omission, course of conduct, decision or contract, by or on behalf of the company to which he has been appointed, its officers, employees, members or creditors or by any other person in relation to the income, assets or liabilities of that company which, in his opinion, is or is likely to be to the detriment of the company, or any interested party, he shall, subject to the rights of parties acquiring an interest in good faith and for value in such income, assets or liabilities, have full power to take whatever steps are necessary to halt, prevent or rectify the effects of such act, omission, course of conduct, decision or contract."

What exactly the examiner is permitted to do under this provision will require judicial elaboration.

Contractual Obligations

17–43 Except where the contract provides otherwise, examiners are personally liable on any contract they enter into in the performance of their functions — whether the contract be in their own name, in the name of the company or otherwise.[80] This is one of the occupational risks of examiners. It is a question of fact whether any particular contract excludes their personal liability. However, an examiner is entitled to an indemnity out of the company's assets in respect of contracts

---

[79] Companies Act 1990, s.181(2), applying s.139 of that Act to the examiner.
[80] s.13(6).

properly entered into by him[81] and that indemnity must be paid, along with remuneration and expenses, before any other debt can be paid.

REPORT ON THE EXAMINATION

17–44 The examiner's principal function is "to conduct an examination of the affairs of the company".[82] It is to enable him to assess the company's financial and trading position, and the true value of its assets and liabilities, that he is given the same powers as are possessed by auditors and additional powers to compel production of certain documents and information. Within 21 days of being appointed, the examiner must present to the court a report on his findings;[83] a longer period may be allowed by the court. At the same time a copy of this report must be given to the company and, on request, copies must be made available to any member or creditor of the company.[84] If the court so directs, there may be omitted, from copies of the report given to members and creditors, information "which would be likely to prejudice the survival of the company, or the whole or any part of its undertaking".[85] Those matters which must be contained in the report are set out in section 16 of the 1990 Act.

17–45 What happens next depends on whether the examiner discovered serious wrong doing and his evaluation of the company's prospects of being rescued from insolvency. If his conclusions are adverse in this sense, the court will direct a prompt hearing into the matters arising from his report.[86] By adverse here is meant where he concludes that there has been a substantial disappearance of company property that has not been adequately accounted for or that there had been other serious irregularities in the company's affairs.[87] Adverse conclusions here also include where the examiner takes the view that neither all nor any part of the company's undertaking would be capable of surviving as a going concern, or that no compromise or scheme which might be adopted would facilitate the survival of the undertaking or

---

[81] s.13(6).
[82] s.15(1). The 1999 proposed amendments will repeal the provisions in this and the following paragraph.
[83] *ibid.*
[84] s.15(3), (4).
[85] s.15(4), (5).
[86] s.17(1). Under the 1999 Amendment Bill, where unaccounted for substantial disappearance of company property is unearthed or some other serious irregularities regarding its affairs, the matter must be referred to the court.
[87] *ibid.*

any part of it, or that winding up the company would be more advantageous to its members as a whole and its creditors as a whole than attempting to continue the whole or part of its business.[88] At this hearing, the examiner, the company, any member and any creditor are entitled to appear and to be heard.[89] So also is any person who is referred to in the report in connection with property disappearing or serious irregularities.[90] What the outcome of that hearing should be is entirely at the court's discretion; it may "make such order or orders as it deems fit".[91] Section 17(4) of the Act lists a whole range of orders which can be made, without prejudice to the court's general discretion.

NEGOTIATING PROPOSALS FOR A RESCUE PACKAGE

17–46 If the examiner's conclusion from his report are favourable or if he is otherwise so directed by the court, having put in his report, he must formulate proposals for rescuing the company.[92] By favourable conclusions here is meant that the examiner takes the view that each of the following three conditions obtain:[93] that all or part of the company's undertaking is capable of surviving as a going concern; that adopting a compromise or scheme would facilitate such survival; that it is more advantageous to all the members and creditors as a whole to carry on and seek to salvage the company rather than wind it up there and then. It is only in the most hopeless circumstances that this last condition would not obtain.

17–47 Just six weeks are allowed, from when the examiner was appointed, for the parties to consider his proposals and to report back to the court on the parties' reaction to those proposals.[94] But an extension of time may be obtained.[95] In drawing up proposals, the creditors must be divided into different classes, but the Act provides no criteria for determining the class composition. Most likely the same approach would be adopted as for schemes of arrangement under section 201 of the Companies Act 1963, for differentiating between the groups of credi-

---

88 *ibid.*
89 s.17(2).
90 *ibid.*
91 s.17(3).
92 ss. 18(1), 17(3).
93 s.18(1).
94 s.18(2); five weeks under the 1999 Amendment Bill.
95 s.18(3).

tors.[96] Usually, there would be at least three classes of creditors — secured, preferred and unsecured creditors. The class composition of the shareholders would be determined by the criteria in the case law for ascertaining members' class rights.[97]

Contents of Proposals

17–48 Among the matters to be dealt with in those proposals are the following:[98]

- each class of members and of creditors must be specified;
- those classes whose interests will be "impaired[99] and those classes whose interest will not be impaired must be specified;
- whatever changes should be made in the management and direction of the company, where the examiner considers such changes would facilitate its survival as a going concern;
- whatever changes should be made in the company's memorandum and articles which the examiner considers would facilitate its survival;
- provisions for implementing the proposals;[100]
- a full account of each class meeting and a copy of the proposals put to that meeting.[101]

The only requirement regarding the proposals' intrinsic merits is equality within classes, *i.e.* except where the class members agree otherwise, all members of the same class must be treated equally.[102] A statement of affairs, as of the date of the proposals, must be attached to them.[103] There must also be attached to them an estimate of how each class of creditor and member would fare in the event of a liquidation.[104] Additional matters must be included where the court so directs and the examiner may include such other matters as he deems appropriate.[105]

---

96 See above, para. 11–59.
97 See above, paras 11–21 *et seq.*
98 s.22(1).
99 Defined in ss. 22(5) and 22(6).
100 *cf. Re Coombe Importers Ltd* (Hamilton P., December 5, 1990).
101 R.S.C. (No.3) Order, 1991, art. 17(2).
102 s.22(1)(d).
103 s.22(2).
104 s.22(3).
105 s.22(4), (1)(h).

Convening Meetings

17–49 The examiner must then convene meetings of such classes of members and of creditors as he deems appropriate to consider these proposals.[106] There is no express requirement to include with the notices of these meetings copies of the actual proposals and of the statement of affairs and estimate of the creditors' position in a liquidation. But the notices must be accompanied by a statement setting out the general effects of the compromise or scheme being put forward;[107] there must be set out, in particular, its effect on any "material interest" of the company's directors, whether those interests are as directors of the company or as its creditors or otherwise. Where the proposals affect debenture-holders whose affairs are in the hands of trustees, the notices must explain the proposals' effects on those trustees and on any "material interest" they may have.[108]

Acceptance of Proposals

17–50 Having duly considered them, the various classes must then vote on the proposals. Votes can be cast either in person or by proxy.[109] Even the Revenue and other State and local authorities, which generally are not permitted by law to compromise obligations due to them, are authorised to vote for and accept proposals they otherwise could not accept.[110] This is one of the main differences between rescue schemes under the 1990 Act and schemes under section 201 of the Companies Act 1963; under the latter the Revenue are not free to accept bonds, securities and other forms of property in lieu of tax which is due and payable.[111] If proposals are agreed and some classes of creditors and members accept them, they are then put before the court to be confirmed and made binding on all classes. If agreement cannot be reached on the proposals, the matter goes back to the court, which may direct that the company be wound up.[112]

COURT CONFIRMATION OF PROPOSALS

17–51 The last stage in the process is the proposals being set down for consideration by the court. From the time of his appointment, the

---

[106] s.23(1).
[107] s.23(8).
[108] s.23(6). *cf. Re Dorman Long & Co.* [1943] Ch. 635.
[109] s.23(3); to be deleted under the 1999 Amendment Bill, which adds that not voting shall not be construed as opposition to the proposals.
[110] s.23(5).
[111] *cf. Re Pye (Ireland) Ltd,* Costello J., March 11, 1985.
[112] s.24(11)(b).

examiner has 42 days (six weeks) within which to have the proposals considered and voted on and report to the court on the outcome of those deliberations.[113] But the court may permit him a longer time to make his report. Four months from the date of the petition being presented is the very maximum period within which a report can be made to the court but, once a report is in by that time, the court may extend the protection period to enable it to decide on the proposals and the court may take so long as it needs for this purpose.[114] There is no statutory deadline although, given the very nature of the issues to be decided, ordinarily the court would give them prompt attention. What the examiner's report must contain is set out in section 19 of the 1990 Act.

17–52 The stage is then set for the high point of the examination. At this hearing, the company and the examiner may appear and be heard;[115] so also may any creditor or member whose interests are impaired if,[116] under the proposals, he is to obtain less than the full amount which was due to him when the protection commenced. A shareholder's interests are impaired if,[117] under the proposals, either the nominal value of his shares is reduced; a fixed dividend to which he is entitled is reduced; his proportionate interest in the entire share capital is diminished; he is otherwise to be deprived of all or part of his rights as a shareholder, like voting rights; or he is to lose his entire shareholding. Proposals can be made and confirmed which do not involve impairing any party's interests in the company. In deciding whether to accept the proposals, with or without modification, the following separate hurdles must be crossed. To use the parlance of American corporate reorganisation law, these are the standards against which any "cram down" of the dissenting creditors and members is to be judged. The impact of schemes on guarantees is provided for in the proposed 1999 amendment to the Act.

Class Acceptance

17–53 First, from the classes whose interests would be impaired in the manner just described, the proposals must have secured acceptance by at least one class of creditors and one class of members.[118] If

---

[113] s.18(2); 35 days in 1999 Amendment Bill.
[114] ss. 18(4), 24(1).
[115] s.24(2).
[116] s.22(5).
[117] s.22(6).
[118] s.24(4)(a); the referance to class of members will go under the 1999 Amendment Bill.

only creditors' rights are impaired, it suffices if one class of them accepted the proposals by a malority in value and in number.

Material Irregularity

17–54 One ground of objection which may be raised at the hearing is that there was a "material irregularity" at or in relation to any of the meetings at which the proposals were considered.[119] What deviations from proper procedure would amount to a material irregularity in this context depends on all the circumstances of the case.

Improper Means and Improper Purpose

17–55 Two other grounds of objection are that acceptance of the proposals was obtained by improper means or that the proposals were made for an improper purpose.[120] Again, what methods and what objectives would be regarded as improper for these purposes will depend on the circumstances of the case. It remains to be seen whether objectives other than tax-avoidance would he deemed to be improper in this context; in the light of the court's general discretion under the Act, the answer would seem to be yes.

Tax Avoidance

17–56 Where the sole or primary purpose of the scheme is to avoid paying tax, it cannot be confirmed by the court.[121] This gives statutory form to several Australian cases where schemes of arrangement, designed primarily to make substantial gains from the tax losses of insolvent companies, were rejected by the courts there.[122] But the mere fact that the proposals, when implemented, will or may give rise to fiscal windfall should not thereby defeat them.

Not Unfairly Prejudicial

17–57 The position of individual creditors and shareholders within the various classes will be considered. A party may object on the grounds that the proposals would "unfairly prejudice" his interests and, if that complaint is sustained, the court cannot give its sanction to the scheme.[123] By unfair prejudice here presumably is meant that, while a party's class in general may be getting fair and equitable treatment,

---

119 s.25(1)(a).
120 s.25(1)(b), (c).
121 s.24(4)(b).
122 *Re Data Homes Property Ltd* [1972] 2 N.Z.W.L..R. 23.
123 ss. 25(1)(d), 24(4)(c)(2).

his special individual circumstances may render that treatment exceptionally harsh. For instance, that person may stand to incur some unique tax penalty with which fellow class members are not confronted.[124] If this is indeed the case, the only way in which the proposals can be salvaged is for the court to permit departure from the equality within the class principle in respect of that person.

Fair and Equitable to Each Class

17–58 As has been observed, within each class the members must be treated equally, save where the members agree or the court directs otherwise.[125] When it comes to comparing each class, whose interests are impaired, with other classes also being impaired, the burdens which the different classes will bear must be "fair and equitable" in relation to each other.[126] In other words, some classes must not be expected to bear far too great a reduction in their rights while others will be sacrificing very little.[127] It depends on all the circumstances whether any particular class is being treated unfairly and inequitably for these purposes. No doubt this is a question which will spawn an abundance of case law in due course. Among the intriguing questions awaiting resolution is whether debts due to the Revenue, which would be priority debts in a liquidation, can be paid off at the same rate or terms as the other unsecured creditors are to be paid.[128] Another vexed question is whether secured creditors must always be paid at least the full value of their security.[129]

17–59 That the proposals are unfair and inequitable to a class of members or of creditors is not enumerated as one of the grounds of objection which can be raised at the confirmation hearing. It is possible, however, that the basis for complaint on these grounds can also be used to demonstrate that the proposals "unfairly prejudice" the objector. In any event, unless the court is satisfied that the proposals are fair and equitable to the affected classes, confirmation will not be forthcoming.

---

124 *cf. Re Hellenic & General Trust Ltd* [1975] 3 All E.R. 382; above, para. 11–59.

125 s.22(1)(d).

126 s.24(4)(c)(i).

127 So far the courts have not elaborated on precisely what is required: above, para. 11–59.

128 The U.S. Chapter 11 procedure permits Revenue priority debts to be spread out over at most six years.

129 This matter raises intriguing constitutional law questions.

Other Considerations

17–60 The court may take account of circumstances other than those set out above in deciding whether to confirm or reject proposals for a scheme of arrangement. Section 24(3) states that the "court may, as it thinks proper", confirm or refuse its confirmation or modify the proposals, subject to sections 24 and 25 of the Act. The very first case in which a set of proposals were presented to the High Court, *Re Coombe Importers Ltd.*[130] is a good example of other considerations causing the court to reject the scheme. The company was heavily insolvent and, if liquidated, it was unlikely that the Revenue's preferential debt would be discharged. Under the proposals made by the examiner and accepted by the overwhelming value and number of the creditors, other than the Revenue, creditors were to be paid 15 pence in pound; the Revenue's preferential debt would be paid at 21 pence in the pound and their pre-preferential debt at 80 pence in the pound but that would be in equal instalments over a five years period. At the time the examiner was negotiating with several investors to put funds into the company, which would finance the proposed settlement and provide working capital for the business, but no binding agreement had been reached to make this investment. Hamilton P. rejected the proposals as being not fair and equitable to the Revenue for several reasons, namely; the company's principal shareholders and directors had been involved in a company in the very same trade some years earlier, which was liquidated with a very large deficiency; the company's accounts had never been audited; there was some evidence which suggested that not all payments made to the company had been retained by the company. Additionally, because there was not yet a contract with a known individual to finance the proposals, the requirement of section 2(1)(e) that the proposals shall "provide for [their] implementation" had not been met.

17–61 Some weeks later Hamilton P. was presented with the proposed scheme in *Re Goodman International Ltd.*[131] and its many related and connected companies. The principal creditors here were banks — the two major Irish banks and also leading British, French and German banks — who were owed hundreds of millions of pounds. Evidence had earlier been given in court by some of these banks which suggested that they had been deceived or at least misled into extending substantial credit facilities to the Goodman group. In the event, the proposals secured very substantial support from the banks and other creditors

---

[130] Hamilton P., December 5, 1990.
[131] Hamilton P., January 28, 1991.

and were approved by the court. One of the terms was that the creditors would not seek to commence civil proceedings against Mr Goodman, the managing director and principal shareholder in managing those companies. Even though the 1990 Act does not expressly authorise a composite across-the-group scheme, Hamilton P. held that the very "purposes of the Act . . . would be nullified if the examiner were not entitled to take into account the position with regard to each and every one of the related companies and to formulate a scheme . . . which would deal with the overall picture."[132]

17–62 Mention has already been made of the *uberrimae fidei* nature of petitions, verified by affidavit, when seeking the appointment of an examiner. If there are major discrepancies between the facts the petitioner deposed to and the true position, as subsequently ascertained, this can be grounds for rejecting the scheme. That the petitioner may no longer be involved in the company, once reorganised, will not necessarily prevent proposals being rejected on those grounds.[133]

Preferential Debts

17–63 There are categories of preferential creditor who are entitled to be paid in a liquidation or in a receivership before a penny can be distributed to the general unsecured creditors, most importantly, the Revenue Commissioners.[134] All that the 1990 Act says about debts to the Revenue is that the tax authorities are empowered to make binding compromises of claims for tax[135] and that, in considering any proposed scheme, the court must reject it if its primary purpose was tax avoidance.[136] Beyond that, the Act is silent. The inference, therefore, would seem to be that there will be no rule of thumb for all companies; each set of proposals will be dealt with on their own merits. The circumstances of a particular case may call for the entire preferential debt being paid off, perhaps in instalments. But the failure to enact an across-the-board rule to this effect suggests that there can be cases where the Revenue will be compelled to forego part of their preferential debts, perhaps even part of a pre-preferential amount as well. Indeed, it could be argued that the omission from the Act of a rule for these debts indicates an intention that the normal principle applicable to unsecured creditors should apply, *i.e.* equality between creditors.

---

[132] At p. 16.
[133] *e.g. Re Wogans (Drogheda) Ltd (No. 2)*, Costello J, May 7, 1992.
[134] See below, paras 18–96 *et seq.*
[135] s.23(5).
[136] s.24(4)(b).

17–64 In *Re Gallaghers Boxty House Ltd.*,[137] the proposals first put by the examiner and which were approved by several classes of creditors included payment of the preferential debts in full over a period of six years and also that the Revenue would waive corporation tax which might be levied on the "write down" under section 24(1) of the Finance Act 1970. These were vigorously opposed by the Revenue. They were then modified during the course of the hearing on the report; the waiver of any tax due under section 24(1) was taken out[138] and, instead, the Revenue were to be treated in much the same way as the general unsecured creditors. During the ensuing argument reference was made *inter alia* to the Dáil Debates; they strongly suggest that the Oireachtas' intention was that schemes of arrangement should be approved even though the full amount of the preferential debts will not be repaid. Denham J. approved the amended proposals because in all the circumstances of the case, she found them fair, reasonable and equitable as between all classes of creditors and the members.[139]

Secured Creditors

17–65 So far the courts have not ruled on perhaps the most important issue in principle under the 1990 Act, the extent to which secured creditors can be impaired. The U.S. Chapter 11 contains detailed rules on this topic; before the 1978 reforms, the principal criterion of fairness was whether those creditors were faring better than they would in a liquidation. For many years the principle was that "if the creditor, in lieu of the return of the property, receives cash in the appraised value of that property, the creditor receives the 'value of the debt'— and the creditor is adequately protected . . . and the plan can be confirmed without [his] consent . . ."[140] Where the amount of debt far exceeds the present value of the security, the post-1978 position has been summarised as follows: "[t]here can be a cash payment cram down requiring the debtor to make cash payments of at least the allowed amount of that claim, and the discounted value of these payments must equal at least the value of the collateral."[141] It remains to be seen whether the value of the security (liquidation or going concern value) will be the benchmark of what is just and equitable for secured creditors.

---

[137] Denham J., *ex tempore*, November 5, 1991.

[138] See below, paras 17–69—17–70.

[139] In *Re Selukwe Ltd*, Costello J., December 20, 1991 the court sanctioned a scheme which also virtually disregarded the Revenue's preferential claims.

[140] *Re Pine Gate Associates Ltd*, 2 B.R.Ct. Dec. (C.R.R.) 1478 (1976).

[141] *Re Griffiths*, 27 B.R. 873 (1983). See generally, Kaplan, "Nonrecourse Unsecured Creditors Under the New Chapter IV, 53 American Bankruptcy L.J. 269 (1979).

Guarantees

17–66 Often the scheme will make express provision concerning debts of the company which have been secured by guarantees — usually personal guarantees given by directors and major shareholders. In one instance, Murphy J. approved proposals that those guarantees should lapse if the company paid the sums falling due under the scheme.[142] But in another instance Costello J. refused to sanction a scheme incorporating similar terms.[143] Instead, he directed that not alone should the guarantees remain in force but that, if the guarantors discharged their obligations to the creditor, they should not have the normal right of subrogation for the company.

17–67 In *Re Wogans (Drogheda) Ltd. (No. 2)*[144] the examiner decided not to include in his scheme a provision about how the directors' personal guarantees should be treated, leaving it entirely to them and the bank to agree on what should be done or to apply to the court as they saw fit. The scheme of arrangement was rejected there, principally because the initial petition had contained deliberate misstatements and also certain tax issues which arose. But Costello J. there explained that in schemes involving creditors with guarantees, some provision should normally be made to deal with the guarantors' right of subrogation against the company in the event of them making payments under their guarantees. If the sums involved are very substantial, the absence of such a provision could seriously jeopardise the company's financial future when the guarantors stand in the shoes of the principal creditor, whom they have paid off.

17–68 If the proposals make no reference to the position of those who have guaranteed the company's debts, it is an open question whether or not approval of a scheme operates to discharge the guarantee. The very terms of a guarantee may provide a clear answer to this question. Where the guarantee does not address the matter, some light may be thrown on the subject by cases on court-approved compositions with bankrupts[145] and on the Official Assignee and liquidators disclaiming leases in which the performance of covenants have been guaranteed.[146] If the guarantee refers to liability in respect of money which "remains due and owing", it would seem that the guarantee would be discharged

---

[142] *Re Presswell Ltd*, Murphy J., *ex tempore*, November 7, 1991.
[143] *Re Selukwe Ltd*, Costello J., December 20, 1991.
[144] Costello J., May 7, 1992.
[145] *e.g. Re London Chartered Bank of Australia* [1893] 3 Ch. 540.
[146] *e.g. Re Farm Machinery Ltd* [1984] I.L.R.M. 273 and below, para. 18–73; *cf. Stacy v. Hill* [1901] 1 I.B. 660.

if the scheme releases the principal debtor.[147] Under the 1999 proposed amendments, detailed provision is made governing the impact of schemes on the liability of guarantors.

Tax Adjustments

17–69 Two years after the U.S. Congress passed the present version of Chapter 11, it enacted a special tax measure to deal with the various tax consequences of reorganisations.[148] No comparable provisions are contained in the Finance Acts.

17–70 In *Re Wogans (Drogheda) Ltd. (No. 2)*[149] the scheme envisaged the ownership of the company passing into entirely new hands, a company in the same general line of business, which would invest approximately £500,000 in the company under protection, much of that money going to pay off the creditors under the examiner's proposals. Since there were no provisions comparable to those in the U.S. Bankruptcy Tax Act 1980, the examiner's revised proposals included provisions to deal with the problems referred to above. The "write down" would not be taxed, in exchange for which the company would not carry forward any of its losses; VAT consequences of the settlement would be treated in the same way as in a receivership or in a liquidation; and the company would not become liable for any outstanding taxes the existence of which was not known at the time the scheme was approved. However, Costello J. declined to make orders along those lines, observing that schemes ought to function within the ordinary tax regime, and rejected the proposals.

Effects of Confirmation

17–71 Court confirmation of the proposals operates to bind the various parties affected by them. According to section 24(6) of the 1990 Act, regarding the creditors, on confirmation "the proposals shall . . . be binding on all the creditors or the class or classes of creditor, as the case may be, affected by the proposals in respect of any claim or claims against the company."

Unlike the position with bankruptcy schemes of arrangement, it is not stipulated that the confirmed scheme binds only those creditors who had notice of the confirmation hearing. All creditors of the af-

---

[147] *cf. Perrott* v. *Newton King Ltd* [1933] N.Z.L.R. 1131.

[148] Bankruptcy Tax Act 1980, 94 Stat. 3389. See generally, Phelan, "Kick 'Em While They're Down — A Taxation and Bankruptcy Critique of the Technical and Policy Aspects of the Bankruptcy Tax Act of 1980" (1981) 35 Sw. L.J. 833.

[149] Costello J, May 7, 1992.

fected class, without qualification, are bound by the scheme. If a creditor who was completely unaware of the proposed scheme can show that the examiner knew of his existence but failed to take reasonable steps to appraise him of the situation, he may possibly have a right of action against the examiner for damages. Confirmation also releases, to the stipulated extent, third parties who are liable for any obligations of the company, like guarantors.

Contesting the Confirmation

17–72 The mere fact that a creditor has not been informed of the examination and thereby was prevented from participating in the decisions is not grounds for setting aside the confirmation. However, if any creditor or member can show that the confirmation was procured by fraud, they can apply to the court within 180 days of the decision to have it revoked. If the court is satisfied that there indeed was fraud, section 27 of the Act empowers it to revoke its confirmation on such terms as it deems fit; but it is required to have regard for the interests of any bona fide purchaser for value of property who relied on the confirmation. Even if there was no fraud or if the 180 days period has expired, a confirmation may always be challenged by an application to have the company wound up on just and equitable grounds.[150] For instance, if the proposals envisaged a certain course of action being taken in respect of the company but without any suggestion of fraud, and that action was not taken, the circumstances may very well warrant the company being wound up on just and equitable grounds.

Priority Status of Examiner's Expenses and Certified Liabilities

17–73 Where a scheme of arrangement is approved by the court, ordinarily it will make adequate provision for paying the examiner's remuneration and expenses and also any liabilities certified under section 10 of the 1990 Act as necessary to ensure the company's survival at the time. Where, however, no scheme is approved or one is approved but the company nevertheless goes into liquidation, the question arises of the priority ranking of what is owing to the examiner and to creditors with his certificates.

17–74 The position is governed by section 29 of the Act. What is being claimed by the examiner and by certified creditors must first be sanctioned by the court, which may want to satisfy itself that the debts were reasonably incurred and there was no extravagance or waste. For

---

[150] 1963 Act, s.213(f).

this purpose, examiners are required to make optimum use of the company's own staff and facilities. The sums so approved must be paid either from the company's revenue or from its assets, when realised, including investments. If the company is forced into receivership or liquidation, section 29(3) provides that those sums "shall be paid in full and shall be paid before any other claim, secured or unsecured, . . . in any receivership or winding up of the company". Three main questions appear to arise from this provision.

17–75 What are the "assets" of the company out of which, when realised, those sums must be paid? For instance, is property which has been mortgaged to a creditor an asset in this context? A strong argument could be made, especially in view of the Constitution's guarantee of private property, that the only company asset is the equity of redemption. Against that, use of the term "asset", as contrasted with the term "property", may have significance.

17–76 If there are insufficient unencumbered assets, must the sums approved be paid from the proceeds of a sale of assets which were the subject of a floating charge and even of a fixed charge? All that section 29(3) says is that there is a priority over "secured" claims. This may include claims that are secured by an outright mortgage. In *Re Atlantic Magnetics Ltd.*,[151] the Supreme Court ruled that certified liabilities have priority over assets which are subject to a fixed charge, a view reiterated by that Court in *Re Holdair Ltd.*[152] It was held that the phrase "before any other claim, secured or unsecured," was unambiguous and must be given its literal meaning. It could be argued that property which is subject to a fixed charge is not an "asset" of the company, on the grounds that, in insolvency, the word "assets" traditionally has meant property which is unencumbered or is only subject to a floating charge.[153] Against that, the legislative intention apparently was to include specific security here. Under the 1999 amendment, however, certified expenses will no longer enjoy priority over fixed charges.

17–77 What liabilities are not "claims" in a receivership or liquidation and, accordingly, are not affected by section 29(3)'s priority? It was held by the Supreme Court in *Re Springline Ltd.*[154] that this word

---

[151] [1993] 2 I.R. 561.
[152] [1994] 1 I.R. 416.
[153] *Re Christonette International Ltd* [1982] 3 All E.R. 225. *cf. MacDonald* v. *Australian Guarantee Corp (N.Z.) Ltd* [1990] 1 N.Z.L.R. 227 and *Re ACL Insurance Ltd* [1991] 1 N.Z.L.R. 211.
[154] [1991] 1 I.L.R.M. 15.

must be given its ordinary meaning and should not be confined to those claims which may be proved in a winding up. In consequence, examination expenses have priority over any remuneration or expenses that may be claimed by a liquidator whenever the examination proves to be a failure and the company is forced into liquidation. The argument that such an interpretation would obstruct the orderly liquidation of such companies was countered by the strong public policy of endeavouring to rescue potentially viable businesses. Their analysis is endorsed by the 1999 proposed amendments.

18

Winding Up — Liquidations

18–01 Companies go out of existence through the formal process of being wound up or put into liquidation; these two terms mean the same thing. The leading work on the subject, B.H. McPherson's *The Law of Company Liquidation*,[1] defines winding up or liquidation as "a process whereby the assets of a company are collected and realised, the resulting proceeds are applied in discharging all its debts and liabilities, and any balance which remains after paying the costs and expenses of winding up is distributed among the members according to their rights and interests, or otherwise dealt with as the constitution of the company directs".[2] A liquidator is appointed (either by the company's members, the creditors or the court, as the case may be) in order to carry out the winding up. One major theme that runs through various rules in this area of company law is protecting creditors' and investors' interests, in the sense of conserving the company's property and asserting rights that the company may possess against persons who have wronged it. Winding up is an almost exclusively statutory regime, governed by Part VI (sections 206-313) of the 1963 Act, as amended. Many of the rules of bankruptcy law either directly or by analogy apply if the company being wound up is insolvent.[3] Order 74 of the Rules of the Superior Courts contains the administrative winding up rules for companies. Company liquidation is a vast and a very complex subject and can only be treated very briefly in a general work on company law.[4]

---

1 J. O'Donovan (ed.), (3rd ed., 1987) (hereinafter referred to as *Company Liquidation*).

2 At p. 1.

3 See generally, M. Forde, *Bankruptcy Law in Ireland* (1990) (hereinafter referred to as *Bankruptcy Law*).

4 As well as McPherson's book, see also M. Forde, *The Law of Company Insolvency* (hereinafter referred to as *Company Insolvency*); Palmer's *Corporate Insolvency* (loose leaf), Chaps 88 and 89, and I. Fletcher, *Law of Insolvency* (2nd ed., 1995).

CATEGORIES OF WINDING UP

18–02 Companies can be wound up in three major ways, namely by the members themselves in a voluntary winding up, by the creditors in a voluntary winding up and by the High Court in a compulsory winding up. Some of the rules are common to all categories of winding up and some are common only to the two kinds of voluntary winding up. Voluntary liquidations are far less expensive and much quicker than winding up by the court. Apart entirely from winding up, the registrar of companies is empowered to strike from the register of companies defunct companies and companies that do not make annual returns.[5]

Members' Voluntary Winding Up

18–03 There are numerous reasons why shareholders may wish to wind up their company. For instance, they may be dissatisfied with the way in which it is being run; they may be unable to raise the additional funds it needs to stay in business; they may want to liquidate their investment in it and there is no ready market for their shares; or they may find that the company is insolvent and is unlikely to become profitable. In order for members themselves voluntarily to wind up their company, a majority of the directors must make a statutory declaration that, upon having made full inquiry, they are of the opinion that the company will be able to pay its debts in full within at least 12 months from when the winding up commences.[6] This declaration must contain a statement of the company's assets and liabilities as of not more than three months before the declaration was made. It must be accompanied by a report by an "independent person" stating that the directors' opinion regarding the company's solvency and the statement of affairs they drew up are reasonable. All that then is required is a special resolution of the company to wind itself up.[7] Notice of that resolution must be given in the *Iris Oifigiúil* and a copy of that resolution and of the declaration of solvency must be delivered to the registrar of companies.[8]

18–04 In *Davidson v. King*[9] it was held that a company cannot bypass the winding up procedures by the simple expedient of realising its entire

---

[5] 1963 Act, s.311 (as amended by 1982 Act, s.11, and 1982 Act, s.12).

[6] 1963 Act, s.256 (as amended by 1990 Act, s.128). *cf. Re Favron Investment Co.* [1993] 1 I.R. 87.

[7] *ibid.*, s.251(1)(b). An ordinary resolution suffices where the fixed duration of a company has expired: *ibid.*, s.251(1)(a).

[8] *ibid.*, ss. 252, 143.

[9] [1928] N.I. 1. *cf. Princess of Reuss v. Bos* (1871) L.R. 5 H.L. 176.

assets, discharging its liabilities and having set aside a sum equal to its nominal capital, then declaring a dividend of what remains. This was described as a fraud on the Act's winding up provisions. Indeed, section 251 of the 1990 Act provides that several of the statutory rules applicable in a winding up also apply where an insolvent company is not being wound up by reason of its lack of assets.

18–05 A voluntary winding up commences from the time the resolution to wind up is passed.[10] The company must then cease to carry on business except in so far as is necessary to facilitate the liquidation.[11] A liquidator must be appointed by the shareholders, who may fix his remuneration.[12] The liquidator's function is "winding up the affairs and distributing the assets of the company . . ."[13] This appointment puts an end to the directors' powers but the shareholders or the liquidator may permit them to continue exercising some or all of their powers.[14] If at any time the liquidator forms the opinion that, contrary to the directors' declaration of insolvency, the company will not be able to pay its debts in full, he must publicly advertise and call a meeting of the company's creditors and provide them with a statement of the company's assets and liabilities and such further information as they may reasonably require.[15] A general meeting of the company must be summoned by the liquidator every year following the decision to wind up;[16] those attending should be given a statement of what the liquidator has done. A copy of this statement should be sent to the registrar of companies.

18–06 When the company's assets have been collected and the creditors and shareholders are paid off, the liquidator must call a publicly advertised general meeting and provide it with an account of the winding up.[17] A copy of this account, together with a return of the holding of the terminal meeting, must be sent to the registrar of companies.[18] The company is deemed to be dissolved three months following the registrar receiving these documents, although the court has power to defer the date of dissolution.[19]

---

[10] 1963 Act, s.253.
[11] *ibid.*, s.254.
[12] *ibid.*, s.258(1).
[13] *ibid.*
[14] *ibid.*, s.258(2).
[15] *ibid.*, s.261 (as amended by 1990 Act, s.129).
[16] *ibid.*, s.262.
[17] *ibid.*, s.263.
[18] *ibid.*, s.263(3)
[19] *ibid.*, s.263(4) and (5).

Creditors' Voluntary Winding Up

18–07 The principal difference between a members' and a creditors' voluntary winding up is that, in the latter, the creditors can choose the liquidator and determine his remuneration. A winding up falls into this category where the members resolve to wind up but the statutory declaration of solvency has not been made. An ordinary resolution suffices where the grounds are the company's insolvency.[20] Alternatively, the declaration of solvency has been made but creditors apply to the court and convince it that the company is unlikely to pay its debts within the twelve months period.[21] Or the liquidator may form the view that the company is insolvent and in consequence convene a creditors' meeting to consider the situation.[22] In a creditors' voluntary winding up, the initiative to wind up is always with the shareholders.

18–08 A publicly advertised meeting of the company's creditors must he called for the day of, or the day following, the members' meeting at which the proposal to wind up is to be put.[23] A full statement of the company's affairs, together with a list of the creditors and the estimated amounts of their claims, must be prepared by the directors and presented to that meeting. While the creditors may accept whoever the shareholders choose as liquidator, they are entitled to put their own nominee in the office;[24] although, on application, the court is empowered to designate somebody else. A liquidator appointed by the members has very limited powers in the period prior to holding the creditors' meeting.[25] The creditors can appoint a committee of inspection[26] whose function is to determine the liquidator's remuneration[27] and to monitor the winding up. Meetings of members and of creditors must be summoned by the liquidator each year following the decision to wind up.[28] The liquidator's account must be presented to terminal meetings of members and of creditors.[29] The company will be deemed to be dissolved three months following delivery of the liquidator's account and a return of these meetings to the registrar of companies, although the court may defer the date of dissolution.[30]

---

[20] 1963 Act, s.251(1)(c).
[21] *ibid.*, s.256(5).
[22] *ibid.*, s.261(3)
[23] *ibid.*, s.266.
[24] *ibid.*, s.267.
[25] 1990 Act, s.131.
[26] 1963 Act, s.268.
[27] *ibid.*, s.269(1).
[28] *ibid.*, s.272.
[29] *ibid.*, s.273.
[30] *ibid.*, s.273(4), (5).

Winding Up by the Court

18–09 The most distinctive features of winding up by order of the High Court are that liquidation can be imposed on the company at the instigation of, *inter alia*, any member or creditor, or by the Minister in appropriate circumstances; it is the court that appoints the liquidator and determines his remuneration; the liquidator is an officer of the court and works very much under its supervision. The fact that a company is already in voluntary liquidation does not prevent the court from ordering that it be wound up.[31] In *Re Downs & Co.*[32] it was held that "if the petitioner proves he will be prejudiced by a continuance of the voluntary winding up then he is entitled to a compulsory order *ex debito justitiae* ... If ... he fails to establish prejudice ... the court still has the power to make the order if the court forms the opinion that the rights of creditors will be prejudiced by a voluntary winding up".[33] The power of the court to order that a company be wound up applies to unregistered companies in the circumstances set out in Part X of the 1963 Act.[34]

Grounds for Ordering a Winding Up — Insolvency

18–10 Section 213 of the 1963 Act sets out the grounds on which the court may order that a company be wound up, namely where, by a special resolution, the company resolves to be wound up in this way; where the company does not commence business within a year of being incorporated or suspends its business for a year; where the membership falls below the statutory minimum of two or seven, as the case may be; where the company is unable to pay its debts; where there is "oppression" and the like that would justify making an order under section 205 of the 1963 Act; and where it is "just and equitable" to order winding up. Some of these grounds are self-explanatory. "Oppression" and the like under section 205 has already been dealt with in considering minority shareholder protection.[35] Some of the principal applications of the "just and equitable" heading are also treated there;[36] other examples include where the main object for which the company was formed has become impracticable[37] where creditors' rights would

---

[31] 1963 Act, s.282.

[32] [1943] I.R. 420.

[33] *ibid.* at 423. See also *Re Wicklow Textile Industries Ltd* (1971) 87 I.L.T.R. 72; *Re Gilt Construction Ltd* [1994] 2 I.L.R.M. 456; *Re Naiad Ltd*, McCracken J., February 13, 1995.

[34] 1963 Act, s.345; see above, para. 14–77.

[35] See above, paras 10–74 *et seq.*

[36] See above, paras 10–89 *et seq.*

[37] *e.g. Re German Date Coffe Co.* (1882) 20 Ch.D. 169.

be seriously prejudiced by a voluntary liquidation that is taking place[38] and where the majority have committed a significant fraud on the company.[39]

18–11 By far the most common ground on which orders for a winding up are sought is under section 213(e), that the company is "unable to pay its debts";[40] a frequent petitioner under this head are the Revenue Commissioners. The mere fact that at the time the company possesses no liquid assets whatsoever,[41] or that its liabilities exceed its assets,[42] is not treated as insolvency. But account will be taken by the court of contingent or prospective liabilities.[43]

18–12 Section 214 of the 1963 Act is most important in this respect because it deems two states of affairs to constitute inability to pay debts, thereby making it much easier to establish that the company is insolvent. One is where execution of a judgment or similar order against the company (notably *fieri facias*) is returned unsatisfied wholly or partly.[44] The other is where a creditor, who is owed at least £1,000 by the company, demands in writing to be paid a liquidated sum and the company fails to pay or to satisfactorily secure or compound the debt within three weeks of that demand being made.[45] However, an order to wind up will not be made on these grounds where there is a bona fide dispute about the existence or the amount of the debt. According to one judge, "the winding up jurisdiction is not for the purpose of deciding a disputed debt (*i.e.*, disputed on substantial and not insubstantial grounds) since, until a creditor is established as a creditor he is not entitled to present the petition. . . ."[46]

Petitioners for a Winding Up Order

18–13 Section 215 of the 1963 Act states who may petition to have a company wound up, namely the company, any creditor, the Minister and any member or contributory. A petition by a contingent or prospective creditor will not be heard unless security for costs is given

---

38 *e.g. Re Downs Co.* [1943] I.R. 420.
39 *e.g. Re Newbridge Sanitary Steam Laundry Ltd* [1917] I.R. 67.
40 See generally *Company Liquidation*, pp. 47–57 and Samuels, "Winding Up a Company for Inability to Pay Its Debts" (1964) 28 *Conv.* 121.
41 *Re Bryant Investment Co.* [1974] 1 W.L.R. 826.
42 *Re Capital Annuities Ltd* [1979] 1 W.L.R. 170.
43 *Re European Life Assurance Society* (1869) 9 Eq. 122.
44 s.214(b); *cf.* Bankruptcy Act 1988, s.7(1)(f) and *Re Alexander* [1966] N.I. 128.
45 s.214(a), as amended by 1990 Act, s.123; *cf.* the bankruptcy summons procedure under Bankruptcy Act 1988, s.7(1)(g).
46 *Stonegate Securities Ltd v. Gregory* [1980] 1 Ch. 576, at p.580. See also *Re Pageboy Couriers Ltd* [1983] I.L.R.M. 510.

and a satisfactory *prima facie* case has been established.[47] As regards a petition by the company itself, unless they have clear authority in its articles of association to do so, the directors may not present a petition without the shareholders' consent;[48] but the general meeting can ratify the directors' unauthorised action in so doing. Following an investigation by inspectors into a company's affairs under Part II of the 1990 Act, the Minister may petition that the company be wound up on just and equitable grounds or for oppression and the like under section 205 of that Act, or both.[49] Any member, or if deceased his personal representative or trustee or legatee, may also petition under this latter ground.[50]

18–14 A contributory, in brief, is an existing member of the company or a previous member who is liable to contribute to the company's assets in the event of it being wound up.[51] There is extensive case law on who precisely are contributories, which deals principally with actual liability to make a contribution. As regards petitioning for a winding up, the contributory must either be an original allottee of the shares or else have been the registered owner of the shares for at least six of the eighteen months before the winding up commences.[52] The purpose of this restriction is to prevent persons seeking to put a company into liquidation by the mere device of acquiring some shares in it and straight away presenting a winding up petition. Where a dispute arises about whether the petitioner is the owner of the shares he has registered in his name or claims to own, the petition to wind up will be postponed until this matter has been resolved.[53]

Procedure

18–15 Sections 216–250 of the 1963 Act, as amended in 1990, set out the procedure governing compulsory winding ups, which, briefly, is as follows; the position of the liquidator, some of the principal rules aimed at creditor and investor protection and priorities among creditors are dealt with separately below. Whoever wishes to wind up the company must present a petition to the High Court for a winding up

---

[47] 1963 Act, s.215(c).
[48] *Re Galway & Salthill Tramways Co.* [1918] 1 I.R. 62; see *Re Emmadart Ltd* [1979] 1 Ch. 540 on petitions by receivers.
[49] 1990 Act, s.12(2).
[50] 1963 Act, s.215(e).
[51] *ibid.*, ss. 207, 208.
[52] *ibid.*, s.215 (a)(ii).
[53] *Re J.N. 2 Ltd* [1978] 1 W.L.R. 183; *Re Garage Door Associates Ltd* [1984] 1 All E.R. 434.

order.[54] The form of the petition, how it is to be dealt with in the Central Office, its advertisement and service, as well as hearings on the petition, are provided for in the Winding Up Rules.[55] In determining all questions relating to a winding up, the court is required to have regard to the creditors' and contributories' wishes, which may be expressed in meetings called by the court.[56] The company or any creditor or contributory may apply to the court to stay the proceedings or to have further proceedings restrained;[57] the court may grant that application on such terms as it thinks fit. The court may dismiss the petition to wind up, adjourn the hearing, make an interim order or make such other order as it thinks fit.[58] In an appropriate case the court may even stay or restrain the very presentation of a winding up petition.[59] A provisional liquidator may be appointed by the court pending appointment of the liquidator proper.[60] Once a compulsory winding up commences, transactions involving the company are frozen,[61] such as dispositions of its property, transfers of its shares, execution against its property and actions and proceedings against the company.

18–16 When a winding up order is made, a copy must be delivered to the registrar of companies.[62] On being appointed, the liquidator must publish that fact in the *Iris Oifigiúil* and deliver to the registrar of companies a copy of the court's appointing order.[63] A statement of the company's affairs that is verified by one or more of the company's officers must be filed by them in the court.[64] It must show the particulars of the company's assets, debts and liabilities; the names, addresses and occupations of its creditors; the securities held by its creditors and the dates when those securities were given; and any additional information that the court may stipulate. Every creditor or contributory is entitled to inspect this statement. The court may order that creditors and contributories may inspect the company's books and papers.[65]

18–17 Conduct of the winding up is then left in the hands of the liq-

---

[54] 1963 Act, s.215.
[55] R.S.C., Ord. 74, rules 7–13.
[56] 1963 Act, s.309.
[57] *ibid.*, s.217.
[58] *ibid.*, s.216.
[59] *e.g. Truck & Machinery Sales Ltd v. Marubeni Komatsu Ltd* [1996] 1 I.R. 12 and *Re Genport Ltd* (McCracken J., November 21, 1997).
[60] 1963 Act, s.226; see below, paras 18–33—18–34.
[61] *ibid.*, ss. 218, 219 and 222; see below, paras 18–20 *et seq.*
[62] *ibid.*, s.221.
[63] *ibid.*, s.227.
[64] *ibid.*, s.224.
[65] *ibid.*, s.243.

uidator, who is an officer of the court and is given extensive powers, but these are subject to the court's control.[66] Usually the court will direct the liquidator to call a meeting of the creditors, or meetings of the creditors and contributories, to appoint a committee of inspection whose function it is to act with the liquidator.[67] Where at any time it is proved to the court's satisfaction that the winding up should be stayed or the winding up order should be annulled, the court may direct a stay or an annulment on such terms as it thinks fit.[68]

18–18 As soon as may be after the winding up order is made, the court must settle a list of contributories with a view to making calls, where shares are not fully paid up, and to adjusting rights between contributories.[69] At the same time, the court must "cause the assets of the company to be collected and applied in discharge of its liabilities."[70] To this end, the court may, *inter alia,* order that any money, property or papers to which the company is prima facie entitled be transferred to the liquidator[71] and order that any money owing to the company be paid into a designated bank account.[72] The court may fix a time or times within which creditors must prove their debts or claims against the company; those not proven in time are excluded from the benefit of any distribution.[73] The court is empowered to order that any officer of the company attend a meeting of the creditors, contributories or committee of inspection in order to give them such information about the company as they need.[74] It moreover may summon before it and examine on oath any company officer or debtor, or person it believes is capable of providing information regarding the company;[75] what may be referred to as the liquidation *inquisitionsprozess.* And where it suspects that any contributory is about to abscond or to remove or conceal property, so as to evade paying calls or avoid being examined about the company, the court may order that he be arrested and detained, and that his property, books and papers be seized.[76]

18–19 Those creditors who proved their debts or claims must be paid off in accordance with the priorities that are explained below. Any rights

---

66 1963 Act, s.231.
67 *ibid.*, ss. 232 and 233.
68 *ibid.*, s.234.
69 *ibid.*, ss. 235, 238 and 237.
70 *ibid.*, s.235(1).
71 *ibid.*, s.236.
72 *ibid.*, s.239; *cf.* s.237.
73 *ibid.*, s.241.
74 *ibid.*, s.246.
75 *ibid.*, s.245; see below, para. 18–37.
76 *ibid.*, s.247.

between the contributories must then be adjusted and, if there is a surplus, it must be distributed among those persons who are entitled to it.[77] On the application of the liquidator and provided that the winding up is complete, the court will order that the company be dissolved and will direct how the company's books and papers are to be disposed of.[78]

EFFECTS OF A WINDING UP

18–20 Commencement of a winding up freezes various transactions that concern the company.[79] As one judge explained with reference to section 218 of the 1963 Act, "[I]t is a basic concept of our law governing the liquidation of insolvent estates, whether in bankruptcy or under the Companies Acts, that the free assets of the insolvent at the commencement of the liquidation shall be distributed rateably amongst the insolvent's unsecured creditors as at that date".[80] A voluntary winding up commences once the appropriate resolution was passed. A compulsory liquidation is deemed to have commenced not when the winding up order is made but when the petition for a winding up was presented in the Central Office of the High Court.[81]

Shareholders

18–21 From the time a winding up commences, any transfer of shares in the company or alteration in the status of any member is void unless the court orders otherwise.[83] Even where a shareholder was defrauded by the company into subscribing for shares in it, rescission is no longer available after the winding up commenced.[83] However, in a voluntary winding up the liquidator may permit shares to be transferred.[84]

Directors

18–22 In a voluntary winding up, once the liquidator is appointed the directors' powers cease except where either the members or the liquidator authorised those directors to continue acting for the com-

---

77 1963 Act, s.242.
78 *ibid.*, s.249 and 305(1)(a).
79 See generally, McPherson, *Company Liquidations*, Chap. 6 and Forde, *Company Insolvency*, Chap. 14.
80 *Re Gray's Inn Construction Co.* [1980] 1 W.L.R. 711 at 717.
81 1963 Act, s.220.
82 *ibid.*, ss. 218 and 255.
83 *Oakes v. Turquand* (1867) L.R. 2 H.L. 325.
84 1963 Act, s.255.

pany.[85] There is no corresponding provision for a compulsory winding up but it seems to be universally accepted that, once a liquidator is appointed, the directors powers come to an end, although it is possible that they continue in office for certain limited purposes.[86]

Contracts

18–23 In general, the advent of liquidation has no immediate effect on contracts persons have with the company. However, there are contracts with express and even implied terms that liquidation either lawfully terminates them or constitutes a repudiatory breach of them. Express provisions to that effect are often contained in leases. Commencement of an official liquidation operates as a notice of immediate termination of employment contracts but those contracts are not immediately terminated by the commencement of a voluntary liquidation.[87] As is explained later, there is a procedure whereby the liquidator may apply to disclaim onerous contracts.[88]

Litigation

18–24 Once the court appoints a provisional liquidator or orders that a company be wound up, all actions against the company are stayed.[89] But the court may allow proceedings to be brought or be continued on such terms as it deems fit.[90] Moreover, once a petition to wind up a company has been presented, either the company or any creditor or contributory may apply to the court to stay or restrain any action or proceeding against the company.[91] In the case of a voluntary winding up, the liquidator may apply to the court to have proceedings being brought against the company stayed; it is for him to show why a stay should be ordered in any particular instance.[92]

Company Property

18–25 Unlike the position in bankruptcies,[93] the company's property does not automatically vest in the liquidator. But he may apply to the

---

85 1963 Act, ss. 258(2) and 269(3).
86 *Madrid Bank Ltd v. Bayley* (1866) 2 Q.B. 37.
87 See generally, M. Forde, *Employment Law* (1991), Chap. 10.
88 1963 Act, s.290; see below, paras 18–73 *et seq*.
89 *ibid.*, s.222; *e.g. Re Belfast Shipowners' Co.* [1894] 1 I.R. 322 and *Pierce v. Wexford Picture House Co.* [1915] 2 I.R. 310.
90 *ibid.*; *e.g. Re Aro Co. Ltd* [1980] 1 Ch. 196. *cf. National Employees Mutual General Insurance Association* [1995] 1 B.C.L.C. 232, where proceedings had been commenced without getting leave.
92 *ibid.*, s.217.
93 *ibid.*, s.280; *e.g. Currie v. Consolidated Kent Colleries Corp.* [1906] 1 K.B. 134.

court to have title to all or part of that property vested in him.[94] Section 218 of the 1963 Act stipulates that any disposition of the company's property following commencement of a compulsory winding up is void unless the court orders otherwise. The principle governing decisions by the court to uphold any such disposition is that "[s]ince the policy of the law is to procure so far as practicable rateable payments of the unsecured creditors' claims, . . . the court should not validate any transaction or series of transactions which might result in one or more pre-liquidation creditors being paid in full at the expense of other creditors, who will receive only a dividend, in the absence of special circumstances making such a course desirable in the interests of the unsecured creditors as a body."[95] In *Re Pat Ruth Ltd.*[96] Costello J. refused to validate payments made into the company's overdrawn bank account between the time the petition was presented and the winding up order was made, on the grounds that to do so would have preferred the bank over other unsecured creditors.[97] But payment into a bank account that is in credit is not caught by section 218.[98]

Creditors' Remedies

18–26 A creditor who has issued execution against a company's property or has attached a debt due by the company is not permitted to retain the benefit of these processes unless enforcement was completed before the winding up commenced or the date the creditor received notice of the proposal to wind up.[99] Furthermore, before goods taken in execution are sold or the execution is completed, the liquidator may demand that the sheriff return those goods.[100] Rights arising under these two powers may be set aside by the court and a purchaser in good faith, under a sale by the sheriff, acquires a good title against the liquidator.[101] Where the company is being wound up compulsorily, any execution, attachment, sequestration or distress put into force against company property after the winding up commences is absolutely void.[102]

---

94 Bankruptcy Act 1988, s.44(1).
95 1963 Act, s.230.
96 *Re Gray's Inn Construction Co.* [1980] 1 W.L.R. 711 at 718.
97 [1981] I.L.R.M. 51.
98 See too *Re Clifton Place Garage Ltd* [1970] 1 Ch. 477, *Re J. Leslie Engineers Co.* [1976] 1 W.L.R. 292, *Ashmark Ltd v. Allied Irish Banks p.l.c.* [1994] 3 I.R. 460, *Ashmark Ltd v. Switzers & Co.* [1994] 3 I.R. 466 and *Mond v. Hammond Suddards* [1996] 2 B.C.L.C. 470.
98 *Re Barn Crown Ltd* [1995] 1 W.L.R. 147.
99 1963 Act, s.291. *cf. Re Lough Neagh Ship Co., ex p. Thompson* [1896] 1 I.R. 29.
100 *ibid.*, s.292.
101 *ibid.*, ss. 291(4), 291(3) and 292(3).
102 *ibid.*, s.219.

18–27 Any judgment mortgage which is registered against the company's land within three months before the winding up commences obtains no "priority or preference over simple contract creditors".[103] Whether a judgment mortgage registered within that period takes priority over tort creditors is debatable; at the time this rule was adopted in bankruptcy law, claims in tort could not be proved against an insolvent's estate.[104]

18–28 Commencement of a winding up is a crystallising event which converts any floating charge on all or part of the company's property into a fixed charge.[105] A winding up does not prevent the appointment of a receiver under a debenture, nor does it affect the receiver's entitlement to dispose of the charged assets. But it puts an end to the receiver's express authority to manage the business and to enter into contracts binding on the company for that purpose.[106]

THE LIQUIDATOR

18–29 Depending on what kind of winding up it is, the members, the creditors or the court will appoint one or more liquidators, whose principal function is to dispose of the company's assets, pay or settle its debts and distribute to the members whatever capital and surplus that may remain. Having a suitable liquidator makes a big difference to creditors and even more so to shareholders, in that they stand to benefit from the price the liquidator obtains for the assets. Liquidators' fees form a significant proportion of accountants' incomes and liquidators can award lucrative conveyancing and other work to legal practitioners. Formerly any person could act as a company liquidator but section 300A of the 1963 Act[107] disqualifies former officers and employees of the company, during the preceding 12 months, any of their partners and any close member of their family. A purported appointment is not effective until the liquidator has signified his written consent.[108] A committee of inspection, comprised of creditors' and contributories' representatives, is usually appointed in creditors' voluntary winding ups and in compulsory winding ups in order to monitor the conduct of the liquidation.

---

[103] 1963 Act, s.284(2); *cf.* Bankruptcy Act 1988, s.51(1).
[104] *i.e.* in 1857. But the position changed in 1961; see below, para. 18–78, n. 221.
[105] See Chap. 16, paras 16–41 *et seq.*
[106] *Sowman v. David Samuel Trusts Ltd* [1978] 1 W.L.R. 22.
[107] Inserted by 1990 Act, s.146.
[108] 1963 Act, s.276A, inserted by 1990 Act, s.133.

Voluntary Winding Up

18–30 Although the liquidator in a voluntary winding up owes certain statutory duties to the creditors and shareholders, he is not strictly speaking a trustee for either of those groups and is best regarded as simply an agent of the company. The 1963 Act confers numerous specific powers on the liquidator, such as to sell company property and to "carry on the business of the company so far as may be necessary for [its] beneficial winding up";[109] also the power to "do all such other things as may be necessary for winding up the affairs of the company and distributing its assets."[110] But the powers to pay any classes of creditors in full and to make compromises with company creditors and debtors, and with members owing outstanding calls, must be exercised with the consent of the members, or with the consent of the creditors or committee of inspection in the case of a creditors' voluntary winding up.[111] The liquidator acts on behalf of the company and is not normally personally liable on contracts made in that capacity.[112] Liquidators frequently apply to the court for directions as to what they are entitled to do.[113] Where cause is shown, the court may remove a liquidator and appoint a replacement.[114]

Official Liquidator

18–31 The liquidator appointed by the court in a compulsory winding up is described as the official liquidator. One consequence of making a winding up order is to terminate the employment contracts of the company's employees[115] and to remove the directors and deprive them of their powers to act for the company.[116] Section 231 of the 1963 Act itemises the liquidator's powers, which include power to "do such . . . things as may be necessary for winding up the affairs of the company and distributing its assets".[117] Some of these powers may be exercised only with the court's or the committee of inspection's consent,[118] namely to bring or defend any action involving the company, to carry on the business for the time being, to appoint a solicitor, to pay any class of creditors and to make compromises with debtors or with mem-

---

109 1963 Act, ss. 231(1)(b) and 276(1)(b).
110 *ibid.*, ss. 231(2)(i) and 276(1)(b).
111 *ibid.*, ss. 231(1)(d)–(f) and 276(1)(a).
112 *Stead Hazel & Co. v. Cooper* [1933] 1 K.B. 840.
113 1963 Act, s.280; *e.g. Re Roche* (1936) 70 I.L.T.R. 134.
114 *ibid.*, s.277(2). *cf. Re Bridgend Goldsmiths Ltd* [1995] 2 B.C.L.C. 208, where the liquidator ceased to be qualified.
115 *Measures Bros. Ltd v. Measures* [1910] 2 Ch. 248.
116 See above, para. 18–22.
117 1963 Act, s.231(2)(i).
118 *ibid.*, s.231(1)(a)–(f).

bers holding not fully-paid shares. Any creditor or contributory may apply to the court in respect of the exercise of the liquidator's powers.[119] Official liquidators often apply to the court for directions as to what they should do or for approval for what they have done. Although official liquidators have a right to resign,[120] the act of resignation does not of itself release them from their obligations.[121]

18–32 A matter that gives rise to great controversy is which of competing bids for company property being offered for sale should be accepted. The liquidator's and the court's primary duty is to get the maximum price obtainable.[122] Although an official liquidator is not obliged to seek the court's consent to the terms of a sale, either prior approval or subsequent confirmation by the court is usually sought for disposals of major properties. In *Van Hool McArdle Ltd. v. Rohan Industrial Estate Ltd.*[123] it was held that, if the sale is subject to the court's prior approval, then the liquidator must accept the highest offer made — even if that offer was made subsequent to the liquidator having agreed with another party to sell him the property, subject to the court's consent. By contrast, in *Re Hibernian Transport Co.*,[124] acting under the court's direction the liquidator accepted one offer but, before the court confirmed the sale, a higher offer was made. It was held that it would be a breach of faith for the court to go back on the earlier bargain. Where the liquidator went about the matter without any prior reference to the court, then if his action is subsequently questioned, the court "would only have been concerned to see whether he acted bona fide and in due discharge of his duties as liquidator."[125]

Provisional Liquidator

18–33 Section 226 of the 1963 Act authorises the court to appoint a provisional liquidator in an appropriate case. An application of this nature may be made *ex parte* unless the court otherwise directs. Where a provisional liquidator is appointed the court will stipulate what his powers and functions shall be and the property over which he is given control. The grounds normally relied upon for seeking such an appointment are that there is a significant danger of the company's assets be-

---

[119] 1963 Act, s.231(3); *e.g. Re Brook Cottage Ltd* [1976] N.I. 78.
[120] *ibid.*, s.228(c).
[121] *Re Northern Waterproof Ltd* [1967] N.I. 17.
[122] *Van Hool McArdle Ltd v. Rohan Industrial Estates Ltd* [1980] I.R. 237 and *Re Brook Cottage Ltd* [1976] N.I. 78.
[123] [1980] I.R. 237.
[124] [1972] I.R. 190; see also *Munster & Leinster Bank v. Munster Motor Co.* [1992] 1 I.R. 15.
[125] *Van Hool* case [1980] I.R. at 240.

ing dissipated by the present directors and shareholders prior to the actual hearing of the petition.[126] An application of this nature may be made at any time up to the date of the hearing and, indeed, also if the court's decision on the petition is being appealed. Once one is appointed, the directors become displaced and control of the company's affairs vests in the provisional liquidator; the practical effect therefore being that the company's business becomes virtually paralysed. However, in special circumstances, the provisional liquidator may be authorised to manage the business for the time being. No action or proceedings may be brought against the company without leave of the court.[127]

18–34 The principal duty of the provisional liquidator is to take into his custody or under his control all the property and things in action to which the company is or appears to be entitled.[128] This is done with a view to protecting and preserving these assets for the benefit of all who will share in the ultimate realisation of them. His primary function therefore is to maintain the status quo pending determination of the winding up proceedings. It has been observed that the term "provisional" here implies a qualification of the tenure of a liquidator's office and not of his powers.[129] Nevertheless, he is confined to the powers which have actually been conferred on him and, even if there are no express restrictions on them, he must not proceed with a *de facto* winding up. In exercising whatever powers were conferred on him, he is always under the control of the court.

ASSET-SWELLING MEASURES

18–35 The whole purpose of winding up a company is to pay off the creditors, according to their priorities, and to distribute what remains among the investors, according to their rights to repayment of capital and to participation in any surplus. Not alone is the machinery of liquidation organised to this end but the 1963 Act contains some major rules that protect creditors and investors against unfair advantage being taken of the company. Several of these are designed to prevent unfair discrimination between creditors. Although section 284 of the 1963 Act applies the general law of bankruptcy to some aspects of wind-

---

126 *E.g. Re Forrester & Lamego Ltd* [1997] 2 B.C.L.C. 155 & *Re Pinstripe Farming Co.* [1996] 2 B.C.L.C. 295.

127 1963 Act, s.222.

128 *ibid.*, s.229(1).

129 *Re A.B.C. Coupler & Engineering Co. Ltd (No. 3)* [1970] 1 W.L.R. 702 at 715.

ing up insolvent companies,[130] in *Re Irish Attested Sales Ltd.*[131] it was held that section 284 does not import into winding ups those bankruptcy rules that have the effect of increasing the insolvent's assets which are available for the creditors. Nevertheless, various other provisions of the 1963 Act either apply or adapt some of those "asset-swelling" rules to company liquidations.

18–36 Curiously, the Companies Acts do not contain an equivalent of section 58 of the Bankruptcy Act 1988, that strikes at what are termed transactions at an undervalue, especially when the British legislation as well as the 1988 Act have similar provisions.[132]

Inquisition

18–37 Sections 245 and 280 of the 1963 Act empower the court to conduct a veritable inquisition into the affairs of the company that is being compulsorily or voluntarily wound up.[133] The court may summon before it any person it knows or suspects possesses company property or is indebted to the company, and any person it deems capable of giving information about the company's formation, promotion, trade, property, dealings or affairs. These persons may be required to produce any documents related to the company that they possess.[134] They may be required to set out in a written statement an account of transactions between themselves and the company. They moreover may be examined on oath.[135] They may not refuse to answer any question on the grounds that they might be incriminating themselves; but any such answer is not admissible in any subsequent proceedings,[136] apart from a prosecution for perjury. Information gained from these examinations frequently provides the foundation for misfeasance suits and for proceedings for fraudulent trading.[137] If in the course of an examination of

---

[130] See generally, *Bankruptcy Law*, Chap. 7 and *Company Insolvency*, Chap. 17 on asset-swelling measures.

[131] [1962] I.R. 70.

[132] Insolvency Act 1986, s.423; see *e.g. Midland Bank v. Wyatt* [1997] 1 B.C.L.C. 242, *National Bank of Kuwait v. Menzies* [1994] 2 B.C.L.C. 306 and *Lloyds Bank v. Marcan* [1973] 1 W.L.R. 1387.

[133] *cf.* Bankruptcy Act 1988, s.21, Bankruptcy Law, pp. 110–114 and *Company Insolvency*, pp. 198–206.

[134] *cf. Soden v. Burns* [1996] 2 B.C.L.C. 636; *Re Bank of Credit & Commerce International S.A. (No. 12)* [1997] 1 B.C.L.C. 526 on the oppressive resort to this power.

[135] *cf. Re PFTZM Ltd* [1995] 2 B.C.L.C. 354 on the oppressive resort to this power.

[136] s.245(6). *cf. Re Jeffry Levitt Ltd* [1992] Ch. 457 and *Bishopgate Investment Management Ltd v. Maxwell* [1993] Ch. 1 holding there is no such principle under a comparable section of the British Act, which does not expressly deal with the point.

[137] *e.g. Re Aluminium Fabricators Ltd* [1984] I.L.R.M. 399.

this nature it appears that any person being questioned owes the company money or holds property belonging to it, the court may direct that the money be paid or the property be delivered up to the liquidator.[138]

Restitution of Assets Fraudulently Disposed Of

18–38 Section 139 of the 1990 Act facilitates recovery of company property which had been disposed of in any way that defrauded the company, its creditors or its members. Any creditor or contributory of the company or the liquidator can apply and, if they satisfy the court that the property was disposed of in that manner, the court is empowered to order its repayment or recovery. That order can be made against any person who appears to have the use, control or possession of such property or of the proceeds from its sale or any development of the property. In deciding to make any order of this nature, account must be taken of the interests of any bona fide purchaser for value of the property.

Fraudulent Conveyance

18–39 Section 10 of the Fraudulent Conveyances Act 1634, declares void a very wide category of transfers of property by a debtor done with the intention to defraud his creditors.[139] The power to set aside transfers of property on these grounds is not an exclusively bankruptcy jurisdiction. In *Re Kill Inn Motel Ltd.*[140] Murphy J. confirmed that this power applies just as much to property transfers made by companies as to transfers by individuals.

Fraudulent Preference

18–40 The Eleventh Schedule of the 1963 Act amended the old Bankruptcy Act's definition of fraudulent preference[141] and section 286 of the 1963 Act applies this bankruptcy rule to companies in liquidation.[142] This rule is based on the principle that it is "unjust to permit a party, on the eve of bankruptcy, to make a voluntary disposition of his property in favour of a particular creditor, leaving the mere husk to the rest, and therefore, that a transfer made at such a period, and under such circumstances, as evidently showed that it was made in contem-

---

138 1963 Act, s.245A, inserted by 1990 Act, s.127.
139 See generally, *Bankruptcy Law*, pp. 115–121.
140 Murphy J., September 16, 1987 (*ex tempore judgment*).
141 Bankruptcy Ireland Amendment Act 1872, s.53.
142 As amended by 1990 Act, s.135. See generally, *Bankruptcy Law*, pp. 121–129 and *Company Insolvency*, pp. 236–246.

plation of bankruptcy and in order to favour a particular creditor, should be void".[143] What section 286 renders void is every transfer and the like by a company of its property, occurring within six months of its being wound up, that was made:

> "in favour of any creditor . . . with a view to giving such creditor, or any surety or guarantor for the debt due to such creditor, a preference over the other creditors. . . ."

18–41 In order for the transfer of property to be caught by this prohibition, the company must have been insolvent at the time the transfer was made, meaning that it was unable to pay its debts as they fell due. It matters not that the directors believed that the company was solvent, or that its financial position would shortly improve and it would not have to be wound up.[144] Although most preferences falling within this section involve cash payments, transfers of any kind of property and, it would seem set-offs,[145] made with the prohibited intention are caught by section 286. A person taking title in good faith and for valuable consideration, through or under a creditor, to property that was fraudulently conveyed is not expressly affected by this rule.

Intention to Prefer

18–42 While fraud in this context does not import moral blame, the courts have narrowly construed the *scienter* requirement.[146] It must be proved that the company's dominant intention was to prefer the transferee over other creditors. The mere fact of preference does not demonstrate this intent; the transaction will be upheld if it was entered into, for example, to withstand pressure being exercised against the company or its directors, or to obtain some advantage for the company.[147] There are certain stock situations where the courts readily infer an improper intention, notably where the company's directors had given personal guarantees for the company's debts and, shortly before the winding up, they arranged to have those debts paid off and the security cancelled.[148] Another is where the company had agreed to give

---

143 *ex p. De Tastet v. Carroll* (1813) 1 Stark 88 at 89.

144 *Re F.P. & C.H. Matthews Ltd* [1982] 1 Ch. 257.

145 *Citroen Sales (Ireland) Ltd v. Ashenhurst Williams & Co.* [1993] 2 I.R. 69.

146 See generally, Farrar, "The Bankruptcy of the Law of Fraudulent Preference" [1983] J. Bus. L. 390 and Coutts, "Proof of Intent to Defeat or Delay Creditors" [1952] Conv. 458.

147 *Sharp v. Jackson* [1899] A.C. 419.

148 *e.g. Re M. Kushler Ltd* [1943] 1 Ch. 248, *Station Motors Ltd v. Allied Irish Banks* [1985] I.R. 756; *Re Agriplant Services Ltd* [1997] 2 B.C.L.C. 598; *cf. Re Welding Plant Ltd* (McWilliam J., June 27, 1984) and *Re Fairway Magazines Ltd* [1993] B.C.L.C. 643.

its creditor a charge once called upon to do so.[149] But there are no hard and fast rules which determine what is improper here; in the end, it depends on all the circumstances of the case whether the company deliberately put one particular creditor at an advantage over all the others for no good business reason in connection with the company's interests.

18–43 In *Re John Daly & Co.*,[150] Porter M.R. said of the *scienter* requirement:

> "A "view to prefer" is produced in one man's mind by the fact that the creditor is his brother or near relation; in another's because the creditor has been kind to him in the past; in that of a third, because he expects that after his bankruptcy the creditor (if now preferred) will aid him in business once again; in that of a fourth, because it is a first transaction with the creditor, and he thinks his a specially hard case; in that of a fifth, because he thinks his other creditors have treated him harshly. There is always some motive behind the "view to prefer". Yet, in cases where there is no trust, no pressure, and no obligation other than contract, neither natural love and affection, gratitude, expectation of benefit, sympathy, vindictiveness, or any other mental condition, can in such cases eliminate the view to prefer, which is the statutory condition of liability, however strongly the debtor may be convinced that he has done what is fair and right in according the preference."[151]

An improper intention was established in that case where the company, which was in serious financial difficulties, borrowed a substantial sum from its auditor. It was understood that the company would then raise funds, from which the auditor would be repaid. In the event, when the shareholders refused to permit the issue of debentures and following remonstrations by the auditor, he was repaid his loan. Shortly afterwards the company was wound up. It was held that the payment to the auditor was unlawful because no actual pressure was exerted on the company to pay him before the other creditors and the reasonable inference, therefore, was to benefit him especially.[152] Little purpose would be served in reciting the facts of the many cases since then where the requisite intent was held either to have been present or not to have been present.[153]

---

149 *e.g. Re Eric Holmes (Property) Ltd* [1965] 1 Ch. 1052; *cf. Re William Hall (Contractors) Ltd* [1967] 1 W.L.R. 948.

150 (1886) 19 L.R. Ir. 83.

151 *ibid.* at 97.

152 *cf. Re Ledingham-Smith* [1993] B.C.L.C. 634.

153 Several of these are considered in *Bankruptcy Law*, pp. 124–129. In addition to cases referred to above see also, *Re F.L.E. Holdings Ltd* [1967] 1 W.L.R. 1409; *Parkes Hotel v. Hong Kong & Shanghai Banking Corp.* [1990] I.L.R.M. 341; *Kelleher v. Continental Irish Meat Ltd* (Costello J., 9 May 1978), *Corran Construction Co. v.*

Payments to Connected Persons

18–44 In many of the instances where payments were challenged on these grounds, the company had discharged a debt owing to one of its officers or some other person or body which was closely connected with them. Even where the circumstances would warrant drawing the inference of an improper intention, if the payment was made more than six months before the winding up had commenced, it could not be challenged on these grounds; the only possibility then would be an attack based on the 1634 Act against fraudulent conveyances.[154] However, in the 1990 Act, section 286 was amended to deal with this kind of situation. Where a payment was made to a "connected person" then the relevant period is extended to two years prior to the liquidation and, additionally, the payment is deemed to be improper unless the contrary is shown. Thus, it is for the connected payee to demonstrate a genuine commercial justification for the company preferring him over all the other creditors. A connected person for these purposes is a director or a shadow director of the company, a person connected with a director as defined in section 26 of the 1990 Act,[155] a "related company" as defined in section 140 of that Act[156] and also a trustee or surety or guarantor for the debt due to any of those parties.

Preferring Secured Creditor

18–45 Section 287 of the 1963 Act is designed to protect, principally, banks that extend credit to a company by an overdraft, that is guaranteed by a director, from unfairly suffering loss in consequence of the fraudulent preference rule. If the company in the circumstances defined in section 286 reduced the overdraft, it may very well thereby prefer the bank; the guarantor and the bank will then be obliged to repay those sums to the liquidator. This provision gives the bank a statutory right of action against the guarantor as if he had undertaken to be personally liable to the extent of the interest in the security given.

Final 12 Months' Floating Charge

18–46 The rule regarding final 12 months' floating charges is an extension of the general principle underlying fraudulent preferences to a particular situation. There is always a danger that, when a company is getting into financial difficulties, one or more unsecured creditors who

---

Bank of Ireland Finance Ltd, McWilliam J, September 8, 1976) and *Countrywide Banking Corp. v. Dean* [1998] 2 W.L.R. 441.

[154] See above, para 18–39.

[155] See above, para. 5–14.

[156] See above, para. 14–36.

are in a very strong bargaining position, like the company's bankers, may be able to obtain a charge over its assets and thereby improve their position if the company proves to be insolvent. Sections 288 and 289 of the 1963 Act[157] strike at this practice in respect of floating charges. A floating charge created by a company within 12 months of its being wound up is invalid unless it is proved that the company was solvent immediately after the charge was given. Where the floating charge is given to a "connected person" as defined in section 288(4) (for instance Mr Saloman in the *Saloman & Co.* case),[158] the relevant period for invalidation is extended to two years.

18–47 In *Crowley v. Northern Bank Finance Corp.*,[159] which is an excellent example of the kind of practice the legislature had in mind, it was held that, once the charge was created within the specified period, it is for the chargee to demonstrate that the company was solvent at the time. Solvency in this context means that the company was able to pay its debts as they fell due — and not that its assets exceeded its liabilities or whether a business person would have regarded the company as solvent. In order to ascertain if the company was solvent, an examination of its financial history, both before and after the charge was given, may be required. Where at that time the directors had intended to carry on the company's business, the company's fixed and movable assets must not be taken into account in determining solvency. But against that, account may be taken of the company's capacity to raise additional funds by borrowing after the charge was given.

18–48 An exception to the above rule is made for a charge that is given in consideration for cash that was paid to the company either when the charge was created or later. In other words, a charge is not invalid where it was given, not to secure existing debts, but to raise additional funds. It was held in *Re Daniel Murphy Ltd.*[160] that the critical time here is not the date the charge was actually executed but when the company agreed to create the charge, provided however that any delay in executing the charge was not intended to deceive creditors and was not unreasonably culpable.[161] However, the 1990 Act's amended version of section 288 would seem to reverse the position as stated there, subject to a *de minimus* delay between getting the money

---

157 As amended by 1990 Act, s.136.
158 [1897] A.C. 22.
159 *Re Creation Printing Co.* [1981] I.R. 353.
160 [1964] I.R. 1.
161 See *Re Olderfleet Shipbuilding Co.* [1922] 1 I.R. 26, *Revere Trust Ltd v. Wellington Handkerchief Works Ltd* [1931] N.I. 55 and *Re Destone Fabrics Ltd* [1941] 1 Ch. 319.

and granting the charge.[162] It was also held there that the rule in *Clayton's Case*[163] applies in this context. For an ordinary overdraft, this means that all subsequent lodgements first pay off the debit balance, and all subsequent withdrawals are fresh payments by the bank. Accordingly, if enough funds are turned over in the bank account during the twelve months period the bank will have obtained a valid charge in respect of substantially what the company owed it at the outset.[164]

18–49 Despite the above rule, if the chargee moves quickly and enforces his security before the company goes into liquidation, he can retain the proceeds of realisation. In *Mace Builders (Glasgow) Ltd. v. Lunn*[165] a company gave the defendant a floating charge and, within twelve months of that time, it went into liquidation. In the meantime, however, the chargee had demanded repayment of the sum owing to him, which was not done. He accordingly appointed a receiver who realised the security and paid off the debt. It was held that section 288 does not operate retrospectively to invalidate what was done under the charge. In this case the chargee was a related company and, being a "connected person", the relevant period would now be two years before the liquidation. But that circumstance would not have effected the outcome in the case.

18–50 Section 289 is an application of the above 12 months rule to floating charges created in favour of an "officer" of the company, but the exception for cash paid on or after the charge being given does not apply here. This provision is designed to prevent evasion of section 288 by directors and the like, to whom the company was indebted, arranging to have the debt discharged and then obtaining a floating charge to secure fresh advances that the officer would make to the company.

Fraudulent Trading

18–51 Sections 297 and 297A of the 1963 Act, which deal with fraudulent trading, were among the most important protections for creditors of insolvent companies.[166] What constitutes fraudulent trading is defined, as:

> "knowingly [being] a party to the carrying on of any business of the com-

---

[162] *Power v. Sharp Investments Ltd* [1994] 1 B.C.L.C. 111.
[163] (1816) 1 Mer. 572.
[164] See *Re Yeovil Glove Co.* [1965] 1 Ch. 148.
[165] [1986] Ch. 459.
[166] See generally, Ussher, "Fraudulent Trading" [1984] D.U.L.J. 58 and Farrar, "Fraudulent Trading" [1980] J. Bus. L. 336.

pany with intent to defraud creditors of the company, or creditors of any other person or for any fraudulent purpose."

Put briefly, if it is shown that the company was being managed with the intention of defrauding its creditors or others, then those who were then running the company can be made responsible. Fraudulent trading is a criminal offence,[167] with a maximum penalty of a £50,000 fine or seven years imprisonment, or both, where there is a conviction on indictment. It is also a civil wrong and proceedings can be instituted by either any creditor or contributory of the company, or by its liquidator, receiver or examiner. The sanction for the civil wrong is imposing unlimited liability for all or part of the company's debts. The contention that the civil part of this section was in substance criminal and accordingly was unconstitutional, because the usual procedures for criminal trials did not apply, was rejected by the Supreme Court.[168]

18–52 *Re Aluminium Fabricators Ltd. (No. 2)*[169] provides an excellent example. In the course of its winding up, it was discovered that all cash payments made to the company were not recorded in the accounts made available to the auditors, but were instead recorded in a secret register which ultimately disappeared unaccountably from the company's premises. The cash was siphoned off by the company's two directors to their bank accounts in the Isle of Man. At the time of the action the company was hopelessly insolvent. O'Hanlon J. had no hesitation in concluding that the directors should be personally liable without limit for all the company's debts and liabilities. He observed that "[t]he privilege of limitation of liability which is afforded by the Companies Act . . . cannot be afforded to those who use a limited company as a cloak or shield beneath which they seek to operate a fraudulent system of carrying on business for their. own personal enrichment and advantage".[170]

Fraud

18–53 In *Re Patrick & Lyon Ltd.*[171] it was said that to come within section 297 requires "actual dishonesty involving, according to current notions of fair trading among commercial men, real moral blame".[172]

---

[167] *e.g. R. v. Smith* [1996] 2 B.C.L.C. 109.
[168] *O'Keefe v. Ferris* [1997] 3 I.R. 463. *cf. Southern Mineral Oil Ltd v. Cooney* [1997] 3 I.R. 549 and *Re Farmizer Products Ltd* [1997] 1 B.C.L.C. 589 on extreme delay in bring proceedings under this section.
[169] O'Hanlon J., May 13, 1983.
[170] At p. 17.
[171] [1933] Ch. 786.
[172] *ibid.* at 790.

In *R. v. Grantham*,[173] which was an appeal against a conviction for fraudulent trading, the requirement of actual dishonesty was stressed:

> "there is nothing wrong in the fact that directors incur credit at a time when, to their knowledge, the company is not able to meet all its liabilities as they fall due. What is manifestly wrong is if directors allow a company to incur credit at a time when the business is being carried on in such circumstances that it is clear that the company will never be able to satisfy its creditors. However, there is nothing to say that directors who genuinely believe that the clouds will roll away and the sunshine of prosperity will shine upon them again and disperse the fog of their depression are not entitled to incur credit to help them to get over the bad time."[174]

Although it was said in *Re W.G Leitch Bros. Ltd.* that "if a company continues to carry on business and incur debts at a time when there is to the knowledge of the directors nó reasonable prospect of the creditors ever receiving payment of those debts, it is, in general, a proper inference that the company is carrying on business with intent to defraud",[175] the court was dealing with what constitutes evidence of fraud. Since usually it is extremely difficult to prove an actual fraudulent intent, a court often can only draw inferences from facts which do not unambiguously constitute fraud. It remains to be seen how section 40 of the 1983 Act on capital haemorrhages[176] will affect establishing liability for fraudulent trading.

18–54 Simply to prefer one creditor of an insolvent company over another does not contravene sections 297-297A, not even when the creditor who is preferred is the company's dominant shareholder or its parent company, provided of course that the indebteness is genuine and bona fide.[177] The tendency to construe the section's *scienter* and *mens rea* requirements narrowly is often criticised because, as a result, it is only in the most blatant instances that individuals are held responsible under this head, for instance, in *Re Aluminium Fabricators Ltd.*[178]

Trading

18–55 As for the other ingredients of this wrong, what amounts to carrying on business has been given an extensive meaning. It includes,

---

173 [1984] 2 W.L.R. 815.
174 *ibid.* at 820. In the same vein, *Re Augustus Barnett & Son Ltd* [1986] B.C.L.C. 170.
175 [1932] 2 Ch. 71 at 77.
176 See above, para. 7–08.
177 *Re Sarflax Ltd* [1979] Ch. 592.
178 See above, para. 18–52; similar instances include *Re Kelly's Carpetdrome Ltd*, Costello J., 1 July 1983 and *Re L. Todd (Swanscombe) Ltd* [1990] B.C.L.C. 454.

for example, engaging in simply one significant commercial transaction,[179] even collecting the assets acquired in the course of the business and distributing the proceeds among the company's debtors.[180] Unlike the new wrong of "reckless trading", liability for fraudulent trading is not confined to officers of the company. Those who can be held responsible under the sections are any person who at the time was involved in carrying on its business and was knowingly a party to the fraud. A company's creditors — even its bankers — can conceivably be caught by sections 297 or 297A. In *Re Cooper (Gerard) Chemicals Ltd.*[181] it was held that "a creditor is party to the carrying on of a business with intent to defraud creditors if he accepts money which he knows full well has in fact been procured by carrying on the business with intent to defraud creditors for the very purpose of making the payment".[182]

Burden of Proof

18–56 Because the civil wrong is also a crime, it was suggested in *Re Kelly's Carpetdrome Ltd. (No.2)*[183] that the burden of proof on plaintiffs is the criminal standard, beyond all reasonable doubt, and not the usual civil standard of the balance of probabilities. It is mainly for this reason and because of the narrow concept of *scienter* in these cases that few claims for fraudulent trading are brought and even fewer succeed. Where a defendant can show any reasonably plausible explanation for his actions, the claim would usually fall.

Unlimited Liability

18–57 One of the few instances where a claim succeeded in this country is *Re Hunting Lodges Ltd.*[184] Directors and the secretary of a company that was insolvent and that owed large sums to the Revenue Commissioners arranged for the sale of the company's principal undertaking, a well known public house called "Durty Nellies". But the full consideration was not paid to the company; part of the consideration was diverted into the directors' and the secretary's own bank accounts. Carroll J. held that disposing of the undertaking constituted carrying on business for these purposes and that, in the circumstances, the defendants had the requisite fraudulent intent. However, the pre-

---

[179] *Re Gerard Cooper (Chemicals) Ltd* [1978] Ch. 262.
[180] *Re Sarflax Ltd* [1979] Ch. 592.
[181] [1978] Ch. 262.
[182] *ibid.* at 268.
[183] O'Hanlon J., July 13, 1984.
[184] [1985] I.L.R.M. 75.

cise extent to which the defendants should be rendered liable for the company's debts was held to depend on their particular circumstances. Two of the defendants were directed to be liable without limit for the company's entire debts, but two others were made jointly liable only for £12,000, which was the amount diverted to their own benefit. So far criteria have not been laid down for determining how extensive a personal liability should be imposed on those who have committed fraudulent trading.[185]

Reckless Trading

18–58 The 1990 Act introduced the concept of "reckless trading", which is intended to answer many of the criticisms against the narrow scope of fraudulent trading.[186] It is probable that henceforth, when creditors or others are seeking to render persons who managed a company personally responsible for its unpaid debts, applications ordinarily will be brought under this heading rather than for fraudulent trading. It is only in the clearest instances of unquestionable fraud that persons would be pursued on that ground rather than for reckless trading. However, where the alleged wrongdoer was not an "officer" of the company, he can only be pursued for fraudulent trading; an officer for these purposes is defined as including "any auditor, liquidator, receiver or shadow director."[187] Mere employees and agents of the company and third parties, therefore, cannot be held accountable for reckless trading.

18–59 These provisions do not expressly purport to apply retrospectively. On account of the drastic consequences of being held liable for reckless trading, section 297A of the Companies Act 1963, will not be applied retrospectively, *i.e.* to events which occurred prior to the enactment of the Companies Act 1990, on the 22nd of December 1990. To apply this section retrospectively might very well contravene Article 15.5 of the Constitution.[188]

18–60 An application to hold a person accountable for reckless trading may be made by any creditor or contributory of the company, or by the liquidator, receiver or examiner. No declaration of personal liability will be made by the court unless the company is insolvent. Also,

---

185 *cf. Re a Company (No. 001418 of 1988)* [1991] B.C.L.C. 197.

186 See observations by Ussher and by Farrar, above, para 18–51, n.1, and *Report — Insolvency Law and Practice* (1982, Cmnd. 8558), Chap. 44 on "wrongful trading".

187 1963 Act, s.297A(10).

188 *Re Heffron Kearns Ltd* [1992] I.L.R.M. 51

the applicant in the proceedings must have suffered loss or damage in consequence of the alleged reckless conduct, or he must be representing someone who has so suffered. Because of this requirement, it will be very exceptionally, if ever at all, that the examiner will make an application under section 297A. The fact that the action being complained of was performed outside the State or that the respondent may be held criminally responsible for what he has done is no bar to a claim for reckless trading by him.

"Reckless"

18–61 The kind of conduct which would constitutes reckless trading is defined by section 297A:

> "any person was, while an officer of the company, knowingly a party to the carrying on of any business of the company in a reckless manner, . . . Without prejudice to the generality of [this definition] an officer of the company shall be deemed to have been knowingly a party to the carrying on of any business of the company in a reckless manner if
>
> (a) he was a party to the carrying on of such business and, having regard to the general knowledge, skill and experience that may reasonably be expected of a person in his position, he ought to have known that his actions or those of the company would cause loss to the creditors or the company or any of them, or
>
> (b) he was a party to the contracting of a debt by the company and did not honestly believe on reasonable grounds that the company would be able to pay the debt when in fell due for payment as well as all its other debts (taking into account the contingent and prospective liabilities)."

18–62 Three categories of situation arise. One ((b) above) is where the officer was directly involved in contracting a debt on behalf of the company, for instance, by ordering supplies. If it can be shown that, at that time, he did not honestly believe on reasonable grounds that the company could repay that debt when in fell due, then he was trading recklessly.[189] The exact significance of the phrase "honestly believe" here is not clear; does it mean that the person did not really believe that the debt could be paid or is it necessary to go further and establish that he had some dishonest intention at the time? Indeed, it is questionable whether a belief can be either honest or dishonest; whether a belief is held is a pure question of fact about which the good or evil intentions of the believer do not have any bearing.

---

[189] *cf. Ross McConnell Kitchen & Co. Pty. Ltd v. Ross (No.2)* [1985] 1 N.S.W.L.R. 238, *Metal Mfrs. Pty. Ltd v. Lewis* [1988] 13 N.S.W.L.R. 315 and *Vinyl Processors (N.Z.) Ltd v. Cant* [1991] N.Z.L.R 416.

18–63 Secondly ((a) above), there is where the officer was directly involved in carrying on the business in circumstances where either his very actions or those of the company damaged the creditors or any one of them. For instance, he may have contracted a large debt which was repaid but at the expense of one or several of the creditors. Here, in order to be made liable, it must be shown that, at the time, he ought to have known that his or the company's actions would damage those creditors. Account will be taken of what general knowledge, skill and experience may reasonably be expected of him in determining whether he should have anticipated that damage.

18–64 Thirdly, there are other situations which do not fall within (a) or (b) which amount to acting recklessly.[190] A possible example may be not keeping proper records or having proper accounts. Indeed, section 204 of the Companies Act 1990, expressly provides for unlimited liability for officers who do not ensure that proper accounts are kept, which contributed to the company's inability to pay its debts.

Unlimited Liability

18–65 If the court finds that the respondent had indeed traded recklessly, it may declare him personally responsible, in whole or in part, for the company's debts. Presumably, in most cases the court would not impose personal liability beyond the amount which was lost as a result of the respondent's activities. No doubt, in time criteria will be adopted for determining the extent to which personal liability should be imposed. It is provided that if in all the circumstances the respondent acted honestly and responsibly in relation to the actions being complained of, the court may relieve him, either wholly or in part, from personal liability for the company's debts.[191] When declaring someone personally liable under this heading, the court may make various ancillary orders.

Misfeasance

18–66 Section 298 of the 1963 Act[192] provides a summary procedure for ensuring that companies being wound up are compensated for losses arising from various wrongs done to them by their directors and other

---

[190] On the meaning of the word "reckless", *cf. Goldman v. Thai Airways Int"l Ltd* [1983] 1 W.L.R. 1186. For a discussion of this term in the criminal law context, see note in (1991) 107 L.Q.R. 187.

[191] *Re Produce Marketing Consortium Ltd* [1989] 1 W.L.R. 745 and *Vinyl Processors case*, see above, n. 189.

[192] As amended by 1990 Act, s.142.

officers. The wrongs for these purposes are where any officer of the company:

> "has misapplied or retained or become liable or accountable for any money or property of the company, or has been guilty of any misfeasance or other breach of trust in relation to the company."

Who is a company "officer" in this context is not defined, so that in principle shadow directors would seem to fall outside section 298, but perhaps not *de facto* directors. Misfeasance can also be committed by any person who took part in forming or promoting the company and its receiver,[193] liquidator or examiner, as well as a director of the subsidiary's holding company.[194] On the application of the liquidator, or of a creditor or contributory, the court may investigate the matter and order restitution and compensation. Any creditor, therefore, can initiate this investigation; but it would appear that a fully paid up shareholder cannot do so if the company is insolvent.[195]

"Misfeasance"

18–67 Section 298 has no application where the damage inflicted was not suffered by the company as such; it provides no remedy for losses caused directly to creditors or shareholders, either individually or collectively.[196] Nor does the section enlarge on the existing substantive law regarding officers' wrongs to the company; it merely provides a special procedure for remedying the more serious of those wrongs when the company is being wound up.[197] Misfeasance in this context is "misfeasance in the nature of a breach of trust, that is to say, it refers to something which the officer . . . has done wrongly by misapplying or retaining in his own hands any moneys of the company, or by which the company's property has been wasted or the company's credit improperly pledged."[198] In *Re George Newman & Co.*,[199] for example, it was held to be misfeasance for directors of a company that was heavily in debt to permit one of their number, without charge, to use company property for his own private ends. According to Lindly L.J., "the presents made by the directors to . . . their chairman were made out of money borrowed by the company for the purposes of its business; and

---

193 Reversing *Re B. Johnson & Co. (Builders) Ltd* [1955] 1 Ch. 634.
194 1990 Act, s.148.
195 *Cavendish Bentbick v. Fenn* (1887) 12 App. Cas. 652 at 664, 667 and 672.
196 *Re Irish Provident Assur. Co.* [1913] 1 I.R. 352.
197 *ibid. cf. Re David Ireland Ltd* [1905] 1 I.R. 133 on awarding costs against officers in misfeasance proceedings.
198 *Walker v. Wimborne*, 50 A.L.T. R. 446 (1976), at 450.
199 [1895] 1 Ch. 674.

this money the directors had no right to apply in making presents to one of themselves. . . . ."[200]

18–68 The misfeasance claim does not provide a remedy for mere negligence. In *Mont Clare Hotels Ltd.*[201] Costello J. reiterated the view that "it is not every error of judgment that amounts to misfeasance in law and it is not every act of negligence that amounts to misfeasance in law . . . [S]omething more than mere carelessness is required, some act that, perhaps, may amount to gross negligence in failing to carry out a duty owed by the director to his company."[202] In this case the director of the company in question had arranged for it to make a substantial loan to another company, of which he was a director, but there was nothing in writing about that loan and no security was given. In the event the borrower failed and, largely because it could not recover the loan, the company got into financial difficulties and eventually had to be wound up. In the light of all the circumstances, it was held that the director was not guilty of misfeasance for not ensuring that the loan was repaid. The misfeasance claim for having actually made the loan and not getting any security was barred by the Statute of Limitations.

18–69 Failure to perform a duty that leads to the company's property being misapplied can constitute misfeasance. Thus in *Re John Fulton & Co.*,[203] the company's auditor who certified erroneous accounts, on the strength of which the company improperly paid dividends, was ordered to compensate the company for those amounts. The company's directors there were made jointly responsible. And it was held that a paid director there could not plead in his defence that he was entirely ignorant of his duties, that he only saw what reports were submitted to the annual general meeting and that he relied entirely on the auditor to look after the company's financial affairs.

Exempting Liability

18–70 It was held by Gavan Duffy P. in *Re S. M. Barker Ltd.*[204] that, where the ex-directors being accused of misfeasance were also the company's sole shareholders and, *qua* shareholders, they consented to the company in effect giving themselves presents of its property, this cannot constitute officer misfeasance. There the directors-owners of a then

---

[200] [1895] 1 Ch. 674 at 685. *cf. West Mercia Safewear Ltd v. Dodd* [1988] B.C.L.C. 250.
[201] Costello J., December 2, 1986.
[202] *ibid.* at 4. *cf. Re Welfab Engineers Ltd* [1990] B.C.L.C. 833.
[203] [1932] N.I. 35.
[204] [1950] I.R. 123.

solvent company had agreed to sell their shares in it and, at the same time, resolved in general meeting that they should be released from a substantial debt they owed the company. That resolution was described as improvident and as regrettable, in that it did not observe various formalities. It nevertheless was concluded that the directors could not be held liable for misfeasance:

> "because they were the owners, they were the complete masters of the company's situation; it is as such that they were in a position to profit and did profit, and not as directors or trustees for the shareholders. [Their release], whether valid in law or void or voidable, was the act of the company in general meeting. . . . There was . . . no concealment by the directors-owners, no trickery and no fraud."[205]

18–71 But the outcome would have been different if at the time of the resolution the company had been heavily in debt to outsiders and probably insolvent. In *Re George Newman & Co.*,[206] it was said that:

> "The shareholders at a meeting duly convened for the purpose, can, if they think proper, . . . make presents to directors out of assets properly divisible amongst the shareholders themselves . . . But to make presents out of profits is one thing and to make them out of capital or out of money borrowed by the company is a very different matter. Such money cannot be lawfully divided amongst the shareholders themselves, nor can it be given away by them for nothing to their directors as to bind the company in its corporate capacity."[207]

And it was held in *Re Greendale Developments Ltd.*[208] that the position is also different, even in the case of a solvent company, where the assent of all the shareholders is given informally rather than by way of a formal resolution, although why the lack of formality should make so significant a difference was not explained.[209]

Related Companies' Contribution

18–72 Where a company's wholly-owned subsidiary company or a closely related company becomes insolvent, a strong economic and moral argument can be made for requiring the holding company or otherwise connected company to pay at least part of the insolvent's debts. This would particularly be so where the insolvent was in fact

---

205 [1950] I.R. 123 at 138. *cf. Multinational Gas & Petrochemical Co. v. Multinational Gas & Petrochemical Services Ltd* [1983] 1 Ch. 258.

206 [1895] 1 Ch. 674.

207 *ibid.* at 686.

208 [1998] 1I.R. 8.

209 See above, paras 3–97 *et seq.* and 14–19 *et seq.*

doing the other company's more risky business and where there were good reasons for believing that the other company would rescue the insolvent if the need ever arose. Provision to this effect is now made in section 140 of the 1990 Act for "related companies" as defined there.[210] Before a contribution to the unpaid debts can be ordered, the court must be satisfied that "the circumstances that gave rise to the winding up of the company are attributable to the actions or omissions of the related company"; in other words, the related company had some decisive role in the events that triggered the winding up. Additionally, the court is required to have regard to certain aspects of the relationship between both companies, notably, involvement of one in the other's management, the conduct of one towards the other's creditors, as well as the effect of a contribution order on the related company's own creditors.

Disclaiming Onerous Obligations

18–73 Section 290 of the 1963 Act applies the somewhat anomalous bankruptcy rule about disclaiming onerous obligations[211] to companies in liquidation. Within 12 months of the winding up commencing and with the court's consent, the liquidator may in a sense discriminate against particular creditors by disclaiming the company's obligations to them, on the grounds that performance would be unduly burdensome for the company. This power is often invoked in order to terminate leases.[212] In one instance the liquidator was permitted to disclaim freehold land constituting a cemetery and contracts relating to the graves in it.[213] The court is empowered to make appropriate orders to give effect to the disclaimer. However, those persons to whom the company owed the disclaimed obligations must not shoulder the entire cost of thereby benefiting the general creditors; any person damaged by the disclaimer is deemed to be a creditor for the amount of that damage and may prove it as a debt in the winding up.[214]

18–74 In *Re Farm Machinery Distributors Ltd.*[215] the position of guarantees of covenants in leases called for consideration when the liquidator sought to disclaim the lease. Keane J. conducted an exhaustive analysis of many authorities on this section and on its analogue in general bankruptcy law, and reached the following conclusions:

---

[210] See above, para. 14–36.
[211] See generally, *Bankruptcy Law*, pp. 106–110.
[212] *e.g. Grant v. Aston Ltd* (1969) 103 I.L.T.R. 39. *cf.* Winding Up Rules, ss. 84(2) and 85(2).
[213] *Re Nottingham General Cemetery Co.* [1955] Ch. 683.
[214] 1963 Act, s.290(9). *cf. Re Park Air Services p.l.c.* [1997] 1 W.L.R. 1376.
[215] *Tempany v. Royal Liver Trustees Ltd* [1984] I.L.R.M. 273.

"1. The exclusive concern of the court in an application for leave to disclaim must be the interests of all persons interested in the liquidation. . .

2. In considering the extent, if any, to which the interests of those interested in the liquidation will be affected by the operation of a disclaimer it is necessary to consider whether the release of third parties such as (in the case of leasehold property) original lessees and sureties, is necessary "for the purpose of releasing the company and the property of the company from liability".

3. In the case of leasehold property which has been assigned by the original lessee to a company in liquidation, the release of the original lessee is not necessary for the purpose of releasing the company and the property of the company from liability. The position of a surety for the payment of the rent and performance of the covenants by a company holding property under a lease which goes into liquidation is no different; the release of the surety is not necessary for the purpose of releasing the company and the property of the company from liability.

4. The release of the surety in [such a] case not being necessary . . . , the liability of the surety is not affected by the disclaimer by the liquidator of the interest of the company in the property."[216]

18–75 In *Re Ranks Ireland Ltd.*,[217] the matter to be determined was the measure of damages payable to a party whose contract was being disclaimed. The contracts there were equipment leases and one of the terms was that, in the event of their being repudiated, a stipulated sum shall become payable as damages. But Murphy J. held that this was not the proper measure of compensation in these circumstances. That measure was the difference between the rent which the company would have paid the lessor and the rent that the lessor is likely to earn during the unexpired residue of the leases.

PAYING OFF CREDITORS

18–76 Before any distribution can be made to the shareholders or members, the liquidator must first pay off the creditors or settle any claims they may have against the company. The intrinsic nature of a winding up, insofar as it concerns company creditors, has been described graphically as follows:

---

216 [1984] I.L.R.M. 273 at pp. 289–190, rejecting *Stacey v. Hill* [1901] 1 Q.B. 66 *and Re Katherine et Cie Ltd* [1932] 1 Ch. 70. The House of Lords followed suit in *Hindcastle Ltd v. Barbara Attenborough Associates Ltd* [1997] A.C. 70.

217 [1989] I.R. 1.

"liquidation is a form of collective enforcement of liabilities under [the] law. . . . Liquidation affects the contractual relationship between debtor and creditor. When the liquidation starts, no further liabilities under contract become payable until such time as it is clear that the pre-liquidation liabilities have been satisfied in full. . . . The beneficial interest in the company's assets is transferred to the liquidator. . . . [T]he making of a winding up order brings into operation a statutory scheme for dealing with the assets of a company which is being wound up. It matters not whether the winding up is by order or pursuant to a resolution. The assets of the company when realised provide a fund which the liquidator administers in many respects, but not in all, as if he were managing a trust fund. Creditors' contractual rights to be paid by the company become under the statutory scheme a statutory right to a share in the trust fund."[218]

18–77 When, as sometimes happens, the company's liabilities exceed its assets, those creditors with various prior and preferential claims must be satisfied first. According to section 284 of the 1963 Act:

"the same rules shall prevail and be observed relating to the respective rights of secured and unsecured creditors and to debts provable and to the valuation of annuities and future and contingent liabilities as are in force . . . under the law of bankruptcy . . ."

This means that if the company is insolvent the bankruptcy rules govern the three matters mentioned here.[219]

Proving Debts

18–78 By proof of debts is meant establishing the sums due to creditors so that they can be paid off in full or given their proper share.[220] The debts that can be proved in a winding up are defined by section 283(1) of the 1963 Act as:

"all debts payable on a contingency, and all claims against the company, present or future, certain or contingent, ascertained or sounding only in damages . . . a just estimate being made, so far as possible, of the value of such debts or claims which may be subject to any contingency or which sound only in damages, or for some other reason do not bear a certain value."

Therefore, every kind of legal claim, be it in contract or tort or other-

---

218 *Re Lines Bros. Ltd* [1983] 1 Ch. 1 at 14.

219 *cf. Re Irish Attested Sales Ltd* [1962] I.R. 70 and *Mersey Steel & Iron Co. v. Naylor, Benzon & Co.* (1882) 9 Q.B.D. 648.

220 See generally, *Bankruptcy Law*, pp.138–150, *Company Insolvency*, Chap. 19 and Winding Up Rules, ss. 102–111.

wise,[221] including future, contingent and unascertained claims, are admissible to proof. All debts are to be computed as of the date the winding up commenced,[222] from which time ceases to run against all creditors for limitations purposes,[223] and foreign currency claims are valued as of that date.[224] Where two or more persons are seeking to prove in respect of what is in substance the same debt, it is the circumstances at the time the dividend is being paid that determine which one will be admitted to proof.[225] The court is empowered to fix a time within which debts must be proved.[226]

Compromises and Arrangements

18–79 The liquidator may make any compromise or arrangement with creditors of the company and with persons claiming to be creditors or alleging that they have a claim against the company.[227] In a compulsory winding up, any such settlement must have the court's approval; in a members' or creditors' winding up, it must be approved by the members or the creditors, respectively. Where the company is solvent, any arrangement sanctioned by a special resolution of the company and by three-fourths in number and value of the creditors binds every creditor and the company; but any member or creditor may appeal to the court against that arrangement.[228] Arrangements under sections 201-203 of the 1963 Act have been dealt with separately above[229] along with reconstructions under section 260 of that Act.[230]

Liability of Contributories

18–80 Where there are insufficient funds to pay all the company's debts and expenses incurred in the winding up, the liquidator will claim against the contributories in respect of the deficiency, and also where it is necessary to adjust the rights of contributories between themselves. Contributories for these purposes in limited companies are, principally, members with amounts unpaid on their shares.[231] Where a company's

---

221 Civil Liability Act 1961, s.61.
222 *cf. Re Ligoniel Spinning Co.* [1900] 1 I.R. 324, *Re Nelson Car Hire Ltd* (1973) 107 I.L.T.R. 97; and *Re Supratone (Eire) Ltd* (1973) 107 I.L.T.R. 105.
223 *Re Cases of Taff Wells Ltd* [1992] Ch. 179.
224 *Re Lines Bros. Ltd* [1983] 1 Ch. l.
225 *Barclays Bank v. T.S.O.G. Trust Fund* [1984] A.C. 626. *cf. Re Polly Peck International p.l.c.* [1996] 2 All E.R. 433 on the rule against "double proof".
226 1963 Act, s.242.
227 *ibid.*, ss. 231(1)(e) and 267(1)(a).
228 *ibid.*, s.279.
229 See above, paras 11–51 *et seq.*
230 See above, paras 11–63 *et seq.*
231 1963 Act, s.207(1)(d).

regulations do not restrict the transferability of its shares, any shareholder with partly paid shares may transfer them up to the last moment before liquidation, even if the objective is simply to avoid liability as a contributory and the transferee happens to be a pauper.[232] It is at this stage in a company's existence that questions about title to shares frequently arise.

Priorities Among Creditors

18–81 There are some categories of creditor whose claims against the company must be satisfied before the claims of others can be met. Except where the 1963 Act otherwise provides, if the company is insolvent the ordinary bankruptcy rules govern the rights of secured as against unsecured creditors and the rights of both of these groups as between themselves.[233] This part of the book deals principally with priorities between creditors in a winding up but some of these priorities may be asserted without the company going into liquidation; indeed some of the circumstances considered here are not strictly priority situations at all. These matters nevertheless are most conveniently dealt with in this context. Since the law on priorities and related questions is extremely complex, only a general outline of the position can be given in a work of this nature.[234]

Retention of Title Clauses

18–82 Since they were first highlighted here in *Re Interview Ltd.*[235] and in the *Romalpa* case[236] in England, retention of title clauses have become a major feature of commercial life and indeed the subject of much litigation. These clauses arise where one firm sells goods to another but stipulates that, until those goods are paid for, the seller retains ownership of them. Often too it is added that, if the buyer sells those goods before they are paid for, the original seller shall become entitled to the proceeds of that sale. Thus in *Re Interview Ltd.*, where an Irish company agreed to import goods from Germany, the contract stipulated that the ownership and property in the goods was to remain in the seller until the goods were paid for. It was held there that in this kind of arrangement the original buyer of the goods does not acquire property or ownership in them, but merely gets possession of them in

---

232 *Re Discoverers Finance Corp.* [1910] 1 Ch. 312; see above, para. 9–30.

233 1963 Act, s.284.

234 See generally, *Company Insolvency*, Part IV, M. Forde, *Commercial Law* (1997), Chap. 5 and J. Breslin, *Banking Law in the Republic of Ireland* (1998), Chaps. 24–38.

235 [1975] I.R. 382.

236 *Aluminium Industrie Vaasen B.V. v. Romalpa Aluminium Ltd* [1976] 1 W.L.R. 676.

the same way as a hirer under a hire purchase agreement until the goods have been paid for. Retention of title stipulations, therefore, provide trade creditors with considerable security, in that suppliers of goods to companies in financial difficulties can retain the right to recapture the goods that are not paid for, and perhaps can follow the proceeds of re-sale if those goods are sold.

18–83 The actual wording of the clause in question is crucial. Thus if the interest reserved by the original seller is not ownership of the goods but is some claim over them, then the goods may only be subject to a charge which, in order to be effective, must be registered under section 99 of the 1963 Act.[237] If the property is reserved not in the original contract but in a later supplementary contract, this may possibly be impeached as an unlawful attempt to contract out of the principle that in a liquidation creditors are entitled to be paid off *pari passu*.[238] Difficulties can arise where the goods are altered physically or are mixed with other goods.[239] In recent years the English courts have tended to read retention of title clauses as narrowly as is reasonably possible. One judge remarked that "this area of the law is presently a maze if not a minefield, and one has to proceed with caution for every step of the way".[240]

18–84 Until recently Irish judges tended to lean in favour of upholding these clauses[241] but the extent to which retention of title clause can capture the proceeds of sub-sales has been substantially diminished by *Carroll Group Distributors Ltd. v. G. & J.F. Bourke Ltd.*[242] The clause there applied to tobacco products purchased by a retailer over a period and it provided that the proceeds from all sub-sales should be held in trust for the supplier in a separate bank account, with the details of that account to be provided to the seller. Murphy J. pointed out that it was very likely that the aggregate amount of those proceeds at various times would exceed the sums actually owing to the supplier, because those proceeds would include the retailer's mark-up on the goods and sums in respect of goods which already had been paid for. Accordingly, it was held, the "substance of the transaction as ascer-

---

237 *e.g. Re Bond Worth Ltd* [1980] 1 Ch. 228.

238 See below, para. 18–111.

239 *e.g. Somers v. James Alien (Ireland) Ltd* [1985] I.R. 340, *Re Peachdart Ltd* [1984] 1 Ch. 131 and *Borden (U.K.) Ltd v. Scottish Timber Products Ltd* [1981] 1 Ch. 25.

240 *Hendy Lennox (Induction Engines) Ltd v. Grahame Puttick Ltd* [1984] 1 W.L.R. 485 at 493.

241 See Maguire, "Romalpa Misinterpreted" (1989) 11 D.U.L.J. 40 and Law Reform Commission Report — *Debt Collection: Retention of Title* (1989).

242 [1990] 1 I.R. 481.

tained from the words used by the parties and the context in which the document [was] executed" was to confer a charge on those proceeds in substitution for the property rights the supplier had retained in the goods".[243] It is not entirely clear from the judgment whether it was this feature of the clause alone or whether it was several other aspects of the clause that proved decisive.

Property Held in Trust

18–85 Property that the company holds in trust for others must be separated from the company's general assets.[244] The existence of a trust depends on whether the "three certainties" are satisfied. In *Re Kayford Ltd.*,[245] a mail order firm that held considerable sums paid by customers, either as a deposit on or as the purchase price for goods ordered, got into financial difficulties. Being concerned about those customers, it instructed its bank to open a separate trust account for them and the money the customers had advanced was lodged in it. In liquidation proceedings, it was held that this money was held in trust for those customers.[246] Where creditors with retention of title have been held entitled to recover the proceeds of sub-sales of the goods affected, it was because that money was being held in trust for them.[247]

Subject to Equities

18–86 It is a principle of bankruptcy law that, when the bankrupt's property vests in the Official Assignee, his title is "subject to equities", meaning all equitable claims against that property continue, despite the change in ownership.[248] An extension of this principle is that where certain contractual rights exist with reference to some of the insolvent's assets, those rights may still be exercisable following commencement of the bankruptcy or winding up. In that event, the person with those rights may gain a distinct advantage over all the other creditors. In *Dempsey v. Bank of Ireland*[249] it was held by the Supreme Court that

---

[243] [1990] 1 I.R. 481 at 486.

[244] See generally, *Bankruptcy Law*, pp. 77–79, *Company Insolvency*, Chap. 22.

[245] [1975] 1 W.L.R. 279.

[246] Similarly, *Barclays Bank Ltd v. Quistclose Investments Ltd* [1970] A.C. 567, *McCann v. Irish Board Mills Ltd* [1980] I.L.R.M. 216, *Carreras Rothmans Ltd v. Freeman Mattkews Treasure Ltd* [1985] 1 Ch. 207, *Re Shanahan's Stamp Auctions Ltd* [1962] I.R. 386 and *Re Eastern Capital Furniture Ltd* [1989] B.C.L.C. 371; *cf. Re Holidays Promotions (Europe) Ltd* [1996] 2 B.C.L.C. 618.

[247] *e.g. Aluminium Industrie* case, above, n. 236; *cf. e.g. Carrolls Group* case, above, n. 242.

[248] See generally, *Bankruptcy Law*, pp. 72–73 and *Company Insolvency*, pp. 330–332.

[249] Supreme Court, December 6, 1985.

contractual rights to apportion a company's funds can be exercised even after the company has gone into liquidation because exercising those rights is not the same as proving a debt. The case concerned the bonding arrangements sponsored by the Irish Travel Agents' Association and the issue was whether a bank, which made payments under one travel agency's bond, could reimburse itself from that agency's bank account even though the agency had by then gone into liquidation. Under the arrangement, the bank entered into a guarantee to pay £75,000 towards the costs of catering for travellers who were stranded because the agency in question had insufficient funds. At the same time, the agency agreed to indemnify the bank against its liability under this guarantee and also agreed that the bank could debit its bank account with whatever was owing to the bank under that indemnity. The agency here, Eurotravel Ltd., had gone into liquidation before the bank sought to debit the account with £75,000, having paid the amount under the guarantee.

18–87 Giving judgment for the court, Henchy J. held that this debit could be

> "made because what was being claimed was not a right to prove a debt in the winding up but an entitlement to enforce a contractual right notwithstanding a winding up. For this reason, several leading cases on set-offs claimed by guarantors, which were applied in the court below,[250] were distinguished. Applying first principles, the bank's claim succeeded because an insolvent company's assets are subject to the same burdens and equities as existed immediately prior to the winding up. Speaking of the situation where the assets vested in the liquidator (under section 230 of the 1963 Act),
>
> The general rule is that he acquires only such title to the assets as the company had — no more, no less. He cannot take any better title to any part of the assets than the company had. This means that he takes the assets subject to any pre-existing enforceable right of a third party in or over them. If that were not so, equities, liabilities and contractual rights validly and enforceably created while the assets were in the hands of the company would be unfairly swept aside and unjust distribution of the assets would result."[251]

18–88 When the travel agency's winding up commenced the bank had paid the £75,000 on the guarantee and, consequently, the company's bank account was subject to the bank's contingent right to debit that sum, which it did shortly afterwards. If, immediately before the

[250] Murphy J., May 28, 1984, *sub nom re Eurotravel Ltd*
[251] At p. 8. See also *Glow Heating Ltd v. Eastern Health Board* [1988] I.R. 110.

winding up, the bank had debited that sum the debit could not have been questioned because "it would have been done under the terms of a guarantee which was entered into in good faith and which in no way offended the statutory provisions applicable in a winding up."[252] It therefore does not matter for these purposes that the bank exercised its contractual right to debit the account after the winding up had commenced.

Third Party Insurance

18–89 Formerly, a most unjust situation could arise where the company was insolvent and had been largely responsible for injuring someone or his property. Where the company was insured for that particular liability, the proceeds of the insurance policy was not payable to the injured party. Instead, the insurance proceeds would form part of the company's general assets and would be distributed in accordance with the priorities and preferences being considered here.[253] Accordingly, if the company were heavily insolvent, the injured party would receive next to nothing. That state of affairs was rectified by section 62 of the Civil Liability Act 1961, which provides that money paid under the insurance must be used to discharge the injured party's claim and none of that money shall form part of the company's assets for the purpose of distribution among its other creditors.[254] It has been held, however, that this form of priority does not apply where the injured party commenced his claim after the company had actually been dissolved.[255]

Set-Off

18–90 The right of set-off in liquidations arises by virtue of bankruptcy law, according to which

> "Where there are mutual credits or debts as between the [insolvent] and any person claiming as a creditor, one debt or demand may be set-off against the other and only the balance found owing shall be recoverable on one side or the other."[256]

Thus where there are "mutual debts" between the company and a creditor, one debt may be set-off against the other.[257] Set-off in this context

---

[252] At p. 10.
[253] *Hood's Trustees v. Southern Union* [1928] Ch. 793.
[254] See generally, *Company Insolvency*, pp. 369–372.
[255] *Bradley v. Eagle Star Insurance Co.* [1989] A.C. 957. The Companies Act was amended in Britain to overrule the position as so held.
[256] Bankruptcy Act 1988, 1st schedule, rule 17(1). See generally, *Bankruptcy Law*, pp. 144–147 and *Company Insolvency*, Chap. 23.
[257] *e.g. M.S. Fashions Ltd v. Bank of Credit & Commerce International S.A.* [1993] Ch. 425.

is not confined to debts arising out of contract but extends, for example, to sums a company is entitled to claim as a tax deduction[258] and to litigation costs.[259] Set-off does not apply to secured debts unless the creditor waives his security and elects to prove in the liquidation instead.[260] In *National Westminister Bank v. Halesowen Presswork & Assemblies Ltd.*,[261] a divided House of Lords held that the rule whereby mutual debts should be set-off and only the balance claimed, was enacted to protect the general public interest and, accordingly, was peremptory and could not be contracted out of.[262] An Irish court almost a hundred years ago came to a contrary conclusion in a bankruptcy case.[263]

18–91 Disputes concerning set-offs frequently involve different bank accounts.[264] For instance, in *Freaney v. Bank of Ireland*,[265] when the bank heard that the company was about to be wound up it opened a suspense account in the company's name. The bank debited to it various cheques drawn by the company and also the amount of the cheques that had been lodged to the company's current account but were returned unpaid. This current account was in credit to a substantial amount and, when the liquidator was appointed, the credit balance was transferred to a new current account and later to a deposit account, each of which were denoted as The Company "in voluntary liquidation". It was held that the bank was entitled to set-off against the amount in this account the sums owing to it on the suspense account. There is no mutuality, and accordingly there can he no set-off, between money borrowed by a company for a particular purpose, which is held by a bank, and debts owed by the company to the bank, where the special purpose was known to the bank.[266]

18–92 The fact that a company's debts or assets are the subject of a floating charge does not prevent its creditors from setting-off against mutual debts incurred by the company, for the company is entitled to

---

258 *Re Harrex Ltd, Murphy v. Revenue Commissioners* [1976] I.R. 15 and *Re D.H.Curtis (Builders) Ltd* [1978] Ch. 162.
259 *Lynch v. Ardmore Studios (Ireland) Ltd* [1966] I.R. 133.
260 *Re Norman Holding Co.* [1991] 1 W.L.R. 10.
261 [1972] A.C. 785.
262 Such contracts are enforcible outside the liquidation context: *Skipskredittforeningen v. Emperor Navigation S.A.* [1997] 2 B.C.L.C. 398.
263 *Deering v. Hyndman* (1886) 18 L.R. Ir. 323 and 467.
264 See generally, M. Hapgood, *Paget's Law of Banking* (11th ed., 1996), Chap. 31.
265 *Re Tailteann Freight Services Ltd* [1975] I.R. 376.
266 *Barclays Bank Ltd v. Quistclose Investments Ltd* [1970] A.C. 567. See also *Re Bank of Credit & Commerce International S.A. (No. 8)* [1997] 3 W.L.R. 909.

carry on its business as if the charge did not exist.[267] But when crystallisation occurs, such as by the chargee appointing a receiver and a manager, other creditors then have no right of set-off against new debts that thereafter are incurred with them on the company's behalf.[268] On crystallisation, the floating security becomes converted into a specific charge, which causes the title in future debts, as they arise, to vest in the chargee. Moreover, the requisite mutuality would not exist where the pre-crystallisation debt was owed to the company alone but the post-crystallisation credit was granted by the receiver-manager, who in reality does not act simply on the company's behalf.

Specifically Secured Debts

18–93 A creditor has specific or fixed security if he possesses a mortgage, charge or lien on the company's property other than a floating charge.[269] Several options are open to the specifically secured creditor,[270] viz. rest on the security and not prove for the debt; realise the security and prove for the deficiency; value the security and prove for the deficiency; or surrender the security and prove for the entire debt. Charges that were duly registered under section 99 of the 1963 Act take priority from their date of creation; except that a later legal charge ranks before an equitable charge where there was neither actual nor constructive notice of the equity or the legal chargee has a better equity. A charge that is not registered as required by section 99 of the 1963 Act is void against any creditor of the company and against the liquidator.[271] Accordingly, any subsequently created charge will take priority over an unregistered one and this is so even where the owner of the registered charge knew, at the time that charge was given or later, of the other charge's existence.[272] A charge that is registered under an extension of time given under section 106 of the 1963 Act will almost invariably be made subject to the rights arising from other charges that were given and duly registered in the intervening period.[273]

Execution Creditors

18–94 Judgment creditors who have taken no active steps to enforce

---

[267] *Murphy v. Revenue Commissioners* [1976] I.R. 15 and *Biggerstaff v. Rowatt's Wharf Ltd* [1896] 2 Ch. 93.

[268] *Lynch v. Ardmore Studios (Ireland) Ltd* [1966] I.R. 133 and *N.W. Robbie & Co. v. Witney Warehouses & Co.* [1963] 1 W.L.R. 1324.

[269] See above, paras 16–09 *et seq.*

[270] See generally, *Bankruptcy Law*, pp. 147–149, *Company Insolvency*, Chap. 24 and W.J. Gough, *Company Charges* (2nd ed., 1996), Chaps. 37–42.

[271] 1963 Act, s.99(1); see above, para. 16–51 *et seq.*

[272] *Re Monolithic Buildings Co.* [1915] 1 Ch. 643.

[273] See above, paras 16–86 *et seq.*

their security are not entitled to be paid in priority to the secured or even the ordinary creditors.[274] A creditor who has issued execution against a company's property or attached a debt due to it is not entitled to retain the benefit of the process unless it was completed before the winding up commenced or, if earlier, the date the creditor received notice of the meeting at which it was proposed to have the company wound up.[275] But the court may override this rule and make such order in favour of the creditor as it thinks fit.

Liquidator's Costs, etc.

18–95 In a voluntary winding up, the liquidator's remuneration, together with all costs, charges and expenses incurred in the winding up, must be paid before the other preferred debts.[276] In *Re Red Breast Preserving Co.*[277] it was held that ordinarily the same rule should apply in a compulsory winding up. A source of dispute in several major cases in recent years has been whether various kinds of taxes which become payable during a winding up should be regarded as costs of the liquidation.[278] Before costs and charges can be paid in an official liquidation, they must have been approved by the Examiner or the Taxing Master, as the case may be.[279]

Preferred Debts

18–96 Legislative provisions give certain categories of creditors the right to be paid off before unsecured creditors and even before those who hold a floating charge on the company's assets. The common law prerogative that gave preference to Crown debts has been held to be inconsistent with the constitutional nature of the State.[280] There are three main categories of preferential creditor today, namely the Revenue Commissioners, company employees and the rating authority. Claims for preferential payment must be made to the liquidator not later than six months after he advertised for claims in at least two daily newspapers.[281]

---

[274] *Re Leinster Contract Corporation* [1903] 1 I.R. 517 and *Re Lough Neagh Ship Co., ex p. Thompson* [1896] 1 I.R. 29.

[275] 1963 Act, ss. 291, 292 and 219.

[276] *ibid.*, s.281.

[277] [1958] I.R. 234.

[278] *E.g. Re Van Hool McArdle Ltd* [1982] I.L.R.M. 340, *Revenue Cmrs. v. Donnelly* [1983] I.L.R.M. 329, *Re Hibernian Transport Companies Ltd* [1984] I.L.R.M. 583 and *Re Noyek & Sons Ltd* [1988] I.R. 772.

[279] Winding Up Rules, r.128(2).

[280] *Re Irish Employers' Mutual Insurance Association* [1955] I.R. 76.

[281] 1963 Act, s.285(14), inserted by 1990 Act, s.134.

The Revenue's Preferences

18–97 The principal basis of the Revenue's preference is section 285 of the 1963 Act, which covers the following matters. All "assessed taxes" up to April 5 before the liquidation commenced are preferred, but not more than any one year's assessed tax in respect of each category of tax of each kind.[282] In other words, as regards all kinds of assessed taxes, a preference exists for any one year's tax of each kind. The Revenue can select which particular year shall be taken for this purpose and it can select different years for the different kinds of assessed taxes.[283] Understandably, the Revenue will select the largest outstanding year of each tax.

18–98 Unpaid value added tax or V.A.T. (less V.A.T. refundable) is preferred in relation to taxable periods ending within 12 months before the company was wound up;[284] preference is also given in respect of any interest payable on outstanding V.A.T. Employers' P.R.S.I. contributions which were payable during the 12 months preceding the winding up are preferred[285] but not interest payable on those sums. Unpaid income tax which a company, as employer, has deducted or should have deducted from its employees' remuneration during the 12 months preceding the liquidation is preferred[286] as is interest payable on those sums. Finally, there is a preference made for deductions made by employers in the construction industry from payments made to non-exempt sub-contractors.[287]

18–99 In 1976 a new category of preference was introduced,[288] the so-called "super" or "pre"-preferential debt, which impresses a form of trust on the funds in question and they rank before all the other preferential debts. That provision is now embodied in section 16 of the Social Welfare (Consolidation) Act 1993, with regard to P.R.S.I. contributions which an employer has or should have deducted from employees' remuneration — as contrasted with the employer's own P.R.S.I. contributions, which are simple preferential debts.[289] According to section 16 of that Act, employees' contributions which have been deducted

---

[282] *ibid.*, s.285(2)(a)(ii); *cf. Gowers v. Walker* [1930] 1 Ch. 262.
[283] *Re Pratt* [1951] 1 Ch. 229.
[284] Finance Act 1976, s.62(2).
[285] 1963 Act, s.285(2)(e) (as amended by Social Welfare (Consolidation) Act 1993, s.15).
[286] 1963 Act, s.285(2)(a)(iii) and Taxes Consolidtion Act 1977, s.995.
[287] Taxes Consolidtion Act, s.1000.
[288] Social Welfare (No. 2) Act 1976, s.7, enacted following *Re Castlemahon Poultry Products Ltd* [1987] I.L.R.M. 222.
[289] 1963 Act, s.285(2)(e).

but not paid over to the social welfare fund and also those contributions which should have been so deducted and paid over shall not form part of the assets:

> "if any company that is being wound up. Further, a sum equal to that amount must be paid the Social Insurance Fund in priority to any of the debts rendered preferential by section 285 of the 1963 Act."[290]

The precise import of section 16 has yet to receive judicial elaboration. Among the matters awaiting resolution are whether this super-preferential debt must be paid before the liquidator's remuneration and expenses and whether any charge on the company's assets is subject to the Revenue's entitlement under section 16.

18–100 As was explained earlier, it was held in *Re Keenan Bros. Ltd.*[291] that it is possible to create a fixed charge over book debts and, in that case, that the bank had succeeded in creating such a charge. The practical consequences of the decision was that banks and other creditors who normally would have a floating charge could rank in front of the Revenue Commissioners by persuading the debtor company to give them a fixed charge over all or some of its book debts. However, the Finance Act 1986, substantially closed off this option for those charges given after 27 May, 1986. Under section 1001 of the Taxes (Consolidation) Act, 1997, where the Revenue are owed outstanding P.A.Y.E. and also value added tax, they are entitled to call on a creditor who has a fixed charge over the debtor company's book debts to pay a sum to the Revenue. The amount that the chargee is made liable to pay is an amount equivalent to that owing by the company to the Revenue under the above heading, subject to the following. The total amount payable should not exceed whatever sums, following receipt of the Revenue's notice, the chargee received from the company, directly or indirectly, in payment of any debts due by the company to the chargee. Thus, following receipt of the Revenue's notice, the secured creditor can be obliged to pay over to the Revenue all or part of whatever funds it obtained from the company in discharging its indebtedness. However, this preference can be departed if particulars of the charge are funished to the Revenue within 21 days of its creation.

18–101 *Employees' Preferences* The main basis for employees' preferred debts also is section 285 of the 1963 Act and, where there is not enough funds to cover all of these and the Revenue's section 285 debts and 12

---

[290] As amended by Social Welfare Act 1991, s.36. See also Social Welfare (Consolidation) Act 1981, s.250(2).

[291] [1985] I.R. 401; see above, para. 16–25.

months rates, they all rank and abate equally. Only those who work with the company under a contract of employment benefit from these preferential debts provisions. Thus in *Re Sunday Tribune Ltd.*,[292] where several journalists with a Sunday newspaper claimed to be preferential creditors, some of their claims were rejected on the grounds that those journalists were independent contractors. In *Stakelum v. Canning*,[293] it was held that executive directors of companies, other than managing directors, can be employees for the purposes of this preference.

18–102 First and foremost are unpaid wages and salaries owing for services rendered to the employer, up to a maximum of £2,500 for every claimant.[294] There is no general definition of what is a "wage" or a "salary" for these purposes but it must mean remuneration for work done; it includes remuneration for periods of absence from work for "good cause" and for holidays.[295] In *Re M.*[296] it was held that amounts deducted from earnings and credited to a holiday stamp scheme in the construction industry were wages, even though the employees were only entitled to have the sums deducted paid into what was described as a suspense account. The services in question must have been rendered during the four months immediately preceding the commencement of the liquidation. Where the arrangement with a "farm labourer" is to pay him a lump sum at the end of the hiring or at the end of the year, the court is empowered to apportion how much of what is owing should be preferred.[297]

18–103 Accrued holiday remuneration at the date of the adjudication is preferred.[298] Outstanding amounts due under an arrangement for sick pay are preferred.[299] Outstanding pension contributions, under any scheme or arrangement made for superannuation, are preferred, whether they are employer's contributions or those deducted from the employee's remuneration.[300] Three major statutory schemes exist for compensating employees who have been dismissed from their jobs in specific circumstances, namely where they were not given the requisite statutory minimum notice, where they were made redundant and

---

[292] Carroll J, September 26, 1984.
[293] [1976] I.R. 314.
[294] s.285(2)(b), (c).
[295] s.285(11).
[296] [1955] N.I. 182.
[297] s.285(4).
[298] s.285(2)(d).
[299] s.285(2)(h).
[300] s.285(2)(i).

where their dismissal was held to be unfair. Compensation which is awarded to a dismissed employee under any of these schemes is a priority debt.[301] Where the employer is unable to pay such compensation, the Protection of Employees (Insolvency) Act 1984, requires those amounts to be paid by the Minister for Labour. In that event, the Minister is subrogated for the employee in respect of the amounts paid.[302]

18–104 If the employee was injured in the course of his employment and has been awarded or stands to be awarded damages and costs in respect of that injury, the amount of those damages and the costs are a preferred debt.[303] However, this preference does not exist where the company is effectively indemnified by insurers against that liability. In such a case, the injured employee is in effect subrogated for the company and is entitled to be paid the full amount forthcoming on the policy.[304]

18–105 Where money was advanced to the company for the purpose of paying employees' wages or salary, holiday remuneration or pension benefits, the lender is preferred to the extent that those employees would have been preferred if they had not been paid what was owing to them.[305] Thus, if a bank lends £20,000 to meet the payroll at the end of the week or the end of the month, it is a preferred creditor for that amount. Any form of "advance" to the employer comes within this preference; it need not strictly be a loan if those wages would have been a preferred debt if unpaid.[306] But the fact that a bank debits wages cheques to a separate wages account does not always entitle it to the preference.[307]

18–106 *Rates* A preference also exists in respect of all local rates which were due and payable during the 12 months preceding the winding up.[308] The term "local rates" is not defined but must mean the rates struck by the local authorities under the various Local Government

---

[301] Minimum Notice and Terms of Employment Act 1973, s.14, Redundancy Payments Act 1979, s.14, Unfair Dismissals Act 1977, s.12.
[302] Protection of Employees (Employers') Insolvency Act 1984, s.10.
[303] s.285(2)(g).
[304] Civil Liability Act 1961, s.62; *cf. Dunne v. P.J. White Construction Co.* [1989] I.L.R.M. 803.
[305] s.285(6).
[306] *Waikato Savings Bank v. Andrews Furniture Ltd* [1982] 2 N.Z.L.R. 520.
[307] *Re E.J. Morel* (1934) Ltd [1962] 1 Ch. 21.
[308] s.285(2)(a)(i).

Acts. It has been held to include levies which the legislature treats in the same way.[309]

Floating Charges[310]

18–107 Mutual debts arising before a floating charge crystallises can be set off;[311] before crystallisation the sheriff may seize and sell property subject to such a charge[312] and a garnishee order may be made against accounts owing to the company.[313] Charges arising out of the general law, like unpaid vendors' liens and solicitors' liens, property held in trust and, subject to what is said below about notice, specific charges and liens, take priority over a floating charge.[314] Although section 285 of the 1963 Act gives preference over the floating charge to certain debts owing to the State and to company employees and rating authorities, those may be defeated by the operation of an "automatic crystallisation" clause that converts the floating security into a fixed charge before winding up commences.[315] As between registered floating charges over the entire undertaking, the first in time prevails.[316] But a subsequent registered floating charge over part of the undertaking gets priority if it was made under a power reserved in the general charge to give such security.[317] The same principles apply to extensions of time under section 106 of the 1963 Act for registering floating charges as apply to specific charges.[318]

18–108 Subsequent legal and equitable specific charges lose their priority where the floating charge prohibited the company from making the charge in question only where the person in whose favour the later charge was given in fact knew or had notice of that prohibition. What constitutes that notice is a complicated matter.[319] But recording, under

---

309 *Re Baker* [1954] 1 W.L.R. 1144, *Re Ellwood* [1927] 1 Ch. 455 and *Re An Arranging Debtor* [1921] 2 I.R. 1.

310 See generally, Farrar, "Floating Charges and Priorities", 38 *Conv.* 315 (1974), W.J. Gough, *Company Charges* (2nd ed., 1996), Chaps. 37–42 and R. Goode, *Legal Problems of Credit and Security* (1988), Chap. 4.

311 *Murphy v. Revenue Comrs.* [1976] I.R. 15.

312 *Robinson v. Burnell's Vienna Bakery Co.* [1904] 2 K.B. 624.

313 *Evans v. Rival Granite Quarries Ltd* [1910] 2 K.B. 979.

314 *De Lorean Motor Cars Ltd v. Northern Ireland Carriers Ltd* [1982] N.I. 163 and *Halpin v. Cremin* [1954] I.R. 19.

315 *Re Manurewa Transport Ltd* [1971] N.Z.L.R. 909.

316 *Re Benjamin Cope &Sons Ltd* [1914] 1 Ch. 800.

317 *Re Automatic Bottle Makers Ltd* [1926] 1 Ch. 412.

318 *Re Farm Fresh Frozen Foods Ltd*[1980] I.L.R.M. 131.

319 See *e.g. English & Scottish Mercantile Investment Co. v. Brunton* [1892] 2 Q.B. 700; *Re Old Bushmills Distillery Co., ex p. Brydon* [1896] 1 I.R. 301; *Cox v. Dublin City Distillery Co.* [1906] 1 I.R. 466 and *Coveney v. Persse Ltd* [1910] 1 I.R. 194.

section 99 of the 1963 Act, in the registry of companies a prohibition against subsequent charges does not of itself amount to notice of that proscription.[320]

18–109 The doctrine of constructive notice of public documents in the company law context has hitherto been confined to questions of the company's capacity to be bound by transactions as opposed to priorities between outsiders claiming the benefit of transactions entered into by the company.[321] It could also be argued that constructive notice, if it applies at all, embraces notice of matters that must be registered; "particulars" under section 99 hardly include details of restrictions on subsequent charges. Even assuming that constructive notice did apply here, if the charge is given by a company "organ" in the sense of S.I. No.163 of 1973,[322] then it could be argued that regulation 6 of this instrument overrides the constructive notice doctrine in favour of persons dealing with the company in good faith. In any event, in *Welch v. Bowmaker (Ireland) Ltd.*,[323] where the company gave a bank an equitable charge by deposit of title deeds over property that was the subject of an earlier floating charge, and the floating charge forbade creating any additional charges, it was held that the specific charge gets priority. According to Henchy J., "it is settled law that there is no duty on the bank in a situation such as this to seek out the precise terms of the debenture [and a]ctual or express notice of the prohibition must be shown before the subsequent mortgagee can be said to be deprived of priority."[324]

Ordinary and Deferred Creditors

18–110 By ordinary creditors here is meant creditors who neither fall into any of the above-mentioned categories nor are members of the company to whom the amount is owed in their "character of . . . member[s] by way of dividends, profits or otherwise".[325] This latter category are known as deferred creditors; they include members who are owed dividends that have been declared and capital that is being repaid[326] but not, for example, shareholder-directors who are voted

320 *Welch v. Bowmaker (Ireland) Ltd* [1980] I.R. 251; see below, para. 18–109.

321 *Ernest v. Nicholls* (1857) 6 H.L.C. 401; see above, para. 13–45.

322 See above, paras 13–56 *et seq.*

323 [1980] I.R. 251.

324 *ibid.* at 256.

325 1963 Act, s.207(1)(g).

326 *e.g. Re Belfast Empire Theatre of Varieties Ltd* [1963] I.R. 41 and *Re Compania de Electricidad de la Provincia de Buenos Aires Ltd* [1980] 1 Ch.146.

directors' remuneration by the shareholders in general meeting,[327] nor members who were deceived by the company into purchasing its shares and in consequence are entitled to damages.[328]

18–111 Ordinary creditors must be paid off before the deferred creditors and before making any payment to the contributories.[329] If the company is insolvent, the ordinary creditors must be paid equally or *pari passu*, *i.e.* the same amount per pound owed to them.[330] This principle, embodied in section 275 of the 1963 Act, is no longer a peremptory rule,[331] since the creditors are permitted to agree that any particular liability may be postponed in favour of or subordinated to other claims against the company.[332]

RESUSCITATING DISSOLVED COMPANIES

18–112 A serious problem, which is not satisfactorily resolved in the legislation, is dealing with circumstances which can arise several years after a company has been wound up and dissolved. For instance, a consumer of products manufactured by a company may discover, years after the company was liquidated, that his health was damaged by that product. What redress then is available to him? Under section 310 of the 1963 Act, the court is empowered to set aside a dissolution within two years of the company having been dissolved. That application may be made by the liquidator or by any other person who seems to the court to be interested. But there is no provision for resuscitation once those two years have elapsed, which can lead to anomalous results.[333]

---

327 *Re Cinnamond Park Ltd* [1930] N.I. 47 and *Re Dale & Plant Ltd* (1889) 43 Ch.D. 255.

328 *Soden v. British & Commonwealth Holdings p.l.c.* [1998] A.C. 298.

329 *Re A.M.F. International Ltd* [1996] 1 W.L.R. 77.

330 *cf. Barlow Clowes International Ltd v. Vaughan* [1992] 4 All E.R. 22, concerning money held in trust for several categories of investor.

331 *cf. British Eagle International Airlines v. Compagnie Nationale Air France* [1975] 1 W.L.R. 758.

332 1990 Act, s.132, amending s.275 of the 1963 Act. *cf. Re Maxwell Commications Corp.* [1993] 1 W.L.R. 1402.

333 *e.g. Butler v. Broadhead* [1975] 1 Ch. 97 and *Bradley v. Eagle Star Insurance Co.* [1989] A.C. 957. *cf.* Note, "Recognising Products Liability Claims at Dissolution: The Compatibility of Corporate and Tort Law Principles", 87 *Columbia L. Rev.* 1048 (1987).

STRIKING COMPANIES OFF THE REGISTER

18–113 Sections 311 of the 1963 Act (as amended by section 11 of the 1982 Act) and 12 of the 1982 Act empower the registrar of companies to dissolve a company by striking it off the register of companies, either on the grounds that it is defunct or that it has failed to make annual returns for two consecutive years.[334] However, de-registration on these grounds does not affect the liability, if any, of every director, officer and member of the company, which may be enforced as if the company had not been dissolved. The power to strike off defunct companies applies in three circumstances,[335] namely where the company appears no longer to be carrying on business, where the company is being wound up but no liquidator appears to be acting, and where the company's affairs are fully wound up but no returns have been made by the liquidator in the preceding six months. The powers given in these sections are circumscribed by extensive procedural requirements, such as the registrar notifying the companies concerned by registered post and publishing notices in the *Iris Oifigiúil*. The fact that a company was de-registered in this manner does not prevent the court from winding it up.[336] Where a p.l.c. was not within a year of its incorporation issued with a certificate under section 6 of the 1983 Act entitling it to do business, the registrar of companies on following certain procedures may de-register it unless it gets that certificate.[337]

18–114 In an appropriate case, the court may restore the name of any such company to the companies' register.[338] An application for re-registration may be made by either the company, any member of the company or any of its creditors at any time up to 20 years from when the company was de-registered. Ordinarily the application will be granted if the court is satisfied that the company was carrying on business when it was struck off or otherwise it is just to restore it to the register. A court application is no longer necessary during the 12 months immediately following the de-registration; instead an application for re-registration can be made directly to the registrar of companies.[339] Once a company is put back on the register it is deemed to have continued in existence throughout the period during which it was struck off.

---

334 1990 Act, s.245.
335 1963 Act, s.311, as amended.
336 1963 Act, ss. 311(7) and 312(5).
337 1983 Act, s.8.
338 1963 Act, ss. 311(8) and 312(6); *e.g. Re Haltone (Cork) Ltd* [1996] 1 I.R. 32. *cf. Re Townreach Ltd* [1995] Ch. 28.
339 1963 Act, s.311A (inserted by 1990 Act, s.246).

Index